Family Maps
of
Butler County, Alabama
Deluxe Edition

With Homesteads, Roads, Waterways, Towns, Cemeteries, Railroads, and More

Family Maps

of

Butler County, Alabama

Deluxe Edition

With Homesteads, Roads, Waterways, Towns, Cemeteries, Railroads, and More

by Gregory A. Boyd, J.D.

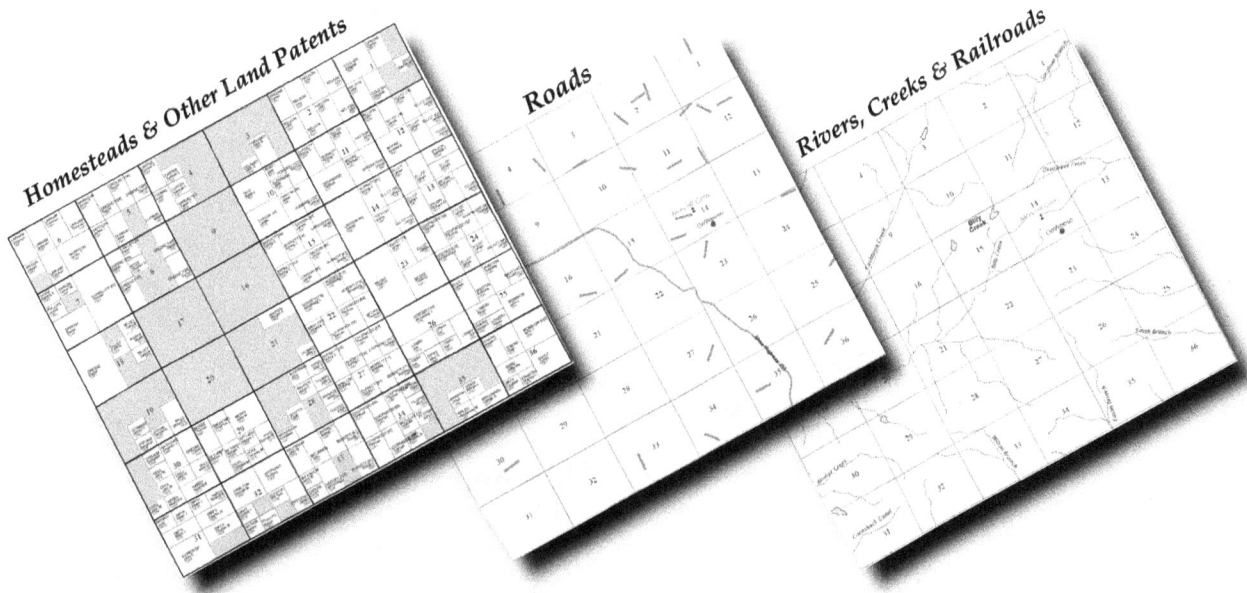

Featuring 3 *Maps Per Township...*

Arphax Publishing Co.
www.arphax.com

Family Maps of Butler County, Alabama, Deluxe Edition: With Homesteads, Roads, Waterways, Towns, Cemeteries, Railroads, and More.
by Gregory A. Boyd, J.D.

ISBN 1-4203-1279-0

Published by Arphax Publishing Co., 2210 Research Park Blvd., Norman, Oklahoma, USA 73069
www.arphax.com

First Edition

ATTENTION HISTORICAL & GENEALOGICAL SOCIETIES, UNIVERSITIES, COLLEGES, CORPORATIONS, FAMILY REUNION COORDINATORS, AND PROFESSIONAL ORGANIZATIONS: Quantity discounts are available on bulk purchases of this book. For information, please contact Arphax Publishing Co., at the address listed above, or at (405) 366-6181, or visit our web-site at www.arphax.com and contact us through the "Bulk Sales" link.

This book is dedicated to my wonderful family:

Vicki, Jordan, & Amy Boyd

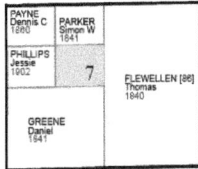

Contents

- Part I -

The Big Picture

- Part II -

Township Map Groups

(each Map Group contains a Patent Index, Patent Map, Road Map, & Historical Map)

Appendices

PAYNE
Dennis C
1860

PARKER
Simon W
1841

PHILLIPS
Jessie
1902

7

FLEWELLEN [96]
Thomas
1840

GREENE
Daniel
1841

Preface

The quest for the discovery of my ancestors' origins, migrations, beliefs, and life-ways has brought me rewards that I could never have imagined. The *Family Maps* series of books is my first effort to share with historical and genealogical researchers, some of the tools that I have developed to achieve my research goals. I firmly believe that this effort will allow many people to reap the same sorts of treasures that I have.

Our Federal government's General Land Office of the Bureau of Land Management (the "GLO") has given genealogists and historians an incredible gift by virtue of its enormous database housed on its web-site at glorecords.blm.gov. Here, you can search for and find millions of parcels of land purchased by our ancestors in about thirty states.

This GLO web-site is one of the best FREE on-line tools available to family researchers. But, it is not for the faint of heart, nor is it for those unwilling or unable to to sift through and analyze the thousands of records that exist for most counties.

My immediate goal with this series is to spare you the hundreds of hours of work that it would take you to map the Land Patents for this county. Every Butler County homestead or land patent that I have gleaned from public GLO databases is mapped here. Consequently, I can usually show you in an instant, where your ancestor's land is located, as well as the names of nearby land-owners.

Originally, that was my primary goal. But after speaking to other genealogists, it became clear that there was much more that they wanted. Taking their advice set me back almost a full year, but I think you will agree it was worth the wait. Because now, you can learn so much more.

Now, this book answers these sorts of questions:

- Are there any variant spellings for surnames that I have missed in searching GLO records?
- Where is my family's traditional home-place?
- What cemeteries are near Grandma's house?
- My Granddad used to swim in such-and-such-Creek—where is that?
- How close is this little community to that one?
- Are there any other people with the same surname who bought land in the county?
- How about cousins and in-laws—did they buy land in the area?

And these are just for starters!

The rules for using the *Family Maps* books are simple, but the strategies for success are many. Some techniques are apparent on first use, but many are gained with time and experience. Please take the time to notice the roads, cemeteries, creek-names, family names, and unique first-names throughout the whole county. You cannot imagine what YOU might be the first to discover.

I hope to learn that many of you have answered age-old research questions within these pages or that you have discovered relationships previously not even considered. When these sorts of things happen to you, will you please let me hear about it? I would like nothing better. My contact information can always be found at www.arphax.com.

One more thing: please read the "How To Use This Book" chapter; it starts on the next page. This will give you the very best chance to find the treasures that lie within these pages.

My family and I wish you the very best of luck, both in life, and in your research.   Greg Boyd

How to Use This Book - A Graphical Summary

Part I
"The Big Picture"

Map A ▸ *Counties in the State*
Map B ▸ *Surrounding Counties*
Map C ▸ *Congressional Townships (Map Groups) in the County*
Map D ▸ *Cities & Towns in the County*
Map E ▸ *Cemeteries in the County*
Surnames in the County ▸ *Number of Land-Parcels for Each Surname*
Surname/Township Index ▸ *Directs you to Township Map Groups in Part II*

*The <u>Surname/Township Index</u> can direct you to any number of **Township Map Groups***

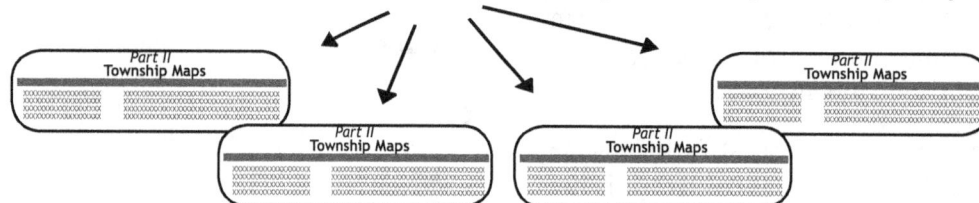

Part II
Township Map Groups
(1 for each Township in the County)

Each Township Map Group contains all four of of the following tools . . .

Land Patent Index ▸ *Every-name Index of Patents Mapped in this Township*
Land Patent Map ▸ *Map of Patents as listed in above Index*
Road Map ▸ *Map of Roads, City-centers, and Cemeteries in the Township*
Historical Map ▸ *Map of Railroads, Lakes, Rivers, Creeks, City-Centers, and Cemeteries*

Appendices

Appendix A ▸ *Congressional Authority enabling Patents within our Maps*
Appendix B ▸ *Section-Parts / Aliquot Parts (a comprehensive list)*
Appendix C ▸ *Multi-patentee Groups (Individuals within Buying Groups)*

How to Use This Book

The two "Parts" of this *Family Maps* volume seek to answer two different types of questions. Part I deals with broad questions like: what counties surround Butler County, are there any ASHCRAFTs in Butler County, and if so, in which Townships or Maps can I find them? Ultimately, though, Part I should point you to a particular Township Map Group in Part II.

Part II concerns itself with details like: where exactly is this family's land, who else bought land in the area, and what roads and streams run through the land, or are located nearby. The Chart on the opposite page, and the remainder of this chapter attempt to convey to you the particulars of these two "parts", as well as how best to use them to achieve your research goals.

Part I
"The Big Picture"

Within Part I, you will find five "Big Picture" maps and two county-wide surname tools.

These include:

• Map A - Where Butler County lies within the state
• Map B - Counties that surround Butler County
• Map C - Congressional Townships of Butler County (+ Map Group Numbers)
• Map D - Cities & Towns of Butler County (with Index)
• Map E - Cemeteries of Butler County (with Index)
• Surnames in Butler County Patents (with Parcel-counts for each surname)
• Surname/Township Index (with Parcel-counts for each surname by Township)

The five "Big-Picture" Maps are fairly self-explanatory, yet should not be overlooked. This is particularly true of Maps "C", "D", and "E", all of which show Butler County and its Congressional Townships (and their assigned Map Group Numbers).

Let me briefly explain this concept of Map Group Numbers. These are a device completely of our own invention. They were created to help you quickly locate maps without having to remember the full legal name of the various Congressional Townships. It is simply easier to remember "Map Group 1" than a legal name like: "Township 9-North Range 6-West, 5th Principal Meridian." But the fact is that the TRUE legal name for these Townships IS terribly important. These are the designations that others will be familiar with and you will need to accurately record them in your notes. This is why both Map Group numbers AND legal descriptions of Townships are almost always displayed together.

Map "C" will be your first intoduction to "Map Group Numbers", and that is all it contains: legal Township descriptions and their assigned Map Group Numbers. Once you get further into your research, and more immersed in the details, you will likely want to refer back to Map "C" from time to time, in order to regain your bearings on just where in the county you are researching.

Remember, township boundaries are a completely artificial device, created to standardize land descriptions. But do not let them become a boundary in your mind when choosing which townships to research. Your relative's in-laws, children, cousins, siblings, and mamas and papas, might just as easily have lived in the township next to the one your grandfather lived in—rather than in the one where he actually lived. So Map "C" can be your guide to which other Townships/ Map Groups you likewise ought to analyze.

Of course, the same holds true for County lines; this is the purpose behind Map "B". It shows you surrounding counties that you may want to consider for further reserarch.

Map "D", the Cities and Towns map, is the first map with an index. Map "E" is the second (Cemeteries). Both, Maps "D" and "E" give you broad views of City (or Cemetery) locations in the County. But they go much further by pointing you toward pertinent Township Map Groups so you can locate the patents, roads, and waterways located near a particular city or cemetery.

Once you are familiar with these *Family Maps* volumes and the county you are researching, the "Surnames In Butler County" chapter (or its sister chapter in other volumes) is where you'll likely start your future research sessions. Here, you can quickly scan its few pages and see if anyone in the county possesses the surnames you are researching. The "Surnames in Butler County" list shows only two things: surnames and the number of parcels of land we have located for that surname in Butler County. But whether or not you immediately locate the surnames you are researching, please do not go any further without taking a few moments to scan ALL the surnames in these very few pages.

You cannot imagine how many lost ancestors are waiting to be found by someone willing to take just a little longer to scan the "Surnames In Butler County" list. Misspellings and typographical errors abound in most any index of this sort. Don't miss out on finding your Kinard that was written Rynard or Cox that was written Lox. If it looks funny or wrong, it very often is. And one of those little errors may well be your relative.

Now, armed with a surname and the knowledge that it has one or more entries in this book, you are ready for the "Surname/Township Index." Unlike the "Surnames In Butler County", which has only one line per Surname, the "Surname/Township Index" contains one line-item for each Township Map Group in which each surname is found. In other words, each line represents a different Township Map Group that you will need to review.

Specifically, each line of the Surname/Township Index contains the following four columns of in-formation:

1. Surname
2. Township Map Group Number (these Map Groups are found in Part II)
3. Parcels of Land (number of them with the given Surname within the Township)
4. Meridian/Township/Range (the legal description for this Township Map Group)

The key column here is that of the Township Map Group Number. While you should definitely record the Meridian, Township, and Range, you can do that later. Right now, you need to dig a little deeper. That Map Group Number tells you where in Part II that you need to start digging.

But before you leave the "Surname/Township Index", do the same thing that you did with the "Surnames in Butler County" list: take a moment to scan the pages of the Index and see if there are similarly spelled or misspelled surnames that deserve your attention. Here again, is an easy opportunity to discover grossly misspelled family names with very little effort. Now you are ready to turn to . . .

Part II
"Township Map Groups"

You will normally arrive here in Part II after being directed to do so by one or more "Map Group Numbers" in the Surname/Township Index of Part I.

Each Map Group represents a set of four tools dedicated to a single Congressional Township that is either wholly or partially within the county. If you are trying to learn all that you can about a particular family or their land, then these tools should usually be viewed in the order they are presented.

These four tools include:

1. a Land Patent Index
2. a Land Patent Map
3. a Road Map, and
4. an Historical Map

As I mentioned earlier, each grouping of this sort is assigned a Map Group Number. So, let's now move on to a discussion of the four tools that make up one of these Township Map Groups.

Land Patent Index

Each Township Map Group's Index begins with a title, something along these lines:

MAP GROUP 1: Index to Land Patents
Township 16-North Range 5-West (2nd PM)

The Index contains seven (7) columns. They are:

1. ID (a unique ID number for this Individual and a corresponding Parcel of land in this Township)
2. Individual in Patent (name)
3. Sec. (Section), and
4. Sec. Part (Section Part, or Aliquot Part)
5. Date Issued (Patent)
6. Other Counties (often means multiple counties were mentioned in GLO records, or the section lies within multiple counties).
7. For More Info . . . (points to other places within this index or elsewhere in the book where you can find more information)

While most of the seven columns are self-explanatory, I will take a few moments to explain the "Sec. Part." and "For More Info" columns.

The "Sec. Part" column refers to what surveryors and other land professionals refer to as an Aliquot Part. The origins and use of such a term mean little to a non-surveyor, and I have chosen to simply call these sub-sections of land what they are: a "Section Part". No matter what we call them, what we are referring to are things like a quarter-section or half-section or quarter-quarter-section. See Appendix "B" for most of the "Section Parts" you will come across (and many you will not) and what size land-parcel they represent.

The "For More Info" column of the Index may seem like a small appendage to each line, but please

recognize quickly that this is not so. And to understand the various items you might find here, you need to become familiar with the Legend that appears at the top of each Land Patent Index.

Here is a sample of the Legend . . .

LEGEND

"For More Info . . . " column

A = Authority (Legislative Act, See Appendix "A")
B = Block or Lot (location in Section unknown)
C = Cancelled Patent
F = Fractional Section
G = Group (Multi-Patentee Patent, see Appendix "C")
V = Overlaps another Parcel
R = Re-Issued (Parcel patented more than once)

Most parcels of land will have only one or two of these items in their "For More Info" columns, but when that is not the case, there is often some valuable information to be gained from further investigation. Below, I will explain what each of these items means to you you as a researcher.

A = Authority
(Legislative Act, See Appendix "A")
All Federal Land Patents were issued because some branch of our government (usually the U.S. Congress) passed a law making such a transfer of title possible. And therefore every patent within these pages will have an "A" item next to it in the index. The number after the "A" indicates which item in Appendix "A" holds the citation to the particular law which authorized the transfer of land to the public. As it stands, most of the Public Land data compiled and released by our government, and which serves as the basis for the patents mapped here, concerns itself with "Cash Sale" homesteads. So in some Counties, the law which authorized cash sales will be the primary, if not the only, entry in the Appendix.

B = Block or Lot (location in Section unknown)
A "B" designation in the Index is a tip-off that the EXACT location of the patent within the map is not apparent from the legal description. This Patent will nonetheless be noted within the proper

Section along with any other Lots purchased in the Section. Given the scope of this project (many states and many Counties are being mapped), trying to locate all relevant plats for Lots (if they even exist) and accurately mapping them would have taken one person several lifetimes. But since our primary goal from the onset has been to establish relationships between neighbors and families, very little is lost to this goal since we can still observe who all lived in which Section.

C = Cancelled Patent

A Cancelled Patent is just that: cancelled. Whether the original Patentee forfeited his or her patent due to fraud, a technicality, non-payment, or whatever, the fact remains that it is significant to know who received patents for what parcels and when. A cancellation may be evidence that the Patentee never physically re-located to the land, but does not in itself prove that point. Further evidence would be required to prove that. *See also*, Re-issued Patents, *below*.

F = Fractional Section

A Fractional Section is one that contains less than 640 acres, almost always because of a body of water. The exact size and shape of land-parcels contained in such sections may not be ascertainable, but we map them nonetheless. Just keep in mind that we are not mapping an actual parcel to scale in such instances. Another point to consider is that we have located some fractional sections that are not so designated by the Bureau of Land Management in their data. This means that not all fractional sections have been so identified in our indexes.

G = Group
(Multi-Patentee Patent, see Appendix "C")

A "G" designation means that the Patent was issued to a GROUP of people (Multi-patentees). The "G" will always be followed by a number. Some such groups were quite large and it was impractical if not impossible to display each individual in our maps without unduly affecting readability. EACH person in the group is named in the Index, but they won't all be found on the Map. You will find the name of the first person in such a Group on the map with the Group number next to it, enclosed in [square brackets].

To find all the members of the Group you can either scan the Index for all people with the same Group Number or you can simply refer to Appendix "C" where all members of the Group are listed next to their number.

O = Overlaps another Parcel

An Overlap is one where PART of a parcel of land gets issued on more than one patent. For genealogical purposes, both transfers of title are important and both Patentees are mapped. If the ENTIRE parcel of land is re-issued, that is what we call it, a Re-Issued Patent (*see below*). The number after the "O" indicates the ID for the overlapping Patent(s) contained within the same Index. Like Re-Issued and Cancelled Patents, Overlaps may cause a map-reader to be confused at first, but for genealogical purposes, all of these parties' relationships to the underlying land is important, and therefore, we map them.

R = Re-Issued (Parcel patented more than once)

The label, "Re-issued Patent" describes Patents which were issued more than once for land with the EXACT SAME LEGAL DESCRIPTION. Whether the original patent was cancelled or not, there were a good many parcels which were patented more than once. The number after the "R" indicates the ID for the other Patent contained within the same Index that was for the same land. A quick glance at the map itself within the relevant Section will be the quickest way to find the other Patentee to whom the Parcel was transferred. They should both be mapped in the same general area.

I have gone to some length describing all sorts of anomalies either in the underlying data or in their representation on the maps and indexes in this book. Most of this will bore the most ardent reseracher, but I do this with all due respect to those researchers who will inevitably (and rightfully) ask: *"Why isn't so-and-so's name on the exact spot that the index says it should be?"*

In most cases it will be due to the existence of a Multi-Patentee Patent, a Re-issued Patent, a Cancelled Patent, or Overlapping Parcels named in separate Patents. I don't pretend that this discussion will answer every question along these lines, but I hope it will at least convince you of the complexity of the subject.

Not to despair, this book's companion web-site will offer a way to further explain "odd-ball" or errant data. Each book (County) will have its own web-page or pages to discuss such situations. You can go to www.arphax.com to find the relevant web-page for Butler County.

Land Patent Map

On the first two-page spread following each Township's Index to Land Patents, you'll find the corresponding Land Patent Map. And here lies the real heart of our work. For the first time anywhere, researchers will be able to observe and analyze, on a grand scale, most of the original land-owners for an area AND see them mapped in proximity to each one another.

We encourage you to make vigorous use of the accompanying Index described above, but then later, to abandon it, and just stare at these maps for a while. This is a great way to catch misspellings or to find collateral kin you'd not known were in the area.

Each Land Patent Map represents one Congressional Township containing approximately 36-square miles. Each of these square miles is labeled by an accompanying Section Number (1 through 36, in most cases). Keep in mind, that this book concerns itself solely with Butler County's patents. Townships which creep into one or more other counties will not be shown in their entirety in any one book. You will need to consult other books, as they become available, in order to view other countys' patents, cities, cemeteries, etc.

But getting back to Butler County: each Land Patent Map contains a Statistical Chart that looks like the following:

Township Statistics

Parcels Mapped	:	173
Number of Patents	:	163
Number of Individuals	:	152
Patentees Identified	:	151
Number of Surnames	:	137
Multi-Patentee Parcels	:	4
Oldest Patent Date	:	11/27/1820
Most Recent Patent	:	9/28/1917
Block/Lot Parcels	:	0
Parcels Re-Issued	:	3
Parcels that Overlap	:	8
Cities and Towns	:	6
Cemeteries	:	6

This information may be of more use to a social statistician or historian than a genealogist, but I think all three will find it interesting.

Most of the statistics are self-explanatory, and what is not, was described in the above discussion of the Index's Legend, but I do want to mention a few of them that may affect your understanding of the Land Patent Maps.

First of all, Patents often contain more than one Parcel of land, so it is common for there to be more Parcels than Patents. Also, the Number of Individuals will more often than not, not match the number of Patentees. A Patentee is literally the person or PERSONS named in a patent. So, a Patent may have a multi-person Patentee or a single-person patentee. Nonetheless, we account for all these individuals in our indexes.

On the lower-righthand side of the Patent Map is a Legend which describes various features in the map, including Section Boundaries, Patent (land) Boundaries, Lots (numbered), and Multi-Patentee Group Numbers. You'll also find a "Helpful Hints" Box that will assist you.

One important note: though the vast majority of Patents mapped in this series will prove to be reasonably accurate representations of their actual locations, we cannot claim this for patents lying along state and county lines, or waterways, or that have been platted (lots).

Shifting boundaries and sparse legal descriptions in the GLO data make this a reality that we have nonetheless tried to overcome by estimating these patents' locations the best that we can.

Road Map

On the two-page spread following each Patent Map you will find a Road Map covering the exact same area (the same Congressional Township).

For me, fully exploring the past means that every once in a while I must leave the library and travel to the actual locations where my ancestors once walked and worked the land. Our Township Road Maps are a great place to begin such a quest.

Keep in mind that the scaling and proportion of these maps was chosen in order to squeeze hundreds of people-names, road-names, and place-names into tinier spaces than you would traditionally see. These are not professional road-maps, and like any secondary genealogical source, should be looked upon as an entry-way to original sources— in this case, original patents and applications, professionally produced maps and surveys, etc.

Both our Road Maps and Historical Maps contain cemeteries and city-centers, along with a listing of these on the left-hand side of the map. I should note that I am showing you city center-points, rather than city-limit boundaries, because in many instances, this will represent a place where settlement began. This may be a good time to mention that many cemeteries are located on private property, Always check with a local historical or genealogical society to see if a particular cemetery is publicly accessible (if it is not obviously so). As a final point, look for your surnames among the road-names. You will often be surprised by what you find.

Historical Map

The third and final map in each Map Group is our attempt to display what each Township might have looked like before the advent of modern roads. In frontier times, people were usually more determined to settle near rivers and creeks than they were near roads, which were often few and far between. As was the case with the Road Map, we've included the same cemeteries and city-centers. We've also included railroads, many of which came along before most roads.

While some may claim "Historical Map" to be a bit of a misnomer for this tool, we settled for this label simply because it was almost as accurate as saying "Railroads, Lakes, Rivers, Cities, and Cemeteries," and it is much easier to remember.

In Closing . . .

By way of example, here is *A Really Good Way to Use a Township Map Group.* First, find the person you are researching in the Township's Index to Land Patents, which will direct you to the proper Section and parcel on the Patent Map. But before leaving the Index, scan all the patents within it, looking for other names of interest. Now, turn to the Patent Map and locate your parcels of land. Pay special attention to the names of patent-holders who own land surrounding your person of interest. Next, turn the page and look at the same Section(s) on the Road Map. Note which roads are closest to your parcels and also the names of nearby towns and cemeteries. Using other resources, you may be able to learn of kin who have been buried here, plus, you may choose to visit these cemeteries the next time you are in the area.

Finally, turn to the Historical Map. Look once more at the same Sections where you found your research subject's land. Note the nearby streams, creeks, and other geographical features. You may be surprised to find family names were used to name them, or you may see a name you haven't heard mentioned in years and years—and a new research possibility is born.

Many more techniques for using these *Family Maps* volumes will no doubt be discovered. If from time to time, you will navigate to Butler County's web-page at www.arphax.com (use the "Research" link), you can learn new tricks as they become known (or you can share ones you have employed). But for now, you are ready to get started. So, go, and good luck.

– Part I –

The Big Picture

Map A - Where Butler County, Alabama Lies Within the State

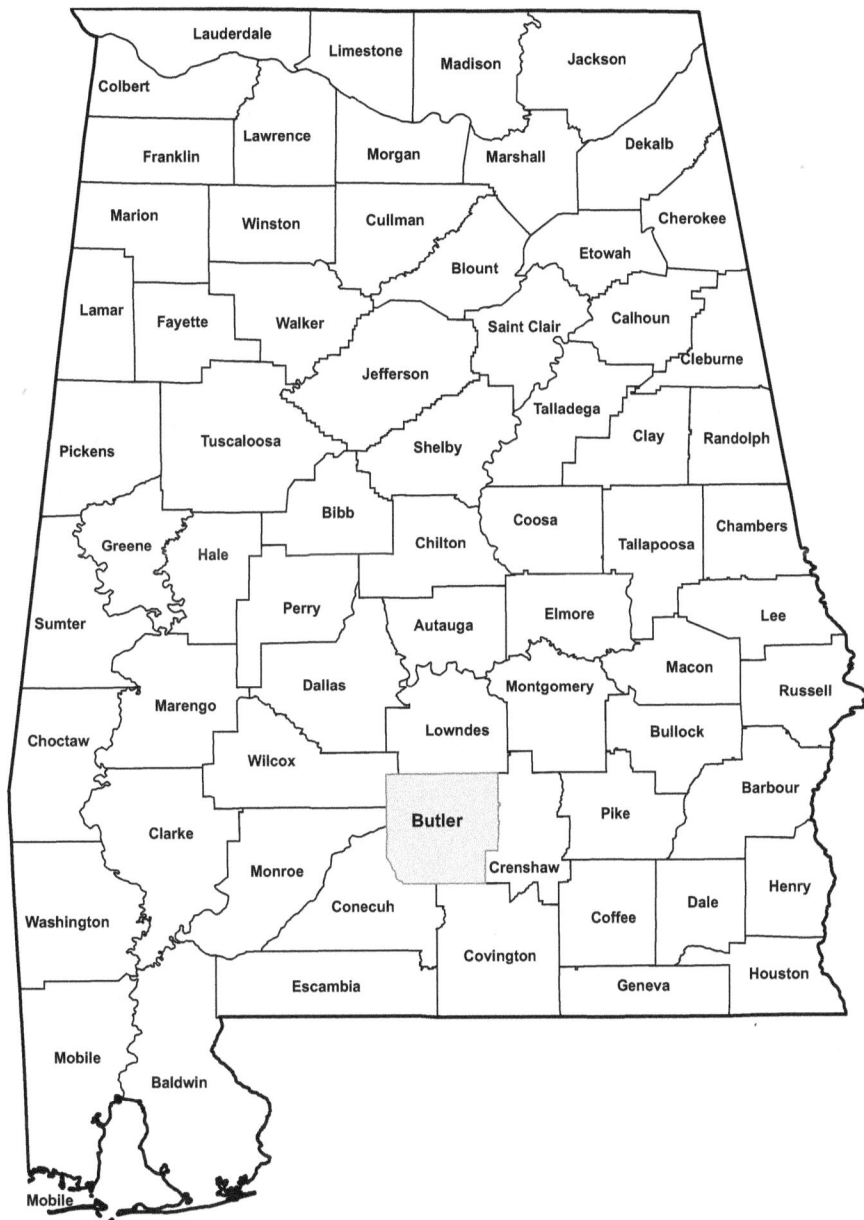

Legend

━━━━━ State Boundary

───── County Boundaries

▢ Butler County, Alabama

Helpful Hints

1 We start with Map "A" which simply shows us where within the State this county lies.

2 Map "B" zooms in further to help us more easily identify surrounding Counties.

3 Map "C" zooms in even further to reveal the Congressional Townships that either lie within or intersect Butler County.

Map B - Butler County, Alabama and Surrounding Counties

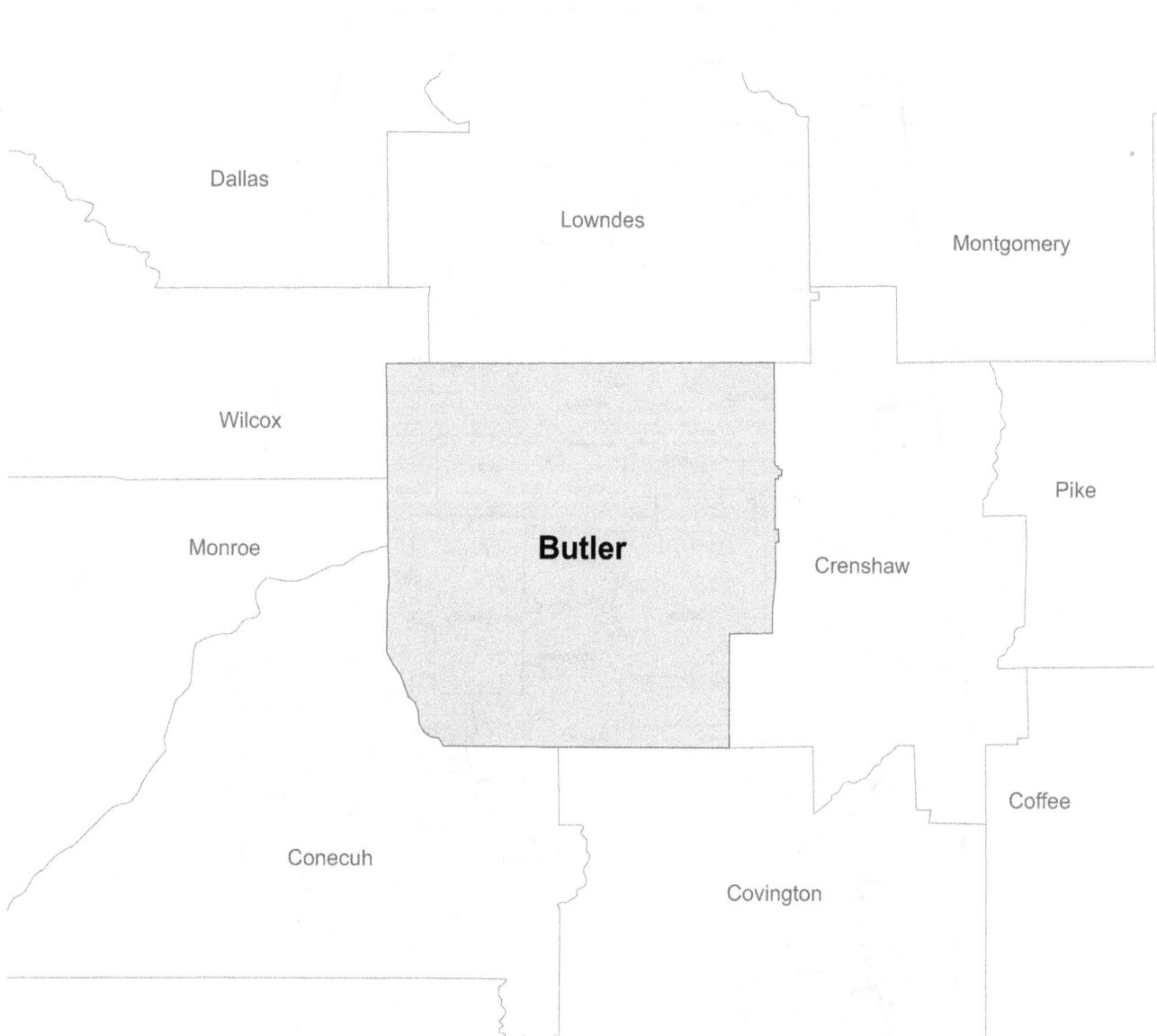

Dallas

Lowndes

Montgomery

Wilcox

Pike

Monroe

Butler

Crenshaw

Coffee

Conecuh

Covington

——— Legend ———

State Boundaries (when applicable)

County Boundary

——— Helpful Hints ———

1 Many Patent-holders and their families settled across county lines. It is always a good idea to check nearby counties for your families.

2 Refer to Map "A" to see a broader view of where this County lies within the State, and Map "C" to see which Congressional Townships lie within Butler County.

Map C - Congressional Townships of Butler County, Alabama

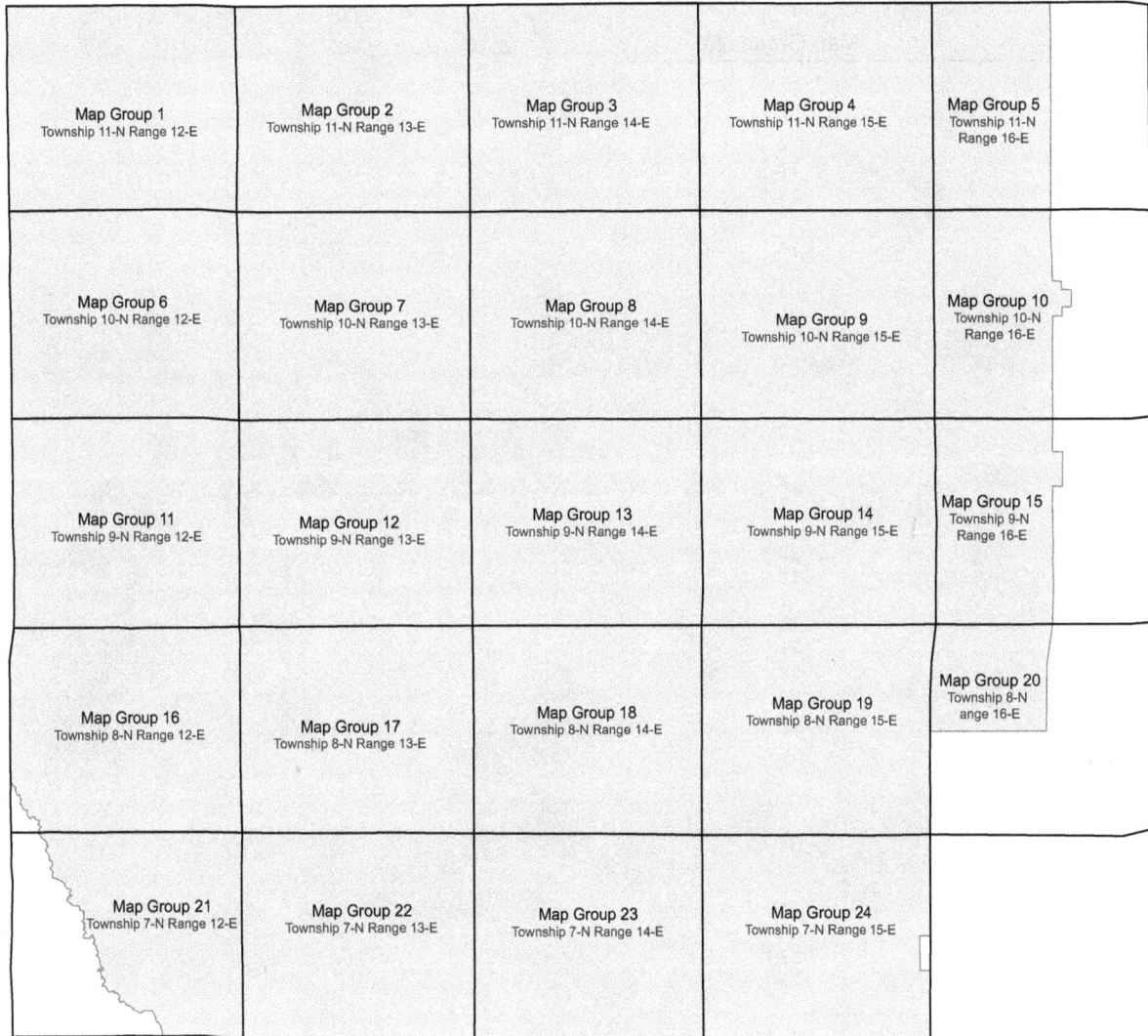

Map Group 1 Township 11-N Range 12-E	Map Group 2 Township 11-N Range 13-E	Map Group 3 Township 11-N Range 14-E	Map Group 4 Township 11-N Range 15-E	Map Group 5 Township 11-N Range 16-E
Map Group 6 Township 10-N Range 12-E	Map Group 7 Township 10-N Range 13-E	Map Group 8 Township 10-N Range 14-E	Map Group 9 Township 10-N Range 15-E	Map Group 10 Township 10-N Range 16-E
Map Group 11 Township 9-N Range 12-E	Map Group 12 Township 9-N Range 13-E	Map Group 13 Township 9-N Range 14-E	Map Group 14 Township 9-N Range 15-E	Map Group 15 Township 9-N Range 16-E
Map Group 16 Township 8-N Range 12-E	Map Group 17 Township 8-N Range 13-E	Map Group 18 Township 8-N Range 14-E	Map Group 19 Township 8-N Range 15-E	Map Group 20 Township 8-N ange 16-E
Map Group 21 Township 7-N Range 12-E	Map Group 22 Township 7-N Range 13-E	Map Group 23 Township 7-N Range 14-E	Map Group 24 Township 7-N Range 15-E	

——— Legend ———

Butler County, Alabama

Congressional Townships

Copyright © 2006 Boyd IT, Inc. All Rights Reserved

——— Helpful Hints ———

1 Many Patent-holders and their families settled across county lines. It is always a good idea to check nearby counties for your families (See Map "B").

2 Refer to Map "A" to see a broader view of where this county lies within the State, and Map "B" for a view of the counties surrounding Butler County.

Map D Index: Cities & Towns of Butler County, Alabama

The following represents the Cities and Towns of Butler County, along with the corresponding Map Group in which each is found. Cities and Towns are displayed in both the Road and Historical maps in the Group.

City/Town	Map Group No.
Avant	18
Beacon	11
Bolling	12
Brushy Creek	18
Butler Springs	6
Chapman	17
Daisy	5
East Chapman	18
Forest Home	6
Fort Dale	3
Garland	21
Georgiana	17
Glasgow	14
Grace	16
Greenville	8
Halso Mill	14
Industry	23
Liberty	8
Manningham	2
Mashville	9
McKenzie	22
Midway	10
Monterey	1
Mount Moriah	1
Mount Olive	21
Oaky Streak	24
Odom Crossroads	22
Pigeon Creek	19
Providence	11
Reddock Springs	8
Rhodes	23
Ridgeville	1
Salter	22
Sand Cut	12
Sardis	19
Saucer	6
Searcy	3
Shacklesville	11
Shell	23
Spring Hill	9
Starlington	16
Wald	13

Map D - Cities & Towns of Butler County, Alabama

Map Group 1 Township 11-N Range 12-E ● Ridgeville ● Mount Moriah ● Monterey	**Map Group 2** Township 11-N Range 13-E ● Manningham	**Map Group 3** Township 11-N Range 14-E Searcy ● ● Fort Dale	**Map Group 4** Township 11-N Range 15-E	**Map Group 5** Township 11-N Range 16-E ● Daisy
Forest Home ● **Map Group 6** Township 10-N Range 12-E ● Saucer ● Butler Springs	**Map Group 7** Township 10-N Range 13-E	**Map Group 8** Township 10-N Range 14-E ● Liberty Greenville ● ● Reddock Springs	● Spring Hill **Map Group 9** Township 10-N Range 15-E ● Mashville	**Map Group 10** Township 10-N Range 16-E Midway ●
Shacklesville ● **Map Group 11** Township 9-N Range 12-E Providence ● Beacon ●	Sand Cut ● **Map Group 12** Township 9-N Range 13-E Bolling ●	● Wald **Map Group 13** Township 9-N Range 14-E	Glasgow ● **Map Group 14** Township 9-N Range 15-E Halso Mill ●	**Map Group 15** Township 9-N Range 16-E
Starlington ● **Map Group 16** Township 8-N Range 12-E Grace ●	Chapman ● **Map Group 17** Township 8-N Range 13-E ● Georgiana	● Brushy Creek ● East Chapman **Map Group 18** Township 8-N Range 14-E ● Avant	Sardis ● Pigeon Creek ● **Map Group 19** Township 8-N Range 15-E	**Map Group 20** Township 8-N Range 16-E
Map Group 21 Township 7-N Range 12-E ● Mount Olive Garland ●	**Map Group 22** Township 7-N Range 13-E ● Salter ● Odom Crossroads McKenzie ●	Shell ● Industry ● ● Rhodes **Map Group 23** Township 7-N Range 14-E	● Oaky Streak **Map Group 24** Township 7-N Range 15-E	

——— Legend ———

▢ Butler County, Alabama

▢ Congressional Townships

——— Helpful Hints ———

1 Cities and towns are marked only at their center-points as published by the USGS and/or NationalAtlas.gov. This often enables us to more closely approximate where these might have existed when first settled.

2 To see more specifically where these Cities & Towns are located within the county, refer to both the Road and Historical maps in the Map-Group referred to above. See also, the Map "D" Index on the opposite page.

Map E Index: Cemeteries of Butler County, Alabama

The following represents many of the Cemeteries of Butler County, along with the corresponding Township Map Group in which each is found. Cemeteries are displayed in both the Road and Historical maps in the Map Groups referred to below.

Cemetery	Map Group No.	Cemetery	Map Group No.
Andress Cem.	9	Pressley Cem.	21
Antioch East Cem.	4	Rhodes Cem.	14
Antioch West Cem.	12	Riley Cem.	23
Bedgood Cem.	15	Saint Paul Cem.	9
Bethel Cem.	5	Sardis Cem.	19
Bragg Cem.	2	Sellers Cem.	22
Brushy Creek Cem.	18	Shacklesville Cem.	11
Butler Cem.	15	Shiloh Cem.	2
Butler Springs Cem.	6	Shiloh Cem.	19
Consolation Cem.	24	South Butler Cem.	22
Crenshaws Cem.	2	Spring Creek Cem.	5
Damascus Cem.	10	Springhill Cem.	4
Ebenezer Cem.	9	Stamps Cem.	16
Ebenezer Cem.	17	Sunrise Cem.	8
Ebenezer Cem.	19	Thompson Cem.	1
Elizabeth Cem.	22	Union Cem.	18
Forest Home Cem.	6	Watts Cem.	6
Fort Dale Cem.	3	Wesley Chapel Cem.	18
Friendship Cem.	17	William Seale Cem.	8
Garland Cem.	21	Wren Cem.	15
Giddens Chapel Cem.	8		
Gravel Hill Cem.	13		
Harrison Cem.	9		
Hartley Cem.	8		
Hickory Grove Cem.	7		
Hopewell Cem.	18		
Howard Cem.	15		
Kilgore Cem.	3		
King Cem.	5		
Liberty Cem.	8		
Macedonia Cem.	23		
Magnolia Cem.	8		
Manningham Cem.	2		
Maye Cem.	21		
McClure Cem.	22		
Miller Cem.	17		
Monterey Cem.	1		
Moriah Cem.	4		
Mount Carmel Cem.	14		
Mount Moriah Cem.	1		
Mount Olive Cem.	9		
Mount Olive East Cem.	14		
Mount Olive West Cem.	21		
Mount Pisgah Cem.	11		
Mount Pleasant Cem.	18		
Mount Zion Cem.	9		
New Prospect Cem.	19		
Oak Bowery Cem.	5		
Oak Grove Cem.	17		
Oakwood Cem.	17		
Oaky Streak Cem.	24		
Old Bethel Cem.	16		
Old Shiloh Cem.	2		
Perdue Cem.	5		
Pine Flat Cem.	6		
Pine Top Cem.	3		
Pioneer Cem.	8		
Pleasant Hill Cem.	22		
Pleasant Home Cem.	7		

Map E - Cemeteries of Butler County, Alabama

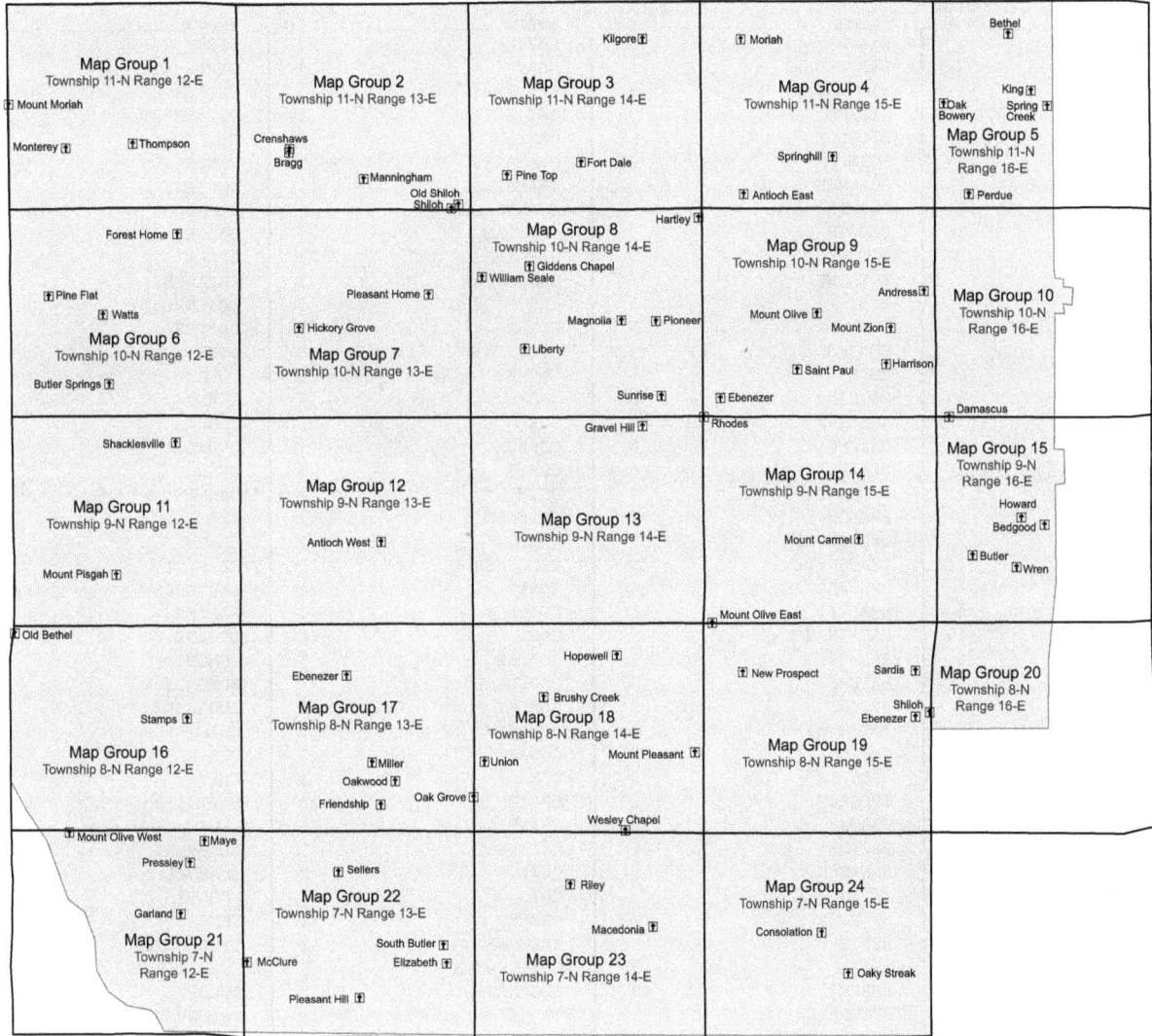

Map Group 1
Township 11-N Range 12-E

⊞ Mount Moriah

Monterey ⊞   ⊞ Thompson

Map Group 2
Township 11-N Range 13-E

Crenshaws ⊞
Bragg
⊞ Manningham
Old Shiloh ⊞
Shiloh ⊞

Map Group 3
Township 11-N Range 14-E

Kilgore ⊞

⊞ Fort Dale
⊞ Pine Top

Map Group 4
Township 11-N Range 15-E

⊞ Moriah

Springhill ⊞

⊞ Antioch East

Bethel ⊞

King ⊞
⊞ Oak   Spring ⊞
Bowery   Creek

Map Group 5
Township 11-N
Range 16-E

⊞ Perdue

Map Group 6
Township 10-N Range 12-E

Forest Home ⊞

⊞ Pine Flat
⊞ Watts

Butler Springs ⊞

Map Group 7
Township 10-N Range 13-E

Pleasant Home ⊞

⊞ Hickory Grove

Map Group 8
Township 10-N Range 14-E

Hartley ⊞
⊞ Giddens Chapel
⊞ William Seale

Magnolia ⊞   ⊞ Pioneer

⊞ Liberty

Sunrise ⊞

Map Group 9
Township 10-N Range 15-E

Andress ⊞

Mount Olive ⊞
Mount Zion ⊞

⊞ Saint Paul   ⊞ Harrison

⊞ Ebenezer

Map Group 10
Township 10-N
Range 16-E

Damascus ⊞

Map Group 11
Township 9-N Range 12-E

Shacklesville ⊞

Mount Pisgah ⊞

Map Group 12
Township 9-N Range 13-E

Antioch West ⊞

Map Group 13
Township 9-N Range 14-E

Gravel Hill ⊞

Map Group 14
Township 9-N Range 15-E

Rhodes ⊞

Mount Carmel ⊞

Mount Olive East ⊞

Map Group 15
Township 9-N
Range 16-E

Howard
⊞
Bedgood

⊞ Butler
⊞ Wren

Map Group 16
Township 8-N Range 12-E

⊞ Old Bethel

Stamps ⊞

Map Group 17
Township 8-N Range 13-E

Ebenezer ⊞

⊞ Miller
Oakwood ⊞
Friendship ⊞   Oak Grove ⊞

Map Group 18
Township 8-N Range 14-E

Hopewell ⊞

⊞ Brushy Creek

⊞ Union   Mount Pleasant ⊞

Wesley Chapel ⊞

Map Group 19
Township 8-N Range 15-E

⊞ New Prospect   Sardis ⊞

Shiloh ⊞
Ebenezer ⊞

Map Group 20
Township 8-N
Range 16-E

Map Group 21
Township 7-N
Range 12-E

⊞ Mount Olive West   ⊞ Maye
Pressley ⊞

Garland ⊞

Map Group 22
Township 7-N Range 13-E

⊞ Sellers

South Butler ⊞
⊞ McClure   Elizabeth ⊞

Pleasant Hill ⊞

Map Group 23
Township 7-N Range 14-E

⊞ Riley

Macedonia ⊞

Map Group 24
Township 7-N Range 15-E

Consolation ⊞

⊞ Oaky Streak

— Legend —

▭ Butler County, Alabama

▭ Congressional Townships

— Helpful Hints —

1 Cemeteries are marked at locations as published by the USGS and/or NationalAtlas.gov.

2 To see more specifically where these Cemeteries are located, refer to the Road & Historical maps in the Map-Group referred to above. See also, the Map "E" Index on the opposite page to make sure you don't miss any of the Cemeteries located within this Congressional township.

Surnames in Butler County, Alabama Patents

The following list represents the surnames that we have located in Butler County, Alabama Patents and the number of parcels that we have mapped for each one. Here is a quick way to determine the existence (or not) of Patents to be found in the subsequent indexes and maps of this volume.

Surname	# of Land Parcels	Surname	# of Land Parcels	Surname	# of Land Parcels	Surname	# of Land Parcels
ABNEY	1	BLAIR	9	CARTER	27	DERNING	1
ACREE	2	BLANKENSHIP	2	CARY	4	DEWBERRY	3
ADAMS	5	BLOCKSOM	1	CASSIDY	1	DICKEN	5
AINESWORTH	1	BLOXOM	2	CATES	1	DICKERSON	2
AINSWORTH	5	BLOXSOM	1	CATLIN	18	DICKSON	1
ALBRITTON	2	BOAN	2	CHAMBERS	1	DIXON	5
ALDAY	7	BOATMUN	3	CHAMBLISS	12	DORIETY	1
ALLEN	16	BOGGAN	20	CHANCELLOR	12	DOUGLASS	1
AMASON	3	BOGGIN	2	CHATHAM	4	DOZIER	6
AMBROSE	3	BOGGUS	3	CHEATHAM	27	DRAKE	7
AMOS	1	BOLLING	37	CHRISTIAN	1	DREADEN	1
ANDERS	1	BOND	1	CHRISTOPHER	1	DRISKELL	3
ANDRESS	12	BONNER	5	CLARK	5	DRIVER	2
ANDREWS	2	BOWDEN	1	CLOPTON	11	DUCK	6
ANSLEY	1	BOWEN	5	CLUTE	5	DUKE	14
ANTONY	5	BOYKIN	2	CODY	2	DUKES	1
ARANT	11	BOZEMAN	3	COE	2	DUNHAM	1
ARDIS	6	BRADEN	8	COHRON	1	DUNKLIN	2
ARMSTRONG	8	BRADLEY	4	COKER	6	DUNN	1
ARNOLD	1	BRAGG	4	COLE	2	DUNNAM	2
ARRINGTON	3	BRANCH	2	COLEMAN	41	DYESS	2
ASHCRAFT	2	BRANSFORD	9	COLLEY	3	EALUM	4
ATKINSON	4	BRASSWELL	5	COLLINS	21	EARNEST	2
AUSTIN	4	BRASWELL	1	CONE	24	EASTERLING	1
BABCOCK	1	BRAZZIL	1	CONOLEY	1	EASTERS	1
BAGGAN	1	BREITHAUPT	3	COOK	25	EDDINS	2
BAILEY	6	BREWER	17	COOPER	5	EDMONDS	1
BAKER	1	BRIERS	2	COPELAND	1	EDMONDSON	2
BALDERREE	5	BRIGHT	2	CORLEY	1	EDWARDS	7
BALDWIN	2	BRIGHTWELL	1	COULSON	1	ELAM	2
BALLARD	6	BRILEY	3	COWART	2	ELDER	5
BANISTER	6	BROGDEN	3	COX	3	ELEY	2
BARGANIEL	1	BROGDON	1	CRAIG	23	ELLINGTON	1
BARGANIER	4	BROOK	2	CRANE	6	ELLIS	12
BARGE	2	BROOKS	36	CRAVEY	1	ELSBERRY	2
BARLOW	2	BROWDER	1	CREECH	2	EMANUEL	1
BARNES	5	BROWN	23	CREG	1	ENGLISH	2
BARRETT	28	BROXSON	2	CREMER	4	ERNEST	12
BARRINGTON	1	BRUCE	1	CRENSHAW	13	ETHEREDGE	9
BARRON	2	BRYAN	13	CRITTENDEN	1	ETHEREGE	2
BASS	1	BRYANT	4	CROCHERON	2	EVANS	7
BATES	1	BUCKELLEW	2	CROCKER	4	EWING	3
BAXLEY	2	BUFFINGTON	2	CROSBY	1	EXUM	7
BAYZIER	1	BURKE	4	CROSS	5	FAIL	42
BEASLEY	6	BURKET	14	CRUM	7	FAILES	3
BECK	4	BURKETT	50	CUNNINGHAM	1	FAILS	13
BECKWORTH	1	BURNETT	10	CURRY	3	FAIN	1
BEDGOOD	1	BURNS	10	DAILEY	1	FARROW	1
BEESLEY	5	BUSH	8	DANIEL	6	FEAGIN	5
BELL	17	BUTLER	23	DARBY	2	FELPS	3
BENDER	1	BUTTS	1	DAVENPORT	18	FERGUSON	19
BENNETT	35	BYRD	2	DAVIDSON	13	FERRELL	2
BENSON	8	CALDWELL	9	DAVIS	23	FIFE	8
BERRY	2	CALLAWAY	3	DAWSON	3	FINDLEY	2
BEVERLY	11	CALLEN	2	DAY	2	FINKLEA	7
BILBERRY	2	CALLIN	2	DEAN	6	FINKLEY	3
BILLINGSLEA	27	CAMP	10	DEASE	4	FLINN	4
BINION	10	CAMPBELL	13	DEEN	16	FLORENCE	3
BISHOP	7	CANTELOO	1	DEES	6	FLOWERS	7
BLACK	27	CARDWELL	1	DEMING	23	FORREST	3
BLACKMAN	9	CARPENTER	3	DENDY	15	FORTUNE	1
BLACKMON	11	CARR	1	DENNIS	1	FOWLER	4

Surname	# of Land Parcels	Surname	# of Land Parcels	Surname	# of Land Parcels	Surname	# of Land Parcels
FOX	5	GWYNN	1	HOLMES	2	LITTLE	13
FRANKLIN	8	HAIGLAR	1	HOMES	4	LIVINGSTON	3
FREEMAN	5	HALIDA	1	HOOD	9	LOGAN	1
FRIDDLE	4	HALL	17	HOPKINS	1	LONG	14
FROST	4	HALLFORD	3	HORN	1	LONTZ	1
FULLER	17	HALLIDAY	1	HORTMAN	4	LOURY	2
FUNDERBURKE	1	HALSO	9	HORTON	1	LOVETT	3
FURGUSON	1	HAM	1	HOWARD	6	LOWERY	1
FUTCH	1	HAMBLETON	3	HOWEL	5	LUCKIE	2
GAFFNEY	4	HAMMETT	2	HOWELL	5	LUDLAM	1
GAFFORD	37	HAMMONDS	18	HUDSON	12	LYNCH	1
GALLAWAY	6	HAMMONS	2	HUGGINS	2	MAHONE	6
GALLOPS	4	HAMN	2	HUGHES	3	MAJORS	7
GALLOWAY	2	HAMPTON	1	HUGHS	13	MANNING	18
GANDY	24	HANDY	1	HUGULEY	8	MARCHANT	1
GANEY	1	HANSON	1	HUMPHREY	1	MARKS	1
GANUS	1	HARALSON	7	HUMPHREYS	1	MARSHALL	16
GARDNER	4	HARBIN	5	HUNTER	1	MARTIN	21
GAREY	3	HARDEE	3	HUSON	13	MASSINGILL	3
GARNER	13	HARDY	2	HUTCHINSON	5	MATHENY	4
GARRETT	10	HARE	2	INGRAM	8	MATHEWS	9
GARRITT	1	HARPER	9	JACKSON	20	MAXCEY	1
GARUM	1	HARRELL	1	JAMES	3	MAXEY	2
GARY	1	HARRISON	45	JAY	25	MAY	11
GASTON	3	HART	5	JEFFERS	3	MCALLISTER	2
GAY	1	HARTLEY	35	JERNIGAN	12	MCBRIDE	7
GAYLE	1	HARVEY	1	JOHNSON	25	MCCALL	5
GENTRY	1	HASE	1	JOHNSTON	4	MCCANN	3
GERRELL	1	HASSEY	3	JOINER	2	MCCLARTY	1
GHOLSON	8	HASTING	2	JOLLIFF	1	MCCLOUD	1
GIBBS	1	HATCHER	7	JONES	56	MCCLURE	13
GIBSON	35	HAWKINS	12	JORDAN	1	MCCONDICHIE	2
GIDDENS	3	HAWTHORN	1	JOSEY	7	MCCORMACK	12
GIDDINGS	2	HAYES	3	JOYNER	2	MCCORMICK	12
GILBERT	10	HAYNIE	4	JUDGE	1	MCCOY	27
GILL	4	HAYS	9	KEEBLER	6	MCCREELESS	1
GILLIAM	1	HEAP	3	KEITH	16	MCCRORY	20
GILLION	7	HEAPE	2	KELLEY	2	MCCULLOUGH	2
GILMER	1	HEATHCOCK	1	KELLY	1	MCCURRY	2
GILMON	2	HEATON	7	KELSOE	3	MCDANIEL	8
GILMORE	7	HECKS	1	KEMP	1	MCDONALD	2
GINGLES	1	HEMPHILL	1	KENDALL	3	MCDUFEE	1
GLASS	11	HENDERSON	18	KENDRICK	2	MCFARLAND	6
GLASSGOW	1	HENDRICKS	1	KENDRICKE	1	MCINEER	1
GLENN	5	HENDRIX	2	KENNEDY	2	MCKEE	3
GLOVER	2	HENRY	2	KENNINGTON	2	MCKEITHEN	1
GODWIN	1	HERBERT	20	KETLER	7	MCKENZIE	9
GOLDSTON	2	HERELONG	1	KETTLER	6	MCKINZIE	12
GONDER	6	HERIN	1	KILLOUGH	3	MCLAIN	6
GOODELL	4	HERINDON	2	KING	6	MCLEAN	1
GOODWIN	1	HERLONG	6	KINSEY	6	MCLEMORE	2
GORUM	2	HERNDON	1	KIRKLAND	1	MCLEOD	6
GOSS	1	HESTER	2	KIRKPATRICK	21	MCMULLEN	1
GRACE	3	HICKMAN	1	KIRVIN	2	MCMULLINS	2
GRAHAM	4	HICKS	1	KITCHENS	1	MCNEILL	10
GRANT	5	HILBUN	19	KITE	10	MCPHERSON	23
GRASON	2	HILL	12	KNOWLES	4	MCPOLLARD	1
GRAVES	3	HILLSON	2	KOLB	3	MCQUEEN	4
GRAY	10	HILSON	5	KORNEGAY	4	MCWHORTER	1
GRAYDON	1	HINSON	10	KUYKENDAL	1	MCWILLIAMS	3
GRAYSON	3	HINTON	1	KUYKENDALL	2	MEALING	7
GREEN	14	HOBBS	9	LANCASTER	1	MENEES	6
GREENE	1	HOBBY	1	LANE	14	MERCER	23
GREGG	2	HODGES	2	LARKINS	3	MERCHANT	1
GREGORY	9	HOLAWAY	1	LE FLORE	2	MIDDLEBROOKS	1
GRIFFIN	5	HOLCOMBE	3	LEE	65	MILLER	12
GRIFFITH	6	HOLDSTON	1	LEONARD	5	MILLS	4
GRIGERS	1	HOLLADAY	6	LEVINGSTON	1	MILNER	51
GRIGGS	2	HOLLIS	1	LEWIS	26	MILTON	3
GRISWOLD	1	HOLLOWAY	3	LILES	6	MIMS	2

Surname	# of Land Parcels	Surname	# of Land Parcels	Surname	# of Land Parcels	Surname	# of Land Parcels
MINIARD	4	PEARMAN	1	RIGSBY	2	SPURLOCK	1
MINTER	1	PEARMON	1	RILEY	16	STAGGERS	13
MINYARD	1	PEARSON	2	ROACH	4	STALLINGS	23
MITCHELL	5	PEARY	2	ROAD	1	STAMPS	2
MIXON	1	PEAVY	14	ROBERSON	6	STANFORD	3
MONTGOMERY	4	PEEVY	11	ROBERTS	6	STANLEY	1
MOORE	33	PERDUE	15	ROBINSON	4	STEANE	1
MOORER	1	PERRITT	15	ROBISON	1	STEINER	2
MOORMAN	5	PERRY	34	ROGERS	21	STEPHENS	1
MORAN	1	PETERGRO	1	ROPER	2	STEVENS	2
MORGAN	26	PETERSON	1	ROSE	6	STEWARD	3
MORRELL	2	PETTY	1	ROSS	2	STEWART	16
MORRIS	4	PEVEY	1	ROUTON	13	STILL	2
MORROW	8	PEVY	2	RUFFIN	1	STINER	1
MOSELEY	9	PHELPS	25	RUGELEY	2	STINSON	25
MOSLEY	2	PHILIPS	2	RUMPH	1	STOCKMAN	7
MOY	1	PHILLIPS	10	RUSHTON	4	STOTT	12
MULLANS	1	PICKENS	16	RUSTIN	2	STRINGER	10
MULLENS	2	PIERCE	3	RYALS	3	STRINGFELLOW	7
MUNCHUS	1	PIGGOT	3	SALTER	4	STUART	6
MUNDY	1	PINGLETON	2	SANDERS	5	STUCKEY	1
MURPHEY	7	PINKERTON	5	SANFORD	7	SULLIVAN	1
MURPHY	11	PIPKIN	3	SARTAIN	1	SWEETEN	1
MURRAY	1	PIRKINS	2	SARTOR	9	TALLENT	2
MURRY	1	PITTS	7	SAUCER	7	TALLEY	23
MURSER	4	PLAYER	1	SAUNDERS	1	TALLY	2
MYERS	6	POLLARD	10	SAVAGE	4	TANKERSLEY	2
MYRES	1	POOL	3	SCARBOROUGH	4	TARVER	4
MYRICK	4	POOLE	4	SCIPPER	3	TATE	2
NEAL	6	PORTER	9	SCONYERS	1	TATOM	3
NELSON	1	PORTERFIELD	1	SEAL	4	TAYLOR	25
NEVILLS	1	POSEY	3	SEALE	25	TEAGLER	2
NEWTON	33	POWELL	33	SEARCY	1	TERRELL	1
NICHOLAS	1	POWERS	3	SEEGAR	5	TERRY	7
NICHOLES	1	PRESLAR	19	SELLARS	1	THAGARD	1
NICHOLS	7	PRESLEY	18	SELLERS	11	THIGPEN	11
NIGHT	2	PRESSLAR	2	SENTELL	4	THIGPIN	2
NIX	5	PRESSLEY	1	SEXTON	2	THOMAS	78
NORMAN	2	PREWETT	1	SHAROCK	6	THOMASON	2
NORRIS	12	PRICE	5	SHAW	6	THOMPSON	64
NORSWORTHY	1	PRUETT	6	SHELL	1	THORINGTON	1
NORTHCUT	4	PRUITT	3	SHEPARD	4	THORNTON	13
NORTHCUTT	1	PUGH	18	SHEPHEARD	1	TIGNER	1
ODOM	12	PULASKI	2	SHEPHERD	18	TILL	2
OFARRELL	3	PURDY	3	SHEPPARD	15	TILLERY	23
OLIVER	14	PURVIS	6	SHIELDS	2	TILLMAN	1
OPRY	1	QUARLES	3	SHINE	18	TILMAN	3
OTT	1	QUINNELLY	4	SHIPP	1	TILMON	4
OUTLAW	3	RABOURN	1	SHOWS	1	TINSLEY	6
OVERSTREET	1	RABUN	11	SHULTZ	2	TIPTON	3
OWEN	1	RABURN	15	SIMMONS	4	TISDALE	1
OWENS	4	RAINEE	1	SIMPSON	6	TOBIAS	1
PACKER	3	RAINER	1	SIMS	46	TOLIN	1
PAGE	17	RAINEY	1	SINGLETARY	3	TORRENCE	2
PALMER	2	RAINS	1	SINGLETON	3	TRAMMEL	4
PARK	1	RAY	4	SIRMON	11	TRAMMELL	2
PARKER	45	RAYBORNE	1	SKINNER	10	TRAWEEK	20
PARKES	10	REAVES	3	SKIPPER	4	TROWELL	1
PARKS	9	REDDOCH	4	SLATER	1	TURNER	16
PARMER	31	REDDOCK	17	SLATON	3	TYNER	7
PARRISH	1	REEVES	3	SMALLWOOD	1	TYNES	7
PARROTT	1	REID	29	SMITH	110	VANN	1
PATTERSON	3	REMLEY	1	SMYTH	49	VARNER	3
PATTILLO	8	REYNOLDS	9	SMYTHE	1	VEAZEY	6
PATTON	12	RHAME	3	SNELGROVE	3	VICKREY	7
PAUL	1	RHOADS	2	SOLOMON	2	VICKRY	3
PAYNE	23	RHODES	62	SORCER	1	VINES	4
PEACOCK	8	RICHARDS	1	SORELL	1	WADE	15
PEAGLER	13	RICHARDSON	4	SORRELLS	4	WADKINS	1
PEARCE	6	RIDDOCK	1	SPEARS	3	WALKER	9

Surname	# of Land Parcels
WALL	6
WALLACE	9
WALLER	9
WALLS	1
WALTERS	3
WARD	20
WARDEN	3
WARE	2
WARREN	3
WASDEN	1
WASDIN	2
WATERS	13
WATSON	13
WATTS	23
WEAVER	3
WEBB	2
WELCH	1
WELLS	3
WEST	8
WHEELER	4
WHIDDON	5
WHITE	7
WHITHERINGTON	1
WHITTED	1
WHITTEN	3
WHITTINGTON	4
WHITTON	1
WIGGINS	6
WIGHT	3
WILKERSON	17
WILLIAMS	45
WILLIAMSON	7
WILLSON	2
WILSON	14
WINBRAY	6
WINDHAM	5
WITHERINGTON	1
WOMACK	30
WOOD	4
WOODS	2
WOODSON	7
WORRELL	6
WREN	6
WRIGHT	33
WYNN	7
YELDELL	24
YOUNG	1

Surname/Township Index

This Index allows you to determine which *Township Map Group(s)* contain individuals with the following surnames. Each *Map Group* has a corresponding full-name index of all individuals who obtained patents for land within its Congressional township's borders. After each index you will find the Patent Map to which it refers, and just thereafter, you can view the township's Road Map and Historical Map, with the latter map displaying streams, railroads, and more.

So, once you find your Surname here, proceed to the Index at the beginning of the **Map Group** indicated below.

Surname	Map Group	Parcels of Land	Meridian/Township/Range
ABNEY	23	1	St Stephens 7-N 14-E
ACREE	10	2	St Stephens 10-N 16-E
ADAMS	18	3	St Stephens 8-N 14-E
" "	22	1	St Stephens 7-N 13-E
" "	24	1	St Stephens 7-N 15-E
AINESWORTH	16	1	St Stephens 8-N 12-E
AINSWORTH	11	3	St Stephens 9-N 12-E
" "	16	1	St Stephens 8-N 12-E
" "	17	1	St Stephens 8-N 13-E
ALBRITTON	11	2	St Stephens 9-N 12-E
ALDAY	9	7	St Stephens 10-N 15-E
ALLEN	8	7	St Stephens 10-N 14-E
" "	19	7	St Stephens 8-N 15-E
" "	10	1	St Stephens 10-N 16-E
" "	20	1	St Stephens 8-N 16-E
AMASON	16	3	St Stephens 8-N 12-E
AMBROSE	15	3	St Stephens 9-N 16-E
AMOS	11	1	St Stephens 9-N 12-E
ANDERS	14	1	St Stephens 9-N 15-E
ANDRESS	10	8	St Stephens 10-N 16-E
" "	9	2	St Stephens 10-N 15-E
" "	4	1	St Stephens 11-N 15-E
" "	5	1	St Stephens 11-N 16-E
ANDREWS	9	1	St Stephens 10-N 15-E
" "	19	1	St Stephens 8-N 15-E
ANSLEY	19	1	St Stephens 8-N 15-E
ANTONY	21	5	St Stephens 7-N 12-E
ARANT	18	8	St Stephens 8-N 14-E
" "	22	3	St Stephens 7-N 13-E
ARDIS	17	3	St Stephens 8-N 13-E
" "	18	3	St Stephens 8-N 14-E
ARMSTRONG	10	5	St Stephens 10-N 16-E
" "	15	2	St Stephens 9-N 16-E
" "	3	1	St Stephens 11-N 14-E
ARNOLD	12	1	St Stephens 9-N 13-E
ARRINGTON	1	2	St Stephens 11-N 12-E
" "	2	1	St Stephens 11-N 13-E
ASHCRAFT	7	1	St Stephens 10-N 13-E
" "	2	1	St Stephens 11-N 13-E
ATKINSON	23	4	St Stephens 7-N 14-E
AUSTIN	6	2	St Stephens 10-N 12-E
" "	22	2	St Stephens 7-N 13-E
BABCOCK	6	1	St Stephens 10-N 12-E
BAGGAN	1	1	St Stephens 11-N 12-E

Surname	Map Group	Parcels of Land	Meridian/Township/Range
BAILEY	**13**	4	St Stephens 9-N 14-E
" "	**22**	1	St Stephens 7-N 13-E
" "	**15**	1	St Stephens 9-N 16-E
BAKER	**22**	1	St Stephens 7-N 13-E
BALDERREE	**7**	3	St Stephens 10-N 13-E
" "	**2**	2	St Stephens 11-N 13-E
BALDWIN	**21**	1	St Stephens 7-N 12-E
" "	**22**	1	St Stephens 7-N 13-E
BALLARD	**4**	6	St Stephens 11-N 15-E
BANISTER	**23**	4	St Stephens 7-N 14-E
" "	**24**	2	St Stephens 7-N 15-E
BARGANIEL	**3**	1	St Stephens 11-N 14-E
BARGANIER	**3**	4	St Stephens 11-N 14-E
BARGE	**6**	2	St Stephens 10-N 12-E
BARLOW	**9**	2	St Stephens 10-N 15-E
BARNES	**13**	3	St Stephens 9-N 14-E
" "	**9**	1	St Stephens 10-N 15-E
" "	**17**	1	St Stephens 8-N 13-E
BARRETT	**10**	15	St Stephens 10-N 16-E
" "	**24**	7	St Stephens 7-N 15-E
" "	**9**	3	St Stephens 10-N 15-E
" "	**23**	1	St Stephens 7-N 14-E
" "	**13**	1	St Stephens 9-N 14-E
" "	**14**	1	St Stephens 9-N 15-E
BARRINGTON	**10**	1	St Stephens 10-N 16-E
BARRON	**11**	2	St Stephens 9-N 12-E
BASS	**13**	1	St Stephens 9-N 14-E
BATES	**6**	1	St Stephens 10-N 12-E
BAXLEY	**7**	1	St Stephens 10-N 13-E
" "	**12**	1	St Stephens 9-N 13-E
BAYZIER	**21**	1	St Stephens 7-N 12-E
BEASLEY	**22**	5	St Stephens 7-N 13-E
" "	**21**	1	St Stephens 7-N 12-E
BECK	**17**	3	St Stephens 8-N 13-E
" "	**18**	1	St Stephens 8-N 14-E
BECKWORTH	**8**	1	St Stephens 10-N 14-E
BEDGOOD	**15**	1	St Stephens 9-N 16-E
BEESLEY	**22**	3	St Stephens 7-N 13-E
" "	**23**	2	St Stephens 7-N 14-E
BELL	**6**	3	St Stephens 10-N 12-E
" "	**9**	3	St Stephens 10-N 15-E
" "	**10**	3	St Stephens 10-N 16-E
" "	**11**	3	St Stephens 9-N 12-E
" "	**15**	2	St Stephens 9-N 16-E
" "	**7**	1	St Stephens 10-N 13-E
" "	**5**	1	St Stephens 11-N 16-E
" "	**17**	1	St Stephens 8-N 13-E
BENDER	**18**	1	St Stephens 8-N 14-E
BENNETT	**23**	11	St Stephens 7-N 14-E
" "	**13**	9	St Stephens 9-N 14-E
" "	**16**	8	St Stephens 8-N 12-E
" "	**11**	3	St Stephens 9-N 12-E
" "	**17**	2	St Stephens 8-N 13-E
" "	**21**	1	St Stephens 7-N 12-E
" "	**18**	1	St Stephens 8-N 14-E
BENSON	**6**	7	St Stephens 10-N 12-E
" "	**1**	1	St Stephens 11-N 12-E
BERRY	**24**	1	St Stephens 7-N 15-E
" "	**18**	1	St Stephens 8-N 14-E
BEVERLY	**6**	5	St Stephens 10-N 12-E

Surname	Map Group	Parcels of Land	Meridian/Township/Range		
BEVERLY (Cont'd)	1	4	St Stephens	11-N	12-E
" "	7	1	St Stephens	10-N	13-E
" "	12	1	St Stephens	9-N	13-E
BILBERRY	11	2	St Stephens	9-N	12-E
BILLINGSLEA	16	19	St Stephens	8-N	12-E
" "	21	8	St Stephens	7-N	12-E
BINION	22	9	St Stephens	7-N	13-E
" "	17	1	St Stephens	8-N	13-E
BISHOP	10	6	St Stephens	10-N	16-E
" "	15	1	St Stephens	9-N	16-E
BLACK	17	9	St Stephens	8-N	13-E
" "	15	5	St Stephens	9-N	16-E
" "	7	4	St Stephens	10-N	13-E
" "	9	3	St Stephens	10-N	15-E
" "	12	2	St Stephens	9-N	13-E
" "	14	2	St Stephens	9-N	15-E
" "	2	1	St Stephens	11-N	13-E
" "	13	1	St Stephens	9-N	14-E
BLACKMAN	11	7	St Stephens	9-N	12-E
" "	18	2	St Stephens	8-N	14-E
BLACKMON	11	9	St Stephens	9-N	12-E
" "	17	1	St Stephens	8-N	13-E
" "	18	1	St Stephens	8-N	14-E
BLAIR	18	8	St Stephens	8-N	14-E
" "	13	1	St Stephens	9-N	14-E
BLANKENSHIP	6	1	St Stephens	10-N	12-E
" "	1	1	St Stephens	11-N	12-E
BLOCKSOM	1	1	St Stephens	11-N	12-E
BLOXOM	1	2	St Stephens	11-N	12-E
BLOXSOM	6	1	St Stephens	10-N	12-E
BOAN	24	2	St Stephens	7-N	15-E
BOATMUN	2	3	St Stephens	11-N	13-E
BOGGAN	1	16	St Stephens	11-N	12-E
" "	17	2	St Stephens	8-N	13-E
" "	12	2	St Stephens	9-N	13-E
BOGGIN	1	2	St Stephens	11-N	12-E
BOGGUS	10	3	St Stephens	10-N	16-E
BOLLING	13	12	St Stephens	9-N	14-E
" "	8	8	St Stephens	10-N	14-E
" "	12	6	St Stephens	9-N	13-E
" "	9	3	St Stephens	10-N	15-E
" "	4	2	St Stephens	11-N	15-E
" "	14	2	St Stephens	9-N	15-E
" "	15	2	St Stephens	9-N	16-E
" "	7	1	St Stephens	10-N	13-E
" "	23	1	St Stephens	7-N	14-E
BOND	1	1	St Stephens	11-N	12-E
BONNER	1	3	St Stephens	11-N	12-E
" "	8	1	St Stephens	10-N	14-E
" "	2	1	St Stephens	11-N	13-E
BOWDEN	21	1	St Stephens	7-N	12-E
BOWEN	6	5	St Stephens	10-N	12-E
BOYKIN	7	2	St Stephens	10-N	13-E
BOZEMAN	2	2	St Stephens	11-N	13-E
" "	14	1	St Stephens	9-N	15-E
BRADEN	14	7	St Stephens	9-N	15-E
" "	10	1	St Stephens	10-N	16-E
BRADLEY	18	3	St Stephens	8-N	14-E
" "	12	1	St Stephens	9-N	13-E
BRAGG	6	1	St Stephens	10-N	12-E

Surname	Map Group	Parcels of Land	Meridian/Township/Range		
BRAGG (Cont'd)	7	1	St Stephens	10-N	13-E
" "	1	1	St Stephens	11-N	12-E
" "	2	1	St Stephens	11-N	13-E
BRANCH	1	1	St Stephens	11-N	12-E
" "	2	1	St Stephens	11-N	13-E
BRANSFORD	17	5	St Stephens	8-N	13-E
" "	16	2	St Stephens	8-N	12-E
" "	1	1	St Stephens	11-N	12-E
" "	22	1	St Stephens	7-N	13-E
BRASSWELL	13	2	St Stephens	9-N	14-E
" "	4	1	St Stephens	11-N	15-E
" "	18	1	St Stephens	8-N	14-E
" "	14	1	St Stephens	9-N	15-E
BRASWELL	13	1	St Stephens	9-N	14-E
BRAZZIL	13	1	St Stephens	9-N	14-E
BREITHAUPT	2	2	St Stephens	11-N	13-E
" "	14	1	St Stephens	9-N	15-E
BREWER	7	9	St Stephens	10-N	13-E
" "	15	6	St Stephens	9-N	16-E
" "	16	1	St Stephens	8-N	12-E
" "	11	1	St Stephens	9-N	12-E
BRIERS	8	2	St Stephens	10-N	14-E
BRIGHT	18	2	St Stephens	8-N	14-E
BRIGHTWELL	19	1	St Stephens	8-N	15-E
BRILEY	24	3	St Stephens	7-N	15-E
BROGDEN	24	3	St Stephens	7-N	15-E
BROGDON	24	1	St Stephens	7-N	15-E
BROOK	24	1	St Stephens	7-N	15-E
" "	19	1	St Stephens	8-N	15-E
BROOKS	22	22	St Stephens	7-N	13-E
" "	21	8	St Stephens	7-N	12-E
" "	17	3	St Stephens	8-N	13-E
" "	2	1	St Stephens	11-N	13-E
" "	23	1	St Stephens	7-N	14-E
" "	16	1	St Stephens	8-N	12-E
BROWDER	20	1	St Stephens	8-N	16-E
BROWN	2	6	St Stephens	11-N	13-E
" "	4	6	St Stephens	11-N	15-E
" "	18	5	St Stephens	8-N	14-E
" "	21	4	St Stephens	7-N	12-E
" "	5	1	St Stephens	11-N	16-E
" "	13	1	St Stephens	9-N	14-E
BROXSON	17	2	St Stephens	8-N	13-E
BRUCE	3	1	St Stephens	11-N	14-E
BRYAN	5	7	St Stephens	11-N	16-E
" "	23	3	St Stephens	7-N	14-E
" "	16	2	St Stephens	8-N	12-E
" "	22	1	St Stephens	7-N	13-E
BRYANT	16	2	St Stephens	8-N	12-E
" "	19	2	St Stephens	8-N	15-E
BUCKELLEW	7	2	St Stephens	10-N	13-E
BUFFINGTON	16	2	St Stephens	8-N	12-E
BURKE	18	4	St Stephens	8-N	14-E
BURKET	11	11	St Stephens	9-N	12-E
" "	12	2	St Stephens	9-N	13-E
" "	16	1	St Stephens	8-N	12-E
BURKETT	11	24	St Stephens	9-N	12-E
" "	16	14	St Stephens	8-N	12-E
" "	17	5	St Stephens	8-N	13-E
" "	12	5	St Stephens	9-N	13-E

Surname	Map Group	Parcels of Land	Meridian/Township/Range
BURKETT (Cont'd)	22	2	St Stephens 7-N 13-E
BURNETT	8	9	St Stephens 10-N 14-E
" "	7	1	St Stephens 10-N 13-E
BURNS	10	5	St Stephens 10-N 16-E
" "	15	3	St Stephens 9-N 16-E
" "	17	2	St Stephens 8-N 13-E
BUSH	18	4	St Stephens 8-N 14-E
" "	14	4	St Stephens 9-N 15-E
BUTLER	3	8	St Stephens 11-N 14-E
" "	21	7	St Stephens 7-N 12-E
" "	4	2	St Stephens 11-N 15-E
" "	16	2	St Stephens 8-N 12-E
" "	18	2	St Stephens 8-N 14-E
" "	7	1	St Stephens 10-N 13-E
" "	2	1	St Stephens 11-N 13-E
BUTTS	2	1	St Stephens 11-N 13-E
BYRD	11	2	St Stephens 9-N 12-E
CALDWELL	17	5	St Stephens 8-N 13-E
" "	14	3	St Stephens 9-N 15-E
" "	9	1	St Stephens 10-N 15-E
CALLAWAY	14	2	St Stephens 9-N 15-E
" "	5	1	St Stephens 11-N 16-E
CALLEN	4	2	St Stephens 11-N 15-E
CALLIN	24	2	St Stephens 7-N 15-E
CAMP	5	4	St Stephens 11-N 16-E
" "	9	3	St Stephens 10-N 15-E
" "	2	2	St Stephens 11-N 13-E
" "	1	1	St Stephens 11-N 12-E
CAMPBELL	19	5	St Stephens 8-N 15-E
" "	13	4	St Stephens 9-N 14-E
" "	7	3	St Stephens 10-N 13-E
" "	20	1	St Stephens 8-N 16-E
CANTELOO	21	1	St Stephens 7-N 12-E
CARDWELL	12	1	St Stephens 9-N 13-E
CARPENTER	23	2	St Stephens 7-N 14-E
" "	22	1	St Stephens 7-N 13-E
CARR	14	1	St Stephens 9-N 15-E
CARTER	6	14	St Stephens 10-N 12-E
" "	10	7	St Stephens 10-N 16-E
" "	4	2	St Stephens 11-N 15-E
" "	7	1	St Stephens 10-N 13-E
" "	2	1	St Stephens 11-N 13-E
" "	5	1	St Stephens 11-N 16-E
" "	17	1	St Stephens 8-N 13-E
CARY	8	4	St Stephens 10-N 14-E
CASSIDY	1	1	St Stephens 11-N 12-E
CATES	3	1	St Stephens 11-N 14-E
CATLIN	24	17	St Stephens 7-N 15-E
" "	23	1	St Stephens 7-N 14-E
CHAMBERS	13	1	St Stephens 9-N 14-E
CHAMBLISS	14	12	St Stephens 9-N 15-E
CHANCELLOR	1	6	St Stephens 11-N 12-E
" "	21	5	St Stephens 7-N 12-E
" "	6	1	St Stephens 10-N 12-E
CHATHAM	8	4	St Stephens 10-N 14-E
CHEATHAM	4	18	St Stephens 11-N 15-E
" "	8	6	St Stephens 10-N 14-E
" "	3	3	St Stephens 11-N 14-E
CHRISTIAN	6	1	St Stephens 10-N 12-E
CHRISTOPHER	2	1	St Stephens 11-N 13-E

Surname	Map Group	Parcels of Land	Meridian/Township/Range		
CLARK	**21**	4	St Stephens	7-N	12-E
" "	**22**	1	St Stephens	7-N	13-E
CLOPTON	**12**	6	St Stephens	9-N	13-E
" "	**7**	3	St Stephens	10-N	13-E
" "	**17**	2	St Stephens	8-N	13-E
CLUTE	**6**	5	St Stephens	10-N	12-E
CODY	**20**	2	St Stephens	8-N	16-E
COE	**15**	2	St Stephens	9-N	16-E
COHRON	**18**	1	St Stephens	8-N	14-E
COKER	**21**	6	St Stephens	7-N	12-E
COLE	**6**	1	St Stephens	10-N	12-E
" "	**7**	1	St Stephens	10-N	13-E
COLEMAN	**11**	13	St Stephens	9-N	12-E
" "	**1**	9	St Stephens	11-N	12-E
" "	**2**	5	St Stephens	11-N	13-E
" "	**21**	4	St Stephens	7-N	12-E
" "	**6**	2	St Stephens	10-N	12-E
" "	**10**	2	St Stephens	10-N	16-E
" "	**24**	2	St Stephens	7-N	15-E
" "	**12**	2	St Stephens	9-N	13-E
" "	**16**	1	St Stephens	8-N	12-E
" "	**17**	1	St Stephens	8-N	13-E
COLLEY	**9**	3	St Stephens	10-N	15-E
COLLINS	**4**	17	St Stephens	11-N	15-E
" "	**3**	2	St Stephens	11-N	14-E
" "	**5**	2	St Stephens	11-N	16-E
CONE	**21**	19	St Stephens	7-N	12-E
" "	**16**	4	St Stephens	8-N	12-E
" "	**22**	1	St Stephens	7-N	13-E
CONOLEY	**6**	1	St Stephens	10-N	12-E
COOK	**15**	10	St Stephens	9-N	16-E
" "	**1**	4	St Stephens	11-N	12-E
" "	**17**	4	St Stephens	8-N	13-E
" "	**24**	3	St Stephens	7-N	15-E
" "	**8**	1	St Stephens	10-N	14-E
" "	**2**	1	St Stephens	11-N	13-E
" "	**4**	1	St Stephens	11-N	15-E
" "	**14**	1	St Stephens	9-N	15-E
COOPER	**7**	3	St Stephens	10-N	13-E
" "	**8**	1	St Stephens	10-N	14-E
" "	**1**	1	St Stephens	11-N	12-E
COPELAND	**16**	1	St Stephens	8-N	12-E`
CORLEY	**17**	1	St Stephens	8-N	13-E
COULSON	**4**	1	St Stephens	11-N	15-E
COWART	**9**	1	St Stephens	10-N	15-E
" "	**13**	1	St Stephens	9-N	14-E
COX	**18**	2	St Stephens	8-N	14-E
" "	**3**	1	St Stephens	11-N	14-E
CRAIG	**8**	7	St Stephens	10-N	14-E
" "	**9**	5	St Stephens	10-N	15-E
" "	**4**	3	St Stephens	11-N	15-E
" "	**23**	3	St Stephens	7-N	14-E
" "	**14**	3	St Stephens	9-N	15-E
" "	**22**	2	St Stephens	7-N	13-E
CRANE	**6**	5	St Stephens	10-N	12-E
" "	**1**	1	St Stephens	11-N	12-E
CRAVEY	**23**	1	St Stephens	7-N	14-E
CREECH	**13**	2	St Stephens	9-N	14-E
CREG	**13**	1	St Stephens	9-N	14-E
CREMER	**11**	4	St Stephens	9-N	12-E

Surname	Map Group	Parcels of Land	Meridian/Township/Range
CRENSHAW	7	7	St Stephens	10-N	13-E
" "	2	5	St Stephens	11-N	13-E
" "	18	1	St Stephens	8-N	14-E
CRITTENDEN	24	1	St Stephens	7-N	15-E
CROCHERON	1	2	St Stephens	11-N	12-E
CROCKER	4	4	St Stephens	11-N	15-E
CROSBY	17	1	St Stephens	8-N	13-E
CROSS	2	4	St Stephens	11-N	13-E
" "	7	1	St Stephens	10-N	13-E
CRUM	1	7	St Stephens	11-N	12-E
CUNNINGHAM	21	1	St Stephens	7-N	12-E
CURRY	24	3	St Stephens	7-N	15-E
DAILEY	2	1	St Stephens	11-N	13-E
DANIEL	16	4	St Stephens	8-N	12-E
" "	22	2	St Stephens	7-N	13-E
DARBY	22	2	St Stephens	7-N	13-E
DAVENPORT	3	16	St Stephens	11-N	14-E
" "	15	2	St Stephens	9-N	16-E
DAVIDSON	8	4	St Stephens	10-N	14-E
" "	2	4	St Stephens	11-N	13-E
" "	18	2	St Stephens	8-N	14-E
" "	12	2	St Stephens	9-N	13-E
" "	1	1	St Stephens	11-N	12-E
DAVIS	9	4	St Stephens	10-N	15-E
" "	2	4	St Stephens	11-N	13-E
" "	23	4	St Stephens	7-N	14-E
" "	24	3	St Stephens	7-N	15-E
" "	12	3	St Stephens	9-N	13-E
" "	6	2	St Stephens	10-N	12-E
" "	3	1	St Stephens	11-N	14-E
" "	22	1	St Stephens	7-N	13-E
" "	11	1	St Stephens	9-N	12-E
DAWSON	7	3	St Stephens	10-N	13-E
DAY	4	1	St Stephens	11-N	15-E
" "	5	1	St Stephens	11-N	16-E
DEAN	10	4	St Stephens	10-N	16-E
" "	16	2	St Stephens	8-N	12-E
DEASE	22	2	St Stephens	7-N	13-E
" "	23	2	St Stephens	7-N	14-E
DEEN	16	9	St Stephens	8-N	12-E
" "	11	6	St Stephens	9-N	12-E
" "	22	1	St Stephens	7-N	13-E
DEES	24	5	St Stephens	7-N	15-E
" "	19	1	St Stephens	8-N	15-E
DEMING	9	8	St Stephens	10-N	15-E
" "	18	6	St Stephens	8-N	14-E
" "	14	6	St Stephens	9-N	15-E
" "	8	2	St Stephens	10-N	14-E
" "	3	1	St Stephens	11-N	14-E
DENDY	23	6	St Stephens	7-N	14-E
" "	24	5	St Stephens	7-N	15-E
" "	18	2	St Stephens	8-N	14-E
" "	19	2	St Stephens	8-N	15-E
DENNIS	1	1	St Stephens	11-N	12-E
DERNING	14	1	St Stephens	9-N	15-E
DEWBERRY	21	3	St Stephens	7-N	12-E
DICKEN	14	3	St Stephens	9-N	15-E
" "	19	2	St Stephens	8-N	15-E
DICKERSON	2	2	St Stephens	11-N	13-E
DICKSON	3	1	St Stephens	11-N	14-E

Surname	Map Group	Parcels of Land	Meridian/Township/Range		
DIXON	**15**	4	St Stephens	9-N	16-E
" "	**4**	1	St Stephens	11-N	15-E
DORIETY	**12**	1	St Stephens	9-N	13-E
DOUGLASS	**6**	1	St Stephens	10-N	12-E
DOZIER	**11**	4	St Stephens	9-N	12-E
" "	**21**	2	St Stephens	7-N	12-E
DRAKE	**1**	3	St Stephens	11-N	12-E
" "	**20**	3	St Stephens	8-N	16-E
" "	**6**	1	St Stephens	10-N	12-E
DREADEN	**12**	1	St Stephens	9-N	13-E
DRISKELL	**22**	3	St Stephens	7-N	13-E
DRIVER	**8**	1	St Stephens	10-N	14-E
" "	**22**	1	St Stephens	7-N	13-E
DUCK	**12**	3	St Stephens	9-N	13-E
" "	**13**	3	St Stephens	9-N	14-E
DUKE	**14**	7	St Stephens	9-N	15-E
" "	**18**	3	St Stephens	8-N	14-E
" "	**21**	2	St Stephens	7-N	12-E
" "	**19**	2	St Stephens	8-N	15-E
DUKES	**13**	1	St Stephens	9-N	14-E
DUNHAM	**6**	1	St Stephens	10-N	12-E
DUNKLIN	**9**	1	St Stephens	10-N	15-E
" "	**2**	1	St Stephens	11-N	13-E
DUNN	**5**	1	St Stephens	11-N	16-E
DUNNAM	**21**	2	St Stephens	7-N	12-E
DYESS	**7**	1	St Stephens	10-N	13-E
" "	**12**	1	St Stephens	9-N	13-E
EALUM	**11**	4	St Stephens	9-N	12-E
EARNEST	**3**	2	St Stephens	11-N	14-E
EASTERLING	**4**	1	St Stephens	11-N	15-E
EASTERS	**16**	1	St Stephens	8-N	12-E
EDDINS	**22**	2	St Stephens	7-N	13-E
EDMONDS	**13**	1	St Stephens	9-N	14-E
EDMONDSON	**1**	2	St Stephens	11-N	12-E
EDWARDS	**6**	4	St Stephens	10-N	12-E
" "	**24**	2	St Stephens	7-N	15-E
" "	**19**	1	St Stephens	8-N	15-E
ELAM	**11**	2	St Stephens	9-N	12-E
ELDER	**1**	5	St Stephens	11-N	12-E
ELEY	**1**	2	St Stephens	11-N	12-E
ELLINGTON	**15**	1	St Stephens	9-N	16-E
ELLIS	**16**	5	St Stephens	8-N	12-E
" "	**21**	4	St Stephens	7-N	12-E
" "	**17**	3	St Stephens	8-N	13-E
ELSBERRY	**13**	2	St Stephens	9-N	14-E
EMANUEL	**21**	1	St Stephens	7-N	12-E
ENGLISH	**17**	2	St Stephens	8-N	13-E
ERNEST	**9**	5	St Stephens	10-N	15-E
" "	**2**	5	St Stephens	11-N	13-E
" "	**3**	2	St Stephens	11-N	14-E
ETHEREDGE	**21**	6	St Stephens	7-N	12-E
" "	**22**	3	St Stephens	7-N	13-E
ETHEREGE	**17**	2	St Stephens	8-N	13-E
EVANS	**8**	3	St Stephens	10-N	14-E
" "	**18**	2	St Stephens	8-N	14-E
" "	**6**	1	St Stephens	10-N	12-E
" "	**5**	1	St Stephens	11-N	16-E
EWING	**9**	3	St Stephens	10-N	15-E
EXUM	**14**	7	St Stephens	9-N	15-E
FAIL	**17**	13	St Stephens	8-N	13-E

Surname	Map Group	Parcels of Land	Meridian/Township/Range
FAIL (Cont'd)	**12**	9	St Stephens 9-N 13-E
" "	**16**	8	St Stephens 8-N 12-E
" "	**18**	6	St Stephens 8-N 14-E
" "	**10**	3	St Stephens 10-N 16-E
" "	**22**	2	St Stephens 7-N 13-E
" "	**4**	1	St Stephens 11-N 15-E
FAILES	**12**	2	St Stephens 9-N 13-E
" "	**17**	1	St Stephens 8-N 13-E
FAILS	**4**	10	St Stephens 11-N 15-E
" "	**17**	3	St Stephens 8-N 13-E
FAIN	**13**	1	St Stephens 9-N 14-E
FARROW	**3**	1	St Stephens 11-N 14-E
FEAGIN	**24**	4	St Stephens 7-N 15-E
" "	**1**	1	St Stephens 11-N 12-E
FELPS	**11**	3	St Stephens 9-N 12-E
FERGUSON	**3**	8	St Stephens 11-N 14-E
" "	**2**	6	St Stephens 11-N 13-E
" "	**8**	3	St Stephens 10-N 14-E
" "	**1**	2	St Stephens 11-N 12-E
FERRELL	**24**	2	St Stephens 7-N 15-E
FIFE	**13**	5	St Stephens 9-N 14-E
" "	**14**	2	St Stephens 9-N 15-E
" "	**9**	1	St Stephens 10-N 15-E
FINDLEY	**5**	2	St Stephens 11-N 16-E
FINKLEA	**11**	5	St Stephens 9-N 12-E
" "	**16**	2	St Stephens 8-N 12-E
FINKLEY	**11**	3	St Stephens 9-N 12-E
FLINN	**4**	3	St Stephens 11-N 15-E
" "	**5**	1	St Stephens 11-N 16-E
FLORENCE	**24**	3	St Stephens 7-N 15-E
FLOWERS	**13**	6	St Stephens 9-N 14-E
" "	**12**	1	St Stephens 9-N 13-E
FORREST	**4**	3	St Stephens 11-N 15-E
FORTUNE	**18**	1	St Stephens 8-N 14-E
FOWLER	**6**	4	St Stephens 10-N 12-E
FOX	**2**	3	St Stephens 11-N 13-E
" "	**7**	2	St Stephens 10-N 13-E
FRANKLIN	**16**	7	St Stephens 8-N 12-E
" "	**19**	1	St Stephens 8-N 15-E
FREEMAN	**17**	5	St Stephens 8-N 13-E
FRIDDLE	**18**	4	St Stephens 8-N 14-E
FROST	**9**	1	St Stephens 10-N 15-E
" "	**10**	1	St Stephens 10-N 16-E
" "	**4**	1	St Stephens 11-N 15-E
" "	**5**	1	St Stephens 11-N 16-E
FULLER	**4**	8	St Stephens 11-N 15-E
" "	**16**	6	St Stephens 8-N 12-E
" "	**3**	2	St Stephens 11-N 14-E
" "	**9**	1	St Stephens 10-N 15-E
FUNDERBURKE	**17**	1	St Stephens 8-N 13-E
FURGUSON	**3**	1	St Stephens 11-N 14-E
FUTCH	**14**	1	St Stephens 9-N 15-E
GAFFNEY	**4**	3	St Stephens 11-N 15-E
" "	**9**	1	St Stephens 10-N 15-E
GAFFORD	**4**	14	St Stephens 11-N 15-E
" "	**3**	10	St Stephens 11-N 14-E
" "	**8**	8	St Stephens 10-N 14-E
" "	**9**	5	St Stephens 10-N 15-E
GALLAWAY	**23**	5	St Stephens 7-N 14-E
" "	**22**	1	St Stephens 7-N 13-E

Surname	Map Group	Parcels of Land	Meridian/Township/Range
GALLOPS	**19**	3	St Stephens 8-N 15-E
" "	**20**	1	St Stephens 8-N 16-E
GALLOWAY	**22**	2	St Stephens 7-N 13-E
GANDY	**16**	10	St Stephens 8-N 12-E
" "	**14**	6	St Stephens 9-N 15-E
" "	**9**	3	St Stephens 10-N 15-E
" "	**19**	3	St Stephens 8-N 15-E
" "	**4**	1	St Stephens 11-N 15-E
" "	**5**	1	St Stephens 11-N 16-E
GANEY	**10**	1	St Stephens 10-N 16-E
GANUS	**22**	1	St Stephens 7-N 13-E
GARDNER	**17**	4	St Stephens 8-N 13-E
GAREY	**3**	2	St Stephens 11-N 14-E
" "	**2**	1	St Stephens 11-N 13-E
GARNER	**16**	13	St Stephens 8-N 12-E
GARRETT	**8**	4	St Stephens 10-N 14-E
" "	**3**	2	St Stephens 11-N 14-E
" "	**7**	1	St Stephens 10-N 13-E
" "	**2**	1	St Stephens 11-N 13-E
" "	**22**	1	St Stephens 7-N 13-E
" "	**20**	1	St Stephens 8-N 16-E
GARRITT	**2**	1	St Stephens 11-N 13-E
GARUM	**22**	1	St Stephens 7-N 13-E
GARY	**2**	1	St Stephens 11-N 13-E
GASTON	**1**	3	St Stephens 11-N 12-E
GAY	**17**	1	St Stephens 8-N 13-E
GAYLE	**6**	1	St Stephens 10-N 12-E
GENTRY	**4**	1	St Stephens 11-N 15-E
GERRELL	**2**	1	St Stephens 11-N 13-E
GHOLSON	**9**	5	St Stephens 10-N 15-E
" "	**5**	3	St Stephens 11-N 16-E
GIBBS	**6**	1	St Stephens 10-N 12-E
GIBSON	**16**	16	St Stephens 8-N 12-E
" "	**17**	10	St Stephens 8-N 13-E
" "	**18**	5	St Stephens 8-N 14-E
" "	**6**	2	St Stephens 10-N 12-E
" "	**9**	1	St Stephens 10-N 15-E
" "	**13**	1	St Stephens 9-N 14-E
GIDDENS	**8**	3	St Stephens 10-N 14-E
GIDDINGS	**13**	2	St Stephens 9-N 14-E
GILBERT	**13**	8	St Stephens 9-N 14-E
" "	**14**	2	St Stephens 9-N 15-E
GILL	**4**	2	St Stephens 11-N 15-E
" "	**3**	1	St Stephens 11-N 14-E
" "	**24**	1	St Stephens 7-N 15-E
GILLIAM	**5**	1	St Stephens 11-N 16-E
GILLION	**5**	7	St Stephens 11-N 16-E
GILMER	**21**	1	St Stephens 7-N 12-E
GILMON	**21**	2	St Stephens 7-N 12-E
GILMORE	**16**	4	St Stephens 8-N 12-E
" "	**21**	3	St Stephens 7-N 12-E
GINGLES	**5**	1	St Stephens 11-N 16-E
GLASS	**4**	9	St Stephens 11-N 15-E
" "	**5**	2	St Stephens 11-N 16-E
GLASSGOW	**14**	1	St Stephens 9-N 15-E
GLENN	**2**	3	St Stephens 11-N 13-E
" "	**1**	2	St Stephens 11-N 12-E
GLOVER	**5**	2	St Stephens 11-N 16-E
GODWIN	**14**	1	St Stephens 9-N 15-E
GOLDSTON	**8**	1	St Stephens 10-N 14-E

Surname	Map Group	Parcels of Land	Meridian/Township/Range
GOLDSTON (Cont'd)	**10**	1	St Stephens 10-N 16-E
GONDER	**7**	5	St Stephens 10-N 13-E
" "	**13**	1	St Stephens 9-N 14-E
GOODELL	**11**	4	St Stephens 9-N 12-E
GOODWIN	**3**	1	St Stephens 11-N 14-E
GORUM	**22**	1	St Stephens 7-N 13-E
" "	**24**	1	St Stephens 7-N 15-E
GOSS	**21**	1	St Stephens 7-N 12-E
GRACE	**16**	3	St Stephens 8-N 12-E
GRAHAM	**9**	1	St Stephens 10-N 15-E
" "	**10**	1	St Stephens 10-N 16-E
" "	**4**	1	St Stephens 11-N 15-E
" "	**22**	1	St Stephens 7-N 13-E
GRANT	**3**	5	St Stephens 11-N 14-E
GRASON	**11**	2	St Stephens 9-N 12-E
GRAVES	**19**	3	St Stephens 8-N 15-E
GRAY	**14**	4	St Stephens 9-N 15-E
" "	**6**	3	St Stephens 10-N 12-E
" "	**1**	3	St Stephens 11-N 12-E
GRAYDON	**9**	1	St Stephens 10-N 15-E
GRAYSON	**11**	2	St Stephens 9-N 12-E
" "	**7**	1	St Stephens 10-N 13-E
GREEN	**6**	3	St Stephens 10-N 12-E
" "	**15**	3	St Stephens 9-N 16-E
" "	**1**	2	St Stephens 11-N 12-E
" "	**22**	2	St Stephens 7-N 13-E
" "	**18**	2	St Stephens 8-N 14-E
" "	**19**	1	St Stephens 8-N 15-E
" "	**11**	1	St Stephens 9-N 12-E
GREENE	**22**	1	St Stephens 7-N 13-E
GREGG	**12**	2	St Stephens 9-N 13-E
GREGORY	**7**	4	St Stephens 10-N 13-E
" "	**24**	3	St Stephens 7-N 15-E
" "	**19**	2	St Stephens 8-N 15-E
GRIFFIN	**10**	3	St Stephens 10-N 16-E
" "	**2**	1	St Stephens 11-N 13-E
" "	**13**	1	St Stephens 9-N 14-E
GRIFFITH	**2**	6	St Stephens 11-N 13-E
GRIGERS	**1**	1	St Stephens 11-N 12-E
GRIGGS	**4**	1	St Stephens 11-N 15-E
" "	**5**	1	St Stephens 11-N 16-E
GRISWOLD	**23**	1	St Stephens 7-N 14-E
GWYNN	**12**	1	St Stephens 9-N 13-E
HAIGLAR	**2**	1	St Stephens 11-N 13-E
HALIDA	**5**	1	St Stephens 11-N 16-E
HALL	**4**	9	St Stephens 11-N 15-E
" "	**22**	3	St Stephens 7-N 13-E
" "	**3**	2	St Stephens 11-N 14-E
" "	**8**	1	St Stephens 10-N 14-E
" "	**18**	1	St Stephens 8-N 14-E
" "	**11**	1	St Stephens 9-N 12-E
HALLFORD	**18**	3	St Stephens 8-N 14-E
HALLIDAY	**9**	1	St Stephens 10-N 15-E
HALSO	**19**	7	St Stephens 8-N 15-E
" "	**14**	2	St Stephens 9-N 15-E
HAM	**4**	1	St Stephens 11-N 15-E
HAMBLETON	**9**	2	St Stephens 10-N 15-E
" "	**5**	1	St Stephens 11-N 16-E
HAMMETT	**21**	2	St Stephens 7-N 12-E
HAMMONDS	**24**	5	St Stephens 7-N 15-E

Surname	Map Group	Parcels of Land	Meridian/Township/Range
HAMMONDS (Cont'd)	**19**	5	St Stephens 8-N 15-E
" "	**18**	4	St Stephens 8-N 14-E
" "	**3**	2	St Stephens 11-N 14-E
" "	**17**	2	St Stephens 8-N 13-E
HAMMONS	**8**	1	St Stephens 10-N 14-E
" "	**4**	1	St Stephens 11-N 15-E
HAMN	**21**	2	St Stephens 7-N 12-E
HAMPTON	**3**	1	St Stephens 11-N 14-E
HANDY	**3**	1	St Stephens 11-N 14-E
HANSON	**15**	1	St Stephens 9-N 16-E
HARALSON	**3**	6	St Stephens 11-N 14-E
" "	**2**	1	St Stephens 11-N 13-E
HARBIN	**15**	5	St Stephens 9-N 16-E
HARDEE	**3**	3	St Stephens 11-N 14-E
HARDY	**14**	2	St Stephens 9-N 15-E
HARE	**21**	2	St Stephens 7-N 12-E
HARPER	**13**	6	St Stephens 9-N 14-E
" "	**17**	3	St Stephens 8-N 13-E
HARRELL	**4**	1	St Stephens 11-N 15-E
HARRISON	**17**	9	St Stephens 8-N 13-E
" "	**10**	8	St Stephens 10-N 16-E
" "	**3**	8	St Stephens 11-N 14-E
" "	**12**	5	St Stephens 9-N 13-E
" "	**15**	5	St Stephens 9-N 16-E
" "	**18**	3	St Stephens 8-N 14-E
" "	**14**	3	St Stephens 9-N 15-E
" "	**9**	2	St Stephens 10-N 15-E
" "	**22**	1	St Stephens 7-N 13-E
" "	**11**	1	St Stephens 9-N 12-E
HART	**24**	5	St Stephens 7-N 15-E
HARTLEY	**3**	31	St Stephens 11-N 14-E
" "	**8**	2	St Stephens 10-N 14-E
" "	**4**	1	St Stephens 11-N 15-E
" "	**13**	1	St Stephens 9-N 14-E
HARVEY	**22**	1	St Stephens 7-N 13-E
HASE	**9**	1	St Stephens 10-N 15-E
HASSEY	**17**	3	St Stephens 8-N 13-E
HASTING	**15**	2	St Stephens 9-N 16-E
HATCHER	**16**	5	St Stephens 8-N 12-E
" "	**3**	2	St Stephens 11-N 14-E
HAWKINS	**6**	11	St Stephens 10-N 12-E
" "	**2**	1	St Stephens 11-N 13-E
HAWTHORN	**1**	1	St Stephens 11-N 12-E
HAYES	**1**	3	St Stephens 11-N 12-E
HAYNIE	**21**	2	St Stephens 7-N 12-E
" "	**16**	2	St Stephens 8-N 12-E
HAYS	**1**	6	St Stephens 11-N 12-E
" "	**21**	2	St Stephens 7-N 12-E
" "	**5**	1	St Stephens 11-N 16-E
HEAP	**17**	3	St Stephens 8-N 13-E
HEAPE	**6**	1	St Stephens 10-N 12-E
" "	**7**	1	St Stephens 10-N 13-E
HEATHCOCK	**18**	1	St Stephens 8-N 14-E
HEATON	**4**	6	St Stephens 11-N 15-E
" "	**3**	1	St Stephens 11-N 14-E
HECKS	**22**	1	St Stephens 7-N 13-E
HEMPHILL	**11**	1	St Stephens 9-N 12-E
HENDERSON	**21**	4	St Stephens 7-N 12-E
" "	**9**	3	St Stephens 10-N 15-E
" "	**22**	3	St Stephens 7-N 13-E

Surname	Map Group	Parcels of Land	Meridian/Township/Range
HENDERSON (Cont'd)	11	3	St Stephens 9-N 12-E
" "	10	2	St Stephens 10-N 16-E
" "	19	2	St Stephens 8-N 15-E
" "	17	1	St Stephens 8-N 13-E
HENDRICKS	7	1	St Stephens 10-N 13-E
HENDRIX	7	1	St Stephens 10-N 13-E
" "	9	1	St Stephens 10-N 15-E
HENRY	22	2	St Stephens 7-N 13-E
HERBERT	8	8	St Stephens 10-N 14-E
" "	1	8	St Stephens 11-N 12-E
" "	3	3	St Stephens 11-N 14-E
" "	2	1	St Stephens 11-N 13-E
HERELONG	5	1	St Stephens 11-N 16-E
HERIN	9	1	St Stephens 10-N 15-E
HERINDON	9	2	St Stephens 10-N 15-E
HERLONG	5	6	St Stephens 11-N 16-E
HERNDON	9	1	St Stephens 10-N 15-E
HESTER	22	1	St Stephens 7-N 13-E
" "	20	1	St Stephens 8-N 16-E
HICKMAN	20	1	St Stephens 8-N 16-E
HICKS	19	1	St Stephens 8-N 15-E
HILBUN	5	19	St Stephens 11-N 16-E
HILL	1	7	St Stephens 11-N 12-E
" "	6	4	St Stephens 10-N 12-E
" "	11	1	St Stephens 9-N 12-E
HILLSON	6	2	St Stephens 10-N 12-E
HILSON	6	3	St Stephens 10-N 12-E
" "	1	1	St Stephens 11-N 12-E
" "	11	1	St Stephens 9-N 12-E
HINSON	18	7	St Stephens 8-N 14-E
" "	23	3	St Stephens 7-N 14-E
HINTON	2	1	St Stephens 11-N 13-E
HOBBS	22	4	St Stephens 7-N 13-E
" "	17	4	St Stephens 8-N 13-E
" "	21	1	St Stephens 7-N 12-E
HOBBY	2	1	St Stephens 11-N 13-E
HODGES	18	2	St Stephens 8-N 14-E
HOLAWAY	12	1	St Stephens 9-N 13-E
HOLCOMBE	1	3	St Stephens 11-N 12-E
HOLDSTON	2	1	St Stephens 11-N 13-E
HOLLADAY	9	6	St Stephens 10-N 15-E
HOLLIS	16	1	St Stephens 8-N 12-E
HOLLOWAY	6	2	St Stephens 10-N 12-E
" "	7	1	St Stephens 10-N 13-E
HOLMES	8	1	St Stephens 10-N 14-E
" "	3	1	St Stephens 11-N 14-E
HOMES	3	4	St Stephens 11-N 14-E
HOOD	13	5	St Stephens 9-N 14-E
" "	11	3	St Stephens 9-N 12-E
" "	17	1	St Stephens 8-N 13-E
HOPKINS	2	1	St Stephens 11-N 13-E
HORN	22	1	St Stephens 7-N 13-E
HORTMAN	19	4	St Stephens 8-N 15-E
HORTON	6	1	St Stephens 10-N 12-E
HOWARD	16	4	St Stephens 8-N 12-E
" "	9	2	St Stephens 10-N 15-E
HOWEL	11	4	St Stephens 9-N 12-E
" "	17	1	St Stephens 8-N 13-E
HOWELL	7	1	St Stephens 10-N 13-E
" "	22	1	St Stephens 7-N 13-E

Surname	Map Group	Parcels of Land	Meridian/Township/Range
HOWELL (Cont'd)	**17**	1	St Stephens 8-N 13-E
" "	**11**	1	St Stephens 9-N 12-E
" "	**13**	1	St Stephens 9-N 14-E
HUDSON	**23**	9	St Stephens 7-N 14-E
" "	**9**	1	St Stephens 10-N 15-E
" "	**19**	1	St Stephens 8-N 15-E
" "	**14**	1	St Stephens 9-N 15-E
HUGGINS	**22**	2	St Stephens 7-N 13-E
HUGHES	**24**	2	St Stephens 7-N 15-E
" "	**23**	1	St Stephens 7-N 14-E
HUGHS	**24**	8	St Stephens 7-N 15-E
" "	**19**	5	St Stephens 8-N 15-E
HUGULEY	**19**	5	St Stephens 8-N 15-E
" "	**20**	3	St Stephens 8-N 16-E
HUMPHREY	**13**	1	St Stephens 9-N 14-E
HUMPHREYS	**13**	1	St Stephens 9-N 14-E
HUNTER	**11**	1	St Stephens 9-N 12-E
HUSON	**21**	11	St Stephens 7-N 12-E
" "	**16**	2	St Stephens 8-N 12-E
HUTCHINSON	**8**	2	St Stephens 10-N 14-E
" "	**4**	2	St Stephens 11-N 15-E
" "	**2**	1	St Stephens 11-N 13-E
INGRAM	**17**	4	St Stephens 8-N 13-E
" "	**12**	4	St Stephens 9-N 13-E
JACKSON	**23**	6	St Stephens 7-N 14-E
" "	**15**	6	St Stephens 9-N 16-E
" "	**18**	4	St Stephens 8-N 14-E
" "	**13**	2	St Stephens 9-N 14-E
" "	**1**	1	St Stephens 11-N 12-E
" "	**16**	1	St Stephens 8-N 12-E
JAMES	**21**	1	St Stephens 7-N 12-E
" "	**22**	1	St Stephens 7-N 13-E
" "	**23**	1	St Stephens 7-N 14-E
JAY	**10**	8	St Stephens 10-N 16-E
" "	**14**	8	St Stephens 9-N 15-E
" "	**21**	6	St Stephens 7-N 12-E
" "	**12**	2	St Stephens 9-N 13-E
" "	**5**	1	St Stephens 11-N 16-E
JEFFERS	**13**	3	St Stephens 9-N 14-E
JERNIGAN	**24**	7	St Stephens 7-N 15-E
" "	**19**	5	St Stephens 8-N 15-E
JOHNSON	**19**	6	St Stephens 8-N 15-E
" "	**12**	6	St Stephens 9-N 13-E
" "	**14**	5	St Stephens 9-N 15-E
" "	**16**	2	St Stephens 8-N 12-E
" "	**18**	2	St Stephens 8-N 14-E
" "	**20**	2	St Stephens 8-N 16-E
" "	**3**	1	St Stephens 11-N 14-E
" "	**17**	1	St Stephens 8-N 13-E
JOHNSTON	**19**	3	St Stephens 8-N 15-E
" "	**14**	1	St Stephens 9-N 15-E
JOINER	**18**	2	St Stephens 8-N 14-E
JOLLIFF	**2**	1	St Stephens 11-N 13-E
JONES	**18**	8	St Stephens 8-N 14-E
" "	**2**	7	St Stephens 11-N 13-E
" "	**11**	6	St Stephens 9-N 12-E
" "	**12**	6	St Stephens 9-N 13-E
" "	**1**	5	St Stephens 11-N 12-E
" "	**23**	5	St Stephens 7-N 14-E
" "	**24**	5	St Stephens 7-N 15-E

Surname	Map Group	Parcels of Land	Meridian/Township/Range		
JONES (Cont'd)	6	4	St Stephens	10-N	12-E
" "	3	4	St Stephens	11-N	14-E
" "	22	3	St Stephens	7-N	13-E
" "	8	1	St Stephens	10-N	14-E
" "	9	1	St Stephens	10-N	15-E
" "	19	1	St Stephens	8-N	15-E
JORDAN	7	1	St Stephens	10-N	13-E
JOSEY	24	7	St Stephens	7-N	15-E
JOYNER	18	2	St Stephens	8-N	14-E
JUDGE	8	1	St Stephens	10-N	14-E
KEEBLER	16	5	St Stephens	8-N	12-E
" "	21	1	St Stephens	7-N	12-E
KEITH	19	12	St Stephens	8-N	15-E
" "	9	3	St Stephens	10-N	15-E
" "	14	1	St Stephens	9-N	15-E
KELLEY	9	1	St Stephens	10-N	15-E
" "	5	1	St Stephens	11-N	16-E
KELLY	7	1	St Stephens	10-N	13-E
KELSOE	18	2	St Stephens	8-N	14-E
" "	23	1	St Stephens	7-N	14-E
KEMP	5	1	St Stephens	11-N	16-E
KENDALL	17	3	St Stephens	8-N	13-E
KENDRICK	21	1	St Stephens	7-N	12-E
" "	16	1	St Stephens	8-N	12-E
KENDRICKE	16	1	St Stephens	8-N	12-E
KENNEDY	24	2	St Stephens	7-N	15-E
KENNINGTON	15	2	St Stephens	9-N	16-E
KETLER	15	7	St Stephens	9-N	16-E
KETTLER	15	6	St Stephens	9-N	16-E
KILLOUGH	4	3	St Stephens	11-N	15-E
KING	5	6	St Stephens	11-N	16-E
KINSEY	7	4	St Stephens	10-N	13-E
" "	12	2	St Stephens	9-N	13-E
KIRKLAND	13	1	St Stephens	9-N	14-E
KIRKPATRICK	5	14	St Stephens	11-N	16-E
" "	4	7	St Stephens	11-N	15-E
KIRVIN	10	1	St Stephens	10-N	16-E
" "	23	1	St Stephens	7-N	14-E
KITCHENS	10	1	St Stephens	10-N	16-E
KITE	19	10	St Stephens	8-N	15-E
KNOWLES	23	2	St Stephens	7-N	14-E
" "	9	1	St Stephens	10-N	15-E
" "	14	1	St Stephens	9-N	15-E
KOLB	2	2	St Stephens	11-N	13-E
" "	1	1	St Stephens	11-N	12-E
KORNEGAY	23	4	St Stephens	7-N	14-E
KUYKENDAL	17	1	St Stephens	8-N	13-E
KUYKENDALL	17	2	St Stephens	8-N	13-E
LANCASTER	18	1	St Stephens	8-N	14-E
LANE	24	7	St Stephens	7-N	15-E
" "	23	3	St Stephens	7-N	14-E
" "	13	2	St Stephens	9-N	14-E
" "	18	1	St Stephens	8-N	14-E
" "	19	1	St Stephens	8-N	15-E
LARKINS	17	3	St Stephens	8-N	13-E
LE FLORE	24	2	St Stephens	7-N	15-E
LEE	17	33	St Stephens	8-N	13-E
" "	16	11	St Stephens	8-N	12-E
" "	14	5	St Stephens	9-N	15-E
" "	22	4	St Stephens	7-N	13-E

Surname	Map Group	Parcels of Land	Meridian/Township/Range		
" "	**24**	4	St Stephens	7-N	15-E
" "	**5**	3	St Stephens	11-N	16-E
" "	**13**	3	St Stephens	9-N	14-E
" "	**12**	2	St Stephens	9-N	13-E
LEONARD	**3**	4	St Stephens	11-N	14-E
" "	**18**	1	St Stephens	8-N	14-E
LEVINGSTON	**1**	1	St Stephens	11-N	12-E
LEWIS	**1**	10	St Stephens	11-N	12-E
" "	**2**	4	St Stephens	11-N	13-E
" "	**19**	4	St Stephens	8-N	15-E
" "	**13**	3	St Stephens	9-N	14-E
" "	**7**	2	St Stephens	10-N	13-E
" "	**20**	2	St Stephens	8-N	16-E
" "	**9**	1	St Stephens	10-N	15-E
LILES	**11**	6	St Stephens	9-N	12-E
LITTLE	**23**	7	St Stephens	7-N	14-E
" "	**1**	6	St Stephens	11-N	12-E
LIVINGSTON	**1**	3	St Stephens	11-N	12-E
LOGAN	**8**	1	St Stephens	10-N	14-E
LONG	**15**	7	St Stephens	9-N	16-E
" "	**19**	6	St Stephens	8-N	15-E
" "	**7**	1	St Stephens	10-N	13-E
LONTZ	**22**	1	St Stephens	7-N	13-E
LOURY	**17**	2	St Stephens	8-N	13-E
LOVETT	**12**	2	St Stephens	9-N	13-E
" "	**7**	1	St Stephens	10-N	13-E
LOWERY	**13**	1	St Stephens	9-N	14-E
LUCKIE	**2**	2	St Stephens	11-N	13-E
LUDLAM	**18**	1	St Stephens	8-N	14-E
LYNCH	**21**	1	St Stephens	7-N	12-E
MAHONE	**16**	6	St Stephens	8-N	12-E
MAJORS	**19**	4	St Stephens	8-N	15-E
" "	**18**	3	St Stephens	8-N	14-E
MANNING	**2**	18	St Stephens	11-N	13-E
MARCHANT	**12**	1	St Stephens	9-N	13-E
MARKS	**10**	1	St Stephens	10-N	16-E
MARSHALL	**12**	13	St Stephens	9-N	13-E
" "	**17**	2	St Stephens	8-N	13-E
" "	**7**	1	St Stephens	10-N	13-E
MARTIN	**6**	4	St Stephens	10-N	12-E
" "	**12**	4	St Stephens	9-N	13-E
" "	**9**	3	St Stephens	10-N	15-E
" "	**19**	3	St Stephens	8-N	15-E
" "	**2**	2	St Stephens	11-N	13-E
" "	**13**	2	St Stephens	9-N	14-E
" "	**14**	2	St Stephens	9-N	15-E
" "	**8**	1	St Stephens	10-N	14-E
MASSINGILL	**17**	3	St Stephens	8-N	13-E
MATHENY	**17**	2	St Stephens	8-N	13-E
" "	**12**	2	St Stephens	9-N	13-E
MATHEWS	**7**	8	St Stephens	10-N	13-E
" "	**2**	1	St Stephens	11-N	13-E
MAXCEY	**24**	1	St Stephens	7-N	15-E
MAXEY	**19**	2	St Stephens	8-N	15-E
MAY	**17**	5	St Stephens	8-N	13-E
" "	**22**	4	St Stephens	7-N	13-E
" "	**5**	1	St Stephens	11-N	16-E
" "	**12**	1	St Stephens	9-N	13-E
MCALLISTER	**14**	1	St Stephens	9-N	15-E
" "	**15**	1	St Stephens	9-N	16-E

Surname	Map Group	Parcels of Land	Meridian/Township/Range
MCBRIDE	**12**	3	St Stephens 9-N 13-E
" "	**10**	2	St Stephens 10-N 16-E
" "	**16**	1	St Stephens 8-N 12-E
" "	**17**	1	St Stephens 8-N 13-E
MCCALL	**19**	3	St Stephens 8-N 15-E
" "	**18**	1	St Stephens 8-N 14-E
" "	**15**	1	St Stephens 9-N 16-E
MCCANN	**18**	3	St Stephens 8-N 14-E
MCCLARTY	**5**	1	St Stephens 11-N 16-E
MCCLOUD	**1**	1	St Stephens 11-N 12-E
MCCLURE	**22**	10	St Stephens 7-N 13-E
" "	**21**	3	St Stephens 7-N 12-E
MCCONDICHIE	**1**	2	St Stephens 11-N 12-E
MCCORMACK	**10**	8	St Stephens 10-N 16-E
" "	**3**	3	St Stephens 11-N 14-E
" "	**15**	1	St Stephens 9-N 16-E
MCCORMICK	**23**	7	St Stephens 7-N 14-E
" "	**3**	3	St Stephens 11-N 14-E
" "	**10**	2	St Stephens 10-N 16-E
MCCOY	**4**	20	St Stephens 11-N 15-E
" "	**5**	7	St Stephens 11-N 16-E
MCCREELESS	**10**	1	St Stephens 10-N 16-E
MCCRORY	**6**	12	St Stephens 10-N 12-E
" "	**11**	7	St Stephens 9-N 12-E
" "	**12**	1	St Stephens 9-N 13-E
MCCULLOUGH	**10**	2	St Stephens 10-N 16-E
MCCURRY	**4**	1	St Stephens 11-N 15-E
" "	**14**	1	St Stephens 9-N 15-E
MCDANIEL	**8**	3	St Stephens 10-N 14-E
" "	**3**	3	St Stephens 11-N 14-E
" "	**23**	2	St Stephens 7-N 14-E
MCDONALD	**4**	1	St Stephens 11-N 15-E
" "	**5**	1	St Stephens 11-N 16-E
MCDUFEE	**6**	1	St Stephens 10-N 12-E
MCFARLAND	**4**	6	St Stephens 11-N 15-E
MCINEER	**5**	1	St Stephens 11-N 16-E
MCKEE	**1**	2	St Stephens 11-N 12-E
" "	**3**	1	St Stephens 11-N 14-E
MCKEITHEN	**13**	1	St Stephens 9-N 14-E
MCKENZIE	**9**	7	St Stephens 10-N 15-E
" "	**10**	2	St Stephens 10-N 16-E
MCKINZIE	**9**	9	St Stephens 10-N 15-E
" "	**10**	2	St Stephens 10-N 16-E
" "	**23**	1	St Stephens 7-N 14-E
MCLAIN	**19**	4	St Stephens 8-N 15-E
" "	**20**	2	St Stephens 8-N 16-E
MCLEAN	**9**	1	St Stephens 10-N 15-E
MCLEMORE	**7**	1	St Stephens 10-N 13-E
" "	**12**	1	St Stephens 9-N 13-E
MCLEOD	**1**	6	St Stephens 11-N 12-E
MCMULLEN	**3**	1	St Stephens 11-N 14-E
MCMULLINS	**21**	2	St Stephens 7-N 12-E
MCNEILL	**11**	10	St Stephens 9-N 12-E
MCPHERSON	**5**	9	St Stephens 11-N 16-E
" "	**22**	6	St Stephens 7-N 13-E
" "	**21**	3	St Stephens 7-N 12-E
" "	**7**	2	St Stephens 10-N 13-E
" "	**23**	2	St Stephens 7-N 14-E
" "	**4**	1	St Stephens 11-N 15-E
MCPOLLARD	**10**	1	St Stephens 10-N 16-E

Surname	Map Group	Parcels of Land	Meridian/Township/Range		
MCQUEEN	**8**	3	St Stephens	10-N	14-E
" "	**9**	1	St Stephens	10-N	15-E
MCWHORTER	**1**	1	St Stephens	11-N	12-E
MCWILLIAMS	**16**	3	St Stephens	8-N	12-E
MEALING	**3**	7	St Stephens	11-N	14-E
MENEES	**23**	6	St Stephens	7-N	14-E
MERCER	**4**	9	St Stephens	11-N	15-E
" "	**19**	4	St Stephens	8-N	15-E
" "	**14**	4	St Stephens	9-N	15-E
" "	**20**	3	St Stephens	8-N	16-E
" "	**18**	2	St Stephens	8-N	14-E
" "	**10**	1	St Stephens	10-N	16-E
MERCHANT	**24**	1	St Stephens	7-N	15-E
MIDDLEBROOKS	**9**	1	St Stephens	10-N	15-E
MILLER	**6**	4	St Stephens	10-N	12-E
" "	**9**	4	St Stephens	10-N	15-E
" "	**7**	2	St Stephens	10-N	13-E
" "	**22**	1	St Stephens	7-N	13-E
" "	**16**	1	St Stephens	8-N	12-E
MILLS	**10**	2	St Stephens	10-N	16-E
" "	**5**	1	St Stephens	11-N	16-E
" "	**22**	1	St Stephens	7-N	13-E
MILNER	**13**	23	St Stephens	9-N	14-E
" "	**17**	12	St Stephens	8-N	13-E
" "	**12**	10	St Stephens	9-N	13-E
" "	**16**	6	St Stephens	8-N	12-E
MILTON	**6**	3	St Stephens	10-N	12-E
MIMS	**21**	2	St Stephens	7-N	12-E
MINIARD	**22**	3	St Stephens	7-N	13-E
" "	**19**	1	St Stephens	8-N	15-E
MINTER	**6**	1	St Stephens	10-N	12-E
MINYARD	**19**	1	St Stephens	8-N	15-E
MITCHELL	**22**	3	St Stephens	7-N	13-E
" "	**23**	2	St Stephens	7-N	14-E
MIXON	**11**	1	St Stephens	9-N	12-E
MONTGOMERY	**19**	2	St Stephens	8-N	15-E
" "	**14**	2	St Stephens	9-N	15-E
MOORE	**18**	6	St Stephens	8-N	14-E
" "	**11**	6	St Stephens	9-N	12-E
" "	**16**	5	St Stephens	8-N	12-E
" "	**17**	5	St Stephens	8-N	13-E
" "	**2**	4	St Stephens	11-N	13-E
" "	**15**	3	St Stephens	9-N	16-E
" "	**7**	1	St Stephens	10-N	13-E
" "	**9**	1	St Stephens	10-N	15-E
" "	**24**	1	St Stephens	7-N	15-E
" "	**19**	1	St Stephens	8-N	15-E
MOORER	**1**	1	St Stephens	11-N	12-E
MOORMAN	**20**	3	St Stephens	8-N	16-E
" "	**15**	2	St Stephens	9-N	16-E
MORAN	**14**	1	St Stephens	9-N	15-E
MORGAN	**9**	15	St Stephens	10-N	15-E
" "	**10**	8	St Stephens	10-N	16-E
" "	**5**	3	St Stephens	11-N	16-E
MORRELL	**7**	2	St Stephens	10-N	13-E
MORRIS	**22**	2	St Stephens	7-N	13-E
" "	**12**	2	St Stephens	9-N	13-E
MORROW	**17**	6	St Stephens	8-N	13-E
" "	**1**	2	St Stephens	11-N	12-E
MOSELEY	**4**	7	St Stephens	11-N	15-E

Surname	Map Group	Parcels of Land	Meridian/Township/Range
MOSELEY (Cont'd)	23	2	St Stephens 7-N 14-E
MOSLEY	4	2	St Stephens 11-N 15-E
MOY	14	1	St Stephens 9-N 15-E
MULLANS	7	1	St Stephens 10-N 13-E
MULLENS	11	2	St Stephens 9-N 12-E
MUNCHUS	19	1	St Stephens 8-N 15-E
MUNDY	2	1	St Stephens 11-N 13-E
MURPHEY	6	6	St Stephens 10-N 12-E
" "	21	1	St Stephens 7-N 12-E
MURPHY	6	9	St Stephens 10-N 12-E
" "	11	1	St Stephens 9-N 12-E
" "	12	1	St Stephens 9-N 13-E
MURRAY	12	1	St Stephens 9-N 13-E
MURRY	4	1	St Stephens 11-N 15-E
MURSER	14	4	St Stephens 9-N 15-E
MYERS	21	5	St Stephens 7-N 12-E
" "	17	1	St Stephens 8-N 13-E
MYRES	21	1	St Stephens 7-N 12-E
MYRICK	11	2	St Stephens 9-N 12-E
" "	12	2	St Stephens 9-N 13-E
NEAL	2	4	St Stephens 11-N 13-E
" "	6	2	St Stephens 10-N 12-E
NELSON	2	1	St Stephens 11-N 13-E
NEVILLS	6	1	St Stephens 10-N 12-E
NEWTON	14	23	St Stephens 9-N 15-E
" "	13	6	St Stephens 9-N 14-E
" "	9	4	St Stephens 10-N 15-E
NICHOLAS	18	1	St Stephens 8-N 14-E
NICHOLES	18	1	St Stephens 8-N 14-E
NICHOLS	19	4	St Stephens 8-N 15-E
" "	18	2	St Stephens 8-N 14-E
" "	24	1	St Stephens 7-N 15-E
NIGHT	1	2	St Stephens 11-N 12-E
NIX	4	2	St Stephens 11-N 15-E
" "	10	1	St Stephens 10-N 16-E
" "	24	1	St Stephens 7-N 15-E
" "	20	1	St Stephens 8-N 16-E
NORMAN	5	2	St Stephens 11-N 16-E
NORRIS	12	9	St Stephens 9-N 13-E
" "	17	2	St Stephens 8-N 13-E
" "	16	1	St Stephens 8-N 12-E
NORSWORTHY	19	1	St Stephens 8-N 15-E
NORTHCUT	23	4	St Stephens 7-N 14-E
NORTHCUTT	22	1	St Stephens 7-N 13-E
ODOM	11	7	St Stephens 9-N 12-E
" "	12	5	St Stephens 9-N 13-E
OFARRELL	12	2	St Stephens 9-N 13-E
" "	1	1	St Stephens 11-N 12-E
OLIVER	8	8	St Stephens 10-N 14-E
" "	10	4	St Stephens 10-N 16-E
" "	9	1	St Stephens 10-N 15-E
" "	3	1	St Stephens 11-N 14-E
OPRY	23	1	St Stephens 7-N 14-E
OTT	4	1	St Stephens 11-N 15-E
OUTLAW	12	3	St Stephens 9-N 13-E
OVERSTREET	18	1	St Stephens 8-N 14-E
OWEN	11	1	St Stephens 9-N 12-E
OWENS	22	2	St Stephens 7-N 13-E
" "	16	2	St Stephens 8-N 12-E
PACKER	22	3	St Stephens 7-N 13-E

Surname	Map Group	Parcels of Land	Meridian/Township/Range		
PAGE	**21**	9	St Stephens	7-N	12-E
" "	**16**	8	St Stephens	8-N	12-E
PALMER	**1**	2	St Stephens	11-N	12-E
PARK	**6**	1	St Stephens	10-N	12-E
PARKER	**23**	10	St Stephens	7-N	14-E
" "	**16**	9	St Stephens	8-N	12-E
" "	**19**	8	St Stephens	8-N	15-E
" "	**12**	6	St Stephens	9-N	13-E
" "	**17**	5	St Stephens	8-N	13-E
" "	**18**	3	St Stephens	8-N	14-E
" "	**7**	1	St Stephens	10-N	13-E
" "	**21**	1	St Stephens	7-N	12-E
" "	**22**	1	St Stephens	7-N	13-E
" "	**11**	1	St Stephens	9-N	12-E
PARKES	**11**	8	St Stephens	9-N	12-E
" "	**6**	2	St Stephens	10-N	12-E
PARKS	**11**	7	St Stephens	9-N	12-E
" "	**6**	2	St Stephens	10-N	12-E
PARMER	**19**	13	St Stephens	8-N	15-E
" "	**12**	6	St Stephens	9-N	13-E
" "	**8**	4	St Stephens	10-N	14-E
" "	**17**	4	St Stephens	8-N	13-E
" "	**10**	1	St Stephens	10-N	16-E
" "	**3**	1	St Stephens	11-N	14-E
" "	**5**	1	St Stephens	11-N	16-E
" "	**13**	1	St Stephens	9-N	14-E
PARRISH	**7**	1	St Stephens	10-N	13-E
PARROTT	**11**	1	St Stephens	9-N	12-E
PATTERSON	**2**	3	St Stephens	11-N	13-E
PATTILLO	**9**	5	St Stephens	10-N	15-E
" "	**4**	3	St Stephens	11-N	15-E
PATTON	**2**	9	St Stephens	11-N	13-E
" "	**7**	2	St Stephens	10-N	13-E
" "	**18**	1	St Stephens	8-N	14-E
PAUL	**2**	1	St Stephens	11-N	13-E
PAYNE	**3**	11	St Stephens	11-N	14-E
" "	**9**	10	St Stephens	10-N	15-E
" "	**8**	1	St Stephens	10-N	14-E
" "	**4**	1	St Stephens	11-N	15-E
PEACOCK	**21**	7	St Stephens	7-N	12-E
" "	**22**	1	St Stephens	7-N	13-E
PEAGLER	**2**	13	St Stephens	11-N	13-E
PEARCE	**3**	5	St Stephens	11-N	14-E
" "	**18**	1	St Stephens	8-N	14-E
PEARMAN	**3**	1	St Stephens	11-N	14-E
PEARMON	**3**	1	St Stephens	11-N	14-E
PEARSON	**1**	2	St Stephens	11-N	12-E
PEARY	**23**	1	St Stephens	7-N	14-E
" "	**24**	1	St Stephens	7-N	15-E
PEAVY	**23**	14	St Stephens	7-N	14-E
PEEVY	**23**	7	St Stephens	7-N	14-E
" "	**8**	2	St Stephens	10-N	14-E
" "	**10**	1	St Stephens	10-N	16-E
" "	**5**	1	St Stephens	11-N	16-E
PERDUE	**5**	9	St Stephens	11-N	16-E
" "	**8**	3	St Stephens	10-N	14-E
" "	**10**	3	St Stephens	10-N	16-E
PERRITT	**6**	10	St Stephens	10-N	12-E
" "	**19**	3	St Stephens	8-N	15-E
" "	**7**	1	St Stephens	10-N	13-E

Surname	Map Group	Parcels of Land	Meridian/Township/Range
PERRITT (Cont'd)	18	1	St Stephens 8-N 14-E
PERRY	14	16	St Stephens 9-N 15-E
" "	9	4	St Stephens 10-N 15-E
" "	13	4	St Stephens 9-N 14-E
" "	19	3	St Stephens 8-N 15-E
" "	20	3	St Stephens 8-N 16-E
" "	7	1	St Stephens 10-N 13-E
" "	3	1	St Stephens 11-N 14-E
" "	23	1	St Stephens 7-N 14-E
" "	15	1	St Stephens 9-N 16-E
PETERGRO	8	1	St Stephens 10-N 14-E
PETERSON	10	1	St Stephens 10-N 16-E
PETTY	18	1	St Stephens 8-N 14-E
PEVEY	23	1	St Stephens 7-N 14-E
PEVY	8	1	St Stephens 10-N 14-E
" "	23	1	St Stephens 7-N 14-E
PHELPS	10	13	St Stephens 10-N 16-E
" "	15	8	St Stephens 9-N 16-E
" "	9	4	St Stephens 10-N 15-E
PHILIPS	6	1	St Stephens 10-N 12-E
" "	4	1	St Stephens 11-N 15-E
PHILLIPS	11	6	St Stephens 9-N 12-E
" "	3	2	St Stephens 11-N 14-E
" "	13	2	St Stephens 9-N 14-E
PICKENS	14	8	St Stephens 9-N 15-E
" "	7	4	St Stephens 10-N 13-E
" "	9	2	St Stephens 10-N 15-E
" "	3	1	St Stephens 11-N 14-E
" "	4	1	St Stephens 11-N 15-E
PIERCE	9	2	St Stephens 10-N 15-E
" "	8	1	St Stephens 10-N 14-E
PIGGOT	16	3	St Stephens 8-N 12-E
PINGLETON	4	2	St Stephens 11-N 15-E
PINKERTON	11	5	St Stephens 9-N 12-E
PIPKIN	21	3	St Stephens 7-N 12-E
PIRKINS	1	2	St Stephens 11-N 12-E
PITTS	24	6	St Stephens 7-N 15-E
" "	19	1	St Stephens 8-N 15-E
PLAYER	4	1	St Stephens 11-N 15-E
POLLARD	9	3	St Stephens 10-N 15-E
" "	10	3	St Stephens 10-N 16-E
" "	16	2	St Stephens 8-N 12-E
" "	17	2	St Stephens 8-N 13-E
POOL	3	3	St Stephens 11-N 14-E
POOLE	2	4	St Stephens 11-N 13-E
PORTER	18	6	St Stephens 8-N 14-E
" "	14	3	St Stephens 9-N 15-E
PORTERFIELD	3	1	St Stephens 11-N 14-E
POSEY	7	1	St Stephens 10-N 13-E
" "	1	1	St Stephens 11-N 12-E
" "	2	1	St Stephens 11-N 13-E
POWELL	1	16	St Stephens 11-N 12-E
" "	12	7	St Stephens 9-N 13-E
" "	22	5	St Stephens 7-N 13-E
" "	7	3	St Stephens 10-N 13-E
" "	17	1	St Stephens 8-N 13-E
" "	13	1	St Stephens 9-N 14-E
POWERS	1	3	St Stephens 11-N 12-E
PRESLAR	23	10	St Stephens 7-N 14-E
" "	21	5	St Stephens 7-N 12-E

Surname	Map Group	Parcels of Land	Meridian/Township/Range
PRESLAR (Cont'd)	**22**	4	St Stephens 7-N 13-E
PRESLEY	**21**	15	St Stephens 7-N 12-E
" "	**23**	2	St Stephens 7-N 14-E
" "	**12**	1	St Stephens 9-N 13-E
PRESSLAR	**23**	2	St Stephens 7-N 14-E
PRESSLEY	**21**	1	St Stephens 7-N 12-E
PREWETT	**24**	1	St Stephens 7-N 15-E
PRICE	**17**	3	St Stephens 8-N 13-E
" "	**22**	1	St Stephens 7-N 13-E
" "	**16**	1	St Stephens 8-N 12-E
PRUETT	**22**	2	St Stephens 7-N 13-E
" "	**23**	2	St Stephens 7-N 14-E
" "	**21**	1	St Stephens 7-N 12-E
" "	**24**	1	St Stephens 7-N 15-E
PRUITT	**2**	2	St Stephens 11-N 13-E
" "	**24**	1	St Stephens 7-N 15-E
PUGH	**12**	15	St Stephens 9-N 13-E
" "	**17**	3	St Stephens 8-N 13-E
PULASKI	**17**	2	St Stephens 8-N 13-E
PURDY	**9**	2	St Stephens 10-N 15-E
" "	**14**	1	St Stephens 9-N 15-E
PURVIS	**16**	6	St Stephens 8-N 12-E
QUARLES	**15**	3	St Stephens 9-N 16-E
QUINNELLY	**22**	2	St Stephens 7-N 13-E
" "	**23**	2	St Stephens 7-N 14-E
RABOURN	**9**	1	St Stephens 10-N 15-E
RABUN	**4**	6	St Stephens 11-N 15-E
" "	**10**	3	St Stephens 10-N 16-E
" "	**15**	2	St Stephens 9-N 16-E
RABURN	**15**	6	St Stephens 9-N 16-E
" "	**9**	4	St Stephens 10-N 15-E
" "	**10**	4	St Stephens 10-N 16-E
" "	**14**	1	St Stephens 9-N 15-E
RAINEE	**24**	1	St Stephens 7-N 15-E
RAINER	**24**	1	St Stephens 7-N 15-E
RAINEY	**7**	1	St Stephens 10-N 13-E
RAINS	**9**	1	St Stephens 10-N 15-E
RAY	**3**	3	St Stephens 11-N 14-E
" "	**2**	1	St Stephens 11-N 13-E
RAYBORNE	**10**	1	St Stephens 10-N 16-E
REAVES	**23**	2	St Stephens 7-N 14-E
" "	**12**	1	St Stephens 9-N 13-E
REDDOCH	**8**	4	St Stephens 10-N 14-E
REDDOCK	**8**	9	St Stephens 10-N 14-E
" "	**19**	8	St Stephens 8-N 15-E
REEVES	**9**	2	St Stephens 10-N 15-E
" "	**12**	1	St Stephens 9-N 13-E
REID	**24**	22	St Stephens 7-N 15-E
" "	**8**	3	St Stephens 10-N 14-E
" "	**9**	2	St Stephens 10-N 15-E
" "	**3**	1	St Stephens 11-N 14-E
" "	**19**	1	St Stephens 8-N 15-E
REMLEY	**9**	1	St Stephens 10-N 15-E
REYNOLDS	**9**	3	St Stephens 10-N 15-E
" "	**6**	2	St Stephens 10-N 12-E
" "	**7**	2	St Stephens 10-N 13-E
" "	**12**	1	St Stephens 9-N 13-E
" "	**13**	1	St Stephens 9-N 14-E
RHAME	**15**	3	St Stephens 9-N 16-E
RHOADS	**13**	2	St Stephens 9-N 14-E

Surname	Map Group	Parcels of Land	Meridian/Township/Range
RHODES	13	42	St Stephens	9-N	14-E
" "	8	5	St Stephens	10-N	14-E
" "	12	4	St Stephens	9-N	13-E
" "	6	3	St Stephens	10-N	12-E
" "	14	3	St Stephens	9-N	15-E
" "	9	2	St Stephens	10-N	15-E
" "	23	2	St Stephens	7-N	14-E
" "	22	1	St Stephens	7-N	13-E
RICHARDS	4	1	St Stephens	11-N	15-E
RICHARDSON	6	1	St Stephens	10-N	12-E
" "	7	1	St Stephens	10-N	13-E
" "	1	1	St Stephens	11-N	12-E
" "	12	1	St Stephens	9-N	13-E
RIDDOCK	19	1	St Stephens	8-N	15-E
RIGSBY	18	2	St Stephens	8-N	14-E
RILEY	17	8	St Stephens	8-N	13-E
" "	23	7	St Stephens	7-N	14-E
" "	16	1	St Stephens	8-N	12-E
ROACH	15	4	St Stephens	9-N	16-E
ROAD	6	1	St Stephens	10-N	12-E
ROBERSON	14	4	St Stephens	9-N	15-E
" "	9	2	St Stephens	10-N	15-E
ROBERTS	21	3	St Stephens	7-N	12-E
" "	9	1	St Stephens	10-N	15-E
" "	22	1	St Stephens	7-N	13-E
" "	14	1	St Stephens	9-N	15-E
ROBINSON	9	1	St Stephens	10-N	15-E
" "	1	1	St Stephens	11-N	12-E
" "	17	1	St Stephens	8-N	13-E
" "	13	1	St Stephens	9-N	14-E
ROBISON	6	1	St Stephens	10-N	12-E
ROGERS	21	9	St Stephens	7-N	12-E
" "	3	8	St Stephens	11-N	14-E
" "	24	3	St Stephens	7-N	15-E
" "	7	1	St Stephens	10-N	13-E
ROPER	5	2	St Stephens	11-N	16-E
ROSE	24	6	St Stephens	7-N	15-E
ROSS	7	1	St Stephens	10-N	13-E
" "	3	1	St Stephens	11-N	14-E
ROUTON	8	8	St Stephens	10-N	14-E
" "	18	3	St Stephens	8-N	14-E
" "	3	1	St Stephens	11-N	14-E
" "	4	1	St Stephens	11-N	15-E
RUFFIN	14	1	St Stephens	9-N	15-E
RUGELEY	8	2	St Stephens	10-N	14-E
RUMPH	6	1	St Stephens	10-N	12-E
RUSHTON	9	2	St Stephens	10-N	15-E
" "	22	2	St Stephens	7-N	13-E
RUSTIN	17	2	St Stephens	8-N	13-E
RYALS	18	3	St Stephens	8-N	14-E
SALTER	4	3	St Stephens	11-N	15-E
" "	21	1	St Stephens	7-N	12-E
SANDERS	19	4	St Stephens	8-N	15-E
" "	17	1	St Stephens	8-N	13-E
SANFORD	20	6	St Stephens	8-N	16-E
" "	22	1	St Stephens	7-N	13-E
SARTAIN	2	1	St Stephens	11-N	13-E
SARTOR	23	8	St Stephens	7-N	14-E
" "	18	1	St Stephens	8-N	14-E
SAUCER	12	5	St Stephens	9-N	13-E

Surname	Map Group	Parcels of Land	Meridian/Township/Range
SAUCER (Cont'd)	17	2	St Stephens 8-N 13-E
SAUNDERS	1	1	St Stephens 11-N 12-E
SAVAGE	11	4	St Stephens 9-N 12-E
SCARBOROUGH	21	2	St Stephens 7-N 12-E
" "	7	1	St Stephens 10-N 13-E
" "	15	1	St Stephens 9-N 16-E
SCIPPER	21	2	St Stephens 7-N 12-E
" "	10	1	St Stephens 10-N 16-E
SCONYERS	2	1	St Stephens 11-N 13-E
SEAL	8	2	St Stephens 10-N 14-E
" "	6	1	St Stephens 10-N 12-E
" "	11	1	St Stephens 9-N 12-E
SEALE	6	12	St Stephens 10-N 12-E
" "	8	12	St Stephens 10-N 14-E
" "	7	1	St Stephens 10-N 13-E
SEARCY	23	1	St Stephens 7-N 14-E
SEEGAR	23	5	St Stephens 7-N 14-E
SELLARS	20	1	St Stephens 8-N 16-E
SELLERS	22	7	St Stephens 7-N 13-E
" "	23	2	St Stephens 7-N 14-E
" "	7	1	St Stephens 10-N 13-E
" "	20	1	St Stephens 8-N 16-E
SENTELL	9	4	St Stephens 10-N 15-E
SEXTON	18	2	St Stephens 8-N 14-E
SHAROCK	1	6	St Stephens 11-N 12-E
SHAW	9	6	St Stephens 10-N 15-E
SHELL	21	1	St Stephens 7-N 12-E
SHEPARD	17	4	St Stephens 8-N 13-E
SHEPHEARD	17	1	St Stephens 8-N 13-E
SHEPHERD	17	12	St Stephens 8-N 13-E
" "	12	5	St Stephens 9-N 13-E
" "	4	1	St Stephens 11-N 15-E
SHEPPARD	4	10	St Stephens 11-N 15-E
" "	9	4	St Stephens 10-N 15-E
" "	17	1	St Stephens 8-N 13-E
SHIELDS	5	2	St Stephens 11-N 16-E
SHINE	24	17	St Stephens 7-N 15-E
" "	18	1	St Stephens 8-N 14-E
SHIPP	13	1	St Stephens 9-N 14-E
SHOWS	15	1	St Stephens 9-N 16-E
SHULTZ	11	2	St Stephens 9-N 12-E
SIMMONS	19	2	St Stephens 8-N 15-E
" "	2	1	St Stephens 11-N 13-E
" "	24	1	St Stephens 7-N 15-E
SIMPSON	21	4	St Stephens 7-N 12-E
" "	6	1	St Stephens 10-N 12-E
" "	17	1	St Stephens 8-N 13-E
SIMS	17	14	St Stephens 8-N 13-E
" "	6	9	St Stephens 10-N 12-E
" "	11	9	St Stephens 9-N 12-E
" "	16	5	St Stephens 8-N 12-E
" "	12	3	St Stephens 9-N 13-E
" "	18	2	St Stephens 8-N 14-E
" "	19	2	St Stephens 8-N 15-E
" "	8	1	St Stephens 10-N 14-E
" "	14	1	St Stephens 9-N 15-E
SINGLETARY	17	3	St Stephens 8-N 13-E
SINGLETON	18	3	St Stephens 8-N 14-E
SIRMON	16	7	St Stephens 8-N 12-E
" "	11	3	St Stephens 9-N 12-E

Surname	Map Group	Parcels of Land	Meridian/Township/Range
SIRMON (Cont'd)	13	1	St Stephens 9-N 14-E
SKINNER	8	9	St Stephens 10-N 14-E
" "	21	1	St Stephens 7-N 12-E
SKIPPER	10	4	St Stephens 10-N 16-E
SLATER	7	1	St Stephens 10-N 13-E
SLATON	20	3	St Stephens 8-N 16-E
SMALLWOOD	23	1	St Stephens 7-N 14-E
SMITH	14	20	St Stephens 9-N 15-E
" "	17	15	St Stephens 8-N 13-E
" "	9	11	St Stephens 10-N 15-E
" "	24	11	St Stephens 7-N 15-E
" "	19	6	St Stephens 8-N 15-E
" "	13	6	St Stephens 9-N 14-E
" "	15	6	St Stephens 9-N 16-E
" "	3	5	St Stephens 11-N 14-E
" "	23	5	St Stephens 7-N 14-E
" "	6	4	St Stephens 10-N 12-E
" "	1	3	St Stephens 11-N 12-E
" "	16	3	St Stephens 8-N 12-E
" "	18	3	St Stephens 8-N 14-E
" "	2	2	St Stephens 11-N 13-E
" "	5	2	St Stephens 11-N 16-E
" "	21	2	St Stephens 7-N 12-E
" "	7	1	St Stephens 10-N 13-E
" "	8	1	St Stephens 10-N 14-E
" "	10	1	St Stephens 10-N 16-E
" "	20	1	St Stephens 8-N 16-E
" "	11	1	St Stephens 9-N 12-E
" "	12	1	St Stephens 9-N 13-E
SMYTH	14	18	St Stephens 9-N 15-E
" "	13	16	St Stephens 9-N 14-E
" "	24	7	St Stephens 7-N 15-E
" "	15	4	St Stephens 9-N 16-E
" "	8	1	St Stephens 10-N 14-E
" "	10	1	St Stephens 10-N 16-E
" "	3	1	St Stephens 11-N 14-E
" "	19	1	St Stephens 8-N 15-E
SMYTHE	13	1	St Stephens 9-N 14-E
SNELGROVE	17	3	St Stephens 8-N 13-E
SOLOMON	24	2	St Stephens 7-N 15-E
SORCER	17	1	St Stephens 8-N 13-E
SORELL	9	1	St Stephens 10-N 15-E
SORRELLS	19	4	St Stephens 8-N 15-E
SPEARS	12	2	St Stephens 9-N 13-E
" "	24	1	St Stephens 7-N 15-E
SPURLOCK	15	1	St Stephens 9-N 16-E
STAGGERS	15	13	St Stephens 9-N 16-E
STALLINGS	24	17	St Stephens 7-N 15-E
" "	8	6	St Stephens 10-N 14-E
STAMPS	17	2	St Stephens 8-N 13-E
STANFORD	23	3	St Stephens 7-N 14-E
STANLEY	23	1	St Stephens 7-N 14-E
STEANE	1	1	St Stephens 11-N 12-E
STEINER	5	2	St Stephens 11-N 16-E
STEPHENS	2	1	St Stephens 11-N 13-E
STEVENS	1	1	St Stephens 11-N 12-E
" "	19	1	St Stephens 8-N 15-E
STEWARD	6	3	St Stephens 10-N 12-E
STEWART	23	10	St Stephens 7-N 14-E
" "	1	2	St Stephens 11-N 12-E

Surname	Map Group	Parcels of Land	Meridian/Township/Range
STEWART (Cont'd)	**9**	1	St Stephens 10-N 15-E
" "	**2**	1	St Stephens 11-N 13-E
" "	**4**	1	St Stephens 11-N 15-E
" "	**12**	1	St Stephens 9-N 13-E
STILL	**21**	2	St Stephens 7-N 12-E
STINER	**5**	1	St Stephens 11-N 16-E
STINSON	**11**	20	St Stephens 9-N 12-E
" "	**21**	4	St Stephens 7-N 12-E
" "	**16**	1	St Stephens 8-N 12-E
STOCKMAN	**6**	5	St Stephens 10-N 12-E
" "	**4**	1	St Stephens 11-N 15-E
" "	**5**	1	St Stephens 11-N 16-E
STOTT	**21**	7	St Stephens 7-N 12-E
" "	**12**	4	St Stephens 9-N 13-E
" "	**17**	1	St Stephens 8-N 13-E
STRINGER	**5**	10	St Stephens 11-N 16-E
STRINGFELLOW	**6**	6	St Stephens 10-N 12-E
" "	**11**	1	St Stephens 9-N 12-E
STUART	**23**	5	St Stephens 7-N 14-E
" "	**22**	1	St Stephens 7-N 13-E
STUCKEY	**16**	1	St Stephens 8-N 12-E
SULLIVAN	**24**	1	St Stephens 7-N 15-E
SWEETEN	**16**	1	St Stephens 8-N 12-E
TALLENT	**22**	2	St Stephens 7-N 13-E
TALLEY	**4**	18	St Stephens 11-N 15-E
" "	**5**	3	St Stephens 11-N 16-E
" "	**1**	2	St Stephens 11-N 12-E
TALLY	**1**	1	St Stephens 11-N 12-E
" "	**4**	1	St Stephens 11-N 15-E
TANKERSLEY	**11**	2	St Stephens 9-N 12-E
TARVER	**1**	4	St Stephens 11-N 12-E
TATE	**11**	2	St Stephens 9-N 12-E
TATOM	**15**	2	St Stephens 9-N 16-E
" "	**14**	1	St Stephens 9-N 15-E
TAYLOR	**8**	6	St Stephens 10-N 14-E
" "	**9**	5	St Stephens 10-N 15-E
" "	**4**	5	St Stephens 11-N 15-E
" "	**10**	2	St Stephens 10-N 16-E
" "	**3**	2	St Stephens 11-N 14-E
" "	**12**	2	St Stephens 9-N 13-E
" "	**2**	1	St Stephens 11-N 13-E
" "	**5**	1	St Stephens 11-N 16-E
" "	**17**	1	St Stephens 8-N 13-E
TEAGLER	**2**	2	St Stephens 11-N 13-E
TERRELL	**7**	1	St Stephens 10-N 13-E
TERRY	**10**	7	St Stephens 10-N 16-E
THAGARD	**11**	1	St Stephens 9-N 12-E
THIGPEN	**2**	5	St Stephens 11-N 13-E
" "	**3**	5	St Stephens 11-N 14-E
" "	**1**	1	St Stephens 11-N 12-E
THIGPIN	**2**	2	St Stephens 11-N 13-E
THOMAS	**14**	22	St Stephens 9-N 15-E
" "	**5**	14	St Stephens 11-N 16-E
" "	**19**	13	St Stephens 8-N 15-E
" "	**13**	12	St Stephens 9-N 14-E
" "	**16**	7	St Stephens 8-N 12-E
" "	**9**	5	St Stephens 10-N 15-E
" "	**22**	2	St Stephens 7-N 13-E
" "	**15**	2	St Stephens 9-N 16-E
" "	**17**	1	St Stephens 8-N 13-E

Surname	Map Group	Parcels of Land	Meridian/Township/Range		
THOMASON	9	1	St Stephens	10-N	15-E
" "	17	1	St Stephens	8-N	13-E
THOMPSON	11	26	St Stephens	9-N	12-E
" "	1	10	St Stephens	11-N	12-E
" "	7	7	St Stephens	10-N	13-E
" "	6	6	St Stephens	10-N	12-E
" "	13	5	St Stephens	9-N	14-E
" "	9	4	St Stephens	10-N	15-E
" "	16	4	St Stephens	8-N	12-E
" "	10	2	St Stephens	10-N	16-E
THORINGTON	2	1	St Stephens	11-N	13-E
THORNTON	5	6	St Stephens	11-N	16-E
" "	10	4	St Stephens	10-N	16-E
" "	9	2	St Stephens	10-N	15-E
" "	2	1	St Stephens	11-N	13-E
TIGNER	8	1	St Stephens	10-N	14-E
TILL	1	2	St Stephens	11-N	12-E
TILLERY	4	23	St Stephens	11-N	15-E
TILLMAN	18	1	St Stephens	8-N	14-E
TILMAN	24	2	St Stephens	7-N	15-E
" "	18	1	St Stephens	8-N	14-E
TILMON	24	4	St Stephens	7-N	15-E
TINSLEY	9	3	St Stephens	10-N	15-E
" "	4	2	St Stephens	11-N	15-E
" "	10	1	St Stephens	10-N	16-E
TIPTON	16	3	St Stephens	8-N	12-E
TISDALE	23	1	St Stephens	7-N	14-E
TOBIAS	18	1	St Stephens	8-N	14-E
TOLIN	22	1	St Stephens	7-N	13-E
TORRENCE	23	2	St Stephens	7-N	14-E
TRAMMEL	11	4	St Stephens	9-N	12-E
TRAMMELL	19	2	St Stephens	8-N	15-E
TRAWEEK	1	16	St Stephens	11-N	12-E
" "	6	4	St Stephens	10-N	12-E
TROWELL	1	1	St Stephens	11-N	12-E
TURNER	14	7	St Stephens	9-N	15-E
" "	18	2	St Stephens	8-N	14-E
" "	13	2	St Stephens	9-N	14-E
" "	6	1	St Stephens	10-N	12-E
" "	10	1	St Stephens	10-N	16-E
" "	1	1	St Stephens	11-N	12-E
" "	2	1	St Stephens	11-N	13-E
" "	3	1	St Stephens	11-N	14-E
TYNER	19	7	St Stephens	8-N	15-E
TYNES	22	3	St Stephens	7-N	13-E
" "	24	2	St Stephens	7-N	15-E
" "	17	1	St Stephens	8-N	13-E
" "	12	1	St Stephens	9-N	13-E
VANN	8	1	St Stephens	10-N	14-E
VARNER	5	2	St Stephens	11-N	16-E
" "	4	1	St Stephens	11-N	15-E
VEAZEY	10	6	St Stephens	10-N	16-E
VICKREY	6	5	St Stephens	10-N	12-E
" "	11	2	St Stephens	9-N	12-E
VICKRY	11	3	St Stephens	9-N	12-E
VINES	13	4	St Stephens	9-N	14-E
WADE	8	8	St Stephens	10-N	14-E
" "	3	4	St Stephens	11-N	14-E
" "	24	2	St Stephens	7-N	15-E
" "	2	1	St Stephens	11-N	13-E

Surname	Map Group	Parcels of Land	Meridian/Township/Range
WADKINS	**13**	1	St Stephens 9-N 14-E
WALKER	**8**	2	St Stephens 10-N 14-E
" "	**17**	2	St Stephens 8-N 13-E
" "	**14**	2	St Stephens 9-N 15-E
" "	**3**	1	St Stephens 11-N 14-E
" "	**4**	1	St Stephens 11-N 15-E
" "	**18**	1	St Stephens 8-N 14-E
WALL	**24**	6	St Stephens 7-N 15-E
WALLACE	**3**	3	St Stephens 11-N 14-E
" "	**21**	2	St Stephens 7-N 12-E
" "	**22**	2	St Stephens 7-N 13-E
" "	**6**	1	St Stephens 10-N 12-E
" "	**9**	1	St Stephens 10-N 15-E
WALLER	**8**	4	St Stephens 10-N 14-E
" "	**7**	3	St Stephens 10-N 13-E
" "	**3**	1	St Stephens 11-N 14-E
" "	**22**	1	St Stephens 7-N 13-E
WALLS	**6**	1	St Stephens 10-N 12-E
WALTERS	**17**	3	St Stephens 8-N 13-E
WARD	**12**	4	St Stephens 9-N 13-E
" "	**13**	4	St Stephens 9-N 14-E
" "	**21**	3	St Stephens 7-N 12-E
" "	**22**	3	St Stephens 7-N 13-E
" "	**1**	2	St Stephens 11-N 12-E
" "	**17**	2	St Stephens 8-N 13-E
" "	**2**	1	St Stephens 11-N 13-E
" "	**15**	1	St Stephens 9-N 16-E
WARDEN	**12**	3	St Stephens 9-N 13-E
WARE	**2**	2	St Stephens 11-N 13-E
WARREN	**6**	3	St Stephens 10-N 12-E
WASDEN	**12**	1	St Stephens 9-N 13-E
WASDIN	**12**	2	St Stephens 9-N 13-E
WATERS	**1**	4	St Stephens 11-N 12-E
" "	**2**	4	St Stephens 11-N 13-E
" "	**7**	3	St Stephens 10-N 13-E
" "	**18**	1	St Stephens 8-N 14-E
" "	**13**	1	St Stephens 9-N 14-E
WATSON	**18**	6	St Stephens 8-N 14-E
" "	**23**	3	St Stephens 7-N 14-E
" "	**3**	2	St Stephens 11-N 14-E
" "	**8**	1	St Stephens 10-N 14-E
" "	**1**	1	St Stephens 11-N 12-E
WATTS	**6**	18	St Stephens 10-N 12-E
" "	**1**	4	St Stephens 11-N 12-E
" "	**7**	1	St Stephens 10-N 13-E
WEAVER	**21**	1	St Stephens 7-N 12-E
" "	**22**	1	St Stephens 7-N 13-E
" "	**24**	1	St Stephens 7-N 15-E
WEBB	**4**	1	St Stephens 11-N 15-E
" "	**5**	1	St Stephens 11-N 16-E
WELCH	**12**	1	St Stephens 9-N 13-E
WELLS	**4**	2	St Stephens 11-N 15-E
" "	**24**	1	St Stephens 7-N 15-E
WEST	**13**	4	St Stephens 9-N 14-E
" "	**21**	3	St Stephens 7-N 12-E
" "	**22**	1	St Stephens 7-N 13-E
WHEELER	**23**	3	St Stephens 7-N 14-E
" "	**24**	1	St Stephens 7-N 15-E
WHIDDON	**10**	2	St Stephens 10-N 16-E
" "	**22**	2	St Stephens 7-N 13-E

Surname	Map Group	Parcels of Land	Meridian/Township/Range		
WHIDDON (Cont'd)	14	1	St Stephens	9-N	15-E
WHITE	4	3	St Stephens	11-N	15-E
" "	11	2	St Stephens	9-N	12-E
" "	12	2	St Stephens	9-N	13-E
WHITHERINGTON	16	1	St Stephens	8-N	12-E
WHITTED	22	1	St Stephens	7-N	13-E
WHITTEN	4	2	St Stephens	11-N	15-E
" "	10	1	St Stephens	10-N	16-E
WHITTINGTON	11	3	St Stephens	9-N	12-E
" "	17	1	St Stephens	8-N	13-E
WHITTON	10	1	St Stephens	10-N	16-E
WIGGINS	22	5	St Stephens	7-N	13-E
" "	12	1	St Stephens	9-N	13-E
WIGHT	4	3	St Stephens	11-N	15-E
WILKERSON	20	5	St Stephens	8-N	16-E
" "	14	5	St Stephens	9-N	15-E
" "	23	3	St Stephens	7-N	14-E
" "	19	3	St Stephens	8-N	15-E
" "	15	1	St Stephens	9-N	16-E
WILLIAMS	19	14	St Stephens	8-N	15-E
" "	23	9	St Stephens	7-N	14-E
" "	22	6	St Stephens	7-N	13-E
" "	18	5	St Stephens	8-N	14-E
" "	17	4	St Stephens	8-N	13-E
" "	21	3	St Stephens	7-N	12-E
" "	24	3	St Stephens	7-N	15-E
" "	12	1	St Stephens	9-N	13-E
WILLIAMSON	15	4	St Stephens	9-N	16-E
" "	9	2	St Stephens	10-N	15-E
" "	24	1	St Stephens	7-N	15-E
WILLSON	3	1	St Stephens	11-N	14-E
" "	4	1	St Stephens	11-N	15-E
WILSON	24	6	St Stephens	7-N	15-E
" "	11	5	St Stephens	9-N	12-E
" "	4	3	St Stephens	11-N	15-E
WINBRAY	13	6	St Stephens	9-N	14-E
WINDHAM	3	5	St Stephens	11-N	14-E
WITHERINGTON	16	1	St Stephens	8-N	12-E
WOMACK	1	15	St Stephens	11-N	12-E
" "	2	13	St Stephens	11-N	13-E
" "	6	2	St Stephens	10-N	12-E
WOOD	20	2	St Stephens	8-N	16-E
" "	6	1	St Stephens	10-N	12-E
" "	19	1	St Stephens	8-N	15-E
WOODS	6	2	St Stephens	10-N	12-E
WOODSON	1	7	St Stephens	11-N	12-E
WORRELL	6	6	St Stephens	10-N	12-E
WREN	5	2	St Stephens	11-N	16-E
" "	14	2	St Stephens	9-N	15-E
" "	15	2	St Stephens	9-N	16-E
WRIGHT	9	29	St Stephens	10-N	15-E
" "	21	3	St Stephens	7-N	12-E
" "	23	1	St Stephens	7-N	14-E
WYNN	14	6	St Stephens	9-N	15-E
" "	12	1	St Stephens	9-N	13-E
YELDELL	1	13	St Stephens	11-N	12-E
" "	6	11	St Stephens	10-N	12-E
YOUNG	4	1	St Stephens	11-N	15-E

– Part II –

Township Map Groups

Map Group 1: Index to Land Patents

Township 11-North Range 12-East (St Stephens)

After you locate an individual in this Index, take note of the Section and Section Part then proceed to the Land Patent map on the pages immediately following. You should have no difficulty locating the corresponding parcel of land.

The "For More Info" Column will lead you to more information about the underlying Patents. See the *Legend* at right, and the "How to Use this Book" chapter, for more information.

```
                    LEGEND
          "For More Info . . . " column
A = Authority (Legislative Act, See Appendix "A")
B = Block or Lot (location in Section unknown)
C = Cancelled Patent
F = Fractional Section
G = Group  (Multi-Patentee Patent, see Appendix "C")
V = Overlaps another Parcel
R = Re-Issued (Parcel patented more than once)

(A & G items require you to look in the Appendixes referred
to above. All other Letter-designations followed by a number
require you to locate line-items in this index that possess
the ID number found after the letter).
```

ID	Individual in Patent	Sec.	Sec. Part	Date Issued	Other Counties	For More Info . . .
29	ARRINGTON, Asa	13	SE	1831-11-30		A1
30	" "	24	NESE	1835-04-15		A1
212	BAGGAN, Solomon	17	E½SE	1843-02-01		A1
130	BENSON, Jim	28	E½SW	1885-03-16		A2
11	BEVERLY, Alexander	36	SESW	1860-08-01		A1
12	" "	36	W½SW	1860-08-01		A1
25	BEVERLY, Anthony	2	SENW	1854-07-15		A1
26	" "	2	SWNE	1854-07-15		A1
132	BLANKENSHIP, John	31	NW	1823-12-01		A1
242	BLOCKSOM, Tinley	21	W½NE	1833-06-04		A1
60	BLOXOM, Ezekiel	32	NWNW	1837-08-09		A1
243	BLOXOM, Tinsley	32	SENW	1838-07-28		A1
46	BOGGAN, Daniel G	24	SESW	1850-04-01		A1
116	BOGGAN, James P	25	NWNE	1858-11-01		A1
118	" "	25	S½SW	1858-11-01		A1
117	" "	25	NWSW	1860-04-02		A1
119	" "	25	SWNW	1860-04-02		A1
120	" "	26	E½NE	1860-04-02		A1
121	" "	26	NESE	1860-04-02		A1
138	BOGGAN, John K	4	S½SW	1837-04-10		A1
195	BOGGAN, Robert L	9	E½SW	1830-11-16		A1
194	" "	4	NWSE	1837-04-10		A1
193	" "	4	NWNW	1837-05-20		A1
215	BOGGAN, Solomon	5	SE	1821-09-27		A1
216	" "	5	W½NE	1821-12-03		A1
217	" "	9	W½SW	1830-11-16		A1
213	" "	17	E½NE	1832-09-10		A1
214	" "	20	E½NW	1837-08-01		A1
180	BOGGIN, Margaret	20	W½NE	1826-05-08		A1
218	BOGGIN, Solomon	9	E½SE	1823-12-01		A1
259	BOND, William	23	E½SE	1841-05-20		A1
261	BONNER, William	20	W½SE	1833-06-04		A1
262	" "	21	W½NW	1833-06-04		A1
260	" "	17	W½SE	1843-02-01		A1
189	BRAGG, Rachel D	36	S½SE	1858-11-01		A1
133	BRANCH, John	25	SESE	1838-07-28		A1
184	BRANSFORD, Nathan	28	NENE	1835-10-08		A1
244	CAMP, Toliver M	1	SENE	1837-08-02		A1 F
126	CASSIDY, Jesse	2	NWNE	1858-11-01		A1
67	CHANCELLOR, George	32	SESW	1858-09-01		A1
79	CHANCELLOR, Gilbert	33	SWSW	1841-05-20		A1
76	" "	33	E½NW	1858-11-01		A1 V43
77	" "	33	S½NE	1858-11-01		A1
78	" "	33	SE	1858-11-01		A1
271	CHANCELLOR, William	32	NESW	1838-07-28		A1
4	COLEMAN, Abraham	23	NWSW	1837-08-14		A1

ID	Individual in Patent	Sec.	Sec. Part	Date Issued	Other Counties	For More Info . . .
15	COLEMAN, Allen W	11	E½SW	1833-09-16		A1
16	" "	14	W½NW	1833-09-16		A1
61	COLEMAN, Francis	13	SW	1831-08-01		A1
85	COLEMAN, Green W	23	SWNE	1835-10-14		A1
86	" "	23	W½SE	1837-08-12		A1
89	COLEMAN, Greene W	14	W½SW	1834-01-21		A1
91	" "	23	W½NW	1834-01-21		A1
90	" "	23	NENW	1835-09-12		A1
31	COOK, Bartlet	24	SWSW	1854-07-15		A1
40	COOK, Charles	21	NESE	1837-04-10		A1
41	" "	21	SWSE	1837-08-07		A1
42	" "	28	W½NE	1837-08-08		A1
257	COOPER, Washington	19	SWNW	1837-08-12		A1
43	CRANE, Charles H	33	SENW	1858-11-01		A1 V76
191	CROCHERON, Richard C	24	W½SE	1850-04-01		A1
192	" "	25	NENW	1850-04-01		A1
62	CRUM, Frederic	9	NWSE	1834-06-12		A1
65	CRUM, Frederick	9	W½NE	1829-07-01		A1
64	" "	9	SWSE	1835-04-02		A1
63	" "	4	S½SE	1837-04-10		A1
93	CRUM, Harman P	4	W½NE	1831-08-01		A1
92	" "	4	NESE	1834-06-12		A1
106	CRUM, Isaac F	3	W½NE	1832-08-08		A1
161	DAVIDSON, Joseph	19	E½SE	1837-08-14		A1
209	DENNIS, Samuel	12	W½NW	1831-08-01		A1
273	DRAKE, William	8	E½SW	1832-08-08		A1 G15
274	" "	8	W½NW	1832-08-08		A1 G15
272	" "	7	E½NE	1843-02-01		A1 G15
37	EDMONDSON, Caleb	1	NESW	1843-02-01		A1
38	" "	1	SWNE	1843-02-01		A1
49	ELDER, David	17	NWSW	1835-04-02		A1
50	" "	21	E½NW	1835-10-08		A1
51	" "	21	NESW	1837-04-10		A1
181	ELDER, Matthew	27	NWNW	1837-08-14		A1
182	" "	29	NWNE	1837-08-14		A1
153	ELEY, John W	15	SESW	1835-10-15		A1
154	" "	22	NWNE	1835-10-15		A1
245	FEAGIN, Tristram E	14	E½NW	1831-08-01		A1
115	FERGUSON, James	18	W½SW	1832-09-10		A1
114	FERGUSON, James F	18	W½NW	1831-12-01		A1
53	GASTON, David	6	W½SE	1832-09-10		A1 G19
52	" "	6	SWNE	1835-09-12		A1
112	GASTON, James A	29	SWNE	1849-09-01		A1
178	GLENN, Lewis R	1	W½NW	1852-02-02		A1
179	" "	2	E½NE	1854-07-15		A1
275	GRAY, William	34	E½SW	1860-12-01		A1
276	" "	34	SE	1860-12-01		A1
277	" "	34	SENW	1860-12-01		A1
80	GREEN, Gilbert	31	W½NE	1826-05-08		A1
113	GREEN, James B	31	E½NE	1826-05-08		A1
226	GRIGERS, Thomas	2	SWSE	1853-11-15		A1
170	HAWTHORN, Kedar	7	E½NW	1828-04-10		A1
228	HAYES, Thomas	9	E½NW	1826-05-12		A1
227	" "	9	E½NE	1826-07-10		A1
229	" "	9	W½NW	1830-11-16		A1
87	HAYS, Greenberry	23	NENE	1835-09-19		A1 R238
88	" "	3	SENE	1845-06-01		A1
137	HAYS, John	10	W½NW	1834-08-20		A1
145	HAYS, John N	2	NESE	1858-09-01		A1
230	HAYS, Thomas	3	W½NW	1834-05-12		A1
246	HAYS, Uriah M	1	NWSW	1845-06-01		A1
56	HERBERT, Edward H	1	NESE	1834-06-12		A1
57	" "	23	NWNE	1837-04-10		A1
72	HERBERT, George P	14	SE	1831-11-30		A1
73	HERBERT, George W	26	SESE	1895-06-28		A2
237	HERBERT, Thomas S	13	NE	1831-08-01		A1
236	" "	13	E½NW	1833-08-02		A1
239	" "	24	NW	1833-08-02		A1
238	" "	23	NENE	1834-06-12		A1 R87
164	HILL, Josiah	18	E½SW	1826-05-08		A1
168	" "	19	W½NE	1826-05-15		A1
166	" "	19	E½NW	1829-05-04		A1
162	" "	18	E½NW	1831-08-01		A1

ID	Individual in Patent	Sec.	Sec. Part	Date Issued	Other Counties	For More Info . . .
163	HILL, Josiah (Cont'd)	18	E½SE	1833-06-04		A1
165	" "	18	W½SE	1837-04-10		A1
167	" "	19	NWNW	1837-04-10		A1
47	HILSON, Daniel	36	SWNW	1884-12-05		A2
34	HOLCOMBE, Benjamin	20	E½NE	1837-08-07		A1
35	" "	20	E½SE	1837-08-07		A1
36	" "	21	W½SW	1837-08-07		A1
66	JACKSON, Frederick	28	NENW	1838-07-28		A1
13	JONES, Allen	1	SENW	1837-08-18		A1
102	JONES, Henry T	23	SENE	1837-04-10		A1
103	" "	24	NWSW	1837-04-10		A1
183	JONES, Matthias	24	NE	1831-08-01		A1
290	JONES, Wilson	29	SENW	1854-07-15		A1
169	KOLB, Josiah	26	NWSW	1843-02-01		A1
1	LEVINGSTON, A	15	NE	1822-01-01		A1
69	LEWIS, George	11	NE	1831-08-01		A1
68	" "	1	SWSW	1834-09-04		A1
71	" "	2	SESE	1834-09-04		A1
70	" "	12	E½NW	1843-02-01		A1
110	LEWIS, Jacob	10	SENW	1834-08-20		A1
111	" "	2	SWSW	1834-09-04		A1
139	LEWIS, John	12	SW	1831-08-01		A1
140	" "	14	E½NE	1833-06-04		A1
141	" "	25	NWNW	1835-10-01		A1
131	LEWIS, John B	2	NWSE	1852-02-02		A1
19	LITTLE, Amos	15	NWSW	1834-06-12		A1
20	" "	15	SWSW	1835-10-15		A1
22	" "	22	NWNW	1835-10-15		A1
21	" "	22	NENW	1837-08-07		A1
17	LITTLE, Amos A	2	N½NW	1852-12-01		A1
18	" "	2	SWNW	1852-12-01		A1
9	LIVINGSTON, Adam	11	NW	1831-11-30		A1
10	" "	11	W½SW	1833-09-16		A1
8	" "	10	NENW	1837-04-10		A1
203	MCCLOUD, Roderick	35	NENW	1858-11-01		A1
143	MCCONDICHIE, John	7	W½NW	1829-05-02		A1
142	" "	7	SW	1829-05-04		A1
105	MCKEE, Hugh	30	W½SW	1825-04-09		A1
104	" "	30	NESE	1858-11-01		A1
204	MCLEOD, Roderick	26	SENW	1858-11-01		A1
205	" "	26	SESW	1858-11-01		A1
206	" "	26	W½NW	1858-11-01		A1 R196
207	" "	35	SENW	1858-11-01		A1
208	" "	35	W½NE	1858-11-01		A1
283	MCLEOD, William	26	W½SE	1838-07-28		A1
144	MCWHORTER, John	28	NWSW	1858-11-01		A1
134	MOORER, John H	27	E½NW	1837-08-18		A1
5	MORROW, Abraham	30	W½NW	1826-05-01		A1
6	MORROW, Abram	20	W½NW	1827-01-08		A1
127	NIGHT, Jesse	30	E½NW	1826-05-08		A1
128	" "	30	E½SW	1826-05-08		A1
155	OFARRELL, John W	2	E½SW	1853-11-15		A1
122	PALMER, James	5	NWNW	1835-10-15		A1
284	PALMER, William	4	SWNW	1852-02-02		A2
263	PEARSON, William C	6	E½NE	1833-11-14		A1
264	" "	6	W½NW	1833-11-14		A1
58	PIRKINS, Elijah	22	SESW	1860-04-02		A1
59	" "	22	SWSE	1860-04-02		A1
196	POSEY, Robert	26	W½NW	1888-02-04		A2 R206
97	POWELL, Henry	32	W½SW	1821-09-27		A1
95	" "	31	E½SW	1821-12-03		A1
96	" "	31	W½SW	1827-01-01		A1
94	" "	17	E½SW	1827-05-15		A1
150	POWELL, John	7	W½NE	1843-02-01		A1
149	" "	32	SWNW	1852-02-02		A1
146	" "	29	S½SE	1858-11-01		A1
147	" "	32	NE	1858-11-01		A1
148	" "	32	NENW	1858-11-01		A1
53	POWELL, William	6	W½SW	1832-09-10		A1 G19
289	" "	5	SWNW	1835-10-14		A1
288	" "	29	NESE	1850-04-01		A1
285	" "	23	SESW	1858-11-01		A1
286	" "	26	NENW	1858-11-01		A1

ID	Individual in Patent	Sec.	Sec. Part	Date Issued	Other Counties	For More Info . . .
287	POWELL, William (Cont'd)	26	NWNE	1858-11-01		A1
291	POWELL, Zachariah	17	W½NE	1833-09-16		A1
151	POWERS, John S	30	SENE	1858-11-01		A1
152	" "	30	SESE	1858-11-01		A1
197	POWERS, Robert	28	SWSW	1882-10-30		A1
190	RICHARDSON, Ransom	28	W½SE	1885-03-16		A2
14	ROBINSON, Allen	24	NESW	1837-04-10		A1
54	SAUNDERS, David N	29	SESW	1849-09-01		A1
265	SHAROCK, William C	27	SESW	1858-11-01		A1
266	" "	27	SWSE	1858-11-01		A1
267	" "	34	NENW	1858-11-01		A1
268	" "	34	NWNE	1858-11-01		A1
269	" "	34	S½NE	1858-11-01		A1
270	" "	35	W½NW	1858-11-01		A1
101	SMITH, Henry	29	NENW	1850-04-01		A1 G42
100	" "	29	NENE	1852-12-01		A1
211	SMITH, Seth	6	W½SW	1843-02-01		A1
188	STEANE, Perry	6	E½SW	1843-02-01		A1
39	STEVENS, Carlton	26	NESW	1837-08-18		A1
28	STEWART, Archibald D	1	S½SE	1853-11-15		A1
27	" "	1	NWSE	1854-07-15		A1
186	TALLEY, Nathan	6	SENW	1834-09-04		A1
185	" "	6	NENW	1837-04-10		A1
187	TALLY, Nathan	6	NWNE	1837-04-10		A1
23	TARVER, Andrew	10	S½	1821-09-27		A1
24	" "	15	E½NW	1821-11-07		A1
32	TARVER, Benjamin H	15	W½NW	1826-05-08		A1
33	" "	4	NENE	1834-06-12		A1
278	THIGPEN, William H	5	E½NE	1845-06-01		A1
247	THOMPSON, Warren A	21	NWSE	1837-04-10		A1
249	" "	21	SESW	1837-05-20		A1
256	" "	4	SENW	1837-08-14		A1
248	" "	21	SESE	1837-08-18		A1
250	" "	27	NESW	1858-11-01		A1
251	" "	27	NWNE	1858-11-01		A1
252	" "	27	SWNW	1858-11-01		A1
253	" "	27	W½SW	1858-11-01		A1
254	" "	28	E½SE	1858-11-01		A1
255	" "	28	SENE	1858-11-01		A1
48	TILL, Daniel	21	E½NE	1837-08-09		A1
210	TILL, Samuel W	1	NWNE	1858-11-01		A1
171	TRAWEEK, Lafayette W	22	SESE	1858-09-01		A1
172	" "	23	SWSW	1858-09-01		A1
173	" "	27	E½NE	1858-09-01		A1
174	" "	27	E½SE	1858-09-01		A1
175	" "	27	NWSE	1858-09-01		A1
176	" "	34	NENE	1858-09-01		A1
231	TRAWEEK, Thomas M	28	S½NW	1858-11-01		A1
232	" "	29	NESW	1858-11-01		A1
233	" "	29	SENE	1858-11-01		A1
234	" "	29	W½NW	1858-11-01		A1
235	" "	29	W½SW	1858-11-01		A1
282	TRAWEEK, William H	8	NWNE	1835-04-15		A1
281	" "	4	N½SW	1837-08-07		A1
280	" "	20	SESW	1848-05-03		A1
101	" "	29	NENW	1850-04-01		A1 G42
279	" "	20	NWSW	1850-08-10		A1
7	TROWELL, Absalom B	25	SWSE	1837-08-15		A1
55	TURNER, David	25	E½NE	1837-08-18		A1
98	WARD, Henry R	17	SWSW	1837-05-15		A1
99	" "	19	E½NE	1837-05-15		A1
177	WATERS, Levi M	22	W½SW	1837-08-15		A1
241	WATERS, Thomas	12	SE	1831-08-01		A1
240	" "	12	NE	1837-08-09		A1
258	WATERS, Wilkes B	14	E½SW	1831-08-01		A1
219	WATSON, Stanmore	1	NENW	1834-08-20		A1
44	WATTS, Comer B	19	W½SE	1826-05-05		A1
45	WATTS, Corner B	30	W½NE	1826-05-05		A1
136	WATTS, John H	19	W½SW	1826-05-05		A1
135	" "	19	E½SW	1826-05-12		A1
75	WOMACK, George	11	SE	1831-11-30		A1 G46
74	" "	14	W½NE	1831-11-30		A1
107	WOMACK, Jacob L	25	NESE	1848-05-03		A1

ID	Individual in Patent	Sec.	Sec. Part	Date Issued	Other Counties	For More Info . . .
108	WOMACK, Jacob L (Cont'd)	36	N½NE	1858-11-01		A1
109	" "	36	NENW	1858-11-01		A1
129	WOMACK, Jesse	15	NESW	1837-04-10		A1
157	WOMACK, John	15	E½SE	1821-09-27		A1
158	" "	15	W½SE	1821-12-03		A1
75	" "	11	SE	1831-11-30		A1 G46
156	" "	13	W½NW	1831-11-30		A1
220	WOMACK, Thaddeus A	25	NWSE	1858-11-01		A1
221	" "	36	N½SE	1858-11-01		A1
222	" "	36	NESW	1858-11-01		A1
223	" "	36	NWNW	1858-11-01		A1
224	" "	36	S½NE	1858-11-01		A1
225	" "	36	SENW	1858-11-01		A1
3	WOODSON, Aaron H	22	NESW	1837-08-07		A1
2	" "	22	NESE	1837-08-18		A1
82	WOODSON, Goodin	22	NWSE	1835-10-08		A1
81	" "	22	NENE	1837-08-07		A1
83	" "	22	SWNE	1837-08-07		A1
84	WOODSON, Goodwin	22	SENE	1835-10-15		A1
125	WOODSON, James	22	S½NW	1835-10-15		A1
101	YELDELL, James R	29	NENW	1850-04-01		A1 G42
124	" "	33	NENE	1858-11-01		A1
123	" "	26	SWSW	1860-09-01		A1
101	YELDELL, Jonathan M	29	NENW	1850-04-01		A1 G42
159	YELDELL, Joseph A	4	NENW	1852-02-02		A1
160	" "	4	SENE	1852-02-02		A1
202	YELDELL, Robert	8	W½SE	1829-05-04		A1
200	" "	8	E½SE	1831-08-01		A1
273	" "	8	E½NW	1832-08-08		A1 G15
274	" "	8	W½NW	1832-08-08		A1 G15
199	" "	8	E½NE	1832-09-10		A1
201	" "	8	SWNE	1837-04-10		A1
272	" "	7	E½NE	1843-02-01		A1 G15
198	" "	20	NESW	1850-08-10		A1

Patent Map

T11-N R12-E
St Stephens Meridian

Map Group 1

Township Statistics

Parcels Mapped	:	291
Number of Patents	:	246
Number of Individuals	:	150
Patentees Identified	:	152
Number of Surnames	:	89
Multi-Patentee Parcels	:	6
Oldest Patent Date	:	9/27/1821
Most Recent Patent	:	6/28/1895
Block/Lot Parcels	:	0
Parcels Re - Issued	:	2
Parcels that Overlap	:	2
Cities and Towns	:	3
Cemeteries	:	3

Section 6
- PEARSON William C 1833
- TALLEY Nathan 1837
- TALLY Nathan 1837
- PEARSON William C 1833
- TALLEY Nathan 1834
- GASTON David 1835
- SMITH Seth 1843
- GASTON David 1832
- GASTON [19]
- STEANE Perry 1843

Section 5
- PALMER James 1835
- POWELL William 1835
- BOGGAN Solomon 1821
- THIGPEN William H 1845
- BOGGAN Solomon 1821

Section 4
- BOGGAN Robert L 1837
- YELDELL Joseph A 1852
- CRUM Harman P 1831
- TARVER Benjamin H 1834
- PALMER William 1852
- THOMPSON Warren A 1837
- YELDELL Joseph A 1852
- TRAWEEK William H 1837
- BOGGAN Robert L 1837
- CRUM Harman P 1834
- BOGGAN John K 1837
- CRUM Frederick 1837

Section 7
- HAWTHORN Kedar 1828
- POWELL John 1843
- DRAKE [15] William 1843
- MCCONDICHIE John 1829
- MCCONDICHIE John 1829

Section 8
- DRAKE [15] William 1832
- DRAKE [15] William 1832
- TRAWEEK William H 1835
- YELDELL Robert 1832
- YELDELL Robert 1837
- YELDELL Robert 1829
- YELDELL Robert 1831

Section 9
- HAYES Thomas 1830
- HAYES Thomas 1826
- CRUM Frederick 1829
- HAYES Thomas 1826
- BOGGAN Solomon 1830
- BOGGAN Robert L 1830
- CRUM Frederic 1834
- CRUM Frederick 1835
- BOGGIN Solomon 1823

Section 18
- FERGUSON James F 1831
- HILL Josiah 1831
- FERGUSON James 1832
- HILL Josiah 1826
- HILL Josiah 1837
- HILL Josiah 1833

Section 17
- POWELL Zachariah 1833
- BOGGAN Solomon 1832
- ELDER David 1835
- WARD Henry R 1837
- POWELL Henry 1827
- BONNER William 1843
- BAGGAN Solomon 1843

Section 16

Section 19
- HILL Josiah 1837
- HILL Josiah 1829
- HILL Josiah 1826
- COOPER Washington 1837
- WARD Henry R 1837
- WATTS John H 1826
- WATTS John H 1826
- WATTS Comer B 1826
- DAVIDSON Joseph 1837

Section 20
- BOGGAN Solomon 1837
- BOGGIN Margaret 1826
- HOLCOMBE Benjamin 1837
- MORROW Abram 1827
- TRAWEEK William H 1850
- YELDELL Robert 1850
- BONNER William 1833
- TRAWEEK William H 1848
- HOLCOMBE Benjamin 1837

Section 21
- BLOCKSOM Tinley 1833
- TILL Daniel 1837
- BONNER William 1833
- ELDER David 1835
- ELDER David 1837
- THOMPSON Warren A 1837
- COOK Charles 1837
- HOLCOMBE Benjamin 1837
- THOMPSON Warren A 1837
- COOK Charles 1837
- THOMPSON Warren A 1837

Section 30
- MORROW Abraham 1826
- NIGHT Jesse 1826
- WATTS Corner B 1826
- POWERS John S 1858
- MCKEE Hugh 1825
- NIGHT Jesse 1826
- MCKEE Hugh 1858
- POWERS John S 1858

Section 29
- SMITH [42] Henry 1850
- ELDER Matthew 1837
- SMITH Henry 1852
- TRAWEEK Thomas M 1858
- JONES Wilson 1854
- GASTON James A 1849
- TRAWEEK Thomas M 1858
- TRAWEEK Thomas M 1858
- POWELL William 1850
- TRAWEEK Thomas M 1858
- SAUNDERS David N 1849
- POWELL John 1858

Section 28
- JACKSON Frederick 1838
- BRANSFORD Nathan 1835
- TRAWEEK Thomas M 1858
- COOK Charles 1837
- THOMPSON Warren A 1858
- MCWHORTER John 1858
- RICHARDSON Ransom 1885
- POWERS Robert 1882
- BENSON Jim 1885
- THOMPSON Warren A 1858

Section 31
- BLANKENSHIP John 1823
- GREEN Gilbert 1826
- GREEN James B 1826
- POWELL Henry 1827
- POWELL Henry 1821

Section 32
- BLOXOM Ezekiel 1837
- POWELL John 1858
- POWELL John 1852
- BLOXOM Tinsley 1838
- POWELL John 1858
- POWELL Henry 1821
- CHANCELLOR William 1838
- CHANCELLOR George 1858

Section 33
- CHANCELLOR Gilbert 1858
- YELDELL James R 1858
- CRANE Charles H 1858
- CHANCELLOR Gilbert 1858
- CHANCELLOR Gilbert 1841
- CHANCELLOR Gilbert 1858

58

HAYS Thomas 1834	CRUM Isaac F 1832	
	HAYS Greenberry 1845	
3		

LITTLE Amos A 1852 | CASSIDY Jesse 1858 | GLENN Lewis R 1854
LITTLE Amos A 1852 | BEVERLY Anthony 1854 | BEVERLY Anthony 1854
2 | LEWIS John B 1852 | HAYS John N 1858
OFARRELL John W 1853 | |
LEWIS Jacob 1834 | GRIGERS Thomas 1853 | LEWIS George 1834

GLENN Lewis R 1852 | WATSON Stanmore 1834 | TILL Samuel W 1858
JONES Allen 1837 | EDMONDSON Caleb 1843 | CAMP Toliver M 1837
1
HAYS Uriah M 1845 | EDMONDSON Caleb 1843 | STEWART Archibald D 1854 | HERBERT Edward H 1834
| | LEWIS George 1834 | STEWART Archibald D 1853

LIVINGSTON Adam 1837 | LEWIS George 1831
HAYS John 1834 | LEWIS Jacob 1834 | LIVINGSTON Adam 1831
10 | **11**
TARVER Andrew 1821 | COLEMAN Allen W 1833
| LIVINGSTON Adam 1833 | WOMACK [46] George 1831

DENNIS Samuel 1831 | LEWIS George 1843 | WATERS Thomas 1837
12
| LEWIS John 1831 | WATERS Thomas 1831

TARVER Benjamin H 1826 | LEVINGSTON A 1822 | COLEMAN Allen W 1833 | WOMACK George 1831 | LEWIS John 1833
TARVER Andrew 1821 | | FEAGIN Tristram E 1831
LITTLE Amos 1834 | WOMACK Jesse 1837 | **15** | WOMACK John 1821 | **14**
LITTLE Amos 1835 | ELEY John W 1835 | WOMACK John 1821 | COLEMAN Greene W 1834 | WATERS Wilkes B 1831 | HERBERT George P 1831

WOMACK John 1831 | HERBERT Thomas S 1831
HERBERT Thomas S 1833 | **13**
COLEMAN Francis 1831 | ARRINGTON Asa 1831

LITTLE Amos 1835 | LITTLE Amos 1837 | ELEY John W 1835 | WOODSON Goodin 1837 | COLEMAN Greene W 1834 | COLEMAN Greene W 1835 | HERBERT Edward H 1837 | HERBERT Thomas S HAYS 1834 Greenberry 1835
WOODSON James 1835 | **22** | WOODSON Goodin 1837 | WOODSON Goodwin 1835 | | | COLEMAN Green W 1835 | JONES Henry T 1837
WOODSON Aaron H 1837 | WOODSON Goodin 1835 | WOODSON Aaron H 1837 | COLEMAN Abraham 1837 | **23** | |
WATERS Levi M 1837 | PIRKINS Elijah 1860 | PIRKINS Elijah 1860 | TRAWEEK Lafayette W 1858 | TRAWEEK Lafayette W 1858 | POWELL William 1858 | COLEMAN Green W 1837 | BOND William 1841

HERBERT Thomas S 1833 | JONES Matthias 1831
24
JONES Henry T 1837 | ROBINSON Allen 1837 | ARRINGTON Asa 1835
COOK Bartlet 1854 | BOGGAN Daniel G 1850 | CROCHERON Richard C 1850

ELDER Matthew 1837 | THOMPSON Warren A 1858 | POSEY Robert 1888 | POWELL William 1858 | POWELL William 1858 | LEWIS John 1835 | CROCHERON Richard C 1850 | BOGGAN James P 1858
MOORER John H 1837 | TRAWEEK Lafayette W 1858 | MCLEOD Roderick 1858 | | BOGGAN James P 1860 | BOGGAN James P 1860 | | TURNER David 1837
THOMPSON Warren A 1858 | **27** | MCLEOD Roderick 1858 | **26** | | | **25**
THOMPSON Warren A 1858 | TRAWEEK Lafayette W 1858 | KOLB Josiah 1843 | STEVENS Carlton 1837 | MCLEOD William 1838 | BOGGAN James P 1860 | BOGGAN James P 1860 | WOMACK Thaddeus A 1858 | WOMACK Jacob L 1848
THOMPSON Warren A 1858 | SHAROCK William C 1858 | SHAROCK William C 1858 | TRAWEEK Lafayette W 1858 | YELDELL James R 1860 | MCLEOD Roderick 1858 | HERBERT George W 1895 | BOGGAN James P 1858 | TROWELL Absalom B 1837 | BRANCH John 1838

SHAROCK William C 1858 | SHAROCK William C 1858 | TRAWEEK Lafayette W 1858 | SHAROCK William C 1858 | MCCLOUD Roderick 1858 | WOMACK Thaddeus A 1858 | WOMACK Jacob L 1858 | WOMACK Jacob L 1858
GRAY William 1860 | SHAROCK William C 1858 | | MCLEOD Roderick 1858 | MCLEOD Roderick 1858 | HILSON Daniel 1884 | WOMACK Thaddeus A 1858 | WOMACK Thaddeus A 1858
34 | | **35** | | WOMACK Thaddeus A 1858 | WOMACK Thaddeus A 1858 | **36**
GRAY William 1860 | GRAY William 1860 | | BEVERLY Alexander 1860 | BEVERLY Alexander 1860 | BRAGG Rachel D 1858

Helpful Hints

1. This Map's INDEX can be found on the preceding pages.

2. Refer to Map "C" to see where this Township lies within Butler County, Alabama.

3. Numbers within square brackets [ ] denote a multi-patentee land parcel (multi-owner). Refer to Appendix "C" for a full list of members in this group.

4. Areas that look to be crowded with Patentees usually indicate multiple sales of the same parcel (Re-issues) or Overlapping parcels. See this Township's Index for an explanation of these and other circumstances that might explain "odd" groupings of Patentees on this map.

Legend

——— Patent Boundary

▬▬▬ Section Boundary

No Patents Found (or Outside County)

1., 2., 3., ... Lot Numbers (when beside a name)

[ ] Group Number (see Appendix "C")

Scale: Section = 1 mile X 1 mile (generally, with some exceptions)

59

Road Map

T11-N R12-E
St Stephens Meridian

Map Group 1

Cities & Towns
Monterey
Mount Moriah
Ridgeville

Cemeteries
Monterey Cemetery
Mount Moriah Cemetery
Thompson Cemetery

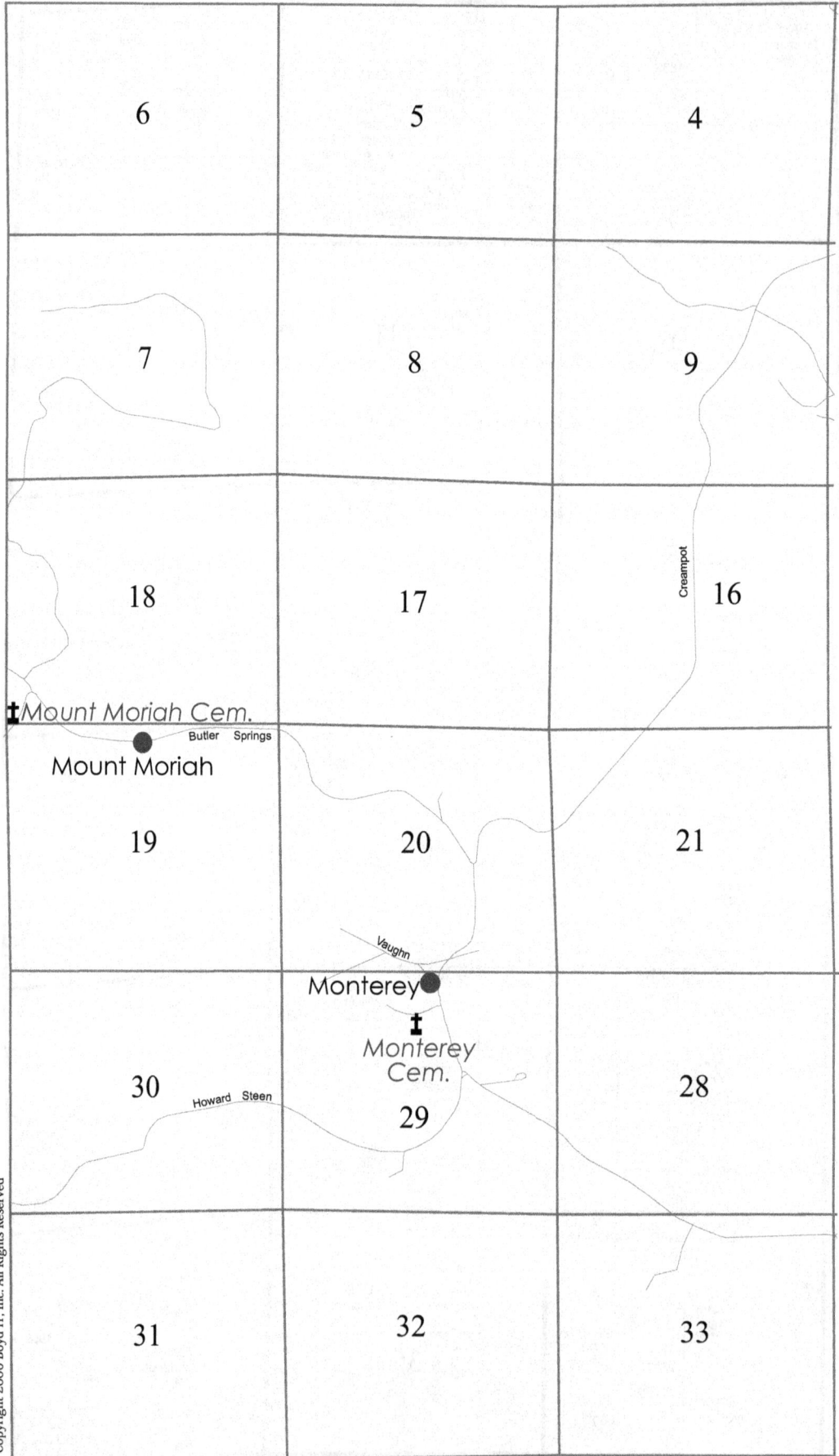

6	5	4
7	8	9
18	17	16

Creampot

✝ *Mount Moriah Cem.*

● **Mount Moriah**

Butler   Springs

| 19 | 20 | 21 |

Vaughn

Monterey ●

✝ *Monterey Cem.*

| 30 | 29 | 28 |

Howard   Steen

| 31 | 32 | 33 |

3

2

1

10

11

12

15

● Ridgeville

14

13

Ridge

Jim   McGowin

22

23

24

Wolf   Creek

✝ Thompson
   Cem.

27

26

Baskin

Broad

Street

25

34

Monterey

Little

35

36

Helpful Hints

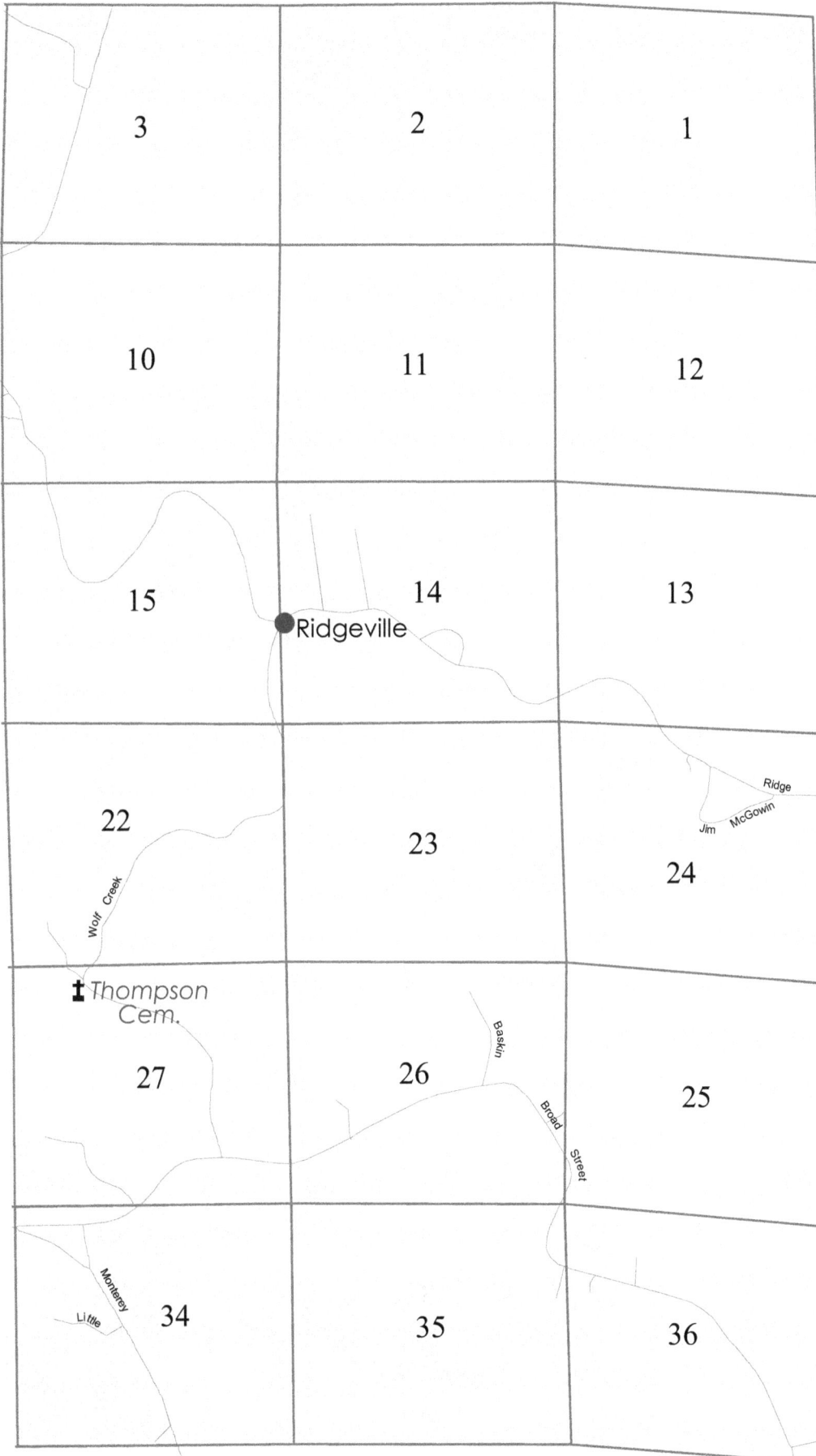

1. This road map has a number of uses, but primarily it is to help you: a) find the present location of land owned by your ancestors (at least the general area), b) find cemeteries and city-centers, and c) estimate the route/roads used by Census-takers & tax-assessors.

2. If you plan to travel to Butler County to locate cemeteries or land parcels, please pick up a modern travel map for the area before you do. Mapping old land parcels on modern maps is not as exact a science as you might think. Just the slightest variations in public land survey coordinates, estimates of parcel boundaries, or road-map deviations can greatly alter a map's representation of how a road either does or doesn't cross a particular parcel of land.

L e g e n d

———————— Section Lines

════════ Interstates

════════ Highways

———————— Other Roads

● Cities/Towns

✝ Cemeteries

Scale: Section = 1 mile X 1 mile
(generally, with some exceptions)

Historical Map

T11-N R12-E
St Stephens Meridian

Map Group 1

Cities & Towns
Monterey
Mount Moriah
Ridgeville

Cemeteries
Monterey Cemetery
Mount Moriah Cemetery
Thompson Cemetery

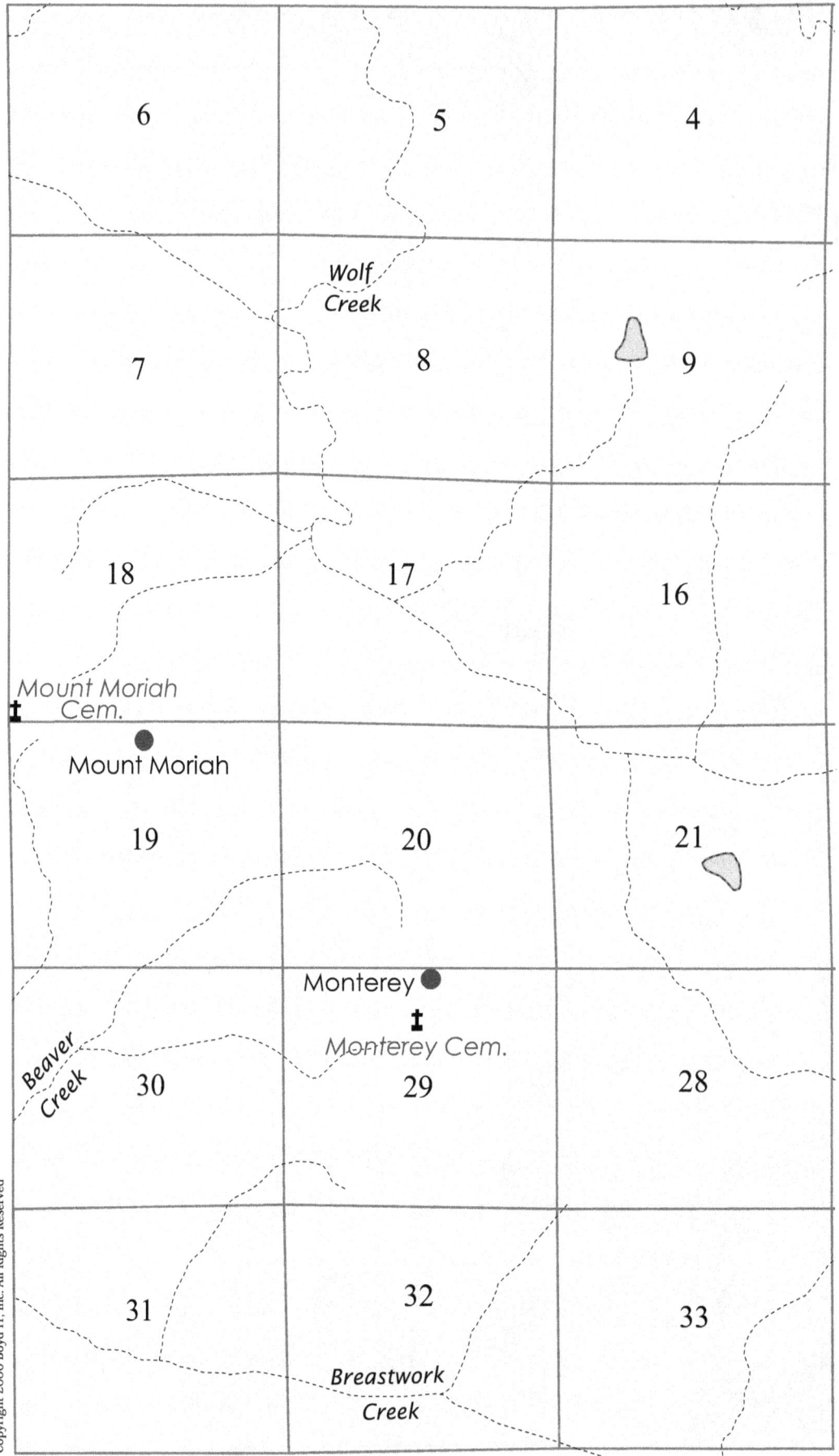

6

5

4

Wolf Creek

7

8

9

18

17

16

✝ *Mount Moriah Cem.*

● Mount Moriah

19

20

21

Monterey ●

✝ *Monterey Cem.*

Beaver Creek

30

29

28

31

32

33

Breastwork Creek

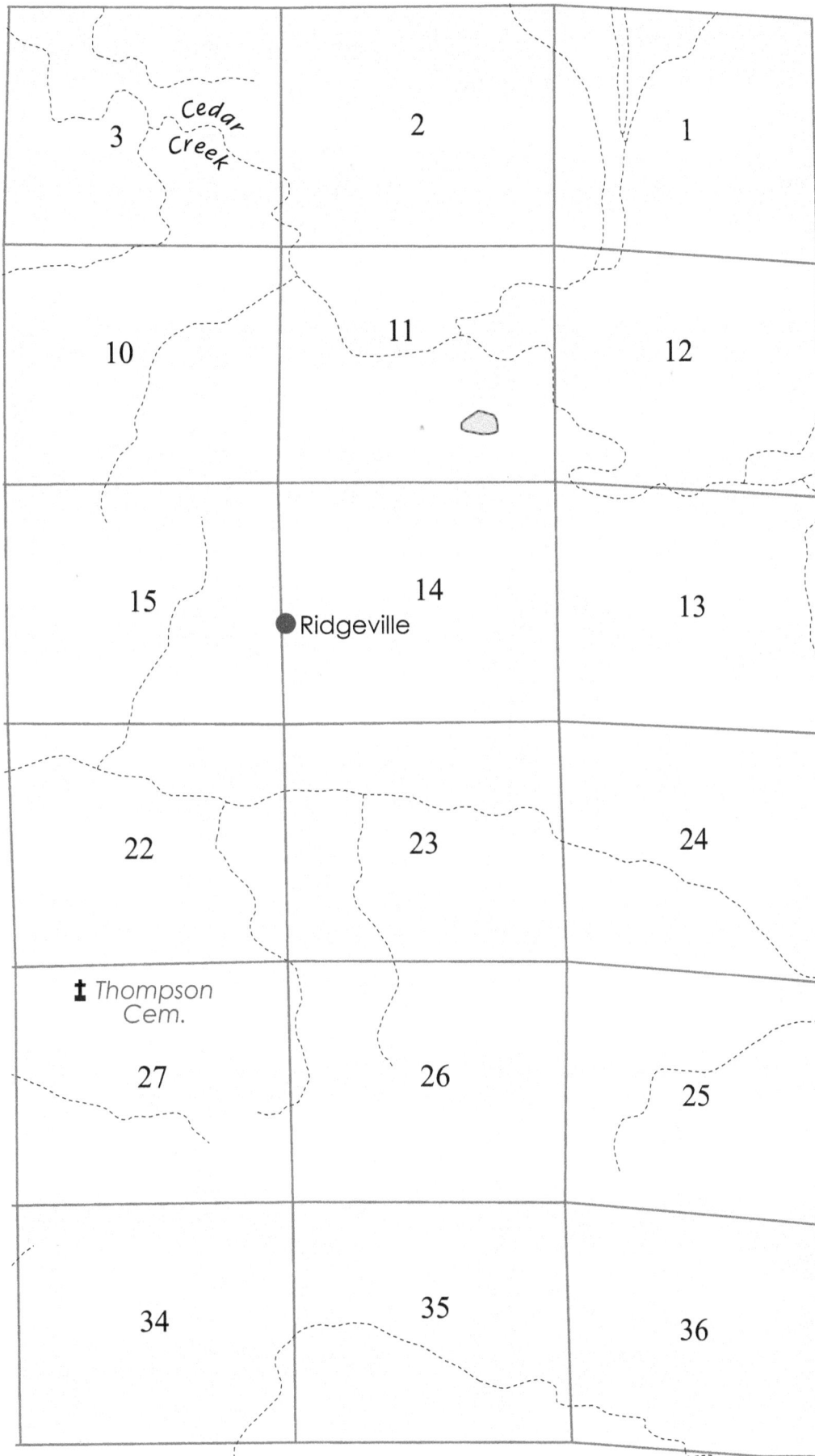

Helpful Hints

1. This Map takes a different look at the same Congressional Township displayed in the preceding two maps. It presents features that can help you better envision the historical development of the area: a) Water-bodies (lakes & ponds), b) Water-courses (rivers, streams, etc.), c) Railroads, d) City/town center-points (where they were oftentimes located when first settled), and e) Cemeteries.

2. Using this "Historical" map in tandem with this Township's Patent Map and Road Map, may lead you to some interesting discoveries. You will often find roads, towns, cemeteries, and waterways are named after nearby landowners: sometimes those names will be the ones you are researching. See how many of these research gems you can find here in Butler County.

Legend

Symbol	Description
———	Section Lines
+++++	Railroads
▭	Large Rivers & Bodies of Water
- - - - -	Streams/Creeks & Small Rivers
●	Cities/Towns
✝	Cemeteries

Scale: Section = 1 mile X 1 mile
(there are some exceptions)

Map Group 2: Index to Land Patents

Township 11-North Range 13-East (St Stephens)

After you locate an individual in this Index, take note of the Section and Section Part then proceed to the Land Patent map on the pages immediately following. You should have no difficulty locating the corresponding parcel of land.

The "For More Info" Column will lead you to more information about the underlying Patents. See the *Legend* at right, and the "How to Use this Book" chapter, for more information.

```
                        LEGEND
             "For More Info . . . " column
A = Authority (Legislative Act, See Appendix "A")
B = Block or Lot (location in Section unknown)
C = Cancelled Patent
F = Fractional Section
G = Group  (Multi-Patentee Patent, see Appendix "C")
V = Overlaps another Parcel
R = Re-Issued (Parcel patented more than once)

(A & G items require you to look in the Appendixes referred
to above. All other Letter-designations followed by a number
require you to locate line-items in this index that possess
the ID number found after the letter).
```

ID	Individual in Patent	Sec.	Sec. Part	Date Issued	Other Counties	For More Info . . .
497	ARRINGTON, West	12	W½SE	1826-05-08		A1
401	ASHCRAFT, John	33	E½SW	1858-11-01		A1
478	BALDERREE, Starling	5	E½NW	1834-09-04		A1
479	" "	5	W½SW	1835-09-19		A1
470	BLACK, Samuel J	10	NWNW	1850-04-01		A1
402	BOATMUN, John	20	NESW	1834-06-12		A1
403	" "	20	NWSW	1834-06-12		A1
404	" "	20	SWSW	1835-04-15		A1
373	BONNER, Henry	25	W½NW	1835-04-02		A1
461	BOZEMAN, Nathan	23	E½NE	1825-04-16		A1
462	" "	23	E½SE	1825-04-16		A1
349	BRAGG, Elizabeth	33	E½NW	1823-10-01		A1
405	BRANCH, John	30	SWSW	1838-07-28		A1
323	BREITHAUPT, Christian	29	E½SE	1826-11-22		A1
324	" "	29	W½SE	1826-11-22		A1
496	BROOKS, Walter W	3	SESW	1848-05-03		A1
382	BROWN, Jabez N	35	S½NW	1858-11-01		A1
383	" "	35	SW	1858-11-01		A1
410	BROWN, John E	31	NESE	1854-07-15		A1
411	" "	31	S½NW	1858-11-01		A1
412	" "	31	SW	1858-11-01		A1
413	" "	31	W½SE	1858-11-01		A1
328	BUTLER, David	35	N½NW	1837-08-12		A1
484	BUTTS, Thomas J	36	NWNE	1852-02-02		A1
443	CAMP, Larkin	6	W½SW	1837-08-12		A1
495	CAMP, Toliver M	6	SWNW	1837-08-15		A1
294	CARTER, Absalom	30	E½NE	1827-01-01		A1
468	CHRISTOPHER, Robert	5	NWSE	1835-10-14		A1
326	COLEMAN, Daniel W	10	S½SW	1834-08-05		A1
369	COLEMAN, Green W	10	W½SE	1831-08-01		A1
407	COLEMAN, John	27	NW	1823-10-01		A1
406	" "	22	E½NW	1826-05-08		A1
481	COLEMAN, Thomas	27	W½SE	1825-04-16		A1
414	COOK, John H	24	E½SW	1831-08-01		A1
297	CRENSHAW, Anderson	29	SW	1823-12-01		A1
298	" "	30	E½SE	1827-07-26		A1
296	" "	20	SESW	1835-04-15		A1
299	" "	30	W½SE	1837-04-10		A1
480	CRENSHAW, Thomas C	8	SE	1858-11-01		A1
352	CROSS, Franklin	31	SESE	1858-11-01		A1
353	" "	32	NESW	1858-11-01		A1
354	" "	32	S½SW	1858-11-01		A1
355	" "	32	SWSE	1858-11-01		A1
434	DAILEY, John S	6	SWNE	1858-11-01		A1
442	DAVIDSON, Joseph	3	SENE	1845-06-01		A1
440	" "	10	NE	1858-11-01		A1

ID	Individual in Patent	Sec.	Sec. Part	Date Issued	Other Counties	For More Info . . .
441	DAVIDSON, Joseph (Cont'd)	3	SE	1858-11-01		A1
469	DAVIDSON, Rufus C	11	NENW	1845-06-01		A1
395	DAVIS, James L	4	NWNE	1858-11-01		A1
396	" "	4	SENW	1858-11-01		A1
409	DAVIS, John	13	E½NE	1825-05-12		A1
408	" "	12	E½NE	1828-04-10		A1
302	DICKERSON, Archillus	23	W½SW	1825-06-06		A1
301	" "	23	W½SE	1826-05-15		A1
325	DUNKLIN, Daniel G	28	NESE	1861-05-01		A1
313	ERNEST, Asa	8	E½NW	1831-08-01		A1
311	" "	2	W½SE	1834-01-21		A1
310	" "	2	SENW	1841-05-20		A1
309	" "	2	NWNW	1858-11-01		A1
312	" "	3	N½NE	1858-11-01		A1
327	FERGUSON, Darius J	34	NWSE	1858-09-01		A1
338	FERGUSON, Elias H	34	SENW	1854-07-15		A1
337	" "	34	NESW	1858-11-01		A1
384	FERGUSON, Jacob	13	E½SW	1833-06-04		A1
385	" "	25	NESE	1838-07-28		A1
506	FERGUSON, William H	27	E½NE	1833-11-14		A1
502	FOX, William	8	W½NW	1831-08-01		A1
501	" "	8	SENE	1835-09-19		A1
503	" "	9	SWNW	1835-09-19		A1
489	GAREY, Thomas W	13	SE	1825-04-09		A1
320	GARRETT, Caswell	13	W½NW	1826-05-12		A1
321	GARRITT, Caswell	11	W½SW	1830-11-16		A1
381	GARY, Isaac H	34	NENW	1837-08-12		A1
315	GERRELL, Bethel D	25	E½NW	1833-11-14		A1
459	GLENN, Mitchell W	7	NWNW	1837-05-15		A1
457	" "	4	NWNW	1837-08-07		A1
458	" "	4	SESW	1854-07-15		A1
329	GRIFFIN, David	26	W½SW	1823-12-01		A1
333	GRIFFITH, Edward	4	SENE	1834-08-20		A1
335	" "	9	NWNE	1834-08-20		A1
334	" "	4	W½SE	1835-04-02		A1
482	GRIFFITH, Thomas	30	W½NE	1823-10-01		A1
486	GRIFFITH, Thomas J	30	E½SW	1827-05-30		A1
485	" "	2	E½SW	1831-05-17		A1
394	HAIGLAR, James	12	SENW	1860-04-02		A1
498	HARALSON, William B	9	E½NW	1837-08-02		A1 R455
295	HAWKINS, Allen	36	SWSW	1858-11-01		A1
336	HERBERT, Edward H	11	SWNW	1834-06-12		A1 V331
356	HINTON, George	4	SWSW	1837-08-18		A1
483	HOBBY, Thomas	22	W½NW	1825-06-06		A1
379	HOLDSTON, Hiram	12	E½SW	1826-05-08		A1
416	HOPKINS, John	34	W½SW	1858-11-01		A1
464	HUTCHINSON, Parr	23	W½NE	1831-08-01		A1
331	JOLLIFF, Davis	11	W½NW	1831-12-01		A1 V336
370	JONES, Grief W	33	NWNW	1837-08-14		A1
375	JONES, Henry T	7	W½NE	1823-12-01		A1
376	" "	7	W½SE	1834-08-12		A1
374	" "	6	SWSE	1834-09-04		A1
474	JONES, Sarah	22	SE	1825-06-06		A1
475	" "	27	E½SE	1825-06-06		A1
476	" "	34	NENE	1837-08-18		A1
487	KOLB, Thomas	36	SENW	1858-11-01		A1
488	" "	36	SWNE	1858-11-01		A1
350	LEWIS, Elizabeth E	6	E½NE	1858-11-01		A1
351	" "	6	NWNE	1858-11-01		A1
417	LEWIS, John	32	NE	1821-09-27		A1
418	" "	5	NENE	1834-09-04		A1
499	LUCKIE, William F	4	SWNW	1841-05-20		A1
500	" "	5	SENE	1841-05-20		A1
314	MANNING, Benjamin	10	E½SE	1831-12-01		A1
340	MANNING, Elijah L	22	SW	1821-09-27		A1
341	" "	28	E½NE	1821-09-27		A1
345	" "	33	NE	1823-10-01		A1
347	" "	34	W½NE	1823-10-01		A1
343	" "	28	W½NE	1826-05-05		A1
339	" "	14	NE	1827-01-08		A1
344	" "	28	W½SE	1832-09-10		A1
342	" "	28	SESE	1837-08-18		A1
346	" "	33	SWNW	1837-08-18		A1

ID	Individual in Patent	Sec.	Sec. Part	Date Issued	Other Counties	For More Info . . .
420	MANNING, John	6	E½SW	1837-08-07		A1
421	" "	6	NWNW	1837-08-07		A1
422	" "	6	SENW	1837-08-15		A1
446	MANNING, Levi	25	SW	1837-08-09		A1
445	" "	14	NW	1837-08-10		A1
449	" "	36	W½NW	1837-08-10		A1
447	" "	36	NENW	1837-08-18		A1
448	" "	36	NWSW	1837-08-18		A1
292	MARTIN, Abram W	34	SESW	1858-11-01		A1
293	" "	34	SWSE	1858-11-01		A1
471	MATHEWS, Samuel M	34	SESE	1858-11-01		A1
424	MOORE, John	35	E½NE	1823-10-01		A1
425	" "	35	W½NE	1823-10-01		A1
423	" "	26	W½SE	1824-03-01		A1
472	MOORE, Samuel	26	E½SE	1826-07-10		A1
378	MUNDY, Hillary C	15	SE	1834-01-21		A1
397	NEAL, James	5	E½SE	1834-08-20		A1
398	" "	5	SWSE	1834-09-04		A1
399	" "	8	NENE	1834-09-04		A1
400	" "	9	NWNW	1837-04-10		A1
473	NELSON, Samuel	6	NENW	1837-08-15		A1
427	PATTERSON, John P	1	SWSE	1852-02-02		A1
428	" "	12	NWNE	1852-02-02		A1
426	" "	1	SESW	1853-11-15		A1
430	PATTON, John	22	NE	1825-06-06		A1
431	" "	35	W½SE	1826-05-08		A1
429	" "	15	NE	1837-08-10		A1
439	PATTON, John W	9	SE	1821-09-27		A1
456	PATTON, Matthew	9	SW	1821-09-27		A1
452	" "	28	SW	1821-12-03		A1
455	" "	9	E½NW	1821-12-03		A1 R498
453	" "	5	NESW	1835-09-19		A1
454	" "	5	SESW	1835-09-19		A1
322	PAUL, Charles	6	E½SE	1826-07-10		A1
303	PEAGLER, Artemas	1	NWSE	1853-11-15		A1
306	" "	12	W½NW	1858-11-01		A1
304	" "	11	SWNE	1896-10-26		A1
305	" "	12	NENW	1896-10-26		A1
307	PEAGLER, Artemous	1	SWSW	1854-07-15		A1 G36
362	PEAGLER, George S	11	S½SE	1837-08-12		A1
363	" "	13	E½NW	1853-11-15		A1
364	" "	13	W½NE	1853-11-15		A1
359	" "	10	NESW	1858-11-01		A1
360	" "	11	E½NE	1858-11-01		A1
361	" "	11	NWNE	1858-11-01		A1
432	PEAGLER, John	1	NESW	1853-11-15		A1
433	" "	12	SWNE	1853-11-15		A1
307	" "	1	SWSW	1854-07-15		A1 G36
316	POOLE, Calvin	3	NESW	1854-07-15		A1
318	" "	4	NENE	1854-07-15		A1
317	" "	3	SWSW	1858-11-01		A1
319	" "	4	SWNE	1858-11-01		A1
460	POSEY, Morgan	30	NWSW	1858-11-01		A1
371	PRUITT, Hardin	3	NENW	1834-08-05		A1
372	" "	3	SENW	1837-05-15		A1
332	RAY, Dempsey J	25	SESE	1837-08-12		A1
308	SARTAIN, Asa B	10	S½NW	1858-11-01		A1
435	SCONYERS, John	2	NENW	1837-08-14		A1
419	SIMMONS, John M	34	NESE	1898-10-04		A2
504	SMITH, William G	35	E½SE	1858-11-01		A1
505	" "	36	NESW	1858-11-01		A1
436	STEPHENS, John	2	W½SW	1834-08-05		A1
393	STEWART, James A	4	NESW	1854-07-15		A1
377	TAYLOR, Herbert B	25	NWSE	1847-05-01		A1
365	TEAGLER, George S	11	NWSE	1852-02-02		A1
366	" "	2	SESE	1852-02-02		A1
368	THIGPEN, Gray	26	W½NE	1832-09-10		A1
367	" "	26	E½NE	1833-09-16		A1
437	THIGPEN, John	27	W½NE	1833-11-14		A1
465	THIGPEN, Reddin	1	SESE	1852-12-01		A1
466	THIGPEN, Redding	1	NESE	1850-08-10		A1
438	THIGPIN, John	23	E½SW	1826-07-10		A1
444	THIGPIN, Lemuel	24	W½SW	1831-10-27		A1

ID	Individual in Patent	Sec.	Sec. Part	Date Issued	Other Counties	For More Info . . .
415	THORINGTON, John H	12	W½SW	1830-11-16		A1
467	THORNTON, Reuben	13	W½SW	1838-07-28		A1
330	TURNER, David	30	SWNW	1837-05-20		A1
490	WADE, Thomas	32	NWSW	1837-05-15		A1
348	WARD, Elisha	36	E½NE	1823-10-01		A1
300	WARE, Andrew J	34	SENE	1837-08-18		A1
380	WARE, Hugh	26	E½SW	1833-11-14		A1
493	WATERS, Thomas	7	E½NE	1834-08-20		A1
494	" "	7	E½SE	1834-08-20		A1
491	" "	5	W½NE	1834-09-04		A1
492	" "	6	NWSE	1834-09-04		A1
358	WOMACK, George L	4	NESE	1835-09-12		A1
357	" "	3	NWSW	1837-05-15		A1
389	WOMACK, Jacob L	30	NENW	1835-04-15		A1
386	" "	19	NESW	1835-10-16		A1
388	" "	19	W½SW	1837-08-07		A1
390	" "	30	NWNW	1837-08-07		A1
387	" "	19	SESW	1858-11-01		A1
391	" "	30	SENW	1858-11-01		A1
392	" "	31	N½NW	1858-11-01		A1
451	WOMACK, Mansel N	9	SWNE	1837-08-08		A1
450	" "	9	E½NE	1837-08-15		A1
463	WOMACK, Noland L	4	SESE	1834-08-20		A1
477	WOMACK, Sarah	5	W½NW	1837-08-14		A1

Patent Map

T11-N R13-E
St Stephens Meridian

Map Group 2

Township Statistics

Parcels Mapped	:	215
Number of Patents	:	194
Number of Individuals	:	118
Patentees Identified	:	118
Number of Surnames	:	84
Multi-Patentee Parcels	:	1
Oldest Patent Date	:	9/27/1821
Most Recent Patent	:	10/4/1898
Block/Lot Parcels	:	0
Parcels Re - Issued	:	1
Parcels that Overlap	:	2
Cities and Towns	:	1
Cemeteries	:	5

Map content (parcels by section):

Section 6:
MANNING John 1837; NELSON Samuel 1837; LEWIS Elizabeth E 1858; CAMP Toliver M 1837; MANNING John 1837; DAILEY John S 1858; LEWIS Elizabeth E 1858; CAMP Larkin 1837; MANNING John 1837; WATERS Thomas 1834; JONES Henry T 1834; PAUL Charles 1826

Section 5:
WOMACK Sarah 1837; BALDERREE Starling 1834; WATERS Thomas 1834; LEWIS John 1834; LUCKIE William F 1841; PATTON Matthew 1835; CHRISTOPHER Robert 1835; BALDERREE Starling 1835; PATTON Matthew 1835; NEAL James 1834; NEAL James 1834

Section 4:
GLENN Mitchell W 1837; DAVIS James L 1858; POOLE Calvin 1854; LUCKIE William F 1841; DAVIS James L 1858; POOLE Calvin 1858; GRIFFITH Edward 1834; STEWART James A 1854; WOMACK George L 1835; HINTON George 1837; GLENN Mitchell W 1854; GRIFFITH Edward 1835; WOMACK Noland L 1834

Section 7:
GLENN Mitchell W 1837; JONES Henry T 1823; WATERS Thomas 1834; JONES Henry T 1834; WATERS Thomas 1834

Section 8:
FOX William 1831; ERNEST Asa 1831; NEAL James 1834; FOX William 1835; CRENSHAW Thomas C 1858

Section 9:
NEAL James 1837; PATTON Matthew 1821; GRIFFITH Edward 1834; WOMACK Mansel N 1837; FOX William 1835; HARALSON William B 1837; WOMACK Mansel N 1837; PATTON Matthew 1821; PATTON John W 1821

Section 18; Section 17; Section 16

Section 19:
WOMACK Jacob L 1837; WOMACK Jacob L 1835; WOMACK Jacob L 1858

Section 20:
BOATMUN John 1834; BOATMUN John 1834; BOATMUN John 1835; CRENSHAW Anderson 1835

Section 21

Section 30:
WOMACK Jacob L 1837; WOMACK Jacob L 1835; GRIFFITH Thomas 1823; CARTER Absalom 1827; TURNER David 1837; WOMACK Jacob L 1858; POSEY Morgan 1858; GRIFFITH Thomas J 1827; CRENSHAW Anderson 1827; CRENSHAW Anderson 1837; BRANCH John 1838

Section 29:
CRENSHAW Anderson 1823; BREITHAUPT Christian 1826; BREITHAUPT Christian 1826

Section 28:
MANNING Elijah L 1826; MANNING Elijah L 1821; PATTON Matthew 1821; MANNING Elijah L 1832; DUNKLIN Daniel G 1861; MANNING Elijah L 1837

Section 31:
WOMACK Jacob L 1858; BROWN John E 1858; BROWN John E 1858; BROWN John E 1858; BROWN John E 1854; CROSS Franklin 1858

Section 32:
WADE Thomas 1837; CROSS Franklin 1858; LEWIS John 1821; CROSS Franklin 1858; CROSS Franklin 1858

Section 33:
JONES Grief W 1837; MANNING Elijah L 1837; BRAGG Elizabeth 1823; MANNING Elijah L 1823; ASHCRAFT John 1858

PRUITT Hardin 1834	ERNEST Asa 1858		ERNEST Asa 1858	SCONYERS John 1837			
PRUITT Hardin 1837		DAVIDSON Joseph 1845		ERNEST Asa 1841	**2**		**1**
WOMACK George L 1837	POOLE Calvin 1854	DAVIDSON Joseph 1858	STEPHENS John 1834	GRIFFITH Thomas J 1831	ERNEST Asa 1834		PEAGLER John 1853

Helpful Hints

1. This Map's INDEX can be found on the preceding pages.

2. Refer to Map "C" to see where this Township lies within Butler County, Alabama.

3. Numbers within square brackets [ ] denote a multi-patentee land parcel (multi-owner). Refer to Appendix "C" for a full list of members in this group.

4. Areas that look to be crowded with Patentees usually indicate multiple sales of the same parcel (Re-issues) or Overlapping parcels. See this Township's Index for an explanation of these and other circumstances that might explain "odd" groupings of Patentees on this map.

L e g e n d

————	Patent Boundary
▬▬▬▬	Section Boundary
(shaded)	No Patents Found (or Outside County)
1., 2., 3., ...	Lot Numbers (when beside a name)
[ ]	Group Number (see Appendix "C")

Scale: Section = 1 mile X 1 mile (generally, with some exceptions)

69

Road Map

T11-N R13-E
St Stephens Meridian

Map Group 2

Cities & Towns
Manningham

Cemeteries
Bragg Cemetery
Crenshaws Cemetery
Manningham Cemetery
Old Shiloh Cemetery
Shiloh Cemetery

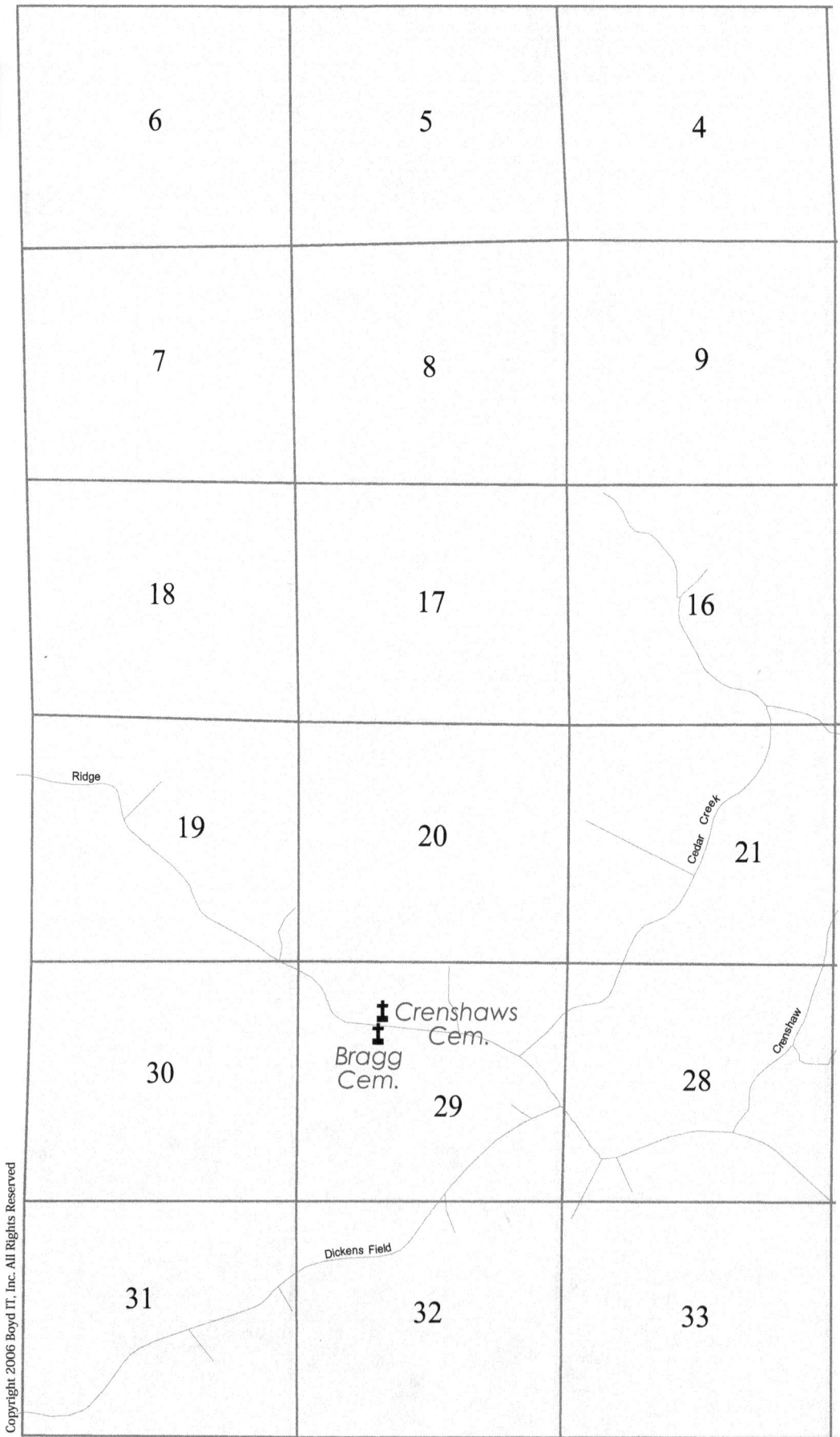

6	5	4
7	8	9
18	17	16
19	20	21
30	29	28
31	32	33

Ridge

Cedar Creek

Crenshaw

Crenshaws Cem.

Bragg Cem.

Dickens Field

3	2	1
10	11	12
15	14	13
22	23	24
27	26	25
34	35	36

Ste Rte 263

✝ Manningham Cem.

● Manningham

Brown

Perry Luckie

Gator

Ridge

Sherling Lake

Old Shiloh Cem ✝

✝ Shiloh Cem.

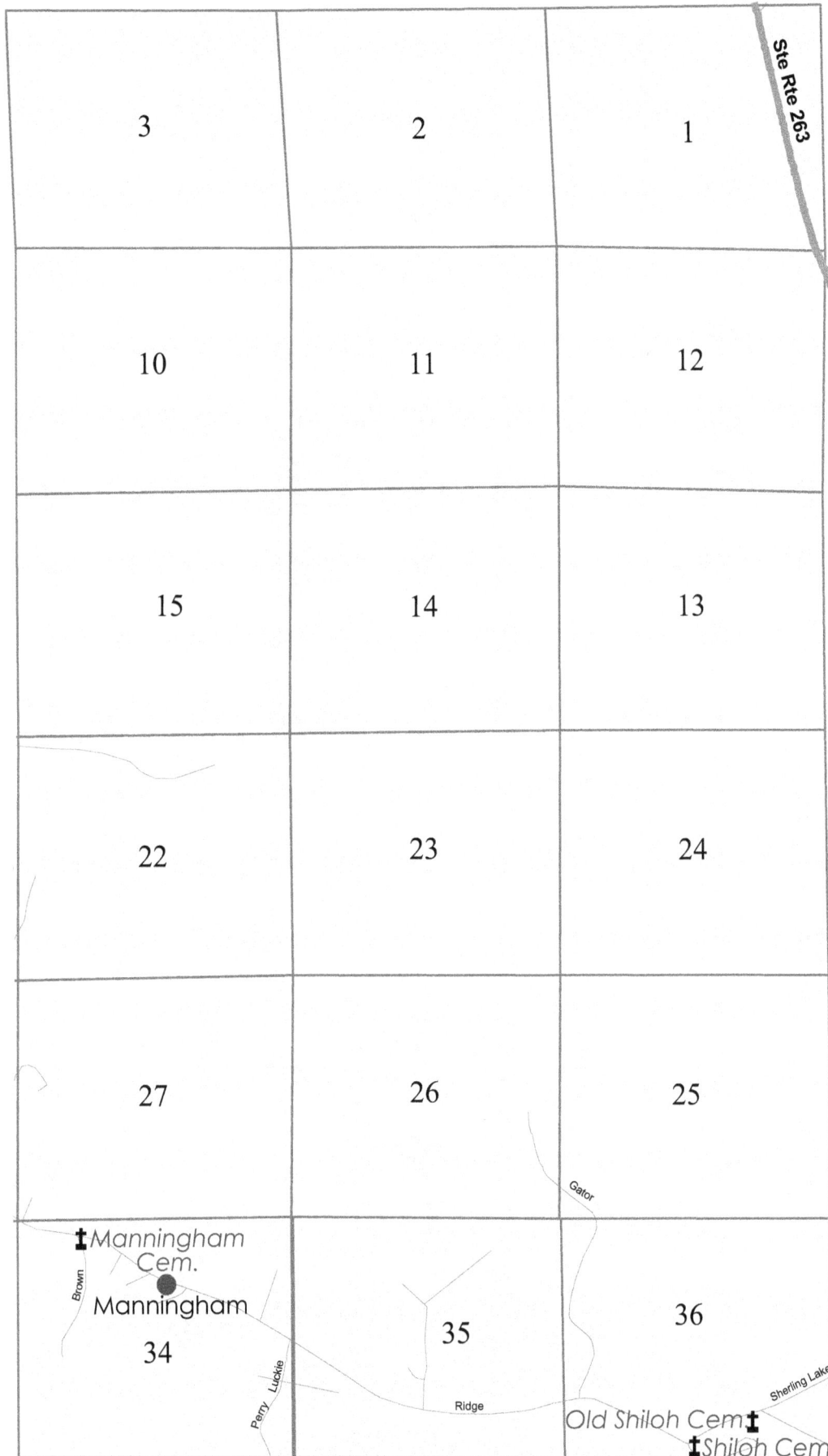

Helpful Hints

1. This road map has a number of uses, but primarily it is to help you: a) find the present location of land owned by your ancestors (at least the general area), b) find cemeteries and city-centers, and c) estimate the route/roads used by Census-takers & tax-assessors.

2. If you plan to travel to Butler County to locate cemeteries or land parcels, please pick up a modern travel map for the area before you do. Mapping old land parcels on modern maps is not as exact a science as you might think. Just the slightest variations in public land survey coordinates, estimates of parcel boundaries, or road-map deviations can greatly alter a map's representation of how a road either does or doesn't cross a particular parcel of land.

Legend

——————— Section Lines

══════════ Interstates

▬▬▬▬▬▬ Highways

——————— Other Roads

● Cities/Towns

✝ Cemeteries

Scale: Section = 1 mile X 1 mile
(generally, with some exceptions)

Historical Map

T11-N R13-E
St Stephens Meridian

Map Group 2

| 6 | 5 | 4 |

Cities & Towns
Manningham

Cemeteries
Bragg Cemetery
Crenshaws Cemetery
Manningham Cemetery
Old Shiloh Cemetery
Shiloh Cemetery

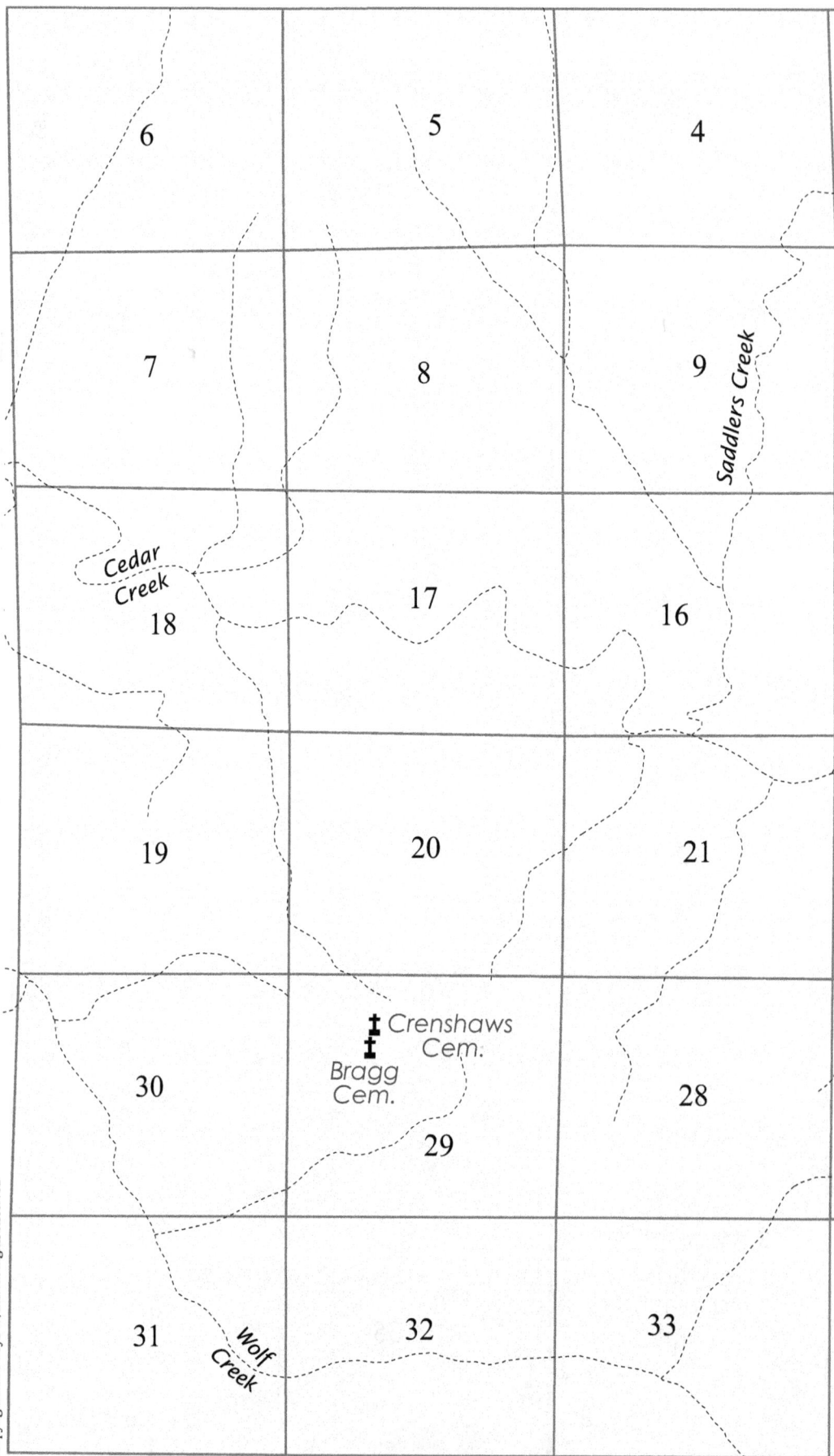

| 7 | 8 | 9 |

Saddlers Creek

Cedar Creek

| 18 | 17 | 16 |

| 19 | 20 | 21 |

Crenshaws Cem.

Bragg Cem.

| 30 | 29 | 28 |

Wolf Creek

| 31 | 32 | 33 |

3

2

1

Mussel
Creek

10

11

12

15

14

13

Cedar
Creek

22

23

24

27

26

25

✝ Manningham
Cem.

● Manningham

34

35

36

Old Shiloh
Cem.
✝

Shiloh Cem. ✝

Helpful Hints

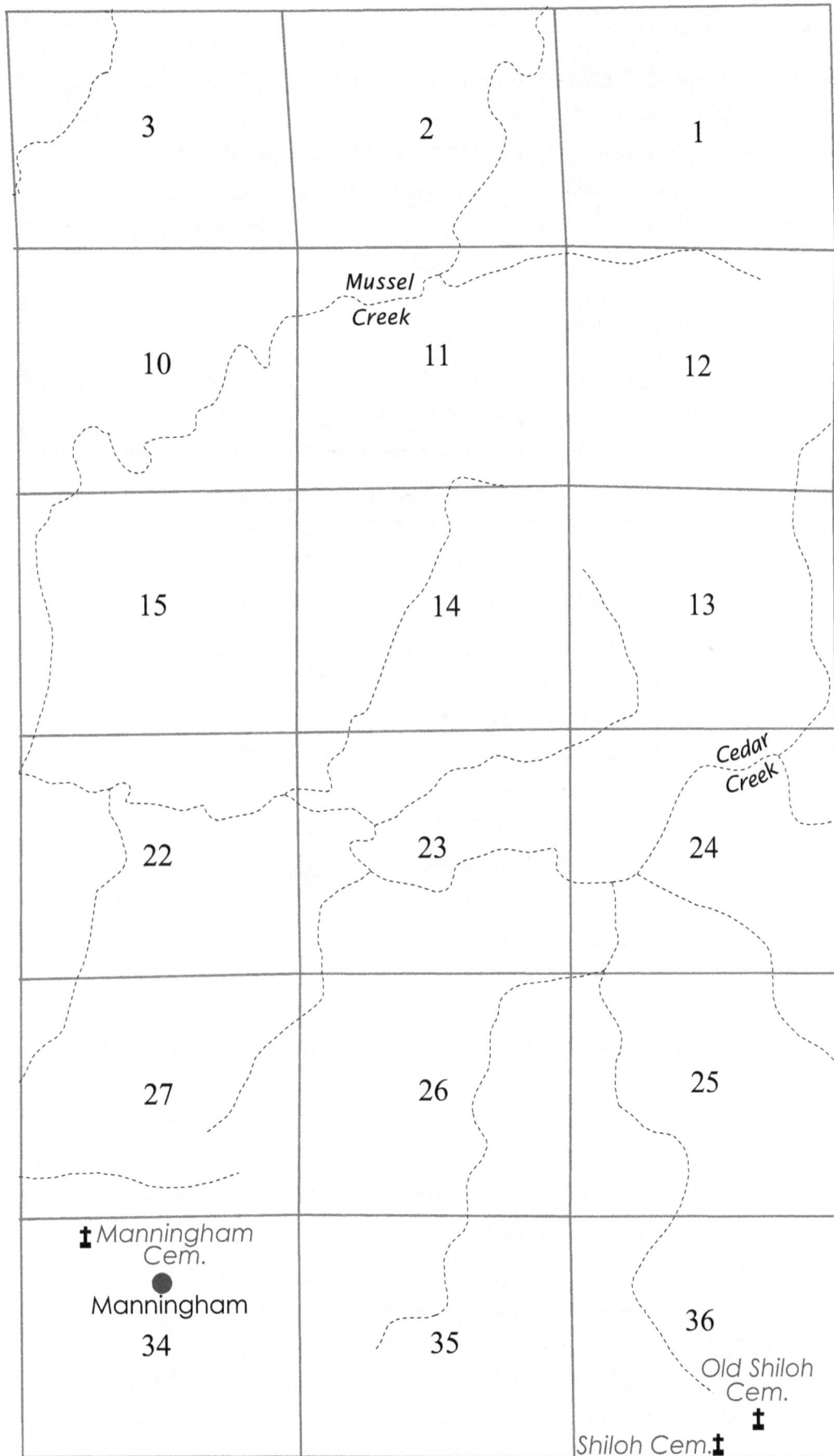

1. This Map takes a different look at the same Congressional Township displayed in the preceding two maps. It presents features that can help you better envision the historical development of the area: a) Water-bodies (lakes & ponds), b) Water-courses (rivers, streams, etc.), c) Railroads, d) City/town center-points (where they were oftentimes located when first settled), and e) Cemeteries.

2. Using this "Historical" map in tandem with this Township's Patent Map and Road Map, may lead you to some interesting discoveries. You will often find roads, towns, cemeteries, and waterways are named after nearby landowners: sometimes those names will be the ones you are researching. See how many of these research gems you can find here in Butler County.

Legend

————	Section Lines
+++++	Railroads
▭	Large Rivers & Bodies of Water
-------	Streams/Creeks & Small Rivers
●	Cities/Towns
✝	Cemeteries

Scale: Section = 1 mile X 1 mile
(there are some exceptions)

Map Group 3: Index to Land Patents

Township 11-North Range 14-East (St Stephens)

After you locate an individual in this Index, take note of the Section and Section Part then proceed to the Land Patent map on the pages immediately following. You should have no difficulty locating the corresponding parcel of land.

The "For More Info" Column will lead you to more information about the underlying Patents. See the *Legend* at right, and the "How to Use this Book" chapter, for more information.

```
                        LEGEND
              "For More Info . . . " column
A = Authority (Legislative Act, See Appendix "A")
B = Block or Lot (location in Section unknown)
C = Cancelled Patent
F = Fractional Section
G = Group  (Multi-Patentee Patent, see Appendix "C")
V = Overlaps another Parcel
R = Re-Issued (Parcel patented more than once)

(A & G items require you to look in the Appendixes referred
to above. All other Letter-designations followed by a number
require you to locate line-items in this index that possess
the ID number found after the letter).
```

ID	Individual in Patent	Sec.	Sec. Part	Date Issued	Other Counties	For More Info . . .
645	ARMSTRONG, Johon W	31	NWNW	1858-11-01		A1
621	BARGANIEL, Jesse	24	SWNE	1837-08-18		A1
622	BARGANIER, Jesse	13	E½SE	1837-08-14		A1
623	" "	24	E½NE	1837-08-15		A1
624	"	24	NWNE	1837-08-15		A1
625	" "	24	W½SE	1838-07-28		A1
626	BRUCE, Jesse	11	SWSE	1837-08-18		A1
508	BUTLER, Aaron	12	NWNE	1835-10-16		A1
507	" "	12	NENE	1838-07-28		A1
570	BUTLER, Edmund	12	E½SW	1837-08-07		A1
571	" "	12	S½NE	1837-08-07		A1
572	" "	12	SE	1837-08-07		A1
589	BUTLER, Isaac	1	SWNE	1835-09-19		A1
684	BUTLER, Magdalene	1	NWNE	1837-08-09		A1
697	BUTLER, Reuben	1	E½NE	1822-01-01		A1
685	CATES, Mahlon	11	N½SW	1837-08-09		A1
690	CHEATHAM, Peter	15	SWSW	1840-10-10		A1
689	" "	15	NESE	1848-05-03		A1
691	" "	17	SENE	1848-05-03		A1
736	COLLINS, William	25	W½SE	1823-10-01		A1
735	" "	25	W½NE	1825-04-02		A1
600	COX, James	29	E½NE	1825-04-16		A1
531	DAVENPORT, Charles	29	E½SE	1833-06-04		A1
539	" "	8	SW	1833-06-04		A1
528	" "	19	W½SE	1834-10-21		A1
529	" "	20	W½NW	1834-10-21		A1
530	" "	20	W½SW	1834-10-21		A1
537	" "	32	NW	1835-10-14		A1
536	" "	32	N½SW	1837-08-12		A1
533	" "	29	W½NE	1837-08-15		A1
534	" "	29	W½SE	1837-08-15		A1
532	" "	29	SENW	1837-08-18		A1
535	" "	32	E½NE	1843-02-01		A1
538	" "	32	W½NE	1843-02-01		A1
602	DAVENPORT, James	5	E½SW	1829-07-06		A1
601	" "	33	E½SW	1835-10-14		A1
737	DAVENPORT, William	17	E½NW	1834-08-20		A1
738	" "	28	NESW	1838-07-28		A1
610	DAVIS, James L	6	NWSW	1835-10-01		A1
713	DEMING, Simeon	6	NW	1854-07-15		A1
628	DICKSON, John	33	NWNW	1835-10-14		A1
590	EARNEST, Isham	7	NE	1822-01-01		A1
635	EARNEST, John J	6	E½SW	1825-06-06		A1
591	ERNEST, Isham	7	E½NW	1826-05-08		A1
636	ERNEST, John J	6	W½SE	1826-05-08		A1
707	FARROW, Samuel W	23	E½SW	1837-08-14		A1

ID	Individual in Patent	Sec.	Sec. Part	Date Issued	Other Counties	For More Info . . .
592	FERGUSON, Jacob	30	NWSW	1834-09-04		A1
595	" "	31	E½SE	1835-09-19		A1
596	" "	31	E½SW	1837-05-20		A1
593	" "	30	SESW	1837-08-12		A1
598	" "	31	W½SE	1837-08-12		A1
594	" "	31	E½NE	1837-08-15		A1
597	" "	31	W½NE	1841-05-20		A1
699	FERGUSON, Robert H	30	NESW	1852-02-02		A1
519	FULLER, Archibald	25	SESE	1852-02-02		A1
525	FULLER, Benjamin	13	E½NE	1837-08-10		A1
599	FURGUSON, Jacob	31	E½NW	1838-07-28		A1
512	GAFFORD, Albert G	26	SENW	1835-09-19		A1
511	" "	26	NENW	1837-08-09		A1
513	" "	26	W½NE	1837-08-14		A1
510	" "	25	E½SW	1858-11-01		A1
556	GAFFORD, Daniel	36	E½NW	1834-03-12		A1
557	" "	36	E½SE	1834-03-12		A1
555	" "	35	SE	1837-08-09		A1
553	" "	15	NESW	1840-10-10		A1
554	" "	15	NWSE	1840-10-10		A1
620	GAFFORD, Jeremiah	36	SENE	1834-09-04		A1
509	GAREY, Absolum	19	E½SW	1825-04-22		A1
717	GAREY, Thomas	19	W½SW	1823-12-01		A1
616	GARRETT, James O	32	SWSW	1834-06-12		A1
615	" "	32	SESW	1837-04-10		A1
683	GILL, Lewis	2	E½SE	1837-08-14		A1
741	GOODWIN, William	15	SESW	1837-08-14		A1
629	GRANT, John	2	W½NE	1837-08-15		A1
631	GRANT, John H	2	NWNW	1837-04-10		A1
630	" "	2	NENW	1837-05-15		A1
632	" "	22	SWSE	1854-07-15		A1
633	" "	27	NWNE	1858-09-01		A1
551	HALL, Daniel D	9	SESE	1837-04-10		A1
552	" "	9	W½NE	1837-05-20		A1
603	HAMMONDS, James	30	SENW	1837-08-12		A1
604	" "	30	SWNE	1837-08-12		A1
686	HAMPTON, Mary F	29	NENW	1858-11-01		A1
718	HANDY, Thomas	11	NE	1837-08-09		A1
729	HARALSON, William B	17	W½NE	1837-08-02		A1
730	" "	5	W½SW	1837-08-02		A1
731	" "	6	E½SE	1837-08-02		A1
732	" "	7	SE	1837-08-02		A1
733	" "	8	W½SE	1837-08-02		A1
734	" "	9	W½NW	1837-08-02		A1
719	HARDEE, Thomas	11	E½NW	1837-05-20		A1
720	" "	2	SESW	1837-08-09		A1
721	" "	2	SWSE	1837-08-09		A1
649	HARRISON, Jonathan	23	NENW	1835-04-15		A1
651	" "	23	W½NE	1835-04-15		A1
650	" "	23	SENW	1837-05-20		A1
646	" "	13	W½NE	1837-08-09		A1
652	" "	24	E½NW	1837-08-09		A1
647	" "	14	SESW	1837-08-15		A1
648	" "	23	E½NE	1838-07-28		A1
682	HARRISON, Levi	13	W½SE	1825-04-16		A1
578	HARTLEY, Henry G	26	SENE	1835-09-12		A1
581	" "	30	W½NW	1837-05-15		A1
576	" "	20	E½SW	1837-08-15		A1
577	" "	20	W½SE	1837-08-15		A1
579	" "	30	NENW	1837-08-15		A1
580	" "	30	NWNE	1837-08-15		A1
642	HARTLEY, John R	34	W½SW	1837-08-02		A1
641	" "	23	W½SW	1837-08-15		A1
640	" "	22	E½SE	1837-08-18		A1
674	HARTLEY, Joseph	26	W½NW	1826-05-01		A1
663	" "	17	E½SE	1834-08-20		A1
679	" "	35	E½NW	1834-10-21		A1 V547
666	" "	21	E½SE	1835-10-15		A1
668	" "	21	SW	1835-10-15		A1
667	" "	21	N½	1837-04-10		A1
669	" "	21	W½SE	1837-04-10		A1
664	" "	17	W½SE	1837-05-15		A1
672	" "	22	W½SW	1837-08-02		A1

ID	Individual in Patent	Sec.	Sec. Part	Date Issued	Other Counties	For More Info . . .
675	HARTLEY, Joseph (Cont'd)	27	E½NW	1837-08-02		A1
665	" "	20	E½NW	1837-08-07		A1
671	" "	22	W½NW	1837-08-12		A1
677	" "	34	NE	1837-08-12		A1
676	" "	27	SE	1837-08-14		A1
678	" "	34	NESE	1837-08-15		A1
680	" "	35	NWSW	1837-08-15		A1
660	" "	15	NWSW	1845-07-01		A1
662	" "	15	SWNW	1845-07-01		A1
661	" "	15	SESE	1848-04-01		A1
670	" "	22	NENE	1848-04-01		A1
673	" "	23	W½NW	1848-04-01		A1
739	HARTLEY, William F	35	SESW	1847-05-01		A1
701	HATCHER, Rutledge	22	NWNE	1837-08-14		A1
702	" "	22	SENE	1837-08-14		A1
634	HEATON, John	12	NW	1837-08-14		A1
582	HERBERT, Hillary	34	SESW	1858-11-01		A1
583	" "	34	SWSE	1858-11-01		A1
584	" "	35	SWSW	1858-11-01		A1
605	HOLMES, James	34	W½NW	1833-08-02		A1
606	HOMES, James	17	E½SW	1825-04-22		A1
609	" "	33	W½NE	1834-08-05		A1
607	" "	28	S½SW	1834-10-21		A1
608	" "	33	NENE	1837-08-12		A1
743	JOHNSON, William	8	NE	1825-04-22		A1
515	JONES, Allen	1	NENW	1837-04-10		A1
516	" "	1	SENW	1837-05-20		A1
518	" "	2	E½NE	1837-08-14		A1
517	" "	1	W½NW	1838-07-28		A1
527	LEONARD, Calvin W	2	SWSW	1849-09-01		A1
573	LEONARD, Elizabeth	11	W½NW	1837-05-20		A1
617	LEONARD, James S	10	NW	1837-05-20		A1
618	" "	3	SESE	1837-08-15		A1
567	MCCORMACK, Dorcas	10	W½SE	1837-08-18		A1
612	MCCORMACK, James	10	E½NE	1823-10-01		A1
613	" "	15	E½NE	1834-09-04		A1
569	MCCORMICK, Dorcas	14	W½NW	1837-05-20		A1
568	" "	11	S½SW	1837-08-12		A1
614	MCCORMICK, James	10	E½SE	1825-04-14		A1
523	MCDANIEL, Bartley	27	E½NE	1837-08-07		A1
524	" "	27	SWNE	1837-08-07		A1
522	" "	22	E½NW	1837-08-14		A1
514	MCKEE, Alexander	33	SENE	1835-10-16		A1
540	MCMULLEN, Charles	6	NE	1831-12-01		A1 G31
655	MEALING, Jonathan	3	SW	1837-05-20		A1
658	" "	9	E½NE	1837-08-09		A1
659	" "	9	NESE	1837-08-09		A1
653	" "	10	SW	1837-08-12		A1
654	" "	10	W½NE	1837-08-12		A1
656	" "	4	S½SW	1837-08-14		A1
657	" "	4	SE	1837-08-14		A1
746	OLIVER, William W	29	NWNW	1847-05-01		A1
681	PARMER, Joseph M	2	SWNW	1850-05-01		A1 G35
681	PARMER, William K	2	SWNW	1850-05-01		A1 G35
542	PAYNE, Claiborn J	9	E½SW	1831-12-01		A1
541	" "	26	W½SE	1837-08-02		A1
543	PAYNE, Claiborne J	26	E½SE	1834-08-05		A1
544	" "	26	SESW	1834-08-05		A1
546	" "	35	E½NE	1834-08-05		A1
547	" "	35	NENW	1834-08-05		A1 V679
548	" "	35	W½NE	1837-08-07		A1
549	" "	35	W½NW	1837-08-07		A1
545	" "	26	W½SW	1838-07-28		A1
706	PAYNE, Samuel	35	SWNW	1837-08-15		A1 C
703	PAYNE, Samuel N	26	NESW	1834-10-21		A1
637	PEARCE, John	11	N½SE	1837-05-20		A1
638	" "	12	W½SW	1837-08-09		A1
639	" "	14	NENW	1837-08-18		A1
709	PEARCE, Seaborn T	11	SESE	1837-08-18		A1
710	" "	14	NENE	1837-08-18		A1
526	PEARMAN, Brittain K	8	SESE	1837-08-02		A1 R695
540	PEARMON, Orrin	6	NE	1831-12-01		A1 G31
700	PERRY, Robert	29	SWNW	1853-11-15		A1

ID	Individual in Patent	Sec.	Sec. Part	Date Issued	Other Counties	For More Info . . .
715	PHILLIPS, Thomas C	1	NWSE	1835-09-19		A1
716	" "	1	SW	1838-07-28		A1 G38
627	PICKENS, John A	22	NWSE	1876-02-01		A2
698	POOL, Richard	24	E½SE	1837-08-18		A1
704	POOL, Samuel P	1	E½SE	1837-08-12		A1
705	" "	1	SWSE	1837-08-12		A1
716	PORTERFIELD, Charles	1	SW	1838-07-28		A1 G38
565	RAY, Dempsey J	30	SWSW	1837-08-12		A1
566	" "	31	SWNW	1838-07-28		A1
742	RAY, William H	35	NESW	1858-11-01		A1
520	REID, Archibald M	9	W½SE	1837-08-15		A1
558	ROGERS, David	23	NESE	1835-09-12		A1
561	" "	23	SWSE	1835-09-12		A1
559	" "	23	NWSE	1837-08-09		A1
560	" "	23	SESE	1837-08-09		A1
562	" "	25	NW	1837-08-09		A1
563	" "	25	NWSW	1837-08-14		A1
564	" "	26	NENE	1837-08-14		A1
575	ROGERS, George W	28	NWSW	1838-07-28		A1
728	ROSS, William A	4	N½SW	1837-08-02		A1
643	ROUTON, John	36	NENE	1837-08-18		A1
725	SMITH, Thomas P	7	W½NW	1833-06-04		A1
723	" "	7	NWSW	1834-08-12		A1
722	" "	7	NESW	1837-08-02		A1
724	" "	7	S½SW	1837-08-07		A1
740	SMITH, William G	6	SWSW	1834-06-12		A1
644	SMYTH, John	3	W½SE	1852-02-02		A1
726	TAYLOR, Ward	17	W½NW	1826-05-01		A1
727	" "	17	W½SW	1826-05-01		A1
695	THIGPEN, Redding	8	SESE	1835-10-15		A1 R526
692	" "	17	NENE	1837-05-15		A1
696	" "	9	W½SW	1837-05-15		A1
693	" "	33	SWNW	1837-08-07		A1
694	" "	33	W½SW	1837-08-07		A1
611	TURNER, James L	22	SWNE	1878-06-13		A2
687	WADE, Micajah	32	SE	1837-08-12		A1
688	"	34	SESE	1838-07-28		A1
744	WADE, William M	34	NESW	1838-07-28		A1
745	" "	34	NWSE	1838-07-28		A1
747	WALKER, William	30	W½SE	1858-11-01		A1
711	WALLACE, Seaborn	14	NESW	1837-05-20		A1
712	" "	14	SENW	1837-05-20		A1
708	WALLACE, Seaborn A	14	SENE	1837-08-18		A1
619	WALLER, James	28	NW	1837-08-10		A1
521	WATSON, Artimus	14	W½NE	1826-05-01		A1
574	WATSON, Emsley	25	SWSW	1834-10-21		A1
550	WILLSON, Cyrus	25	E½NE	1858-11-01		A1
587	WINDHAM, Huston	15	NWNW	1834-10-21		A1
588	" "	15	SWSE	1834-10-21		A1
585	" "	14	W½SW	1837-08-14		A1
586	" "	15	E½NW	1837-08-14		A1
714	WINDHAM, Thomas B	15	W½NE	1826-05-01		A1

Patent Map

T11-N R14-E
St Stephens Meridian

Map Group 3

Township Statistics

Parcels Mapped	:	241
Number of Patents	:	221
Number of Individuals	:	110
Patentees Identified	:	108
Number of Surnames	:	75
Multi-Patentee Parcels	:	3
Oldest Patent Date	:	1/1/1822
Most Recent Patent	:	6/13/1878
Block/Lot Parcels	:	0
Parcels Re - Issued	:	1
Parcels that Overlap	:	2
Cities and Towns	:	2
Cemeteries	:	3

Section 6
DEMING Simeon 1854
MCMULLEN [31] Charles 1831
DAVIS James L 1835
EARNEST John J 1825
ERNEST John J 1826
HARALSON William B 1837
SMITH William G 1834

Section 5
HARALSON William B 1837
DAVENPORT James 1829

Section 4
ROSS William A 1837
MEALING Jonathan 1837
MEALING Jonathan 1837

Section 7
SMITH Thomas P 1833
ERNEST Isham 1826
EARNEST Isham 1822
SMITH Thomas P 1834
SMITH Thomas P 1837
HARALSON William B 1837
SMITH Thomas P 1837

Section 8
JOHNSON William 1825
DAVENPORT Charles 1833
HARALSON William B 1837
PEARMAN Brittain K 1837
THIGPEN Redding 1835

Section 9
HARALSON William B 1837
HALL Daniel D 1837
MEALING Jonathan 1837
THIGPEN Redding 1837
PAYNE Claiborn J 1831
REID Archibald M 1837
MEALING Jonathan 1837
HALL Daniel D 1837

Section 18

Section 17
TAYLOR Ward 1826
DAVENPORT William 1834
HARALSON William B 1837
THIGPEN Redding 1837
CHEATHAM Peter 1848
TAYLOR Ward 1826
HOMES James 1825
HARTLEY Joseph 1837
HARTLEY Joseph 1834

Section 16

Section 19

Section 20
DAVENPORT Charles 1834
HARTLEY Joseph 1837
DAVENPORT Charles 1834
HARTLEY Henry G 1837
HARTLEY Henry G 1837

Section 21
HARTLEY Joseph 1837
HARTLEY Joseph 1835
HARTLEY Joseph 1837
HARTLEY Joseph 1835

Section 30
GAREY Thomas 1823
GAREY Absolum 1825
DAVENPORT Charles 1834
HARTLEY Henry G 1837
HARTLEY Henry G 1837
HARTLEY Henry G 1837
HAMMONDS James 1837
HAMMONDS James 1837
FERGUSON Jacob 1834
FERGUSON Robert H 1852
WALKER William 1858
FERGUSON Jacob 1837
RAY Dempsey J 1837

Section 29
OLIVER William W 1847
HAMPTON Mary F 1858
DAVENPORT Charles 1837
COX James 1825
PERRY Robert 1853
DAVENPORT Charles 1837
DAVENPORT Charles 1833
DAVENPORT Charles 1837

Section 28
WALLER James 1837
ROGERS George W 1838
DAVENPORT William 1838
HOMES James 1834

Section 31
ARMSTRONG John W 1858
RAY Dempsey J 1838
FURGUSON Jacob 1838
FERGUSON Jacob 1837
FERGUSON Jacob 1841
FERGUSON Jacob 1837
FERGUSON Jacob 1835
FERGUSON Jacob 1837

Section 32
DAVENPORT Charles 1835
DAVENPORT Charles 1843
DAVENPORT Charles 1843
DAVENPORT Charles 1837
WADE Micajah 1837
GARRETT James O 1834
GARRETT James O 1837

Section 33
DICKSON John 1835
THIGPEN Redding 1837
HOMES James 1834
HOMES James 1837
MCKEE Alexander 1835
DAVENPORT James 1835
THIGPEN Redding 1837

3

MEALING
Jonathan
1837

SMYTH
John
1852

LEONARD
James S
1837

2

GRANT
John H
1837

GRANT
John H
1837

PARMER [35]
Joseph M
1850

GRANT
John
1837

JONES
Allen
1837

LEONARD
Calvin W
1849

HARDEE
Thomas
1837

HARDEE
Thomas
1837

GILL
Lewis
1837

JONES
Allen
1838

JONES
Allen
1837

BUTLER
Magdalene
1837

JONES
Allen
1837

BUTLER
Isaac
1835

BUTLER
Reuben
1822

1

PHILLIPS
Thomas C
1838

PHILLIPS
Thomas C
1835

POOL
Samuel P
1837

POOL
Samuel P
1837

10

LEONARD
James S
1837

MEALING
Jonathan
1837

MCCORMACK
James
1823

MEALING
Jonathan
1837

MCCORMACK
Dorcas
1837

MCCORMICK
James
1825

11

LEONARD
Elizabeth
1837

HARDEE
Thomas
1837

HANDY
Thomas
1837

CATES
Mahlon
1837

MCCORMICK
Dorcas
1837

PEARCE
John
1837

BRUCE
Jesse
1837

PEARCE
Seaborn T
1837

12

HEATON
John
1837

BUTLER
Aaron
1835

BUTLER
Aaron
1838

BUTLER
Edmund
1837

BUTLER
Edmund
1837

PEARCE
John
1837

BUTLER
Edmund
1837

15

WINDHAM
Huston
1834

WINDHAM
Thomas B
1826

WINDHAM
Huston
1837

MCCORMACK
James
1834

HARTLEY
Joseph
1845

GAFFORD
Daniel
1840

GAFFORD
Daniel
1840

CHEATHAM
Peter
1848

HARTLEY
Joseph
1845

CHEATHAM
Peter
1840

GOODWIN
William
1837

WINDHAM
Huston
1834

HARTLEY
Joseph
1848

14

MCCORMICK
Dorcas
1837

PEARCE
John
1837

WATSON
Artimus
1826

WALLACE
Seaborn
1837

WALLACE
Seaborn
1837

WINDHAM
Huston
1837

HARRISON
Jonathan
1837

PEARCE
Seaborn T
1837

WALLACE
Seaborn A
1837

13

HARRISON
Jonathan
1837

HARRISON
Levi
1825

FULLER
Benjamin
1837

BARGANIER
Jesse
1837

22

MCDANIEL
Bartley
1837

HATCHER
Rutledge
1837

TURNER
James L
1878

HARTLEY
Joseph
1848

HATCHER
Rutledge
1837

HARTLEY
Joseph
1837

HARTLEY
Joseph
1837

PICKENS
John A
1876

HARTLEY
John R
1837

GRANT
John H
1854

23

HARTLEY
Joseph
1848

HARRISON
Jonathan
1835

HARRISON
Jonathan
1837

HARTLEY
John R
1837

FARROW
Samuel W
1837

HARRISON
Jonathan
1835

HARRISON
Jonathan
1838

ROGERS
David
1837

ROGERS
David
1835

ROGERS
David
1835

ROGERS
David
1837

24

HARRISON
Jonathan
1837

BARGANIER
Jesse
1837

BARGANIER
Jesse
1837

BARGANIEL
Jesse
1837

BARGANIER
Jesse
1838

BARGANIER
Jesse
1838

POOL
Richard
1837

27

HARTLEY
Joseph
1837

GRANT
John H
1858

MCDANIEL
Bartley
1837

MCDANIEL
Bartley
1837

HARTLEY
Joseph
1837

HARTLEY
Joseph
1826

HARTLEY
Joseph
1837

26

GAFFORD
Albert G
1837

GAFFORD
Albert G
1837

GAFFORD
Albert G
1835

PAYNE
Samuel N
1834

PAYNE
Claiborne J
1838

PAYNE
Claiborne J
1834

GAFFORD
Albert G
1837

ROGERS
David
1837

HARTLEY
Henry G
1835

PAYNE
Claiborne J
1834

PAYNE
Claiborn J
1837

25

ROGERS
David
1837

ROGERS
David
1837

WATSON
Emsley
1834

COLLINS
William
1825

COLLINS
William
1823

GAFFORD
Albert G
1858

WILLSON
Cyrus
1858

FULLER
Archibald
1852

34

HOLMES
James
1833

HARTLEY
Joseph
1837

HARTLEY
John R
1837

WADE
William M
1838

WADE
William M
1838

HARTLEY
Joseph
1837

HERBERT
Hillary
1858

HERBERT
Hillary
1858

WADE
Micajah
1838

35

PAYNE
Claiborne J
1837

PAYNE
Samuel
1837

PAYNE
Claiborne J
1834

HARTLEY
Joseph
1834

PAYNE
Claiborne J
1837

HARTLEY
Joseph
1837

RAY
William H
1858

HERBERT
Hillary
1858

HARTLEY
William F
1847

PAYNE
Claiborne J
1834

GAFFORD
Daniel
1837

36

GAFFORD
Daniel
1834

ROUTON
John
1837

GAFFORD
Jeremiah
1834

GAFFORD
Daniel
1834

Helpful Hints

1. This Map's INDEX can be found on the preceding pages.

2. Refer to Map "C" to see where this Township lies within Butler County, Alabama.

3. Numbers within square brackets [ ] denote a multi-patentee land parcel (multi-owner). Refer to Appendix "C" for a full list of members in this group.

4. Areas that look to be crowded with Patentees usually indicate multiple sales of the same parcel (Re-issues) or Overlapping parcels. See this Township's Index for an explanation of these and other circumstances that might explain "odd" groupings of Patentees on this map.

Legend

Patent Boundary

Section Boundary

No Patents Found
(or Outside County)

1., 2., 3., ... Lot Numbers
(when beside a name)

[ ] Group Number
(see Appendix "C")

Scale: Section = 1 mile X 1 mile
(generally, with some exceptions)

Road Map

T11-N R14-E
St Stephens Meridian

Map Group 3

Cities & Towns
Fort Dale
Searcy

Cemeteries
Fort Dale Cemetery
Kilgore Cemetery
Pine Top Cemetery

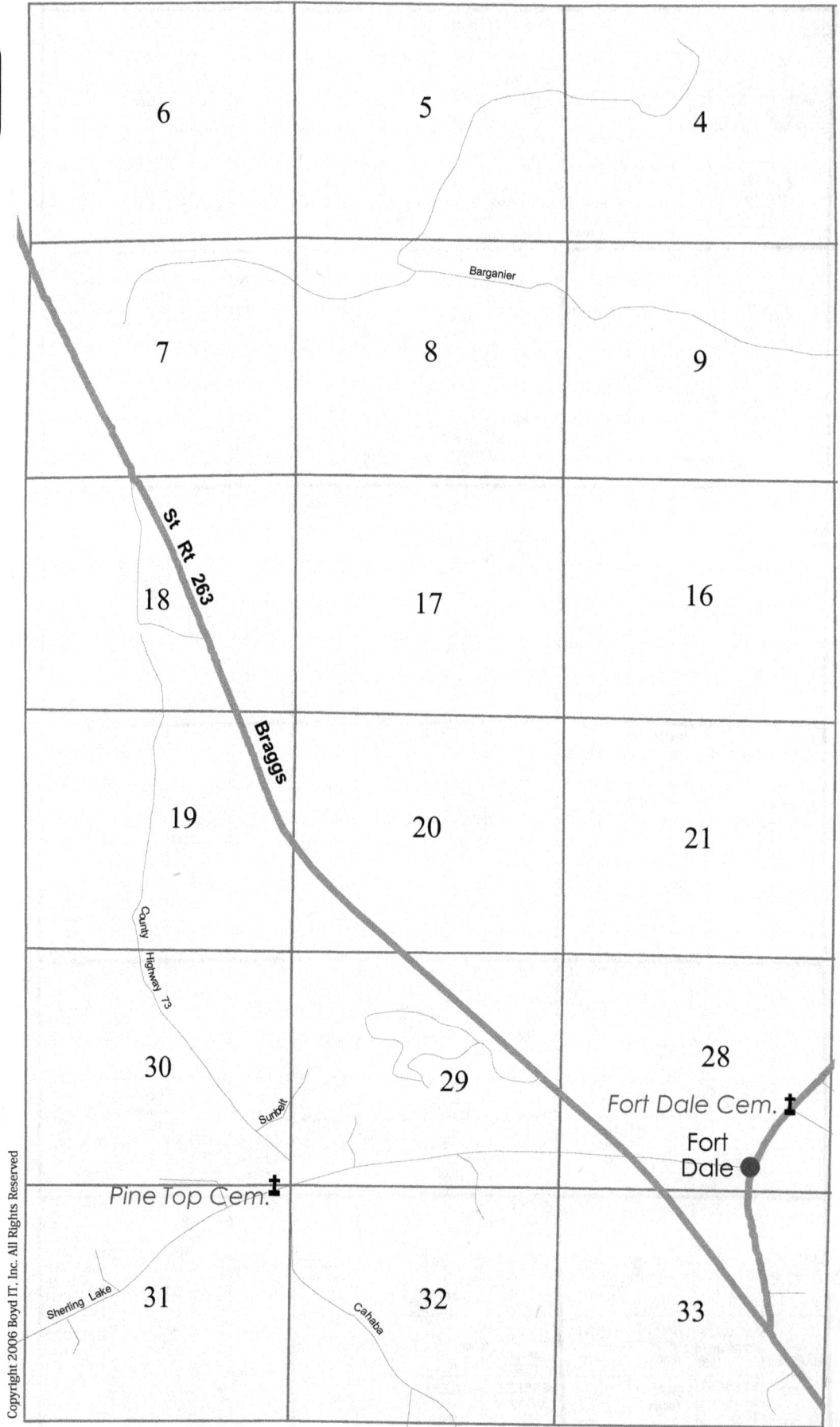

6	5	4
7	8	9
18	17	16
19	20	21
30	29	28
31	32	33

Barganier

St Rt 263

Braggs

County Highway 73

Sunbelt

Pine Top Cem.

Fort Dale Cem.

Fort Dale

Sherling Lake

Cahaba

3

2

1

Fort Dale

✝ Kilgore Cem.

Mitchell

10

11

12

Old Stage

15

14

13

Cates

County Road 41

22

23

24

Searcy ● Wite

Harmony

Cotton Blossom

New Searcy

27

26

25

Airport

Fort Dale

I-65

Old Searcy

34

35

36

Airport

Helpful Hints

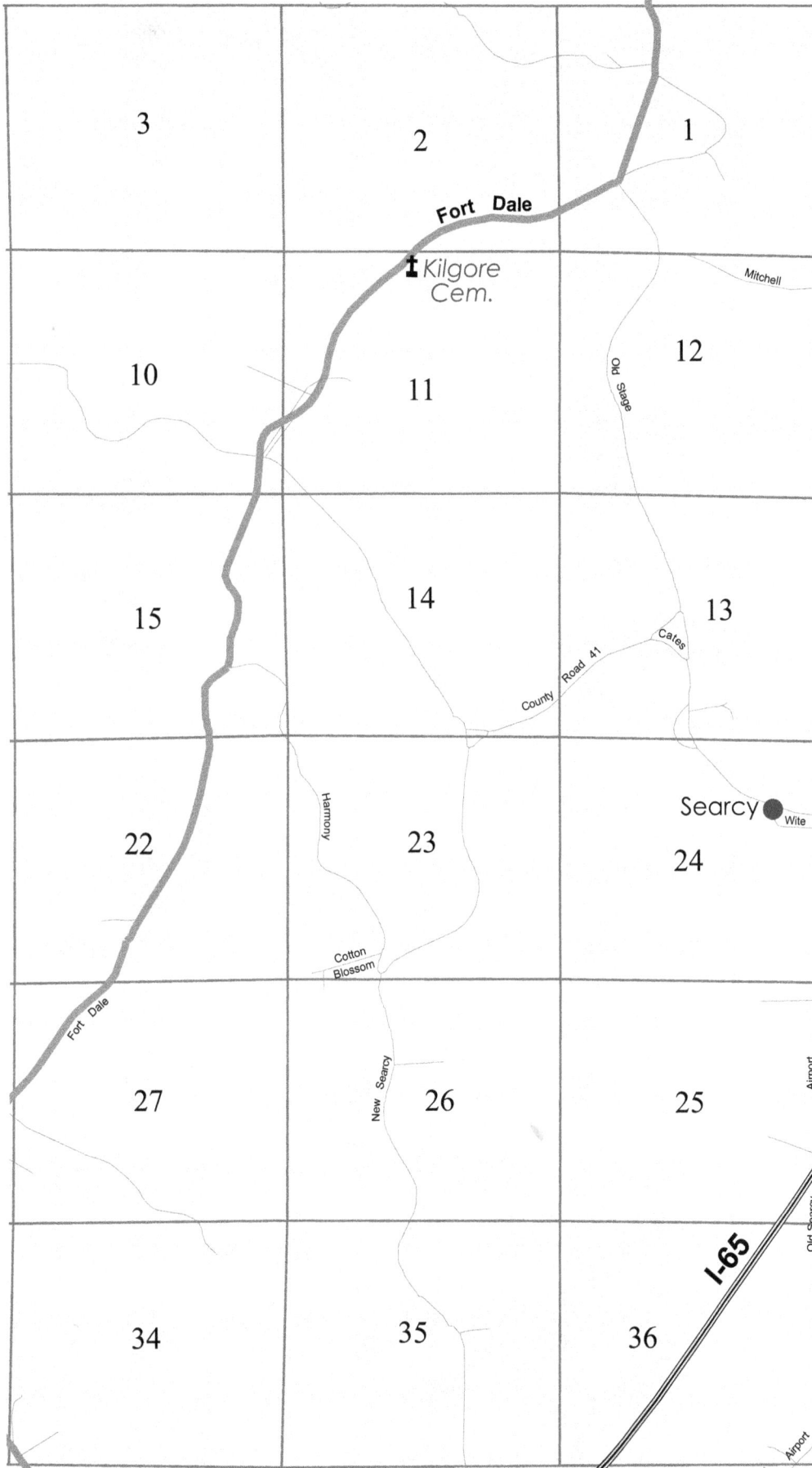

1. This road map has a number of uses, but primarily it is to help you: a) find the present location of land owned by your ancestors (at least the general area), b) find cemeteries and city-centers, and c) estimate the route/roads used by Census-takers & tax-assessors.

2. If you plan to travel to Butler County to locate cemeteries or land parcels, please pick up a modern travel map for the area before you do. Mapping old land parcels on modern maps is not as exact a science as you might think. Just the slightest variations in public land survey coordinates, estimates of parcel boundaries, or road-map deviations can greatly alter a map's representation of how a road either does or doesn't cross a particular parcel of land.

Legend

————	Section Lines
▬▬▬▬	Interstates
▬▬▬▬	Highways
————	Other Roads
●	Cities/Towns
✝	Cemeteries

Scale: Section = 1 mile X 1 mile
(generally, with some exceptions)

Historical Map

T11-N R14-E
St Stephens Meridian

Map Group 3

Cities & Towns
Fort Dale
Searcy

Cemeteries
Fort Dale Cemetery
Kilgore Cemetery
Pine Top Cemetery

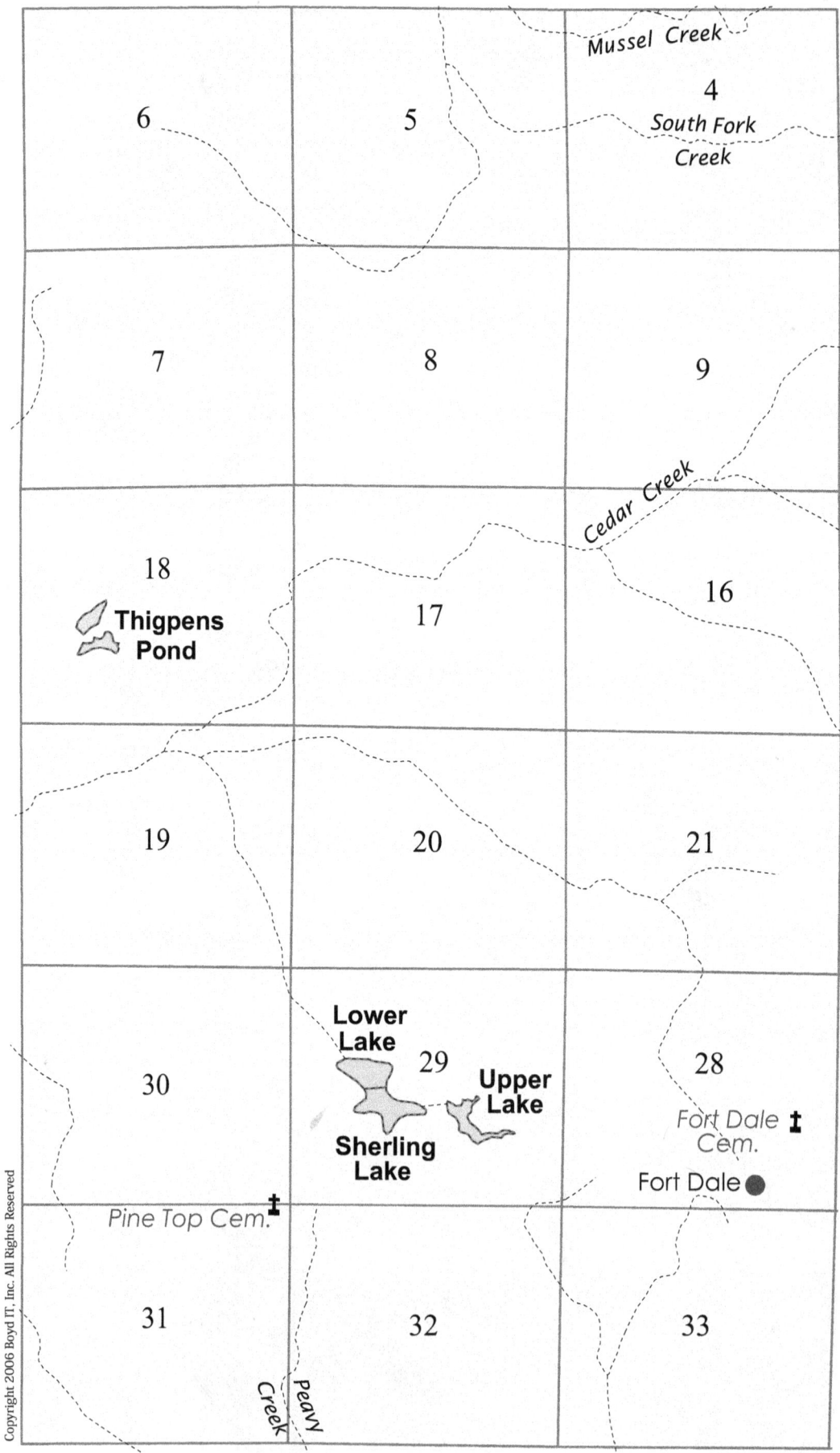

Mussel Creek

6

5

4

South Fork
Creek

7

8

9

Cedar Creek

18

Thigpens
Pond

17

16

19

20

21

Lower
Lake

30

29

Upper
Lake

28

Sherling
Lake

Fort Dale
Cem.

Fort Dale

Pine Top Cem.

31

32

33

Peavy Creek

3

2

1

✝
Kilgore Cem.

10

11

12

Persimmon Creek

15

14

13

22

23

Searcy ●

24

27

26

25

34

35

36

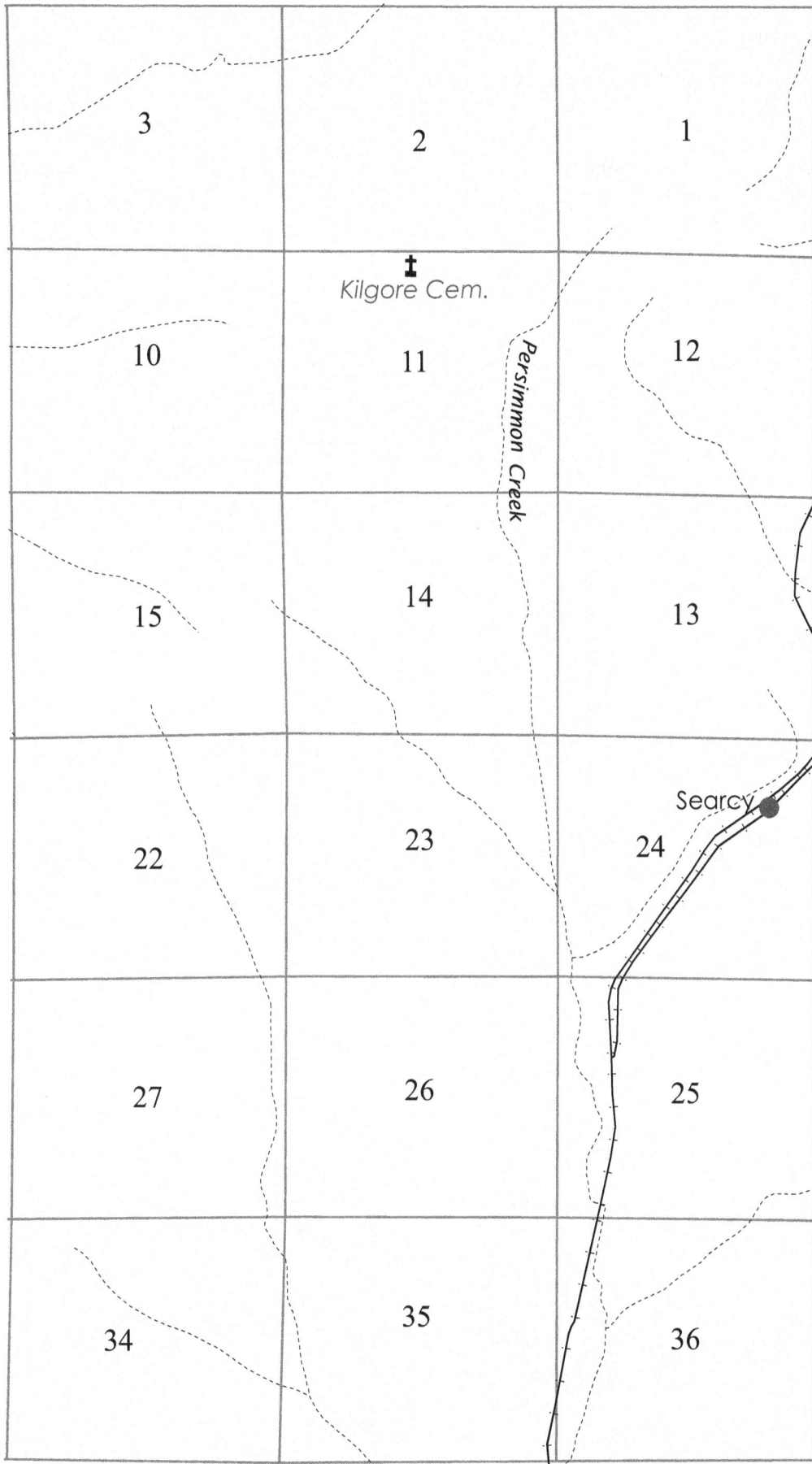

Helpful Hints

1. This Map takes a different look at the same Congressional Township displayed in the preceding two maps. It presents features that can help you better envision the historical development of the area: a) Water-bodies (lakes & ponds), b) Water-courses (rivers, streams, etc.), c) Railroads, d) City/town center-points (where they were oftentimes located when first settled), and e) Cemeteries.

2. Using this "Historical" map in tandem with this Township's Patent Map and Road Map, may lead you to some interesting discoveries. You will often find roads, towns, cemeteries, and waterways are named after nearby landowners: sometimes those names will be the ones you are researching. See how many of these research gems you can find here in Butler County.

Legend

— Section Lines

+++++ Railroads

▭ Large Rivers & Bodies of Water

----- Streams/Creeks & Small Rivers

● Cities/Towns

✝ Cemeteries

Scale: Section = 1 mile X 1 mile
(there are some exceptions)

Map Group 4: Index to Land Patents

Township 11-North Range 15-East (St Stephens)

After you locate an individual in this Index, take note of the Section and Section Part then proceed to the Land Patent map on the pages immediately following. You should have no difficulty locating the corresponding parcel of land.

The "For More Info" Column will lead you to more information about the underlying Patents. See the *Legend* at right, and the "How to Use this Book" chapter, for more information.

ID	Individual in Patent	Sec.	Sec. Part	Date Issued	Other Counties	For More Info . . .
891	ANDRESS, John N	1	SESW	1837-08-12		A1
990	BALLARD, Theophilus	4	E½NW	1837-04-15		A1
992	" "	4	NWSE	1837-04-15		A1
991	" "	4	E½SW	1837-05-15		A1
993	" "	4	W½NE	1837-05-15		A1
994	BALLARD, Theopholus	10	SWNW	1854-10-02		A1
995	" "	9	SENE	1854-10-02		A1
868	BOLLING, John	35	NWNW	1850-08-10		A1
869	" "	35	SWNW	1851-04-10		A1
831	BRASSWELL, James	1	SENW	1837-08-09		A1
832	BROWN, James	24	NE	1826-05-01		A1
866	BROWN, Joel	24	E½NW	1826-05-01		A1
867	" "	24	E½SW	1826-05-01		A1
913	BROWN, Joseph	25	E½NE	1832-09-10		A1
987	BROWN, Squire	24	SE	1826-05-01		A1
988	" "	24	W½SW	1832-09-10		A1
790	BUTLER, Edmund	7	NWSW	1837-05-15		A1
791	" "	7	SWSW	1837-08-07		A1 R956
976	CALLEN, Ross	1	NENW	1847-05-01		A1
977	" "	11	SENE	1858-11-01		A1
853	CARTER, Jarrett	10	N½NW	1837-05-15		A1
854	" "	4	E½SE	1837-05-15		A1
781	CHEATHAM, Daniel A	5	SENE	1837-08-08		A1
784	CHEATHAM, Daniel H	4	SWSE	1838-07-28		A1
785	CHEATHAM, David	5	NENE	1837-05-15		A1
786	CHEATHAM, David H	4	NWSW	1837-08-02		A1
801	CHEATHAM, Gattridge	9	W½SW	1826-07-10		A1
808	CHEATHAM, Guteridge	15	NENW	1854-10-02		A1
809	CHEATHAM, Gutridge	22	W½SE	1837-08-14		A1
812	CHEATHAM, Gutteridge	22	NWSW	1837-05-15		A1
814	" "	22	SWNW	1837-05-15		A1
813	" "	22	SENW	1837-08-01		A1
810	" "	21	E½NE	1837-08-02		A1
811	" "	22	E½SW	1837-08-02		A1
815	" "	22	SWSW	1837-08-02		A1
816	" "	9	W½SE	1837-08-02		A1
817	CHEATHAM, Guttridge	15	W½NE	1838-07-28		A1
818	" "	9	E½SW	1838-07-28		A1
819	" "	9	NW	1838-07-28		A1
949	CHEATHAM, Peter	4	W½NW	1831-05-19		A1
822	COLLINS, Isaac	10	E½SE	1831-06-01		A1
823	" "	14	NWSW	1834-08-05		A1
824	" "	14	SENW	1834-08-05		A1
825	" "	15	SWSE	1834-08-12		A1
828	" "	27	W½SE	1837-08-02		A1
826	" "	27	E½NW	1837-08-07		A1

ID	Individual in Patent	Sec.	Sec. Part	Date Issued	Other Counties	For More Info . . .
827	COLLINS, Isaac (Cont'd)	27	E½SE	1837-08-08		A1
829	" "	34	E½NE	1838-07-28		A1
830	" "	22	N½NW	1843-02-01		A1 G10
1020	COLLINS, William	14	W½NW	1831-05-17		A1
1024	" "	26	SW	1831-08-01		A1 G11
1018	" "	10	W½SE	1833-09-16		A1
1021	" "	15	SENW	1834-08-20		A1
1017	" "	10	E½SW	1837-05-15		A1
1019	" "	14	NENW	1837-08-12		A1
1022	" "	2	SESW	1837-08-18		A1
1023	" "	3	SESE	1837-08-18		A1
802	COOK, George H	28	NE	1837-08-15		A1
997	COULSON, Thomas	36	NWSW	1837-08-18		A1
833	CRAIG, James D	34	E½SE	1837-08-18		A1 R803
834	" "	35	W½SW	1837-08-18		A1
940	CRAIG, Nathan H	12	NWSW	1845-07-01		A1
770	CROCKER, Benjamin	11	NENW	1837-08-07		A1 G14
771	" "	11	W½NW	1837-08-07		A1 G14
769	" "	2	SWSW	1837-08-12		A1
768	" "	1	NESW	1838-07-28		A1
800	DAY, Frederick	8	E½SE	1837-05-15		A1
870	DIXON, John	13	E½NE	1837-08-18		A1
777	EASTERLING, Bennett	34	W½NE	1854-07-15		A1
794	FAIL, Ellsberry	36	SENW	1854-07-15		A1
871	FAILS, John	35	SENE	1837-08-12		A1
872	" "	36	NENW	1837-08-12		A1
873	" "	36	SWNW	1837-08-12		A1
999	FAILS, Thomas	25	SWSE	1834-10-21		A1
1000	" "	25	W½SW	1834-10-21		A1
1003	" "	36	SENE	1834-10-21		A1
998	" "	25	E½SW	1837-05-20		A1
1002	" "	35	E½SE	1837-08-08		A1
1004	" "	36	W½NE	1837-08-08		A1
1001	" "	26	E½SE	1837-08-12		A1
932	FLINN, Leander W	14	SESW	1852-02-02		A1
931	" "	14	NESW	1852-12-01		A1
933	" "	14	SWSW	1852-12-01		A1
874	FORREST, John	29	W½NW	1837-08-18		A1
875	" "	30	E½NE	1837-08-18		A1
876	" "	30	SWNE	1837-08-18		A1
820	FROST, Henry	35	SESW	1850-08-10		A1
748	FULLER, Abner J	19	NESE	1837-08-10		A1
749	" "	20	NWSW	1837-08-10		A1
756	FULLER, Archibald	30	SWSW	1852-02-02		A1
774	FULLER, Benjamin	20	NENW	1837-08-10		A1
776	" "	20	W½NW	1837-08-10		A1
772	" "	19	NESW	1838-07-28		A1
773	" "	19	NWSE	1838-07-28		A1
775	" "	20	SENW	1838-07-28		A1
787	GAFFNEY, Davis F	34	NWSW	1858-11-01		A1
788	" "	34	S½NW	1858-11-01		A1
789	GAFFNEY, Drury A	1	E½SE	1845-07-01		A1
757	GAFFORD, Augustus P	32	SE	1838-07-28		A1
758	" "	33	SW	1838-07-28		A1
783	GAFFORD, Daniel	30	SE	1837-08-15		A1
859	GAFFORD, Jeremiah	31	E½SE	1834-09-04		A1
860	" "	31	SWNE	1834-09-04		A1
861	" "	31	W½NW	1834-09-04		A1
863	" "	32	W½SW	1837-05-15		A1
862	" "	32	E½SW	1837-08-01		A1
856	" "	29	W½SW	1837-08-12		A1
858	" "	31	E½NE	1837-08-12		A1
864	" "	33	E½SE	1837-08-12		A1
857	" "	30	E½SW	1837-08-18		A1
855	" "	27	E½SW	1838-07-28		A1
989	GAFFORD, Stephen F	31	NWNE	1838-07-28		A1
750	GANDY, Achsa	1	NENE	1837-08-09		A1
865	GENTRY, Jesse	1	SWSW	1837-05-20		A1
936	GILL, Lewis	7	NWSE	1837-04-10		A1
935	" "	7	NESW	1837-08-12		A1
767	GLASS, Benjamin A	2	W½SE	1837-05-15		A1
764	" "	2	E½SE	1837-05-20		A1
765	" "	2	NESW	1837-08-07		A1

ID	Individual in Patent	Sec.	Sec. Part	Date Issued	Other Counties	For More Info . . .
766	GLASS, Benjamin A (Cont'd)	2	S½NW	1837-08-07		A1
759	" "	1	NWSW	1837-08-08		A1
760	" "	1	W½NW	1837-08-08		A1
761	" "	11	NENE	1837-08-12		A1
762	" "	12	NENW	1837-08-12		A1
763	" "	12	SWNW	1837-08-12		A1
979	GRAHAM, Samuel N	2	NENW	1837-05-20		A1
937	GRIGGS, Lewis	1	SENE	1838-07-28		A1
919	HALL, Joseph	29	E½SE	1823-10-01		A1
918	" "	29	E½NE	1826-05-01		A1
915	" "	28	E½SW	1834-01-21		A1
916	" "	28	W½NW	1835-11-20		A1
921	" "	33	E½NW	1835-11-20		A1
914	" "	28	E½NW	1837-04-10		A1
917	" "	28	W½SW	1837-08-10		A1
920	" "	32	E½NE	1837-08-10		A1
922	" "	33	W½NW	1837-08-10		A1
1025	HAM, William	12	W½SE	1837-05-20		A1
928	HAMMONS, Larkin	1	W½NE	1837-08-18		A1
807	HARRELL, German B	2	NE	1837-08-12		A1 G23
821	HARTLEY, Henry G	30	NENW	1837-08-15		A1 G25
880	HEATON, John	7	NWNE	1837-08-07		A1 R837
881	" "	7	SENW	1837-08-07		A1
877	" "	6	E½SE	1837-08-09		A1
879	" "	7	NENW	1837-08-09		A1
878	" "	6	W½SE	1837-08-12		A1
882	" "	7	SWNE	1837-08-12		A1
948	HUTCHINSON, Parr	5	SE	1837-08-02		A1
947	" "	4	SWSW	1841-05-20		A1
929	KILLOUGH, Lawson	36	SESW	1852-12-01		A1
930	" "	36	SWSE	1854-07-15		A1
978	KILLOUGH, Samuel	36	NESW	1850-08-10		A1
836	KIRKPATRICK, James	11	SWNE	1834-10-21		A1
837	" "	7	NWNE	1837-08-10		A1 R880
835	" "	11	SESE	1837-08-12		A1
844	KIRKPATRICK, James P	12	SWNE	1837-08-18		A1
969	KIRKPATRICK, Robert H	11	NESE	1848-05-03		A1
1026	KIRKPATRICK, William	11	W½SW	1833-09-16		A1
1027	" "	27	SWNW	1854-07-15		A1
889	MCCOY, John	24	W½NW	1832-09-10		A1
886	" "	23	SENW	1837-05-20		A1
887	" "	23	W½NE	1837-05-20		A1
884	" "	22	SWNE	1837-08-12		A1
885	" "	23	E½NE	1837-08-12		A1
888	" "	23	W½SW	1838-07-28		A1
893	MCCOY, John R	22	SENE	1854-07-15		A1
892	" "	22	NENE	1858-11-01		A1
894	" "	23	NENW	1858-11-01		A1
895	" "	23	W½NW	1858-11-01		A1
923	MCCOY, Joseph	23	NESW	1837-08-08		A1
924	" "	23	SESE	1837-08-08		A1
925	" "	23	W½SE	1837-08-08		A1
938	MCCOY, Mary	23	NESE	1854-10-02		A1
971	MCCOY, Robert J	13	SWSE	1835-10-14		A1
970	" "	13	NWSE	1837-08-01		A1
973	" "	32	E½NW	1837-08-01		A1
974	" "	32	W½NE	1837-08-01		A1
975	" "	32	W½NW	1837-08-02		A1
972	" "	29	SWSE	1837-08-18		A1
1028	MCCURRY, William	12	NWNW	1835-09-12		A1
782	MCDONALD, Daniel B	12	NESE	1852-12-01		A1
843	MCFARLAND, James	5	W½NE	1837-08-09		A1
838	" "	3	E½NE	1837-08-12		A1
839	" "	3	NW	1837-08-12		A1
840	" "	3	NWNE	1837-08-12		A1
841	" "	3	NWSW	1837-08-12		A1
842	" "	4	E½NE	1837-08-12		A1
890	MCPHERSON, John	25	NWNE	1854-07-15		A1
942	MERCER, Noah	15	E½SW	1837-08-12		A1
944	" "	15	NWSW	1837-08-12		A1
943	" "	15	NWSE	1837-08-14		A1
945	" "	15	SWNW	1838-07-28		A1
946	" "	27	S½NE	1854-07-15		A1

ID	Individual in Patent	Sec.	Sec. Part	Date Issued	Other Counties	For More Info . . .
983	MERCER, Seth	26	W½NW	1837-08-12		A1
984	" "	27	NENE	1837-08-12		A1
985	" "	27	NWNE	1837-08-14		A1
982	" "	15	SWSW	1850-04-01		A1
1030	MOSELEY, William	18	SE	1826-07-10		A1
1031	" "	19	E½NE	1837-08-09		A1 V1033
1034	" "	19	NWNW	1837-08-09		A1
1029	" "	18	E½SW	1837-08-15		A1
1032	" "	19	E½NW	1837-08-15		A1
1033	" "	19	N½NE	1837-08-15		A1 V1031
1015	MOSELEY, William B	18	W½SW	1837-08-01		A1
1035	MOSLEY, William	19	NWSW	1837-05-15		A1
1036	" "	19	SWNW	1837-05-15		A1
1046	MURRY, William W	28	NWSE	1854-10-02		A1
1050	NIX, Zacheus	5	W½NW	1837-05-20		A1
1049	" "	5	SW	1837-08-09		A1
845	OTT, James P	33	S½NE	1858-11-01		A1
805	PATTILLO, George H	34	SWSW	1835-10-08		A1
804	" "	34	E½SW	1837-08-07		A1
803	" "	34	E½SE	1838-07-28		A1 R833
1005	PAYNE, Thomas G	23	SESW	1854-10-02		A1
996	PHILIPS, Thomas C	6	W½SW	1823-12-01		A1
849	PICKENS, James V	25	SWNE	1837-08-08		A1
980	PINGLETON, Samuel	35	NENE	1837-08-12		A1
981	" "	36	NWNW	1837-08-12		A1
939	PLAYER, Mary S	20	E½SW	1837-08-02		A1
778	RABUN, Bud	30	NWNE	1837-08-08		A1
779	" "	30	SENW	1837-08-08		A1
821	" "	30	NENW	1837-08-15		A1 G25
901	RABUN, John	21	W½SW	1837-08-08		A1
899	" "	19	S½SE	1838-07-28		A1
900	" "	19	S½SW	1838-07-28		A1
1037	RICHARDS, William	20	SWSW	1858-11-01		A1
902	ROUTON, John	29	E½SW	1838-07-28		A1
846	SALTER, James	6	E½SW	1837-05-20		A1
848	" "	6	S½NW	1837-08-07		A1
847	" "	6	N½NW	1837-08-15		A1
795	SHEPHERD, Francis	33	W½SE	1830-11-16		A1
755	SHEPPARD, Andrew	25	NENW	1838-07-28		A1
830	" "	22	N½NW	1843-02-01		A1 G10
799	SHEPPARD, Francis	35	W½NE	1837-08-02		A1
798	" "	35	NESW	1838-07-28		A1
796	" "	12	NWNE	1854-07-15		A1
797	" "	12	SENE	1854-07-15		A1
1039	SHEPPARD, William	25	W½NW	1831-08-01		A1
1038	" "	25	SENW	1837-05-15		A1
1041	" "	26	SENE	1837-05-15		A1
1040	" "	26	E½NE	1837-08-08		A1
1016	STEWART, William B	27	NWNW	1837-08-12		A1
806	STOCKMAN, George	1	NWSE	1845-07-01		A1
903	TALLEY, John	21	NENW	1835-10-01		A1
905	" "	21	SENW	1837-08-01		A1
904	" "	21	NWNE	1837-08-14		A1
941	TALLEY, Nathan	21	W½NW	1823-10-01		A1
959	TALLEY, Reuben	8	SW	1823-10-01		A1
961	" "	8	W½SE	1825-05-12		A1
951	" "	18	N½	1837-08-01		A1
958	" "	8	SENW	1837-08-01		A1
960	" "	8	W½NW	1837-08-01		A1
955	" "	7	SESW	1837-08-08		A1
956	" "	7	SWSW	1837-08-08		A1 R791
957	" "	8	NENW	1837-08-08		A1
954	" "	7	E½SE	1837-08-14		A1
950	" "	10	W½SW	1837-08-18		A1
953	" "	29	W½NE	1837-08-18		A1
952	" "	29	E½NW	1838-07-28		A1
1043	TALLEY, William	8	W½NE	1825-04-20		A1
1042	" "	8	E½NE	1826-07-10		A1
906	TALLY, John	21	NESW	1854-07-15		A1
752	TAYLOR, Andrew J	25	E½SE	1838-07-28		A1
753	" "	25	NWSE	1838-07-28		A1
754	" "	36	NENE	1838-07-28		A1
1024	TAYLOR, Joseph M	26	SW	1831-08-01		A1 G11

ID	Individual in Patent	Sec.	Sec. Part	Date Issued	Other Counties	For More Info . . .
1008	TAYLOR, Ward	26	W½SE	1827-01-08		A1
910	TILLERY, John	10	SWNE	1837-05-20		A1
912	" "	3	NESE	1837-05-20		A1
909	" "	10	SENW	1837-08-08		A1
907	" "	10	NWNE	1858-11-01		A1
908	" "	10	SENE	1858-11-01		A1
911	" "	2	NWSW	1858-11-01		A1
897	TILLERY, John R	11	SESW	1852-02-02		A1
896	" "	11	NESW	1858-11-01		A1
898	" "	11	SWSE	1858-11-01		A1
965	TILLERY, Richard	3	SWSW	1837-05-15		A1
966	" "	3	W½SE	1837-05-15		A1
964	" "	3	SWNE	1837-05-20		A1
963	" "	3	E½SW	1837-08-08		A1
962	" "	15	NWNW	1852-02-02		A1
967	" "	9	NESE	1852-02-02		A1
968	" "	9	SESE	1852-02-02		A1
1009	TILLERY, Washington	10	NENE	1843-02-01		A1
1011	" "	9	NWNE	1845-06-01		A1
1010	" "	9	NENE	1858-11-01		A1
1045	TILLERY, William	11	SENW	1837-05-20		A1
770	" "	11	NENW	1837-08-07		A1 G14
771	" "	11	W½NW	1837-08-07		A1 G14
1044	" "	11	NWSE	1837-08-12		A1
1006	TINSLEY, Thomas	15	E½NE	1833-08-02		A1
1007	" "	35	W½SE	1837-08-02		A1
883	VARNER, John L	13	NESE	1838-07-28		A1
751	WALKER, Anderson	12	NENE	1841-05-20		A1
934	WEBB, Leonard	2	NWNW	1835-10-08		A1
926	WELLS, Kinneth W	26	NENW	1837-08-18		A1
927	" "	26	W½NE	1837-08-18		A1
792	WHITE, Elihu M	13	SESE	1837-08-02		A1
793	WHITE, Elihue M	13	W½NE	1837-08-15		A1
807	WHITE, John P	2	NE	1837-08-12		A1 G23
1047	WHITTEN, William	12	NESW	1837-05-20		A1
1048	" "	12	SENW	1837-05-20		A1
850	WIGHT, James W	28	S½SE	1858-11-01		A1
851	" "	33	N½NE	1858-11-01		A1
852	" "	34	N½NW	1858-11-01		A1
780	WILLSON, Cyrus	30	NWNW	1858-11-01		A1
1014	WILSON, William A	36	SWSW	1854-07-15		A1
1013	" "	36	NWSE	1858-09-01		A1
1012	" "	36	E½SE	1858-11-01		A1
986	YOUNG, Simeon	6	NE	1837-08-07		A1

Patent Map

T11-N R15-E
St Stephens Meridian

Map Group 4

Township Statistics

Parcels Mapped	:	303
Number of Patents	:	265
Number of Individuals	:	126
Patentees Identified	:	127
Number of Surnames	:	80
Multi-Patentee Parcels	:	6
Oldest Patent Date	:	10/1/1823
Most Recent Patent	:	11/1/1858
Block/Lot Parcels	:	0
Parcels Re - Issued	:	3
Parcels that Overlap	:	2
Cities and Towns	:	0
Cemeteries	:	3

Section 6
SALTER James 1837
SALTER James 1837
YOUNG Simeon 1837
PHILIPS Thomas C 1823
SALTER James 1837
HEATON John 1837
HEATON John 1837

Section 5
NIX Zacheus 1837
MCFARLAND James 1837
CHEATHAM David 1837
CHEATHAM Daniel A 1837
NIX Zacheus 1837
HUTCHINSON Parr 1837

Section 4
CHEATHAM Peter 1831
BALLARD Theophilus 1837
BALLARD Theophilus 1837
MCFARLAND James 1837
CHEATHAM David H 1837
BALLARD Theophilus 1837
BALLARD Theophilus 1837
CARTER Jarrett 1837
HUTCHINSON Parr 1841
CHEATHAM Daniel H 1838

Section 7
HEATON John 1837
KIRKPATRICK James 1837
HEATON John 1837
HEATON John 1837
HEATON John 1837
BUTLER Edmund 1837
GILL Lewis 1837
GILL Lewis 1837
TALLEY Reuben 1837
BUTLER Edmund 1837
TALLEY Reuben 1837
TALLEY Reuben 1837

Section 8
TALLEY Reuben 1837
TALLEY Reuben 1837
TALLEY Reuben 1837
TALLEY Reuben 1823
TALLEY Reuben 1825

Section 9
TALLEY William 1825
TALLEY William 1826
CHEATHAM Guttridge 1838
DAY Frederick 1837
CHEATHAM Gattridge 1826
CHEATHAM Guttridge 1838
TILLERY Washington 1845
TILLERY Washington 1858
BALLARD Theopholus 1854
CHEATHAM Gutteridge 1837
TILLERY Richard 1852
TILLERY Richard 1852

Section 18
TALLEY Reuben 1837
MOSELEY William B 1837
MOSELEY William 1826
MOSELEY William 1837

Section 17
(blank)

Section 16
(blank)

Section 19
MOSELEY William 1837
MOSELEY William 1837
MOSELEY William 1837
MOSELEY William 1837
MOSLEY William 1837
MOSELEY William 1837
MOSLEY William 1837
FULLER Benjamin 1838
FULLER Benjamin 1838
FULLER Abner J 1837
RABUN John 1838
RABUN John 1838

Section 20
FULLER Benjamin 1837
FULLER Benjamin 1837
FULLER Benjamin 1838
FULLER Abner J 1837
RICHARDS William 1858
PLAYER Mary S 1837

Section 21
TALLEY Nathan 1823
TALLEY John 1835
TALLEY John 1837
TALLEY John 1837
TALLY John 1854
RABUN John 1837
CHEATHAM Gutteridge 1837

Section 30
WILLSON Cyrus 1858
HARTLEY Henry G 1837
[25] RABUN Bud 1837
FORREST John 1837
RABUN Bud 1837
FORREST John 1837
GAFFORD Jeremiah 1837
GAFFORD Daniel 1837
FULLER Archibald 1852

Section 29
FORREST John 1837
TALLEY Reuben 1838
TALLEY Reuben 1837
HALL Joseph 1826
GAFFORD Jeremiah 1837
ROUTON John 1838

Section 28
HALL Joseph 1835
HALL Joseph 1837
COOK George H 1837
HALL Joseph 1837
HALL Joseph 1834
MURRY William W 1854
WIGHT James W 1858

Section 31
GAFFORD Jeremiah 1834
GAFFORD Stephen F 1838
GAFFORD Jeremiah 1834
GAFFORD Jeremiah 1837
GAFFORD Jeremiah 1834

Section 32
MCCOY Robert J 1837
MCCOY Robert J 1837
MCCOY Robert J 1837
MCCOY Robert J 1837
HALL Joseph 1823
HALL Joseph 1837
MCCOY Robert J 1837
GAFFORD Jeremiah 1837
GAFFORD Jeremiah 1837

Section 33
HALL Joseph 1837
HALL Joseph 1835
WIGHT James W 1858
OTT James P 1858
GAFFORD Augustus P 1838
GAFFORD Augustus P 1838
SHEPHERD Francis 1830
GAFFORD Jeremiah 1837
GAFFORD Augustus P 1838

Section 3 / 2 / 1 (top row)

MCFARLAND James 1837	MCFARLAND James 1837		WEBB Leonard 1835	GRAHAM Samuel N 1837	HARRELL [23] German B 1837	GLASS Benjamin A 1837	CALLEN Ross 1847	HAMMONS Larkin 1837	GANDY Achsa 1837

Section 3
- MCFARLAND James 1837
- MCFARLAND James 1837 / MCFARLAND James 1837
- TILLERY Richard 1837
- MCFARLAND James 1837 / TILLERY Richard 1837 / TILLERY Richard 1837
- TILLERY John 1837 / TILLERY Richard 1837
- COLLINS William 1837

Section 2
- WEBB Leonard 1835 / GRAHAM Samuel N 1837
- GLASS Benjamin A 1837
- TILLERY John 1858 / GLASS Benjamin A 1837 / GLASS Benjamin A 1837
- CROCKER Benjamin 1837 / COLLINS William 1837 / GLASS Benjamin A 1837

Section 1
- GLASS Benjamin A 1837 / CALLEN Ross 1847 / HAMMONS Larkin 1837 / GANDY Achsa 1837
- BRASSWELL James 1837 / GRIGGS Lewis 1838
- GLASS Benjamin A 1837 / CROCKER Benjamin 1838 / STOCKMAN George 1845
- ANDRESS John N 1837 / GAFFNEY Drury A 1845
- GENTRY Jesse 1837

Section 10
- CARTER Jarrett 1837 / TILLERY John 1858 / TILLERY Washington 1843
- BALLARD Theopholus 1854 / TILLERY John 1837 / TILLERY John 1837 / TILLERY John 1858
- TALLEY Reuben 1837 / COLLINS William 1837 / 10
- COLLINS William 1833 / COLLINS Isaac 1831

Section 11
- CROCKER [14] Benjamin 1837 / GLASS Benjamin A 1837 / MCCURRY William 1835 / GLASS Benjamin A 1837
- CROCKER [14] Benjamin 1837 / KIRKPATRICK James 1834 / CALLEN Ross 1858 / 11
- TILLERY William 1837
- TILLERY John R 1858 / TILLERY William 1837 / KIRKPATRICK Robert H 1848
- KIRKPATRICK William 1833 / TILLERY John R 1852 / KIRKPATRICK James 1837

Section 12
- SHEPPARD Francis 1854 / WALKER Anderson 1841
- GLASS Benjamin A 1837 / WHITTEN William 1837 / KIRKPATRICK James P 1837 / SHEPPARD Francis 1854 / 12
- CRAIG Nathan H 1845 / WHITTEN William 1837 / HAM William 1837 / MCDONALD Daniel B 1852

Section 15
- TILLERY Richard 1852 / CHEATHAM Guteridge 1854 / CHEATHAM Guttridge 1838 / TINSLEY Thomas 1833
- MERCER Noah 1838 / COLLINS William 1834 / 15
- COLLINS William 1831 / COLLINS William 1837 / COLLINS Isaac 1834
- MERCER Noah 1837 / MERCER Noah 1837 / MERCER Noah 1837 / COLLINS Isaac 1834
- MERCER Seth 1850 / COLLINS Isaac 1834 / FLINN Leander W 1852
- FLINN Leander W 1852 / FLINN Leander W 1852

Section 14
- COLLINS William 1831 / COLLINS William 1837
- COLLINS Isaac 1834
- 14

Section 13
- 13
- WHITE Elihue M 1837 / DIXON John 1837
- MCCOY Robert J 1837 / VARNER John L 1838
- MCCOY Robert J 1835 / WHITE Elihu M 1837

Section 22
- COLLINS [10] Isaac 1843
- CHEATHAM Gutteridge 1837 / CHEATHAM Gutteridge 1837
- CHEATHAM Gutteridge 1837 / 22 / CHEATHAM Gutridge 1837
- CHEATHAM Gutteridge 1837 / CHEATHAM Gutteridge 1837

Section 23
- MCCOY John R 1858 / MCCOY John R 1858 / MCCOY John R 1854
- MCCOY John R 1858 / MCCOY John 1837
- MCCOY John R 1858 / MCCOY John 1837 / MCCOY John 1837
- MCCOY John 1838 / MCCOY Joseph 1837 / 23
- PAYNE Thomas G 1854 / MCCOY Joseph 1837
- MCCOY Mary 1854 / MCCOY Joseph 1837

Section 24
- MCCOY John 1832 / BROWN Joel 1826 / BROWN James 1826
- 24
- BROWN Squire 1832 / BROWN Squire 1826
- BROWN Joel 1826

Section 27
- STEWART William B 1837 / MERCER Seth 1837 / MERCER Seth 1837
- COLLINS Isaac 1837 / MERCER Noah 1854
- KIRKPATRICK William 1854
- 27
- GAFFORD Jeremiah 1838 / COLLINS Isaac 1837 / COLLINS Isaac 1837

Section 26
- MERCER Seth 1837 / WELLS Kinneth W 1837
- SHEPPARD William 1837 / WELLS Kinneth W 1837
- 26
- COLLINS [11] William 1831 / TAYLOR Ward 1827 / FAILS Thomas 1837

Section 25
- SHEPPARD Andrew 1838 / MCPHERSON John 1854
- SHEPPARD William 1831 / SHEPPARD William 1837 / PICKENS James V 1837 / BROWN Joseph 1832
- 25
- TAYLOR Andrew J 1838
- FAILS Thomas 1834 / FAILS Thomas 1837 / FAILS Thomas 1834 / TAYLOR Andrew J 1838

Section 34
- WIGHT James W 1858 / EASTERLING Bennett 1854
- COLLINS Isaac 1838
- GAFFNEY Davis F 1858 / 34
- GAFFNEY Davis F 1858 / PATTILLO George H 1837
- PATTILLO George H 1835
- PATTILLO George H 1838 / CRAIG James D 1837

Section 35
- BOLLING John 1850 / PINGLETON Samuel 1837
- SHEPPARD Francis 1837 / FAILS John 1837
- BOLLING John 1851 / 35 / FAILS John 1837
- SHEPPARD Francis 1838 / TINSLEY Thomas 1837 / FAILS Thomas 1837
- CRAIG James D 1837 / FROST Henry 1850

Section 36
- PINGLETON Samuel 1837 / FAILS John 1837 / TAYLOR Andrew J 1838
- FAILS Thomas 1837 / FAILS Thomas 1837
- FAIL Ellsberry 1854 / 36 / FAILS Thomas 1834
- COULSON Thomas 1837 / KILLOUGH Samuel 1850 / WILSON William A 1858
- WILSON William A 1854 / KILLOUGH Lawson 1852 / KILLOUGH Lawson 1854 / WILSON William A 1858

Helpful Hints

1. This Map's INDEX can be found on the preceding pages.

2. Refer to Map "C" to see where this Township lies within Butler County, Alabama.

3. Numbers within square brackets [ ] denote a multi-patentee land parcel (multi-owner). Refer to Appendix "C" for a full list of members in this group.

4. Areas that look to be crowded with Patentees usually indicate multiple sales of the same parcel (Re-issues) or Overlapping parcels. See this Township's Index for an explanation of these and other circumstances that might explain "odd" groupings of Patentees on this map.

Legend

— Patent Boundary

— Section Boundary

No Patents Found (or Outside County)

1., 2., 3., ... Lot Numbers (when beside a name)

[ ] Group Number (see Appendix "C")

Scale: Section = 1 mile X 1 mile (generally, with some exceptions)

Road Map

T11-N R15-E
St Stephens Meridian

Map Group 4

Cities & Towns
None

Cemeteries
Antioch East Cemetery
Moriah Cemetery
Springhill Cemetery

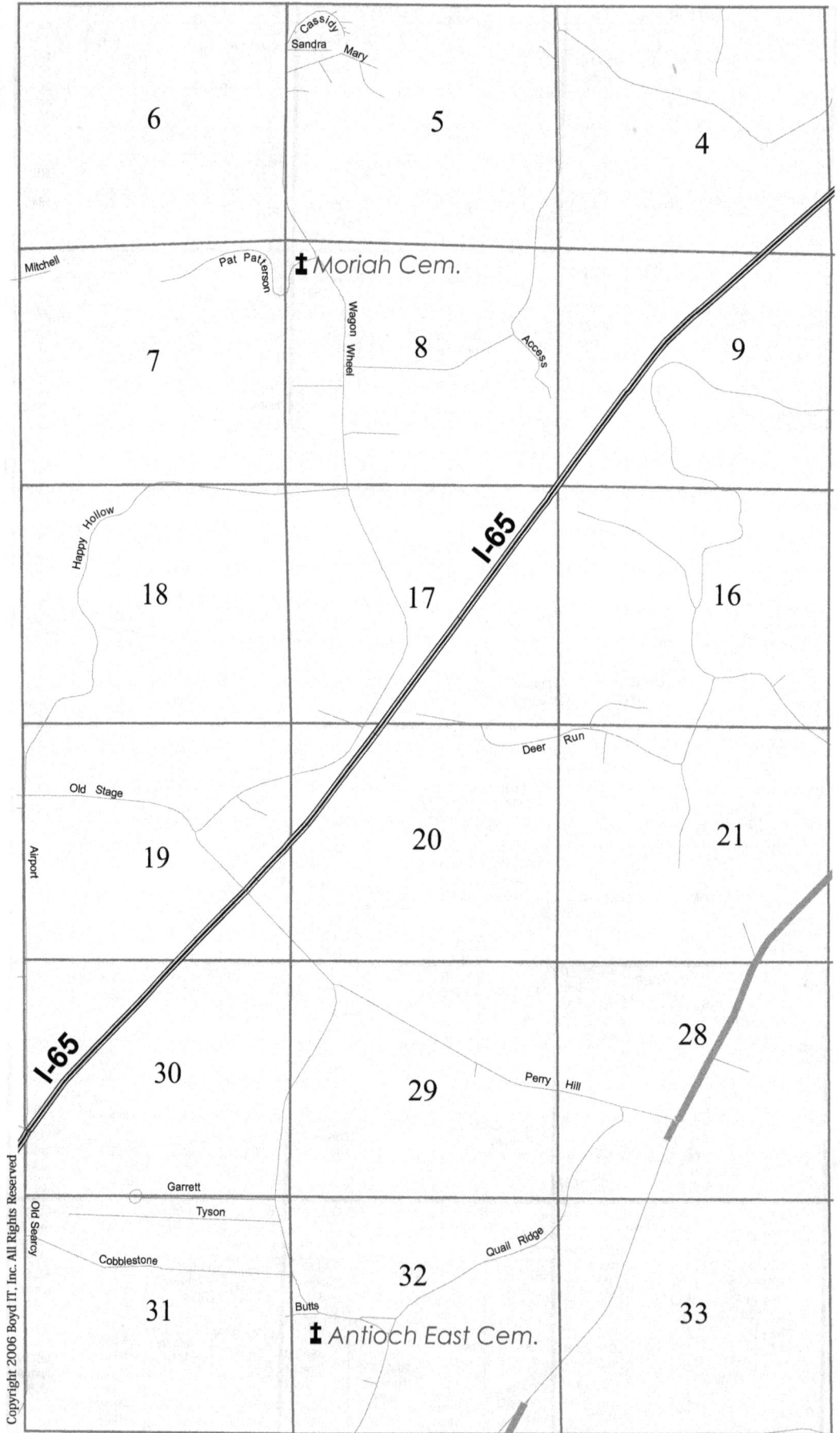

6	5	4
7	8	9
18	17	16
19	20	21
30	29	28
31	32	33

Cassidy
Sandra
Mary

Mitchell
Pat Patterson
✝ Moriah Cem.
Wagon Wheel
Access

Happy Hollow

I-65

Deer Run

Old Stage
Airport

Perry Hill

Garrett
Tyson
Old Searcy
Cobblestone
Butts
Quail Ridge

✝ Antioch East Cem.

Golson

3

Fort Deposit

2

1

Kirkville

10

11

12

Nickquenum

15

Montgomery

14

Philen

13

Jasmine

Hill

22

Green Oaks

23

24

County Road 77

27

Springhill Cem.

26

25

34

Gibson

35

Mt Zion

36

Farmstead

Helpful Hints

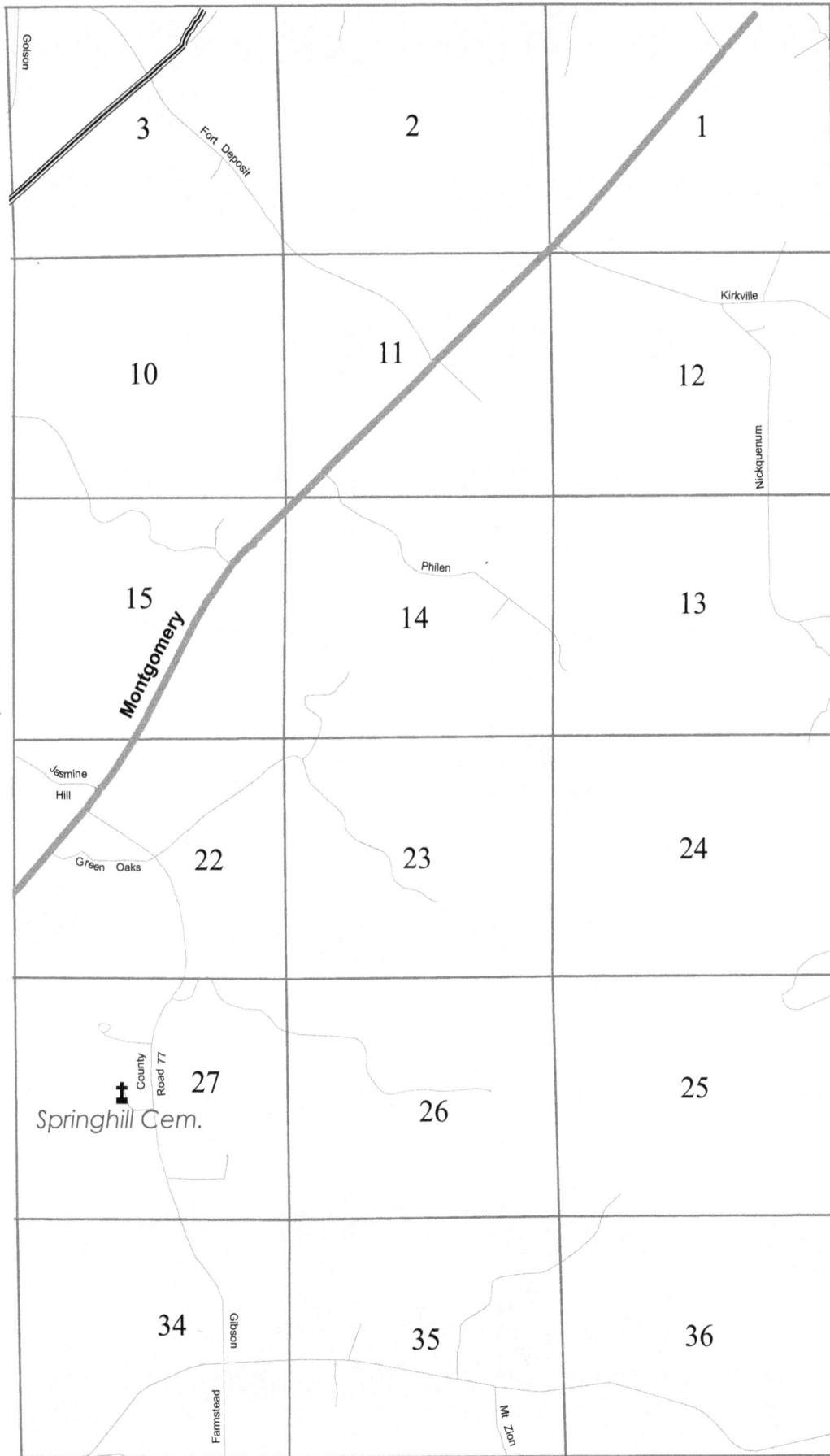

1. This road map has a number of uses, but primarily it is to help you: a) find the present location of land owned by your ancestors (at least the general area), b) find cemeteries and city-centers, and c) estimate the route/roads used by Census-takers & tax-assessors.

2. If you plan to travel to Butler County to locate cemeteries or land parcels, please pick up a modern travel map for the area before you do. Mapping old land parcels on modern maps is not as exact a science as you might think. Just the slightest variations in public land survey coordinates, estimates of parcel boundaries, or road-map deviations can greatly alter a map's representation of how a road either does or doesn't cross a particular parcel of land.

L e g e n d

———— Section Lines

════ Interstates

▬▬▬▬ Highways

——— Other Roads

● Cities/Towns

✝ Cemeteries

Scale: Section = 1 mile X 1 mile
(generally, with some exceptions)

Historical Map

T11-N R15-E
St Stephens Meridian

Map Group 4

Cities & Towns
None

Cemeteries
Antioch East Cemetery
Moriah Cemetery
Springhill Cemetery

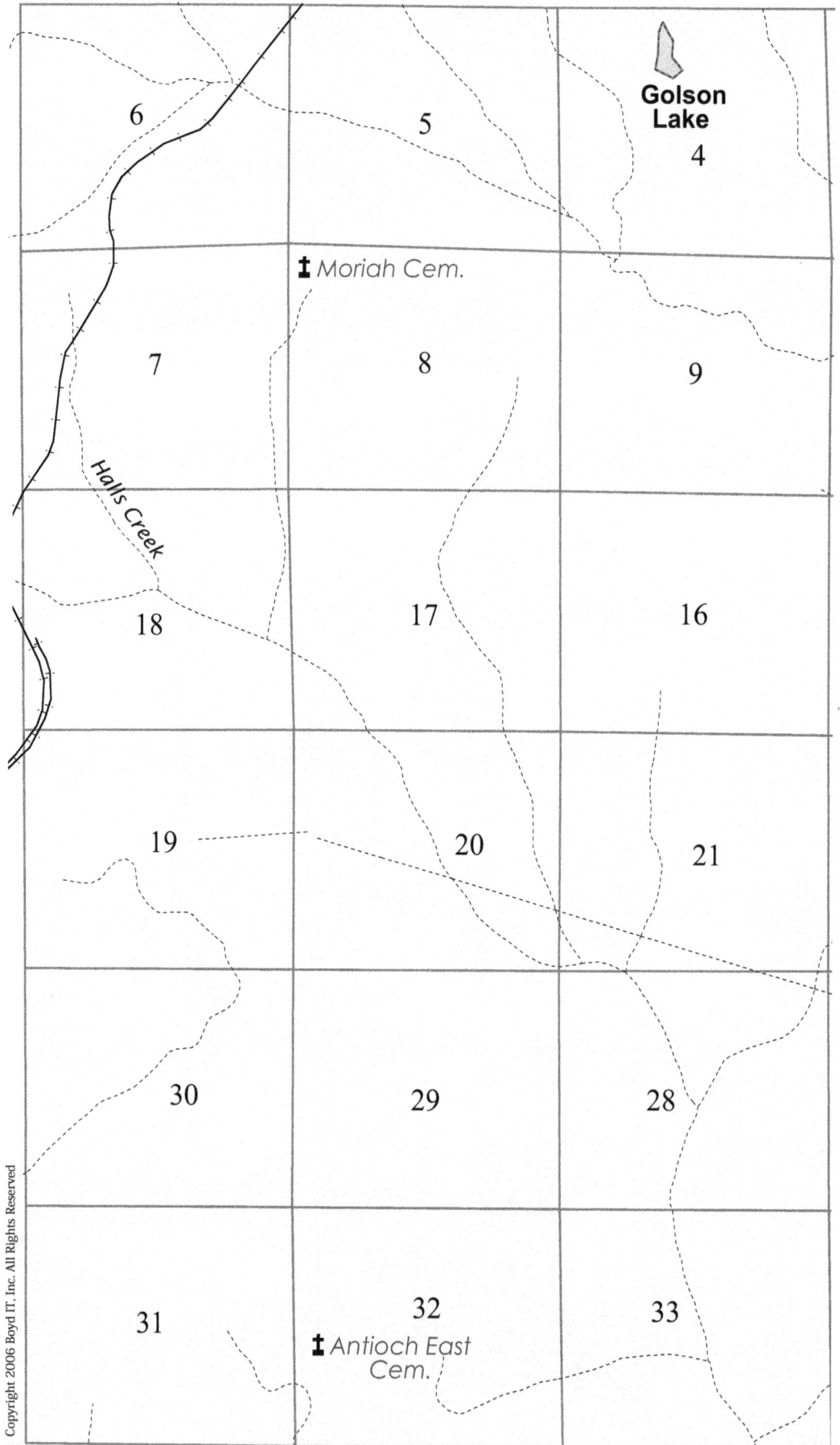

6

5

Golson
Lake

4

✝ *Moriah Cem.*

7

8

9

Halls Creek

18

17

16

19

20

21

30

29

28

31

32

33

✝ *Antioch East
Cem.*

3

2

1

Piney Woods Creek

Pigeon Creek

11

12

10

14

13

15

Indian Creek

22

23

24

26

Mill Branch

25

27
Springhill Cem.

34

35

36

Helpful Hints

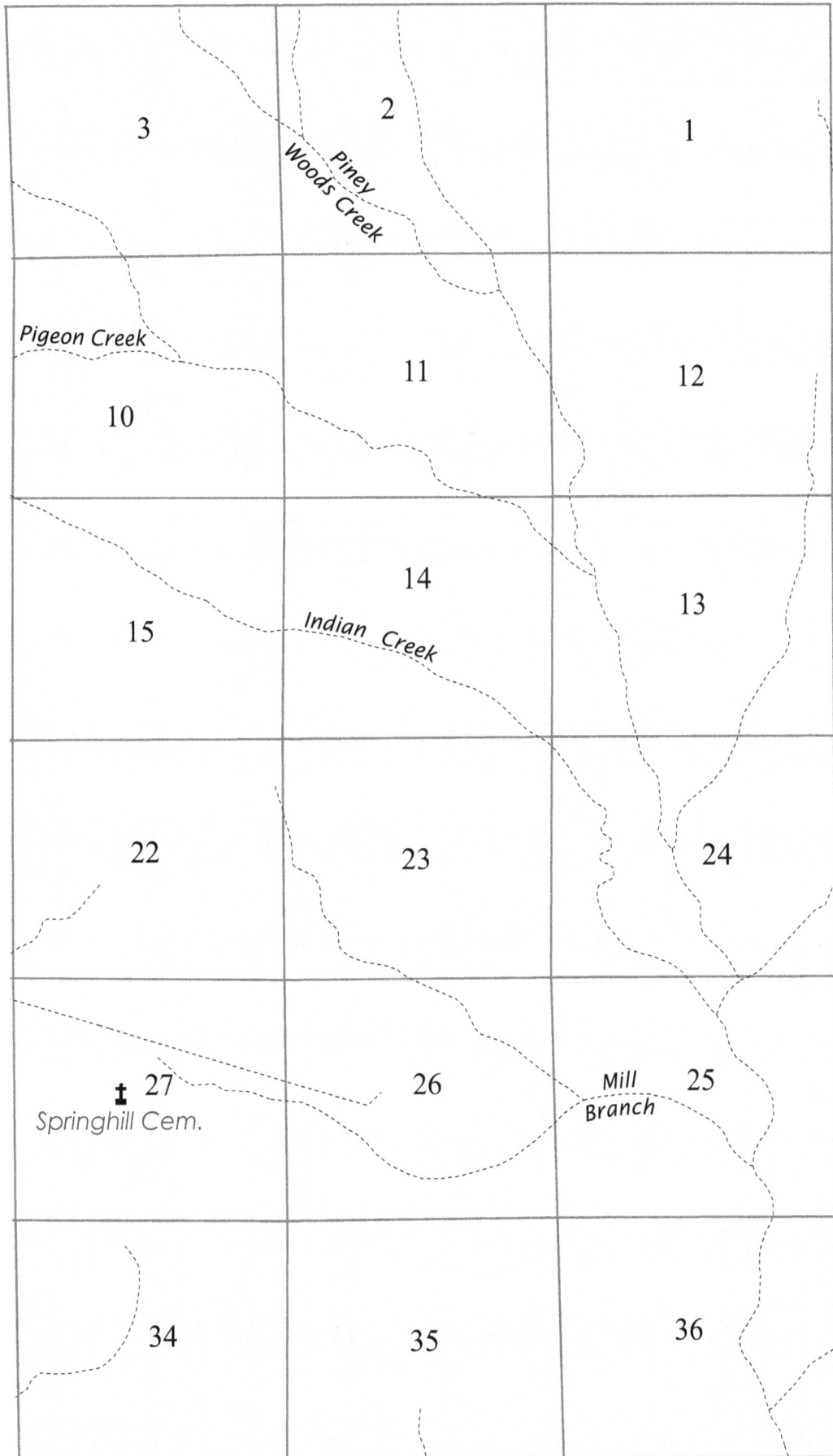

1. This Map takes a different look at the same Congressional Township displayed in the preceding two maps. It presents features that can help you better envision the historical development of the area: a) Water-bodies (lakes & ponds), b) Water-courses (rivers, streams, etc.), c) Railroads, d) City/town center-points (where they were oftentimes located when first settled), and e) Cemeteries.

2. Using this "Historical" map in tandem with this Township's Patent Map and Road Map, may lead you to some interesting discoveries. You will often find roads, towns, cemeteries, and waterways are named after nearby landowners: sometimes those names will be the ones you are researching. See how many of these research gems you can find here in Butler County.

Legend

——————————	Section Lines
+‑+‑+‑+‑+‑+‑+	Railroads
▭	Large Rivers & Bodies of Water
- - - - - - -	Streams/Creeks & Small Rivers
●	Cities/Towns
✝	Cemeteries

Scale: Section = 1 mile X 1 mile
(there are some exceptions)

Map Group 5: Index to Land Patents

Township 11-North Range 16-East (St Stephens)

After you locate an individual in this Index, take note of the Section and Section Part then proceed to the Land Patent map on the pages immediately following. You should have no difficulty locating the corresponding parcel of land.

The "For More Info" Column will lead you to more information about the underlying Patents. See the *Legend* at right, and the "How to Use this Book" chapter, for more information.

<table>
<tr><td colspan="3">LEGEND</td></tr>
<tr><td colspan="3">"For More Info . . . " column</td></tr>
</table>

A = Authority (Legislative Act, See Appendix "A")
B = Block or Lot (location in Section unknown)
C = Cancelled Patent
F = Fractional Section
G = Group (Multi-Patentee Patent, see Appendix "C")
V = Overlaps another Parcel
R = Re-Issued (Parcel patented more than once)

(A & G items require you to look in the Appendixes referred to above. All other Letter-designations followed by a number require you to locate line-items in this index that possess the ID number found after the letter).

ID	Individual in Patent	Sec.	Sec. Part	Date Issued	Other Counties	For More Info . . .
1206	ANDRESS, William J	32	NWNW	1852-02-02		A1
1134	BELL, John W	32	SWSW	1849-09-01		A1
1135	BROWN, John W	7	SESW	1854-10-02		A1
1153	BRYAN, Nicholas	8	NENW	1837-05-15		A1
1154	" "	8	NWNE	1837-05-15		A1
1188	BRYAN, Waid	6	E½SW	1837-08-02		A1
1192	" "	6	W½SE	1837-08-02		A1
1189	" "	6	NW	1837-08-08		A1
1190	" "	6	SESE	1837-08-08		A1
1191	" "	6	SWNE	1837-08-08		A1
1057	CALLAWAY, Claborn N	31	NWSE	1860-04-02		A1
1145	CAMP, Larkin G	29	SENW	1858-11-01		A1
1180	CAMP, Thomas M	29	NENE	1837-08-18		A1
1182	" "	29	W½NE	1837-08-18		A1
1181	" "	29	NENW	1843-02-01		A1
1051	CARTER, Absalom	31	SWSE	1838-07-28		A1
1232	COLLINS, William W	7	NWNE	1841-05-20		A1
1233	" "	7	W½NW	1841-05-20		A1
1177	DAY, Thomas C	31	SW	1837-08-15		A1
1178	DUNN, Thomas	19	W½SW	1837-08-18		A1
1187	EVANS, Uriah	7	NESW	1850-08-10		A1
1199	FINDLEY, William	17	NESE	1852-02-02		A1
1200	" "	17	SENE	1852-02-02		A1
1146	FLINN, Leander W	5	SWNE	1837-05-15		A1
1234	FROST, Young H	30	SWSE	1858-11-01		A1 V1224
1052	GANDY, Augustus	33	E½SW	1858-11-01		A1
1224	GHOLSON, William S	30	W½SE	1848-05-03		A1 V1123, 1234
1226	" "	33	SESE	1848-05-03		A1
1225	" "	33	NESE	1852-02-02		A1
1072	GILLIAM, Isaac	21	SWSW	1854-10-02		A1
1075	GILLION, Isaac	32	N½SE	1837-05-20		A1
1074	" "	32	E½SW	1837-08-02		A1 V1186, 1076
1077	" "	32	S½SE	1837-08-02		A1
1076	" "	32	NESW	1838-07-28		A1 V1074
1078	" "	32	W½NE	1843-02-01		A1
1079	" "	33	NWSW	1848-05-03		A1
1073	" "	20	E½NE	1858-09-01		A1
1168	GINGLES, Samuel	5	W½NW	1837-04-10		A1
1053	GLASS, Benjamin A	18	E½SW	1837-08-02		A1
1065	GLASS, Francis	19	NESW	1837-08-09		A1
1201	GLOVER, William	17	S½NW	1838-07-28		A1
1202	" "	20	NENW	1843-02-01		A1
1147	GRIGGS, Lewis	6	NWSW	1838-07-28		A1
1088	HALIDA, James	17	NESW	1838-07-28		A1
1179	HAMBLETON, Thomas	18	E½NW	1838-07-28		A1
1093	HAYS, Jesse	7	SWSE	1852-12-01		A1

ID	Individual in Patent	Sec.	Sec. Part	Date Issued	Other Counties	For More Info . . .
1058	HERELONG, Daniel D	7	NENW	1841-05-20		A1
1059	HERLONG, Daniel	9	NENW	1852-02-02		A1
1194	HERLONG, William F	17	N½NE	1858-11-01		A1
1195	" "	17	NWSE	1858-11-01		A1
1196	" "	17	SWNE	1858-11-01		A1
1197	" "	8	SESE	1858-11-01		A1
1198	" "	9	SWSW	1858-11-01		A1
1070	HILBUN, Frederick	9	E½NE	1837-08-08		A1
1071	" "	9	NWNE	1837-08-10		A1
1069	" "	8	SENE	1837-08-12		A1
1101	HILBUN, John	4	E½SW	1837-05-15		A1
1102	" "	4	NWSW	1837-05-15		A1
1105	" "	5	NESE	1837-05-15		A1
1104	" "	4	W½NW	1837-05-20		A1
1103	" "	4	SWSW	1837-08-01		A1
1106	" "	9	W½NW	1837-08-12		A1
1100	" "	17	SESW	1845-06-01		A1
1136	HILBUN, Joseph	5	E½NE	1837-05-15		A1
1139	" "	5	NWNE	1837-05-15		A1
1141	" "	5	SWSE	1837-05-15		A1
1138	" "	5	NESW	1837-05-20		A1
1140	" "	5	NWSE	1837-05-20		A1
1137	" "	5	E½NW	1837-08-01		A1
1204	HILBUN, William	4	SWNE	1837-05-15		A1
1205	" "	4	W½SE	1837-05-15		A1
1203	" "	4	E½NW	1837-05-20		A1
1094	JAY, Jesse	8	NWSE	1841-05-20		A1
1107	KELLEY, John	8	E½SW	1858-09-01		A1
1183	KEMP, Thomas M	29	SWNW	1849-09-01		A1
1055	KING, Calvin D	9	NWSE	1838-07-28		A1
1056	" "	9	SENW	1838-07-28		A1
1109	KING, John	21	SWNE	1837-08-09		A1
1108	" "	21	NWSW	1858-11-01		A1
1110	" "	21	W½NW	1858-11-01		A1
1184	KING, Thomas M	8	NENE	1860-10-01		A1
1068	KIRKPATRICK, Francis	6	SENE	1834-10-21		A1
1066	" "	6	NESE	1837-08-01		A1
1067	" "	6	NWNE	1837-08-01		A1
1091	KIRKPATRICK, James P	7	SENW	1837-08-10		A1
1111	KIRKPATRICK, John L	18	SE	1837-05-20		A1
1171	KIRKPATRICK, Samuel	5	SWSW	1841-05-20		A1
1167	KIRKPATRICK, Samuel A	17	NWSW	1845-06-01		A1
1212	KIRKPATRICK, William	7	E½NE	1831-11-30		A1
1215	" "	8	W½NW	1831-11-30		A1
1216	" "	8	W½SW	1833-11-14		A1
1214	" "	7	SWNE	1834-08-05		A1
1211	" "	28	SWNW	1834-08-12		A1
1213	" "	7	NESE	1837-08-18		A1
1220	KIRKPATRICK, William P	18	W½NW	1837-08-02		A1
1164	LEE, Robert S	17	SWSW	1848-04-01		A1
1165	" "	29	NESW	1848-05-03		A1
1166	" "	29	NWSW	1852-12-01		A1
1173	MAY, Seth S	17	NENW	1858-11-01		A1
1185	MCCLARTY, Thomas P	7	SESE	1837-08-01		A1
1116	MCCOY, John	29	SESE	1837-05-20		A1
1118	" "	32	E½NE	1837-05-20		A1
1115	" "	29	NESE	1837-08-08		A1
1117	" "	29	W½SE	1837-08-08		A1
1150	MCCOY, Mary	19	NWNE	1852-02-02		A1
1152	" "	19	SWNE	1852-02-02		A1
1151	" "	19	NWSE	1852-12-01		A1
1219	MCDONALD, William	20	SWNW	1848-05-03		A1
1099	MCINEER, John C	17	NWNW	1837-05-20		A1
1121	MCPHERSON, John	30	NW	1837-08-08		A1
1122	" "	30	NWNE	1837-08-08		A1
1126	" "	30	W½SW	1837-08-08		A1
1124	" "	30	SENE	1838-07-28		A1
1119	" "	30	NENE	1850-04-01		A1
1125	" "	30	SWNE	1852-02-02		A1
1127	" "	31	NWNW	1852-02-02		A1
1120	" "	30	NESW	1858-11-01		A1
1123	" "	30	NWSE	1858-11-01		A1 V1224
1161	MILLS, Ramsey M	8	SWSE	1920-01-19		A1

ID	Individual in Patent	Sec.	Sec. Part	Date Issued	Other Counties	For More Info . . .
1095	MORGAN, John A	31	SWNW	1837-08-15		A1
1217	MORGAN, William M	31	SENW	1837-08-15		A1
1218	" "	31	W½NE	1837-08-15		A1
1089	NORMAN, James	19	NENW	1850-04-01		A1
1090	" "	19	SENW	1852-02-02		A1
1054	PARMER, Benjamin W	30	E½SE	1852-02-02		A1
1186	PEEVY, Thomas	32	SESW	1837-05-20		A1 V1074
1092	PERDUE, James	5	NWSW	1841-05-20		A1
1085	PERDUE, James E	31	SESE	1850-08-10		A1
1084	" "	20	SENW	1852-02-02		A1
1086	PERDUE, James H	31	SENE	1852-02-02		A1
1087	" "	32	SWNW	1852-02-02		A1
1174	PERDUE, Sovereign	9	E½SE	1843-02-01		A1
1175	" "	9	SWSE	1843-02-01		A1
1176	PERDUE, Sovereign T	9	NESW	1852-02-02		A1
1193	PERDUE, William E	32	NWSW	1843-02-01		A1
1114	ROPER, John M	4	E½SE	1837-08-02		A1
1113	" "	4	E½NE	1837-08-08		A1
1169	SHIELDS, Samuel J	8	SENW	1858-11-01		A1
1170	" "	8	SWNE	1858-11-01		A1
1060	SMITH, Daniel	20	NWSW	1852-12-01		A1
1172	SMITH, Samuel	6	NENE	1835-09-12		A1
1143	STEINER, Joseph	20	SWSW	1850-05-01		A1
1142	" "	17	SWSE	1858-11-01		A1
1144	STINER, Joseph	19	E½NE	1852-02-02		A1
1083	STOCKMAN, Jacob E	5	SESW	1845-07-01		A1
1128	STRINGER, John	21	E½NE	1831-11-30		A1
1129	" "	21	E½NW	1837-08-12		A1
1131	" "	21	NWSE	1837-08-12		A1
1130	" "	21	NWNE	1849-09-01		A1
1096	STRINGER, John A	28	E½NW	1848-05-03		A1
1097	" "	28	NESW	1860-10-01		A1
1098	" "	28	SENE	1860-10-01		A1
1223	STRINGER, William R	21	SWSE	1837-05-20		A1
1222	" "	21	SESE	1837-08-12		A1
1221	" "	21	NESE	1858-09-01		A1
1155	TALLEY, Obadiah	18	E½NE	1837-08-12		A1
1157	" "	7	NWSE	1837-08-12		A1
1156	" "	18	W½NE	1837-08-18		A1
1162	TAYLOR, Robert B	9	NWSW	1837-08-10		A1
1132	THOMAS, John	20	SE	1837-08-02		A1
1133	" "	33	NENE	1837-08-14		A1
1158	THOMAS, Phillip	28	W½SW	1837-08-02		A1
1159	" "	33	NWNE	1837-08-02		A1
1160	" "	33	SENW	1837-08-02		A1
1227	THOMAS, William	21	E½SW	1831-11-30		A1
1229	" "	28	W½NE	1837-05-20		A1
1230	" "	29	SENE	1837-08-02		A1
1231	" "	5	SESE	1837-08-10		A1
1228	" "	28	E½SE	1837-08-18		A1
1207	THOMAS, William J	20	E½SW	1837-08-02		A1
1210	" "	28	NWNW	1837-08-02		A1
1208	" "	20	NWNE	1837-08-14		A1
1209	" "	20	SWNE	1843-02-01		A1
1061	THORNTON, Eli	28	SESW	1858-11-01		A1
1062	" "	28	SWSE	1858-11-01		A1
1063	" "	33	SWNW	1858-11-01		A1
1081	THORNTON, Jacob A	33	SENE	1852-12-01		A1
1080	" "	33	NENW	1858-11-01		A1
1082	THORNTON, Jacob D	33	SWNE	1854-07-15		A1
1112	VARNER, John L	18	W½SW	1837-08-08		A1
1163	VARNER, Robert H	19	W½NW	1837-08-07		A1
1064	WEBB, Foster C	4	NWNE	1852-12-01		A1
1148	WREN, Mack	30	SESW	1837-08-08		A1
1149	" "	31	NENW	1837-08-15		A1

Copyright 2006 Boyd IT, Inc. All Rights Reserved

Patent Map

T11-N R16-E
St Stephens Meridian

Map Group 5

Township Statistics

Parcels Mapped	:	184
Number of Patents	:	160
Number of Individuals	:	91
Patentees Identified	:	91
Number of Surnames	:	60
Multi-Patentee Parcels	:	0
Oldest Patent Date	:	11/30/1831
Most Recent Patent	:	1/19/1920
Block/Lot Parcels	:	0
Parcels Re - Issued	:	0
Parcels that Overlap	:	6
Cities and Towns	:	1
Cemeteries	:	5

Note: the area contained in this map amounts to far less than a full Township. Therefore, its contents are completely on this single page (instead of a "normal" 2-page spread).

Legend

—— Patent Boundary

━━ Section Boundary

No Patents Found
(or Outside County)

1., 2., 3., ... Lot Numbers
(when beside a name)

[ ] Group Number
(see Appendix "C")

Scale: Section = 1 mile X 1 mile
(generally, with some exceptions)

Section 6
KIRKPATRICK Francis 1837
SMITH Samuel 1835
BRYAN Waid 1837
BRYAN Waid 1837
KIRKPATRICK Francis 1834
GRIGGS Lewis 1838
BRYAN Waid 1837
KIRKPATRICK Francis 1837
BRYAN Waid 1837
BRYAN Waid 1837

Section 5
GINGLES Samuel 1837
HILBUN Joseph 1837
HILBUN Joseph 1837
FLINN Leander W 1837
HILBUN Joseph 1837
PERDUE James 1841
HILBUN Joseph 1837
HILBUN Joseph 1837
HILBUN John 1837
KIRKPATRICK Samuel 1841
STOCKMAN Jacob E 1845
HILBUN Joseph 1837
THOMAS William 1837

Section 4
HILBUN John 1837
HILBUN William 1837
WEBB Foster C 1852
ROPER John M 1837
HILBUN William 1837
HILBUN John 1837
HILBUN John 1837
HILBUN John 1837
HILBUN William 1837
ROPER John M 1837

Section 7
COLLINS William W 1841
HERELONG Daniel D 1841
COLLINS William W 1841
KIRKPATRICK William 1831
KIRKPATRICK James P 1837
KIRKPATRICK William 1834
EVANS Uriah 1850
TALLEY Obadiah 1837
KIRKPATRICK William 1837
BROWN John W 1854
HAYS Jesse 1852
MCCLARTY Thomas F 1837

Section 8
KIRKPATRICK William 1831
SHIELDS Samuel 1858
KIRKPATRICK William 1833
KELLEY John 1858
JAY Jesse 1841
MILLS Ramsey M 1920
BRYAN Nicholas 1837
BRYAN Nicholas 1837
SHIELDS Samuel J 1858
KING Thomas M 1860
HILBUN Frederick 1837
HERLONG William F 1858

Section 9
HILBUN John 1837
HERLONG Daniel 1852
HILBUN Frederick 1837
KING Calvin D 1838
HILBUN Frederick 1837
TAYLOR Robert B 1837
PERDUE Sovereign T 1852
KING Calvin D 1838
PERDUE Sovereign 1843
HERLONG William F 1858
PERDUE Sovereign 1843

Section 18
HAMBLETON Thomas 1838
KIRKPATRICK William P 1837
TALLEY Obadiah 1837
TALLEY Obadiah 1837
VARNER John L 1837
GLASS Benjamin A 1837
KIRKPATRICK John L 1837

Section 17
MCINEER John C 1837
MAY Seth S 1858
HERLONG William F 1858
GLOVER William 1838
HERLONG William F 1858
FINDLEY William 1852
KIRKPATRICK Samuel A 1845
HALIDA James 1838
HERLONG William F 1858
FINDLEY William 1852
LEE Robert S 1848
HILBUN John 1845
STEINER Joseph 1858

Section 16

Section 19
VARNER Robert H 1837
NORMAN James 1850
MCCOY Mary 1852
STINER Joseph 1852
NORMAN James 1852
MCCOY Mary 1852
DUNN Thomas 1837
GLASS Francis 1837
MCCOY Mary 1852

Section 20
GLOVER William 1843
THOMAS William J 1837
MCDONALD William 1848
PERDUE James E 1852
THOMAS William J 1843
GILLION Isaac 1858
SMITH Daniel 1852
THOMAS William J 1837
STEINER Joseph 1850
THOMAS John 1837

Section 21
KING John 1858
STRINGER John 1837
STRINGER John 1849
STRINGER John 1831
KING John 1837
KING John 1858
THOMAS William 1831
STRINGER John 1837
STRINGER William R 1858
GILLIAM Isaac 1854
STRINGER William R 1837
STRINGER William R 1837

Section 30
MCPHERSON John 1837
MCPHERSON John 1837
MCPHERSON John 1850
MCPHERSON John 1838
MCPHERSON John 1852
MCPHERSON John 1858
MCPHERSON John 1837
MCPHERSON John 1858
GHOLSON William S 1848
PARMER Benjamin W 1852
WREN Mack 1837
FROST Young H 1858

Section 29
CAMP Thomas M 1843
CAMP Thomas M 1837
KEMP Thomas M 1849
CAMP Thomas M 1837
CAMP Larkin G 1858
THOMAS William 1837
LEE Robert S 1852
LEE Robert S 1848
MCCOY John 1837
MCCOY John 1837
MCCOY John 1837

Section 28
THOMAS William J 1837
STRINGER John A 1848
THOMAS William 1837
KIRKPATRICK William 1834
STRINGER John A 1860
STRINGER John A 1860
THOMAS William 1837
THOMAS Phillip 1837
THORNTON Eli 1858
THORNTON Eli 1858

Section 31
MCPHERSON John 1852
WREN Mack 1837
MORGAN William M 1837
MORGAN John A 1837
MORGAN William M 1837
PERDUE James H 1852
DAY Thomas C 1837
CALLAWAY Claborn N 1860
CARTER Absalom 1838
PERDUE James E 1850

Section 32
ANDRESS William J 1852
PERDUE James H 1852
GILLION Isaac 1843
PERDUE William E 1843
GILLION Isaac 1838
GILLION Isaac 1837
BELL John W 1849
PEEVY Thomas 1837
GILLION Isaac 1837
GILLION Isaac 1837

Section 33
THORNTON Jacob A 1858
THOMAS Phillip 1837
THOMAS John 1837
THORNTON Eli 1858
THOMAS Phillip 1837
THORNTON Jacob D 1854
THORNTON Jacob A 1852
GILLION Isaac 1848
GANDY Augustus 1858
GHOLSON William S 1852
GHOLSON William S 1848
MCCOY John 1837

Road Map

T11-N R16-E
St Stephens Meridian

Map Group 5

Note: the area contained in this map amounts to far less than a full Township. Therefore, its contents are completely on this single page (instead of a "normal" 2-page spread).

Cities & Towns
Daisy

Cemeteries
Bethel Cemetery
King Cemetery
Oak Bowery Cemetery
Perdue Cemetery
Spring Creek Cemetery

Legend

———————	Section Lines
═══════════	Interstates
━━━━━━━━━	Highways
———————	Other Roads
●	Cities/Towns
✝	Cemeteries

Scale: Section = 1 mile X 1 mile
(generally, with some exceptions)

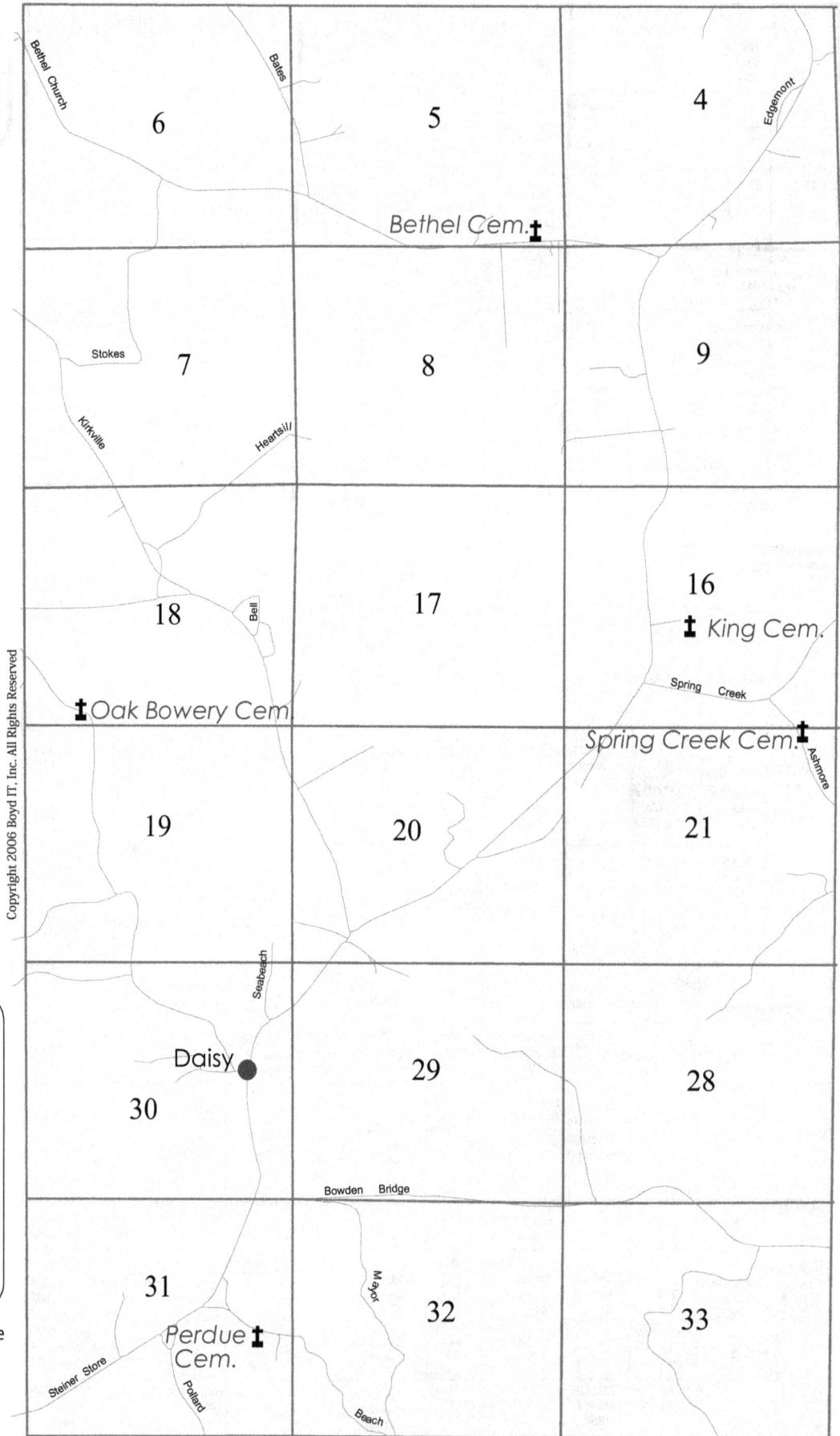

Bethel Church

Bates

6

5

4

Edgemont

Bethel Cem. ✝

Stokes

7

8

9

Kirkville

Heartsill

18

Bell

17

16

✝ King Cem.

Spring Creek

✝ Oak Bowery Cem.

Spring Creek Cem. ✝

Ashmore

19

20

21

Seabeach

Daisy ●

29

28

30

Bowden Bridge

31

Major

32

33

Perdue Cem. ✝

Steiner Store

Pollard

Beach

6

5

4

Bethel Cem

7

8

Three Run Creek

9

Historical Map
T11-N R16-E
St Stephens Meridian
Map Group 5

Note: the area contained in this map amounts to far less than a full Township. Therefore, its contents are completely on this single page (instead of a "normal" 2-page spread).

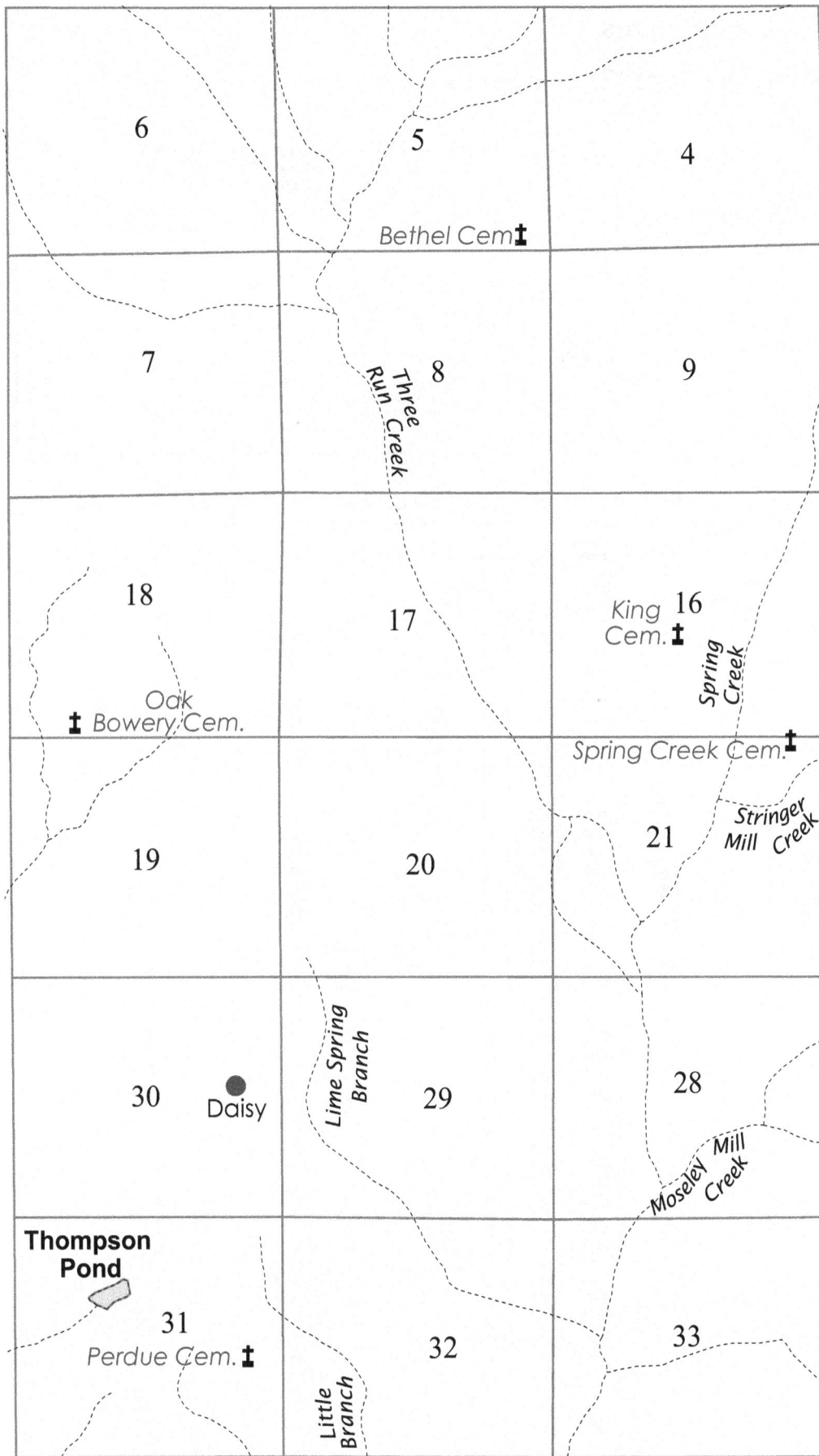

Cities & Towns
Daisy

18

17

King Cem.

16

Spring Creek

Oak Bowery Cem.

Cemeteries
Bethel Cemetery
King Cemetery
Oak Bowery Cemetery
Perdue Cemetery
Spring Creek Cemetery

Spring Creek Cem.

19

20

21

Stringer Mill Creek

30

Daisy

Lime Spring Branch

29

28

Moseley Mill Creek

Legend
——— Section Lines
+++ Railroads
▭ Large Rivers & Bodies of Water
----- Streams/Creeks & Small Rivers
● Cities/Towns
✝ Cemeteries

Thompson Pond

31

Perdue Cem.

32

33

Little Branch

Scale: Section = 1 mile X 1 mile
(there are some exceptions)

Map Group 6: Index to Land Patents

Township 10-North Range 12-East (St Stephens)

After you locate an individual in this Index, take note of the Section and Section Part then proceed to the Land Patent map on the pages immediately following. You should have no difficulty locating the corresponding parcel of land.

The "For More Info" Column will lead you to more information about the underlying Patents. See the *Legend* at right, and the "How to Use this Book" chapter, for more information.

```
                    LEGEND
          "For More Info . . . " column
A = Authority (Legislative Act, See Appendix "A")
B = Block or Lot (location in Section unknown)
C = Cancelled Patent
F = Fractional Section
G = Group (Multi-Patentee Patent, see Appendix "C")
V = Overlaps another Parcel
R = Re-Issued (Parcel patented more than once)

(A & G items require you to look in the Appendixes referred
to above. All other Letter-designations followed by a number
require you to locate line-items in this index that possess
the ID number found after the letter).
```

ID	Individual in Patent	Sec.	Sec. Part	Date Issued	Other Counties	For More Info . . .
1276	AUSTIN, Davis	7	W½SW	1837-08-08		A1
1275	" "	18	E½NW	1837-08-18		A1
1412	BABCOCK, Joseph	28	S½NE	1848-05-03		A1 G1
1284	BARGE, Edward W	6	SESW	1853-11-15		A1
1407	BARGE, John R	19	E½NW	1858-11-01		A1
1322	BATES, James M	9	SESW	1858-11-01		A1
1447	BELL, Robert H	5	S½SE	1858-11-01		A1
1448	" "	8	NE	1858-11-01		A1
1449	" "	9	W½NW	1858-11-01		A1
1320	BENSON, James K	6	NWSW	1835-10-14		A1
1321	" "	6	W½NW	1837-08-12		A1
1332	BENSON, James R	6	NESW	1834-10-21		A1
1408	BENSON, John W	4	NWSW	1858-11-01		A1
1409	" "	5	N½SE	1858-11-01		A1
1410	" "	5	SW	1858-11-01		A1
1411	" "	6	NESE	1858-11-01		A1
1244	BEVERLY, Alexander	13	SWNE	1852-12-01		A1
1241	" "	13	SENE	1858-09-01		A1
1242	" "	13	SENW	1858-09-01		A1
1240	" "	13	N½SE	1858-11-01		A1
1243	" "	13	SESE	1858-11-01		A1
1358	BLANKENSHIP, John	18	E½NE	1827-07-26		A1
1472	BLOXSOM, Washington	6	NWNE	1841-05-20		A1
1281	BOWEN, Edward	11	E½SW	1854-10-02		A1
1282	" "	19	W½NW	1854-10-02		A1
1283	" "	25	W½NW	1854-10-02		A1
1285	BOWEN, Edwin	18	W½SE	1835-04-02		A1
1286	" "	18	W½SW	1835-04-02		A1
1431	BRAGG, Rachel D	1	NENE	1858-11-01		A1
1236	CARTER, Adeline	10	SESW	1858-11-01		A1
1237	" "	10	SWSE	1858-11-01		A1
1238	" "	15	N½NW	1858-11-01		A1
1239	" "	15	NWSW	1858-11-01		A1
1261	CARTER, Charles B	1	NW	1858-11-01		A1
1262	" "	1	SENE	1858-11-01		A1
1263	" "	1	W½NE	1858-11-01		A1
1264	" "	2	NENE	1858-11-01		A1
1300	CARTER, Harris E	22	W½NW	1860-12-01		A1
1365	CARTER, John	18	W½NE	1823-10-01		A1
1364	" "	17	NE	1837-04-10		A1
1366	" "	19	E½SE	1837-08-01		A1 F
1367	" "	30	W½NE	1837-08-01		A1 F
1486	CARTER, William	33	W½NE	1823-10-01		A1
1298	CHANCELLOR, Gillum	4	NWNW	1837-04-10		A1
1442	CHRISTIAN, Rhoda G	4	SE	1860-12-01		A1
1374	CLUTE, John H	24	N½SE	1858-11-01		A1

ID	Individual in Patent	Sec.	Sec. Part	Date Issued	Other Counties	For More Info . . .
1375	CLUTE, John H (Cont'd)	24	N½SW	1858-11-01		A1
1376	" "	24	S½NE	1858-11-01		A1
1377	" "	24	SENW	1858-11-01		A1
1378	" "	24	SESW	1858-11-01		A1
1446	COLE, Robert	24	NENE	1858-11-01		A1
1299	COLEMAN, Green W	3	W½NW	1837-08-08		A1
1353	COLEMAN, Jesse	4	SENE	1837-05-15		A1
1412	CONOLEY, John F	28	S½NE	1848-05-03		A1 G1
1269	CRANE, Charles H	4	E½SW	1858-11-01		A1
1270	" "	4	SWNW	1858-11-01		A1
1271	" "	4	SWSW	1858-11-01		A1
1272	" "	9	E½NW	1858-11-01		A1
1273	" "	9	NESW	1858-11-01		A1
1487	DAVIS, William	13	SESW	1837-08-15		A1
1488	" "	24	NENW	1837-08-15		A1
1319	DOUGLASS, James	18	SESW	1834-10-21		A1
1489	DRAKE, William	18	E½SE	1832-08-08		A1
1494	DUNHAM, William P	33	SWSW	1848-05-03		A1
1265	EDWARDS, Charles G	28	E½SE	1848-05-03		A1
1266	" "	28	NWSE	1848-05-03		A1
1267	" "	33	E½SE	1848-05-03		A1
1268	" "	33	E½SW	1848-05-03		A1
1412	EVANS, George R	28	S½NE	1848-05-03		A1 G1
1277	FOWLER, Duncan C	5	NENE	1858-11-01		A1
1278	" "	5	NW	1858-11-01		A1
1279	" "	5	W½NE	1858-11-01		A1
1280	" "	6	NENE	1858-11-01		A1
1412	GAYLE, Matt	28	S½NE	1848-05-03		A1 G1
1287	GIBBS, Elhannon	23	W½NW	1825-04-09		A1
1421	GIBSON, Obadiah D	4	NENE	1837-08-15		A1
1422	" "	4	W½NE	1837-08-15		A1
1295	GRAY, George	7	SESW	1837-08-08		A1
1294	" "	7	NESW	1838-07-28		A1
1293	" "	14	NESE	1858-11-01		A1
1288	GREEN, Elijah	8	SESE	1858-11-01		A1
1289	" "	9	SWSW	1858-11-01		A1
1490	GREEN, William	8	NESE	1860-09-01		A1
1469	HAWKINS, Thomas W	11	E½SE	1858-11-01		A1
1470	" "	11	NE	1858-11-01		A1
1471	" "	11	NWSE	1858-11-01		A1
1478	HAWKINS, Wiley	11	NENW	1854-07-15		A1
1483	" "	2	SESW	1854-07-15		A1
1479	" "	11	SENW	1858-11-01		A1
1480	" "	15	SENW	1858-11-01		A1
1481	" "	2	SE	1858-11-01		A1
1482	" "	2	SENE	1858-11-01		A1
1484	" "	2	W½NE	1858-11-01		A1
1485	HAWKINS, Wiley W	15	SWNW	1852-12-01		A1
1491	HEAPE, William H	13	NENE	1837-08-18		A1
1305	HILL, Isaac	23	NE	1858-11-01		A1
1306	" "	23	NENW	1858-11-01		A1
1307	" "	23	SESE	1858-11-01		A1
1308	" "	23	W½SE	1858-11-01		A1
1248	HILLSON, Anny	35	NWSE	1858-11-01		A1
1249	" "	35	SWNE	1858-11-01		A1
1430	HILSON, Pinckney W	35	SENW	1835-09-19		A1
1428	" "	27	NWNE	1837-08-18		A1
1429	" "	27	SESE	1837-08-18		A1
1459	HOLLOWAY, Templeton M	9	S½NE	1858-11-01		A1
1460	" "	9	SE	1858-11-01		A1
1274	HORTON, Daniel	11	SWSE	1852-02-02		A1
1235	JONES, Abner	12	SWSE	1850-04-01		A1
1246	JONES, Amos	36	SWNE	1861-05-01		A1
1247	" "	36	W½SE	1861-05-01		A1
1500	JONES, Willis	12	E½NE	1891-01-15		A2
1423	MARTIN, Peter F	24	S½SE	1858-09-01		A1
1424	" "	25	E½NW	1858-09-01		A1
1425	" "	25	N½NE	1858-09-01		A1
1426	" "	25	NESW	1858-09-01		A1
1392	MCCRORY, John	26	SESE	1834-10-21		A1
1394	" "	26	SWSE	1837-08-07		A1
1393	" "	26	SESW	1847-05-01		A1
1391	" "	26	NESE	1848-04-01		A1

ID	Individual in Patent	Sec.	Sec. Part	Date Issued	Other Counties	For More Info . . .
1395	MCCRORY, John (Cont'd)	35	N½NE	1858-11-01		A1
1396	" "	35	SENE	1858-11-01		A1
1397	" "	36	N½NW	1858-11-01		A1
1398	" "	36	S½NW	1858-11-01		A1
1390	" "	26	NENE	1860-08-01		A1
1464	MCCRORY, Thomas	26	NWSE	1837-08-07		A1
1465	" "	26	S½NE	1858-11-01		A1
1466	" "	26	SENW	1896-10-26		A1
1399	MCDUFEE, John	7	SENE	1837-04-10		A1
1302	MILLER, Hiram	14	NWSE	1838-07-28		A1
1303	" "	14	SWSW	1838-07-28		A1
1304	" "	23	SENW	1838-07-28		A1
1493	MILLER, William	14	SWSE	1837-08-15		A1
1314	MILTON, Jacob C	2	E½NW	1861-05-01		A1
1315	" "	2	NESW	1861-05-01		A1
1316	" "	2	NWNW	1861-05-01		A1 V1338
1497	MINTER, William T	33	NWSW	1848-05-03		A1
1401	MURPHEY, John	34	E½SW	1858-11-01		A1
1402	" "	34	W½NW	1858-11-01		A1
1400	" "	34	E½NW	1860-08-01		A1
1502	MURPHEY, Wilson	22	SE	1858-09-01		A1
1503	" "	23	W½SW	1858-09-01		A1
1504	" "	26	W½NW	1858-09-01		A1
1405	MURPHY, John	30	NWSE	1835-04-08		A1
1403	" "	21	SE	1835-10-16		A1
1404	" "	29	E½NE	1837-08-08		A1
1413	MURPHY, Julius S	28	SWSE	1848-05-03		A1
1505	MURPHY, Wilson	26	W½SW	1826-11-22		A1
1507	" "	33	NENE	1835-04-08		A1
1509	" "	34	W½SW	1837-05-15		A1
1508	" "	33	NWSE	1837-08-18		A1
1506	" "	33	E½NW	1848-05-03		A1
1323	NEAL, James	12	W½NW	1837-08-15		A1
1324	" "	12	W½SW	1837-08-15		A1
1406	NEVILLS, John	31	E½SW	1858-11-01		A1
1467	PARK, Thomas	6	SWNE	1843-02-01		A1
1301	PARKES, Henry D	33	SWSE	1858-09-01		A1
1317	PARKES, James D	31	SWSW	1858-09-01		A1
1325	PARKS, James	24	NWNW	1837-08-14		A1
1318	PARKS, James D	14	SESE	1837-08-14		A1
1327	PERRITT, James	14	NWNW	1835-10-01		A1
1330	" "	14	SWNW	1835-10-01		A1
1331	" "	15	SENE	1835-10-01		A1
1326	" "	14	NENW	1858-11-01		A1
1328	" "	14	NWSW	1858-11-01		A1
1329	" "	14	S½NE	1858-11-01		A1
1416	PERRITT, Needham	15	SWSE	1835-10-01		A1
1415	" "	15	NWSE	1837-08-09		A1
1417	" "	15	SWSW	1837-08-15		A1
1495	PERRITT, William	14	SENW	1837-08-15		A1
1311	PHILIPS, Isam	32	SESW	1854-07-15		A1
1256	REYNOLDS, Austin L	7	SENW	1852-12-01		A1
1496	REYNOLDS, William	7	W½NW	1852-12-01		A1
1258	RHODES, Benjamin	27	NESE	1834-10-21		A1
1257	" "	27	E½NE	1837-08-18		A1
1259	" "	33	SENE	1837-08-18		A1
1457	RICHARDSON, Stephen C	36	SESE	1860-09-01		A1
1260	ROAD, Benjamin	27	SWNE	1837-08-07		A1
1388	ROBISON, John L	22	NE	1860-12-01		A1
1492	RUMPH, William M	33	W½NW	1848-05-03		A1
1468	SEAL, Thomas	35	E½SW	1825-04-02		A1
1250	SEALE, Arnold	29	NESE	1858-11-01		A1
1251	" "	29	W½SE	1858-11-01		A1
1252	" "	29	W½SW	1858-11-01		A1
1253	" "	30	E½SW	1858-11-01		A1
1254	" "	30	SWSE	1858-11-01		A1
1437	SEALE, Ransom	29	SESE	1837-08-18		A1
1438	" "	32	E½NE	1837-08-18		A1
1432	" "	27	E½NW	1858-09-01		A1
1433	" "	27	N½SW	1858-09-01		A1
1434	" "	27	NWSE	1858-09-01		A1
1436	" "	27	SWNW	1858-09-01		A1
1435	" "	27	S½SW	1858-11-01		A1

ID	Individual in Patent	Sec.	Sec. Part	Date Issued	Other Counties	For More Info . . .
1450	SIMPSON, Robert H	7	NENE	1858-11-01		A1
1255	SIMS, Arthur	23	NESE	1843-02-01		A1
1309	SIMS, Isaac	12	E½NW	1858-11-01		A1
1310	" "	12	W½NE	1858-11-01		A1
1312	SIMS, Jackson	26	NENW	1860-09-01		A1
1313	" "	26	NWNE	1860-09-01		A1
1344	SIMS, James	25	W½SW	1837-08-15		A1
1455	SIMS, Sherod	13	SWSE	1837-08-15		A1
1456	" "	14	NENE	1838-07-28		A1
1458	SIMS, Stephen	25	S½SE	1837-08-15		A1
1355	SMITH, John A	24	NWNE	1882-12-20		A1
1356	SMITH, John B	35	NENW	1835-10-16		A1
1357	" "	35	W½NW	1837-08-15		A1
1501	SMITH, Willis	14	NWNE	1837-08-09		A1
1419	STEWARD, Nimrod	13	W½SW	1837-08-14		A1
1420	" "	24	SWNW	1838-07-28		A1
1418	" "	13	NESW	1840-10-10		A1
1477	STOCKMAN, Wesley	13	W½NW	1853-08-01		A1
1476	" "	13	NWNE	1854-07-15		A1
1473	" "	12	E½SE	1858-11-01		A1
1474	" "	12	NWSE	1858-11-01		A1
1475	" "	13	NENW	1858-11-01		A1
1345	STRINGFELLOW, Jefferson W	32	NWNE	1854-07-15		A1
1346	" "	32	S½NW	1858-11-01		A1
1347	" "	32	SWNE	1858-11-01		A1
1441	STRINGFELLOW, Reuben	32	W½SW	1843-02-01		A1
1440	" "	32	NESW	1854-07-15		A1
1439	" "	31	SE	1858-11-01		A1
1359	THOMPSON, John C	15	E½SE	1858-11-01		A1
1360	" "	25	N½SE	1858-11-01		A1
1361	" "	25	S½NE	1858-11-01		A1
1362	" "	25	SESW	1858-11-01		A1
1363	" "	36	NWNE	1858-11-01		A1
1498	THOMPSON, William	30	E½SE	1826-11-22		A1
1451	TRAWEEK, Robert	10	E½NE	1821-11-07		A1
1445	TRAWEEK, Robert C	3	W½NE	1825-04-02		A1
1463	TRAWEEK, Thomas M	7	E½SE	1837-08-15		A1 G45
1462	" "	7	SWNE	1837-08-18		A1
1452	TURNER, Samuel	8	NWSW	1858-11-01		A1
1290	VICKREY, Franklin	35	E½SE	1858-11-01		A1
1291	" "	36	N½SW	1858-11-01		A1
1292	" "	36	S½SW	1858-11-01		A1
1296	VICKREY, George W	35	NWSW	1860-04-02		A1
1297	" "	35	SWSE	1860-04-02		A1
1499	WALLACE, William	3	SWSE	1835-10-15		A1
1379	WALLS, John H	21	W½NE	1832-09-13		A1
1245	WARREN, Alfred	24	SWSW	1895-06-19		A2
1443	WARREN, Richard	30	W½SW	1835-04-15		A1
1444	" "	31	W½NW	1835-10-01		A1
1349	WATTS, Jeremiah	17	E½NW	1826-05-08		A1
1351	" "	8	S½SW	1837-05-15		A1
1463	" "	7	E½SE	1837-08-15		A1 G45
1350	" "	8	NW	1837-08-15		A1
1352	" "	8	W½SE	1837-08-15		A1
1348	WATTS, Jeremiah B	7	NWNE	1837-08-18		A1
1380	WATTS, John H	17	W½NW	1823-10-01		A1
1383	" "	22	E½SW	1835-10-01		A1
1384	" "	22	SENW	1835-10-01		A1
1385	" "	27	NWNW	1837-04-15		A1
1386	" "	28	NW	1837-04-15		A1
1382	" "	21	E½NE	1837-08-02		A1
1381	" "	18	NESW	1837-08-12		A1
1387	" "	7	W½SE	1837-08-15		A1
1414	WATTS, Monroe P	8	NESW	1838-07-28		A1
1461	WATTS, Thomas H	28	N½NE	1835-10-01		A1
1510	WATTS, Winson	6	SENE	1838-07-28		A1
1511	" "	6	W½SE	1838-07-28		A1
1354	WOMACK, Jesse	4	E½NW	1827-01-08		A1
1389	WOMACK, John M	6	SESE	1858-11-01		A1
1427	WOOD, Phoeby A	1	S½	1858-11-01		A1
1453	WOODS, Sarah	2	NWSW	1858-11-01		A1
1454	" "	2	SWNW	1858-11-01		A1 V1338
1368	WORRELL, John D	10	E½SE	1858-11-01		A1

ID	Individual in Patent	Sec.	Sec. Part	Date Issued	Other Counties	For More Info . . .
1369	WORRELL, John D (Cont'd)	10	NESW	1858-11-01		A1
1370	" "	10	NWSE	1858-11-01		A1
1371	" "	10	SENW	1858-11-01		A1
1372	" "	15	NENE	1858-11-01		A1
1373	" "	15	W½NE	1858-11-01		A1
1335	YELDELL, James R	10	W½SW	1858-09-01		A1
1338	" "	2	W½NW	1858-09-01		A1 V1454, 1316
1339	" "	3	NESW	1858-09-01		A1
1340	" "	3	NWSE	1858-09-01		A1
1341	" "	3	SESE	1858-09-01		A1
1343	" "	3	SWSW	1858-09-01		A1
1333	" "	10	NENW	1858-11-01		A1
1334	" "	10	W½NE	1858-11-01		A1
1336	" "	11	W½NW	1858-11-01		A1
1337	" "	2	SWSW	1858-11-01		A1
1342	" "	3	SESW	1858-11-01		A1

Patent Map

T10-N R12-E
St Stephens Meridian

Map Group 6

Township Statistics

Parcels Mapped	:	277
Number of Patents	:	198
Number of Individuals	:	125
Patentees Identified	:	123
Number of Surnames	:	81
Multi-Patentee Parcels	:	2
Oldest Patent Date	:	11/7/1821
Most Recent Patent	:	10/26/1896
Block/Lot Parcels	:	0
Parcels Re - Issued	:	0
Parcels that Overlap	:	3
Cities and Towns	:	3
Cemeteries	:	4

Map grid (Section 6): BENSON James K 1837; BLOXSOM Washington 1841; FOWLER Duncan C; BENSON James K 1835; BENSON James R 1834; PARK Thomas 1843; WATTS Winson 1838; BENSON John W 1858; WATTS Winson 1838; BARGE Edward W 1853; WOMACK John M 1858

Section 5: FOWLER Duncan C 1858; FOWLER Duncan C 1858; FOWLER Duncan C 1858; BENSON John W 1858; BENSON John W 1858; BENSON John W 1858; BELL Robert H 1858

Section 4: CHANCELLOR Gillum 1837; GIBSON Obadiah D 1837; GIBSON Obadiah D 1837; CRANE Charles H 1858; WOMACK Jesse 1827; COLEMAN Jesse 1837; BENSON John W 1858; CRANE Charles H 1858; CRANE Charles H 1858; CHRISTIAN Rhoda G 1860

Section 7: REYNOLDS William 1852; WATTS Jeremiah B 1837; SIMPSON Robert H 1858; REYNOLDS Austin L 1852; TRAWEEK Thomas M 1837; MCDUFEE John 1837; AUSTIN Davis 1837; GRAY George 1838; TRAWEEK [45] Thomas M 1837; GRAY George 1837; WATTS John H 1837

Section 8: WATTS Jeremiah 1837; BELL Robert H 1858; TURNER Samuel 1858; WATTS Monroe P 1838; GREEN William 1860; WATTS Jeremiah 1837; WATTS Jeremiah 1837; GREEN Elijah 1858

Section 9: BELL Robert H 1858; CRANE Charles H 1858; HOLLOWAY Templeton M 1858; CRANE Charles H 1858; GREEN Elijah 1858; BATES James M 1858; HOLLOWAY Templeton M 1858

Section 18: AUSTIN Davis 1837; CARTER John 1823; BLANKENSHIP John 1827; WATTS John H 1823; WATTS Jeremiah 1826; CARTER John 1837; WATTS John H 1837; DRAKE William 1832; BOWEN Edwin 1835; BOWEN Edwin 1835; DOUGLASS James 1834

Section 17: (17)

Section 16: (16)

Section 19: BARGE John R 1858; BOWEN Edward 1854; CARTER John 1837

Section 20: (20)

Section 21: WALLS John H 1832; WATTS John H 1837; MURPHY John 1835

Section 30: (30); CARTER John 1837; MURPHY John 1835; WARREN Richard 1835; SEALE Arnold 1858; SEALE Arnold 1858; THOMPSON William 1826; WARREN Richard 1835; (31)

Section 29: (29); SEALE Arnold 1858; SEALE Arnold 1858; MURPHY John 1837; SEALE Arnold 1858; SEALE Ransom 1837

Section 28: WATTS John H 1837; (28); WATTS Thomas H 1835; BABCOCK [1] Joseph 1848; EDWARDS Charles G 1848; EDWARDS Charles G 1848; MURPHY Julius S 1848

Section 31: NEVILLS John 1858; STRINGFELLOW Reuben 1858; PARKES James D 1858

Section 32: STRINGFELLOW Jefferson W 1854; STRINGFELLOW Jefferson W 1858; STRINGFELLOW Jefferson W 1858; SEALE Ransom 1837; STRINGFELLOW Reuben 1854; STRINGFELLOW Reuben 1843; (32); PHILIPS Isam 1854

Section 33: RUMPH William M 1848; MURPHY Wilson 1848; CARTER William 1823; MURPHY Wilson 1835; RHODES Benjamin 1837; MINTER William T 1848; (33); MURPHY Wilson 1837; DUNHAM William P 1848; EDWARDS Charles G 1848; PARKES Henry D 1858; EDWARDS Charles G 1848

COLEMAN Green W 1837		TRAWEEK Robert C 1825		MILTON Jacob C 1861	MILTON Jacob C 1861	HAWKINS Wiley 1858	CARTER Charles B 1858	CARTER Charles B 1858	CARTER Charles B 1858	BRAGG Rachel D 1858

3 / **2** / **1** — section layout

Section 3:
- COLEMAN Green W 1837
- TRAWEEK Robert C 1825
- YELDELL James R 1858
- YELDELL James R 1858
- YELDELL James R 1858
- YELDELL James R 1858
- WALLACE William 1835
- YELDELL James R 1858

Section 2:
- MILTON Jacob C 1861
- YELDELL James R 1858
- WOODS Sarah 1858
- MILTON Jacob C 1861
- HAWKINS Wiley 1858
- CARTER Charles B 1858
- WOODS Sarah 1858
- MILTON Jacob C 1861
- YELDELL James R 1858
- HAWKINS Wiley 1854
- HAWKINS Wiley 1858

Section 1:
- CARTER Charles B 1858
- CARTER Charles B 1858
- BRAGG Rachel D 1858
- CARTER Charles B 1858
- WOOD Phoeby A 1858

Section 10:
- YELDELL James R 1858
- YELDELL James R 1858
- TRAWEEK Robert 1821
- WORRELL John D 1858
- YELDELL James R 1858
- WORRELL John D 1858
- WORRELL John D 1858
- YELDELL James R 1858
- CARTER Adeline 1858
- CARTER Adeline 1858

Section 11:
- HAWKINS Wiley 1854
- HAWKINS Thomas W 1858
- YELDELL James R 1858
- HAWKINS Wiley 1858
- BOWEN Edward 1854
- HAWKINS Thomas W 1858
- HAWKINS Thomas W 1858
- HORTON Daniel 1852

Section 12:
- NEAL James 1837
- SIMS Isaac 1858
- SIMS Isaac 1858
- JONES Willis 1891
- STOCKMAN Wesley 1858
- STOCKMAN Wesley 1858
- NEAL James 1837
- JONES Abner 1850

Section 15:
- CARTER Adeline 1858
- WORRELL John D 1858
- WORRELL John D 1858
- HAWKINS Wiley W 1852
- HAWKINS Wiley 1858
- CARTER Adeline 1858
- PERRITT Needham 1837
- THOMPSON John C 1858
- PERRITT Needham 1837
- PERRITT Needham 1835

Section 14:
- PERRITT James 1835
- PERRITT James 1835
- SMITH Willis 1858
- SIMS Sherod 1838
- PERRITT James 1835
- PERRITT William 1837
- PERRITT James 1858
- PERRITT James 1858
- MILLER Hiram 1838
- GRAY George 1858
- MILLER Hiram 1838
- MILLER William 1837
- PARKS James D 1837

Section 13:
- STOCKMAN Wesley 1858
- STOCKMAN Wesley 1854
- HEAPE William H 1837
- STOCKMAN Wesley 1853
- BEVERLY Alexander 1858
- BEVERLY Alexander 1852
- BEVERLY Alexander 1858
- STEWARD Nimrod 1840
- BEVERLY Alexander 1858
- STEWARD Nimrod 1837
- DAVIS William 1837
- SIMS Sherod 1837
- BEVERLY Alexander 1858

Section 22:
- CARTER Harris E 1860
- ROBISON John L 1860
- WATTS John H 1835
- WATTS John H 1835
- MURPHEY Wilson 1858

Section 23:
- GIBBS Elhannon 1825
- HILL Isaac 1858
- MILLER Hiram 1838
- HILL Isaac 1858
- MURPHEY Wilson 1858
- HILL Isaac 1858

Section 24:
- PARKS James 1837
- DAVIS William 1837
- SMITH John A 1882
- COLE Robert 1858
- STEWARD Nimrod 1838
- CLUTE John H 1858
- CLUTE John H 1858
- CLUTE John H 1858
- CLUTE John H 1858
- WARREN Alfred 1895
- CLUTE John H 1858
- MARTIN Peter F 1858
- SIMS Arthur 1843
- HILL Isaac 1858

Section 27:
- WATTS John H 1837
- HILSON Pinckney W 1837
- RHODES Benjamin 1837
- SEALE Ransom 1858
- ROAD Benjamin 1837
- SEALE Ransom 1858
- SEALE Ransom 1858
- SEALE Ransom 1858
- RHODES Benjamin 1834
- SEALE Ransom 1858
- HILSON Pinckney W 1837

Section 26:
- MURPHEY Wilson 1858
- SIMS Jackson 1860
- SIMS Jackson 1860
- MCCRORY John 1860
- MCCRORY Thomas 1896
- MCCRORY Thomas 1858
- MURPHY Wilson 1826
- MCCRORY Thomas 1837
- MCCRORY John 1848
- MCCRORY John 1847
- MCCRORY John 1837
- MCCRORY John 1834

Section 25:
- BOWEN Edward 1854
- MARTIN Peter F 1858
- MARTIN Peter F 1858
- SIMS James 1837
- MARTIN Peter F 1858
- THOMPSON John C 1858
- THOMPSON John C 1858
- THOMPSON John C 1858
- SIMS Stephen 1837

Section 34:
- MURPHEY John 1858
- MURPHEY John 1860
- MURPHEY John 1858
- MURPHY Wilson 1837

Section 35:
- SMITH John B 1835
- MCCRORY John 1858
- SMITH John B 1837
- HILSON Pinckney W 1835
- HILLSON Anny 1858
- MCCRORY John 1858
- VICKREY George W 1860
- HILLSON Anny 1858
- VICKREY Franklin 1858
- SEAL Thomas 1825
- VICKREY George W 1860

Section 36:
- MCCRORY John 1858
- THOMPSON John C 1858
- MCCRORY John 1858
- JONES Amos 1861
- VICKREY Franklin 1858
- JONES Amos 1861
- VICKREY Franklin 1858
- RICHARDSON Stephen C 1860

Helpful Hints

1. This Map's INDEX can be found on the preceding pages.

2. Refer to Map "C" to see where this Township lies within Butler County, Alabama.

3. Numbers within square brackets [ ] denote a multi-patentee land parcel (multi-owner). Refer to Appendix "C" for a full list of members in this group.

4. Areas that look to be crowded with Patentees usually indicate multiple sales of the same parcel (Re-issues) or Overlapping parcels. See this Township's Index for an explanation of these and other circumstances that might explain "odd" groupings of Patentees on this map.

Legend

— Patent Boundary

▬ Section Boundary

No Patents Found (or Outside County)

1., 2., 3., ... Lot Numbers (when beside a name)

[ ] Group Number (see Appendix "C")

Scale: Section = 1 mile X 1 mile (generally, with some exceptions)

Road Map

T10-N R12-E
St Stephens Meridian

Map Group 6

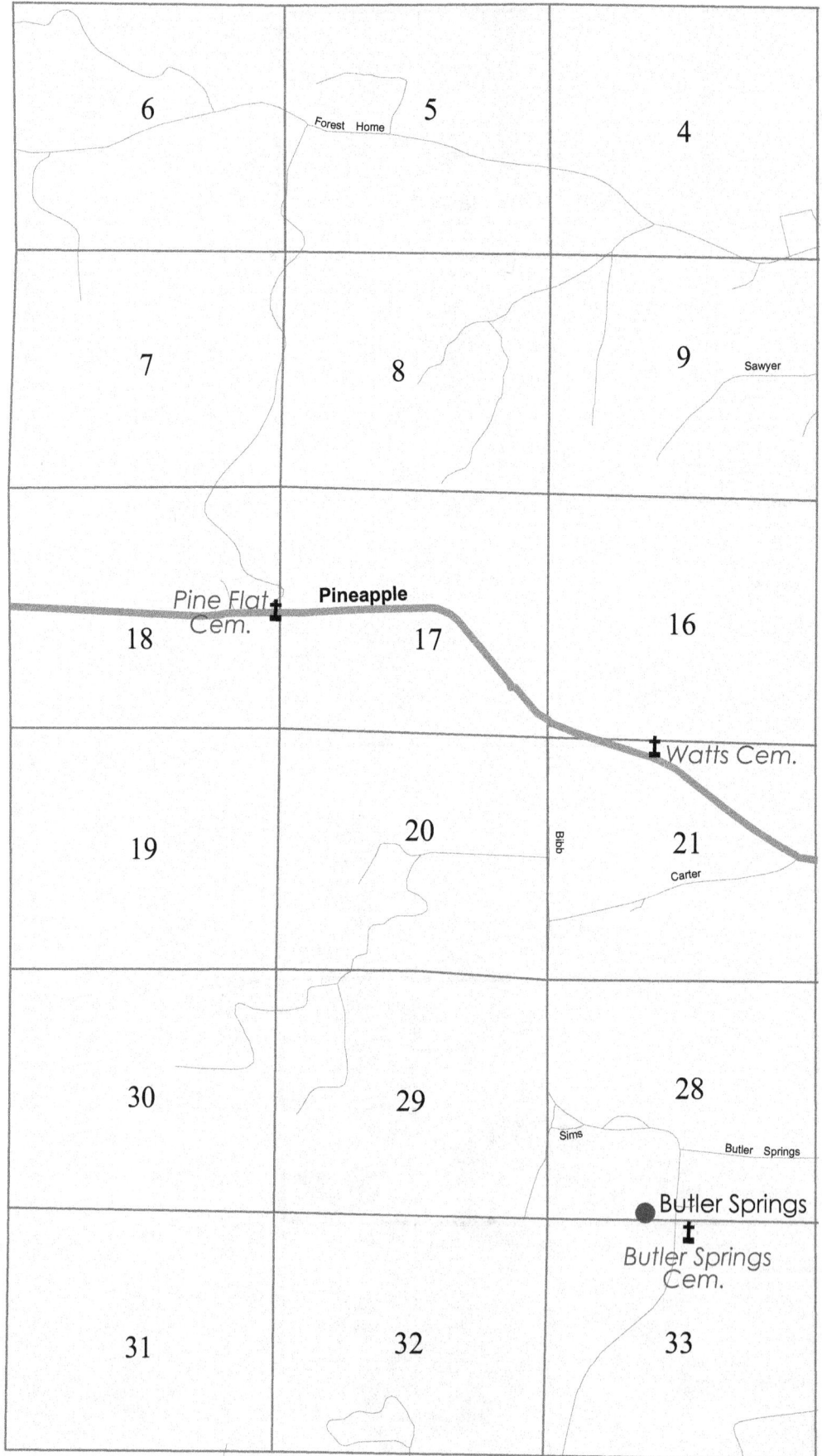

6

5

Forest Home

4

7

8

9

Sawyer

Pine Flat Cem.

Pineapple

18

17

16

Watts Cem.

19

20

Bibb

21

Carter

30

29

28

Sims

Butler Springs

Butler Springs

Butler Springs Cem.

31

32

33

3

2

Forest Home ●

1

Monterey

Forest Home

Broad Street

♱
Forest Home Cem.

Sunset

11

Boutwell

12

10

7th

15

Yelder

14

13

22

23

24

Pineapple

● Saucer

Murphy

27

26

Cole

25

34

35

36

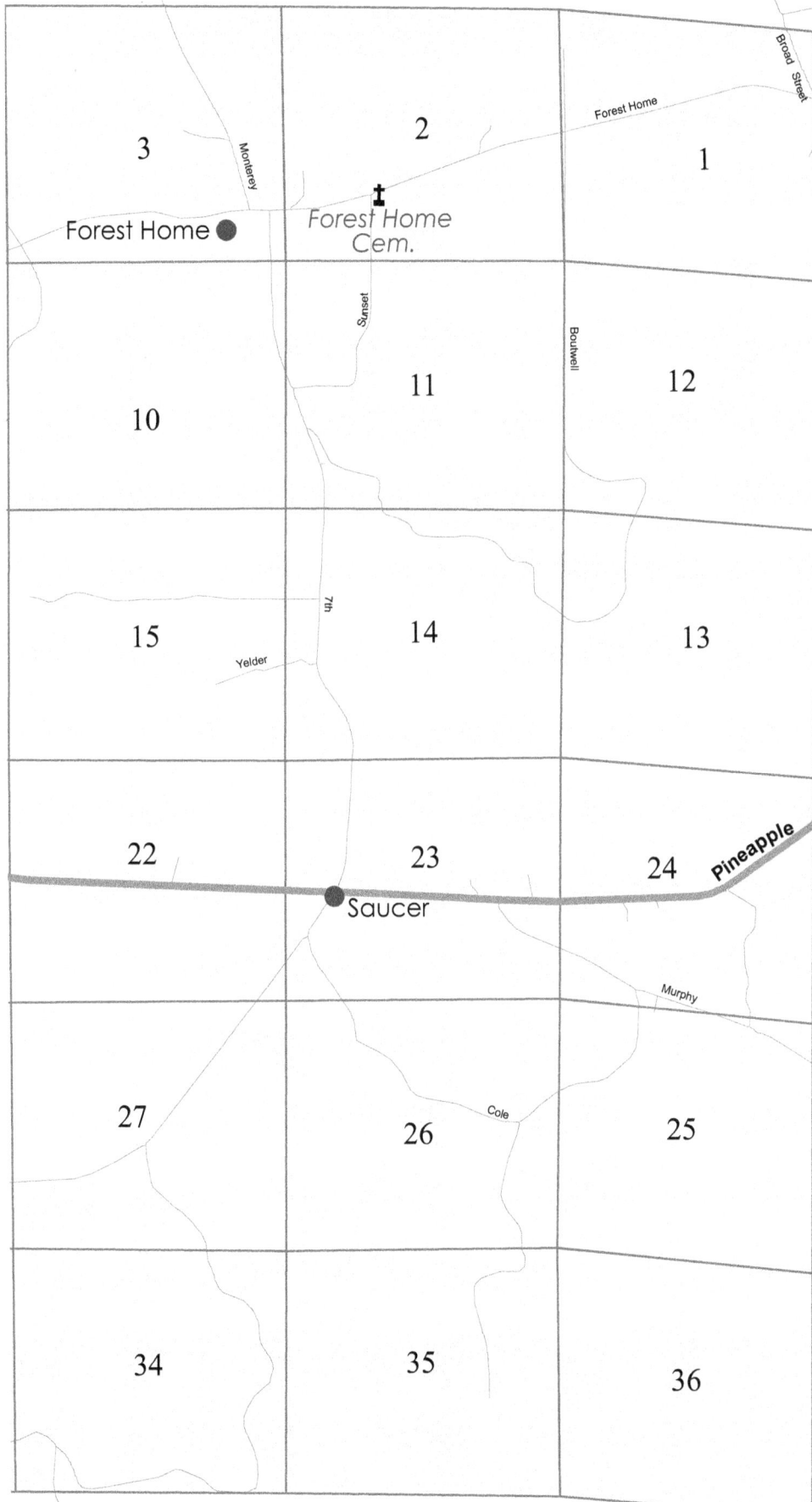

Helpful Hints

1. This road map has a number of uses, but primarily it is to help you: a) find the present location of land owned by your ancestors (at least the general area), b) find cemeteries and city-centers, and c) estimate the route/roads used by Census-takers & tax-assessors.

2. If you plan to travel to Butler County to locate cemeteries or land parcels, please pick up a modern travel map for the area before you do. Mapping old land parcels on modern maps is not as exact a science as you might think. Just the slightest variations in public land survey coordinates, estimates of parcel boundaries, or road-map deviations can greatly alter a map's representation of how a road either does or doesn't cross a particular parcel of land.

L e g e n d

——————— Section Lines

═══════ Interstates

▬▬▬▬▬ Highways

——————— Other Roads

● Cities/Towns

♱ Cemeteries

Scale: Section = 1 mile X 1 mile
(generally, with some exceptions)

Historical Map

T10-N R12-E
St Stephens Meridian

Map Group 6

Cities & Towns
Butler Springs
Forest Home
Saucer

Cemeteries
Butler Springs Cemetery
Forest Home Cemetery
Pine Flat Cemetery
Watts Cemetery

6

5

4

Breastwork Creek

7

8

9

Pine Barren Creek

18

Pine Flat Cem.

17

16

Watts Cem.

19

20

21

Redicks Creek

30

29

28

Butler Springs

Butler Springs Cem.

31

32

33

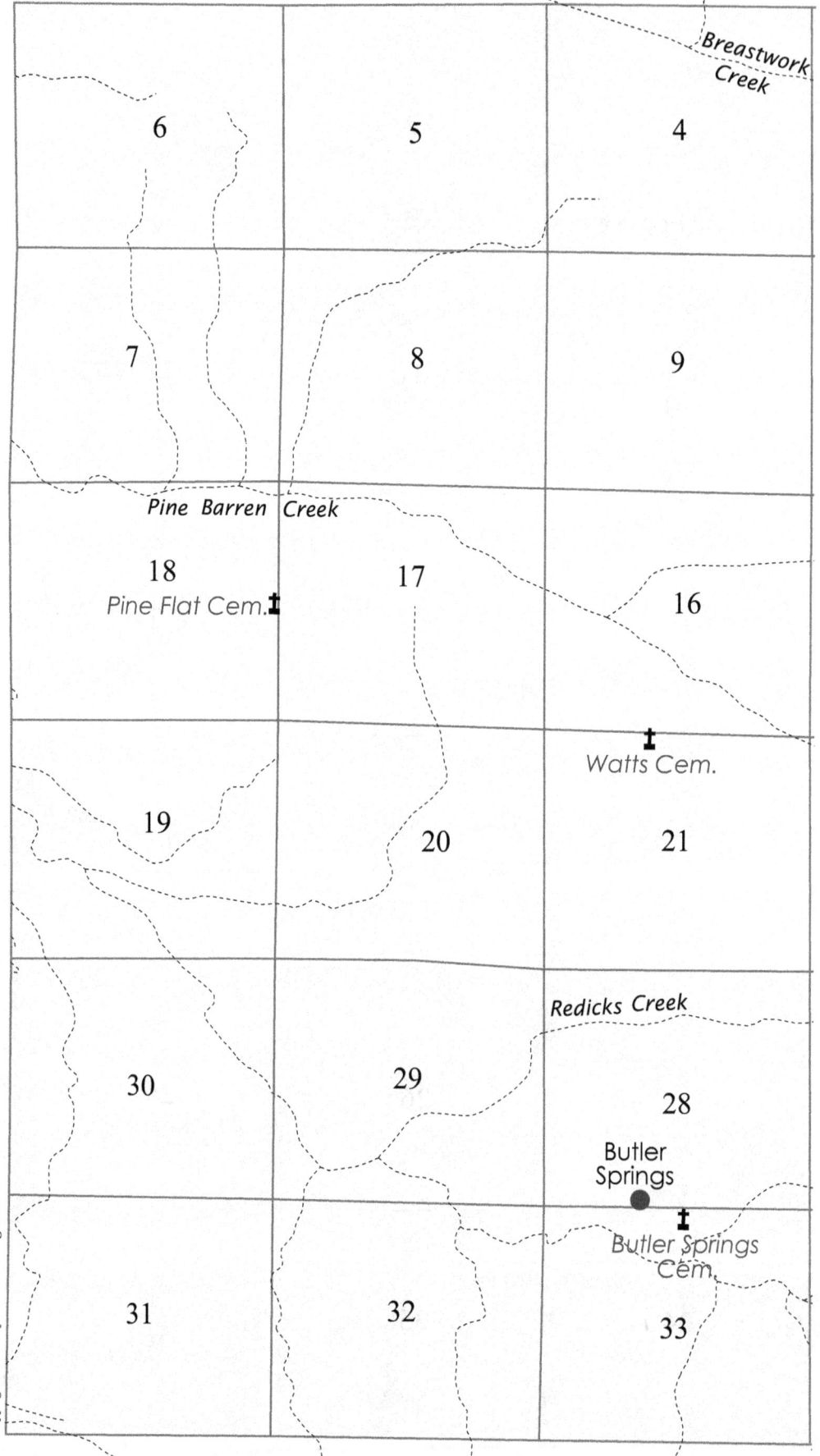

3

2

*Forest Home
Cem.*
✝

1

Forest Home ●

10

11

12

15

14

13

Pine Barren Creek

23

● Saucer

22

Black Branch

24

27

26

25

34

35

36

Redicks Creek

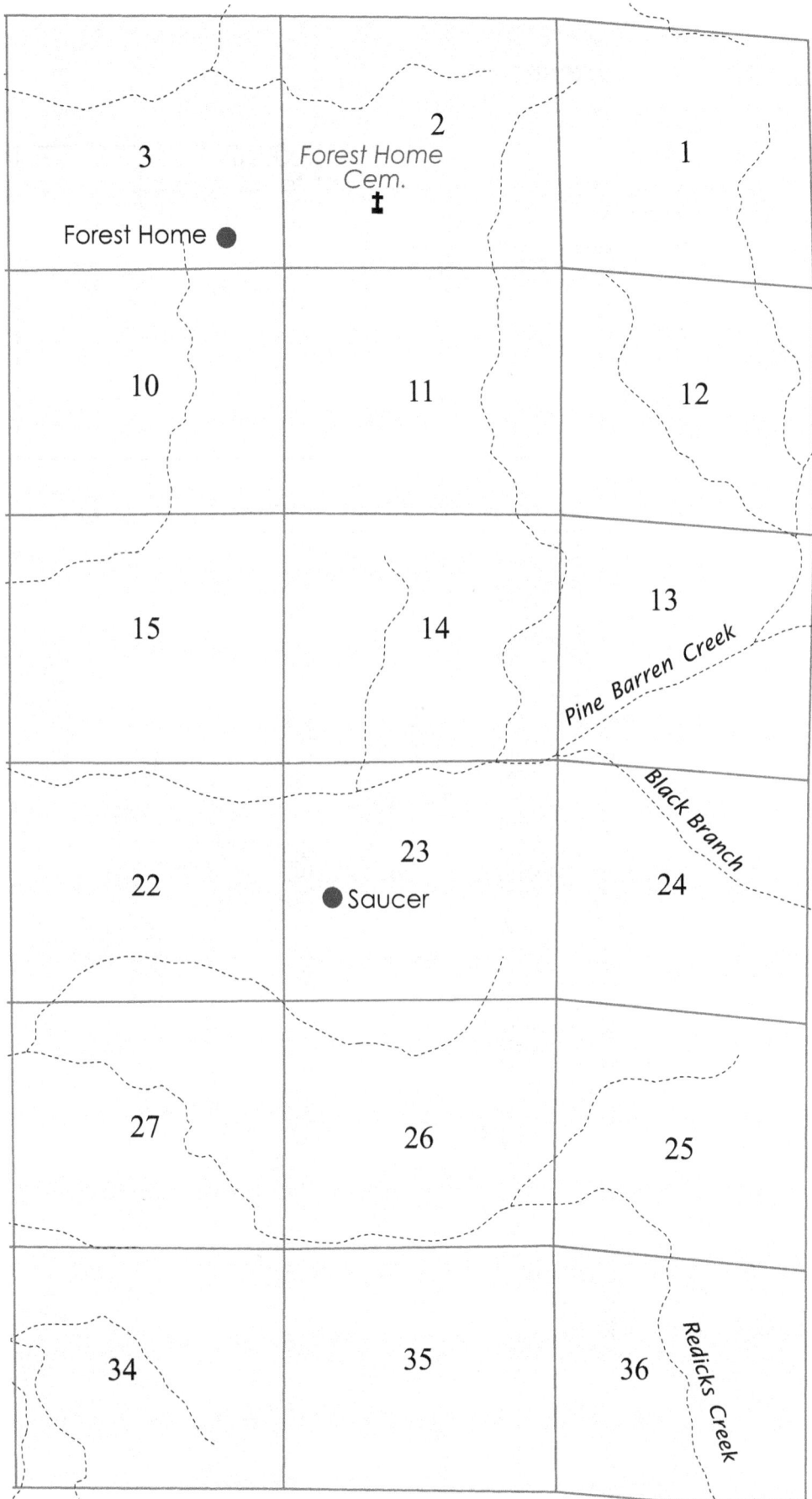

Helpful Hints

1. This Map takes a different look at the same Congressional Township displayed in the preceding two maps. It presents features that can help you better envision the historical development of the area: a) Water-bodies (lakes & ponds), b) Water-courses (rivers, streams, etc.), c) Railroads, d) City/town center-points (where they were oftentimes located when first settled), and e) Cemeteries.

2. Using this "Historical" map in tandem with this Township's Patent Map and Road Map, may lead you to some interesting discoveries. You will often find roads, towns, cemeteries, and waterways are named after nearby landowners: sometimes those names will be the ones you are researching. See how many of these research gems you can find here in Butler County.

Legend

——————	Section Lines
┼┼┼┼┼┼┼	Railroads
▨	Large Rivers & Bodies of Water
- - - - - - -	Streams/Creeks & Small Rivers
●	Cities/Towns
✝	Cemeteries

Scale: Section = 1 mile X 1 mile
(there are some exceptions)

113

Map Group 7: Index to Land Patents

Township 10-North Range 13-East (St Stephens)

After you locate an individual in this Index, take note of the Section and Section Part then proceed to the Land Patent map on the pages immediately following. You should have no difficulty locating the corresponding parcel of land.

The "For More Info" Column will lead you to more information about the underlying Patents. See the *Legend* at right, and the "How to Use this Book" chapter, for more information.

```
                        LEGEND
              "For More Info . . . " column

A = Authority (Legislative Act, See Appendix "A")
B = Block or Lot (location in Section unknown)
C = Cancelled Patent
F = Fractional Section
G = Group  (Multi-Patentee Patent, see Appendix "C")
V = Overlaps another Parcel
R = Re-Issued (Parcel patented more than once)

(A & G items require you to look in the Appendixes referred
to above. All other Letter-designations followed by a number
require you to locate line-items in this index that possess
the ID number found after the letter).
```

ID	Individual in Patent	Sec.	Sec. Part	Date Issued	Other Counties	For More Info . . .
1567	ASHCRAFT, John	4	N½NE	1858-11-01		A1
1615	BALDERREE, Robert	20	NENW	1858-11-01		A1
1616	" "	23	SWSE	1858-11-01		A1
1617	" "	26	NWNE	1858-11-01		A1
1592	BAXLEY, Martha A	26	W½SW	1883-03-01		A2 G3
1537	BELL, Edward W	22	SWNE	1878-04-09		A2
1565	BEVERLY, John A	14	E½NE	1891-06-29		A2
1569	BLACK, John	19	W½NW	1837-08-18		A1
1630	BLACK, Thomas M	18	SWNW	1858-09-01		A1
1629	" "	18	NENW	1858-11-01		A1
1631	" "	7	SESW	1858-11-01		A1
1619	BOLLING, Samuel J	14	E½NW	1860-10-01		A1 G5
1563	BOYKIN, Jesse	1	SESW	1837-08-15		A1
1564	" "	12	NWSE	1837-08-15		A1
1544	BRAGG, George B	3	S½NE	1837-08-18		A1
1579	BREWER, John W	2	SESW	1860-09-01		A1
1580	" "	2	SWNW	1860-09-01		A1
1581	" "	20	E½SW	1860-09-01		A1
1582	" "	22	SWSW	1860-09-01		A1
1583	" "	32	S½	1860-09-01		A1
1584	" "	32	SENW	1860-09-01		A1
1585	" "	32	W½NW	1860-09-01		A1
1586	" "	8	E½SE	1860-09-01		A1
1587	" "	8	SENE	1860-09-01		A1
1570	BUCKELLEW, John	22	SESW	1858-11-01		A1
1571	" "	22	SWSE	1858-11-01		A1
1628	BURNETT, Thomas J	12	W½	1858-11-01		A1
1545	BUTLER, Henry H	14	W½NW	1890-03-19		A2
1547	CAMPBELL, James H	34	NENW	1880-02-20		A2
1548	" "	34	NWNE	1880-02-20		A2
1549	" "	34	NWNW	1890-07-03		A2
1635	CARTER, William B	2	SWSW	1860-12-01		A1
1515	CLOPTON, Allford	33		1858-11-01		A1
1604	CLOPTON, Nathaniel V	25		1858-11-01		A1
1605	" "	36	N½	1858-11-01		A1
1637	COLE, William E	18	SWNE	1858-11-01		A1
1524	COOPER, Augustin	12	E½SE	1858-11-01		A1
1525	" "	12	NE	1858-11-01		A1
1526	" "	12	SWSE	1858-11-01		A1
1530	CRENSHAW, Charles E	17	S½SW	1851-04-10		A1
1535	" "	8	NENW	1851-04-10		A1 G13
1531	" "	18	S½SE	1852-02-02		A1
1532	" "	19	N½NE	1852-02-02		A1
1533	" "	19	NENW	1852-02-02		A1
1534	" "	8	NWSW	1852-02-02		A1
1535	CRENSHAW, Frederick W	8	NENW	1851-04-10		A1 G13

ID	Individual in Patent	Sec.	Sec. Part	Date Issued	Other Counties	For More Info . . .
1633	CRENSHAW, Walter H	20	NWNW	1852-02-02		A1
1543	CROSS, Franklin	6	E½NE	1858-11-01		A1
1528	DAWSON, Benjamin G	14	W½SW	1889-08-16		A2
1592	DAWSON, Martha A	26	W½SW	1883-03-01		A2 G3
1644	DAWSON, William R	14	S½SE	1858-11-01		A1
1646	DYESS, Winfield S	34	S½SE	1885-03-30		A2
1552	FOX, James M	10	SW	1860-10-01		A1
1553	" "	10	W½SE	1860-10-01		A1
1529	GARRETT, Caswell	3	SENW	1837-05-15		A1
1557	GONDER, Jasper M	23	E½SE	1858-11-01		A1
1558	" "	23	N½	1858-11-01		A1
1559	" "	23	NWSE	1858-11-01		A1
1560	" "	23	SW	1858-11-01		A1
1561	" "	24		1858-11-01		A1
1538	GRAYSON, Emily S	8	SESW	1895-06-19		A2 G21
1538	GRAYSON, James T	8	SESW	1895-06-19		A2 G21
1608	GREGORY, Ossian	5	NESE	1858-11-01		A1 G22
1609	" "	5	S½SE	1858-11-01		A1 G22
1610	" "	5	SW	1858-11-01		A1 G22
1611	" "	6	SESE	1858-11-01		A1 G22
1608	GREGORY, Susan	5	NESE	1858-11-01		A1 G22
1609	" "	5	S½SE	1858-11-01		A1 G22
1610	" "	5	SW	1858-11-01		A1 G22
1611	" "	6	SESE	1858-11-01		A1 G22
1638	HEAPE, William H	18	NWNW	1837-08-18		A1
1523	HENDRICKS, Asa	14	N½SW	1884-12-05		A2
1588	HENDRIX, Josiah S	26	E½SW	1890-07-03		A2
1593	HOLLOWAY, Martha A	26	S½SE	1883-03-01		A2
1640	HOWELL, William	19	SWNE	1838-07-28		A1
1620	JORDAN, Samuel	14	NWNE	1890-07-03		A2
1607	KELLY, Osborne	6	SWSW	1848-04-01		A1
1595	KINSEY, Martin	26	E½NE	1858-11-01		A1
1596	" "	26	NW	1858-11-01		A1
1597	" "	26	NWSE	1858-11-01		A1
1598	" "	26	SWNE	1858-11-01		A1
1641	LEWIS, William L	19	E½SW	1858-11-01		A1
1642	" "	19	W½SE	1858-11-01		A1
1572	LONG, John C	26	NESE	1889-08-16		A2
1514	LOVETT, Allen	34	S½SW	1858-11-01		A1
1619	MARSHALL, William B	14	E½NW	1860-10-01		A1 G5
1555	MATHEWS, James S	3	NENW	1854-07-15		A1
1556	" "	3	NWNE	1858-11-01		A1
1573	MATHEWS, John D	2	N½NW	1858-11-01		A1
1574	" "	2	SENW	1858-11-01		A1
1622	MATHEWS, Samuel M	2	NWSW	1854-07-15		A1
1623	" "	3	N½SE	1854-07-15		A1
1624	" "	3	NENE	1858-11-01		A1
1625	" "	3	SESE	1858-11-01		A1
1550	MCLEMORE, James J	36	E½SE	1858-11-01		A1
1577	MCPHERSON, John T	36	N½SW	1883-04-10		A2
1578	" "	36	S½SW	1883-07-03		A2
1546	MILLER, Hiram	6	SESW	1848-04-01		A1
1643	MILLER, William	18	SENW	1840-10-10		A1
1516	MOORE, Andrew	22	E½NE	1891-06-29		A2
1602	MORRELL, Nancy	34	NESW	1891-05-29		A2
1603	" "	34	SENW	1891-05-29		A2
1594	MULLANS, Martha	28	N½SE	1884-03-20		A2
1599	PARKER, Mason	28	E½NE	1888-02-04		A2
1551	PARRISH, James J	28	S½SE	1883-10-01		A2
1600	PATTON, Matthew	17	NE	1858-11-01		A1
1601	" "	8	SWSE	1858-11-01		A1
1562	PERRITT, Jehu H	32	NWNE	1901-10-08		A2
1618	PERRY, Robert	11	S½SW	1852-02-02		A1
1542	PICKENS, Ezekiel H	20	NE	1860-09-01		A1
1539	" "	18	E½NE	1896-11-21		A1
1540	" "	18	N½SE	1896-11-21		A1
1541	" "	18	SW	1896-11-21		A1
1513	POSEY, Addison J	11	E½	1858-11-01		A1
1554	POWELL, James R	14	SWNE	1854-07-15		A1
1621	POWELL, Samuel L	34	N½SE	1891-06-10		A2
1636	POWELL, William B	34	NENE	1884-03-20		A2
1645	RAINEY, William	21	NWNW	1854-07-15		A1
1575	REYNOLDS, John P	34	NWSW	1891-06-19		A2

ID	Individual in Patent	Sec.	Sec. Part	Date Issued	Other Counties	For More Info . . .
1576	REYNOLDS, John P (Cont'd)	34	SWNW	1891-06-19		A2
1627	RICHARDSON, Stephen C	28	W½NE	1860-09-01		A1
1634	ROGERS, Walter H	7	NWNW	1909-10-07		A1
1536	ROSS, Charles	22	NWNE	1883-07-03		A2
1512	SCARBOROUGH, Addison B	2	NESW	1861-05-01		A1
1632	SEALE, Thomas	18	NWNE	1837-08-14		A1
1566	SELLERS, John A	8	NENE	1896-04-23		A2
1626	SLATER, Sandom	34	S½NE	1885-04-27		A2
1568	SMITH, John B	32	NENW	1837-08-18		A1
1639	TERRELL, William H	36	W½SE	1882-12-20		A1
1518	THOMPSON, Andrew P	8	NWSE	1860-09-01		A1
1520	" "	8	SWSW	1860-09-01		A1
1521	" "	8	W½NE	1860-09-01		A1
1517	" "	8	NESW	1923-05-03		A1
1519	" "	8	SENW	1923-05-03		A1
1522	" "	8	W½NW	1923-05-03		A1
1527	THOMPSON, Augustus H	30	N½	1860-09-01		A1
1589	WALLER, Levin S	1	NE	1858-11-01		A1
1590	" "	1	SESE	1858-11-01		A1
1591	" "	1	W½SE	1858-11-01		A1
1614	WATERS, Philemon B	3	SESW	1850-08-10		A1
1612	" "	10	NW	1878-07-15		A1
1613	" "	10	W½NE	1878-07-15		A1
1606	WATTS, Noah	22	E½SE	1880-02-20		A2

Patent Map

T10-N R13-E
St Stephens Meridian

Map Group 7

Township Statistics

Parcels Mapped	:	135
Number of Patents	:	103
Number of Individuals	:	83
Patentees Identified	:	79
Number of Surnames	:	69
Multi-Patentee Parcels	:	8
Oldest Patent Date	:	5/15/1837
Most Recent Patent	:	5/3/1923
Block/Lot Parcels	:	0
Parcels Re - Issued	:	0
Parcels that Overlap	:	0
Cities and Towns	:	0
Cemeteries	:	2

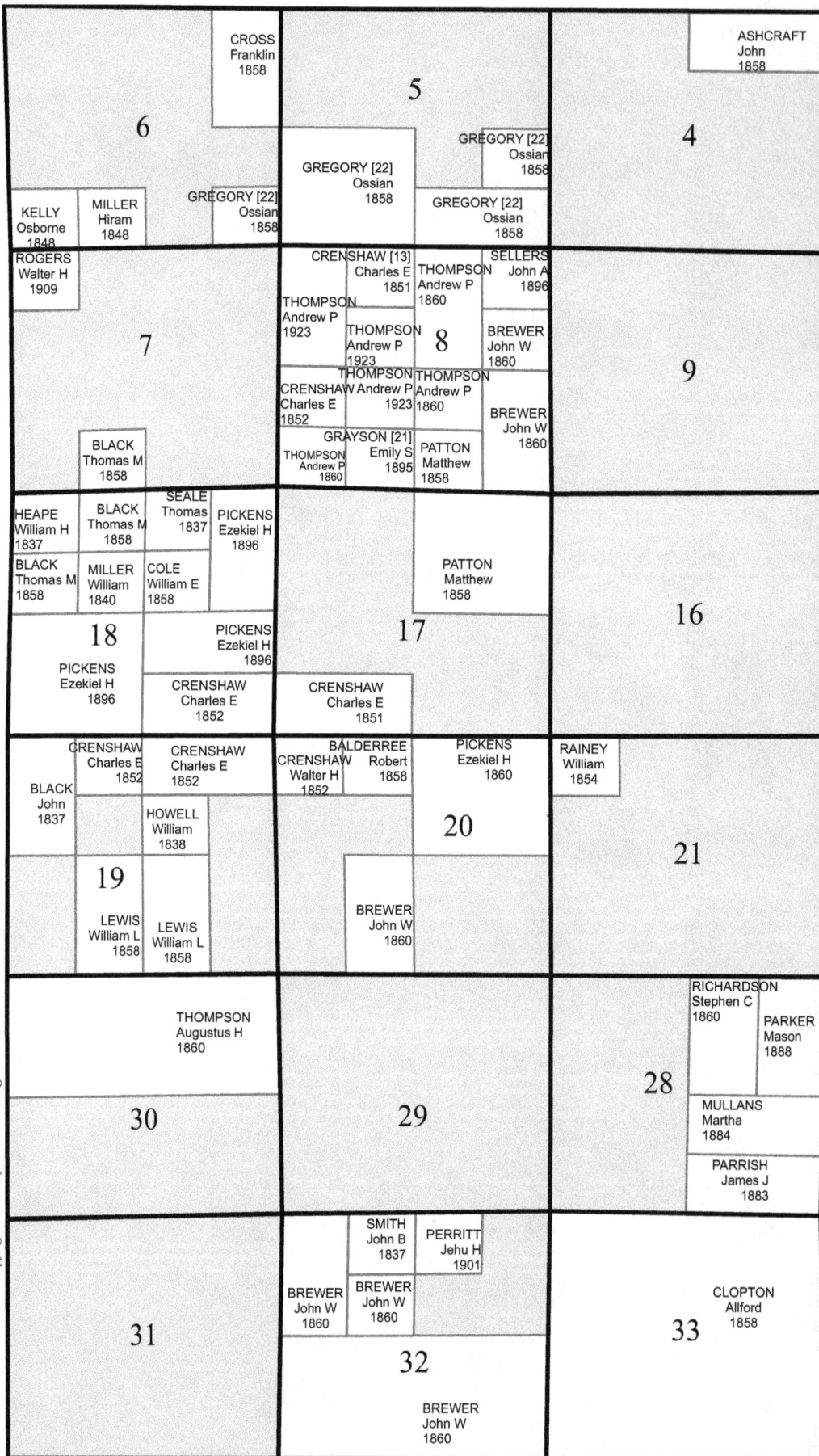

6

CROSS
Franklin
1858

5

ASHCRAFT
John
1858

GREGORY [22]
Ossian
1858

4

KELLY
Osborne
1848

MILLER
Hiram
1848

GREGORY [22]
Ossian
1858

GREGORY [22]
Ossian
1858

GREGORY [22]
Ossian
1858

ROGERS
Walter H
1909

7

CRENSHAW [13]
Charles E
1851

THOMPSON
Andrew P
1860

SELLERS
John A
1896

THOMPSON
Andrew P
1923

THOMPSON
Andrew P
1923

8

BREWER
John W
1860

9

CRENSHAW
Charles E
1852

THOMPSON
Andrew P
1923

THOMPSON
Andrew P
1860

BREWER
John W
1860

BLACK
Thomas M
1858

GRAYSON [21]
Emily S
1895

THOMPSON
Andrew P
1860

PATTON
Matthew
1858

HEAPE
William H
1837

BLACK
Thomas M
1858

SEALE
Thomas
1837

PICKENS
Ezekiel H
1896

BLACK
Thomas M
1858

MILLER
William
1840

COLE
William E
1858

PATTON
Matthew
1858

16

18

PICKENS
Ezekiel H
1896

17

PICKENS
Ezekiel H
1896

CRENSHAW
Charles E
1852

CRENSHAW
Charles E
1851

CRENSHAW
Charles E
1852

CRENSHAW
Charles E
1852

BALDERREE
Robert
1858

PICKENS
Ezekiel H
1860

RAINEY
William
1854

BLACK
John
1837

CRENSHAW
Walter H
1852

HOWELL
William
1838

20

21

19

LEWIS
William L
1858

LEWIS
William L
1858

BREWER
John W
1860

THOMPSON
Augustus H
1860

RICHARDSON
Stephen C
1860

PARKER
Mason
1888

30

29

28

MULLANS
Martha
1884

PARRISH
James J
1883

31

SMITH
John B
1837

PERRITT
Jehu H
1901

CLOPTON
Allford
1858

BREWER
John W
1860

BREWER
John W
1860

33

32

BREWER
John W
1860

MATHEWS James S 1854	MATHEWS James S 1858	MATHEWS Samuel M 1858	MATHEWS John D 1858		WALLER Levin S 1858
GARRETT Caswell 1837	BRAGG George B 1837	BREWER John W 1860	MATHEWS John D 1858	2	
3	MATHEWS Samuel M 1854	MATHEWS Samuel M 1854	SCARBOROUGH Addison B 1861		1
					WALLER Levin S 1858
WATERS Philemon B 1850	MATHEWS Samuel M 1858	CARTER William B 1860	BREWER John W 1860	BOYKIN Jesse 1837	WALLER Levin S 1858

Helpful Hints

1. This Map's INDEX can be found on the preceding pages.

2. Refer to Map "C" to see where this Township lies within Butler County, Alabama.

3. Numbers within square brackets [ ] denote a multi-patentee land parcel (multi-owner). Refer to Appendix "C" for a full list of members in this group.

4. Areas that look to be crowded with Patentees usually indicate multiple sales of the same parcel (Re-issues) or Overlapping parcels. See this Township's Index for an explanation of these and other circumstances that might explain "odd" groupings of Patentees on this map.

WATERS Philemon B 1878	WATERS Philemon B 1878	POSEY Addison J 1858	BURNETT Thomas J 1858 / COOPER Augustin 1858
FOX James M 1860 / 10	FOX James M 1860	11	12 / BOYKIN Jesse 1837
		PERRY Robert 1852	COOPER Augustin 1858 / COOPER Augustin 1858

15	BUTLER Henry H 1890	BOLLING [5] Samuel J 1860 / JORDAN Samuel 1890 / POWELL James R 1854 / BEVERLY John A 1891	13
	DAWSON Benjamin G 1889 / 14	HENDRICKS Asa 1884 / DAWSON William R 1858	

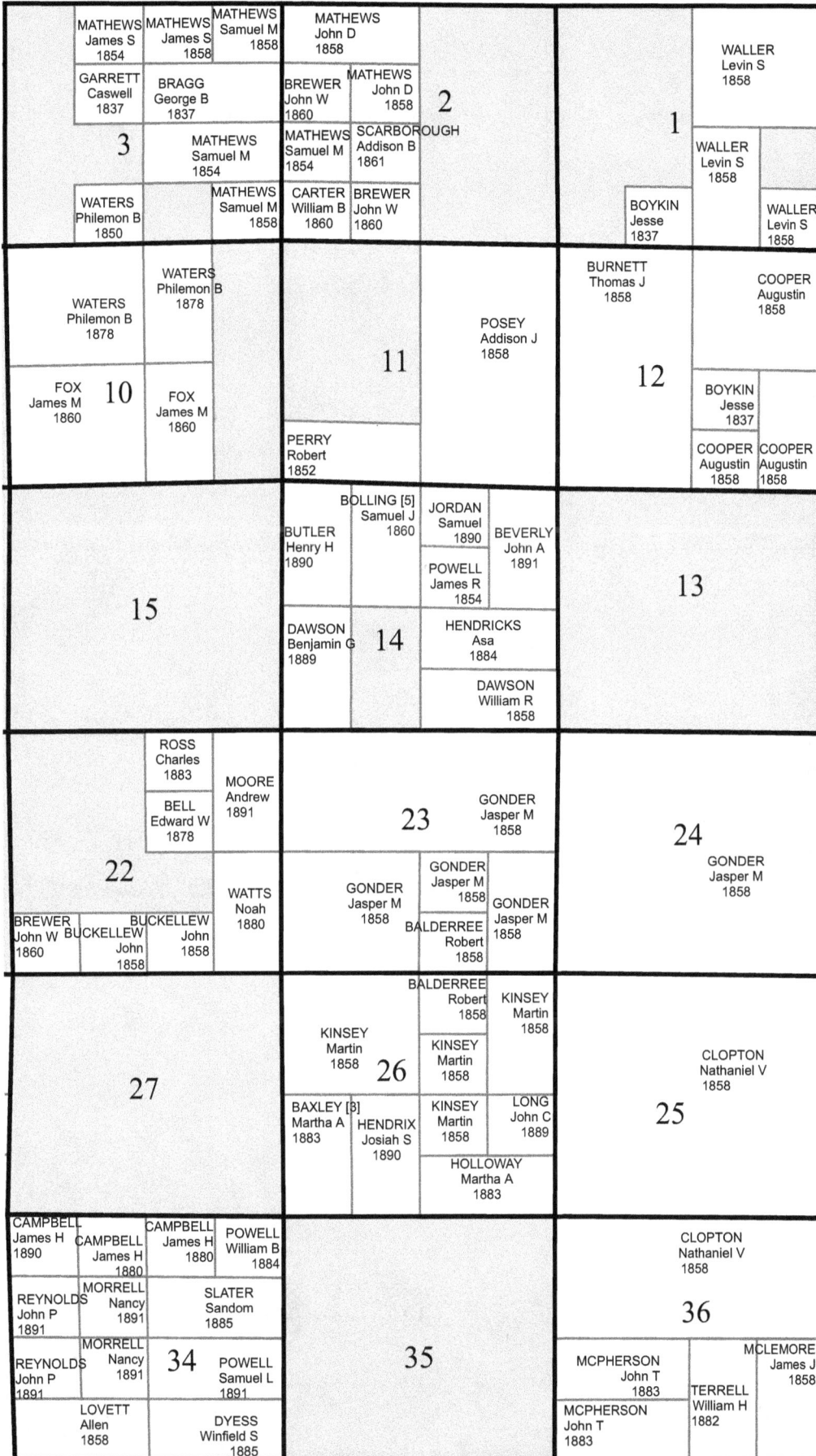

	ROSS Charles 1883 / BELL Edward W 1878 / MOORE Andrew 1891	GONDER Jasper M 1858	24
22	WATTS Noah 1880	23 / GONDER Jasper M 1858 / GONDER Jasper M 1858 / BALDERREE Robert 1858 / GONDER Jasper M 1858	GONDER Jasper M 1858
BREWER John W 1860 / BUCKELLEW John 1858 / BUCKELLEW John 1858			

27	KINSEY Martin 1858 / 26	BALDERREE Robert 1858 / KINSEY Martin 1858 / KINSEY Martin 1858 / KINSEY Martin 1858	CLOPTON Nathaniel V 1858
	BAXLEY [3] Martha A 1883 / HENDRIX Josiah S 1890	LONG John C 1889 / HOLLOWAY Martha A 1883	25

CAMPBELL James H 1890 / CAMPBELL James H 1880	CAMPBELL James H 1880 / POWELL William B 1884		CLOPTON Nathaniel V 1858
REYNOLDS John P 1891 / MORRELL Nancy 1891	SLATER Sandom 1885	35	36
REYNOLDS John P 1891 / MORRELL Nancy 1891 / 34	POWELL Samuel L 1891		MCPHERSON John T 1883 / MCLEMORE James J 1858
LOVETT Allen 1858	DYESS Winfield S 1885		MCPHERSON John T 1883 / TERRELL William H 1882

Legend

Patent Boundary

Section Boundary

No Patents Found (or Outside County)

1., 2., 3., ... Lot Numbers (when beside a name)

[ ] Group Number (see Appendix "C")

Scale: Section = 1 mile X 1 mile (generally, with some exceptions)

Road Map

T10-N R13-E
St Stephens Meridian

Map Group 7

Cities & Towns
None

Cemeteries
Hickory Grove Cemetery
Pleasant Home Cemetery

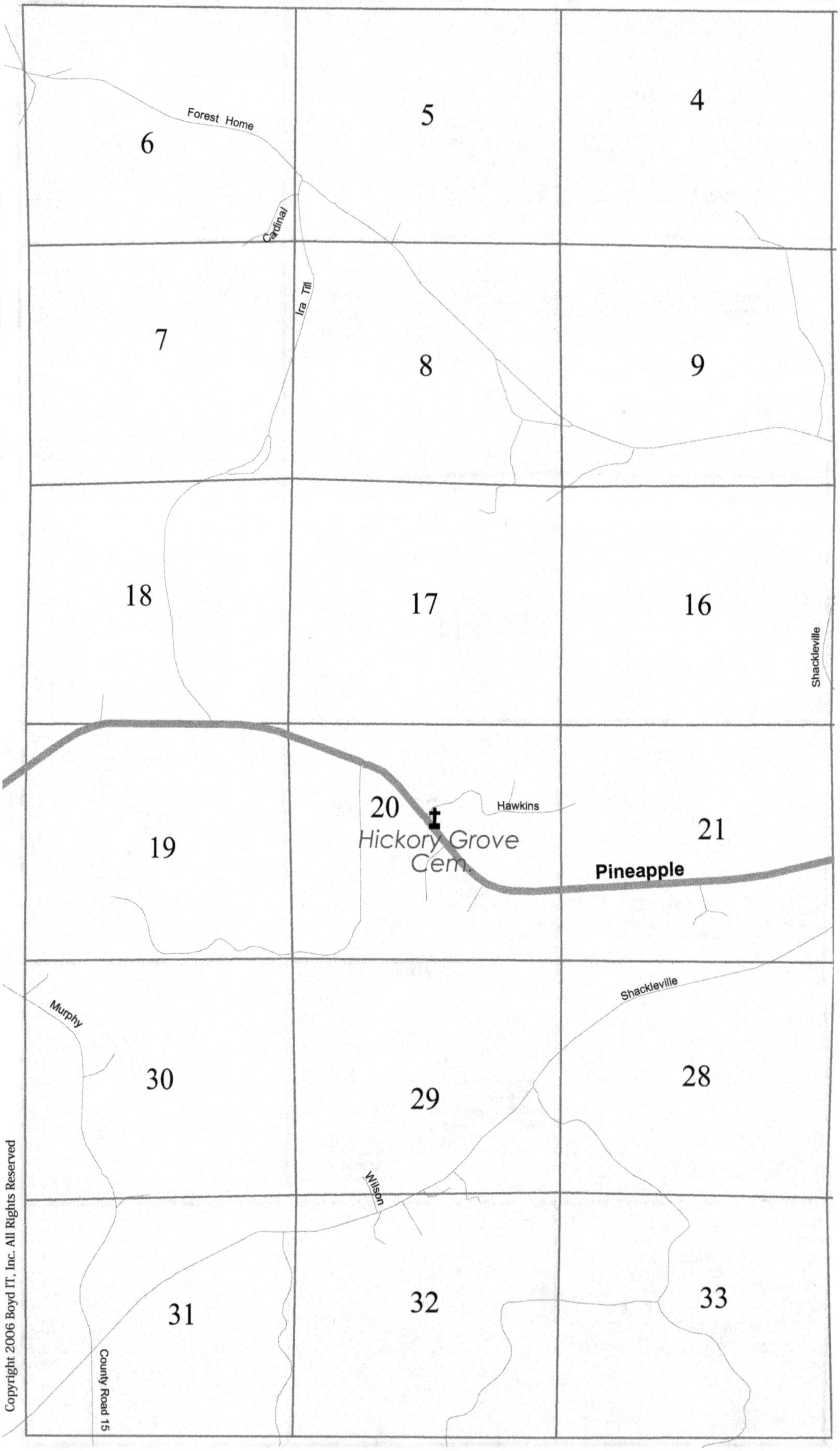

6

5

4

Forest Home

Cardinal

Ira Till

7

8

9

18

17

16

Shackleville

20

Hickory Grove Cem.

Hawkins

21

Pineapple

19

Murphy

Shackleville

30

29

28

Wilson

31

32

33

County Road 15

3

2

1

Manningham

Perry Luckie

Sandy Lane

Ridge

10

11

12

Forest Home

Forest Home

Conservation

14

13

Pleasant Home ✝ Cem.

15

Smith

High

Coach

Atchison

Car Lot

22

23

24

County Road 25

26

27

25

Wasden

Sandcutt

Vickery

34

35

36

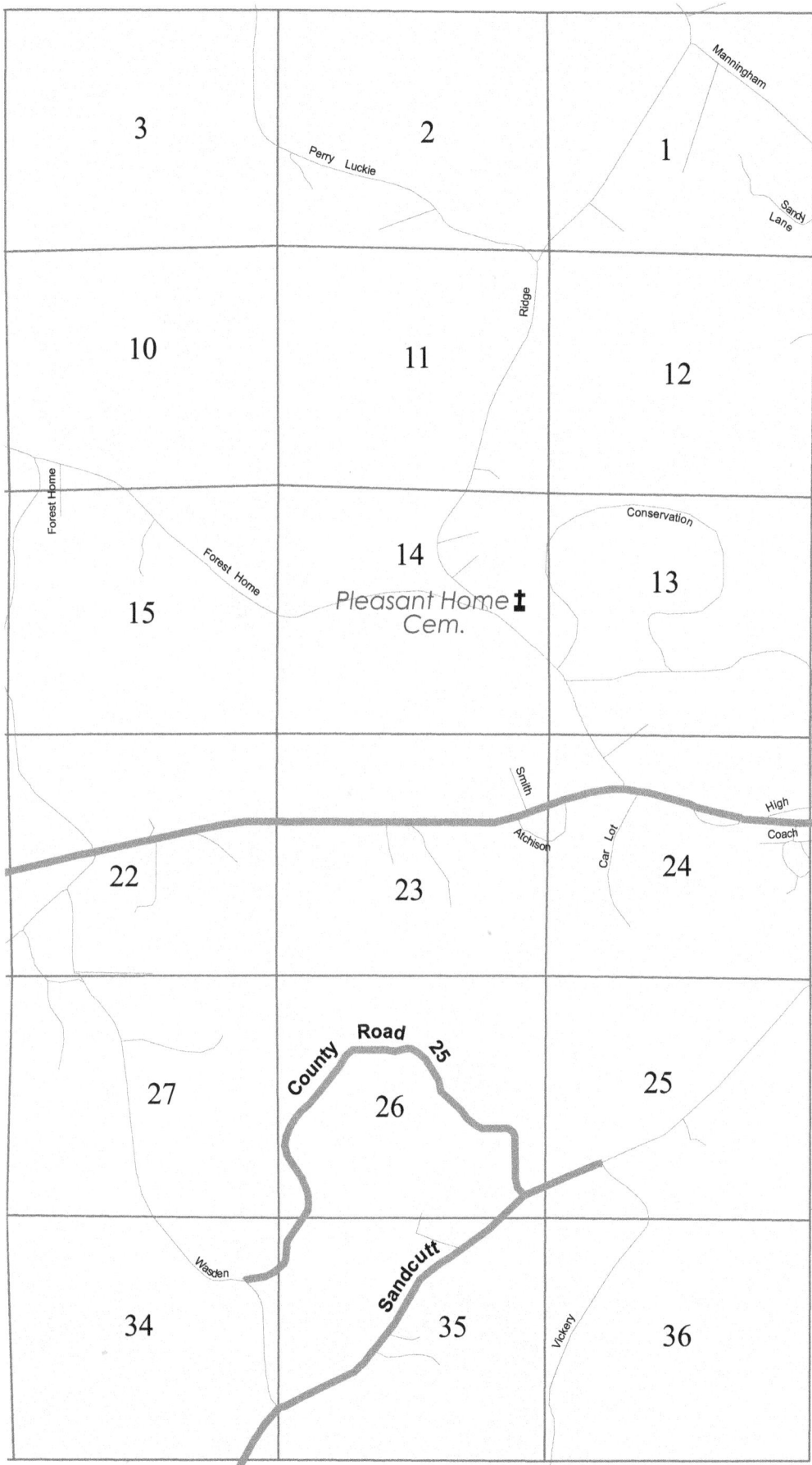

Helpful Hints

1. This road map has a number of uses, but primarily it is to help you: a) find the present location of land owned by your ancestors (at least the general area), b) find cemeteries and city-centers, and c) estimate the route/roads used by Census-takers & tax-assessors.

2. If you plan to travel to Butler County to locate cemeteries or land parcels, please pick up a modern travel map for the area before you do. Mapping old land parcels on modern maps is not as exact a science as you might think. Just the slightest variations in public land survey coordinates, estimates of parcel boundaries, or road-map deviations can greatly alter a map's representation of how a road either does or doesn't cross a particular parcel of land.

Legend

Section Lines
Interstates
Highways
Other Roads
● Cities/Towns
✝ Cemeteries

Scale: Section = 1 mile X 1 mile
(generally, with some exceptions)

Historical Map

T10-N R13-E
St Stephens Meridian

Map Group 7

Cities & Towns
None

Cemeteries
Hickory Grove Cemetery
Pleasant Home Cemetery

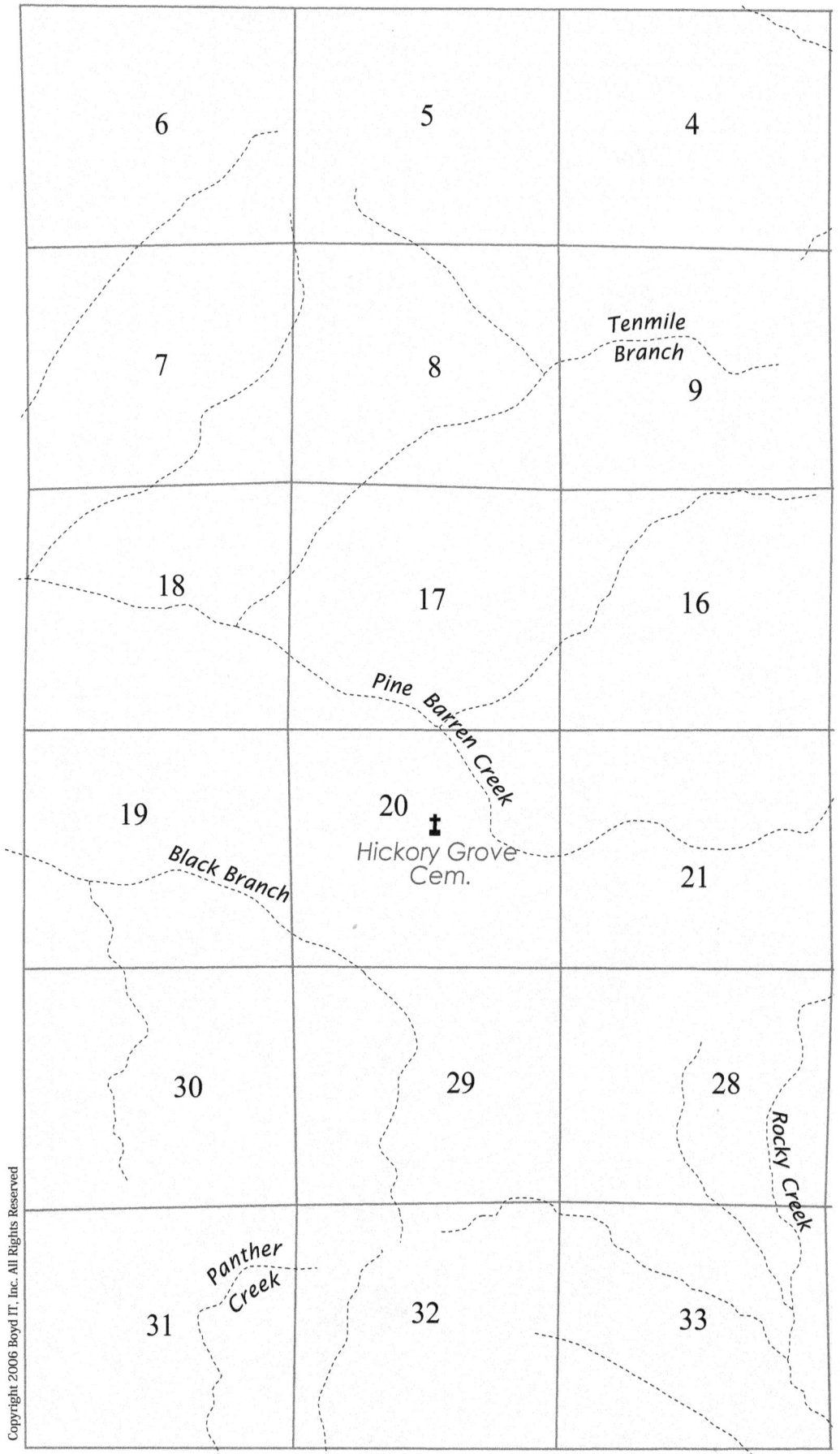

6	5	4
7	8	Tenmile Branch 9
18	17	16
19	20 ✝ Hickory Grove Cem.	21
30	29	28
31	32	33

Pine Barren Creek

Black Branch

Panther Creek

Rocky Creek

122

3

2

Wolf Creek

1

10

11

12

15

14

Pleasant Home ✝ Cem.

13

22

23

24

27

26

25

Beaver Creek

34

35

Clear Creek

36

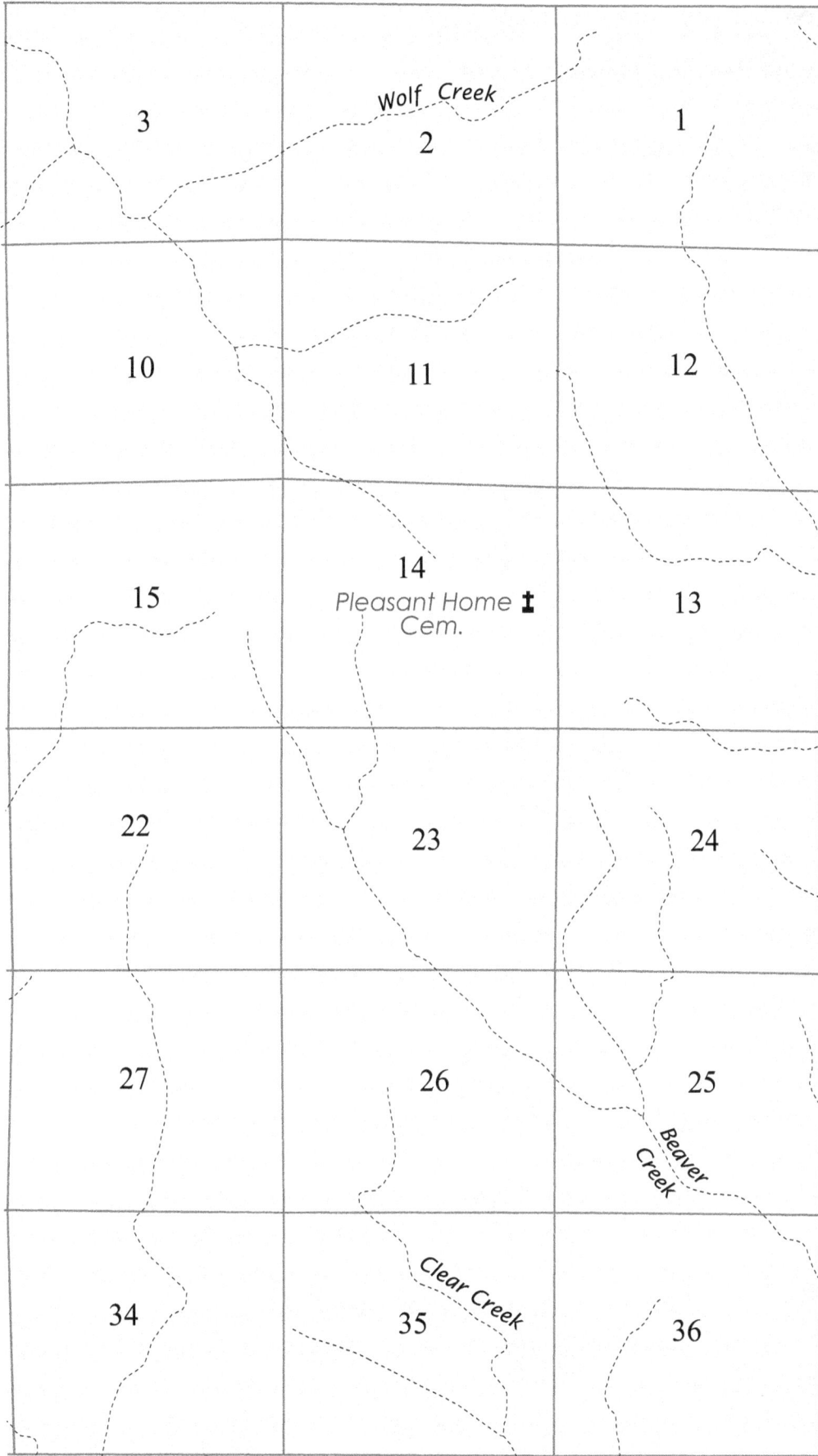

Helpful Hints

1. This Map takes a different look at the same Congressional Township displayed in the preceding two maps. It presents features that can help you better envision the historical development of the area: a) Water-bodies (lakes & ponds), b) Water-courses (rivers, streams, etc.), c) Railroads, d) City/town center-points (where they were oftentimes located when first settled), and e) Cemeteries.

2. Using this "Historical" map in tandem with this Township's Patent Map and Road Map, may lead you to some interesting discoveries. You will often find roads, towns, cemeteries, and waterways are named after nearby landowners: sometimes those names will be the ones you are researching. See how many of these research gems you can find here in Butler County.

L e g e n d

―――――― Section Lines

+++++++ Railroads

Large Rivers & Bodies of Water

------------ Streams/Creeks & Small Rivers

● Cities/Towns

✝ Cemeteries

Scale: Section = 1 mile X 1 mile
(there are some exceptions)

Map Group 8: Index to Land Patents

Township 10-North Range 14-East (St Stephens)

After you locate an individual in this Index, take note of the Section and Section Part then proceed to the Land Patent map on the pages immediately following. You should have no difficulty locating the corresponding parcel of land.

The "For More Info" Column will lead you to more information about the underlying Patents. See the *Legend* at right, and the "How to Use this Book" chapter, for more information.

```
                          LEGEND
             "For More Info . . . " column
A = Authority (Legislative Act, See Appendix "A")
B = Block or Lot (location in Section unknown)
C = Cancelled Patent
F = Fractional Section
G = Group  (Multi-Patentee Patent, see Appendix "C")
V = Overlaps another Parcel
R = Re-Issued (Parcel patented more than once)

(A & G items require you to look in the Appendixes referred
to above. All other Letter-designations followed by a number
require you to locate line-items in this index that possess
the ID number found after the letter).
```

ID	Individual in Patent	Sec.	Sec. Part	Date Issued	Other Counties	For More Info . . .
1703	ALLEN, Gideon	28	NWNE	1835-10-01		A1
1708	" "	29	SENE	1835-10-01		A1
1705	" "	28	SWNE	1852-02-02		A1
1704	" "	28	NWSW	1858-11-01		A1
1706	" "	28	W½NW	1858-11-01		A1
1707	" "	29	E½SE	1858-11-01		A1
1709	" "	29	SWSE	1858-11-01		A1
1653	BECKWORTH, Amos	36	SESW	1838-07-28		A1
1744	BOLLING, John	34	SE	1858-11-01		A1
1745	" "	34	SENE	1858-11-01		A1
1746	" "	35	SESW	1858-11-01		A1
1747	" "	35	SWNW	1858-11-01		A1
1748	" "	35	W½SW	1858-11-01		A1
1786	BOLLING, Samuel J	24	NENE	1835-04-02		A1
1787	" "	24	NESE	1852-02-02		A1
1788	" "	29	NENE	1854-07-15		A1
1814	BONNER, William	5	W½SE	1826-05-08		A1
1670	BRIERS, Bazzillia L	31	N½	1858-11-01		A1
1830	BRIERS, William K	30	S½	1858-11-01		A1
1702	BURNETT, George M	2	SWSW	1838-07-28		A1
1816	BURNETT, William	10	NWNE	1834-06-12		A1
1819	" "	15	NWSE	1835-04-02		A1
1821	" "	3	SESE	1835-04-02		A1
1817	" "	10	SWNE	1837-04-10		A1
1818	" "	11	E½NE	1837-04-10		A1
1822	" "	3	W½SE	1837-08-02		A1
1815	" "	10	E½NE	1837-08-07		A1
1820	" "	2	E½SW	1837-08-12		A1
1810	CARY, William A	20	NESW	1838-07-28		A1
1811	" "	20	SENW	1838-07-28		A1
1812	" "	24	SWNE	1838-07-28		A1
1813	" "	26	SWNE	1838-07-28		A1
1682	CHATHAM, Daniel H	19	NENE	1858-11-01		A1
1683	" "	19	NWNW	1858-11-01		A1
1684	" "	19	S½NW	1858-11-01		A1
1685	" "	19	SWNE	1858-11-01		A1
1673	CHEATHAM, Daniel	19	SENE	1854-10-02		A1
1674	" "	19	SESE	1854-10-02		A1
1686	CHEATHAM, Daniel H	19	NWSE	1858-11-01		A1
1687	" "	20	NESE	1858-11-01		A1
1688	" "	30	NENE	1858-11-01		A1
1689	" "	30	SWNE	1858-11-01		A1
1802	COOK, Thomas F	32	S½	1858-11-01		A1
1669	COOPER, Augustin	7	SWNW	1858-11-01		A1
1727	CRAIG, James	36	W½NE	1832-09-10		A1
1723	" "	35	E½NE	1837-08-14		A1

ID	Individual in Patent	Sec.	Sec. Part	Date Issued	Other Counties	For More Info . . .
1724	CRAIG, James (Cont'd)	35	NWNE	1837-08-14		A1
1726	" "	36	NWSE	1837-08-14		A1
1725	" "	36	NESW	1849-09-01		A1
1827	CRAIG, William G	35	NWSE	1858-11-01		A1
1828	" "	35	SWNE	1858-11-01		A1
1823	DAVIDSON, William	27	NESW	1858-09-01		A1
1824	" "	27	S½SW	1858-11-01		A1
1825	" "	27	W½SE	1858-11-01		A1
1826	" "	34	NWNE	1858-11-01		A1
1800	DEMING, Simeon	23	SENW	1834-10-21		A1
1801	" "	23	SWNW	1834-10-21		A1
1764	DRIVER, Leroy	31	S½	1858-11-01		A1
1647	EVANS, Alexander B	30	NWNE	1848-04-01		A1
1762	EVANS, Joshua W	28	SESE	1858-11-01		A1
1763	" "	33	SW	1858-11-01		A1
1692	FERGUSON, Darius J	7	SWNE	1850-04-01		A1
1690	" "	7	E½NW	1858-11-01		A1
1691	" "	7	NWNW	1858-11-01		A1
1675	GAFFORD, Daniel	1	SW	1834-10-21		A1
1678	" "	12	NE	1834-10-21		A1
1680	" "	2	E½SE	1834-10-21		A1
1676	" "	11	W½NE	1837-08-07		A1
1679	" "	12	W½NW	1837-08-07		A1
1681	" "	2	W½NE	1837-08-07		A1
1677	" "	12	E½NW	1837-08-15		A1
1729	GAFFORD, James M	6	SWNW	1852-02-02		A1
1700	GARRETT, George A	5	W½NW	1841-05-20		A1
1722	GARRETT, James C	6	E½NW	1837-08-12		A1
1730	GARRETT, James O	5	E½NW	1837-08-12		A1
1832	GARRETT, William P	6	NWNW	1848-05-03		A1
1841	GIDDENS, William R	18	NWSE	1858-11-01		A1
1842	" "	18	S½NW	1858-11-01		A1
1843	" "	18	SWNE	1858-11-01		A1
1699	GOLDSTON, Elizabeth	26	E½SW	1823-10-01		A1
1829	HALL, William	19	NESE	1838-07-28		A1
1852	HAMMONS, William W	19	SWSE	1848-05-03		A1
1752	HARTLEY, John R	3	W½NE	1837-08-02		A1
1753	" "	3	W½NW	1837-08-02		A1
1715	HERBERT, Hillary	11	W½SE	1834-05-12		A1
1716	" "	14	NW	1834-05-12		A1
1720	" "	3	SW	1834-05-12		A1
1714	" "	11	NW	1835-09-19		A1
1717	" "	2	NWSW	1858-11-01		A1
1718	" "	3	NESE	1858-11-01		A1
1719	" "	3	SENE	1858-11-01		A1
1807	HERBERT, Thomas S	22	E½NE	1834-06-12		A1
1728	HOLMES, James	15	E½SE	1833-08-02		A1
1777	HUTCHINSON, Parr	7	NWNE	1838-07-28		A1
1778	" "	7	SENE	1838-07-28		A1
1756	JONES, Joseph	22	SESE	1850-08-10		A1
1768	JUDGE, Mary H	17	NESE	1835-04-02		A1
1701	LOGAN, George A	19	SESW	1848-04-01		A1 G27
1831	MARTIN, William	19	NENW	1858-11-01		A1
1805	MCDANIEL, Thomas	24	W½SW	1825-04-09		A1 G30
1804	" "	28	W½SE	1825-04-09		A1
1803	" "	28	E½SW	1825-06-06		A1
1696	MCQUEEN, Eliza	19	N½SW	1858-11-01		A1
1697	" "	30	SENW	1858-11-01		A1
1698	" "	30	W½NW	1858-11-01		A1
1710	OLIVER, Henry	22	SWSW	1852-02-02		A1 G34
1711	" "	27	NWNW	1852-02-02		A1 G34
1712	OLIVER, Henry P	27	SWNW	1852-12-01		A1 G33
1790	OLIVER, Samuel	15	S½NE	1837-04-10		A1
1793	" "	23	NWNW	1837-04-10		A1
1789	" "	13	E½SE	1837-08-12		A1
1791	" "	15	W½SW	1843-02-01		A1
1792	" "	22	W½SE	1848-04-01		A1
1710	" "	22	SWSW	1852-02-02		A1 G34
1711	" "	27	NWNW	1852-02-02		A1 G34
1712	" "	27	SWNW	1852-12-01		A1 G33
1758	PARMER, Joseph M	23	W½SW	1837-08-12		A1
1759	" "	26	E½NW	1837-08-12		A1
1757	" "	13	NWSE	1838-07-28		A1

ID	Individual in Patent	Sec.	Sec. Part	Date Issued	Other Counties	For More Info . . .
1776	PARMER, Milton	11	E½SE	1837-08-09		A1
1701	PAYNE, William	19	SESW	1848-04-01		A1 G27
1774	PEEVY, Michael	5	E½SE	1825-06-06		A1
1806	PEEVY, Thomas	7	SESE	1849-09-01		A1
1749	PERDUE, John	22	E½SW	1823-10-01		A1
1750	" "	27	E½NW	1823-10-01		A1
1751	" "	27	NE	1823-10-01		A1
1731	PETERGRO, James	25	NWSE	1837-08-12		A1
1775	PEVY, Michael	7	NENE	1834-09-04		A1 G37
1721	PIERCE, Hubbell	25	SW	1837-08-10		A1
1649	REDDOCH, Alexander	20	SESW	1835-10-15		A1
1650	" "	30	SENE	1835-10-15		A1
1648	" "	17	SESE	1837-08-08		A1
1754	REDDOCH, John	24	SESE	1837-08-02		A1
1652	REDDOCK, Alexander	20	W½SW	1824-03-01		A1
1651	" "	20	W½SE	1826-07-10		A1
1755	REDDOCK, John	28	E½NW	1825-04-09		A1
1798	REDDOCK, Sarah M	28	SWSW	1858-11-01		A1
1799	" "	33	NWNW	1858-11-01		A1
1844	REDDOCK, William	17	SESW	1838-07-28		A1
1845	" "	20	NENW	1838-07-28		A1
1854	REDDOCK, William W	30	NENW	1848-05-03		A1
1853	" "	19	SWSW	1850-04-01		A1
1657	REID, Archibald M	26	W½NW	1837-08-12		A1 C R1733
1783	REID, Robert	22	NESE	1837-08-12		A1
1784	" "	22	SWNE	1837-08-12		A1
1671	RHODES, Berry	20	SESE	1858-11-01		A1
1672	" "	29	SENW	1858-11-01		A1
1795	RHODES, Sanford	35	E½SE	1858-09-01		A1
1796	" "	35	SWSE	1858-09-01		A1
1797	" "	36	W½SW	1858-09-01		A1
1833	ROUTON, William P	26	NENE	1835-09-12		A1
1835	" "	26	SE	1837-08-12		A1
1834	" "	26	NWNE	1837-08-14		A1
1836	" "	26	SENE	1858-11-01		A1
1837	" "	26	W½SW	1858-11-01		A1
1838	" "	27	E½SE	1858-11-01		A1
1839	" "	34	NENE	1858-11-01		A1
1840	" "	35	N½NW	1858-11-01		A1
1805	RUGELEY, Henry	24	W½SW	1825-04-09		A1 G30
1713	" "	24	E½SW	1825-04-16		A1
1732	SEAL, James	18	E½SE	1822-01-01		A1
1779	SEAL, Ranson	20	W½NW	1825-06-06		A1
1656	SEALE, Anderson	17	W½SE	1835-11-20		A1 V1655, 1847
1654	" "	17	E½NE	1837-05-15		A1
1655	" "	17	NWSE	1841-05-20		A1 V1656
1780	SEALE, Reuben H	18	NWNW	1858-11-01		A1
1781	" "	7	S½SW	1858-11-01		A1
1782	" "	7	SWSE	1858-11-01		A1
1846	SEALE, William	17	NESW	1852-02-02		A1
1847	" "	17	SWSE	1858-11-01		A1 V1656
1848	" "	18	E½NE	1858-11-01		A1
1849	" "	18	NENW	1858-11-01		A1
1850	" "	18	NWNE	1858-11-01		A1
1855	SEALE, Wilson M	17	SWSW	1858-11-01		A1
1851	SIMS, William	25	SWSE	1835-09-12		A1
1660	SKINNER, Ariss	18	SWSE	1858-11-01		A1
1661	" "	19	NWNE	1858-11-01		A1
1662	SKINNER, Asa	17	NWSW	1854-10-02		A1
1663	" "	29	N½SW	1858-11-01		A1
1664	" "	29	NENW	1858-11-01		A1
1665	" "	29	NWSE	1858-11-01		A1
1666	" "	29	SESW	1858-11-01		A1
1667	" "	29	SWNW	1858-11-01		A1
1668	" "	29	W½NE	1858-11-01		A1
1785	SMITH, Robert	36	SWSE	1848-05-03		A1
1761	SMYTH, Joseph	36	E½SE	1826-05-05		A1
1658	STALLINGS, Archy R	7	N½SW	1858-11-01		A1
1659	" "	7	NWSE	1858-11-01		A1
1742	STALLINGS, Jesse	15	NWNE	1834-05-12		A1
1740	" "	10	W½SW	1835-04-02		A1
1741	" "	15	NENE	1837-08-02		A1
1743	" "	7	NESE	1849-09-01		A1

ID	Individual in Patent	Sec.	Sec. Part	Date Issued	Other Counties	For More Info . . .
1693	TAYLOR, Elias	21	E½NE	1835-04-02		A1
1694	" "	22	NWNE	1835-04-02		A1
1695	" "	22	W½NW	1835-04-02		A1
1760	TAYLOR, Joseph M	24	W½SE	1826-05-05		A1
1808	TAYLOR, Ward	13	SWSE	1834-09-04		A1
1809	" "	24	NWNE	1834-09-04		A1
1733	TIGNER, James	26	W½NW	1837-08-12		A1 R1657
1794	VANN, Sanders R	32	N½	1858-11-01		A1
1734	WADE, James W	23	E½SW	1835-04-15		A1
1735	" "	23	NENW	1835-09-19		A1
1736	" "	5	SENE	1835-09-19		A1
1771	WADE, Micajah	4	W½SE	1835-04-02		A1
1772	" "	5	NENE	1835-10-16		A1
1770	" "	4	E½SW	1837-05-15		A1
1773	" "	5	W½NE	1837-05-15		A1
1769	" "	3	NENE	1837-08-12		A1
1737	WALKER, James	18	N½SW	1858-11-01		A1
1738	" "	18	S½SW	1858-11-01		A1
1775	WALLER, James	7	NENE	1834-09-04		A1 G37
1765	WALLER, Leven	6	NESW	1837-08-12		A1
1766	" "	6	NWSW	1838-07-28		A1
1767	WALLER, Levin S	6	S½SW	1854-07-15		A1
1739	WATSON, James	15	SWSE	1835-10-16		A1

Patent Map

T10-N R14-E
St Stephens Meridian

Map Group 8

Township Statistics

Parcels Mapped	:	209
Number of Patents	:	168
Number of Individuals	:	94
Patentees Identified	:	93
Number of Surnames	:	61
Multi-Patentee Parcels	:	6
Oldest Patent Date	:	1/1/1822
Most Recent Patent	:	11/1/1858
Block/Lot Parcels	:	0
Parcels Re - Issued	:	1
Parcels that Overlap	:	3
Cities and Towns	:	3
Cemeteries	:	7

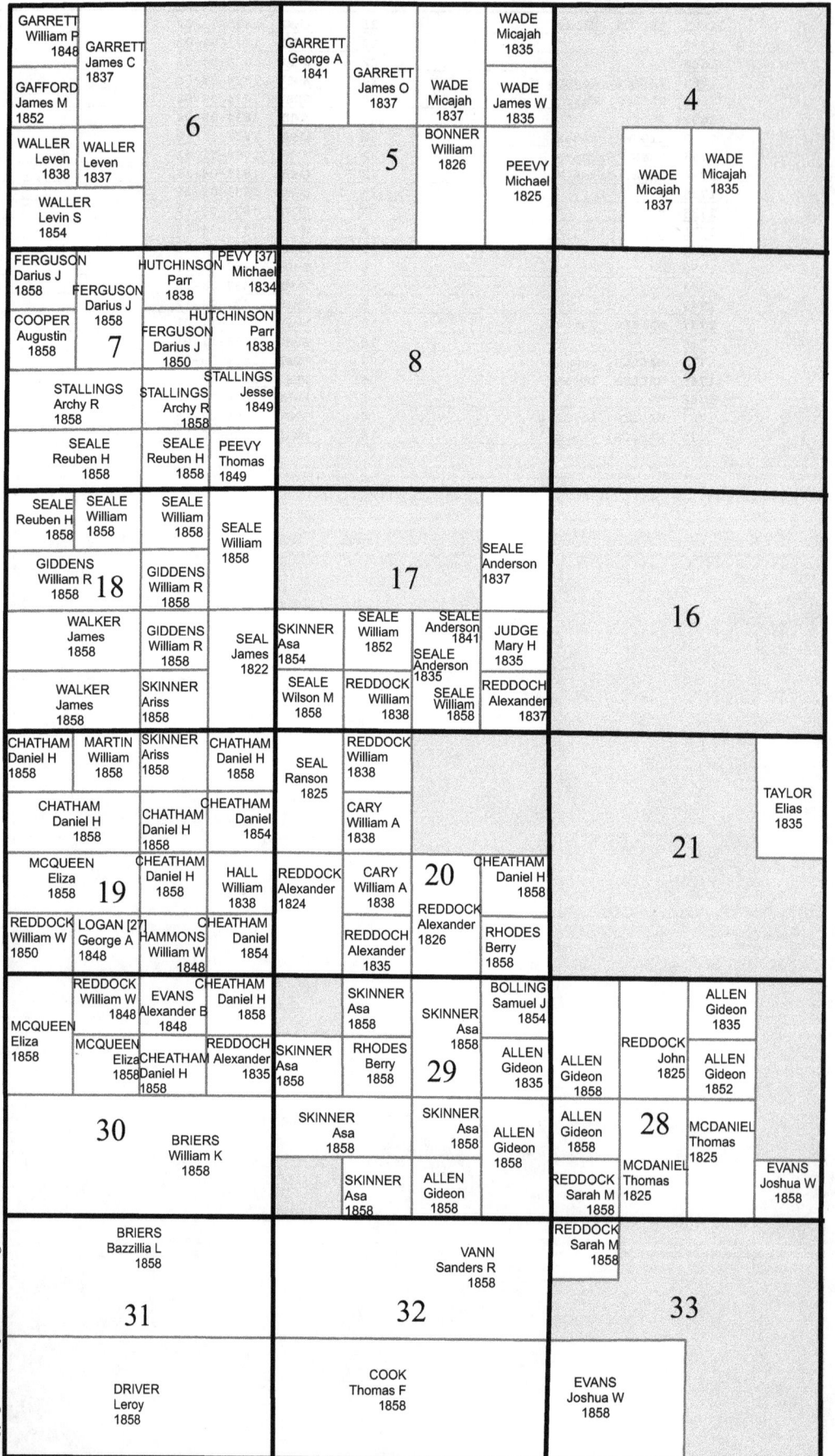

Section 6:
GARRETT William P 1848
GARRETT James C 1837
GAFFORD James M 1852
WALLER Leven 1838
WALLER Leven 1837
WALLER Levin S 1854

Section 5:
GARRETT George A 1841
GARRETT James O 1837
WADE Micajah 1835
WADE Micajah 1837
WADE James W 1835
BONNER William 1826
PEEVY Michael 1825

Section 4:
WADE Micajah 1837
WADE Micajah 1835

Section 7:
FERGUSON Darius J 1858
FERGUSON Darius J 1858
COOPER Augustin 1858
HUTCHINSON Parr 1838
PEVY [37] Michael 1834
FERGUSON Darius J 1850
HUTCHINSON Parr 1838
STALLINGS Archy R 1858
STALLINGS Archy R 1858
STALLINGS Jesse 1849
SEALE Reuben H 1858
SEALE Reuben H 1858
PEEVY Thomas 1849

Section 8

Section 9

Section 18:
SEALE Reuben H 1858
SEALE William 1858
SEALE William 1858
SEALE William 1858
GIDDENS William R 1858
GIDDENS William R 1858
WALKER James 1858
GIDDENS William R 1858
SEAL James 1822
WALKER James 1858
SKINNER Ariss 1858

Section 17:
SEALE Anderson 1837
SKINNER Asa 1854
SEALE William 1852
SEALE Anderson 1841
SEALE Anderson 1835
JUDGE Mary H 1835
SEALE Wilson M 1858
REDDOCK William 1838
SEALE William 1858
REDDOCH Alexander 1837

Section 16

Section 19:
CHATHAM Daniel H 1858
MARTIN William 1858
SKINNER Ariss 1858
CHATHAM Daniel H 1858
CHATHAM Daniel H 1858
CHATHAM Daniel H 1858
CHEATHAM Daniel 1854
MCQUEEN Eliza 1858
CHEATHAM Daniel H 1858
HALL William 1838
REDDOCK William W 1850
LOGAN [27] George A 1848
HAMMONS William W 1848
CHEATHAM Daniel 1854

Section 20:
SEAL Ranson 1825
REDDOCK William 1838
CARY William A 1838
REDDOCK Alexander 1824
CARY William A 1838
REDDOCH Alexander 1835
CHEATHAM Daniel H 1858
REDDOCK Alexander 1826
RHODES Berry 1858

Section 21:
TAYLOR Elias 1835

Section 30:
REDDOCK William W 1848
EVANS Alexander B 1848
CHEATHAM Daniel H 1858
MCQUEEN Eliza 1858
MCQUEEN Eliza 1858
CHEATHAM Daniel H 1858
REDDOCH Alexander 1835

Section 29:
SKINNER Asa 1858
SKINNER Asa 1858
BOLLING Samuel J 1854
SKINNER Asa 1858
RHODES Berry 1858
ALLEN Gideon 1835
SKINNER Asa 1858
SKINNER Asa 1858
SKINNER Asa 1858
ALLEN Gideon 1858

Section 28:
ALLEN Gideon 1835
REDDOCK John 1825
ALLEN Gideon 1852
ALLEN Gideon 1858
ALLEN Gideon 1858
REDDOCK Sarah M 1858
MCDANIEL Thomas 1825
MCDANIEL Thomas 1825
EVANS Joshua W 1858

Section 31:
BRIERS William K 1858
BRIERS Bazzillia L 1858
DRIVER Leroy 1858

Section 32:
VANN Sanders R 1858
COOK Thomas F 1858

Section 33:
REDDOCK Sarah M 1858
EVANS Joshua W 1858

Section 3
HARTLEY John R 1837
HARTLEY John R 1837
WADE Micajah 1837
HERBERT Hillary 1858
HERBERT Hillary 1834
BURNETT William 1837
HERBERT Hillary 1858
HERBERT Hillary 1858
BURNETT William 1835
BURNETT George M 1838

Section 2
GAFFORD Daniel 1837
BURNETT William 1837

Section 1
GAFFORD Daniel 1834
GAFFORD Daniel 1834

Section 10
BURNETT William 1834
BURNETT William 1837
BURNETT William 1837
HERBERT Hillary 1835
STALLINGS Jesse 1835

Section 11
GAFFORD Daniel 1837
PARMER Milton 1837
HERBERT Hillary 1834

Section 12
BURNETT William 1837
GAFFORD Daniel 1837
GAFFORD Daniel 1837
GAFFORD Daniel 1834

Section 15
STALLINGS Jesse 1834
STALLINGS Jesse 1837
OLIVER Samuel 1837
OLIVER Samuel 1843
BURNETT William 1835
HOLMES James 1833
WATSON James 1835

Section 14
HERBERT Hillary 1834

Section 13
PARMER Joseph M 1838
TAYLOR Ward 1834
OLIVER Samuel 1837

Section 22
TAYLOR Elias 1835
REID Robert 1837
HERBERT Thomas S 1834
TAYLOR Elias 1835
PERDUE John 1823
REID Robert 1837
OLIVER [34] Henry 1852
OLIVER Samuel 1848
JONES Joseph 1850

Section 23
OLIVER Samuel 1837
WADE James W 1835
DEMING Simeon 1834
DEMING Simeon 1834
WADE James W 1835
PARMER Joseph M 1837

Section 24
TAYLOR Ward 1834
BOLLING Samuel J 1835
CARY William A 1838
MCDANIEL Thomas 1825
[30]
RUGELEY Henry 1825
TAYLOR Joseph M 1826
BOLLING Samuel J 1852
REDDOCH John 1837

Section 27
OLIVER [34] Henry 1852
PERDUE John 1823
OLIVER [33] Henry P 1852
PERDUE John 1823
DAVIDSON William 1858
DAVIDSON William 1858
DAVIDSON William 1858
ROUTON William P 1858

Section 26
PARMER Joseph M 1837
REID Archibald M 1837
TIGNER James 1837
ROUTON William P 1837
CARY William A 1838
ROUTON William P 1858
ROUTON William P 1858
GOLDSTON Elizabeth 1823

Section 25
ROUTON William P 1835
ROUTON William P 1837
PETERGRO James 1837
PIERCE Hubbell 1837
SIMS William 1835

Section 34
DAVIDSON William 1858
ROUTON William P 1858
BOLLING John 1858
BOLLING John 1858

Section 35
ROUTON William P 1858
BOLLING John 1858
BOLLING John 1858
CRAIG James 1837
CRAIG William G 1858
CRAIG William G 1858
RHODES Sanford 1858

Section 36
CRAIG James 1837
CRAIG James 1832
CRAIG James 1849
CRAIG James 1837
SMYTH Joseph 1826
RHODES Sanford 1858
BECKWORTH Amos 1838
SMITH Robert 1848

Copyright 2006 Boyd IT, Inc. All Rights Reserved

Helpful Hints

1. This Map's INDEX can be found on the preceding pages.

2. Refer to Map "C" to see where this Township lies within Butler County, Alabama.

3. Numbers within square brackets [ ] denote a multi-patentee land parcel (multi-owner). Refer to Appendix "C" for a full list of members in this group.

4. Areas that look to be crowded with Patentees usually indicate multiple sales of the same parcel (Re-issues) or Overlapping parcels. See this Township's Index for an explanation of these and other circumstances that might explain "odd" groupings of Patentees on this map.

Legend

—————— Patent Boundary

━━━━━━ Section Boundary

No Patents Found (or Outside County)

1., 2., 3., ... Lot Numbers (when beside a name)

[ ] Group Number (see Appendix "C")

Scale: Section = 1 mile X 1 mile (generally, with some exceptions)

Road Map

T10-N R14-E
St Stephens Meridian

Map Group 8

Cities & Towns
Greenville
Liberty
Reddock Springs

Cemeteries
Giddens Chapel Cemetery
Hartley Cemetery
Liberty Cemetery
Magnolia Cemetery
Pioneer Cemetery
Sunrise Cemetery
William Seale Cemetery

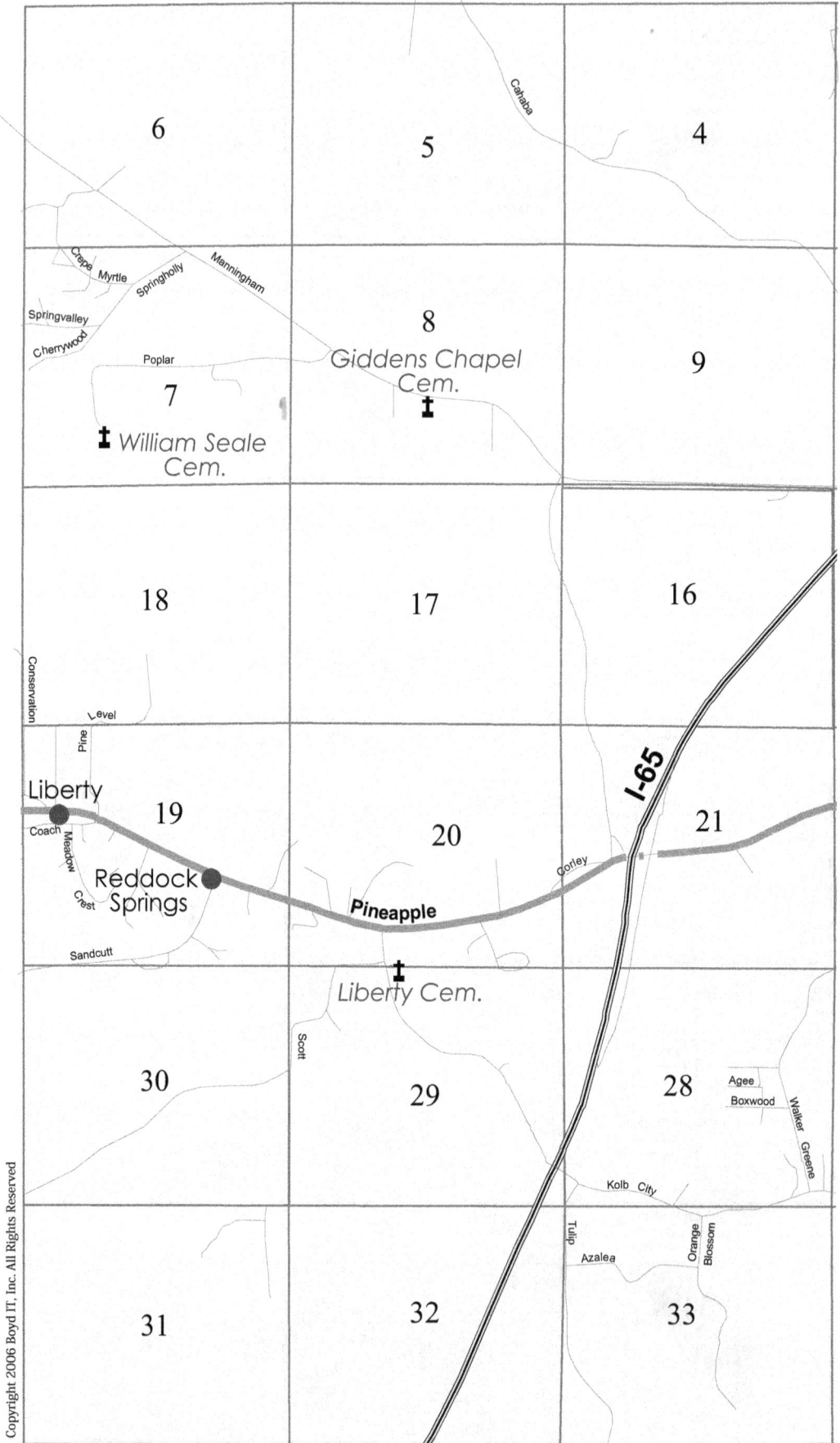

3

2

1

Hartley Cem. ✝

Cole Tr

Pine Dale

Airport

Haygood

New Searcy

Searcy Cut Off

Cloverdale

10

Interstate

11

12

Gateway

Shannon Hill

Willow

Butler

Chalet

Logans

Hardscramble

Greenville

Forest

Country Club

Glendale

14

Lake

Flowers

13

Terrell

Boutwell

Wood Valley

Balaclava

Hillcrest

Gamble

15

Fort

Dale

Overlook

Shanks

Steele Hill

Thames

Beeland

2nd

1st

Merrimac

Commerce

Westwood

Oak

Oliver

Burnett

Linda

Cedar

Wimberly

Perry

Waters

South

Pioneer Cem. ✝

Chestnut

● **Greenville**

Walnut

Grant

Burger

Chaudron

Tiger

Magnolia Cem. ✝

Dohrmer

Milner

Herbert

✝ Dunklin

Bell

Cunningham

West End

Mountain View

Long

Lucile

College

King

Bolling

Hicks

Winkler

Harrison

Oglesby

Church

Park

Pine

Hickory

Wright

22

Industrial

Norvel

Fields

East Fields

24

Crum

World

Government

Perdue

Aztec

23

Carver

Lincoln

School Highland

Montezuma

Valley

Dunbar Pk

26

Conecuh

25

Mobile

Iris

27

Gravel Hill

Pole

Crosby

Rhodes

Sunrise Cem. ✝

Halso Mill

34

Lake Greenville

35

36

Marshy

Borton

Simpson

Colfax

Elm

Helpful Hints

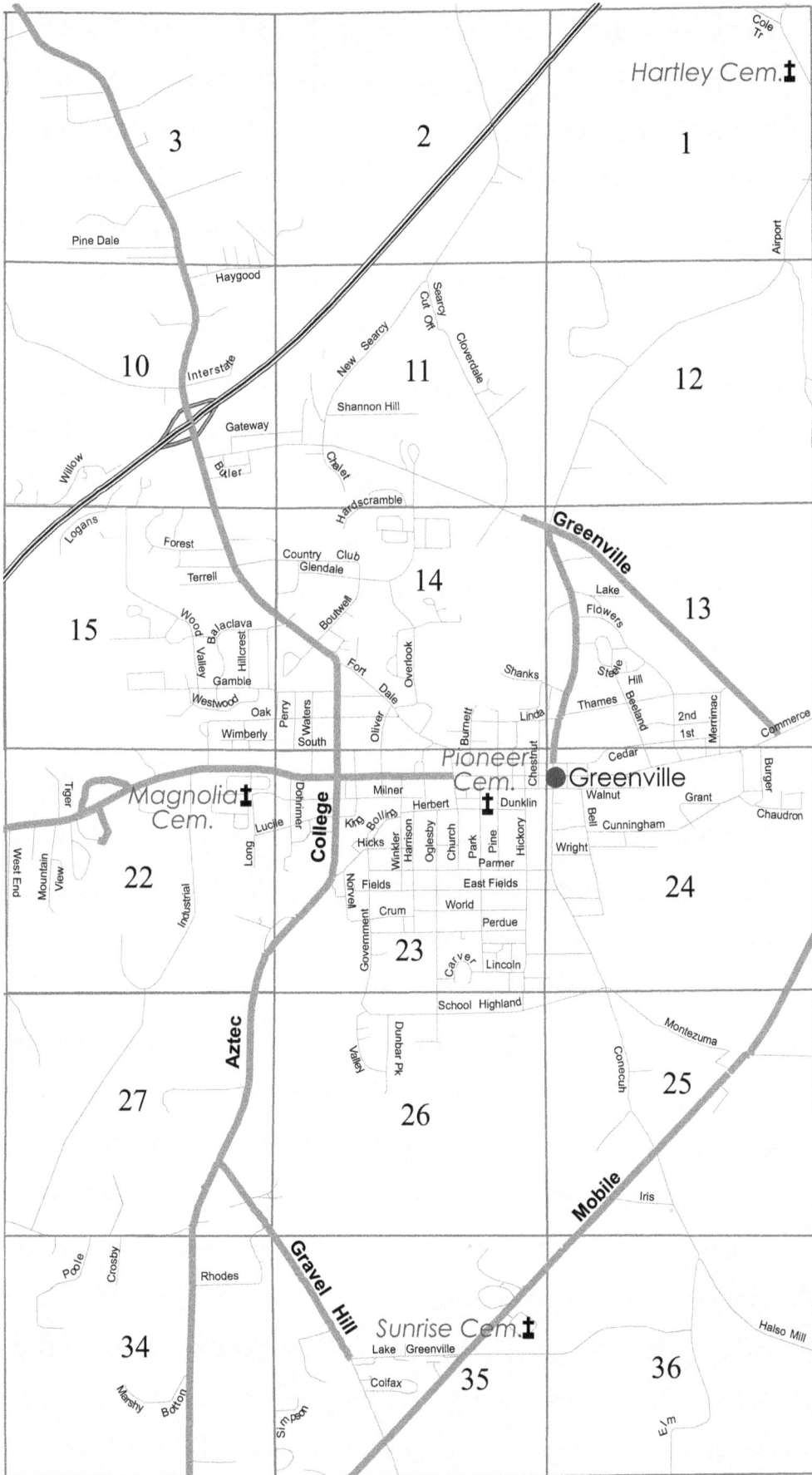

1. This road map has a number of uses, but primarily it is to help you: a) find the present location of land owned by your ancestors (at least the general area), b) find cemeteries and city-centers, and c) estimate the route/roads used by Census-takers & tax-assessors.

2. If you plan to travel to Butler County to locate cemeteries or land parcels, please pick up a modern travel map for the area before you do. Mapping old land parcels on modern maps is not as exact a science as you might think. Just the slightest variations in public land survey coordinates, estimates of parcel boundaries, or road-map deviations can greatly alter a map's representation of how a road either does or doesn't cross a particular parcel of land.

Legend

————	Section Lines
≡≡≡≡	Interstates
▬▬▬▬	Highways
————	Other Roads
●	Cities/Towns
✝	Cemeteries

Scale: Section = 1 mile X 1 mile
(generally, with some exceptions)

Historical Map
T10-N R14-E
St Stephens Meridian
Map Group 8

Cities & Towns
Greenville
Liberty
Reddock Springs

Cemeteries
Giddens Chapel Cemetery
Hartley Cemetery
Liberty Cemetery
Magnolia Cemetery
Pioneer Cemetery
Sunrise Cemetery
William Seale Cemetery

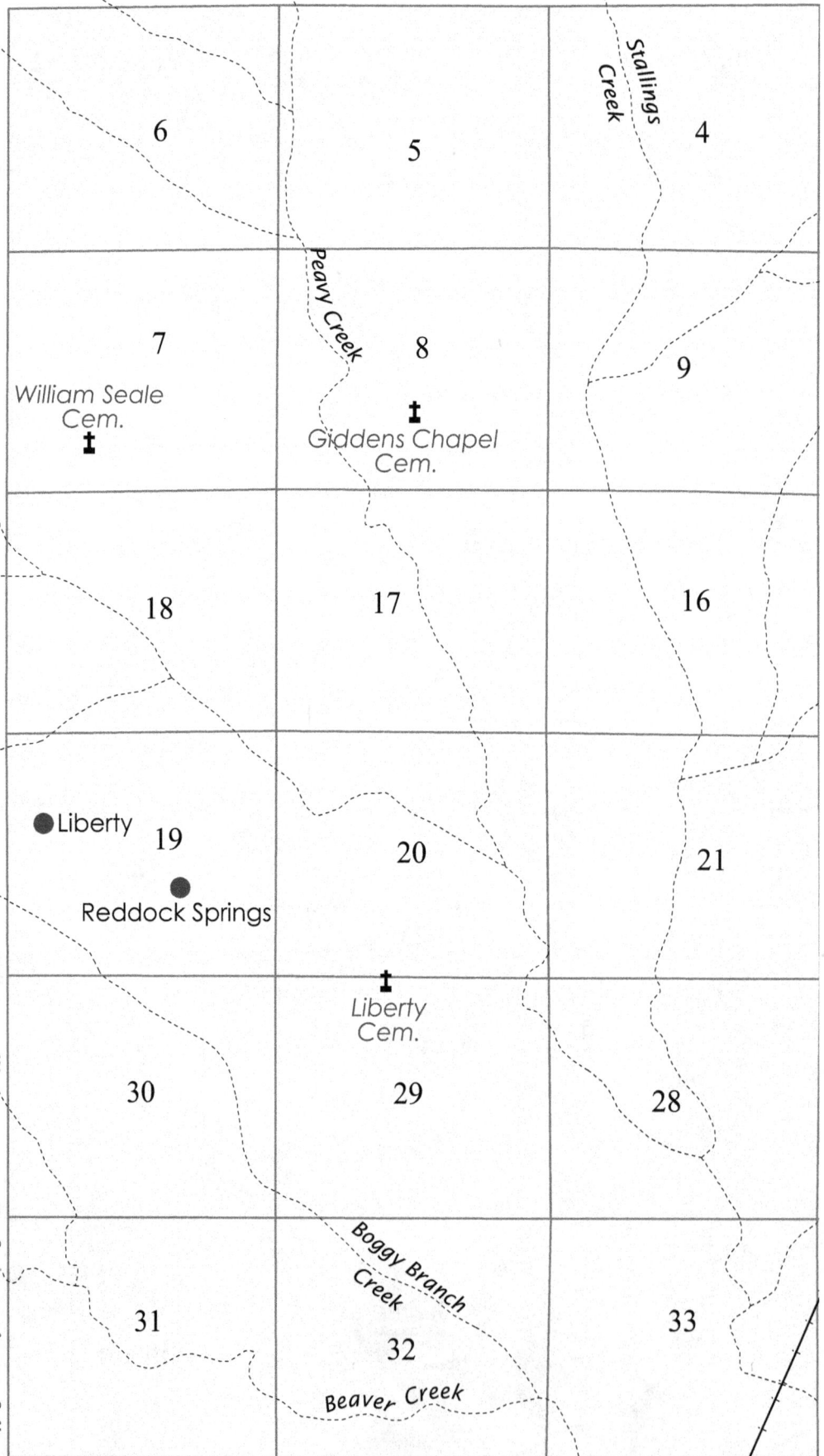

6

5

Stallings Creek

4

Peavy Creek

7

William Seale Cem.

8

✝

Giddens Chapel Cem.

9

18

17

16

●Liberty

19

●Reddock Springs

20

21

✝

Liberty Cem.

30

29

28

31

Boggy Branch Creek

32

33

Beaver Creek

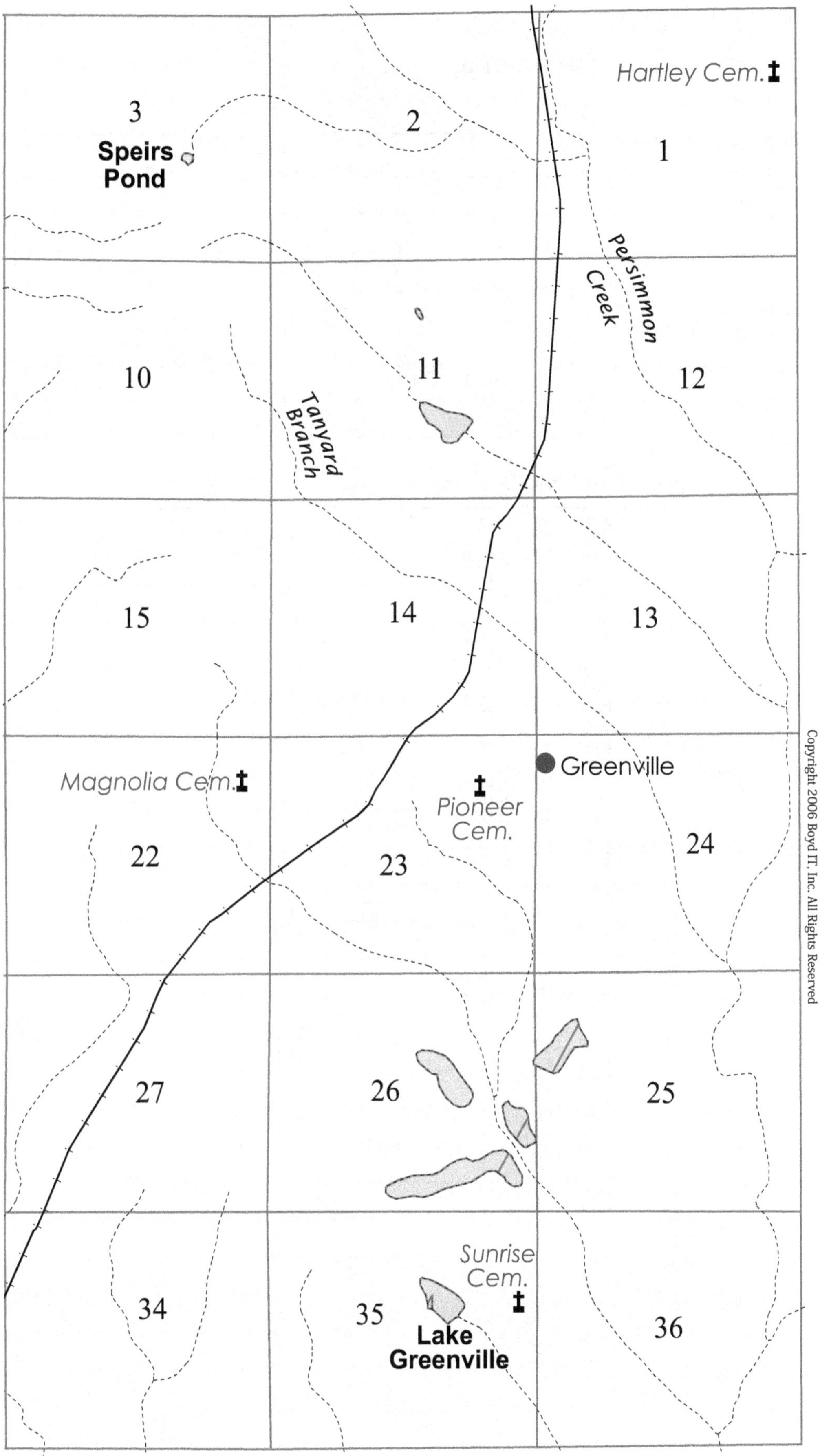

Hartley Cem.
3
Speirs Pond
2
1
Persimmon Creek
10
Tanyard Branch
11
12
15
14
13
Magnolia Cem.
Greenville
Pioneer Cem.
22
23
24
27
26
25
Sunrise Cem.
34
35
Lake Greenville
36

Helpful Hints

1. This Map takes a different look at the same Congressional Township displayed in the preceding two maps. It presents features that can help you better envision the historical development of the area: a) Water-bodies (lakes & ponds), b) Water-courses (rivers, streams, etc.), c) Railroads, d) City/town center-points (where they were oftentimes located when first settled), and e) Cemeteries.
2. Using this "Historical" map in tandem with this Township's Patent Map and Road Map, may lead you to some interesting discoveries. You will often find roads, towns, cemeteries, and waterways are named after nearby landowners: sometimes those names will be the ones you are researching. See how many of these research gems you can find here in Butler County.

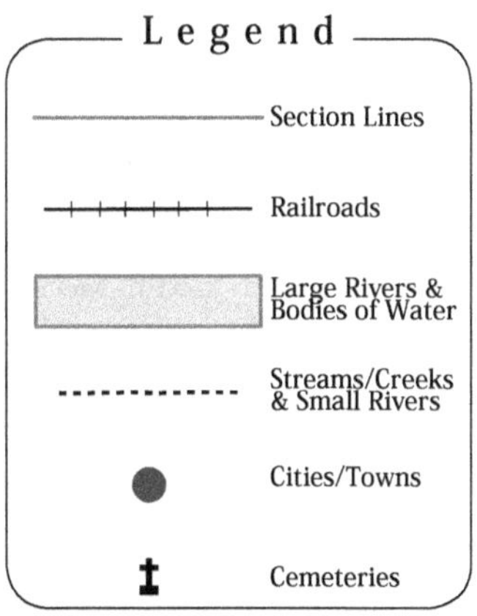

Legend
Section Lines
Railroads
Large Rivers & Bodies of Water
Streams/Creeks & Small Rivers
Cities/Towns
Cemeteries

Scale: Section = 1 mile X 1 mile
(there are some exceptions)

Map Group 9: Index to Land Patents

Township 10-North Range 15-East (St Stephens)

After you locate an individual in this Index, take note of the Section and Section Part then proceed to the Land Patent map on the pages immediately following. You should have no difficulty locating the corresponding parcel of land.

The "For More Info" Column will lead you to more information about the underlying Patents. See the *Legend* at right, and the "How to Use this Book" chapter, for more information.

```
                        LEGEND
              "For More Info . . . " column
A = Authority (Legislative Act, See Appendix "A")
B = Block or Lot (location in Section unknown)
C = Cancelled Patent
F = Fractional Section
G = Group  (Multi-Patentee Patent, see Appendix "C")
V = Overlaps another Parcel
R = Re-Issued (Parcel patented more than once)

(A & G items require you to look in the Appendixes referred
to above. All other Letter-designations followed by a number
require you to locate line-items in this index that possess
the ID number found after the letter).
```

ID	Individual in Patent	Sec.	Sec. Part	Date Issued	Other Counties	For More Info . . .
1891	ALDAY, Benjamin	13	NESW	1835-11-20		A1
1893	" "	14	E½NE	1837-05-20		A1 F
1892	"	13	SENW	1837-08-10		A1
1894	ALDAY, Benjamin J	13	SWNW	1840-10-10		A1
2102	ALDAY, William	5	SWSW	1837-05-15		A1
2100	" "	15	SESW	1838-07-28		A1
2101	" "	22	E½NW	1838-07-28		A1
1979	ANDRESS, Jeremiah	12	SESE	1858-11-01		A1
2075	ANDRESS, Stephen F	12	NESW	1858-11-01		A1
2103	ANDREWS, William	13	NENE	1837-08-02		A1
1985	BARLOW, John	10	NESW	1837-08-12		A1
1986	" "	10	NWSE	1837-08-12		A1
1990	BARNES, John C	20	S½SW	1838-07-28		A1 G2
1935	BARRETT, Gatsey	23	E½SW	1858-09-01		A1
1936	" "	23	W½SE	1858-09-01		A1
1953	BARRETT, James	15	NWSE	1837-08-10		A1
2030	BELL, Joseph	9	NESE	1838-07-28		A1
2031	" "	9	SWNE	1838-07-28		A1
2032	" "	9	SWSE	1838-07-28		A1
1908	BLACK, Columbus	35	SWSW	1835-10-14		A1
1954	BLACK, James	27	E½SW	1823-10-01		A1
2033	BLACK, Joseph	35	SWSE	1835-10-14		A1
1987	BOLLING, John	17	E½NW	1837-08-08		A1
1988	" "	17	NWNW	1837-08-08		A1
1989	" "	21	NENE	1837-08-12		A1 V1995
2104	CALDWELL, William	34	SWNW	1848-05-03		A1
1898	CAMP, Bradick	4	NESW	1858-11-01		A1
1899	" "	4	W½SW	1858-11-01		A1
1900	" "	9	NW	1858-11-01		A1
1862	COLLEY, Allen	4	W½SE	1854-07-15		A1
1864	" "	9	SENE	1858-09-01		A1
1863	" "	9	N½NE	1858-11-01		A1
1952	COWART, James A	12	SWSW	1853-11-15		A1
1955	CRAIG, James	21	SWSE	1837-08-18		A1
1956	" "	31	NWSE	1854-07-15		A1
1957	" "	31	SWSE	1858-09-01		A1
2106	CRAIG, William G	21	SENE	1837-08-18		A1
2107	" "	28	NENE	1837-08-18		A1
1976	DAVIS, Jane M	30	NWSE	1834-10-21		A1
1977	" "	30	SWSE	1834-10-21		A1 V2016
1975	" "	28	SWSE	1858-11-01		A1
1978	" "	33	S½SW	1858-11-01		A1
2067	DEMING, Simeon	29	SE	1858-11-01		A1
2068	" "	29	SESW	1858-11-01		A1
2069	" "	32	E½SW	1858-11-01		A1
2070	" "	32	N½SE	1858-11-01		A1

ID	Individual in Patent	Sec.	Sec. Part	Date Issued	Other Counties	For More Info . . .
2071	DEMING, Simeon (Cont'd)	32	NE	1858-11-01		A1
2072	" "	32	NENW	1858-11-01		A1
2073	" "	32	SENW	1858-11-01		A1
2074	" "	32	SESE	1858-11-01		A1
1965	DUNKLIN, James L	24	SWSW	1860-10-01		A1
1865	ERNEST, Amanda R	28	N½SE	1858-09-01		A1
1866	" "	28	SESW	1858-09-01		A1
2016	ERNEST, John R	30	S½SE	1837-04-10		A1 V1977
2017	" "	34	NWNW	1854-07-15		A1
2018	" "	34	SENW	1854-07-15		A1
2026	EWING, Jonathan	2	SESE	1858-11-01		A1
2027	" "	2	W½SE	1858-11-01		A1
2063	EWING, Samuel T	3	NWSE	1852-02-02		A1
1997	FIFE, John	34	S½SW	1837-08-12		A1
2105	FROST, William	2	SWNE	1838-07-28		A1
2079	FULLER, Thomas	10	SWNW	1854-07-15		A1
1915	GAFFNEY, Davis F	4	E½NE	1858-11-01		A1
1909	GAFFORD, Daniel	6	W½NW	1834-10-21		A1
1981	GAFFORD, Jeremiah	6	E½NW	1834-09-04		A1
1982	" "	6	NE	1834-09-04		A1
1983	" "	6	SW	1834-09-04		A1
1980	" "	4	NW	1838-07-28		A1
1888	GANDY, Augustus	11	NESW	1837-08-08		A1
1889	" "	11	NWSE	1837-08-08		A1
1890	" "	3	NESW	1849-09-01		A1
2120	GHOLSON, William P	14	NWNW	1858-09-01		A1
2121	" "	14	SENW	1858-09-01		A1
2122	GHOLSON, William S	11	NWNE	1854-07-15		A1
2123	" "	11	SWNE	1854-07-15		A1
2124	" "	14	NENW	1858-09-01		A1
1958	GIBSON, James	24	E½SW	1837-08-09		A1
2108	GRAHAM, William	12	NWSE	1849-09-01		A1
2109	GRAYDON, William	18	SWNE	1837-08-08		A1
1998	HALLIDAY, John	29	SENE	1837-08-01		A1
1930	HAMBLETON, Everet	4	W½NE	1837-08-09		A1
1929	" "	4	E½SE	1837-08-15		A1
1959	HARRISON, James J	23	SESE	1849-09-01		A1
2143	HARRISON, Williamson	24	NESE	1860-10-01		A1
1984	HASE, Jesse	9	NWSE	1837-08-09		A1
1945	HENDERSON, Herndon L	24	SESE	1837-08-09		A1
1947	" "	25	SENE	1837-08-09		A1
1946	" "	25	NENE	1852-02-02		A1
1920	HENDRIX, Elhanan	24	SENW	1837-08-12		A1
1999	HERIN, John	34	NWSW	1837-08-18		A1
2110	HERINDON, William	10	NENW	1896-10-26		A1
2111	" "	3	SESW	1896-11-21		A1
2000	HERNDON, John	10	NWNE	1837-08-18		A1
2116	HOLLADAY, William	29	SENW	1837-08-18		A1
2117	" "	30	SENE	1837-08-18		A1
2112	" "	15	SWSE	1858-11-01		A1
2113	" "	22	E½NE	1858-11-01		A1
2114	" "	22	N½SE	1858-11-01		A1
2115	" "	22	NWNE	1858-11-01		A1
2007	HOWARD, John P	27	SENW	1858-09-01		A1
2008	" "	28	SWNE	1858-09-01		A1
1921	HUDSON, Eli	33	SESE	1837-08-15		A1
1991	JONES, John C	23	SWNE	1853-11-15		A1
2043	KEITH, Nathaniel	12	SENE	1837-08-08		A1
2042	" "	12	NWNE	1838-07-28		A1
2041	" "	1	SWSE	1840-10-10		A1
1964	KELLEY, James	27	NWNE	1837-08-08		A1
1916	KNOWLES, Edmund	33	NESE	1837-08-12		A1
2001	LEWIS, John	22	SWNE	1843-02-01		A1
2002	MARTIN, John	33	E½NE	1823-10-01		A1
2049	MARTIN, Peter	17	W½SE	1825-04-22		A1
2050	" "	34	N½SE	1837-08-14		A1
1902	MCKENZIE, Charles	23	NESE	1858-09-01		A1
1904	" "	25	W½NE	1858-09-01		A1
1905	" "	25	W½SE	1858-09-01		A1
1903	" "	24	NWSW	1858-11-01		A1
1928	MCKENZIE, Elias	14	SWNW	1838-07-28		A1
1927	" "	13	SWSW	1845-06-01		A1
2003	MCKENZIE, John	23	NWNE	1853-11-15		A1

ID	Individual in Patent	Sec.	Sec. Part	Date Issued	Other Counties	For More Info . . .
1906	MCKINZIE, Charles	24	NENW	1858-11-01		A1
1907	" "	24	SWSE	1858-11-01		A1
1922	MCKINZIE, Elias G	11	SESE	1853-11-15		A1
1923	" "	14	E½SW	1858-11-01		A1
1924	" "	14	SESE	1858-11-01		A1
1925	" "	14	SWSW	1858-11-01		A1
1926	" "	14	W½SE	1858-11-01		A1
2004	MCKINZIE, John	13	NWNW	1845-07-01		A1
2127	MCKINZIE, William T	11	NESE	1858-11-01		A1
2005	MCLEAN, John	10	SWSE	1837-08-15		A1
1910	MCQUEEN, Daniel	14	NESE	1858-11-01		A1
2006	MIDDLEBROOKS, John	21	NWNW	1837-08-14		A1
1932	MILLER, Ezra	34	NWNE	1854-07-15		A1
1968	MILLER, James	22	SWSE	1837-04-10		A1
1966	" "	22	SESE	1837-08-02		A1
1967	" "	22	SW	1837-08-02		A1
2036	MOORE, Lewis	31	SENE	1835-04-15		A1 V1869
2040	MORGAN, Michael S	2	SENW	1852-12-01		A1
2039	" "	2	NENW	1860-04-02		A1
2080	MORGAN, Thomas R	1	E½SW	1837-08-10		A1
2082	" "	1	NWSE	1837-08-15		A1
2091	" "	2	NWSW	1838-07-28		A1
2092	" "	2	W½NW	1838-07-28		A1
2081	" "	1	NESE	1849-09-01		A1
2084	" "	1	SWNE	1854-10-02		A1
2085	" "	1	W½SW	1854-10-02		A1
2086	" "	12	NENE	1854-10-02		A1
2088	" "	12	NWNW	1854-10-02		A1
2090	" "	2	NESE	1854-10-02		A1
2083	" "	1	SESE	1858-11-01		A1
2087	" "	12	NENW	1858-11-01		A1
2089	" "	12	SWNE	1858-11-01		A1
1897	NEWTON, Benjamin	18	SESW	1835-04-15		A1
1895	" "	18	NESW	1837-08-02		A1
1896	" "	18	NWSW	1837-08-12		A1
1901	NEWTON, Caswell	32	SWSE	1854-07-15		A1
2062	OLIVER, Samuel	1	E½NE	1838-07-28		A1
1939	PATTILLO, George H	3	NWNW	1835-10-08		A1
1938	" "	3	E½NW	1837-08-07		A1
1940	" "	3	SWNW	1837-08-07		A1
1937	" "	3	E½NE	1838-07-28		A1
1941	" "	3	W½SW	1838-07-28		A1
2011	PAYNE, John	18	E½SE	1833-06-04		A1
2010	" "	17	W½SW	1834-07-23		A1
2013	" "	19	W½NE	1834-09-04		A1
2012	" "	18	W½SE	1834-10-21		A1
2009	" "	17	SESW	1837-08-07		A1
2133	PAYNE, William W	15	NESW	1858-11-01		A1
2134	" "	15	NWNW	1858-11-01		A1
2135	" "	15	SENW	1858-11-01		A1
2136	" "	15	SWNE	1858-11-01		A1
2137	" "	15	SWNW	1858-11-01		A1
1970	PERRY, James	34	NESW	1848-04-01		A1
1969	" "	27	SWSW	1858-09-01		A1
2014	PERRY, John	29	NWSW	1835-11-20		A1
2015	" "	30	NESE	1835-11-20		A1
1919	PHELPS, Edward A	3	W½NE	1852-02-02		A1
1918	" "	25	NESE	1853-11-15		A1
1917	" "	10	NWNW	1854-07-15		A1
2037	PHELPS, Lorenzo D	10	NWSW	1852-02-02		A1
1931	PICKENS, Ezekiel H	27	NWSW	1850-08-10		A1
1992	PICKENS, John C	28	SESE	1848-05-03		A1
1949	PIERCE, Hubbell	8	NWSW	1835-11-20		A1
1948	" "	18	NWNE	1837-08-12		A1
1856	POLLARD, Albert	17	SWNW	1835-10-14		A1
1858	" "	18	SENE	1837-05-15		A1
1857	" "	18	NENE	1837-08-07		A1
1943	PURDY, Henry	34	SESE	1835-10-14		A1
1942	" "	21	SWNW	1837-08-02		A1
1913	RABOURN, David	35	E½SE	1832-08-08		A1
1914	RABURN, David	35	NWSE	1843-02-01		A1
2019	RABURN, John	35	E½SW	1835-10-14		A1
2051	RABURN, Richard	25	SESE	1858-09-01		A1

ID	Individual in Patent	Sec.	Sec. Part	Date Issued	Other Counties	For More Info . . .
2052	RABURN, Richard (Cont'd)	36	NWNE	1862-01-01		A1
2038	RAINS, Mary	15	SENE	1858-11-01		A1
1911	REEVES, David P	15	NENW	1858-11-01		A1
1912	" "	15	NWNE	1858-11-01		A1
1859	REID, Alexander	20	NW	1833-11-14		A1
1882	REID, Archibald M	11	SWSE	1834-06-12		A1
1944	REMLEY, Henry	2	NESW	1838-07-28		A1
2048	REYNOLDS, Overton	10	S½SW	1858-09-01		A1
2047	REYNOLDS, Overton H	9	SESE	1858-11-01		A1
2061	REYNOLDS, Robert	10	SWNE	1852-02-02		A1
2034	RHODES, Kinchin	36	SESE	1850-05-01		A1
2035	" "	36	SWSE	1858-11-01		A1
2045	ROBERSON, Nathaniel	35	NWSW	1837-08-02		A1
2044	" "	34	SWNE	1837-08-14		A1
2099	ROBERTS, William A	34	SENE	1854-07-15		A1
2046	ROBINSON, Nathaniel	34	SWSE	1837-08-15		A1
1861	RUSHTON, Alfred A	12	SWSE	1837-08-18		A1
1860	" "	12	NESE	1838-07-28		A1
1995	SENTELL, John E	21	N½NE	1837-04-10		A1 V1989
1996	" "	21	SWNE	1837-08-10		A1
1993	" "	15	E½SE	1838-07-28		A1
1994	" "	15	W½SW	1838-07-28		A1
2028	SHAW, Jonathan J	2	SESW	1837-08-09		A1
2029	" "	2	SWSW	1837-08-09		A1
2095	SHAW, Thomas	11	W½SW	1835-04-15		A1
2094	" "	11	SESE	1837-05-20		A1
2093	" "	10	E½SE	1837-08-08		A1
2096	" "	15	NENE	1838-07-28		A1
1880	SHEPPARD, Andrew	2	E½NE	1837-08-07		A1
1881	" "	2	NWNE	1837-08-07		A1
1878	" "	1	SENW	1837-08-12		A1
1879	" "	1	W½NW	1837-08-12		A1
1868	SMITH, Ambrose	30	NWNE	1835-09-12		A1
1871	" "	31	NWNE	1835-10-16		A1 V1869
1867	" "	29	SWSW	1837-08-12		A1
1869	" "	31	NE	1837-08-12		A1 V2036, 1871, 1873
1873	" "	31	SWNE	1837-08-12		A1 V1869
1874	" "	32	NWNW	1852-12-01		A1
1870	" "	31	NESE	1854-10-02		A1
1872	" "	31	SESE	1854-10-02		A1
1875	" "	32	SWNW	1854-10-02		A1
1876	" "	32	W½SW	1854-10-02		A1
2125	SMITH, William	29	W½NW	1823-10-01		A1
2020	SORELL, John	14	W½NE	1833-06-04		A1
2126	STEWART, William	3	SWSE	1837-08-15		A1
2128	TAYLOR, William	17	E½SE	1825-04-16		A1
2132	" "	20	W½NE	1825-04-20		A1
2131	" "	20	SENE	1835-10-16		A1
2130	" "	20	NWSE	1837-08-02		A1
2129	" "	20	NESE	1837-08-10		A1
2021	THOMAS, John	36	NWSE	1838-07-28		A1
2022	" "	36	SWNE	1838-07-28		A1
2023	" "	36	W½SW	1838-07-28		A1
2118	THOMAS, William J	36	NESW	1835-10-14		A1
2119	" "	36	SESW	1852-02-02		A1
1877	THOMASON, Anderson	21	E½NW	1825-04-20		A1
1960	THOMPSON, James K	10	E½NE	1837-08-09		A1
1961	" "	3	E½SE	1837-08-09		A1
1963	" "	5	NWSW	1837-08-12		A1
1962	" "	5	E½SW	1838-07-28		A1
1950	THORNTON, Jacob	36	NESE	1860-10-01		A1
1951	" "	36	SENE	1860-10-01		A1
1971	TINSLEY, James	11	NW	1837-08-10		A1 G44
1971	TINSLEY, Mary	11	NW	1837-08-10		A1 G44
2097	TINSLEY, Thomas	13	SENE	1835-10-14		A1
2098	" "	13	W½NE	1837-05-20		A1 F
2024	WALLACE, John	29	NESW	1835-11-20		A1
1933	WILLIAMSON, Francis M	13	NWSW	1840-10-10		A1
1934	" "	13	SESW	1840-10-10		A1
1883	WRIGHT, Asa	22	W½NW	1823-10-01		A1
1884	" "	23	W½SW	1837-08-10		A1
1885	" "	27	E½NE	1837-08-10		A1
1886	" "	27	SWNE	1837-08-10		A1

ID	Individual in Patent	Sec.	Sec. Part	Date Issued	Other Counties	For More Info . . .
1887	WRIGHT, Asa (Cont'd)	34	NENE	1837-08-10		A1
1972	WRIGHT, James	27	NENW	1837-08-02		A1
1974	" "	28	SENE	1837-08-02		A1
1973	" "	27	W½NW	1837-08-10		A1
2025	WRIGHT, Johnson	17	NESW	1837-04-10		A1
2054	WRIGHT, Robert R	21	S½SW	1854-07-15		A1
2055	" "	28	NENW	1854-07-15		A1
2053	" "	20	SESE	1858-11-02		A1
2056	" "	28	NESW	1858-11-02		A1
2057	" "	28	NWNE	1858-11-02		A1
2058	" "	28	SENW	1858-11-02		A1
2059	" "	28	W½NW	1858-11-02		A1
2060	" "	28	W½SW	1858-11-02		A1
2064	WRIGHT, Samuel	21	E½SE	1837-04-10		A1
2065	" "	21	NESW	1837-08-02		A1
2066	" "	21	NWSE	1837-08-02		A1
2076	WRIGHT, Stephen M	33	N½SW	1858-09-01		A1
2077	" "	33	NW	1858-09-01		A1
2078	" "	33	W½NE	1858-09-01		A1
2138	WRIGHT, William	20	N½SW	1835-04-02		A1
1990	" "	20	S½SW	1838-07-28		A1 G2
2139	" "	29	N½NE	1858-09-01		A1
2140	" "	29	NENW	1858-09-01		A1
2141	" "	29	SWNE	1858-09-01		A1
2142	" "	30	NENE	1858-09-01		A1

Patent Map

T10-N R15-E
St Stephens Meridian

Map Group 9

Township Statistics

Parcels Mapped	:	288
Number of Patents	:	233
Number of Individuals	:	133
Patentees Identified	:	132
Number of Surnames	:	92
Multi-Patentee Parcels	:	2
Oldest Patent Date	:	10/1/1823
Most Recent Patent	:	11/21/1896
Block/Lot Parcels	:	0
Parcels Re - Issued	:	0
Parcels that Overlap	:	8
Cities and Towns	:	2
Cemeteries	:	6

Section 5
- GAFFORD Daniel 1834
- GAFFORD Jeremiah 1834
- GAFFORD Jeremiah 1834
- GAFFORD Jeremiah 1834
- 6
- THOMPSON James K 1837
- THOMPSON James K 1838
- ALDAY William 1837

Section 4
- GAFFORD Jeremiah 1838
- HAMBLETON Everet 1837
- GAFFNEY Davis F 1858
- CAMP Bradick 1858
- CAMP Bradick 1858
- HAMBLETON Everet 1837
- COLLEY Allen 1854

Section 7

Section 8
- PIERCE Hubbell 1835

Section 9
- CAMP Bradick 1858
- COLLEY Allen 1858
- BELL Joseph 1838
- COLLEY Allen 1858
- HASE Jesse 1837
- BELL Joseph 1838
- BELL Joseph 1838
- REYNOLDS Overton H 1858

Section 18
- PIERCE Hubbell 1837
- POLLARD Albert 1837
- BOLLING John 1837
- BOLLING John 1837
- GRAYDON William 1837
- POLLARD Albert 1837
- POLLARD Albert 1835
- NEWTON Benjamin 1837
- NEWTON Benjamin 1837
- PAYNE John 1834
- PAYNE John 1833
- NEWTON Benjamin 1835

Section 17
- PAYNE John 1834
- WRIGHT Johnson 1837
- PAYNE John 1837
- MARTIN Peter 1825
- TAYLOR William 1825

Section 16

Section 19
- PAYNE John 1834

Section 20
- REID Alexander 1833
- TAYLOR William 1825
- TAYLOR William 1835
- WRIGHT William 1835
- TAYLOR William 1837
- TAYLOR William 1837
- BARNES [2] John C 1838
- WRIGHT Robert R 1858

Section 21
- MIDDLEBROOKS John 1837
- THOMASON Anderson 1825
- SENTELL John E 1837
- BOLLING John 1837
- PURDY Henry 1837
- SENTELL John E 1837
- CRAIG William G 1837
- WRIGHT Robert R 1854
- WRIGHT Samuel 1837
- WRIGHT Samuel 1837
- WRIGHT Samuel 1837
- CRAIG James 1837

Section 30
- SMITH Ambrose 1835
- WRIGHT William 1858
- HOLLADAY William 1837
- DAVIS Jane M 1834
- PERRY John 1835
- DAVIS Jane M 1834
- ERNEST John R 1837

Section 29
- SMITH William 1823
- WRIGHT William 1858
- WRIGHT William 1858
- HOLLADAY William 1837
- WRIGHT William 1858
- HALLIDAY John 1858
- PERRY John 1835
- WALLACE John 1835
- SMITH Ambrose 1837
- DEMING Simeon 1858
- DEMING Simeon 1858

Section 28
- WRIGHT Robert R 1858
- WRIGHT Robert R 1854
- WRIGHT Robert R 1858
- CRAIG William G 1837
- WRIGHT Robert R 1858
- HOWARD John P 1858
- WRIGHT James 1837
- WRIGHT Robert R 1858
- ERNEST Amanda R 1858
- WRIGHT Robert R 1858
- ERNEST Amanda R 1858
- DAVIS Jane M 1858
- PICKENS John C 1848

Section 31
- SMITH Ambrose 1835
- SMITH Ambrose 1837
- SMITH Ambrose 1837
- MOORE Lewis 1835
- CRAIG James 1854
- SMITH Ambrose 1854
- CRAIG James 1858
- SMITH Ambrose 1854

Section 32
- SMITH Ambrose 1852
- DEMING Simeon 1858
- DEMING Simeon 1858
- SMITH Ambrose 1854
- DEMING Simeon 1858
- DEMING Simeon 1858
- SMITH Ambrose 1854
- DEMING Simeon 1858
- NEWTON Caswell 1854
- DEMING Simeon 1858

Section 33
- WRIGHT Stephen M 1858
- MARTIN John 1823
- WRIGHT Stephen M 1858
- WRIGHT Stephen M 1858
- DAVIS Jane M 1858
- KNOWLES Edmund 1837
- HUDSON Eli 1837

Section 3
PATTILLO George H 1835
PATTILLO George H 1837
PATTILLO George H 1837 **3**
PATTILLO George H 1838
GANDY Augustus 1849
HERINDON William 1896
PATTILLO George H 1837
PHELPS Edward A 1852
EWING Samuel T 1852
THOMPSON James K 1837
STEWART William 1837
PATTILLO George H 1838

Section 2
MORGAN Thomas R 1838
MORGAN Michael S 1860
MORGAN Michael S 1852 **2**
SHEPPARD Andrew 1837
FROST William 1838
MORGAN Thomas R 1838
REMLEY Henry 1838
SHAW Jonathan J 1837
SHAW Jonathan J 1837
EWING Jonathan 1858

Section 1
SHEPPARD Andrew 1837
SHEPPARD Andrew 1837
SHEPPARD Andrew 1837
MORGAN Thomas R 1854 **1**
MORGAN Thomas R 1837
MORGAN Thomas R 1854
OLIVER Samuel 1838
MORGAN Thomas R 1854
MORGAN Thomas R 1849
KEITH Nathaniel 1840
MORGAN Thomas R 1858
MORGAN Thomas R 1854
EWING Jonathan 1858

Section 10
PHELPS Edward A 1854
HERINDON William 1896
HERNDON John 1837
THOMPSON James K 1837
FULLER Thomas 1854 **10**
REYNOLDS Robert 1852
PHELPS Lorenzo D 1852
BARLOW John 1837
BARLOW John 1837
REYNOLDS Overton 1858
MCLEAN John 1837
SHAW Thomas 1837

Section 11
TINSLEY [44] James 1837 **11**
GHOLSON William S 1854
GHOLSON William S 1854
GANDY Augustus 1837
GANDY Augustus 1837
MCKINZIE William T 1858
SHAW Thomas 1835
SHAW Thomas 1837
REID Archibald M 1834
MCKINZIE Elias G 1853

Section 12
MORGAN Thomas R 1854
MORGAN Thomas R 1858
KEITH Nathaniel 1838
MORGAN Thomas R 1854 **12**
MORGAN Thomas R 1858
KEITH Nathaniel 1837
ANDRESS Stephen F 1858
GRAHAM William 1849
RUSHTON Alfred A 1838
COWART James A 1853
RUSHTON Alfred A 1837
ANDRESS Jeremiah 1858

Section 15
PAYNE William W 1858
REEVES David P 1858
REEVES David P 1858
SHAW Thomas 1838
PAYNE William W 1858 **15**
PAYNE William W 1858
RAINS Mary 1858
PAYNE William W 1858
BARRETT James 1837
SENTELL John E 1838
SENTELL John E 1838
ALDAY William 1838
HOLLADAY William 1858

Section 14
GHOLSON William P 1858
GHOLSON William S 1858
SORELL John 1833
ALDAY Benjamin 1837
MCKENZIE Elias 1838
GHOLSON William P 1858 **14**
MCKINZIE Elias G 1858
MCKINZIE Elias G 1858
MCKINZIE Elias G 1858
MCQUEEN Daniel 1858
MCKINZIE Elias 1845

Section 13
MCKINZIE John 1845
ALDAY Benjamin J 1840
ALDAY Benjamin 1837
TINSLEY Thomas 1837
ANDREWS William 1837
TINSLEY Thomas 1835
WILLIAMSON Francis M 1840
ALDAY Benjamin 1835 **13**
WILLIAMSON Francis M 1840

Section 22
WRIGHT Asa 1823
ALDAY William 1838
HOLLADAY William 1858
HOLLADAY William 1858
LEWIS John 1843
MILLER James 1837 **22**
HOLLADAY William 1858
MILLER James 1837
MILLER James 1837

Section 23
MCKENZIE John 1853
JONES John C 1853 **23**
WRIGHT Asa 1837
BARRETT Gatsey 1858
BARRETT Gatsey 1858
MCKENZIE Charles 1858
HARRISON James J 1849
MCKENZIE Charles 1858
DUNKLIN James L 1860

Section 24
MCKINZIE Charles 1858
HENDRIX Elhanan 1837 **24**
GIBSON James 1837
HARRISON Williamson 1860
MCKINZIE Charles 1858
HENDERSON Herndon L 1837

Section 27
WRIGHT James 1837
WRIGHT James 1837
KELLEY James 1837
WRIGHT Asa 1837
HOWARD John P 1858
WRIGHT Asa 1837
PICKENS Ezekiel H 1850
BLACK James 1823 **27**
PERRY James 1858

Section 26
26

Section 25
25
MCKENZIE Charles 1858
HENDERSON Herndon L 1852
HENDERSON Herndon L 1837
PHELPS Edward A 1853
MCKENZIE Charles 1858
RABURN Richard 1858

Section 34
ERNEST John R 1854
MILLER Ezra 1854
WRIGHT Asa 1837
CALDWELL William 1848
ERNEST John R 1854
ROBERSON Nathaniel 1837
ROBERTS William A 1854
HERIN John 1837
PERRY James 1848 **34**
MARTIN Peter 1837
FIFE John 1837
ROBINSON Nathaniel 1837
PURDY Henry 1835

Section 35
35
ROBERSON Nathaniel 1837
BLACK Columbus 1835
RABURN John 1835
RABURN David 1843
RABOURN David 1832
BLACK Joseph 1835

Section 36
RABURN Richard 1862
THOMAS John 1838
THORNTON Jacob 1860
THORNTON Jacob 1860
THOMAS John 1838
THOMAS William J 1835 **36**
THOMAS John 1838
THOMAS William J 1852
RHODES Kinchin 1858
RHODES Kinchin 1850

Helpful Hints

1. This Map's INDEX can be found on the preceding pages.

2. Refer to Map "C" to see where this Township lies within Butler County, Alabama.

3. Numbers within square brackets [ ] denote a multi-patentee land parcel (multi-owner). Refer to Appendix "C" for a full list of members in this group.

4. Areas that look to be crowded with Patentees usually indicate multiple sales of the same parcel (Re-issues) or Overlapping parcels. See this Township's Index for an explanation of these and other circumstances that might explain "odd" groupings of Patentees on this map.

Legend

———— Patent Boundary

━━━━ Section Boundary

▨ No Patents Found (or Outside County)

1., 2., 3., ... Lot Numbers (when beside a name)

[ ] Group Number (see Appendix "C")

Scale: Section = 1 mile X 1 mile (generally, with some exceptions)

Road Map

T10-N R15-E
St Stephens Meridian

Map Group 9

Cities & Towns
Mashville
Spring Hill

Cemeteries
Andress Cemetery
Ebenezer Cemetery
Harrison Cemetery
Mount Olive Cemetery
Mount Zion Cemetery
Saint Paul Cemetery

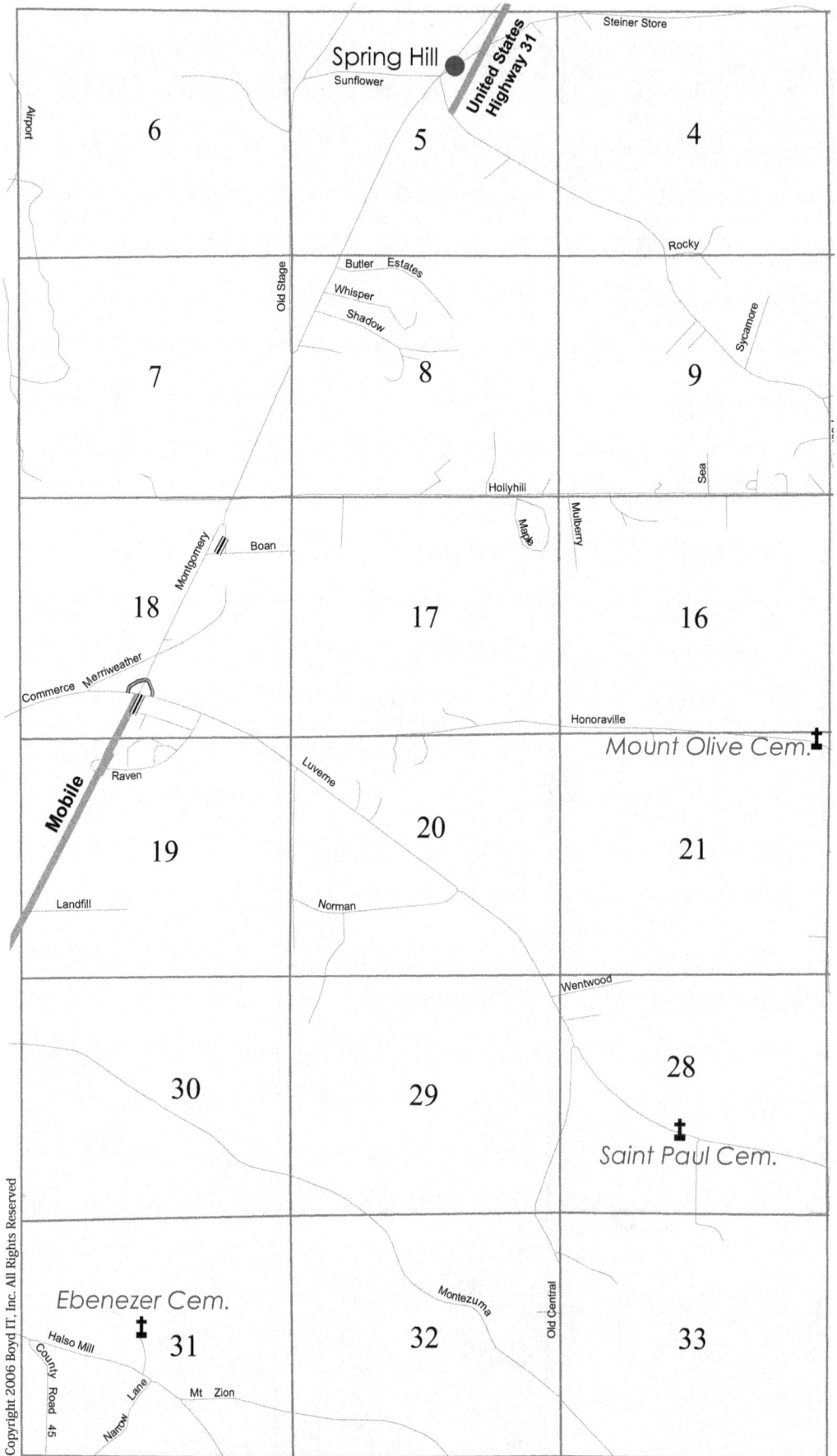

Spring Hill

Steiner Store

United States Highway 31

Sunflower

6

5

4

Rocky

Old Stage

Butler Estates

Whisper

Shadow

Sycamore

7

8

9

Hollyhill

Sea

Maple

Mulberry

Montgomery

Boan

18

17

16

Commerce Merriweather

Honoraville

Mount Olive Cem.

Mobile

Raven

Luverne

19

20

21

Landfill

Norman

Wentwood

28

30

29

Saint Paul Cem.

Old Central

Ebenezer Cem.

Montezuma

Halso Mill

County Road 45

Narrow Lane

Mt Zion

31

32

33

3	2	1
10	11	12
15	14	13
22	23	24
27	26	25
34	35	36

Gandy

Farmstead
Poor House
Union
Henderson
Andress Cem. ✝
Tyler
Dunn
Mashville
Heartsill
Mount Zion Cem. ✝
Mt Zion
Honoraville
Harrison Cem. ✝
Mashville
Beulah
Bluebird
McCall
Whitney
Rolling Hills
Luverne
Falcon

Copyright 2006 Boyd IT, Inc. All Rights Reserved

Helpful Hints

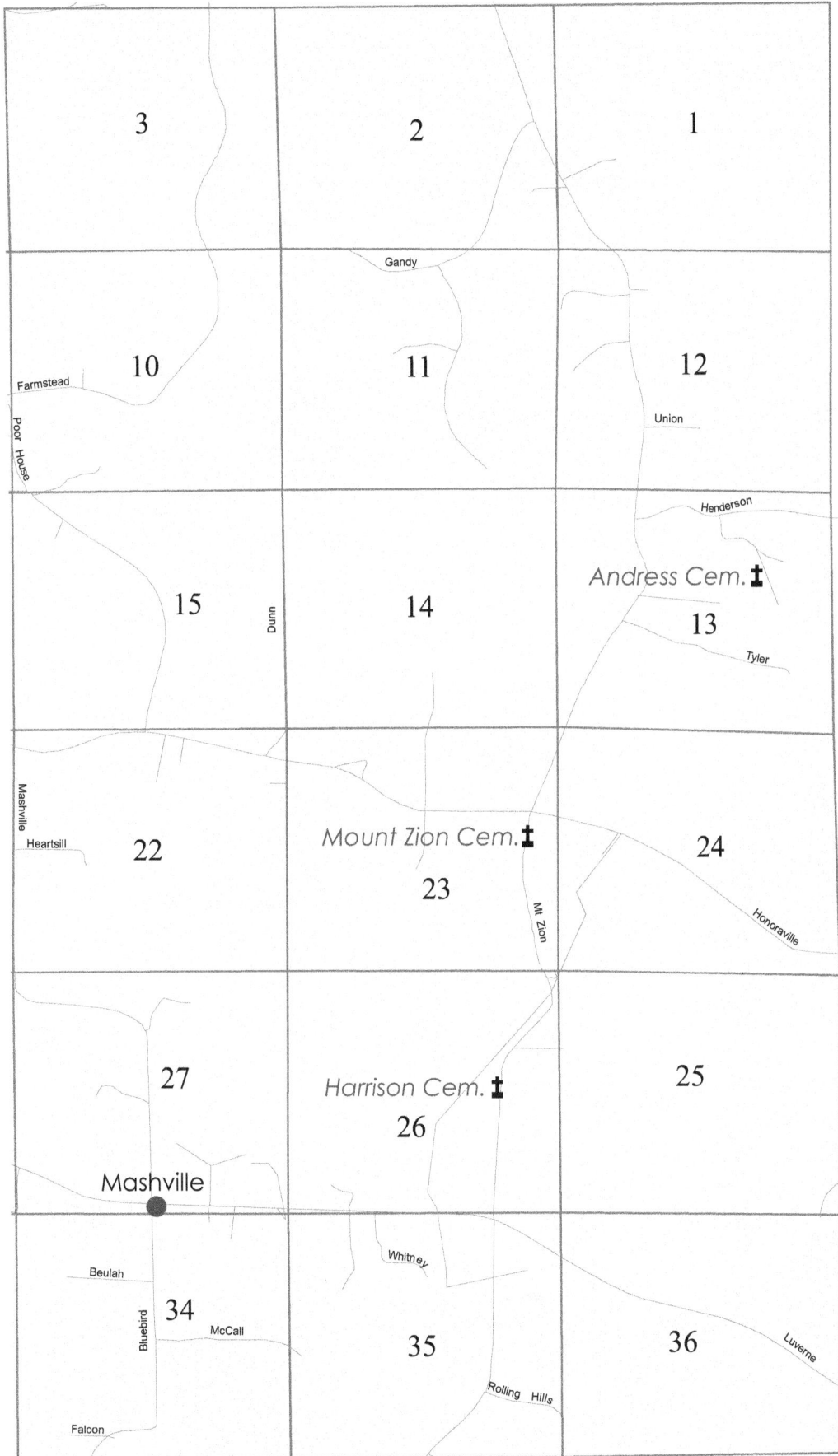

1. This road map has a number of uses, but primarily it is to help you: a) find the present location of land owned by your ancestors (at least the general area), b) find cemeteries and city-centers, and c) estimate the route/roads used by Census-takers & tax-assessors.

2. If you plan to travel to Butler County to locate cemeteries or land parcels, please pick up a modern travel map for the area before you do. Mapping old land parcels on modern maps is not as exact a science as you might think. Just the slightest variations in public land survey coordinates, estimates of parcel boundaries, or road-map deviations can greatly alter a map's representation of how a road either does or doesn't cross a particular parcel of land.

Legend

Section Lines
Interstates
Highways
Other Roads
● Cities/Towns
✝ Cemeteries

Scale: Section = 1 mile X 1 mile
(generally, with some exceptions)

143

Historical Map

T10-N R15-E
St Stephens Meridian

Map Group 9

Cities & Towns
Mashville
Spring Hill

Cemeteries
Andress Cemetery
Ebenezer Cemetery
Harrison Cemetery
Mount Olive Cemetery
Mount Zion Cemetery
Saint Paul Cemetery

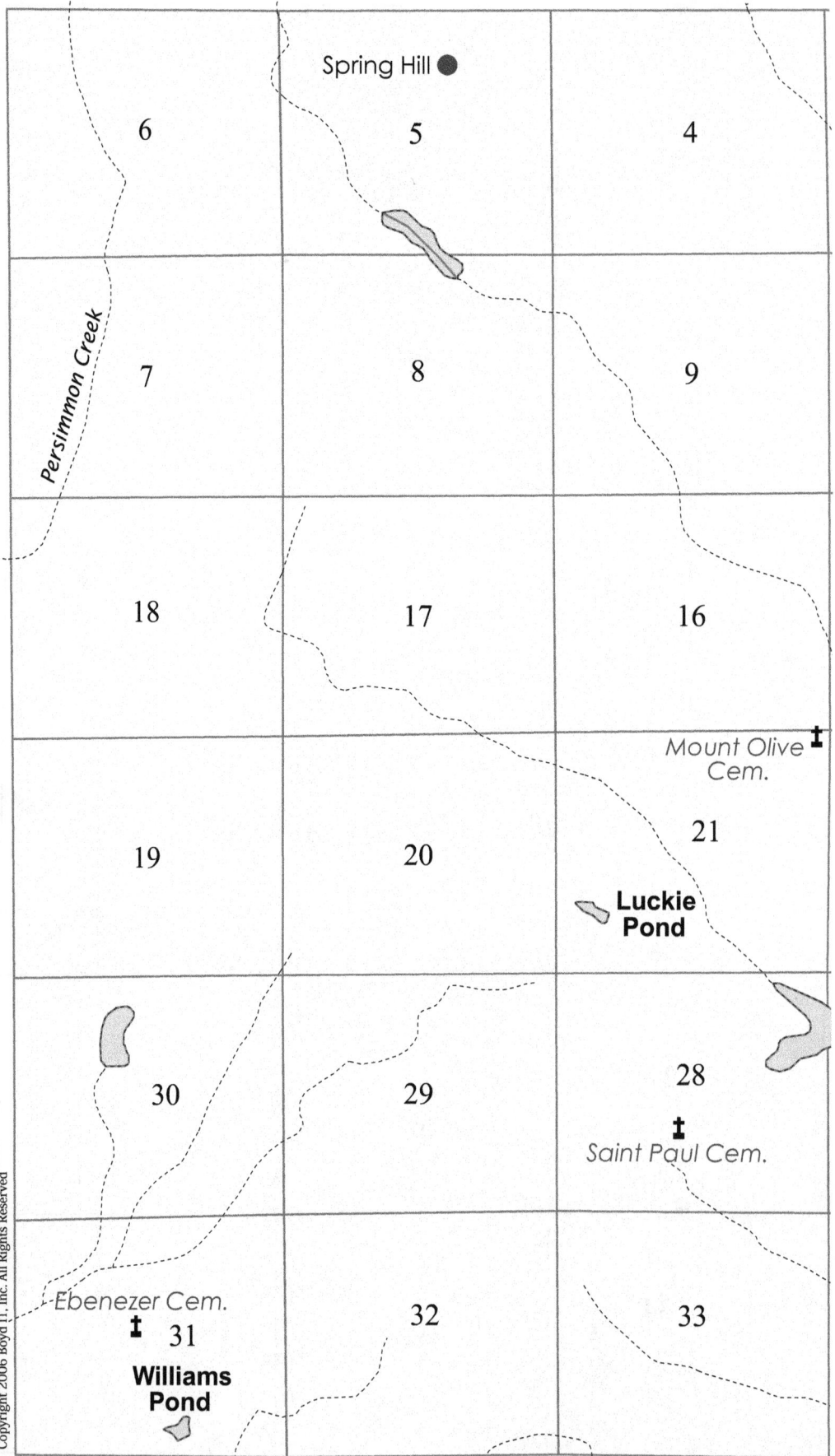

Spring Hill ●

6

5

4

7

8

9

Persimmon Creek

18

17

16

Mount Olive
Cem. ✝

19

20

21

Luckie
Pond

30

29

28

✝ Saint Paul Cem.

Ebenezer Cem.
✝ 31

32

33

Williams
Pond

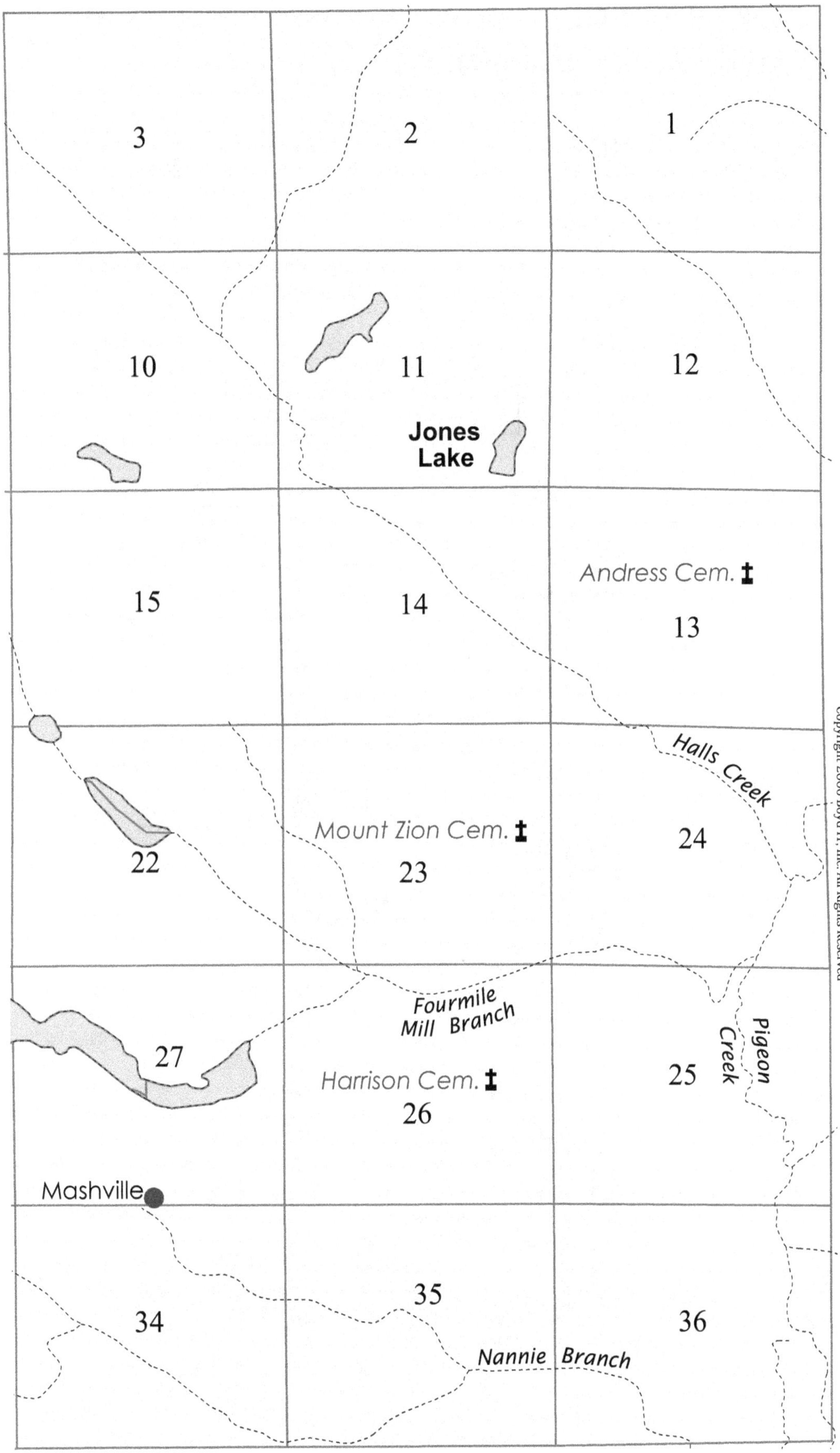
3
2
1
10
11
12
Jones Lake
15
14
Andress Cem.
13
22
Mount Zion Cem.
23
Halls Creek
24
27
Fourmile Mill Branch
Harrison Cem.
26
25
Pigeon Creek
Mashville
34
35
36
Nannie Branch

Helpful Hints

1. This Map takes a different look at the same Congressional Township displayed in the preceding two maps. It presents features that can help you better envision the historical development of the area: a) Water-bodies (lakes & ponds), b) Water-courses (rivers, streams, etc.), c) Railroads, d) City/town center-points (where they were oftentimes located when first settled), and e) Cemeteries.
2. Using this "Historical" map in tandem with this Township's Patent Map and Road Map, may lead you to some interesting discoveries. You will often find roads, towns, cemeteries, and waterways are named after nearby landowners: sometimes those names will be the ones you are researching. See how many of these research gems you can find here in Butler County.

Legend

- Section Lines
- Railroads
- Large Rivers & Bodies of Water
- Streams/Creeks & Small Rivers
- Cities/Towns
- Cemeteries

Scale: Section = 1 mile X 1 mile
(there are some exceptions)

Map Group 10: Index to Land Patents

Township 10-North Range 16-East (St Stephens)

After you locate an individual in this Index, take note of the Section and Section Part then proceed to the Land Patent map on the pages immediately following. You should have no difficulty locating the corresponding parcel of land.

The "For More Info" Column will lead you to more information about the underlying Patents. See the *Legend* at right, and the "How to Use this Book" chapter, for more information.

```
                              LEGEND
                 "For More Info . . . " column
A = Authority (Legislative Act, See Appendix "A")
B = Block or Lot (location in Section unknown)
C = Cancelled Patent
F = Fractional Section
G = Group (Multi-Patentee Patent, see Appendix "C")
V = Overlaps another Parcel
R = Re-Issued (Parcel patented more than once)

(A & G items require you to look in the Appendixes referred
to above. All other Letter-designations followed by a number
require you to locate line-items in this index that possess
the ID number found after the letter).
```

ID	Individual in Patent	Sec.	Sec. Part	Date Issued	Other Counties	For More Info . . .
2209	ACREE, John E	15	NESE	1858-11-01	Crenshaw	A1
2210	" "	15	SENE	1858-11-01	Crenshaw	A1
2314	ALLEN, Washington W	33	SENE	1858-11-01		A1
2196	ANDRESS, Jeremiah	18	NENW	1845-07-01		A1
2197	" "	18	NWNW	1852-02-02		A1
2198	" "	18	SENW	1852-02-02		A1
2284	ANDRESS, Stephen F	18	E½SW	1858-11-01		A1
2285	" "	19	NW	1858-11-01		A1
2323	ANDRESS, William J	18	NWNE	1848-05-03		A1
2324	" "	7	SWSE	1848-05-03		A1
2325	" "	7	W½NE	1848-05-03		A1
2207	ARMSTRONG, Jesse M	20	NWSE	1843-02-01		A1
2254	ARMSTRONG, Maximilian	21	SWNE	1837-08-08		A1
2255	" "	21	SWNW	1837-08-08		A1
2256	ARMSTRONG, Mitchell	18	SESE	1837-08-08		A1
2257	" "	21	SENW	1837-08-08		A1
2233	BARRETT, Joshua	17	E½NW	1835-04-15		A1
2235	" "	17	NWSE	1837-08-09		A1
2236	" "	17	SWNE	1837-08-09		A1
2237	" "	17	W½NW	1837-08-09		A1
2234	" "	17	NWNE	1848-04-01		A1
2240	" "	20	NENE	1849-09-01		A1
2241	" "	8	SWSE	1849-09-01		A1
2232	" "	17	E½NE	1852-02-02		A1
2239	" "	18	W½SE	1858-09-01		A1
2242	" "	8	SWSW	1858-09-01		A1
2243	" "	9	E½SW	1858-09-01		A1
2244	" "	9	SWSE	1858-09-01		A1
2238	" "	18	NESE	1858-11-01		A1
2312	BARRETT, Timothy	17	SWSE	1835-04-15		A1
2313	" "	20	NWNE	1835-04-15		A1
2333	BARRINGTON, William W	28	W½SE	1858-11-01		A1
2190	BELL, James	8	NESE	1835-10-14		A1
2191	" "	8	SENE	1838-07-28		A1
2208	BELL, John	6	NESE	1837-08-10		A1
2248	BISHOP, Mathew	32	E½NW	1854-07-15		A1
2249	" "	32	N½SW	1854-07-15		A1
2250	BISHOP, Matthew	31	E½SE	1852-02-02		A1
2251	" "	32	S½SW	1858-11-01		A1
2252	" "	32	W½NE	1858-11-01		A1
2253	" "	32	W½SE	1858-11-01		A1
2278	BOGGUS, Silus	28	N½NW	1858-11-01		A1
2279	" "	28	SENW	1858-11-01		A1
2280	" "	28	SW	1858-11-01		A1
2171	BRADEN, Harvey C	31	SENE	1852-02-02		A1
2150	BURNS, Archibald	29	NWSW	1854-10-02		A1

ID	Individual in Patent	Sec.	Sec. Part	Date Issued	Other Counties	For More Info . . .
2151	BURNS, Archibald (Cont'd)	29	SWSW	1858-11-01		A1
2152	" "	30	NESE	1858-11-01		A1
2272	BURNS, Samuel	29	SWNW	1854-07-15		A1
2273	"	30	SENE	1854-07-15		A1
2144	CARTER, Abner	4	NENE	1852-02-02		A1
2146	CARTER, Absalom	5	E½SW	1837-08-15		A1
2147	" "	5	NENW	1837-08-15		A1
2149	" "	5	W½NW	1837-08-15		A1
2148	" "	5	NWSE	1838-07-28		A1
2145	" "	4	SENE	1852-12-01		A1
2260	CARTER, Nancy	6	NENE	1849-09-01		A1
2318	COLEMAN, William	20	NENW	1835-10-01		A1
2319	" "	20	SWNE	1835-10-01		A1
2292	DEAN, Thomas	20	SENW	1854-07-15		A1
2293	" "	20	SESW	1854-07-15		A1
2294	" "	20	SWSE	1854-07-15		A1
2295	" "	20	W½SW	1854-07-15		A1
2164	FAIL, Dixon N	15	NENE	1858-11-01	Crenshaw	A1
2165	" "	15	NENW	1858-11-01	Crenshaw	A1
2166	" "	15	W½NE	1858-11-01	Crenshaw	A1
2172	FROST, Henry	7	NENE	1850-08-10		A1
2310	GANEY, Thomas T	17	NESE	1849-09-01		A1
2320	GOLDSTON, William	4	NWNE	1850-08-10		A1
2321	GRAHAM, William	18	SWSW	1849-09-01		A1
2296	GRIFFIN, Thomas	15	NWSE	1858-11-01	Crenshaw	A1
2297	"	15	SESE	1858-11-01	Crenshaw	A1
2315	GRIFFIN, Wesley	31	NENE	1852-02-02		A1
2154	HARRISON, Augustus	8	NWSE	1849-09-01		A1
2155	" "	8	SESE	1852-02-02		A1
2156	" "	8	SWNE	1858-09-01		A1
2157	" "	9	W½SW	1858-09-01		A1
2334	HARRISON, Williamson	18	SWNW	1854-07-15		A1
2335	" "	30	NWSW	1858-11-01		A1
2336	" "	30	SESE	1858-11-01		A1
2337	" "	30	SESW	1858-11-01		A1
2180	HENDERSON, Herndon L	19	W½SW	1837-08-09		A1
2326	HENDERSON, William M	19	W½SE	1843-02-01		A1
2215	JAY, John	8	NENE	1843-02-01		A1
2218	" "	9	NWNW	1848-04-01		A1
2214	" "	6	SENE	1849-09-01		A1
2216	" "	8	NWNW	1849-09-01		A1
2217	" "	8	SWNW	1849-09-01		A1
2211	" "	5	NWSW	1850-08-10		A1
2213	" "	5	SWSW	1851-04-10		A1
2212	" "	5	SWSE	1858-11-01		A1
2219	KIRVIN, John	4	W½SW	1837-08-15		A1
2193	KITCHENS, James	32	NWNW	1858-11-01		A1
2262	MARKS, Nicholas M	5	E½NE	1837-08-15		A1
2206	MCBRIDE, Jesse J	21	NENW	1850-08-10		A1
2205	" "	20	SENE	1854-07-15		A1
2182	MCCORMACK, Isabella	21	NWNE	1850-08-10		A1
2298	MCCORMACK, Thomas	21	NESE	1850-05-01		A1
2299	" "	21	NESW	1852-02-02		A1
2300	" "	21	NWSE	1852-02-02		A1
2301	" "	21	S½SE	1858-11-01		A1
2302	" "	28	E½NE	1858-11-01		A1
2303	" "	28	E½SE	1858-11-01		A1
2304	" "	28	SWNE	1858-11-01		A1
2183	MCCORMICK, Isabella	20	NESE	1852-02-02		A1
2184	" "	21	NWSW	1852-02-02		A1
2170	MCCREELESS, George	9	NE	1821-12-03		A1
2226	MCCULLOUGH, Jonathan C	28	SWNW	1837-08-02		A1 F
2227	" "	29	SENE	1837-08-02		A1 F
2160	MCKENZIE, Charles	6	SWSE	1850-08-10		A1
2245	MCKENZIE, Kinith	6	SESW	1852-02-02		A1
2162	MCKINZIE, Charles	7	SESE	1848-05-03		A1
2161	" "	6	SESE	1849-09-01		A1
2271	MCPOLLARD, Roderick	8	NWSW	1852-02-02		A1
2331	MERCER, William	5	NESE	1858-11-01		A1
2258	MILLS, Morgan	29	E½SW	1838-07-28		A1
2259	" "	29	SE	1838-07-28		A1
2181	MORGAN, Ira B	9	NWSE	1854-07-15		A1
2307	MORGAN, Thomas R	6	W½NW	1835-10-08		A1

ID	Individual in Patent	Sec.	Sec. Part	Date Issued	Other Counties	For More Info . . .
2306	MORGAN, Thomas R (Cont'd)	6	NENW	1837-08-10		A1
2308	" "	7	SENW	1858-11-01		A1
2309	" "	7	W½NW	1858-11-01		A1
2328	MORGAN, William M	5	SENW	1837-08-10		A1
2327	" "	4	SWSE	1838-07-28		A1
2329	" "	9	NENW	1850-08-10		A1
2322	NIX, William H	32	E½NE	1858-11-01		A1
2275	OLIVER, Samuel	6	SENW	1837-08-15		A1
2276	" "	6	W½NE	1837-08-15		A1
2277	" "	6	W½SW	1837-08-15		A1
2274	" "	6	NESW	1848-05-03		A1
2228	PARMER, Joseph M	4	NW	1838-07-28		A1
2305	PEEVY, Thomas	5	W½NE	1837-05-20		A1
2230	PERDUE, Joshua A	8	NENW	1848-05-03		A1
2229	" "	5	SESE	1858-11-01		A1
2231	" "	8	NWNE	1858-11-01		A1
2291	PETERSON, Thomas B	30	E½NW	1858-11-01		A1
2153	PHELPS, Ardin J	33	W½SW	1837-08-02		A1
2168	PHELPS, Edward A	33	NWNW	1852-12-01		A1
2169	" "	33	SENW	1852-12-01		A1
2167	" "	30	SWNW	1853-11-15		A1
2194	PHELPS, James	33	NENW	1837-08-15		A1
2195	" "	33	NWNE	1837-08-15		A1
2247	PHELPS, Lorenzo D	31	NWSE	1852-02-02		A1
2246	" "	30	NWSE	1854-07-15		A1
2286	PHELPS, Terel	33	E½SE	1858-11-01		A1
2289	PHELPS, Terrel	33	SESW	1854-07-15		A1
2288	" "	33	NESW	1854-10-02		A1
2290	" "	33	SWSE	1858-09-01		A1
2287	" "	32	E½SE	1858-11-01		A1
2268	POLLARD, Roderick M	7	N½SE	1858-11-01		A1
2269	" "	7	SENE	1858-11-01		A1
2270	" "	8	SENW	1858-11-01		A1
2163	RABUN, David	30	NESW	1852-12-01		A1
2221	RABUN, John	31	SWSE	1837-08-15		A1
2265	RABUN, Richard	31	NWNE	1853-08-01		A1
2263	RABURN, Reuben	30	SWSE	1850-08-10		A1
2264	" "	31	NENW	1850-08-10		A1
2266	RABURN, Richard	30	SWSW	1835-10-14		A1
2267	" "	31	W½NW	1837-05-20		A1
2222	RAYBORNE, John	31	SESW	1849-09-01		A1
2281	SCIPPER, Sion	21	SENE	1850-05-01		A1
2158	SKIPPER, Barnabas	15	SESW	1837-08-18	Crenshaw	A1
2159	" "	15	SWSE	1838-07-28	Crenshaw	A1
2282	SKIPPER, Sion	21	NENE	1852-02-02		A1
2283	" "	28	NWNE	1852-02-02		A1
2330	SMITH, William M	30	NWNW	1838-07-28		A1
2223	SMYTH, John	17	SESE	1849-09-01		A1
2224	TAYLOR, John	19	E½SW	1825-04-09		A1
2332	TAYLOR, William	30	W½NE	1825-04-02		A1
2174	TERRY, Henry	19	SESE	1852-02-02		A1
2176	" "	29	NWNE	1852-02-02		A1
2173	" "	19	NESE	1858-11-01		A1
2175	" "	29	E½NW	1858-11-01		A1
2177	" "	29	NWNW	1858-11-01		A1
2178	" "	29	SWNE	1858-11-01		A1
2179	" "	30	NENE	1858-11-01		A1
2192	THOMPSON, James K	7	NENW	1852-02-02		A1
2220	THOMPSON, John P	6	NWSE	1852-02-02		A1
2186	THORNTON, Jacob	31	NWSW	1849-09-01		A1
2188	" "	31	SWSW	1850-05-01		A1
2185	" "	31	NESW	1852-02-02		A1
2187	" "	31	SENW	1852-02-02		A1
2311	TINSLEY, Thomas	18	NWSW	1835-10-01		A1
2189	TURNER, Jacob	21	NWNW	1852-02-02		A1
2202	VEAZEY, Jesse H	15	SWNW	1852-02-02	Crenshaw	A1
2199	" "	15	N½SW	1858-11-01	Crenshaw	A1
2200	" "	15	NWNW	1858-11-01	Crenshaw	A1
2201	" "	15	SENW	1858-11-01	Crenshaw	A1
2203	" "	15	SWSW	1858-11-01	Crenshaw	A1
2204	" "	9	E½SE	1858-11-01		A1
2316	WHIDDON, Wester	4	NESE	1845-07-01		A1
2317	" "	4	SESE	1847-05-01		A1

ID	Individual in Patent	Sec.	Sec. Part	Date Issued	Other Counties	For More Info . . .
2225	WHITTEN, John	4	SWNE	1838-07-28		A1
2261	WHITTON, Nancy	4	NWSE	1841-05-20		A1

Patent Map

T10-N R16-E
St Stephens Meridian

Map Group 10

Township Statistics

Parcels Mapped	:	194
Number of Patents	:	158
Number of Individuals	:	90
Patentees Identified	:	90
Number of Surnames	:	62
Multi-Patentee Parcels	:	0
Oldest Patent Date	:	12/3/1821
Most Recent Patent	:	11/1/1858
Block/Lot Parcels	:	0
Parcels Re - Issued	:	0
Parcels that Overlap	:	0
Cities and Towns	:	1
Cemeteries	:	1

Patent map grid (Sections 4–9, 16–21, 28–33):

Section 6: MORGAN Thomas R 1835; MORGAN Thomas R 1837; OLIVER Samuel 1837; CARTER Nancy 1849; OLIVER Samuel 1837; JAY John 1849; OLIVER Samuel 1837; OLIVER Samuel 1848; THOMPSON John P 1852; BELL John 1837; MCKENZIE Kinith 1852; MCKENZIE Charles 1850; MCKINZIE Charles 1849

Section 5: CARTER Absalom 1837; CARTER Absalom 1837; MORGAN William M 1837; JAY John 1850; JAY John 1851; CARTER Absalom 1838; CARTER Absalom 1837

Section 4: PEEVY Thomas 1837; MARKS Nicholas M 1837; MERCER William 1858; JAY John 1858; PERDUE Joshua A 1858; KIRVIN John 1837; PARMER Joseph M 1838; GOLDSTON William 1850; CARTER Abner 1852; WHITTEN John 1838; CARTER Absalom 1852; WHITTON Nancy 1841; WHIDDON Wester 1845; MORGAN William M 1838; WHIDDON Wester 1847

Section 7: THOMPSON James K 1852; ANDRESS William J 1848; FROST Henry 1850; MORGAN Thomas R 1858; MORGAN Thomas R 1858; POLLARD Roderick M 1858; POLLARD Roderick M 1858; ANDRESS William J 1848; MCKINZIE Charles 1848

Section 8: JAY John 1849; PERDUE Joshua A 1848; JAY John 1849; PERDUE Joshua A 1858; POLLARD Roderick M 1858; MCPOLLARD Roderick 1852; BARRETT Joshua 1858; HARRISON Augustus 1858; HARRISON Augustus 1849; BELL James 1838; BELL James 1835; BARRETT Joshua 1849; HARRISON Augustus 1852

Section 9: PERDUE Joshua A 1858; JAY John 1843; JAY John 1848; MORGAN William M 1850; MCCREELESS George 1821; HARRISON Augustus 1858; MORGAN Ira B 1854; BARRETT Joshua 1858; BARRETT Joshua 1858; VEAZEY Jesse H 1858

Section 18: ANDRESS Jeremiah 1852; ANDRESS Jeremiah 1845; ANDRESS William J 1848; HARRISON Williamson 1854; ANDRESS Jeremiah 1852; TINSLEY Thomas 1835; BARRETT Joshua 1858; ANDRESS Stephen F 1858; GRAHAM William 1849; BARRETT Joshua 1858; ARMSTRONG Mitchell 1837

Section 17: BARRETT Joshua 1837; BARRETT Joshua 1858

Section 16: Butler County

Section 19: ANDRESS Stephen F 1858; HENDERSON Herndon L 1837; TAYLOR John 1825; HENDERSON William M 1843; TERRY Henry 1858; TERRY Henry 1852

Section 20: COLEMAN William 1835; DEAN Thomas 1854; ARMSTRONG Jesse M 1843; MCCORMICK Isabella 1843; DEAN Thomas 1854; COLEMAN William 1835; MCBRIDE Jesse J 1854; BARRETT Timothy 1835; BARRETT Joshua 1849; DEAN Thomas 1854; DEAN Thomas 1854

Section 21: TURNER Jacob 1852; MCBRIDE Jesse J 1850; MCCORMACK Isabella 1850; SKIPPER Sion 1852; ARMSTRONG Maximilian 1837; ARMSTRONG Mitchell 1837; ARMSTRONG Maximilian 1837; SCIPPER Sion 1850; MCCORMICK Isabella 1852; MCCORMACK Thomas 1852; MCCORMACK Thomas 1850; MCCORMACK Thomas 1858

Section 30: SMITH William M 1838; TAYLOR William 1825; TERRY Henry 1858; PETERSON Thomas B 1858; PHELPS Edward A 1853; BURNS Samuel 1854; HARRISON Williamson 1858; RABUN David 1852; PHELPS Lorenzo D 1854; BURNS Archibald 1858; RABURN Richard 1835; HARRISON Williamson 1858; RABURN Reuben 1850; HARRISON Williamson 1858

Section 29: TERRY Henry 1858; TERRY Henry 1852; TERRY Henry 1858; BURNS Samuel 1854; MILLS Morgan 1838; MILLS Morgan 1838; BURNS Archibald 1854; MCCULLOUGH Jonathan C 1837

Section 28: MCCULLOUGH Jonathan C 1837; BOGGUS Silus 1858; BOGGUS Silus 1858; SKIPPER Sion 1852; MCCORMACK Thomas 1858; MCCORMACK Thomas 1858; BOGGUS Silus 1858; BARRINGTON William W 1858

Section 31: RABURN Richard 1837; RABURN Reuben 1850; RABUN Richard 1853; GRIFFIN Wesley 1852; THORNTON Jacob 1852; BRADEN Harvey C 1852; THORNTON Jacob 1849; THORNTON Jacob 1852; PHELPS Lorenzo D 1852; THORNTON Jacob 1850; RAYBORNE John 1849; RABUN John 1837

Section 32: KITCHENS James 1858; BISHOP Mathew 1854; BISHOP Matthew 1858; NIX William H 1858; BISHOP Mathew 1854; BISHOP Matthew 1852; BISHOP Matthew 1858; BISHOP Matthew 1858; PHELPS Terrel 1858

Section 33: PHELPS Edward A 1852; PHELPS James 1837; PHELPS James 1837; PHELPS Edward A 1852; ALLEN Washington W 1858; PHELPS Terrel 1854; PHELPS Ardin J 1837; PHELPS Terrel 1854; PHELPS Terrel 1858; PHELPS Terel 1858

| 3 | 2 | 1 |
| 10 | 11 | 12 |

VEAZEY Jesse H 1858	FAIL Dixon N 1858	FAIL Dixon N 1858	FAIL Dixon N 1858
VEAZEY Jesse H 1852	VEAZEY Jesse H 1858	15	ACREE John E 1858
VEAZEY Jesse H 1858		GRIFFIN Thomas 1858	ACREE John E 1858
VEAZEY Jesse H 1858	SKIPPER Barnabas 1837	SKIPPER Barnabas 1838	GRIFFIN Thomas 1858

| 14 | 13 |

Crenshaw County

22 | 23 | 24
27 | 26 | 25
34 | 35 | 36

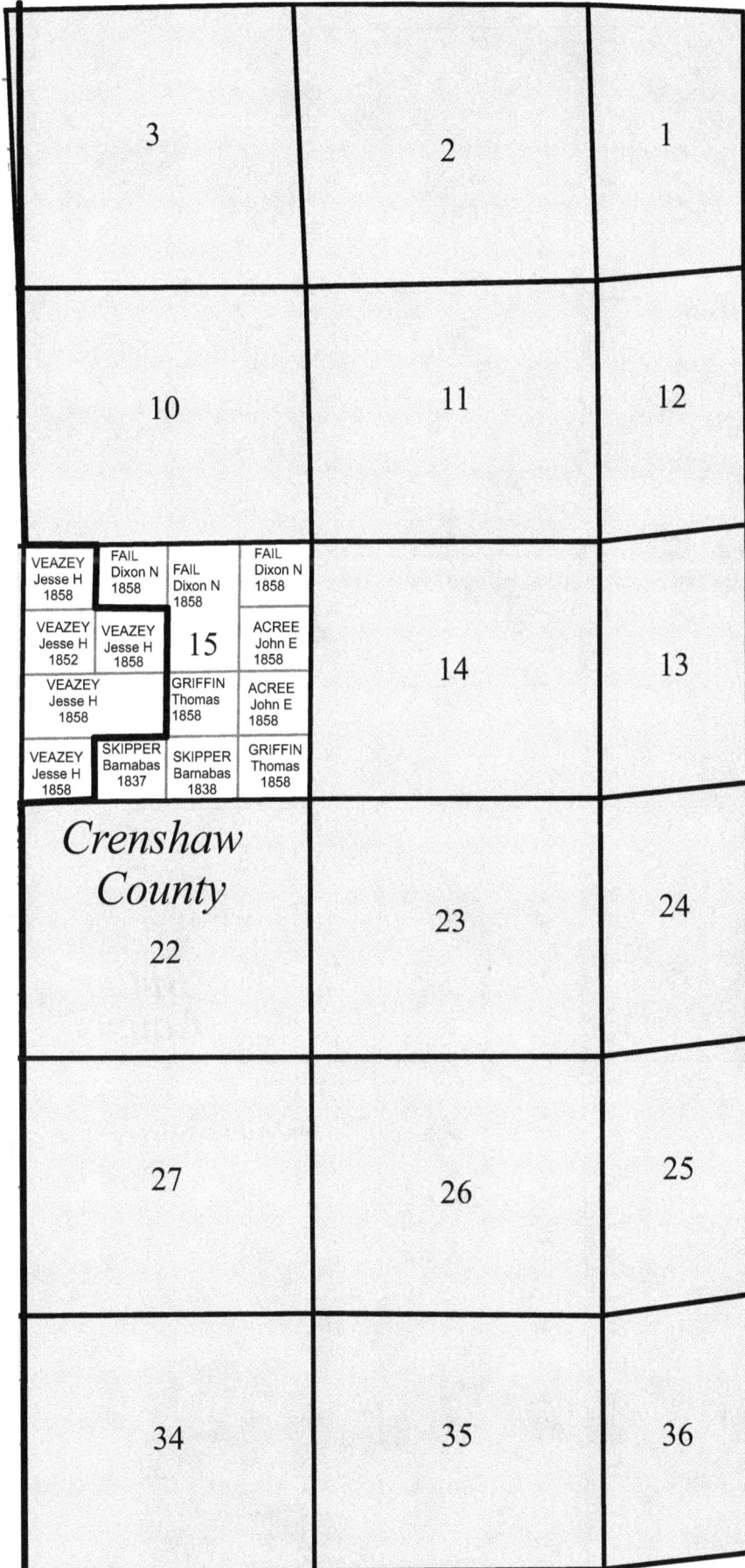

Helpful Hints

1. This Map's INDEX can be found on the preceding pages.

2. Refer to Map "C" to see where this Township lies within Butler County, Alabama.

3. Numbers within square brackets [ ] denote a multi-patentee land parcel (multi-owner). Refer to Appendix "C" for a full list of members in this group.

4. Areas that look to be crowded with Patentees usually indicate multiple sales of the same parcel (Re-issues) or Overlapping parcels. See this Township's Index for an explanation of these and other circumstances that might explain "odd" groupings of Patentees on this map.

Legend

- Patent Boundary
- Section Boundary
- No Patents Found (or Outside County)
- 1., 2., 3., ... Lot Numbers (when beside a name)
- [ ] Group Number (see Appendix "C")

Scale: Section = 1 mile X 1 mile (generally, with some exceptions)

Road Map

T10-N R16-E
St Stephens Meridian

Map Group 10

Cities & Towns
Midway

Cemeteries
Damascus Cemetery

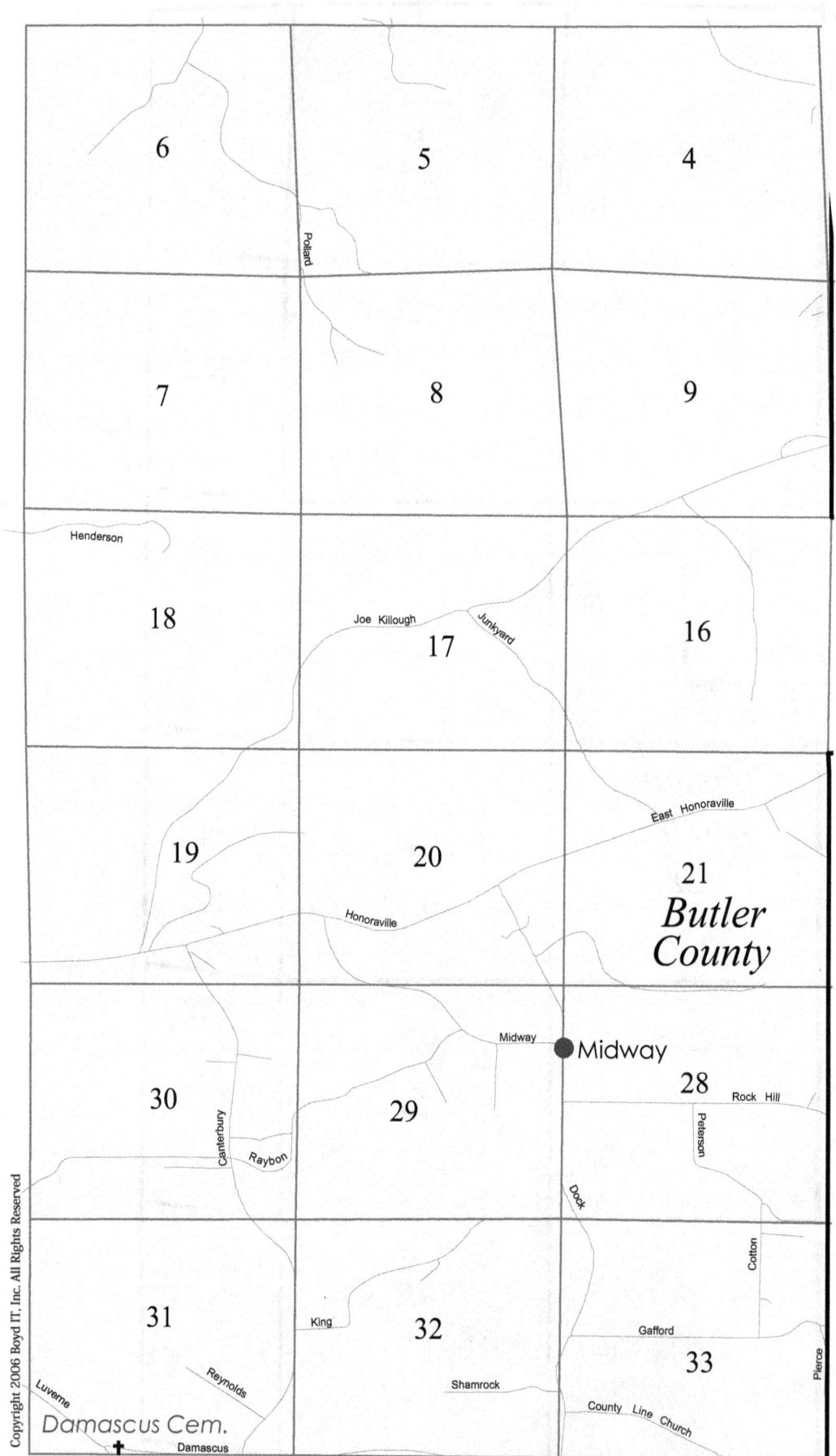

6

5

4

Pollard

7

8

9

Henderson

18

Joe Killough

Junkyard

17

16

East Honoraville

19

20

21

Butler County

Honoraville

Midway ● Midway

30

Canterbury

Raybon

29

28

Rock Hill

Peterson

Dock

Cotton

31

King

32

Gafford

33

Reynolds

Luverne

Shamrock

County Line Church

Pierce

Damascus Cem.

✝

Damascus

3

2

1

10

11

12

Greenleaf

15

14

13

22

Crenshaw County

23

24

27

26

25

34

35

36

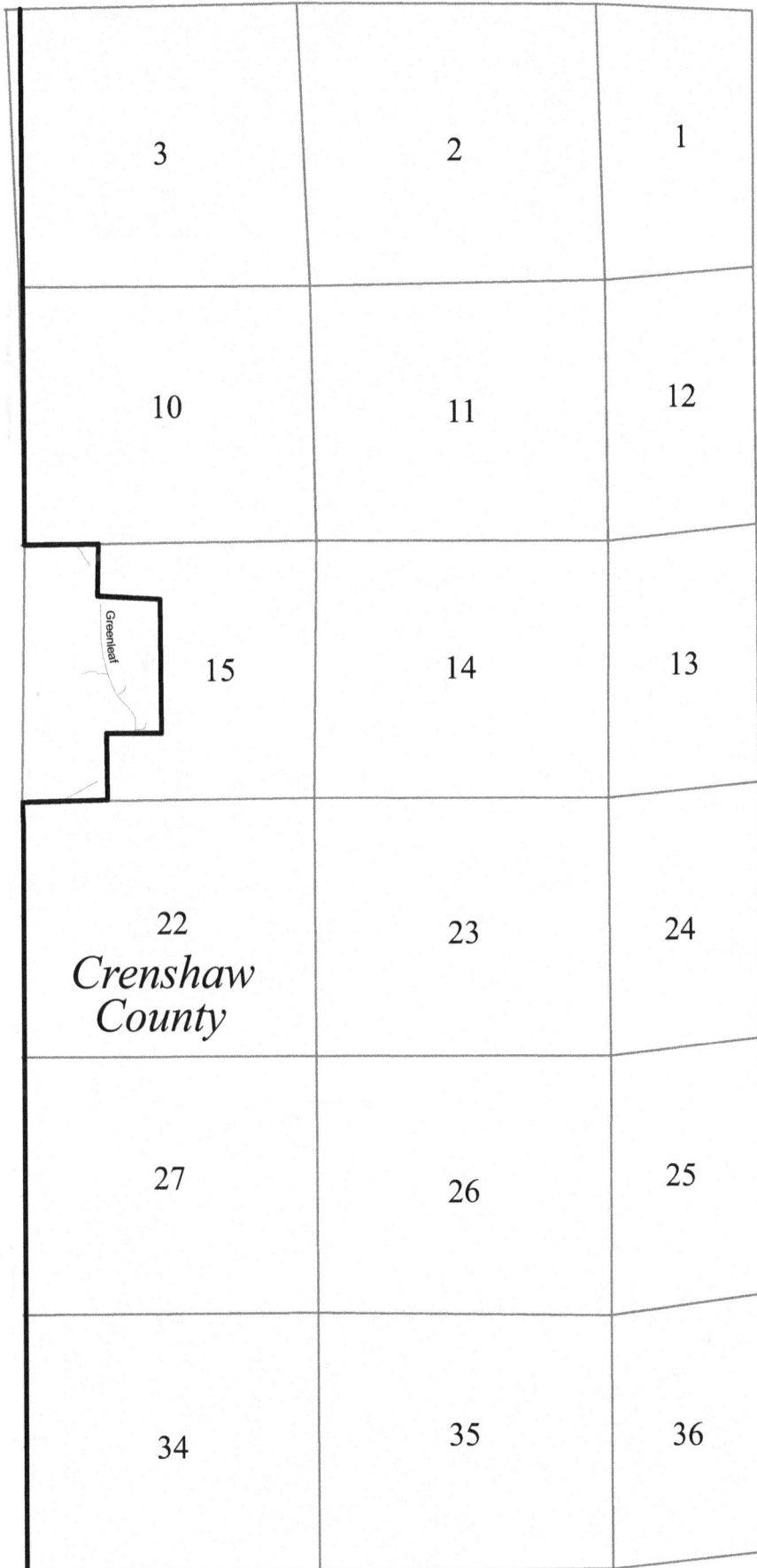

Helpful Hints

1. This road map has a number of uses, but primarily it is to help you: a) find the present location of land owned by your ancestors (at least the general area), b) find cemeteries and city-centers, and c) estimate the route/roads used by Census-takers & tax-assessors.

2. If you plan to travel to Butler County to locate cemeteries or land parcels, please pick up a modern travel map for the area before you do. Mapping old land parcels on modern maps is not as exact a science as you might think. Just the slightest variations in public land survey coordinates, estimates of parcel boundaries, or road-map deviations can greatly alter a map's representation of how a road either does or doesn't cross a particular parcel of land.

L e g e n d

	Section Lines
	Interstates
	Highways
	Other Roads
●	Cities/Towns
✝	Cemeteries

Scale: Section = 1 mile X 1 mile
(generally, with some exceptions)

Historical Map

T10-N R16-E
St Stephens Meridian

Map Group 10

Cities & Towns
Midway

Cemeteries
Damascus Cemetery

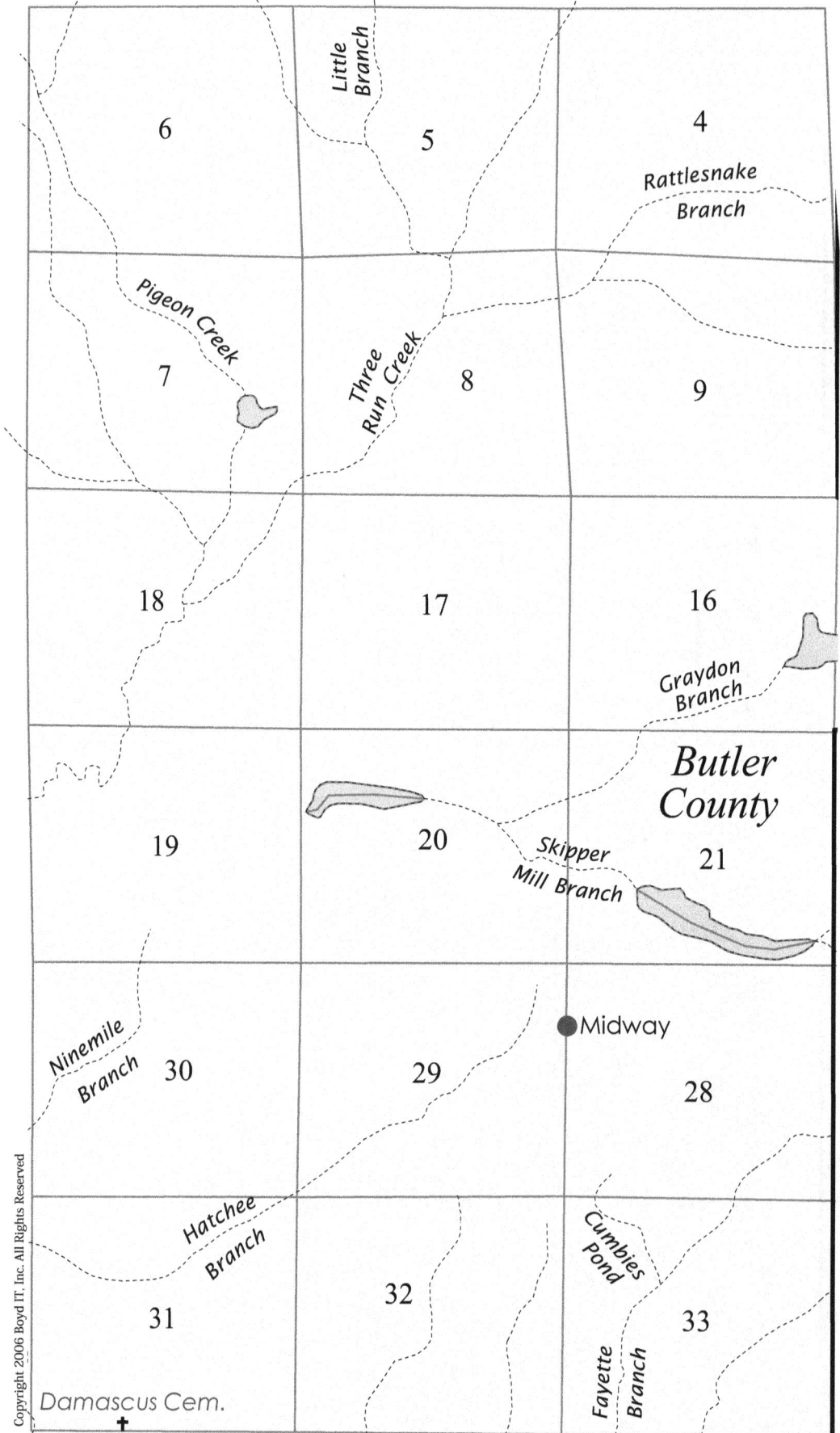

6

5

4

Little Branch

Rattlesnake Branch

Pigeon Creek

7

Three Run Creek

8

9

18

17

16

Graydon Branch

Butler County

19

20

21

Skipper Mill Branch

Ninemile Branch

30

29

●Midway

28

Hatchee Branch

31

32

33

Cumbies Pond

Fayette Branch

Damascus Cem.
✝

154

3	2	1
10	11	12
15	14	13
22	23	24
27	26	25
34	35	36

Crenshaw County

Helpful Hints

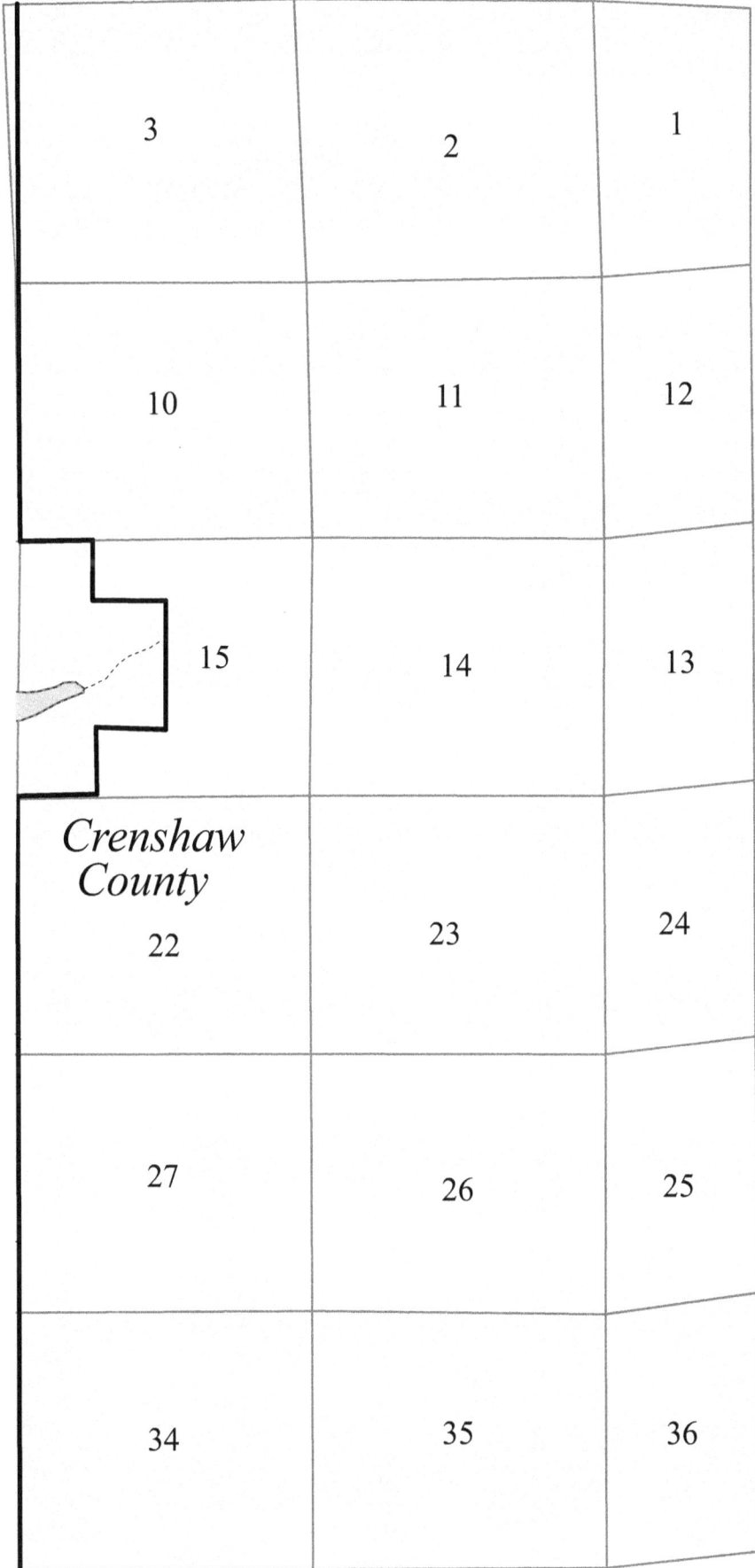

1. This Map takes a different look at the same Congressional Township displayed in the preceding two maps. It presents features that can help you better envision the historical development of the area: a) Water-bodies (lakes & ponds), b) Water-courses (rivers, streams, etc.), c) Railroads, d) City/town center-points (where they were oftentimes located when first settled), and e) Cemeteries.

2. Using this "Historical" map in tandem with this Township's Patent Map and Road Map, may lead you to some interesting discoveries. You will often find roads, towns, cemeteries, and waterways are named after nearby landowners: sometimes those names will be the ones you are researching. See how many of these research gems you can find here in Butler County.

Legend

————————	Section Lines
—+—+—+—+—	Railroads
▭	Large Rivers & Bodies of Water
- - - - - - - -	Streams/Creeks & Small Rivers
●	Cities/Towns
✝	Cemeteries

Scale: Section = 1 mile X 1 mile
(there are some exceptions)

Map Group 11: Index to Land Patents

Township 9-North Range 12-East (St Stephens)

After you locate an individual in this Index, take note of the Section and Section Part then proceed to the Land Patent map on the pages immediately following. You should have no difficulty locating the corresponding parcel of land.

The "For More Info" Column will lead you to more information about the underlying Patents. See the *Legend* at right, and the "How to Use this Book" chapter, for more information.

```
                          LEGEND
              "For More Info . . . " column
A = Authority (Legislative Act, See Appendix "A")
B = Block or Lot (location in Section unknown)
C = Cancelled Patent
F = Fractional Section
G = Group  (Multi-Patentee Patent, see Appendix "C")
V = Overlaps another Parcel
R = Re-Issued (Parcel patented more than once)

(A & G items require you to look in the Appendixes referred
to above. All other Letter-designations followed by a number
require you to locate line-items in this index that possess
the ID number found after the letter).
```

ID	Individual in Patent	Sec.	Sec. Part	Date Issued	Other Counties	For More Info . . .
2457	AINSWORTH, James P	28	NENW	1850-08-10		A1
2542	AINSWORTH, Joseph C	12	SESW	1858-11-01		A1
2543	" "	20	SE	1858-11-01		A1
2597	ALBRITTON, Silas W	4	N½SW	1858-11-01		A1
2598	" "	4	S½NW	1858-11-01		A1
2624	AMOS, William	17	E½NW	1858-11-01		A1
2431	BARRON, Jacob	27	SWSW	1849-09-01		A1
2430	" "	27	NWSW	1858-09-01		A1
2625	BELL, William	13	S½NE	1858-11-01		A1
2626	" "	13	SE	1858-11-01		A1
2627	" "	24	N½NE	1858-11-01		A1
2432	BENNETT, James A	5	S½SW	1858-11-01		A1
2433	" "	5	SESE	1858-11-01		A1
2434	" "	5	W½SE	1858-11-01		A1
2478	BILBERRY, John	24	NW	1858-11-01		A1
2479	" "	24	S½NE	1858-11-01		A1
2435	BLACKMAN, James	19	SENW	1845-07-01		A1
2486	BLACKMAN, John C	11	NESW	1858-11-01		A1
2487	" "	11	NWSE	1858-11-01		A1
2488	" "	11	SESE	1858-11-01		A1
2489	" "	12	NESW	1858-11-01		A1
2490	" "	12	W½SW	1858-11-01		A1
2628	BLACKMAN, William	20	NWNW	1852-02-02		A1
2491	BLACKMON, John C	11	NENE	1858-11-01		A1 R2366
2492	" "	11	NESE	1858-11-01		A1
2633	BLACKMON, William	20	NWNE	1845-07-01		A1
2630	" "	17	SESE	1858-11-01		A1
2631	" "	20	E½NW	1858-11-01		A1
2634	" "	20	SENE	1858-11-01		A1
2635	" "	20	SWNW	1858-11-01		A1
2629	" "	17	E½SW	1860-04-02		A1
2632	" "	20	NENE	1860-04-02		A1
2525	BREWER, John W	20	SWNE	1860-09-01		A1
2338	BURKET, Alfred	34	E½NW	1858-11-01		A1
2339	" "	34	SESW	1858-11-01		A1
2340	" "	34	SWSE	1858-11-01		A1
2363	BURKET, Caleb	13	NW	1858-09-01		A1
2386	BURKET, Emanuel	25	NESE	1858-11-01		A1
2387	" "	25	SESE	1858-11-01		A1
2388	" "	25	W½SE	1858-11-01		A1
2389	" "	36	NENE	1858-11-01		A1
2636	BURKET, William	25	E½SW	1858-11-01		A1
2637	" "	36	NENW	1858-11-01		A1
2638	" "	36	NWNE	1858-11-01		A1
2341	BURKETT, Alfred	33	NESE	1858-11-01		A1
2342	" "	34	N½SW	1858-11-01		A1

ID	Individual in Patent	Sec.	Sec. Part	Date Issued	Other Counties	For More Info . . .
2364	BURKETT, Caleb	12	S½NW	1875-04-20		A1
2408	BURKETT, Henry	35	N½SW	1858-11-01		A1
2409	" "	35	SWNE	1858-11-01		A1 V2552
2427	BURKETT, Ivin	25	W½SW	1858-09-01		A1
2428	" "	26	SE	1858-09-01		A1
2429	" "	35	N½NE	1858-09-01		A1
2482	BURKETT, John	33	NWSE	1850-08-10		A1
2483	" "	33	SENE	1850-08-10		A1
2480	" "	28	S½SE	1858-11-01		A1
2481	" "	33	NENE	1858-11-01		A1
2484	" "	33	W½NE	1858-11-01		A1
2485	" "	34	W½NW	1858-11-01		A1
2536	BURKETT, Joseph	27	S½SE	1858-11-01		A1
2537	" "	27	SESW	1858-11-01		A1
2538	" "	34	N½SE	1858-11-01		A1
2539	" "	34	NWNE	1858-11-01		A1
2540	" "	34	S½NE	1858-11-01		A1
2541	" "	34	SESE	1858-11-01		A1
2614	BURKETT, Thomas	35	NWNW	1838-07-28		A1
2611	" "	26	S½SW	1858-11-01		A1
2612	" "	34	NENE	1858-11-01		A1
2613	" "	35	E½NW	1858-11-01		A1
2555	BYRD, Martin	31	SE	1858-11-01		A1
2556	" "	31	W½NE	1858-11-01		A1
2473	COLEMAN, Jesse	36	SENE	1858-09-01		A1
2475	" "	36	SWNE	1858-09-01		A1
2474	" "	36	SENW	1858-11-01		A1
2476	" "	36	W½NW	1858-11-01		A1
2494	COLEMAN, John	23	N½SE	1860-04-02		A1
2495	" "	23	NE	1860-04-02		A1
2496	" "	23	SWSE	1860-04-02		A1
2497	" "	26	NWNE	1860-04-02		A1
2570	COLEMAN, Philip	27	E½NE	1858-11-01		A1
2571	" "	27	N½SE	1858-11-01		A1
2572	" "	27	NESW	1858-11-01		A1
2575	COLEMAN, Rachael	36	SE	1858-11-01		A1
2576	" "	36	SW	1858-11-01		A1
2560	CREMER, Michael	5	E½NW	1858-09-01		A1
2562	" "	5	W½NE	1858-09-01		A1
2559	" "	5	E½NE	1858-11-01		A1
2561	" "	5	N½SW	1858-11-01		A1
2601	DAVIS, Sinie A	23	W½	1858-09-01		A1
2379	DEEN, Drury	31	E½SW	1837-08-08		A1 R2521
2380	" "	31	NWSW	1837-08-08		A1
2620	DEEN, Thomas M	31	SENW	1837-08-18		A1
2617	" "	30	SESW	1858-11-01		A1
2618	" "	30	W½SW	1858-11-01		A1
2619	" "	31	NENW	1858-11-01		A1
2381	DOZIER, Edmond	9	N½SE	1858-11-01		A1
2382	" "	9	NENW	1858-11-01		A1
2383	" "	9	SENW	1858-11-01		A1
2384	" "	9	W½NE	1858-11-01		A1
2503	EALUM, John	21	E½NW	1858-11-01		A1
2504	" "	21	NENE	1858-11-01		A1
2505	" "	21	NWNW	1858-11-01		A1
2506	" "	21	W½NE	1858-11-01		A1
2507	ELAM, John	21	NESE	1858-11-01		A1
2508	" "	21	SENE	1858-11-01		A1
2586	FELPS, Samuel	23	SESE	1858-11-01		A1
2587	" "	25	W½NW	1858-11-01		A1
2588	" "	26	NENE	1858-11-01		A1
2415	FINKLEA, Hugh	29	W½SE	1837-08-18		A1
2416	" "	32	SWNE	1837-08-18		A1
2417	" "	32	W½SE	1837-08-18		A1
2418	" "	33	SWNW	1837-08-18		A1
2616	FINKLEA, Thomas	31	W½NW	1824-03-01		A1
2419	FINKLEY, Hugh	31	E½NE	1858-11-01		A1
2420	" "	32	NW	1858-11-01		A1
2421	" "	32	W½SW	1858-11-01		A1
2639	GOODELL, William C	7	NE	1858-11-01		A1
2640	" "	7	NENW	1858-11-01		A1
2641	" "	7	NESE	1858-11-01		A1
2642	" "	8	N½NW	1858-11-01		A1

ID	Individual in Patent	Sec.	Sec. Part	Date Issued	Other Counties	For More Info . . .
2377	GRASON, David	25	SENW	1858-11-01		A1
2378	" "	25	SWNE	1858-11-01		A1
2590	GRAYSON, Sarah	25	NENW	1858-11-01		A1
2591	" "	25	SENE	1858-11-01		A1
2414	GREEN, Howard P	18	NWNE	1837-08-15		A1
2362	HALL, Benton	17	W½SE	1858-11-01		A1
2532	HARRISON, Jonathan A	6	W½	1858-11-01		A1
2370	HEMPHILL, Cornelius M	18	W½NW	1827-01-08		A1
2444	HENDERSON, James	7	W½SE	1843-02-01		A1
2443	" "	7	SESE	1858-11-01		A1
2445	" "	8	SWSW	1858-11-01		A1
2569	HILL, Peter E	4	E½SE	1837-08-15		A1
2574	HILSON, Pinckney W	10	NWNW	1837-08-18		A1
2514	HOOD, John	26	N½SW	1858-09-01		A1
2515	" "	26	NW	1858-09-01		A1
2516	" "	26	S½NE	1858-09-01		A1
2446	HOWEL, James	22	E½SE	1858-11-01		A1
2447	" "	22	W½SE	1858-11-01		A1
2448	" "	27	E½NW	1858-11-01		A1
2449	" "	27	W½NE	1858-11-01		A1
2643	HOWELL, William	19	SWNE	1848-05-03		A1
2544	HUNTER, Joseph C	30	E½NE	1837-08-18		A1
2343	JONES, Allen	12	N½SE	1858-11-01		A1
2344	" "	12	NE	1858-11-01		A1
2345	" "	12	SWSE	1858-11-01		A1
2589	JONES, Samuel	31	SWSW	1858-11-01		A1
2602	JONES, Sterling	30	NENW	1858-11-01		A1
2603	" "	30	NWNE	1858-11-01		A1
2392	LILES, Francis A	11	SWSE	1858-11-01		A1
2393	" "	11	SWSW	1858-11-01		A1
2394	" "	14	NENW	1858-11-01		A1
2395	" "	14	NWNE	1858-11-01		A1
2396	" "	14	W½NW	1858-11-01		A1
2397	" "	15	E½NE	1858-11-01		A1
2346	MCCRORY, Andrew J	28	SWNW	1843-02-01		A1
2422	MCCRORY, Hugh	28	SENW	1848-05-03		A1
2501	MCCRORY, John E	1	SWNW	1858-09-01		A1
2502	" "	2	E½NE	1858-09-01		A1
2498	" "	1	N½SW	1858-11-01		A1
2499	" "	1	S½SW	1858-11-01		A1
2500	" "	1	SENW	1858-11-01		A1
2371	MCNEILL, Daniel	9	NESW	1858-11-01		A1
2372	" "	9	NWNW	1858-11-01		A1
2373	" "	9	NWSW	1858-11-01		A1
2374	" "	9	S½SE	1858-11-01		A1
2375	" "	9	S½SW	1858-11-01		A1
2376	" "	9	SWNW	1858-11-01		A1
2519	MCNEILL, John	15	W½NW	1858-11-01		A1
2520	" "	15	W½SW	1858-11-01		A1
2526	MCNEILL, John W	2	NWSW	1875-04-20		A1
2527	" "	2	W½NW	1875-04-20		A1
2361	MIXON, Anthony W	6	E½	1858-11-01		A1
2450	MOORE, James J	21	N½SW	1858-11-01		A1
2451	" "	21	SWNW	1858-11-01		A1
2452	" "	21	W½SE	1858-11-01		A1
2453	" "	28	NENE	1860-04-02		A1
2454	" "	28	W½NE	1860-04-02		A1
2615	MOORE, Thomas D	34	SWSW	1858-11-01		A1
2547	MULLENS, Josiah	4	S½SW	1858-11-01		A1
2548	" "	4	W½SE	1858-11-01		A1
2549	MURPHY, Julius B	1	SE	1860-04-02		A1
2564	MYRICK, Moses	25	NWNE	1858-11-01		A1
2563	" "	24	S½	1875-04-20		A1
2477	ODOM, Jethro J	21	S½SW	1858-11-01		A1
2509	ODOM, John H	17	NENE	1858-11-01		A1
2510	" "	17	NESE	1858-11-01		A1
2511	" "	17	SENE	1858-11-01		A1
2512	" "	17	W½NE	1858-11-01		A1
2513	" "	8	S½SE	1858-11-01		A1
2644	ODOM, William	5	NESE	1837-08-15		A1
2573	OWEN, Phillip	30	NESW	1860-08-01		A1
2521	PARKER, John	31	E½SW	1837-08-18		A1 R2379
2410	PARKES, Henry D	4	W½NE	1858-09-01		A1

ID	Individual in Patent	Sec.	Sec. Part	Date Issued	Other Counties	For More Info . . .
2440	PARKES, James D	3	NWNW	1852-12-01		A1
2436	" "	10	NENW	1858-09-01		A1
2437	" "	10	SWNW	1858-09-01		A1
2438	" "	3	E½NW	1858-09-01		A1
2439	" "	3	E½SW	1858-09-01		A1
2441	" "	3	SWSW	1858-09-01		A1
2442	" "	9	NENE	1858-09-01		A1
2411	PARKS, Henry D	3	SWNW	1858-11-01		A1
2412	" "	4	E½NE	1858-11-01		A1
2413	" "	4	N½NW	1858-11-01		A1
2607	PARKS, Tempy D	10	NE	1858-11-01		A1
2608	" "	10	SENW	1858-11-01		A1
2609	" "	3	W½SE	1858-11-01		A1
2610	" "	9	SENE	1858-11-01		A1
2585	PARROTT, Robert	1	NENE	1837-08-18		A1
2423	PHILLIPS, Isham	17	W½NW	1858-11-01		A1
2424	" "	17	W½SW	1858-11-01		A1
2425	" "	18	E½SE	1858-11-01		A1
2426	" "	19	E½NE	1862-01-01		A1
2622	PHILLIPS, Wiley	11	NWNW	1858-11-01		A1
2623	" "	3	NE	1858-11-01		A1
2458	PINKERTON, James	18	W½SE	1858-11-01		A1
2459	" "	19	NWNE	1858-11-01		A1
2460	" "	29	W½SW	1858-11-01		A1
2461	" "	30	NWSE	1858-11-01		A1
2462	" "	30	S½SE	1858-11-01		A1
2565	SAVAGE, Nathan L	15	E½NW	1858-11-01		A1
2566	" "	15	E½SW	1858-11-01		A1
2567	" "	15	W½NE	1858-11-01		A1
2568	" "	22	N½NW	1858-11-01		A1
2621	SEAL, Thomas	2	E½SW	1825-04-02		A1
2599	SHULTZ, Simeon	1	SENE	1858-11-01		A1
2600	" "	1	W½NE	1858-11-01		A1
2463	SIMS, James	30	NESE	1850-08-10		A1
2592	SIMS, Sherrod	19	NESW	1850-08-10		A1
2593	" "	19	NWSW	1850-08-10		A1
2595	" "	30	NWNW	1850-08-10		A1
2594	" "	19	S½SW	1858-09-01		A1
2596	" "	30	S½NW	1858-09-01		A1
2604	SIMS, Susan	29	NWNW	1858-09-01		A1
2605	" "	29	SWNW	1858-09-01		A1
2606	" "	30	SWNE	1858-09-01		A1
2522	SIRMON, John R	19	E½SE	1858-11-01		A1
2523	" "	20	SW	1858-11-01		A1
2524	" "	29	E½NW	1858-11-01		A1
2385	SMITH, Elizabeth	27	SWNW	1858-11-01		A1
2403	STINSON, George	10	E½SE	1858-11-01		A1
2404	" "	10	E½SW	1858-11-01		A1
2405	" "	10	W½SE	1858-11-01		A1
2406	" "	10	W½SW	1858-11-01		A1
2528	STINSON, John W	21	SESE	1858-09-01		A1
2529	" "	22	S½NW	1858-09-01		A1
2530	" "	22	SW	1858-09-01		A1
2531	" "	27	NWNW	1858-09-01		A1
2545	STINSON, Joseph H	18	SW	1858-11-01		A1
2546	" "	19	N½NW	1858-11-01		A1
2552	STINSON, Leander	35	S½NE	1858-09-01		A1 V2409
2553	" "	35	SE	1858-09-01		A1
2554	" "	35	SESW	1858-09-01		A1
2579	STINSON, Reuben	28	SENE	1845-07-01		A1
2578	" "	19	SWNW	1849-09-01		A1
2577	" "	18	NENW	1850-04-01		A1
2581	STINSON, Rheubin	18	E½NE	1858-11-01		A1
2582	" "	18	SENW	1858-11-01		A1
2583	" "	18	SWNE	1858-11-01		A1
2584	" "	7	SW	1858-11-01		A1
2580	STRINGFELLOW, Reuben	5	W½NW	1858-11-01		A1
2550	TANKERSLEY, L	7	SENW	1837-08-15		A1
2551	" "	7	W½NW	1837-08-15		A1
2645	TATE, William W	13	SW	1860-04-02		A1
2646	" "	14	SE	1860-04-02		A1
2407	THAGARD, George W	25	NENE	1858-11-01		A1
2360	THOMPSON, Andrew	33	W½SW	1831-12-01		A1

ID	Individual in Patent	Sec.	Sec. Part	Date Issued	Other Counties	For More Info . . .
2355	THOMPSON, Andrew (Cont'd)	32	NESE	1835-09-12		A1
2354	" "	32	E½NE	1835-10-01		A1
2356	" "	32	NWNE	1837-08-12		A1
2352	" "	29	E½SE	1838-07-28		A1
2353	" "	29	E½SW	1838-07-28		A1
2357	" "	33	E½NW	1838-07-28		A1
2358	" "	33	E½SW	1838-07-28		A1
2359	" "	33	NWNW	1838-07-28		A1
2347	THOMPSON, Andrew P	19	W½SE	1858-09-01		A1
2348	" "	28	NWNW	1858-11-01		A1
2349	" "	28	NWSE	1858-11-01		A1
2350	" "	28	SW	1858-11-01		A1
2351	" "	29	NE	1858-11-01		A1
2470	THOMPSON, James	8	SENW	1848-04-01		A1
2464	" "	8	NENE	1858-11-01		A1
2467	" "	8	NWSE	1858-11-01		A1
2468	" "	8	NWSW	1858-11-01		A1
2472	" "	8	SWNW	1858-11-01		A1
2466	" "	8	NWNE	1860-04-02		A1
2465	" "	8	NESE	1896-10-26		A1
2469	" "	8	SENE	1896-10-26		A1
2471	" "	8	SESW	1896-10-26		A1
2493	THOMPSON, John C	32	SESE	1837-08-15		A1
2557	THOMPSON, Mary	8	NESW	1848-04-01		A1
2558	" "	8	SWNE	1848-04-01		A1
2399	TRAMMEL, George A	14	E½NE	1858-11-01		A1
2400	" "	14	SENW	1858-11-01		A1
2401	" "	14	SW	1858-11-01		A1
2402	" "	14	SWNE	1858-11-01		A1
2398	VICKREY, Franklin	1	N½NW	1858-11-01		A1
2517	VICKREY, John J	2	S½SE	1858-11-01		A1
2390	VICKRY, Fanny	2	E½NW	1858-11-01		A1
2391	" "	2	W½NE	1858-11-01		A1
2518	VICKRY, John J	2	N½SE	1858-11-01		A1
2455	WHITE, James M	15	SE	1858-11-01		A1
2456	" "	22	NE	1858-11-01		A1
2533	WHITTINGTON, Jonathan	12	SESE	1858-11-01		A1
2534	" "	13	NENE	1858-11-01		A1
2535	" "	13	NWNE	1858-11-01		A1
2365	WILSON, Calvin	11	E½NW	1858-11-01		A1
2366	" "	11	NENE	1858-11-01		A1 R2491
2367	" "	11	SWNW	1858-11-01		A1
2368	" "	11	W½NE	1858-11-01		A1
2369	" "	12	N½NW	1858-11-01		A1

Patent Map

T9-N R12-E
St Stephens Meridian

Map Group 11

Township Statistics

Parcels Mapped	:	309
Number of Patents	:	170
Number of Individuals	:	115
Patentees Identified	:	115
Number of Surnames	:	72
Multi-Patentee Parcels	:	0
Oldest Patent Date	:	3/1/1824
Most Recent Patent	:	10/26/1896
Block/Lot Parcels	:	0
Parcels Re - Issued	:	2
Parcels that Overlap	:	2
Cities and Towns	:	3
Cemeteries	:	2

Section 6
MIXON Anthony W 1858
HARRISON Jonathan A 1858

Section 5
STRINGFELLOW Reuben 1858
CREMER Michael 1858
CREMER Michael 1858
CREMER Michael 1858
CREMER Michael 1858
BENNETT James A 1858
ODOM William 1837
BENNETT James A 1858
BENNETT James A 1858

Section 4
PARKS Henry D 1858
PARKES Henry D 1858
PARKS Henry D 1858
ALBRITTON Silas W 1858
ALBRITTON Silas W 1858
MULLENS Josiah 1858
MULLENS Josiah 1858
HILL Peter E 1837

Section 7
TANKERSLEY L 1837
GOODELL William C 1858
TANKERSLEY L 1837
GOODELL William C 1858
HENDERSON James 1843
GOODELL William C 1858
STINSON Rheubin 1858
HENDERSON James 1858

Section 8
GOODELL William C 1858
THOMPSON James 1860
THOMPSON James 1858
THOMPSON James 1848
THOMPSON Mary 1848
THOMPSON James 1858
THOMPSON Mary 1848
HENDERSON James 1858
THOMPSON James 1896
THOMPSON James 1896
THOMPSON James 1858
THOMPSON James 1896
ODOM John H 1858

Section 9
THOMPSON James 1858
MCNEILL Daniel 1858
DOZIER Edmond 1858
DOZIER Edmond 1858
PARKES James D 1858
MCNEILL Daniel 1858
DOZIER Edmond 1858
PARKS Tempy D 1858
MCNEILL Daniel 1858
MCNEILL Daniel 1858
DOZIER Edmond 1858
MCNEILL Daniel 1858
MCNEILL Daniel 1858

Section 18
HEMPHILL Cornelius M 1827
STINSON Reuben 1850
GREEN Howard P 1837
STINSON Rheubin 1858
STINSON Rheubin 1858
STINSON Rheubin 1858
STINSON Joseph H 1858
PINKERTON James 1858

Section 17
STINSON Rheubin 1858
AMOS William 1858
PHILLIPS Isham 1858
PHILLIPS Isham 1858
PHILLIPS Isham 1858

Section 16

ODOM John H 1858
ODOM John H 1858
ODOM John H 1858
HALL Benton 1858
ODOM John H 1858
BLACKMON William 1858

Section 19
STINSON Joseph H 1858
PINKERTON James 1858
PHILLIPS Isham 1862
STINSON Reuben 1849
BLACKMAN James 1845
HOWELL William 1848
SIMS Sherrod 1850
SIMS Sherrod 1850
THOMPSON Andrew P 1858
SIMS Sherrod 1858
SIRMON John R 1858

Section 20
BLACKMAN William 1852
BLACKMON William 1858
BLACKMON William 1858
BLACKMON William 1845
BLACKMON William 1860
BREWER John W 1860
BLACKMON William 1858
SIRMON John R 1858
SIRMON John R 1858
AINSWORTH Joseph C 1858

Section 21
EALUM John 1858
EALUM John 1858
EALUM John 1858
EALUM John 1858
MOORE James J 1858
MOORE James J 1858
MOORE James J 1858
ODOM Jethro J 1858
ELAM John 1858
ELAM John 1858
STINSON John W 1858

Section 30
SIMS Sherrod 1850
JONES Sterling 1858
JONES Sterling 1858
HUNTER Joseph C 1837
SIMS Sherrod 1858
SIMS Susan 1858
OWEN Phillip 1860
PINKERTON James 1858
SIMS James 1850
DEEN Thomas M 1858
DEEN Thomas M 1858
PINKERTON James 1858

Section 29
SIMS Susan 1858
SIMS Susan 1858
SIRMON John R 1858
THOMPSON Andrew P 1858
PINKERTON James 1858
THOMPSON Andrew 1838
FINKLEA Hugh 1837
THOMPSON Andrew 1838

Section 28
THOMPSON Andrew P 1858
AINSWORTH James P 1850
MCCRORY Andrew J 1843
MCCRORY Hugh 1848
MOORE James J 1860
THOMPSON Andrew P 1858
THOMPSON Andrew P 1858
MOORE James J 1860
STINSON Reuben 1845
THOMPSON Andrew P 1858
BURKETT John 1858

Section 31
DEEN Thomas M 1858
FINKLEA Thomas 1824
DEEN Thomas M 1837
BYRD Martin 1858
FINKLEY Hugh 1858
DEEN Drury 1837
DEEN Drury 1837
BYRD Martin 1858
JONES Samuel 1858
PARKER John 1837

Section 32
FINKLEY Hugh 1858
FINKLEY Hugh 1858
FINKLEY Hugh 1858

Section 33
THOMPSON Andrew 1835
THOMPSON Andrew 1838
FINKLEA Hugh 1837
THOMPSON Andrew 1838
THOMPSON Andrew 1838
FINKLEA Hugh 1837
FINKLEA Hugh 1837
THOMPSON Andrew 1838
THOMPSON Andrew 1835
THOMPSON John C 1837
THOMPSON Andrew 1831
THOMPSON Andrew 1838
BURKETT John 1858
BURKETT John 1858
BURKETT John 1858
BURKETT John 1850
BURKETT John 1850
BURKETT Alfred 1858

Map Grid

Section 3
PARKES James D 1852
PARKS Henry D 1858
PARKES James D 1858
PHILLIPS Wiley 1858
3
PARKES James D 1858
PARKES James D 1858
PARKS Tempy D 1858

Section 2
MCNEILL John W 1875
VICKRY Fanny 1858
MCCRORY John E 1858
MCNEILL John W 1875
SEAL Thomas 1825
2
VICKRY John J 1858
VICKREY John J 1858

Section 1
VICKREY Franklin 1858
MCCRORY John E 1858
MCCRORY John E 1858
SHULTZ Simeon 1858
PARROTT Robert 1837
SHULTZ Simeon 1858
MCCRORY John E 1858
MCCRORY John E 1858
1
MURPHY Julius B 1860

Section 10
HILSON Pinckney W 1837
PARKES James D 1858
PARKES Tempy D 1858
PARKS Tempy D 1858
PARKS Tempy D 1858
10
STINSON George 1858
STINSON George 1858
STINSON George 1858
STINSON George 1858

Section 11
PHILLIPS Wiley 1858
WILSON Calvin 1858
WILSON Calvin 1858
WILSON Calvin 1858
11
BLACKMAN John C 1858
LILES Francis A 1858

Section 12
BLACKMON John C 1858 WILSON Calvin
WILSON Calvin 1858
BURKETT Caleb 1875
BLACKMON John C 1858
BLACKMAN John C 1858
BLACKMAN John C 1858
12
JONES Allen 1858
JONES Allen 1858
AINSWORTH Joseph C 1858
WHITTINGTON Jonathan 1858
WHITTINGTON JONES Allen 1858

Section 15
MCNEILL John 1858
SAVAGE Nathan L 1858
SAVAGE Nathan L 1858
LILES Francis A 1858
MCNEILL John 1858
15
WHITE James M 1858
SAVAGE Nathan L 1858

Section 14
LILES Francis A 1858
LILES Francis A 1858
TRAMMEL George A 1858
LILES Francis A 1858
14
TRAMMEL George A 1858
TATE William W 1860

Section 13
BURKET Caleb 1858
WHITTINGTON Jonathan 1858 WHITTINGTON Jonathan 1858
BELL William 1858
13
TATE William W 1860
BELL William 1858

Section 22
SAVAGE Nathan L 1858
STINSON John W 1858
WHITE James M 1858
22
STINSON John W 1858
HOWEL James 1858
HOWEL James 1858

Section 23
DAVIS Sinie A 1858
COLEMAN John 1860
23
COLEMAN John 1860
COLEMAN John 1860
FELPS Samuel 1858

Section 24
BILBERRY John 1858
BELL William 1858
BILBERRY John 1858
24
MYRICK Moses 1875

Section 27
STINSON John W 1858
HOWEL James 1858
SMITH Elizabeth 1858
HOWEL James 1858
COLEMAN Philip 1858
27
BARRON Jacob 1858
COLEMAN Philip 1858
COLEMAN Philip 1858
BARRON Jacob 1849
BURKETT Joseph 1858
BURKETT Joseph 1858

Section 26
COLEMAN John 1860
FELPS Samuel 1858
HOOD John 1858
26
HOOD John 1858
HOOD John 1858
BURKETT Thomas 1858

Section 25
GRAYSON Sarah 1858
MYRICK Moses 1858
THAGARD George W 1858
FELPS Samuel 1858
GRASON David 1858
GRASON David 1858
GRAYSON Sarah 1858
BURKETT Ivin 1858
BURKET William 1858
25
BURKET Emanuel 1858
BURKETT Ivin 1858
BURKET William 1858
BURKET Emanuel 1858
BURKET Emanuel 1858

Section 34
BURKETT John 1858
BURKET Alfred 1858
BURKETT Joseph 1858
BURKETT Thomas 1858
34
BURKETT Joseph 1858
BURKETT Alfred 1858
BURKETT Joseph 1858
MOORE Thomas D 1858
BURKET Alfred 1858
BURKET Alfred 1858
BURKETT Joseph 1858

Section 35
BURKETT Thomas 1838
BURKETT Thomas 1858
BURKETT Ivin 1858
BURKETT Henry 1858
STINSON Leander 1858
BURKETT Thomas 1858
BURKETT Henry 1858
35
STINSON Leander 1858
STINSON Leander 1858

Section 36
BURKET William 1858
BURKET Emanuel 1858
COLEMAN Jesse 1858
BURKET William 1858
COLEMAN Jesse 1858
BURKET Emanuel 1858
COLEMAN Jesse 1858
COLEMAN Jesse 1858
COLEMAN Rachael 1858
36
COLEMAN Rachael 1858

Helpful Hints

1. This Map's INDEX can be found on the preceding pages.

2. Refer to Map "C" to see where this Township lies within Butler County, Alabama.

3. Numbers within square brackets [ ] denote a multi-patentee land parcel (multi-owner). Refer to Appendix "C" for a full list of members in this group.

4. Areas that look to be crowded with Patentees usually indicate multiple sales of the same parcel (Re-issues) or Overlapping parcels. See this Township's Index for an explanation of these and other circumstances that might explain "odd" groupings of Patentees on this map.

Legend

———	Patent Boundary
▬▬▬	Section Boundary
(shaded)	No Patents Found (or Outside County)
1., 2., 3., ...	Lot Numbers (when beside a name)
[ ]	Group Number (see Appendix "C")

Scale: Section = 1 mile X 1 mile (generally, with some exceptions)

Road Map

T9-N R12-E
St Stephens Meridian

Map Group 11

Cities & Towns

Beacon
Providence
Shacklesville

Cemeteries

Mount Pisgah Cemetery
Shacklesville Cemetery

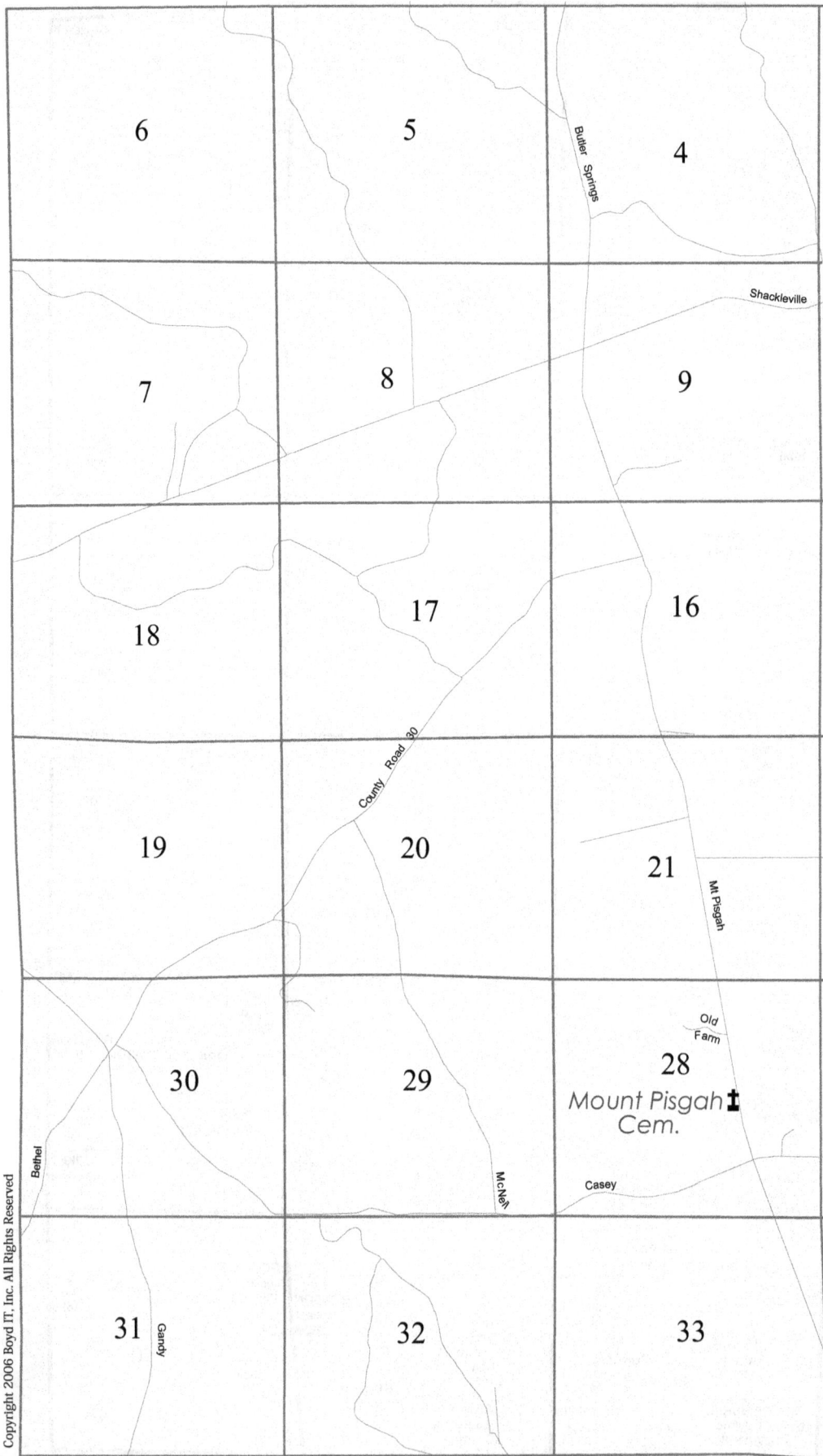

6	5	4
7	8	9
18	17	16
19	20	21
30	29	28 Mount Pisgah Cem.
31	32	33

Butler Springs

Shackleville

County Road 30

Mt Pisgah

Old Farm

Bethel

McNeil

Casey

Gandy

3

2

1

Murphy

✝ *Shacklesville Cem.*

● Shacklesville

10

Wilkinson

11

12

Pettibone

Smith

15

14

13

22

30th

23

24

Starlington

27

Beasley

Pine

Providence ●
26

Deer Track

25

Beacon ●

Burkett

34

35

36

Stinson

Planters

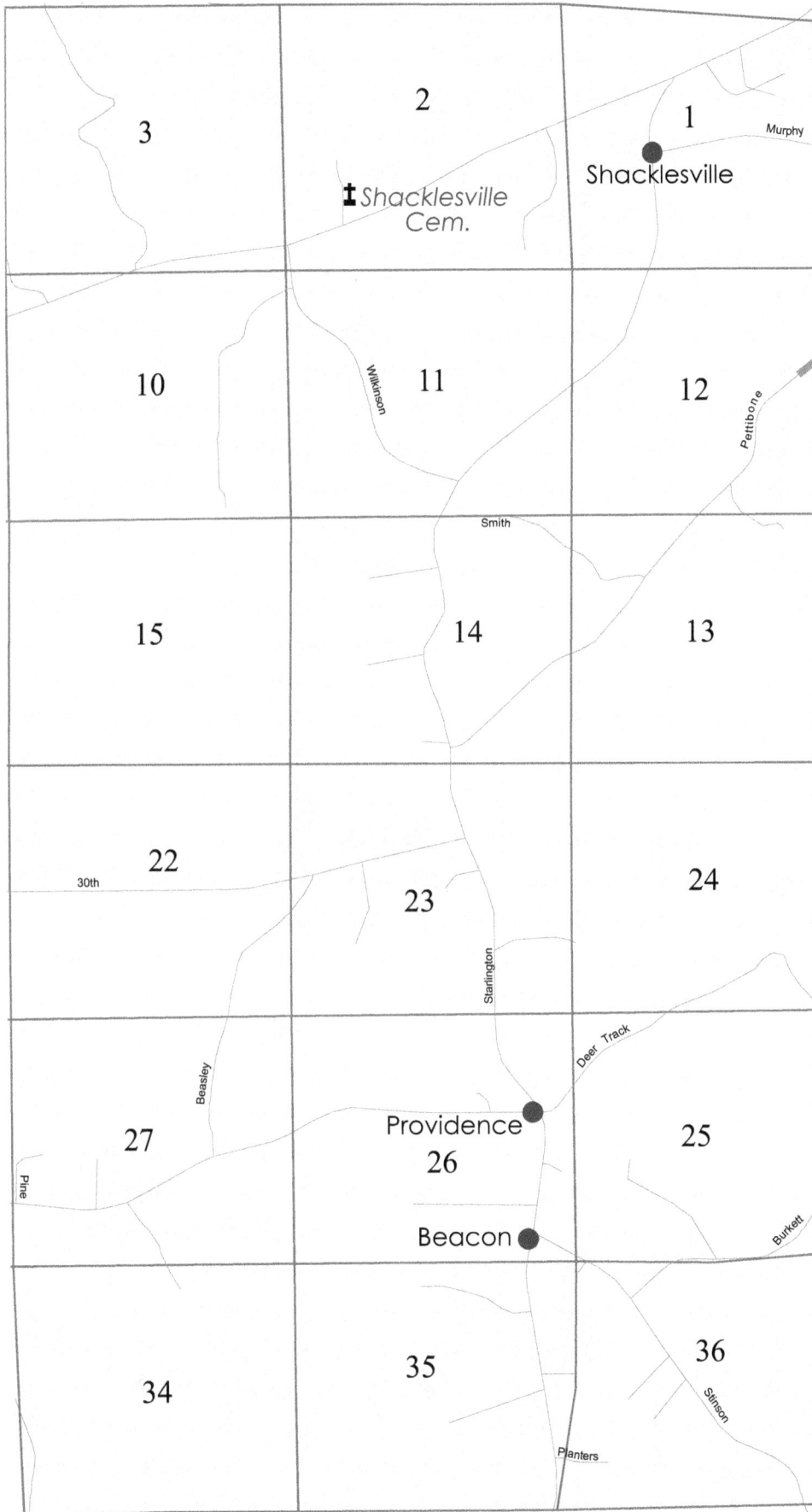

Helpful Hints

1. This road map has a number of uses, but primarily it is to help you: a) find the present location of land owned by your ancestors (at least the general area), b) find cemeteries and city-centers, and c) estimate the route/roads used by Census-takers & tax-assessors.

2. If you plan to travel to Butler County to locate cemeteries or land parcels, please pick up a modern travel map for the area before you do. Mapping old land parcels on modern maps is not as exact a science as you might think. Just the slightest variations in public land survey coordinates, estimates of parcel boundaries, or road-map deviations can greatly alter a map's representation of how a road either does or doesn't cross a particular parcel of land.

L e g e n d

——— Section Lines

══ Interstates

══ Highways

——— Other Roads

● Cities/Towns

✝ Cemeteries

Scale: Section = 1 mile X 1 mile
(generally, with some exceptions)

Historical Map

T9-N R12-E
St Stephens Meridian

Map Group 11

Cities & Towns
Beacon
Providence
Shacklesville

Cemeteries
Mount Pisgah Cemetery
Shacklesville Cemetery

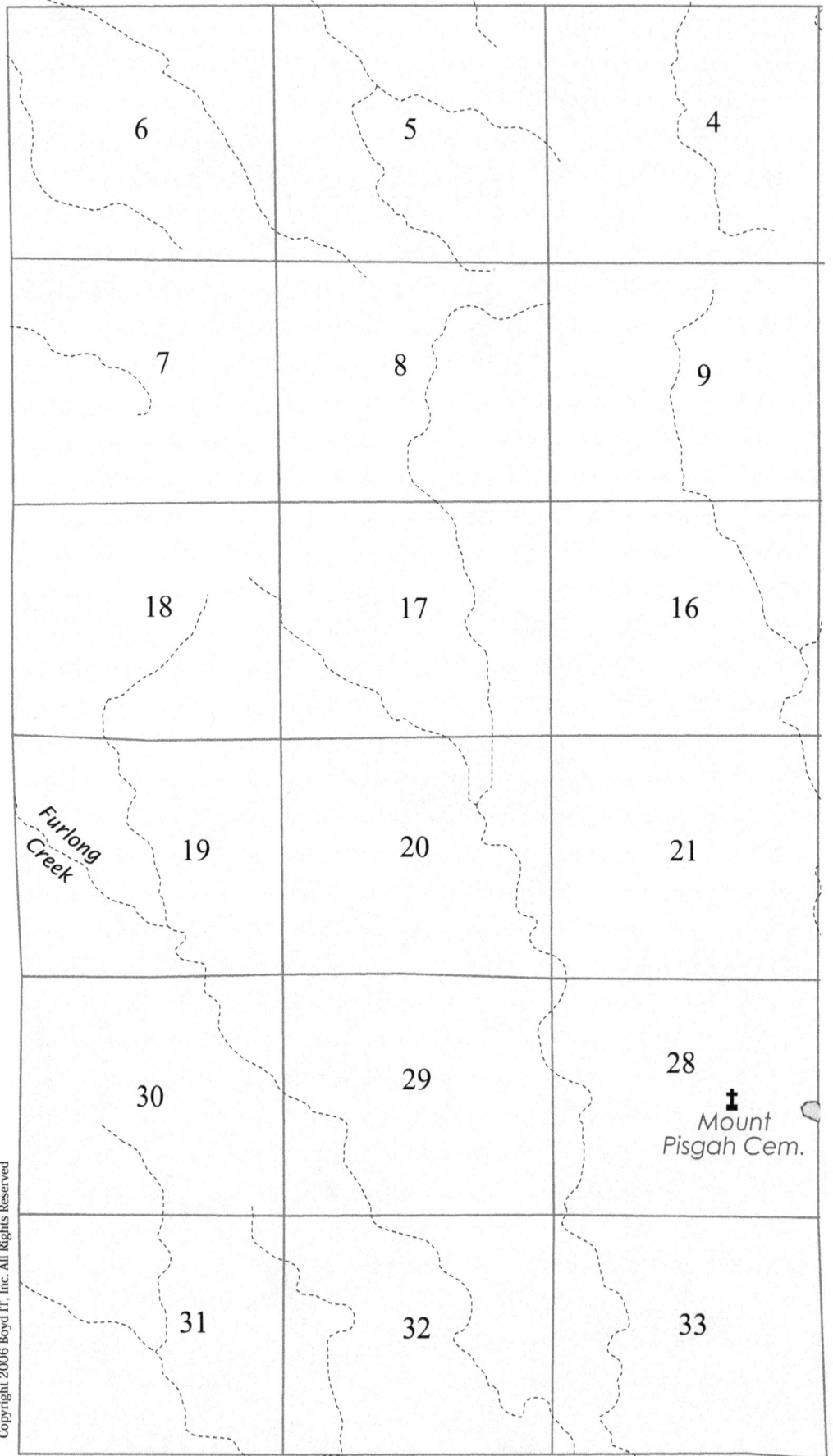

6	5	4
7	8	9
18	17	16
19	20	21
30	29	28
31	32	33

Furlong Creek

Mount
Pisgah Cem.

3

2

1

●Shacklesville

‡ *Shacklesville*
Cem.

10

Long Creek

11

12

15

14

13

22

23

24

Casey
Pond

Providence ●

26

25

27

Beacon ●

34

35

36

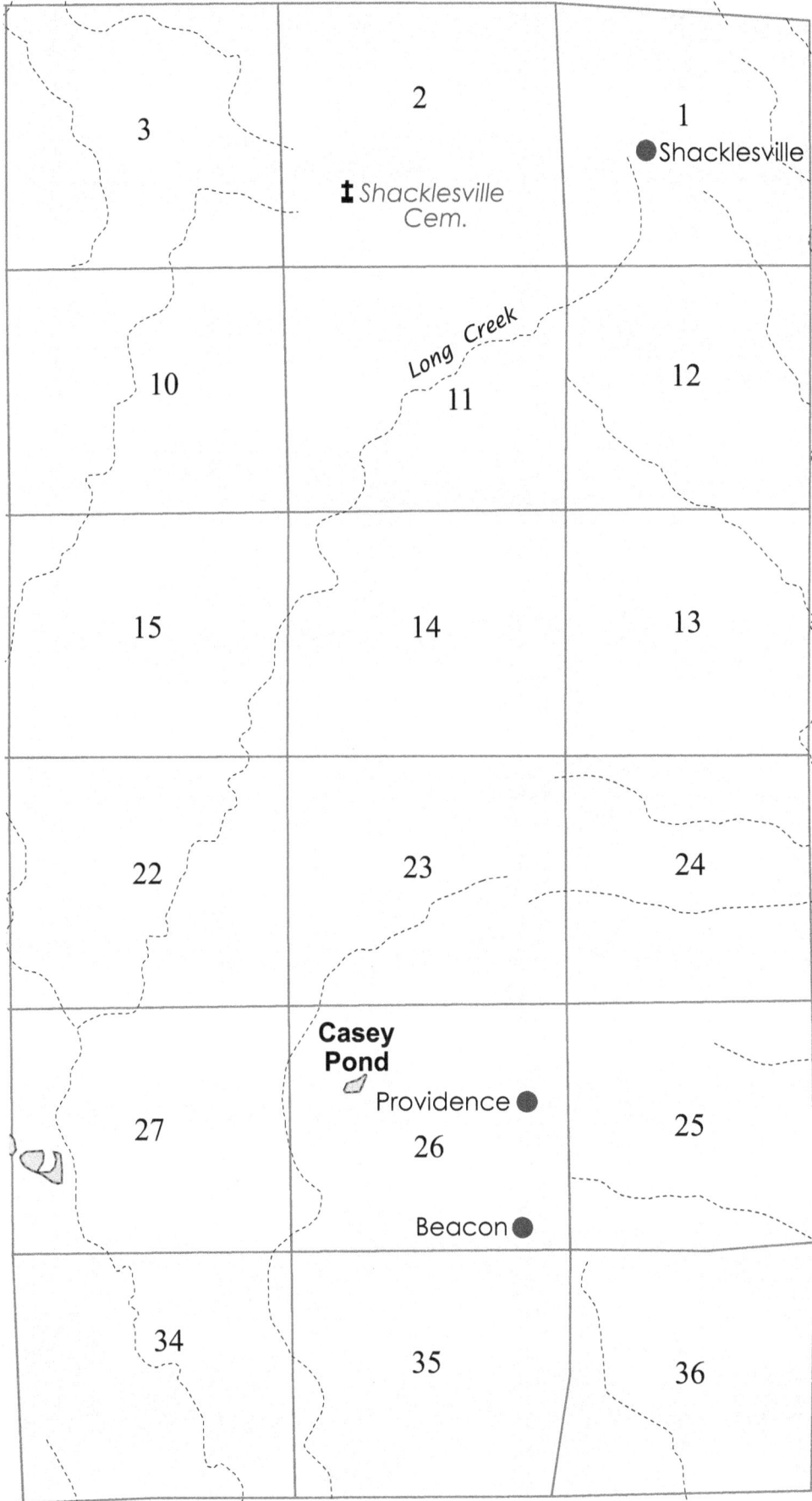

Helpful Hints

1. This Map takes a different look at the same Congressional Township displayed in the preceding two maps. It presents features that can help you better envision the historical development of the area: a) Water-bodies (lakes & ponds), b) Water-courses (rivers, streams, etc.), c) Railroads, d) City/town center-points (where they were oftentimes located when first settled), and e) Cemeteries.

2. Using this "Historical" map in tandem with this Township's Patent Map and Road Map, may lead you to some interesting discoveries. You will often find roads, towns, cemeteries, and waterways are named after nearby landowners: sometimes those names will be the ones you are researching. See how many of these research gems you can find here in Butler County.

Legend

————	Section Lines
+++++	Railroads
▭	Large Rivers & Bodies of Water
- - - - -	Streams/Creeks & Small Rivers
●	Cities/Towns
‡	Cemeteries

Scale: Section = 1 mile X 1 mile
(there are some exceptions)

Map Group 12: Index to Land Patents

Township 9-North Range 13-East (St Stephens)

After you locate an individual in this Index, take note of the Section and Section Part then proceed to the Land Patent map on the pages immediately following. You should have no difficulty locating the corresponding parcel of land.

The "For More Info" Column will lead you to more information about the underlying Patents. See the *Legend* at right, and the "How to Use this Book" chapter, for more information.

```
                        LEGEND
            "For More Info . . . " column
A = Authority (Legislative Act, See Appendix "A")
B = Block or Lot (location in Section unknown)
C = Cancelled Patent
F = Fractional Section
G = Group  (Multi-Patentee Patent, see Appendix "C")
V = Overlaps another Parcel
R = Re-Issued (Parcel patented more than once)

(A & G items require you to look in the Appendixes referred
to above. All other Letter-designations followed by a number
require you to locate line-items in this index that possess
the ID number found after the letter).
```

ID	Individual in Patent	Sec.	Sec. Part	Date Issued	Other Counties	For More Info . . .
2662	ARNOLD, Anderson S	22	NE	1885-06-20		A2
2769	BAXLEY, Martha A	2	E½SE	1885-08-05		A1
2668	BEVERLY, Anthony	26	NESE	1837-08-14		A1
2687	BLACK, Eli J	19	N½	1858-11-01		A1
2688	BLACK, Elijah	36	SWSW	1858-11-01		A1
2721	BOGGAN, James E	35	SENW	1912-06-27		A2
2868	BOGGAN, Willie J	35	N½NW	1919-10-04		A2
2809	BOLLING, Samuel J	36	E½NW	1860-10-01		A1 G5
2810	" "	36	E½SE	1860-10-01		A1 G5
2811	" "	36	E½SW	1860-10-01		A1 G5
2812	" "	36	NWSW	1860-10-01		A1 G5
2813	" "	36	SENE	1860-10-01		A1 G5
2814	" "	36	W½SE	1860-10-01		A1 G5
2703	BRADLEY, George W	27	NE	1858-11-01		A1
2689	BURKET, Emanuel	30	NWSW	1858-11-01		A1
2690	" "	30	SWSW	1858-11-01		A1
2647	BURKETT, Abdel P	8	SWSW	1891-11-23		A2
2691	BURKETT, Emanuel	31	NWNW	1858-11-01		A1
2692	BURKETT, Florence L	8	E½SE	1898-08-15		A2 G7
2707	BURKETT, Huey	30	SENW	1885-04-27		A2
2708	" "	30	SWNE	1885-04-27		A2
2841	CARDWELL, William	20	W½SW	1858-09-01		A1
2656	CLOPTON, Allford	11	E½NW	1858-11-01		A1 G9
2657	" "	11	E½SW	1858-11-01		A1 G9
2658	" "	11	NWNE	1858-11-01		A1 G9
2792	CLOPTON, Nathaniel V	34	NESW	1858-11-01		A1
2793	" "	34	NWSE	1858-11-01		A1
2794	" "	34	W½SW	1858-11-01		A1
2656	CLOPTON, Sally	11	E½NW	1858-11-01		A1 G9
2657	" "	11	E½SW	1858-11-01		A1 G9
2658	" "	11	NWNE	1858-11-01		A1 G9
2728	COLEMAN, Joab	31	SESW	1852-02-02		A1
2727	" "	31	NWSW	1858-11-01		A1
2790	DAVIDSON, Moses H	14	NESE	1876-04-01		A2
2791	" "	14	SENE	1876-04-01		A2
2842	DAVIS, William	21	E½NE	1860-04-02		A1
2843	" "	22	SENW	1860-04-02		A1
2844	" "	22	W½NW	1860-04-02		A1
2664	DORIETY, Andrew J	22	NESE	1892-06-10		A2
2692	DREADEN, Florence L	8	E½SE	1898-08-15		A2 G7
2825	DUCK, Timothy	25	NWSE	1858-11-01		A1
2826	" "	25	SWNE	1858-11-01		A1
2827	" "	25	SWSE	1858-11-01		A1
2869	DYESS, Winfield	10	SE	1885-03-30		A2
2736	FAIL, John J	8	NWSW	1884-03-10		A2
2737	" "	8	SWNW	1884-03-10		A2

ID	Individual in Patent	Sec.	Sec. Part	Date Issued	Other Counties	For More Info . . .
2735	FAIL, John J (Cont'd)	8	N½NW	1888-02-04		A2
2808	FAIL, Rufus D	8	NE	1889-08-13		A2
2845	FAIL, William	17	NE	1858-11-01		A1
2848	" "	8	SESW	1858-11-01		A1
2849	" "	8	W½SE	1858-11-01		A1
2846	" "	8	NESW	1889-08-02		A2
2847	" "	8	SENW	1889-08-02		A2
2775	FAILES, Mary	2	NWSE	1888-01-18		A2
2776	" "	2	SWNE	1888-01-18		A2
2738	FLOWERS, John J	4	N½NW	1883-10-20		A1
2685	GREGG, Edmond W	17	NW	1858-11-01		A1
2686	" "	18	NE	1858-11-01		A1
2681	GWYNN, Coleman O	34	E½NW	1858-11-01		A1
2722	HARRISON, James E	24	W½NW	1880-02-20		A2
2734	HARRISON, John H	36	W½NE	1858-11-01		A1
2739	HARRISON, John K	12	N½NW	1885-03-16		A2 R2682
2815	HARRISON, Sarah J	20	E½SW	1885-05-25		A2
2816	" "	20	W½SE	1885-05-25		A2
2733	HOLAWAY, John F	10	NE	1884-12-05		A2 G26
2733	HOLAWAY, Mary J	10	NE	1884-12-05		A2 G26
2764	INGRAM, Marshall	34	NESE	1858-11-01		A1
2765	" "	34	SENE	1858-11-01		A1
2766	" "	35	NWSW	1858-11-01		A1
2767	" "	35	SWNW	1858-11-01		A1
2770	JAY, Martha A	2	E½NE	1885-04-27		A2
2771	" "	2	NWNE	1885-04-27		A2
2802	JOHNSON, Robert	21	S½SE	1858-11-01		A1
2803	" "	22	SESW	1858-11-01		A1
2804	" "	22	SWSW	1858-11-01		A1
2805	" "	27	SENW	1858-11-01		A1
2807	" "	28	NWSE	1858-11-01		A1 V2799
2806	" "	27	W½NW	1898-08-15		A1
2753	JONES, Levi	11	NESE	1858-11-01		A1
2754	" "	11	S½NE	1858-11-01		A1
2755	" "	11	W½SE	1858-11-01		A1
2756	" "	3	E½NW	1858-11-01		A1
2757	" "	3	W½NE	1858-11-01		A1
2758	" "	4	NE	1858-11-01		A1
2773	KINSEY, Martin	14	NWSE	1888-11-08		A1
2774	" "	14	SWNE	1888-11-08		A1
2729	LEE, Joel W	26	E½NW	1858-11-01		A1
2730	" "	26	W½NE	1858-11-01		A1
2750	LOVETT, Joseph	4	SESW	1885-12-10		A2
2751	" "	4	W½SW	1885-12-10		A2
2855	MARCHANT, William J	20	W½NW	1896-06-15		A2
2828	MARSHALL, William B	28	W½	1858-11-01		A1
2829	" "	29	NE	1858-11-01		A1
2830	" "	31	N½SE	1858-11-01		A1
2831	" "	32	NW	1858-11-01		A1
2832	" "	32	W½NE	1858-11-01		A1
2833	" "	33	NW	1858-11-01		A1
2834	" "	33	W½NE	1858-11-01		A1
2809	" "	36	E½NW	1860-10-01		A1 G5
2810	" "	36	E½SE	1860-10-01		A1 G5
2811	" "	36	E½SW	1860-10-01		A1 G5
2812	" "	36	NWSW	1860-10-01		A1 G5
2813	" "	36	SENE	1860-10-01		A1 G5
2814	" "	36	W½SE	1860-10-01		A1 G5
2799	MARTIN, Robert H	28	N½SE	1858-11-01		A1 V2807
2800	" "	28	NENE	1858-11-01		A1
2801	" "	28	S½NE	1858-11-01		A1
2798	" "	27	NENW	1898-08-15		A1
2851	MATHENY, William H	2	SESW	1883-10-01		A2
2852	" "	2	SWSE	1883-10-01		A2
2663	MAY, Andrew C	2	NW	1891-06-29		A2
2795	MCBRIDE, Richard	30	E½NE	1858-11-01		A1
2796	" "	30	NENW	1858-11-01		A1
2797	" "	30	NWNE	1858-11-01		A1
2709	MCCRORY, Hugh	36	W½NW	1840-10-10		A1
2724	MCLEMORE, James J	1	NENE	1858-11-01		A1
2675	MILNER, Benjamin C	13	SESE	1858-11-01		A1
2676	" "	24	E½NE	1858-11-01		A1
2677	" "	24	E½SE	1858-11-01		A1

ID	Individual in Patent	Sec.	Sec. Part	Date Issued	Other Counties	For More Info . . .
2678	MILNER, Benjamin C (Cont'd)	25	NENE	1858-11-01		A1
2748	MILNER, John T	25	SESE	1858-11-01		A1
2749	" "	36	NENE	1858-11-01		A1
2744	" "	24	E½NW	1860-10-01		A1
2745	" "	24	E½SW	1860-10-01		A1
2746	" "	24	W½NE	1860-10-01		A1
2747	" "	24	W½SE	1860-10-01		A1
2858	MORRIS, William	27	NESW	1858-11-01		A1
2859	" "	27	NWSE	1858-11-01		A1
2752	MURPHY, Julius B	6	W½SW	1860-04-02		A1
2682	MURRAY, Daniel	12	N½NW	1885-03-30		A2 R2739
2853	MYRICK, William H	30	E½SE	1885-03-30		A2
2854	" "	30	W½SE	1885-03-30		A2
2648	NORRIS, Abud	17	W½SW	1858-11-01		A1
2649	" "	18	E½SE	1858-11-01		A1
2650	" "	18	N½NW	1858-11-01		A1
2651	" "	18	NWSE	1858-11-01		A1
2652	" "	18	SW	1858-11-01		A1
2683	NORRIS, David A	21	NW	1858-11-01		A1
2684	" "	21	W½SW	1858-11-01		A1
2710	NORRIS, Ingram	21	NWSE	1862-01-01		A1
2711	" "	21	SWNE	1862-01-01		A1
2679	ODOM, Benjamin C	10	SWSW	1858-11-01		A1
2725	ODOM, James W	23	NESE	1858-11-01		A1
2726	" "	23	SENE	1858-11-01		A1
2860	ODOM, William	26	E½NE	1858-11-01		A1
2861	" "	26	NWSE	1858-11-01		A1
2693	OFARRELL, Franklin P	27	W½SW	1875-04-20		A1
2694	" "	28	S½SE	1875-04-20		A1
2696	OUTLAW, George	17	E½SW	1858-11-01		A1
2697	" "	20	E½NW	1858-11-01		A1
2698	" "	20	W½NE	1858-11-01		A1
2669	PARKER, Arthur	25	W½SW	1837-04-10		A1
2671	" "	26	SESW	1837-08-18		A1
2674	" "	35	NENE	1837-08-18		A1
2670	" "	26	N½SW	1858-11-01		A1
2672	" "	26	SWNW	1858-11-01		A1
2673	" "	26	SWSE	1858-11-01		A1
2740	PARMER, John M	12	E½SW	1858-11-01		A1
2741	" "	12	S½NE	1858-11-01		A1
2742	" "	12	SE	1858-11-01		A1
2787	PARMER, Milton K	13	N½SE	1858-11-01		A1
2788	" "	13	NE	1858-11-01		A1
2789	" "	13	S½NW	1858-11-01		A1
2701	POWELL, George	4	SWNW	1858-11-01		A1
2699	" "	4	NESW	1860-04-02		A1
2700	" "	4	SENW	1860-04-02		A1
2702	" "	4	W½SE	1860-04-02		A1
2835	POWELL, William B	3	NESW	1860-04-02		A1
2836	" "	3	W½SW	1860-04-02		A1
2837	" "	4	NESE	1860-04-02		A1
2704	PRESLEY, Green	30	E½SW	1896-04-23		A2
2653	PUGH, Albert	29	E½SE	1858-11-01		A1
2654	" "	29	W½SE	1858-11-01		A1
2655	" "	32	E½NE	1858-11-01		A1
2712	PUGH, Ira	26	SWSW	1858-11-01		A1
2713	" "	27	NESE	1858-11-01		A1
2714	" "	27	S½SE	1858-11-01		A1
2715	" "	27	SESW	1858-11-01		A1
2716	" "	34	N½NE	1858-11-01		A1
2717	" "	34	SWNE	1858-11-01		A1
2781	PUGH, Masten B	32	N½SE	1858-11-01		A1
2782	" "	32	NESW	1858-11-01		A1
2783	" "	32	SESW	1858-11-01		A1
2784	" "	33	NWSW	1858-11-01		A1
2785	" "	33	SWSW	1858-11-01		A1
2786	PUGH, Mastin B	32	S½SE	1858-11-01		A1
2772	REAVES, Martha E	20	SESE	1889-03-01		A2
2661	REEVES, Amanda C	24	W½SW	1880-02-20		A2
2706	REYNOLDS, Hines H	2	NESE	1885-06-20		A2
2862	RHODES, William	11	SESE	1858-11-01		A1
2863	" "	12	W½SW	1858-11-01		A1
2864	" "	13	NWNW	1858-11-01		A1

ID	Individual in Patent	Sec.	Sec. Part	Date Issued	Other Counties	For More Info . . .
2865	RHODES, William (Cont'd)	14	N½NE	1858-11-01		A1
2823	RICHARDSON, Stephen C	6	W½NW	1860-09-01		A1
2680	SAUCER, Benjamin F	6	SWNE	1860-10-01		A1
2777	SAUCER, Mary	6	E½SW	1896-10-28		A1
2778	" "	6	W½SE	1896-10-28		A1
2779	" "	7	N½NW	1896-10-28		A1
2780	" "	7	W½NE	1896-10-28		A1
2718	SHEPHERD, James C	35	SESW	1858-11-01		A1
2719	" "	35	SWSW	1858-11-01		A1
2838	SHEPHERD, William C	34	SESE	1858-11-01		A1
2839	" "	34	SESW	1858-11-01		A1
2840	" "	34	SWSE	1858-11-01		A1
2759	SIMS, Lucretia	22	NESW	1895-12-14		A2
2760	" "	22	NWSW	1895-12-14		A2
2818	SIMS, Sherrod	10	NW	1888-02-04		A2
2824	SMITH, Thomas M	30	SWNW	1909-12-27		A2
2731	SPEARS, John C	10	E½SW	1888-02-04		A2
2732	" "	10	NWSW	1888-02-04		A2
2817	STEWART, Seabron W	9	S½SW	1860-04-02		A1
2761	STOTT, Marshal	33	E½NE	1858-11-01		A1
2762	" "	33	E½SE	1858-11-01		A1
2763	" "	34	NWNW	1858-11-01		A1
2768	STOTT, Marshall	34	SWNW	1858-11-01		A1
2866	TAYLOR, William	22	SESE	1894-12-07		A2
2867	" "	22	W½SE	1894-12-07		A2
2705	TYNES, Henry	23	SWSE	1860-04-02		A1
2819	WARD, Solomon	26	SESE	1838-07-28		A1
2820	" "	35	SE	1838-07-28		A1
2821	" "	35	SENE	1838-07-28		A1
2822	" "	35	W½NE	1838-07-28		A1
2665	WARDEN, Andrew S	14	N½NW	1885-06-20		A2
2666	" "	14	NWSW	1885-06-20		A2
2667	" "	14	SWNW	1885-06-20		A2
2720	WASDEN, James C	2	W½SW	1889-08-02		A2
2856	WASDIN, William J	14	S½SE	1885-06-20		A2
2857	" "	14	S½SW	1885-06-20		A2
2695	WELCH, George E	22	NENW	1888-02-04		A2
2659	WHITE, Allien D	14	NESW	1891-05-29		A2
2660	" "	14	SENW	1891-05-29		A2
2723	WIGGINS, James E	29	SENW	1858-11-01		A1
2743	WILLIAMS, John P	35	NESW	1912-06-27		A2
2850	WYNN, William G	7	S½NW	1858-11-01		A1

Patent Map

T9-N R13-E
St Stephens Meridian

Map Group 12

Township Statistics

Parcels Mapped	:	223
Number of Patents	:	138
Number of Individuals	:	104
Patentees Identified	:	101
Number of Surnames	:	77
Multi-Patentee Parcels	:	11
Oldest Patent Date	:	4/10/1837
Most Recent Patent	:	10/4/1919
Block/Lot Parcels	:	0
Parcels Re - Issued	:	1
Parcels that Overlap	:	2
Cities and Towns	:	2
Cemeteries	:	1

Section 6: RICHARDSON Stephen C 1860; SAUCER Benjamin F 1860; MURPHY Julius B 1860; SAUCER Mary 1896; SAUCER Mary 1896

Section 5

Section 4: FLOWERS John J 1883; POWELL George 1858; POWELL George 1860; JONES Levi 1858; LOVETT Joseph 1885; POWELL George 1860; LOVETT Joseph 1885; POWELL George 1860; POWELL William B 1860

Section 7: SAUCER Mary 1896; WYNN William G 1858; SAUCER Mary 1896

Section 8: FAIL John J 1888; FAIL Rufus D 1889; FAIL John J 1884; FAIL William 1889; FAIL John J 1884; FAIL William 1889; BURKETT Abdel P 1891; FAIL William 1858; FAIL William 1858; BURKETT [7] Florence L 1898

Section 9: STEWART Seabron W 1860

Section 18: NORRIS Abud 1858; GREGG Edmond W 1858; NORRIS Abud 1858; NORRIS Abud 1858; NORRIS Abud 1858

Section 17: GREGG Edmond W 1858; FAIL William 1858; NORRIS Abud 1858; OUTLAW George 1858

Section 16

Section 19: BLACK Eli J 1858

Section 20: MARCHANT William J 1896; OUTLAW George 1858; OUTLAW George 1858; CARDWELL William 1858; HARRISON Sarah J 1885; HARRISON Sarah J 1885; REAVES Martha E 1889

Section 21: NORRIS David A 1858; NORRIS Ingram 1862; DAVIS William 1860; NORRIS Ingram 1862; NORRIS David A 1858; JOHNSON Robert 1858

Section 30: MCBRIDE Richard 1858; MCBRIDE Richard 1858; MCBRIDE Richard 1858; SMITH Thomas M 1909; BURKETT Huey 1885; BURKETT Huey 1885; BURKET Emanuel 1858; PRESLEY Green 1896; MYRICK William H 1885; BURKET Emanuel 1858; MYRICK William H 1885

Section 29: WIGGINS James E 1858

Section 28: MARSHALL William B 1858; PUGH Albert 1858; MARSHALL William B 1858; PUGH Albert 1858; MARTIN Robert H 1858; MARTIN Robert H 1858; JOHNSON Robert 1858; MARTIN Robert H 1858; OFARRELL Franklin P 1875

Section 31: BURKETT Emanuel 1858; COLEMAN Joab 1858; MARSHALL William B 1858; COLEMAN Joab 1852

Section 32: MARSHALL William B 1858; PUGH Albert 1858; PUGH Masten B 1858; PUGH Masten B 1858; PUGH Masten B 1858; PUGH Mastin B 1858

Section 33: MARSHALL William B 1858; MARSHALL William B 1858; STOTT Marshal 1858; PUGH Masten B 1858; PUGH Masten B 1858; STOTT Marshal 1858

172

Section 3
JONES Levi 1858
JONES Levi 1858
3
POWELL William B 1860
POWELL William B 1860

Section 2
MAY Andrew C 1891
JAY Martha A 1885
FAILES Mary 1888
JAY Martha A 1885
2
REYNOLDS Hines H 1885
FAILES Mary 1888
BAXLEY Martha A 1885
WASDEN James C 1889
MATHENY William H 1883
MATHENY William H 1883

Section 1
MCLEMORE James J 1858
1

Section 10
SIMS Sherrod 1888
HOLAWAY [26] John F 1884
10
SPEARS John C 1888
SPEARS John C 1888
DYESS Winfield 1885
ODOM Benjamin C 1858

Section 11 / 12
CLOPTON [9] Allford 1858
CLOPTON [9] Allford 1858
MURRAY Daniel 1885
HARRISON John K 1885
PARMER John M 1858
12
JONES Levi 1858
CLOPTON [9] Allford 1858
11
JONES Levi 1858
RHODES William 1858
PARMER John M 1858
JONES Levi 1858
RHODES William 1858

Section 15 / 14 / 13
WARDEN Andrew S 1885
RHODES William 1858
RHODES William 1858
PARMER Milton K 1858
WARDEN Andrew S 1885
WHITE Allien D 1891
14
KINSEY Martin 1888
DAVIDSON Moses H 1876
PARMER Milton K 1858
13
15
WARDEN Andrew S 1885
WHITE Allien D 1891
KINSEY Martin 1888
DAVIDSON Moses H 1876
PARMER Milton K 1858
WASDIN William J 1885
WASDIN William J 1885
MILNER Benjamin C 1858

Section 22 / 23 / 24
WELCH George E 1888
ARNOLD Anderson S 1885
HARRISON James E 1880
MILNER Benjamin C 1858
DAVIS William 1860
DAVIS William 1860
22
ODOM James W 1858
MILNER John T 1860
MILNER John T 1860
24
23
SIMS Lucretia 1895
SIMS Lucretia 1895
DORIETY Andrew J 1892
ODOM James W 1858
REEVES Amanda C 1880
MILNER John T 1860
MILNER John T 1860
MILNER Benjamin C 1858
TAYLOR William 1894
JOHNSON Robert 1858
JOHNSON Robert 1858
TAYLOR William 1894
TYNES Henry 1860

Section 27 / 26 / 25
MARTIN Robert H 1898
BRADLEY George W 1858
LEE Joel W 1858
MILNER Benjamin C 1858
JOHNSON Robert 1898
JOHNSON Robert 1858
LEE Joel W 1858
ODOM William 1858
27
PARKER Arthur 1858
26
DUCK Timothy 1858
25
OFARRELL Franklin P 1875
MORRIS William 1858
MORRIS William 1858
PUGH Ira 1858
PARKER Arthur 1858
ODOM William 1858
BEVERLY Anthony 1837
PARKER Arthur 1837
DUCK Timothy 1858
PUGH Ira 1858
PUGH Ira 1858
PUGH Ira 1858
PARKER Arthur 1837
PARKER Arthur 1858
WARD Solomon 1838
DUCK Timothy 1858
MILNER John T 1858

Section 34 / 35 / 36
STOTT Marshal 1858
GWYNN Coleman O 1858
PUGH Ira 1858
BOGGAN Willie J 1919
PARKER Arthur 1837
MCCRORY Hugh 1840
HARRISON John H 1858
MILNER John T 1858
STOTT Marshall 1858
WARD Solomon 1838
BOLLING [5] Samuel J 1860
BOLLING [5] Samuel J 1860
PUGH Ira 1858
INGRAM Marshall 1858
INGRAM Marshall 1858
BOGGAN James E 1912
34
35
36
CLOPTON Nathaniel V 1858
CLOPTON Nathaniel V 1858
INGRAM Marshall 1858
INGRAM Marshall 1858
WILLIAMS John P 1912
BOLLING [5] Samuel J 1860
BOLLING [5] Samuel J 1860
CLOPTON Nathaniel V 1858
WARD Solomon 1838
BOLLING [5] Samuel J 1860
BOLLING [5] Samuel J 1860
SHEPHERD William C 1858
SHEPHERD William C 1858
SHEPHERD William C 1858
SHEPHERD James C 1858
SHEPHERD James C 1858
BLACK Elijah 1858

Helpful Hints

1. This Map's INDEX can be found on the preceding pages.

2. Refer to Map "C" to see where this Township lies within Butler County, Alabama.

3. Numbers within square brackets [ ] denote a multi-patentee land parcel (multi-owner). Refer to Appendix "C" for a full list of members in this group.

4. Areas that look to be crowded with Patentees usually indicate multiple sales of the same parcel (Re-issues) or Overlapping parcels. See this Township's Index for an explanation of these and other circumstances that might explain "odd" groupings of Patentees on this map.

Legend

- Patent Boundary
- Section Boundary
- No Patents Found (or Outside County)
- 1., 2., 3., ... Lot Numbers (when beside a name)
- [ ] Group Number (see Appendix "C")

Scale: Section = 1 mile X 1 mile (generally, with some exceptions)

Road Map

T9-N R13-E
St Stephens Meridian

Map Group 12

Cities & Towns
Bolling
Sand Cut

Cemeteries
Antioch West Cemetery

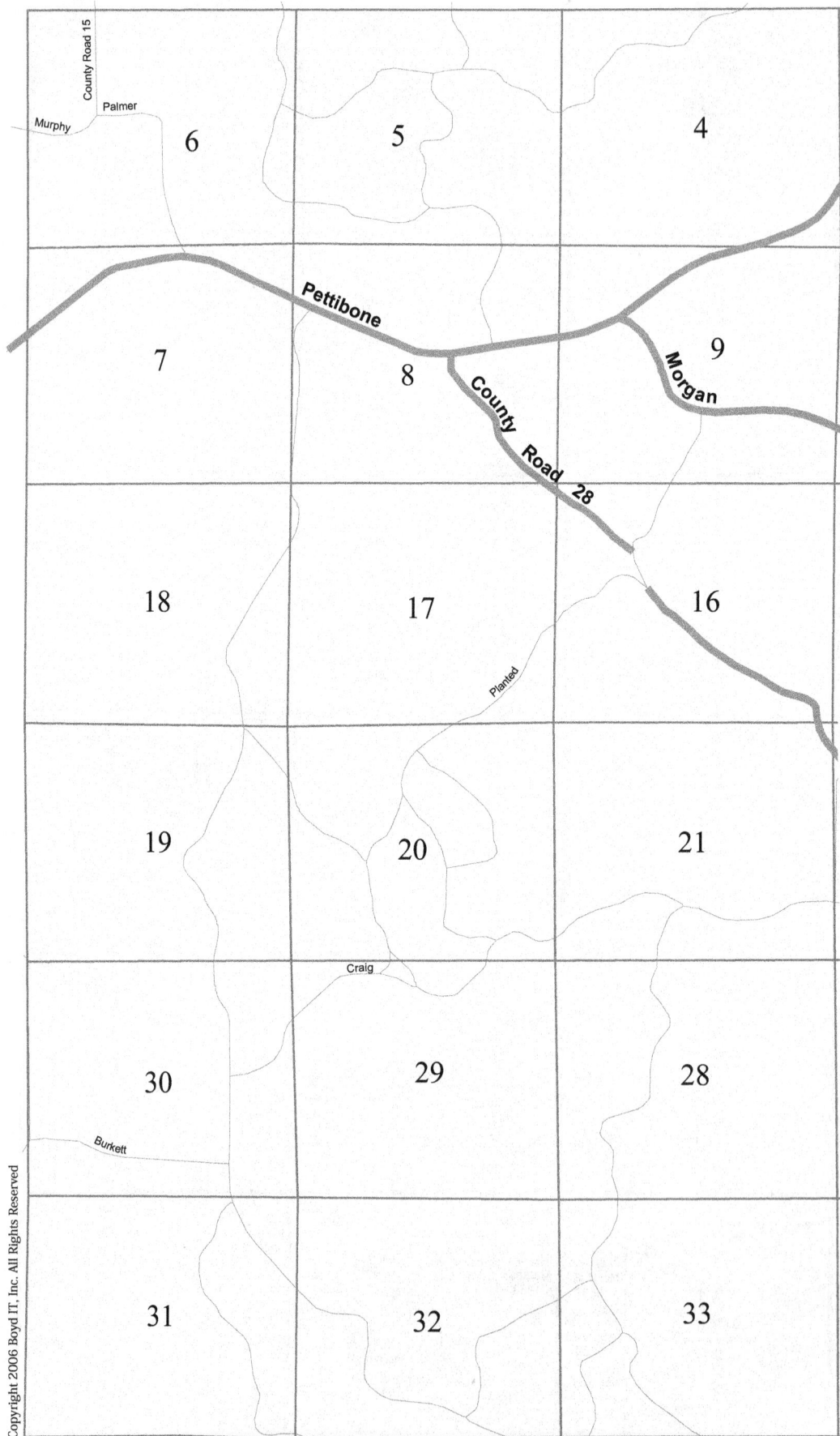

County Road 15

Murphy

Palmer

6

5

4

Pettibone

7

8

County Road 28

Morgan

9

18

17

16

Planted

19

20

21

Craig

30

29

28

Burkett

31

32

33

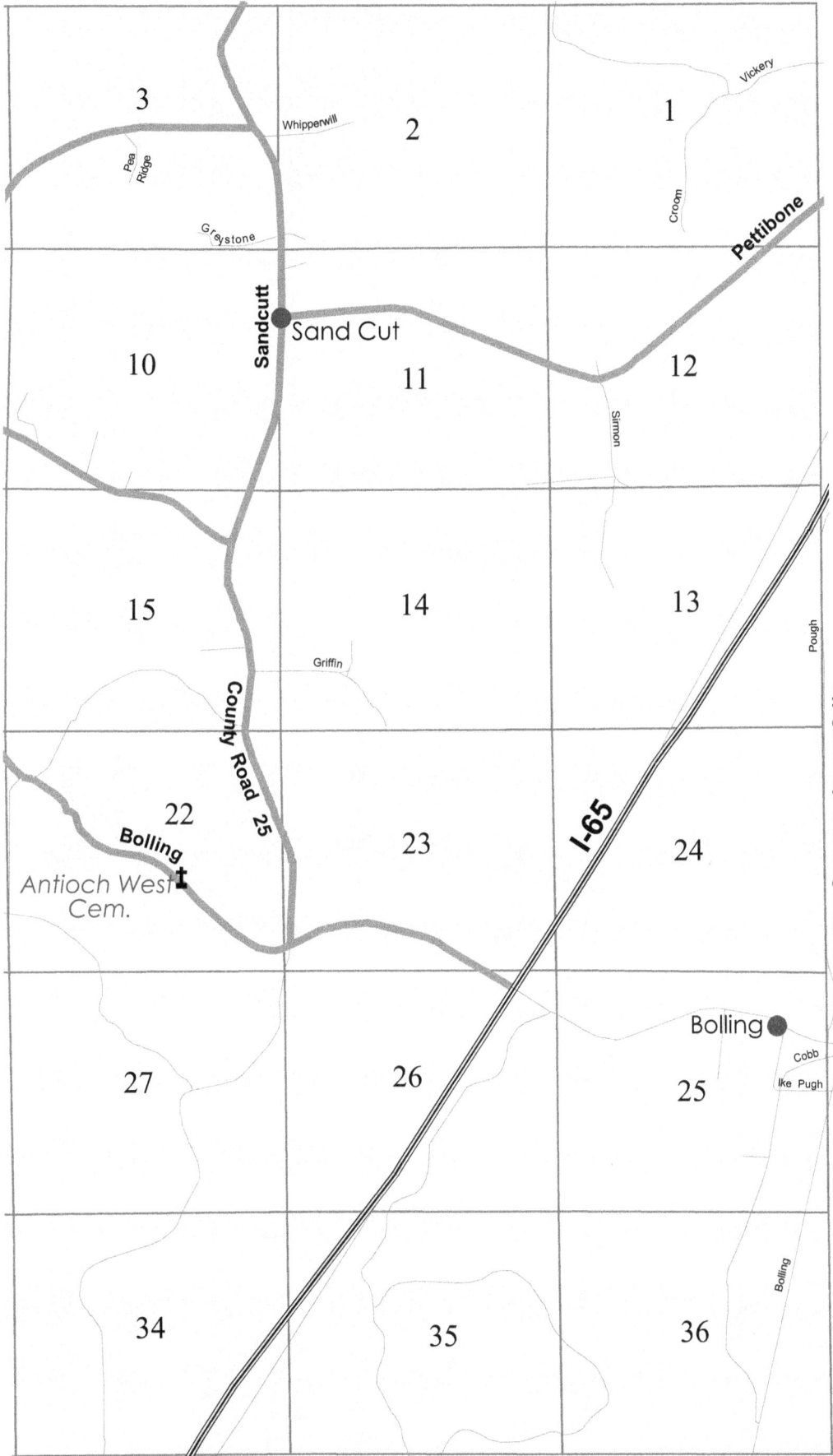

3

Whipperwill

2

1

Vickery

Pea Ridge

Croom

Greystone

Pettibone

Sandcutt

Sand Cut

10

11

12

Sirmon

15

14

13

Pugh

Griffin

County Road 25

22

Bolling

23

I-65

24

Antioch West Cem.

Bolling

Cobb

27

26

Ike Pugh

25

Bolling

34

35

36

Helpful Hints

1. This road map has a number of uses, but primarily it is to help you: a) find the present location of land owned by your ancestors (at least the general area), b) find cemeteries and city-centers, and c) estimate the route/roads used by Census-takers & tax-assessors.

2. If you plan to travel to Butler County to locate cemeteries or land parcels, please pick up a modern travel map for the area before you do. Mapping old land parcels on modern maps is not as exact a science as you might think. Just the slightest variations in public land survey coordinates, estimates of parcel boundaries, or road-map deviations can greatly alter a map's representation of how a road either does or doesn't cross a particular parcel of land.

Legend

——————— Section Lines

════════ Interstates

▬▬▬▬▬▬ Highways

——————— Other Roads

● Cities/Towns

✝ Cemeteries

Scale: Section = 1 mile X 1 mile
(generally, with some exceptions)

Historical Map

T9-N R13-E
St Stephens Meridian

Map Group 12

Cities & Towns
Bolling
Sand Cut

Cemeteries
Antioch West Cemetery

6	5	4
7	8	9
18	17	16
19	20	21
30	29	28
31	32	33

Oaklog Creek

Panther Creek

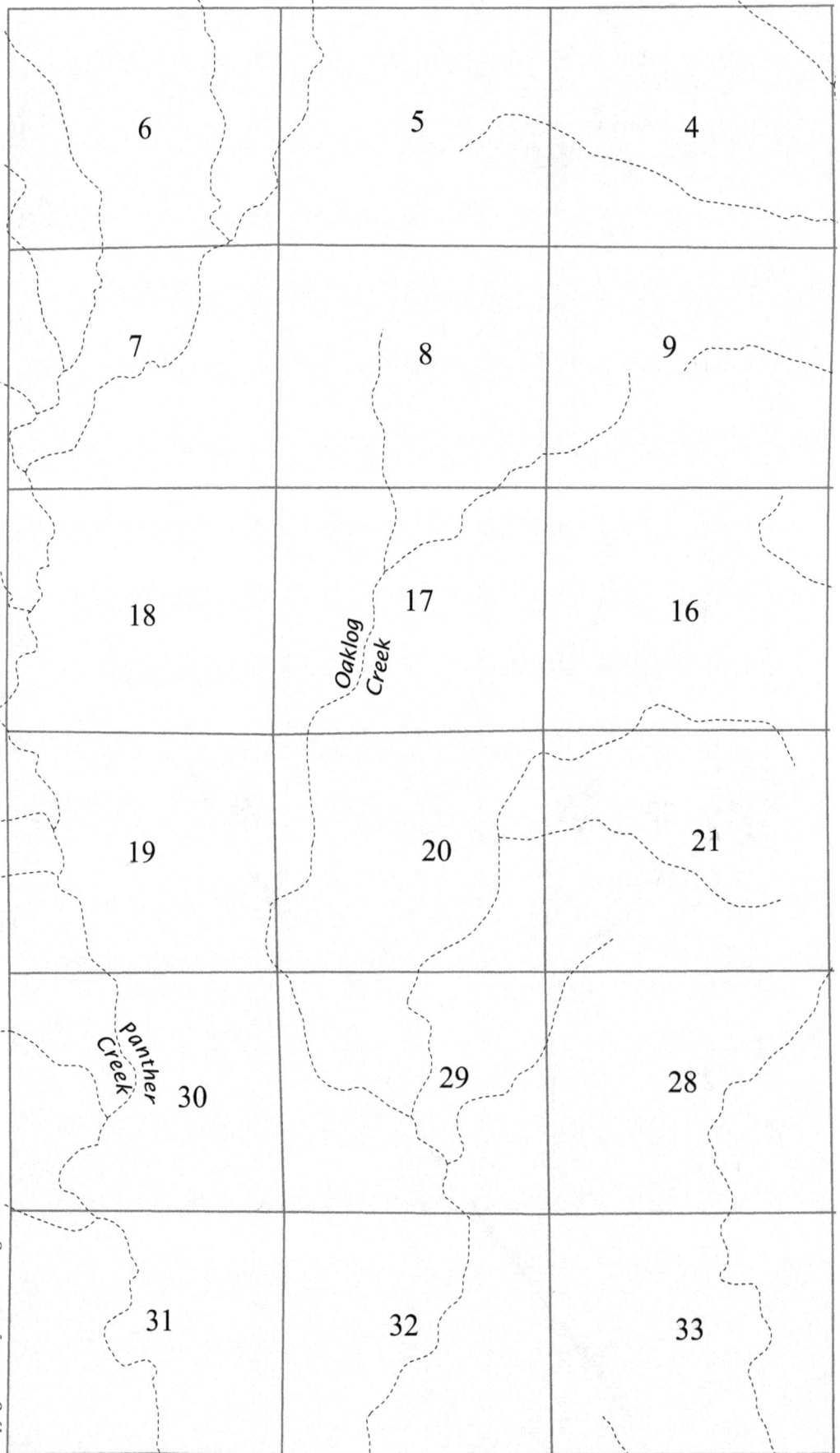

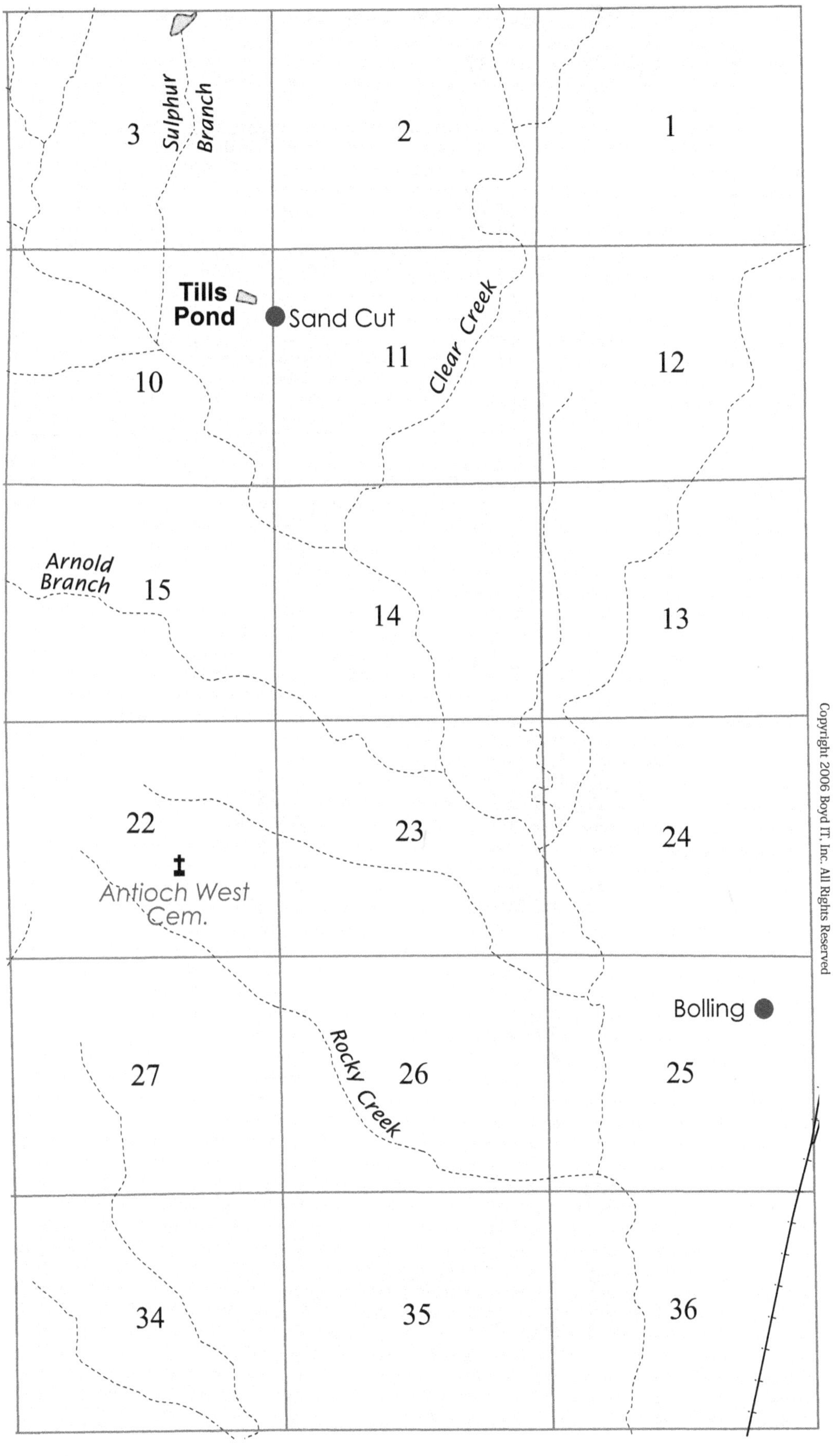
3
Sulphur Branch
2
1
Tills Pond
Sand Cut
11
Clear Creek
12
10
Arnold Branch
15
14
13
22
23
24
Antioch West Cem.
Bolling
27
Rocky Creek
26
25
34
35
36

Helpful Hints

1. This Map takes a different look at the same Congressional Township displayed in the preceding two maps. It presents features that can help you better envision the historical development of the area: a) Water-bodies (lakes & ponds), b) Water-courses (rivers, streams, etc.), c) Railroads, d) City/town center-points (where they were oftentimes located when first settled), and e) Cemeteries.

2. Using this "Historical" map in tandem with this Township's Patent Map and Road Map, may lead you to some interesting discoveries. You will often find roads, towns, cemeteries, and waterways are named after nearby landowners: sometimes those names will be the ones you are researching. See how many of these research gems you can find here in Butler County.

Legend

- Section Lines
- Railroads
- Large Rivers & Bodies of Water
- Streams/Creeks & Small Rivers
- Cities/Towns
- Cemeteries

Scale: Section = 1 mile X 1 mile
(there are some exceptions)

Map Group 13: Index to Land Patents

Township 9-North Range 14-East (St Stephens)

After you locate an individual in this Index, take note of the Section and Section Part then proceed to the Land Patent map on the pages immediately following. You should have no difficulty locating the corresponding parcel of land.

The "For More Info" Column will lead you to more information about the underlying Patents. See the *Legend* at right, and the "How to Use this Book" chapter, for more information.

```
                         LEGEND
             "For More Info . . . " column
_____
A = Authority (Legislative Act, See Appendix "A")
B = Block or Lot (location in Section unknown)
C = Cancelled Patent
F = Fractional Section
G = Group  (Multi-Patentee Patent, see Appendix "C")
V = Overlaps another Parcel
R = Re-Issued (Parcel patented more than once)

(A & G items require you to look in the Appendixes referred
to above. All other Letter-designations followed by a number
require you to locate line-items in this index that possess
the ID number found after the letter).
```

ID	Individual in Patent	Sec.	Sec. Part	Date Issued	Other Counties	For More Info . . .
2907	BAILEY, Isaac	24	SESW	1849-09-01		A1
2908	" "	24	SWSE	1858-11-01		A1
2906	" "	24	NWSE	1862-01-01		A1
3061	BAILEY, Sarah	25	E½SW	1858-11-01		A1
3065	BARNES, Solomon	2	NW	1858-11-01		A1
3066	" "	3	E½NE	1858-11-01		A1
3067	" "	3	E½SE	1858-11-01		A1 R3088
2915	BARRETT, James	32	S½NE	1883-07-03		A2
3101	BASS, William F	34	S½SW	1883-03-10		A1
3042	BENNETT, Ryan	10	E½NE	1858-11-01		A1
3043	" "	11	E½SW	1858-11-01		A1
3044	" "	11	NW	1858-11-01		A1
3045	" "	14	E½NW	1858-11-01		A1
3046	" "	14	NE	1858-11-01		A1
3047	" "	15	SESE	1858-11-01		A1
3049	" "	2	W½SW	1858-11-01		A1 V3087
3048	" "	2	SESW	1861-05-01		A1
3050	" "	22	NENE	1861-05-01		A1
3078	BLACK, Thomas J	24	NESE	1845-06-01		A1
3090	BLAIR, William	31	NW	1858-11-01		A1
2942	BOLLING, John	4	E½NE	1845-06-01		A1
2943	" "	4	NESE	1845-06-01		A1
2940	" "	3	SESW	1848-05-03		A1
2941	" "	3	SWSE	1848-05-03		A1
2939	" "	3	NWNE	1858-11-01		A1
3051	BOLLING, Samuel J	3	NWSW	1845-06-01		A1
3055	" "	3	N½NW	1858-11-01		A1 G4
3052	" "	3	SWSW	1858-11-01		A1
3054	" "	4	SESE	1858-11-01		A1
3056	" "	4	SWSE	1858-11-01		A1 G4
3057	" "	9	NWNE	1858-11-01		A1 G4
3053	" "	4	NWNE	1860-10-01		A1
2916	BRASSWELL, James	36	NESW	1897-03-18		A1
2917	" "	36	SENW	1897-03-18		A1
2918	BRASWELL, James	36	SESE	1858-11-01		A1
3031	BRAZZIL, Robert	3	NESW	1837-08-18		A1
2894	BROWN, Francis M	35	SWSE	1875-04-20		A1
2897	CAMPBELL, Henry E	21	NESW	1858-11-01		A1
2898	" "	21	NWSE	1858-11-01		A1
2899	" "	21	SENW	1858-11-01		A1
2900	" "	21	SWNE	1858-11-01		A1
2870	CHAMBERS, Andy	6	NENW	1889-03-02		A1
3069	COWART, Stephen D	2	NESW	1889-10-07		A1
3091	CREECH, William C	10	SE	1858-11-01		A1
3092	" "	11	W½SW	1858-11-01		A1
3084	CREG, Wade	32	SE	1891-09-01		A2 V3074

ID	Individual in Patent	Sec.	Sec. Part	Date Issued	Other Counties	For More Info . . .
2965	DUCK, John R	30	SESW	1858-11-01		A1
2966	" "	30	SWSE	1858-11-01		A1
2967	" "	31	N½NE	1858-11-01		A1 F
2997	DUKES, Joseph L	28	SWSW	1904-12-20		A2
2944	EDMONDS, John	34	N½SW	1882-06-10		A1
2919	ELSBERRY, James	34	E½NE	1882-06-10		A1
3100	ELSBERRY, William	34	W½SE	1882-06-10		A1
2914	FAIN, James B	18	E½	1858-11-01		A1
2946	FIFE, John	13	E½SW	1848-05-03		A1
2945	" "	11	SESE	1849-09-01		A1
2947	" "	13	NWNE	1858-11-01		A1
2948	" "	13	SENE	1858-11-01		A1
2949	" "	13	W½SW	1858-11-01		A1
2893	FLOWERS, Francis A	28	SESW	1884-03-20		A1
2950	FLOWERS, John J	28	NESW	1883-10-20		A1
2951	" "	28	S½SE	1883-10-20		A1
3104	FLOWERS, William H	29	S½SW	1858-11-01		A1
3105	" "	32	N½SW	1858-11-01		A1 V3075
3106	" "	32	NW	1858-11-01		A1
2920	GIBSON, James G	19	NWNE	1858-11-01		A1
3076	GIDDINGS, Thomas	13	NWNW	1848-04-01		A1
3077	" "	13	SWNW	1848-04-01		A1
2887	GILBERT, Eliza	8	N½	1858-11-01		A1
2928	GILBERT, John A	5	E½NW	1858-11-01		A1
2929	" "	5	NESW	1858-11-01		A1
2930	" "	5	NWNW	1858-11-01		A1
2931	" "	6	E½NE	1858-11-01		A1
2932	" "	6	E½SE	1858-11-01		A1
3085	GILBERT, Webster	10	W½NW	1858-11-01		A1
3086	" "	9	E½NE	1858-11-01		A1
3008	GONDER, Mark F	8	S½	1858-11-01		A1
3103	GRIFFIN, William	34	W½NW	1882-06-10		A1
2901	HARPER, Henry S	35	NESW	1858-11-01		A1
2902	" "	35	NW	1858-11-01		A1
2903	" "	35	NWSE	1858-11-01		A1
2904	" "	35	W½NE	1858-11-01		A1
3107	HARPER, William	1	NWNW	1838-07-28		A1
3089	HARPER, William B	1	SENW	1837-08-02		A1 V3009
3102	HARTLEY, William F	30	SESE	1860-10-01		A1
2909	HOOD, Isaac F	18	N½NW	1858-11-01		A1
2910	" "	7	E½SE	1858-11-01		A1
2911	" "	7	N½SW	1858-11-01		A1
2912	" "	7	NWSE	1858-11-01		A1
2913	" "	7	SWSW	1858-11-01		A1
3002	HOWELL, Joseph W	26	SW	1885-03-16		A2
3014	HUMPHREY, Mary E	18	W½SW	1885-06-12		A2 V2872
2886	HUMPHREYS, Elijah J	6	W½SW	1891-06-19		A2
2881	JACKSON, Cleton	35	SESE	1858-11-01		A1
2882	" "	36	W½SW	1858-11-01		A1
2952	JEFFERS, John	22	N½SE	1860-04-02		A1
2954	" "	22	S½NE	1860-04-02		A1
2953	" "	22	NW	1875-04-20		A1
3093	KIRKLAND, William C	12	SWNE	1860-12-01		A1
3006	LANE, Marcus C	24	E½NW	1860-10-01		A1
3007	" "	24	NWNW	1860-10-01		A1
3062	LEE, Seaborn A	31	S½NE	1858-11-01		A1
3063	" "	31	SE	1858-11-01		A1
3064	" "	32	S½SW	1858-11-01		A1
3055	LEWIS, John B	3	N½NW	1858-11-01		A1 G4
3056	" "	4	SWSE	1858-11-01		A1 G4
3057	" "	9	NWNE	1858-11-01		A1 G4
3041	LOWERY, Rubin B	22	S½SE	1889-11-21		A2
2895	MARTIN, Green	36	SENE	1852-02-02		A1
2896	" "	36	SWNE	1852-02-02		A1
3070	MCKEITHEN, Stephen H	34	E½SE	1884-03-20		A1
2872	MILNER, Benjamin C	18	S½SW	1858-11-01		A1 V3014
2876	MILNER, Bonita M	19	E½NE	1858-11-01		A1
2877	" "	19	E½SW	1858-11-01		A1
2878	" "	19	NESE	1858-11-01		A1
2879	" "	19	SWNE	1858-11-01		A1
2880	" "	19	W½SE	1858-11-01		A1
2982	MILNER, John T	19	SWSW	1858-11-01		A1
2983	" "	29	SWNW	1858-11-01		A1

ID	Individual in Patent	Sec.	Sec. Part	Date Issued	Other Counties	For More Info . . .
2984	MILNER, John T (Cont'd)	30	NENE	1858-11-01		A1
2985	" "	30	NENW	1858-11-01		A1
2989	" "	30	SWNE	1858-11-01		A1
2990	" "	30	W½NW	1858-11-01		A1
2991	" "	30	W½SW	1858-11-01		A1
2986	" "	30	NWNE	1860-10-01		A1
2987	" "	30	SENE	1860-10-01		A1
2988	" "	30	SENW	1860-10-01		A1
3068	MILNER, Solomon	6	W½NW	1882-06-10		A1
3119	MILNER, Willis J	4	SESW	1858-11-01		A1
3120	" "	4	SWSW	1858-11-01		A1
3121	" "	5	S½SE	1858-11-01		A1
3122	" "	5	S½SW	1858-11-01		A1
3123	" "	9	NENW	1858-11-01		A1
3124	" "	9	W½NW	1858-11-01		A1
2871	NEWTON, Angus	26	S½SE	1888-11-08		A1
3080	NEWTON, Thomas	26	NWNE	1883-10-20		A1
3079	" "	26	NESE	1891-06-29		A2
3081	" "	26	NWSE	1891-06-29		A2
3082	" "	26	SENE	1891-06-29		A2
3083	" "	26	SWNE	1891-06-29		A2
2892	PARMER, Foster R	18	S½NW	1886-04-10		A2
2873	PERRY, Benjamin	1	NWSE	1848-04-01		A1
2874	" "	13	SENW	1848-04-01		A1
2963	PERRY, John	24	SESE	1858-09-01		A1
2964	" "	25	NENE	1858-11-01		A1
3087	PHILLIPS, Wiley	2	SWSW	1858-11-01		A1 V3049
3088	" "	3	E½SE	1858-11-01		A1 R3067
3003	POWELL, Mack	34	W½NE	1882-06-10		A1
2883	REYNOLDS, Daniel A	2	SWSE	1885-03-16		A1
2921	RHOADS, Jared	1	NWNE	1837-08-14		A1
2922	" "	1	SWSW	1837-08-14		A1
2875	RHODES, Benjamin	20	S½	1858-11-01		A1
2885	RHODES, Eli	7	N½	1858-11-01		A1
2923	RHODES, Jared	1	SWNE	1834-06-12		A1
2926	RHODES, Jarred	24	E½NE	1845-06-01		A1
2924	" "	1	SWSE	1848-04-01		A1
2925	" "	12	NENW	1849-09-01		A1
2968	RHODES, John	1	NESE	1858-11-01		A1
2969	" "	1	NESW	1858-11-01		A1
2970	" "	10	E½SW	1858-11-01		A1
2971	" "	10	NWSW	1858-11-01		A1
2972	" "	10	SWSW	1858-11-01		A1
2974	" "	12	NWSW	1858-11-01		A1
2975	" "	15	W½NW	1858-11-01		A1
2973	" "	12	NWNW	1860-10-01		A1
2992	RHODES, Jonathan	17	W½	1858-11-01		A1
3005	RHODES, Mansel	20	N½	1858-11-01		A1
3004	" "	12	SWSW	1860-10-01		A1
3009	RHODES, Martha	1	S½NW	1858-11-01		A1 V3089
3010	" "	11	E½NE	1858-11-01		A1
3011	" "	12	SWNW	1858-11-01		A1
3012	" "	2	E½SE	1858-11-01		A1
3013	" "	2	NWSE	1858-11-01		A1
3015	RHODES, Reddin	1	E½NE	1833-06-04		A1
3021	" "	24	SWSW	1852-02-02		A1
3016	" "	23	E½NE	1858-11-01		A1
3017	" "	23	E½SE	1858-11-01		A1
3018	" "	24	NESW	1858-11-01		A1
3019	" "	24	NWSW	1858-11-01		A1
3020	" "	24	SWNW	1858-11-01		A1
3022	" "	26	NENE	1858-11-01		A1
3023	RHODES, Redding	25	SWSE	1838-07-28		A1
3032	RHODES, Robert	14	S½SW	1858-11-01		A1
3033	" "	23	E½NW	1858-11-01		A1
3034	" "	23	W½NE	1858-11-01		A1
3035	" "	23	W½SE	1858-11-01		A1
3058	RHODES, Sanford	2	NENE	1858-09-01		A1
3059	" "	2	SENE	1858-09-01		A1
3060	" "	2	W½NE	1858-11-01		A1
3115	RHODES, William	1	NWSW	1848-04-01		A1
3116	" "	12	SENW	1848-05-03		A1
3117	" "	24	NWNE	1848-05-03		A1

ID	Individual in Patent	Sec.	Sec. Part	Date Issued	Other Counties	For More Info . . .
3118	RHODES, William (Cont'd)	25	NWSE	1849-09-01		A1
2884	ROBINSON, Eldridge	34	E½NW	1882-06-10		A1
3040	SHIPP, Robert W	3	S½NW	1841-05-20		A1
3027	SIRMON, Richard P	17	E½	1858-11-01		A1
2976	SMITH, John	12	E½SE	1848-05-03		A1
2955	SMITH, John P	1	SESW	1845-06-01		A1
2956	" "	12	NESW	1848-05-03		A1
3108	SMITH, William M	25	W½NE	1858-11-01		A1
3109	" "	27	N½SW	1858-11-01		A1
3110	" "	28	N½SE	1858-11-01		A1
2978	SMYTH, John	13	NENE	1848-04-01		A1
2979	" "	13	NENW	1848-04-01		A1
2980	" "	13	NWSE	1848-04-01		A1
2981	" "	13	SWNE	1848-04-01		A1
2977	" "	13	E½SE	1848-05-03		A1
2958	SMYTH, John P	12	NENE	1858-09-01		A1
2960	" "	12	SESW	1858-09-01		A1
2957	" "	1	SESE	1858-11-01		A1
2959	" "	12	SENE	1858-11-01		A1
2961	" "	12	W½SE	1858-11-01		A1
3036	SMYTH, Robert	27	W½NW	1858-11-01		A1
3037	" "	28	E½NE	1858-11-01		A1
3038	" "	28	E½NW	1858-11-01		A1
3039	" "	28	W½NE	1858-11-01		A1
3111	SMYTH, William M	25	NWNW	1858-09-01		A1
3112	" "	25	SENW	1858-09-01		A1
2962	SMYTHE, John P	12	NWNE	1852-02-02		A1
2994	THOMAS, Joseph G	9	SW	1858-11-01		A1
2993	" "	9	SENW	1862-01-01		A1
2995	" "	9	SWNE	1862-01-01		A1
2996	" "	9	W½SE	1862-01-01		A1
3028	THOMAS, Richard	25	E½SE	1858-11-01		A1
3029	" "	25	SENE	1858-11-01		A1
3030	" "	36	NENE	1858-11-01		A1
3024	THOMAS, Richard C	36	NENW	1858-11-01		A1
3025	" "	36	NWNE	1858-11-01		A1
3026	" "	36	W½NW	1858-11-01		A1
3113	THOMAS, William R	22	E½SW	1858-11-01		A1
3114	" "	22	W½SW	1858-11-01		A1
3071	THOMPSON, Thomas A	29	N½SW	1858-11-01		A1
3072	" "	29	NWSE	1858-11-01		A1
3073	" "	29	W½NE	1858-11-01		A1
3074	" "	32	N½SE	1858-11-01		A1 V3084
3075	" "	32	NESW	1858-11-01		A1 V3105
3094	TURNER, William D	36	SESW	1858-11-01		A1
3095	" "	36	SWSE	1858-11-01		A1
2998	VINES, Joseph	4	NW	1858-11-01		A1
2999	" "	4	NWSE	1858-11-01		A1
3000	" "	4	SWNE	1858-11-01		A1
3001	" "	5	S½NE	1858-11-01		A1
2927	WADKINS, Jesse	31	SW	1858-11-01		A1
3096	WARD, William E	15	NESE	1858-11-01		A1
3097	" "	15	SENW	1858-11-01		A1
3098	" "	15	SW	1858-11-01		A1
3099	" "	15	W½SE	1858-11-01		A1
2905	WATERS, Ibbin	32	N½NE	1894-11-12		A2
2891	WEST, Elizabeth	15	NENW	1854-07-15		A1
2888	" "	14	N½SW	1858-11-01		A1
2889	" "	14	W½NW	1858-11-01		A1
2890	" "	15	NE	1858-11-01		A1
2933	WINBRAY, John A	21	NENW	1858-11-01		A1
2934	" "	21	NWNE	1858-11-01		A1
2935	" "	21	SESW	1858-11-01		A1
2936	" "	21	SWSE	1858-11-01		A1
2937	" "	21	W½NW	1858-11-01		A1
2938	" "	21	W½SW	1858-11-01		A1

Patent Map

T9-N R14-E
St Stephens Meridian

Map Group 13

Township Statistics

Parcels Mapped	:	255
Number of Patents	:	161
Number of Individuals	:	103
Patentees Identified	:	103
Number of Surnames	:	68
Multi-Patentee Parcels	:	3
Oldest Patent Date	:	6/4/1833
Most Recent Patent	:	12/20/1904
Block/Lot Parcels	:	0
Parcels Re - Issued	:	1
Parcels that Overlap	:	10
Cities and Towns	:	1
Cemeteries	:	1

Section 6
CHAMBERS Andy 1889
MILNER Solomon 1882
HUMPHREYS Elijah J 1891
GILBERT John A 1858
GILBERT John A 1858

Section 5
GILBERT John A 1858
GILBERT John A 1858
VINES Joseph 1858
GILBERT John A 1858
MILNER Willis J 1858
MILNER Willis J 1858

Section 4
VINES Joseph 1858
BOLLING Samuel J 1860
BOLLING John 1845
VINES Joseph 1858
VINES Joseph 1858
BOLLING John 1845
MILNER Willis J 1858
MILNER Willis J 1858
BOLLING [4] Samuel J 1858
BOLLING Samuel J 1858

Section 7
RHODES Eli 1858
HOOD Isaac F 1858
HOOD Isaac F 1858
HOOD Isaac F 1858
HOOD Isaac F 1858

Section 8
GILBERT Eliza 1858
HOOD Isaac F 1858
GONDER Mark F 1858

Section 9
MILNER Willis J 1858
MILNER Willis J 1858
BOLLING [4] Samuel J 1858
GILBERT Webster 1858
THOMAS Joseph G 1862
THOMAS Joseph G 1862
THOMAS Joseph G 1858
THOMAS Joseph G 1862

Section 18
HOOD Isaac F 1858
PARMER Foster R 1886
HUMPHREY Mary E 1885
FAIN James B 1858
MILNER Benjamin C 1858

Section 17
RHODES Jonathan 1858
SIRMON Richard P 1858

Section 16

Section 19
GIBSON James G 1858
MILNER Bonita M 1858
MILNER Bonita M 1858
MILNER Bonita M 1858
MILNER John T 1858
MILNER Bonita M 1858
MILNER Bonita M 1858

Section 20
RHODES Mansel 1858
RHODES Benjamin 1858

Section 21
WINBRAY John A 1858
WINBRAY John A 1858
WINBRAY John A 1858
CAMPBELL Henry E 1858
CAMPBELL Henry E 1858
CAMPBELL Henry E 1858
WINBRAY John A 1858
WINBRAY John A 1858
WINBRAY John A 1858

Section 30
MILNER John T 1858
MILNER John T 1858
MILNER John T 1860
MILNER John T 1858
MILNER John T 1860
MILNER John T 1858
MILNER John T 1860
MILNER John T 1858
DUCK John R 1858
DUCK John R 1858
HARTLEY William F 1860

Section 29
MILNER John T 1858
THOMPSON Thomas A 1858
THOMPSON Thomas A 1858
THOMPSON Thomas A 1858
FLOWERS William H 1858

Section 28
SMYTH Robert 1858
SMYTH Robert 1858
SMYTH Robert 1858
FLOWERS John J 1883
SMITH William M 1858
DUKES Joseph L 1904
FLOWERS Francis A 1884
FLOWERS John J 1883

Section 31
BLAIR William 1858
WADKINS Jesse 1858
DUCK John R 1858
LEE Seaborn A 1858
LEE Seaborn A 1858

Section 32
FLOWERS William H 1858
WATERS Ibbin 1894
BARRETT James 1883
FLOWERS William H 1858
THOMPSON Thomas A 1858
THOMPSON Thomas A 1858
LEE Seaborn A 1858
CREG Wade 1891

Section 33

BOLLING [4] Samuel J 1858	BOLLING John 1858	BARNES Solomon 1858	BARNES Solomon 1858	RHODES Sanford 1858	RHODES Sanford 1858	HARPER William 1838	RHOADS Jared 1837	RHODES Reddin 1833

Section 3 / 2 / 1 area:

- BOLLING [4] Samuel J 1858
- SHIPP Robert W 1841
- BOLLING Samuel J 1845
- BRAZZIL Robert 1837
- BOLLING Samuel J 1858
- BOLLING John 1848
- BOLLING John 1848
- BOLLING John 1858
- BARNES Solomon 1858
- PHILLIPS Wiley 1858
- PHILLIPS Wiley 1858

3

- BARNES Solomon 1858
- BENNETT Ryan 1858
- COWART Stephen D 1889
- BENNETT Ryan 1861

2

- RHODES Sanford 1858
- RHODES Sanford 1858
- RHODES Martha 1858
- RHODES Martha 1858
- REYNOLDS Daniel A 1885

1

- HARPER William 1838
- RHODES Martha 1858
- HARPER William B 1837
- RHODES William 1848
- RHODES John 1858
- RHOADS Jared 1837
- RHOADS Jared 1837
- RHODES Jared 1834
- PERRY Benjamin 1848
- SMITH John P 1845
- RHODES Reddin 1833
- RHODES John 1858
- RHODES Jarred 1848
- SMYTH John P 1858

Section 10 / 11 / 12:

- GILBERT Webster 1858
- BENNETT Ryan 1858

10

- RHODES John 1858
- RHODES John 1858
- RHODES John 1858
- CREECH William C 1858

- BENNETT Ryan 1858
- CREECH William C 1858
- BENNETT Ryan 1858

11

- RHODES Martha 1858
- FIFE John 1849

- RHODES John 1860
- RHODES Martha 1858
- RHODES John 1858
- RHODES Mansel 1860
- RHODES Jarred 1849
- RHODES William 1848
- SMITH John P 1848
- SMYTH John P 1858
- SMYTHE John P 1852
- KIRKLAND William C 1860
- SMYTH John P 1858

12

- SMYTH John P 1858
- SMYTH John P 1858
- SMITH John 1848

Section 15 / 14 / 13:

- RHODES John 1858
- WEST Elizabeth 1854
- WEST Elizabeth 1858
- WARD William E 1858

15

- WARD William E 1858
- WARD William E 1858
- WARD William E 1858
- BENNETT Ryan 1858

- WEST Elizabeth 1858
- BENNETT Ryan 1858
- WEST Elizabeth 1858
- RHODES Robert 1858

14

- BENNETT Ryan 1858

- GIDDINGS Thomas 1848
- GIDDINGS Thomas 1848
- SMYTH John 1848
- PERRY Benjamin 1848
- FIFE John 1858
- SMYTH John 1848
- SMYTH John 1848
- FIFE John 1858
- SMYTH John 1848

13

- FIFE John 1858
- FIFE John 1848
- SMYTH John 1848

Section 22 / 23 / 24:

- JEFFERS John 1875
- BENNETT Ryan 1861
- JEFFERS John 1860

22

- THOMAS William R 1858
- THOMAS William R 1858
- JEFFERS John 1860
- LOWERY Rubin B 1889

- RHODES Robert 1858
- RHODES Robert 1858
- RHODES Robert 1858

23

- RHODES Robert 1858
- RHODES Reddin 1858
- RHODES Reddin 1858

- LANE Marcus C 1860
- LANE Marcus C 1860
- RHODES Reddin 1858
- RHODES William 1848
- RHODES Jarred 1845
- RHODES Reddin 1858
- RHODES Reddin 1858
- RHODES Reddin 1852
- BAILEY Isaac 1862
- BAILEY Isaac 1849
- BAILEY Isaac 1858
- BLACK Thomas J 1845
- PERRY John 1858

24

Section 27 / 26 / 25:

- SMYTH Robert 1858
- SMITH William M 1858

27

- NEWTON Thomas 1883
- NEWTON Thomas 1891
- NEWTON Thomas 1891
- RHODES Reddin 1858
- NEWTON Thomas 1891
- NEWTON Thomas 1891
- HOWELL Joseph W 1885
- NEWTON Angus 1888

26

- SMYTH William M 1858
- SMYTH William M 1858
- SMITH William M 1858
- BAILEY Sarah 1858
- PERRY John 1858
- THOMAS Richard 1858
- RHODES William 1849
- RHODES Redding 1838
- THOMAS Richard 1858

25

Section 34 / 35 / 36:

- ROBINSON Eldridge 1882
- POWELL Mack 1882
- GRIFFIN William 1882

34

- ELSBERRY James 1882
- EDMONDS John 1882
- ELSBERRY William 1882
- BASS William F 1883
- MCKEITHEN Stephen H 1884

- HARPER Henry S 1858
- HARPER Henry S 1858

35

- HARPER Henry S 1858
- HARPER Henry S 1858
- BROWN Francis M 1875
- JACKSON Cleton 1858

- THOMAS Richard C 1858
- THOMAS Richard C 1858
- THOMAS Richard C 1858
- THOMAS Richard 1858
- BRASSWELL James 1897
- MARTIN Green 1852
- MARTIN Green 1852
- BRASSWELL James 1897
- JACKSON Cleton 1858
- TURNER William D 1858
- TURNER William D 1858
- BRASWELL James 1858

36

Helpful Hints

1. This Map's INDEX can be found on the preceding pages.

2. Refer to Map "C" to see where this Township lies within Butler County, Alabama.

3. Numbers within square brackets [ ] denote a multi-patentee land parcel (multi-owner). Refer to Appendix "C" for a full list of members in this group.

4. Areas that look to be crowded with Patentees usually indicate multiple sales of the same parcel (Re-issues) or Overlapping parcels. See this Township's Index for an explanation of these and other circumstances that might explain "odd" groupings of Patentees on this map.

Legend

————————	Patent Boundary
▬▬▬▬▬▬	Section Boundary
	No Patents Found (or Outside County)
1., 2., 3., ...	Lot Numbers (when beside a name)
[ ]	Group Number (see Appendix "C")

Scale: Section = 1 mile X 1 mile (generally, with some exceptions)

Road Map

T9-N R14-E
St Stephens Meridian

Map Group 13

Cities & Towns
Wald

Cemeteries
Gravel Hill Cemetery

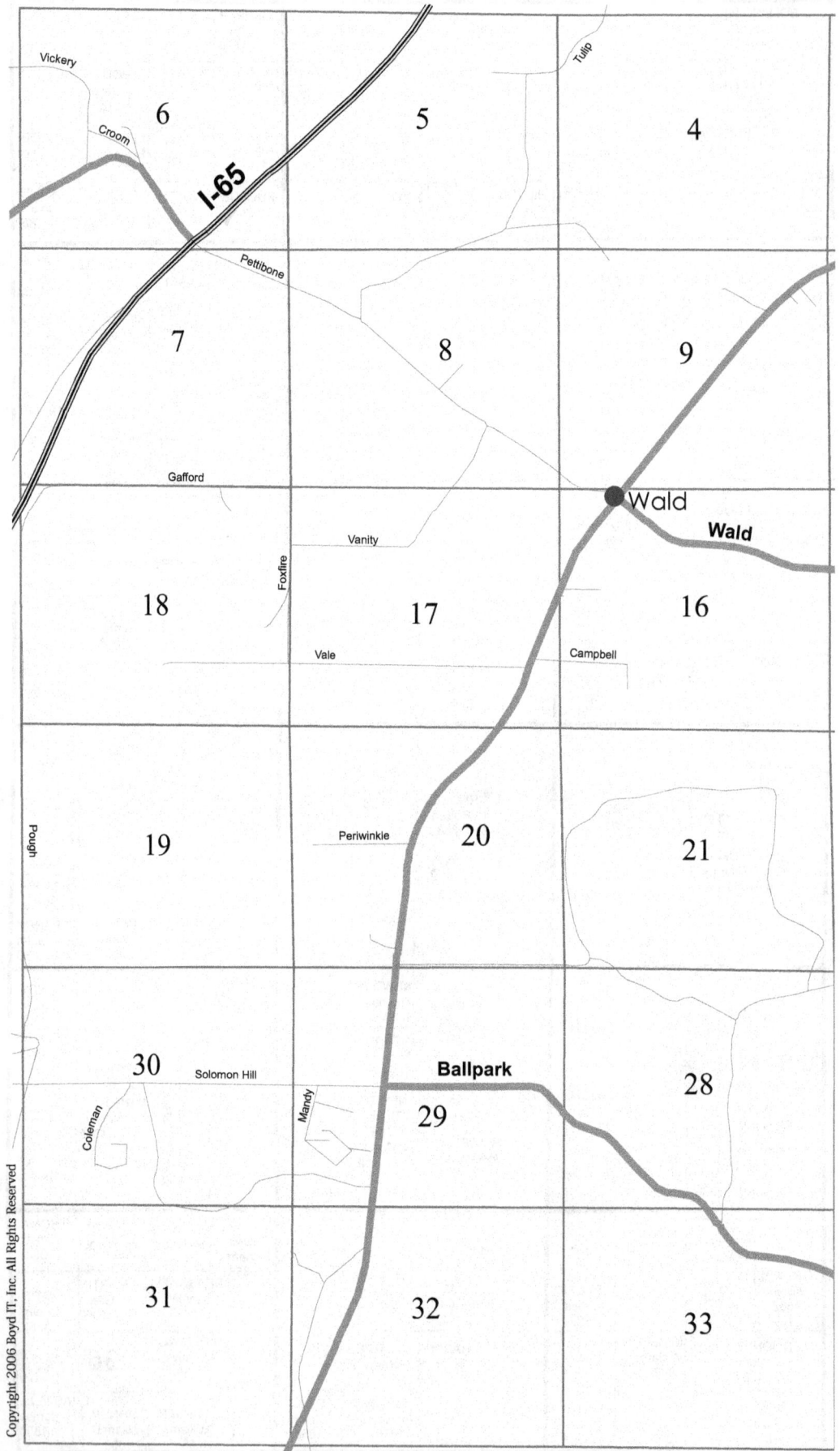

Vickery

Croom

I-65

6

5

Tulip

4

Pettibone

7

8

9

Gafford

Wald

Wald

Vanity

Foxfire

18

17

16

Vale

Campbell

Pough

19

Periwinkle

20

21

30

Solomon Hill

Coleman

Mandy

Ballpark

29

28

31

32

33

Vandiver

Aztec

Simpson

Mobile

Elm

✝ *Gravel Hill Cem.*

3

Mt Ida

Rason

County Road 45

2

1

Dogwood

Industry

10

11

12

County Road 165

Gravel Hill

15

14

13

County Road 30

22

23

24

27

26

25

Dogwood

34

Green Briar

35

36

Copyright 2006 Boyd IT, Inc. All Rights Reserved

Helpful Hints

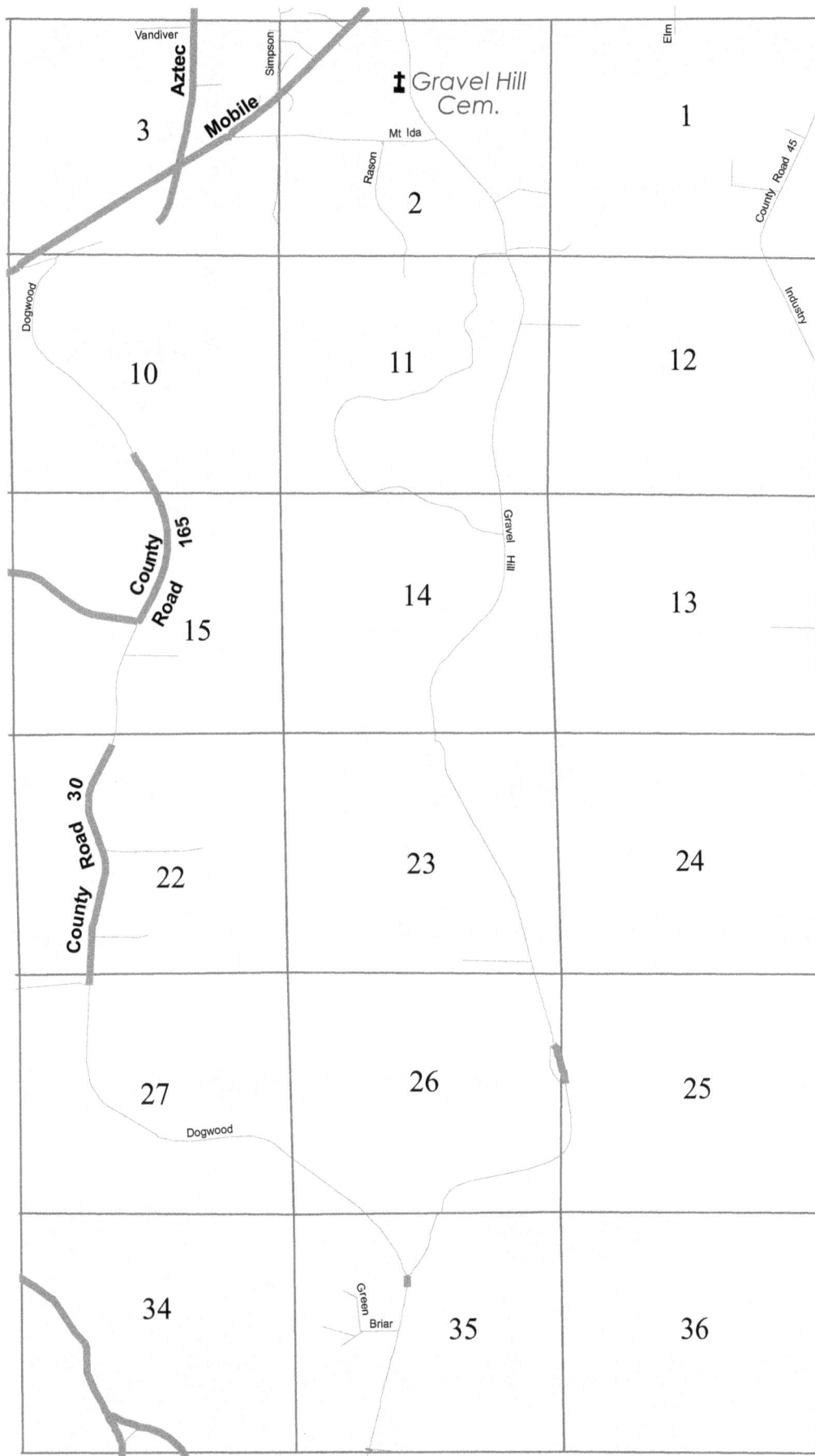

1. This road map has a number of uses, but primarily it is to help you: a) find the present location of land owned by your ancestors (at least the general area), b) find cemeteries and city-centers, and c) estimate the route/roads used by Census-takers & tax-assessors.

2. If you plan to travel to Butler County to locate cemeteries or land parcels, please pick up a modern travel map for the area before you do. Mapping old land parcels on modern maps is not as exact a science as you might think. Just the slightest variations in public land survey coordinates, estimates of parcel boundaries, or road-map deviations can greatly alter a map's representation of how a road either does or doesn't cross a particular parcel of land.

L e g e n d

———————— Section Lines

══════════ Interstates

━━━━━━━━━━ Highways

———————— Other Roads

● Cities/Towns

✝ Cemeteries

Scale: Section = 1 mile X 1 mile
(generally, with some exceptions)

Historical Map

T9-N R14-E
St Stephens Meridian

Map Group 13

Cities & Towns
Wald

Cemeteries
Gravel Hill Cemetery

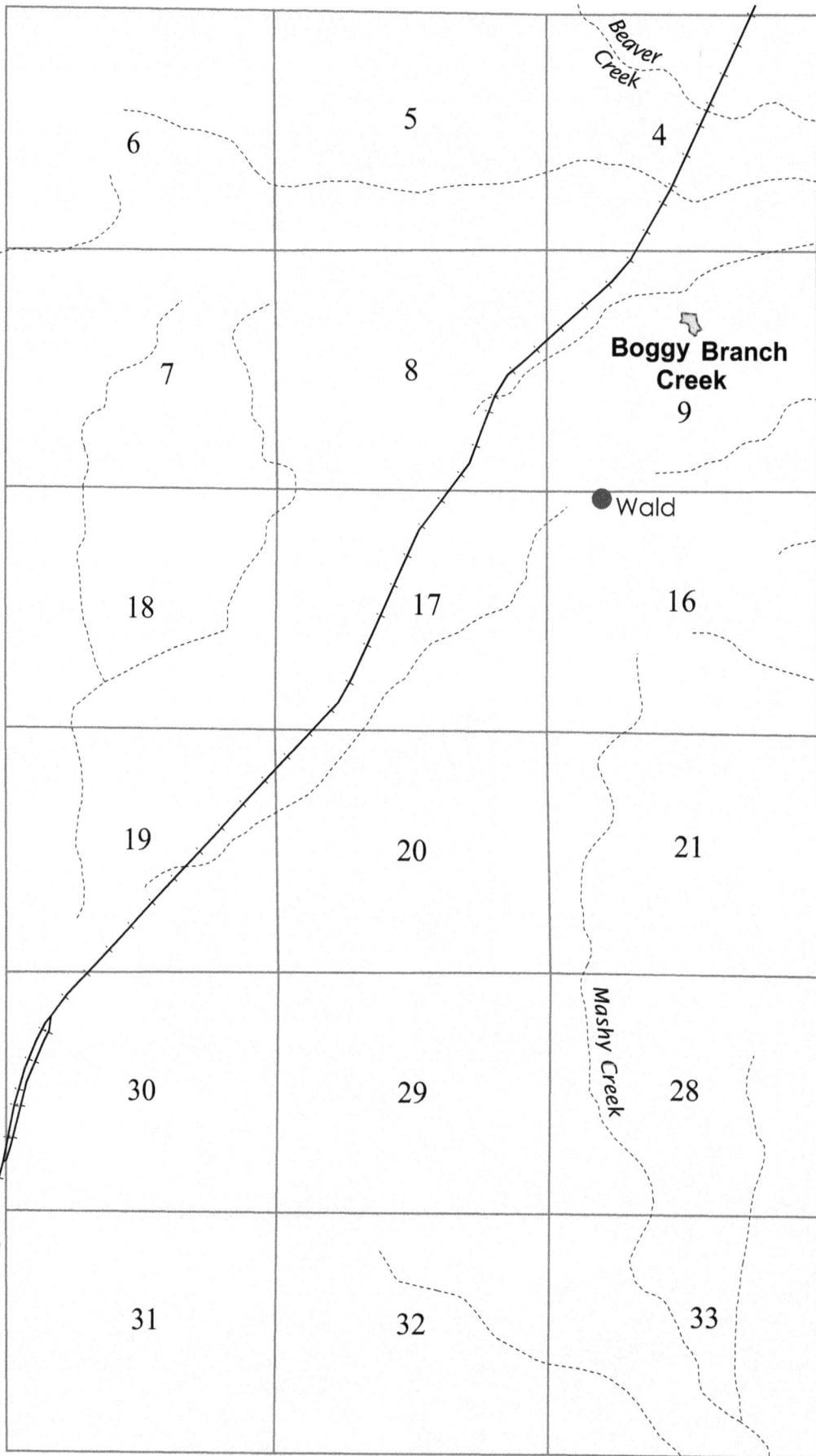

Beaver Creek

6

5

4

7

8

Boggy Branch Creek

9

Wald

18

17

16

19

20

21

Mashy Creek

30

29

28

31

32

33

Stallings Creek 3	✝ Gravel Hill Cem. 2	1
10	11	12 Piney Woods Creek
15	14 Hawkins Creek	13
22	23	24
27	26	25 Persimmon Creek
34	35 Deep Step Creek	36

Helpful Hints

1. This Map takes a different look at the same Congressional Township displayed in the preceding two maps. It presents features that can help you better envision the historical development of the area: a) Water-bodies (lakes & ponds), b) Water-courses (rivers, streams, etc.), c) Railroads, d) City/town center-points (where they were oftentimes located when first settled), and e) Cemeteries.

2. Using this "Historical" map in tandem with this Township's Patent Map and Road Map, may lead you to some interesting discoveries. You will often find roads, towns, cemeteries, and waterways are named after nearby landowners: sometimes those names will be the ones you are researching. See how many of these research gems you can find here in Butler County.

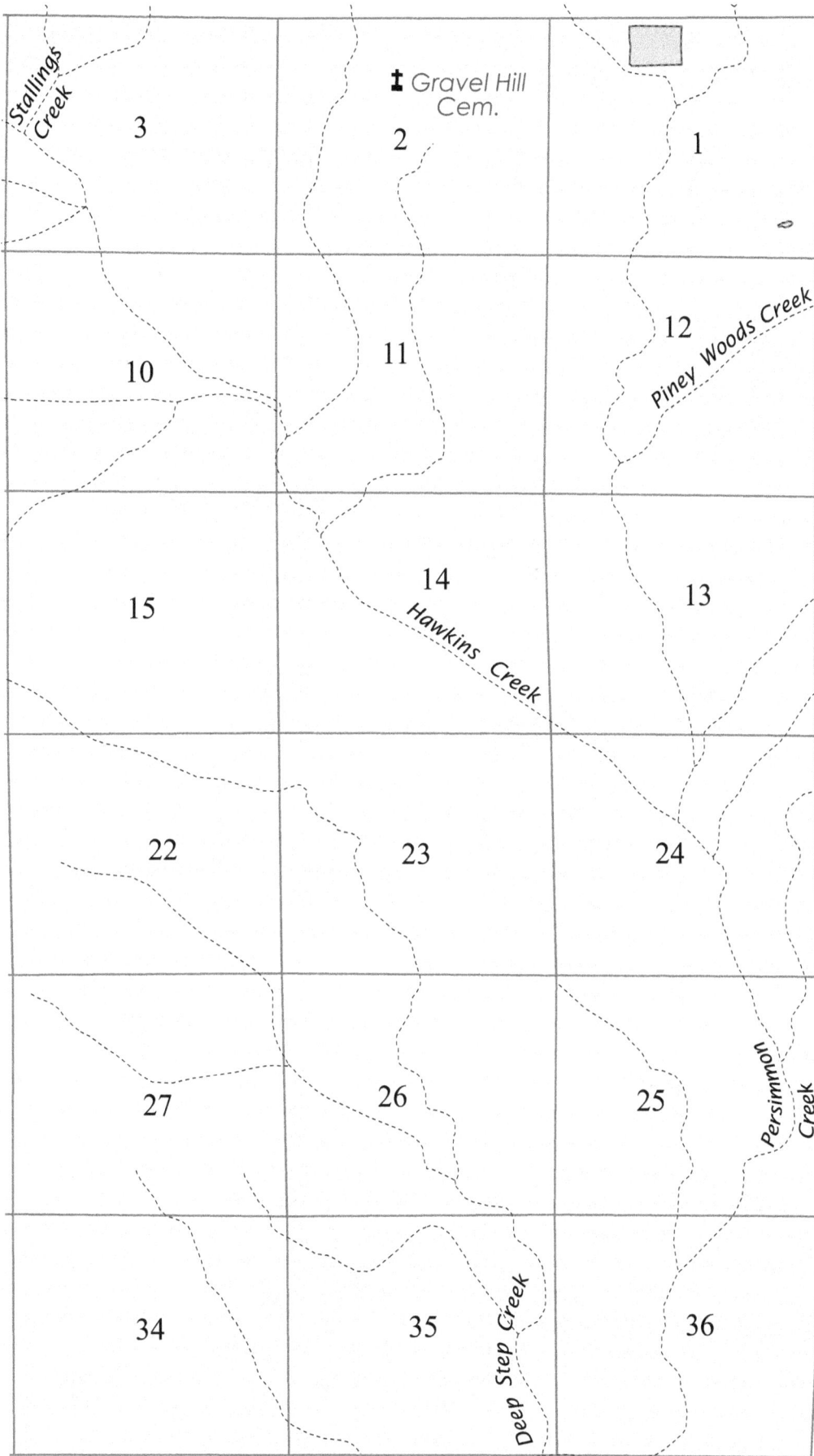

Legend

————————	Section Lines
＋＋＋＋＋＋	Railroads
▭	Large Rivers & Bodies of Water
- - - - - - - -	Streams/Creeks & Small Rivers
●	Cities/Towns
✝	Cemeteries

Scale: Section = 1 mile X 1 mile
(there are some exceptions)

Map Group 14: Index to Land Patents

Township 9-North Range 15-East (St Stephens)

After you locate an individual in this Index, take note of the Section and Section Part then proceed to the Land Patent map on the pages immediately following. You should have no difficulty locating the corresponding parcel of land.

The "For More Info" Column will lead you to more information about the underlying Patents. See the *Legend* at right, and the "How to Use this Book" chapter, for more information.

ID	Individual in Patent	Sec.	Sec. Part	Date Issued	Other Counties	For More Info . . .
3164	ANDERS, Daniel	21	E½NE	1858-11-01		A1
3385	BARRETT, William R	22	E½SE	1860-04-02		A1
3310	BLACK, Joseph	2	NENW	1835-10-14		A1
3348	BLACK, Robert	4	SWNE	1837-08-15		A1
3265	BOLLING, John	15	W½NE	1858-11-01		A1
3358	BOLLING, Samuel J	10	W½SE	1858-11-01		A1
3332	BOZEMAN, Nathan	15	E½NE	1823-10-01		A1
3220	BRADEN, Harvey C	30	NESW	1858-09-01		A1
3221	" "	30	NWSE	1858-09-01		A1
3223	" "	30	SENW	1858-09-01		A1
3224	" "	30	SWNE	1858-09-01		A1
3218	" "	29	NWSW	1858-11-01		A1
3219	" "	30	E½SE	1858-11-01		A1
3222	" "	30	SENE	1858-11-01		A1
3244	BRASSWELL, James	31	W½SW	1897-03-18		A1
3162	BREITHAUPT, Christian	14	E½SW	1826-11-22		A1
3338	BUSH, Richard H	28	SW	1858-11-01		A1
3339	" "	28	SWNW	1858-11-01		A1
3340	" "	28	W½SE	1858-11-01		A1
3341	" "	29	SENE	1858-11-01		A1
3266	CALDWELL, John C	3	W½NE	1823-10-01		A1
3368	CALDWELL, William H	22	NWSE	1837-08-12		A1
3369	" "	22	SWNE	1837-08-12		A1
3211	CALLAWAY, Francis	15	SE	1859-12-09		A1
3212	" "	22	NENE	1859-12-09		A1
3135	CARR, Allen	10	E½SE	1837-08-10		A1
3187	CHAMBLISS, David E	29	SESE	1852-02-02		A1
3190	" "	32	NENE	1852-02-02		A1
3193	" "	33	NWNW	1852-02-02		A1
3195	" "	33	SWNW	1852-02-02		A1
3189	" "	29	SWSE	1858-11-01		A1
3184	" "	29	E½SW	1859-07-15		A1
3185	" "	29	N½SE	1859-07-15		A1
3186	" "	29	SENW	1859-07-15		A1
3188	" "	29	SWNE	1859-07-15		A1
3192	" "	33	NESW	1859-07-15		A1
3194	" "	33	SENW	1859-07-15		A1
3191	" "	33	NENW	1911-02-23		A1
3243	COOK, James B	25	NWNE	1849-09-01		A1
3247	CRAIG, James	6	W½NW	1837-08-14		A1
3245	" "	6	E½NW	1854-10-02		A1
3246	" "	6	NESW	1854-10-02		A1
3128	DEMING, Albert	23	NENE	1854-10-02		A1
3129	" "	23	NESE	1854-10-02		A1
3132	" "	23	SWNE	1854-10-02		A1
3127	" "	14	W½SW	1858-09-01		A1

ID	Individual in Patent	Sec.	Sec. Part	Date Issued	Other Counties	For More Info . . .
3130	DEMING, Albert (Cont'd)	23	NW	1858-09-01		A1
3131	" "	23	NWNE	1858-09-01		A1
3133	DERNING, Albert	23	SENE	1852-02-02		A1
3200	DICKEN, Elisha T	28	E½SE	1858-11-01		A1
3201	" "	33	E½NE	1858-11-01		A1
3202	" "	34	N½NW	1858-11-01		A1
3261	DUKE, Joel	6	NWSE	1854-07-15		A1
3258	" "	6	E½NE	1858-11-01		A1
3259	" "	6	NESE	1858-11-01		A1
3260	" "	6	NWNE	1858-11-01		A1
3262	" "	6	SESW	1858-11-01		A1
3263	" "	6	SWSE	1858-11-01		A1
3264	" "	6	W½SW	1858-11-01		A1
3225	EXUM, Henry	8	E½SW	1858-11-01		A1
3226	" "	8	NWSW	1858-11-01		A1
3227	" "	8	SE	1858-11-01		A1
3327	EXUM, Mathew	4	SWSW	1860-04-02		A1
3328	" "	5	S½SE	1860-04-02		A1
3329	" "	9	NW	1860-04-02		A1
3330	" "	9	SWNE	1860-04-02		A1
3320	FIFE, Malind M	10	SESW	1858-09-01		A1
3321	" "	10	W½SW	1858-09-01		A1
3236	FUTCH, Isaac	3	NW	1831-08-01		A1 G17
3236	FUTCH, Jacob	3	NW	1831-08-01		A1 G17
3126	GANDY, Abijah	22	SENE	1837-08-12		A1
3203	GANDY, Evander	34	NENE	1848-04-01		A1
3322	GANDY, Marina	32	SE	1858-11-01		A1
3323	" "	32	SENE	1858-11-01		A1
3324	" "	33	SESW	1858-11-01		A1
3325	" "	33	W½SW	1858-11-01		A1
3253	GILBERT, James	21	NWSE	1858-11-01		A1
3254	" "	21	SWNE	1858-11-01		A1
3319	GLASSGOW, Lewis	6	SESE	1891-11-23		A2
3168	GODWIN, Daniel	20	NENE	1884-03-20		A2 G20
3168	GODWIN, Jane	20	NENE	1884-03-20		A2 G20
3312	GRAY, Joseph P	30	SWSE	1858-11-01		A1
3313	" "	31	NE	1858-11-01		A1
3314	" "	31	NESE	1858-11-01		A1
3315	" "	31	W½SE	1858-11-01		A1
3360	HALSO, Stephen	26	E½SE	1858-11-01		A1
3361	" "	36	N½NW	1858-11-01		A1
3213	HARDY, Freeman	25	E½NE	1825-04-16		A1
3214	" "	25	E½SE	1825-04-16		A1 R3270
3256	HARRISON, James	12	NWNW	1835-10-14		A1
3255	" "	1	W½SW	1837-08-15		A1
3270	HARRISON, John H	25	E½SE	1858-11-01		A1 R3214
3331	HUDSON, Max	35	N½SE	1843-02-01		A1
3272	JAY, John	20	S½SE	1858-09-01		A1
3273	" "	20	S½SW	1858-09-01		A1
3274	" "	29	NENW	1858-09-01		A1
3275	" "	29	NWNE	1858-09-01		A1
3276	" "	29	W½NW	1858-09-01		A1
3311	JAY, Joseph	20	NESW	1858-11-01		A1
3374	JAY, William	32	SENW	1861-05-01		A1
3375	" "	32	SWNE	1861-05-01		A1
3248	JOHNSON, James E	21	S½SW	1858-11-01		A1
3249	" "	28	E½NW	1858-11-01		A1
3250	" "	28	NWNW	1858-11-01		A1
3251	" "	28	W½NE	1858-11-01		A1
3252	" "	29	NENE	1858-11-01		A1
3292	JOHNSTON, John S	14	W½SE	1825-04-16		A1
3359	KEITH, Silas	35	NWNW	1845-07-01		A1
3198	KNOWLES, Edmund	4	NWNE	1837-08-12		A1
3229	LEE, Hillary	26	E½SW	1858-11-01		A1
3230	" "	26	N½NW	1858-11-01		A1
3231	" "	26	SENW	1858-11-01		A1
3232	" "	26	SWNE	1858-11-01		A1
3233	" "	26	W½SE	1858-11-01		A1
3216	MARTIN, Green	31	NW	1858-09-01		A1
3376	MARTIN, William	31	E½SW	1858-11-01		A1
3163	MCALLISTER, Colin	12	NENE	1852-02-02		A1
3370	MCCURRY, William J	10	NESW	1837-08-10		A1
3377	MERCER, William	25	SWNE	1834-10-21		A1

ID	Individual in Patent	Sec.	Sec. Part	Date Issued	Other Counties	For More Info . . .
3380	MERCER, William (Cont'd)	36	SWNE	1843-02-01		A1
3378	" "	25	SWSE	1849-09-01		A1
3379	" "	35	SWSE	1849-09-01		A1
3234	MONTGOMERY, Hugh B	34	SENE	1861-09-10		A1
3235	" "	34	SWNW	1861-09-10		A1
3366	MORAN, Washington B	33	SE	1858-11-01		A1
3277	MOY, John	9	S½	1858-11-01		A1
3381	MURSER, William	25	NWSE	1858-11-01		A1
3382	" "	36	N½NE	1858-11-01		A1
3383	" "	36	N½SE	1858-11-01		A1
3384	" "	36	SENE	1858-11-01		A1
3137	NEWTON, Amos	4	E½SW	1858-09-01		A1
3138	" "	4	NW	1858-09-01		A1
3139	" "	4	NWSE	1858-09-01		A1
3140	" "	4	NWSW	1858-09-01		A1
3142	NEWTON, Benjamin	15	SW	1858-09-01		A1
3144	" "	22	NENW	1858-09-01		A1
3146	" "	22	NWNE	1858-09-01		A1
3148	" "	22	SENW	1858-11-01		A1
3145	" "	22	NESW	1860-10-01		A1
3149	" "	22	SWNW	1860-10-01		A1
3143	" "	15	SWNW	1862-01-01		A1
3147	" "	22	NWNW	1862-01-01		A1
3158	NEWTON, Caswell	5	W½NE	1849-09-01		A1
3154	" "	5	NESW	1854-07-15		A1
3160	" "	7	NENW	1854-10-02		A1
3161	" "	7	NWNW	1854-10-02		A1
3151	" "	5	E½NE	1858-09-01		A1
3152	" "	5	E½NW	1858-09-01		A1
3153	" "	5	NESE	1858-09-01		A1
3155	" "	5	NWSE	1858-09-01		A1
3157	" "	5	SESW	1858-09-01		A1
3156	" "	5	NWSW	1858-11-01		A1
3159	" "	7	NENE	1858-11-01		A1
3150	PERRY, Benjamin	2	SWNW	1858-11-01		A1
3257	PERRY, James	30	SESW	1852-02-02		A1
3282	PERRY, John	19	NWSW	1848-04-01		A1
3286	" "	19	SWSW	1852-02-02		A1
3284	" "	19	SESW	1858-09-01		A1
3285	" "	19	SWSE	1858-09-01		A1
3290	" "	30	NENW	1858-09-01		A1
3291	" "	30	NWNE	1858-09-01		A1
3278	" "	17	E½SW	1858-11-01		A1
3279	" "	17	SENW	1858-11-01		A1
3280	" "	17	SWNE	1858-11-01		A1
3281	" "	17	W½SE	1858-11-01		A1
3283	" "	19	SESE	1858-11-01		A1
3287	" "	20	NENW	1858-11-01		A1
3288	" "	20	NWNE	1858-11-01		A1
3289	" "	30	NENE	1858-11-01		A1
3141	PICKENS, Andrew	3	NWSE	1837-08-14		A1
3206	PICKENS, Ezekiel H	3	E½SW	1837-08-12		A1
3208	" "	4	SWSE	1854-07-15		A1
3204	" "	2	W½SW	1858-11-01		A1 V3269
3205	" "	3	E½SE	1858-11-01		A1
3207	" "	3	SWSE	1858-11-01		A1
3209	" "	9	E½NE	1858-11-01		A1
3210	" "	9	NWNE	1858-11-01		A1
3371	PORTER, William J	12	SESE	1860-10-01		A1
3372	" "	12	W½NE	1860-10-01		A1
3373	" "	12	W½SE	1860-10-01		A1
3228	PURDY, Henry	3	E½NE	1823-10-01		A1
3386	RABURN, William	2	NWNW	1837-08-18		A1
3316	RHODES, Kinchin	1	E½SE	1858-11-01		A1
3317	" "	1	NE	1858-11-01		A1
3318	" "	1	NWSE	1858-11-01		A1
3333	ROBERSON, Nathaniel J	18	E½SW	1858-11-01		A1
3334	" "	18	SE	1858-11-01		A1
3335	" "	19	NENW	1858-11-01		A1
3336	" "	19	NWNE	1858-11-01		A1
3367	ROBERTS, William A	6	SWNE	1850-04-01		A1
3134	RUFFIN, Alexander	2	SESW	1858-11-01		A1 V3269
3387	SIMS, William	4	E½NE	1821-12-03		A1

ID	Individual in Patent	Sec.	Sec. Part	Date Issued	Other Counties	For More Info . . .
3136	SMITH, Ambrose	5	W½NW	1858-11-01		A1
3173	SMITH, Daniel	2	NESW	1852-02-02		A1
3174	" "	2	SENW	1852-02-02		A1
3165	SMITH, Daniel C	1	SESW	1858-09-01		A1
3166	" "	12	E½NW	1858-09-01		A1
3167	" "	12	SWNW	1858-09-01		A1
3169	SMITH, Daniel L	20	N½SE	1858-11-01		A1
3170	" "	20	S½NE	1858-11-01		A1
3171	" "	21	N½SW	1858-11-01		A1
3172	" "	21	S½NW	1858-11-01		A1
3294	SMITH, John	14	E½SE	1825-04-16		A1
3296	" "	24	W½SE	1834-01-21		A1
3295	" "	18	W½NW	1848-05-03		A1
3293	" "	12	SENE	1852-02-02		A1
3391	SMITH, William	4	E½SE	1821-12-03		A1
3388	" "	17	N½NW	1858-11-01		A1
3389	" "	17	NWNE	1858-11-01		A1
3390	" "	18	N½NE	1858-11-01		A1
3392	" "	7	S½SE	1858-11-01		A1
3393	" "	8	SWSW	1858-11-01		A1
3196	SMYTH, David J	30	W½SW	1858-11-01		A1
3238	SMYTH, Jacob A	7	NESW	1858-09-01		A1
3239	" "	7	NWSW	1858-09-01		A1
3240	" "	7	S½NW	1858-09-01		A1
3242	" "	7	W½NE	1858-09-01		A1
3237	" "	7	NESE	1858-11-01		A1
3241	" "	7	SENE	1858-11-01		A1
3297	SMYTH, John	18	W½SW	1848-04-01		A1
3298	" "	19	NWSE	1848-04-01		A1
3300	" "	19	W½NW	1848-05-03		A1
3299	" "	19	SENE	1849-09-01		A1
3301	" "	20	NWSW	1849-09-01		A1
3342	SMYTH, Robert B	19	E½NE	1858-11-01		A1
3343	" "	19	NESE	1858-11-01		A1
3344	" "	19	NESW	1858-11-01		A1
3345	" "	19	SWNE	1858-11-01		A1
3346	" "	20	SENW	1858-11-01		A1
3347	" "	20	W½NW	1858-11-01		A1
3125	TATOM, Abel	36	S½SE	1858-11-01		A1
3175	THOMAS, Daniel	34	E½SE	1852-02-02		A1
3176	" "	34	NWNE	1852-02-02		A1
3181	" "	35	SWNW	1852-02-02		A1
3177	" "	34	SENW	1858-11-01		A1
3178	" "	34	SW	1858-11-01		A1
3179	" "	34	SWNE	1858-11-01		A1
3180	" "	34	W½SE	1858-11-01		A1
3182	" "	35	SWSW	1858-11-01		A1
3217	THOMAS, Harriett M	27	W½	1858-11-01		A1
3302	THOMAS, John	1	W½NW	1837-08-14		A1
3305	" "	27	NESE	1854-10-02		A1
3308	" "	35	NENW	1854-10-02		A1
3303	" "	26	W½SW	1858-11-01		A1
3304	" "	27	E½NE	1858-11-01		A1
3306	" "	27	SESE	1858-11-01		A1
3307	" "	27	W½SE	1858-11-01		A1
3309	" "	35	SENW	1858-11-01		A1
3337	THOMAS, Patrick	8	N½	1858-11-01		A1
3354	THOMAS, Robert	17	SWNW	1858-11-01		A1
3355	" "	18	E½NW	1858-11-01		A1
3356	" "	18	S½NE	1858-11-01		A1
3357	" "	7	S½SW	1858-11-01		A1
3267	TURNER, John E	11	NE	1858-11-01		A1
3268	" "	2	S½SE	1858-11-01		A1
3269	" "	2	S½SW	1858-11-01		A1 V3134, 3204
3362	TURNER, Thomas	32	NENW	1858-11-01		A1
3363	" "	32	NWNE	1858-11-01		A1
3364	" "	32	SW	1858-11-01		A1
3365	" "	32	W½NW	1858-11-01		A1
3183	WALKER, Daniel	35	SWNE	1843-02-01		A1
3326	WALKER, Mary	35	SENE	1843-02-01		A1
3199	WHIDDON, Elias	26	E½NE	1858-11-01		A1
3394	WILKERSON, William	35	N½NE	1858-11-01		A1
3395	" "	35	SESE	1858-11-01		A1

ID	Individual in Patent	Sec.	Sec. Part	Date Issued	Other Counties	For More Info . . .
3396	WILKERSON, William (Cont'd)	36	E½SW	1858-11-01		A1
3397	" "	36	S½NW	1858-11-01		A1
3398	" "	36	SWSW	1858-11-01		A1
3197	WREN, Davis B	12	NESE	1858-11-01		A1
3215	WREN, George	1	NESW	1852-12-01		A1
3271	WYNN, John J	23	NWSE	1858-11-01		A1
3349	WYNN, Robert P	21	S½SE	1858-11-01		A1
3350	" "	22	NWSW	1858-11-01		A1
3351	" "	22	S½SW	1858-11-01		A1
3352	" "	22	SWSE	1858-11-01		A1
3353	" "	28	E½NE	1858-11-01		A1

Patent Map

T9-N R15-E
St Stephens Meridian

Map Group 14

Township Statistics

Parcels Mapped	:	274
Number of Patents	:	145
Number of Individuals	:	99
Patentees Identified	:	97
Number of Surnames	:	66
Multi-Patentee Parcels	:	2
Oldest Patent Date	:	12/3/1821
Most Recent Patent	:	2/23/1911
Block/Lot Parcels	:	0
Parcels Re - Issued	:	1
Parcels that Overlap	:	3
Cities and Towns	:	2
Cemeteries	:	3

Section 6: CRAIG James 1837; CRAIG James 1854; DUKE Joel 1858; ROBERTS William A 1850; DUKE Joel 1858; DUKE Joel 1858; CRAIG James 1854; DUKE Joel 1854; DUKE Joel 1858; DUKE Joel 1858; DUKE Joel 1858; GLASSGOW Lewis 1891

Section 5: SMITH Ambrose 1858; NEWTON Caswell 1858; NEWTON Caswell 1849; NEWTON Caswell 1858; NEWTON Caswell 1858; NEWTON Caswell 1854; NEWTON Caswell 1858; NEWTON Caswell 1858; NEWTON Caswell 1858; EXUM Mathew 1860

Section 4: NEWTON Amos 1858; KNOWLES Edmund 1837; BLACK Robert 1837; SIMS William 1821; NEWTON Amos 1858; NEWTON Amos 1858; SMITH William 1821; EXUM Mathew 1860; NEWTON Amos 1858; PICKENS Ezekiel H 1854

Section 7: NEWTON Caswell 1854; NEWTON Caswell 1854; SMYTH Jacob A 1858; NEWTON Caswell 1858; SMYTH Jacob A 1858; SMYTH Jacob A 1858; SMYTH Jacob A 1858; SMYTH Jacob A 1858; SMYTH Jacob A 1858; THOMAS Robert 1858; SMITH William 1858

Section 8: THOMAS Patrick 1858; EXUM Henry 1858; EXUM Henry 1858; EXUM Henry 1858; SMITH William 1858

Section 9: EXUM Mathew 1860; PICKENS Ezekiel H 1858; EXUM Mathew 1860; PICKENS Ezekiel H 1858; MOY John 1858

Section 18: SMITH John 1848; THOMAS Robert 1858; SMITH William 1858; THOMAS Robert 1858; ROBERSON Nathaniel J 1858; ROBERSON Nathaniel J 1858; SMYTH John 1848

Section 17: SMITH William 1858; THOMAS Robert 1858; PERRY John 1858; SMITH William 1858; PERRY John 1858; PERRY John 1858; PERRY John 1858

Section 16

Section 19: SMYTH John 1848; ROBERSON Nathaniel J 1858; ROBERSON Nathaniel J 1858; SMYTH John 1849; SMYTH Robert B 1858; SMYTH Robert B 1858; PERRY John 1848; SMYTH Robert B 1848; SMYTH John 1848; SMYTH Robert B 1858; PERRY John 1852; PERRY John 1858; PERRY John 1858; PERRY John 1858

Section 20: SMYTH Robert B 1858; SMYTH Robert B 1858; PERRY John 1858; SMITH Daniel L 1858; SMITH Daniel L 1858; SMYTH John 1849; JAY Joseph 1858; JAY John 1858; JAY John 1858

Section 21: GODWIN [20] Daniel 1884; SMITH Daniel L 1858; GILBERT James 1858; SMITH Daniel L 1858; GILBERT James 1858; JOHNSON James E 1858; ANDERS Daniel 1858; WYNN Robert P 1858

Section 30: PERRY John 1858; PERRY John 1858; PERRY John 1858; BRADEN Harvey C 1858; BRADEN Harvey C 1858; BRADEN Harvey C 1858; BRADEN Harvey C 1858; BRADEN Harvey C 1858; SMYTH David J 1858; PERRY James 1852; GRAY Joseph P 1858; BRADEN Harvey C 1858

Section 29: JAY John 1858; JAY John 1858; JAY John 1858; CHAMBLISS David E 1859; CHAMBLISS David E 1859; BRADEN Harvey C 1858; CHAMBLISS David E 1859; CHAMBLISS David E 1859; CHAMBLISS David E 1852

Section 28: JOHNSON James E 1858; JOHNSON James E 1858; BUSH Richard H 1858; JOHNSON James E 1858; JOHNSON James E 1858; WYNN Robert P 1858; BUSH Richard H 1858; BUSH Richard H 1858; DICKEN Elisha T 1858

Section 31: MARTIN Green 1858; GRAY Joseph P 1858; BRASSWELL James 1897; MARTIN William 1858; GRAY Joseph P 1858; GRAY Joseph P 1858

Section 32: TURNER Thomas 1858; TURNER Thomas 1858; JAY William 1861; JAY William 1861; TURNER Thomas 1858; GANDY Marina 1858

Section 33: TURNER Thomas 1858; CHAMBLISS David E 1852; CHAMBLISS David E 1852; CHAMBLISS David E 1911; GANDY Marina 1858; CHAMBLISS David E 1852; CHAMBLISS David E 1859; CHAMBLISS David E 1859; GANDY Marina 1858; DICKEN Elisha T 1858; MORAN Washington B 1858

194

FUTCH [17] Isaac 1831	CALDWELL John C 1823		RABURN William 1837	BLACK Joseph 1835		THOMAS John 1837		RHODES Kinchin 1858

3

PURDY Henry 1823

PERRY Benjamin 1858

SMITH Daniel 1852

2

1

PICKENS Ezekiel H 1837

PICKENS Andrew 1837

PICKENS Ezekiel H 1858

PICKENS Ezekiel H 1858

SMITH Daniel 1852

HARRISON James 1837

WREN George 1852

RHODES Kinchin 1858

RHODES Kinchin 1858

PICKENS Ezekiel H 1858

TURNER John E 1858

RUFFIN Alexander 1858

TURNER John E 1858

SMITH Daniel C 1858

10

TURNER John E 1858

HARRISON James 1835

SMITH Daniel C 1858

SMITH Daniel C 1858

PORTER William J 1860

MCALLISTER Colin 1852

SMITH John 1852

FIFE Malind M 1858

MCCURRY William J 1837

FIFE Malind M 1858

BOLLING Samuel J 1858

CARR Allen 1837

11

12

PORTER William J 1860

WREN Davis B 1858

PORTER William J 1860

BOLLING John 1858

BOZEMAN Nathan 1823

NEWTON Benjamin 1862

15

14

13

NEWTON Benjamin 1858

CALLAWAY Francis 1859

DEMING Albert 1858

BREITHAUPT Christian 1826

JOHNSTON John S 1825

SMITH John 1825

NEWTON Benjamin 1862

NEWTON Benjamin 1858

NEWTON Benjamin 1858

CALLAWAY Francis 1859

DEMING Albert 1858

DEMING Albert 1854

NEWTON Benjamin 1860

NEWTON Benjamin 1858

CALDWELL William H 1837

22

GANDY Abijah 1837

DEMING Albert 1858

DEMING Albert 1854

DERNING Albert 1852

24

WYNN Robert P 1858

NEWTON Benjamin 1860

CALDWELL William H 1837

BARRETT William R 1860

23

WYNN John J 1858

DEMING Albert 1854

SMITH John 1834

WYNN Robert P 1858

WYNN Robert P 1858

27

THOMAS John 1858

LEE Hillary 1858

LEE Hillary 1858

LEE Hillary 1858

WHIDDON Elias 1858

COOK James B 1849

HARDY Freeman 1825

THOMAS Harriett M 1858

THOMAS John 1854

26

LEE Hillary 1858

MERCER William 1834

25

THOMAS John 1858

THOMAS John 1858

THOMAS John 1858

LEE Hillary 1858

LEE Hillary 1858

HALSO Stephen 1858

MURSER William 1858

HARRISON John H 1858

MERCER William 1849

HARDY Freeman 1825

DICKEN Elisha T 1858

THOMAS Daniel 1852

GANDY Evander 1848

KEITH Silas 1845

THOMAS John 1854

WILKERSON William 1858

HALSO Stephen 1858

MURSER William 1858

MONTGOMERY Hugh B 1861

THOMAS Daniel 1858

MONTGOMERY THOMAS Daniel 1858

MONTGOMERY Hugh B 1861

THOMAS Daniel 1852

THOMAS John 1858

WALKER Daniel 1843

WALKER Mary 1843

WILKERSON William 1858

36

MERCER William 1843

MURSER William 1858

34

THOMAS Daniel 1852

MURSER William 1858

THOMAS Daniel 1858

THOMAS Daniel 1858

35

HUDSON Max 1843

WILKERSON William 1858

THOMAS Daniel 1858

MERCER William 1849

WILKERSON William 1858

WILKERSON William 1858

TATOM Abel 1858

Helpful Hints

1. This Map's INDEX can be found on the preceding pages.

2. Refer to Map "C" to see where this Township lies within Butler County, Alabama.

3. Numbers within square brackets [ ] denote a multi-patentee land parcel (multi-owner). Refer to Appendix "C" for a full list of members in this group.

4. Areas that look to be crowded with Patentees usually indicate multiple sales of the same parcel (Re-issues) or Overlapping parcels. See this Township's Index for an explanation of these and other circumstances that might explain "odd" groupings of Patentees on this map.

Legend

— Patent Boundary

━ Section Boundary

No Patents Found (or Outside County)

1., 2., 3., ... Lot Numbers (when beside a name)

[ ] Group Number (see Appendix "C")

Scale: Section = 1 mile X 1 mile (generally, with some exceptions)

Road Map

T9-N R15-E
St Stephens Meridian

Map Group 14

Cities & Towns

Glasgow
Halso Mill

Cemeteries

Mount Carmel Cemetery
Mount Olive East Cemetery
Rhodes Cemetery

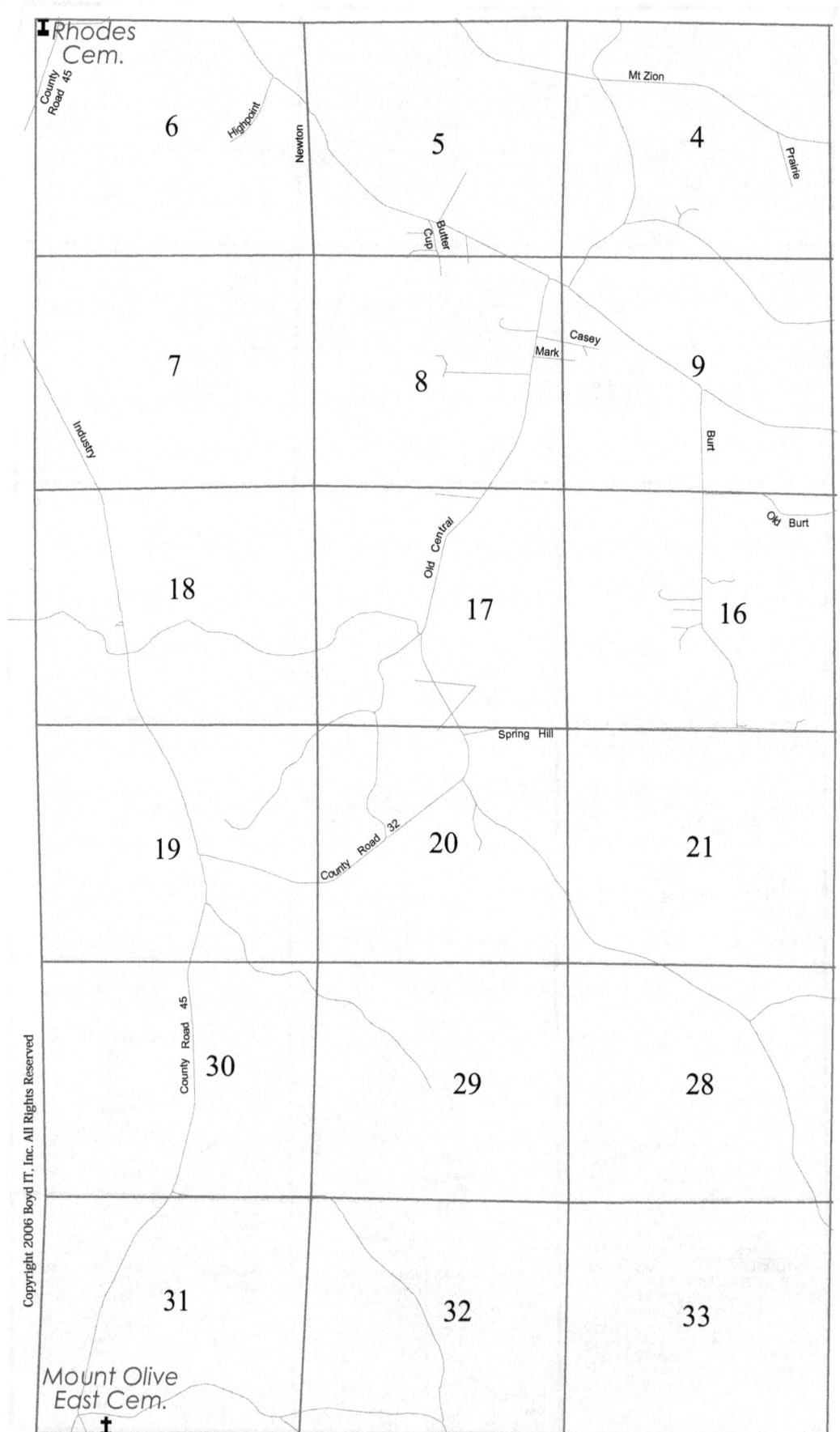

Rhodes Cem.

County Road 45

6

Highpoint

Newton

5

Mt Zion

4

Prairie

Butter Cup

7

8

Mark

Casey

9

Burt

Industry

Old Central

18

17

Old Burt

16

Spring Hill

19

County Road 32

20

21

County Road 45

30

29

28

31

32

33

Mount Olive East Cem.

3	2	1
10	11 ● Glasgow	12
15	14	13
22	23 ‡ Mount Carmel Cem.	24
27	26	25
34	35 Halso Mill ●	36

Roads/labels: Bluebird, Blue Bird, Falls, Rolling Hills, Williams, Hermitage, Edgeview, Heights, Mossy Oak, Halso Mill, St Francis Church, Davenport, Hugely, Bridge, Maye

Helpful Hints

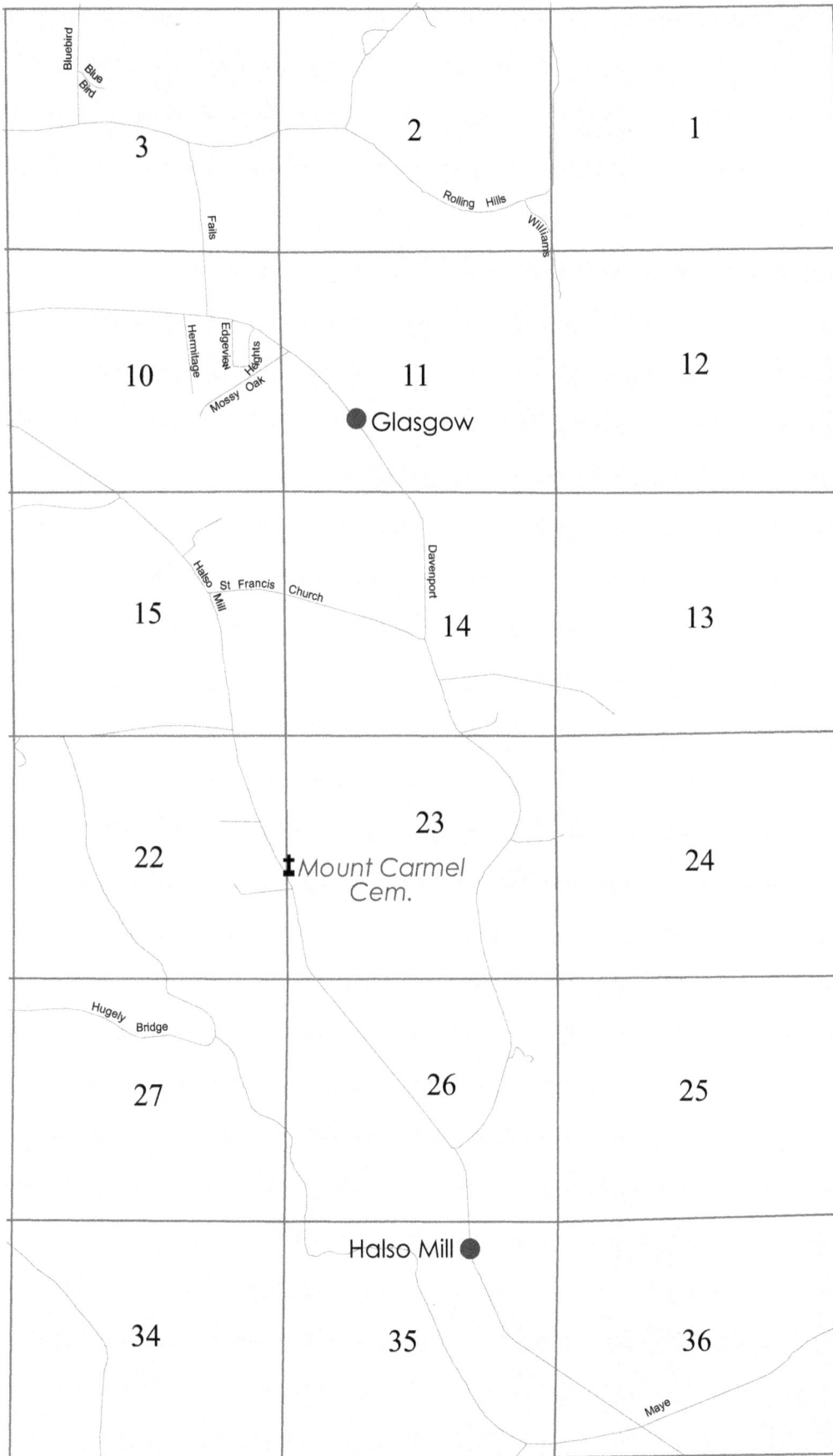

1. This road map has a number of uses, but primarily it is to help you: a) find the present location of land owned by your ancestors (at least the general area), b) find cemeteries and city-centers, and c) estimate the route/roads used by Census-takers & tax-assessors.

2. If you plan to travel to Butler County to locate cemeteries or land parcels, please pick up a modern travel map for the area before you do. Mapping old land parcels on modern maps is not as exact a science as you might think. Just the slightest variations in public land survey coordinates, estimates of parcel boundaries, or road-map deviations can greatly alter a map's representation of how a road either does or doesn't cross a particular parcel of land.

Legend

————	Section Lines
≡≡≡≡	Interstates
▬▬▬▬	Highways
————	Other Roads
●	Cities/Towns
‡	Cemeteries

Scale: Section = 1 mile X 1 mile
(generally, with some exceptions)

Historical Map

T9-N R15-E
St Stephens Meridian

Map Group 14

Cities & Towns
Glasgow
Halso Mill

Cemeteries
Mount Carmel Cemetery
Mount Olive East Cemetery
Rhodes Cemetery

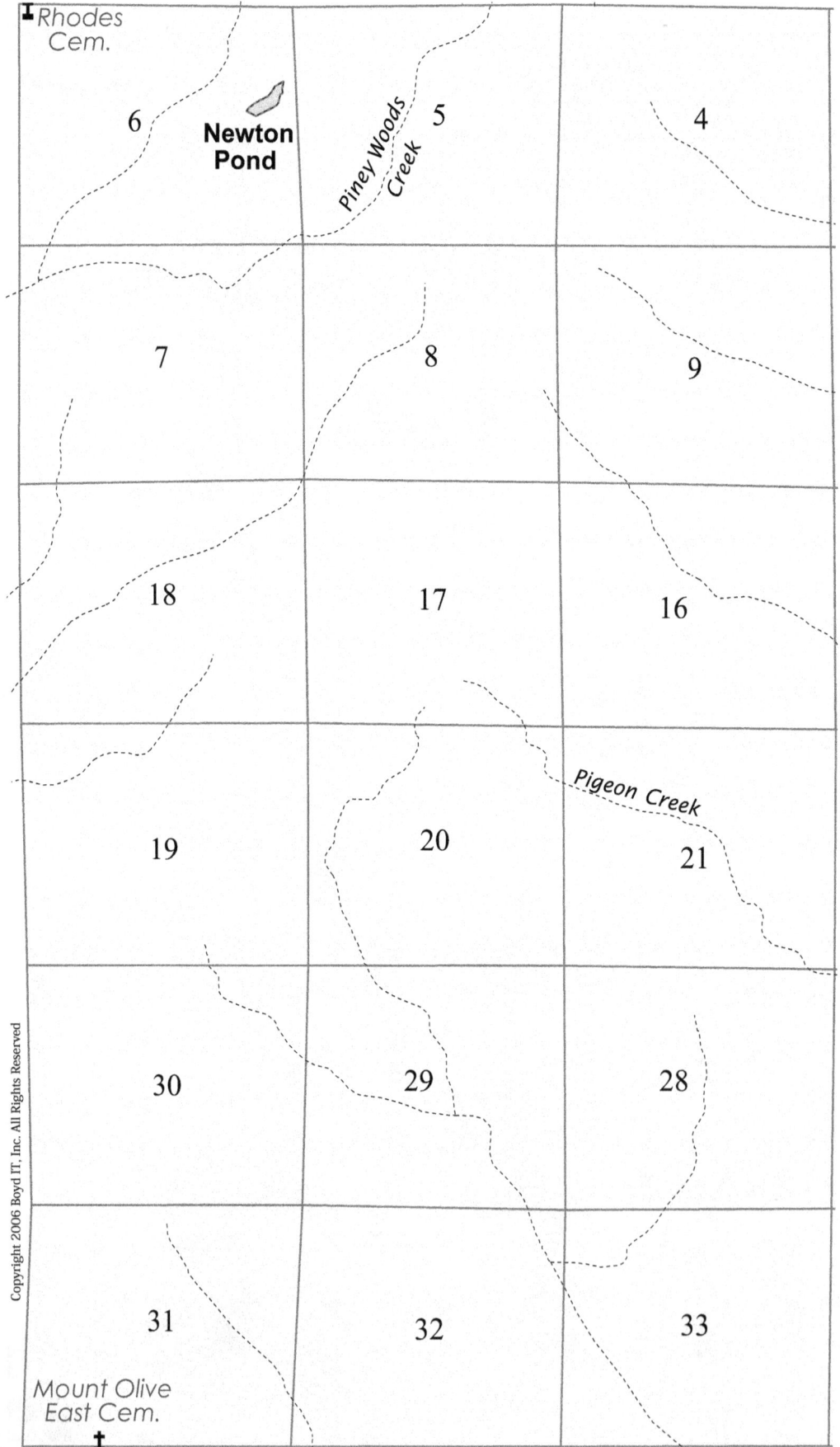

Rhodes Cem.

Newton Pond

Piney Woods Creek

6

5

4

7

8

9

18

17

16

Pigeon Creek

19

20

21

30

29

28

31

32

33

Mount Olive East Cem.

3

2

1

Nannie Branch

10

11

● Glasgow

12

15

14

13

22

23

✝ *Mount Carmel Cem.*

24

27

26

25

Harrigan Creek

34

Halso Mill ●

35

Hard Labor Creek

36

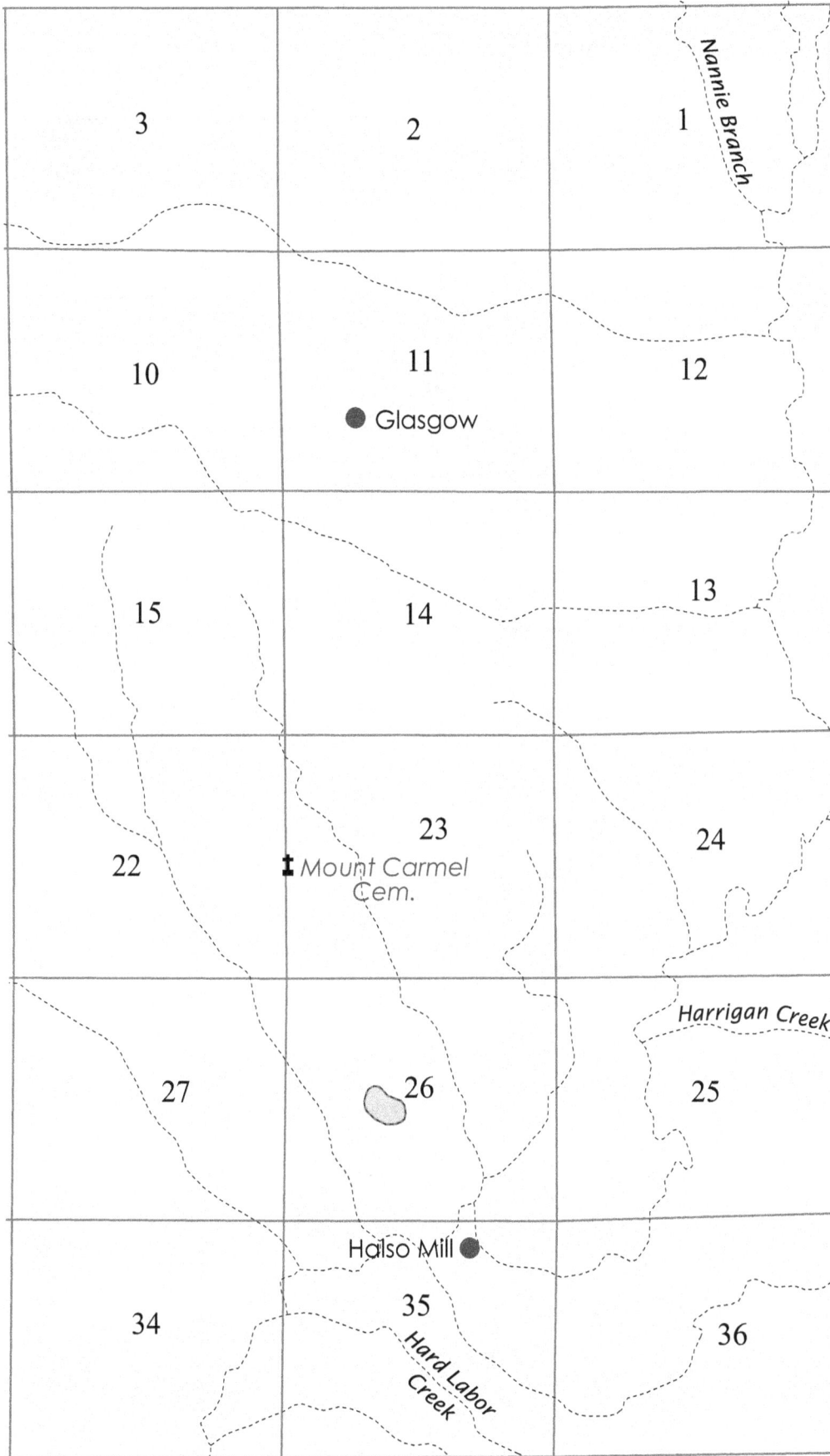

Helpful Hints

1. This Map takes a different look at the same Congressional Township displayed in the preceding two maps. It presents features that can help you better envision the historical development of the area: a) Water-bodies (lakes & ponds), b) Water-courses (rivers, streams, etc.), c) Railroads, d) City/town center-points (where they were oftentimes located when first settled), and e) Cemeteries.

2. Using this "Historical" map in tandem with this Township's Patent Map and Road Map, may lead you to some interesting discoveries. You will often find roads, towns, cemeteries, and waterways are named after nearby landowners: sometimes those names will be the ones you are researching. See how many of these research gems you can find here in Butler County.

Legend

————	Section Lines
✛✛✛✛✛✛	Railroads
▭	Large Rivers & Bodies of Water
- - - - - - -	Streams/Creeks & Small Rivers
●	Cities/Towns
✝	Cemeteries

Scale: Section = 1 mile X 1 mile
(there are some exceptions)

Map Group 15: Index to Land Patents

Township 9-North Range 16-East (St Stephens)

After you locate an individual in this Index, take note of the Section and Section Part then proceed to the Land Patent map on the pages immediately following. You should have no difficulty locating the corresponding parcel of land.

The "For More Info" Column will lead you to more information about the underlying Patents. See the *Legend* at right, and the "How to Use this Book" chapter, for more information.

```
                          LEGEND
              "For More Info . . . " column

A = Authority (Legislative Act, See Appendix "A")
B = Block or Lot (location in Section unknown)
C = Cancelled Patent
F = Fractional Section
G = Group  (Multi-Patentee Patent, see Appendix "C")
V = Overlaps another Parcel
R = Re-Issued (Parcel patented more than once)

(A & G items require you to look in the Appendixes referred
to above. All other Letter-designations followed by a number
require you to locate line-items in this index that possess
the ID number found after the letter).
```

ID	Individual in Patent	Sec.	Sec. Part	Date Issued	Other Counties	For More Info . . .
3408	AMBROSE, Ashley	6	NWSW	1848-04-01		A1
3409	" "	6	SENE	1852-12-01		A1
3407	" "	6	NWSE	1858-11-01		A1
3426	ARMSTRONG, Elisha J	4	NWSW	1852-12-01		A1
3448	ARMSTRONG, Jesse M	4	E½SE	1858-11-01		A1
3518	BAILEY, Singleton	17	NESE	1837-08-12		A1
3510	BEDGOOD, Richmond	21	NWNE	1843-02-01		A1
3446	BELL, James W	4	SWSW	1852-12-01		A1
3447	" "	5	SENE	1852-12-01		A1
3500	BISHOP, Matthew	6	NWNE	1852-02-02		A1
3404	BLACK, Andrew M	8	NENE	1852-12-01		A1
3427	BLACK, Francis M	10	SESE	1858-09-01	Crenshaw	A1
3428	" "	10	SW	1858-09-01	Crenshaw	A1
3429	" "	10	W½SE	1858-09-01	Crenshaw	A1
3524	BLACK, Thomas J	5	W½SE	1858-11-01		A1
3449	BOLLING, John	6	NESW	1848-04-01		A1
3450	" "	7	NWNE	1848-04-01		A1
3420	BREWER, Edward	29	E½SW	1858-11-01		A1
3421	" "	29	SWSW	1858-11-01		A1
3422	" "	30	SESE	1858-11-01		A1
3423	" "	31	N½NE	1858-11-01		A1
3424	" "	31	SWNE	1858-11-01		A1
3425	" "	32	NWNW	1858-11-01		A1
3484	BURNS, Lauchlin	10	NENE	1858-11-01	Crenshaw	A1
3485	" "	10	NW	1858-11-01	Crenshaw	A1
3486	" "	10	W½NE	1858-11-01	Crenshaw	A1
3541	COE, William A	28	NWSE	1858-11-01		A1
3542	" "	28	S½NE	1858-11-01		A1
3430	COOK, Francis M	20	NESE	1841-05-20		A1
3431	" "	20	SWNE	1841-05-20		A1
3437	COOK, Isaac	19	E½SW	1832-08-08		A1
3440	" "	20	W½NW	1832-08-08		A1
3442	" "	20	W½SW	1832-08-08		A1
3438	" "	19	N½SE	1835-09-12		A1
3439	" "	20	E½NW	1837-08-09		A1
3441	" "	20	W½SE	1837-08-12		A1
3443	COOK, Isaac M	20	E½SW	1848-05-03		A1
3519	COOK, Stephen H	6	SWNW	1848-04-01		A1
3502	DAVENPORT, Palmore P	30	NENW	1858-11-01		A1
3503	" "	30	SWNW	1858-11-01		A1
3557	DIXON, Zebulon	32	N½SE	1858-09-01		A1
3558	" "	32	NE	1858-09-01		A1
3559	" "	32	NESW	1858-09-01		A1
3560	" "	32	SENW	1858-09-01		A1
3477	ELLINGTON, Joseph	8	W½NE	1837-08-15		A1
3511	GREEN, Rolla A	17	W½SE	1848-05-03		A1

ID	Individual in Patent	Sec.	Sec. Part	Date Issued	Other Counties	For More Info . . .
3513	GREEN, Rolla A (Cont'd)	20	NWNE	1848-05-03		A1
3512	" "	20	NENE	1849-09-01		A1
3435	HANSON, Herndon	9	NWNW	1849-09-01		A1
3543	HARBIN, William P	33	E½SW	1858-11-01		A1
3544	" "	33	NWSW	1858-11-01		A1
3545	" "	33	SESE	1858-11-01		A1
3546	" "	33	W½NE	1858-11-01		A1
3547	" "	33	W½SE	1858-11-01		A1
3453	HARRISON, John H	29	NWSW	1858-11-01		A1
3454	" "	30	NESE	1858-11-01		A1
3455	" "	30	S½SW	1858-11-01		A1
3456	" "	30	W½SE	1858-11-01		A1
3556	HARRISON, Williamson	21	N½NW	1837-08-18		A1
3410	HASTING, Benjamin	28	NENE	1858-11-01		A1
3462	HASTING, John P	28	NWNE	1854-07-15		A1
3487	JACKSON, Littleberry	31	E½SE	1858-11-01		A1
3488	" "	31	NWSE	1858-11-01		A1
3489	" "	31	SENE	1858-11-01		A1
3490	" "	32	SESW	1858-11-01		A1
3491	" "	32	SWNW	1858-11-01		A1
3492	" "	32	W½SW	1858-11-01		A1
3405	KENNINGTON, Arnold	33	NESE	1858-11-01		A1
3406	" "	33	SENE	1858-11-01		A1
3504	KETLER, Peter	29	NWNE	1858-11-01		A1
3525	KETLER, Thomas S	18	E½SW	1858-09-01		A1
3527	" "	19	S½SE	1858-09-01		A1
3528	" "	29	SENW	1858-09-01		A1
3529	" "	30	NWNE	1858-09-01		A1
3530	" "	30	SENE	1858-09-01		A1
3526	" "	18	SWSW	1860-10-01		A1
3533	KETTLER, Thomas S	29	NENW	1852-12-01		A1
3534	" "	30	NENE	1852-12-01		A1
3535	" "	30	SENW	1852-12-01		A1
3536	" "	30	SWNE	1852-12-01		A1
3532	" "	28	NENW	1854-07-15		A1
3531	" "	18	NWSW	1858-11-01		A1
3445	LONG, Jacob	21	S½NW	1843-02-01		A1
3444	" "	20	SENE	1852-02-02		A1
3551	LONG, William T	28	E½SE	1858-11-01		A1
3552	" "	28	E½SW	1858-11-01		A1
3553	" "	28	SWSE	1858-11-01		A1
3554	" "	33	E½NW	1858-11-01		A1
3555	" "	33	SWNW	1858-11-01		A1
3411	MCALLISTER, Colin	5	SWSW	1852-02-02		A1
3508	MCCALL, Reuel E	30	N½SW	1858-11-01		A1
3501	MCCORMACK, Maxfield	5	E½SE	1837-08-12		A1
3495	MOORE, Littleton J	29	SWNE	1854-07-15		A1
3493	" "	29	N½SE	1858-09-01		A1
3494	" "	29	SENE	1858-09-01		A1
3416	MOORMAN, David J	32	S½SE	1858-11-01		A1
3417	" "	33	SWSW	1858-11-01		A1
3436	PERRY, Hiram	21	NWSW	1837-08-01		A1 F
3498	PHELPS, Lorenzo D	5	NW	1858-09-01		A1
3499	" "	5	W½NE	1858-09-01		A1
3496	" "	4	SWNW	1858-11-01		A1
3497	" "	5	NENE	1858-11-01		A1
3520	PHELPS, Terrel	4	N½NW	1858-09-01		A1
3521	" "	4	NWNE	1858-09-01		A1
3523	PHELPS, Terrell	6	NWNW	1848-04-01		A1
3522	" "	6	NENW	1849-09-01		A1
3516	QUARLES, Samuel	29	W½NW	1826-07-10		A1
3514	" "	19	E½NE	1832-08-08		A1
3515	" "	19	W½NE	1832-08-08		A1
3481	RABUN, Joseph	6	SENW	1840-10-10		A1
3509	RABUN, Richard	21	NENE	1848-04-01		A1
3463	RABURN, John	4	E½NE	1858-09-01		A1
3464	" "	4	E½SW	1858-09-01		A1
3465	" "	4	SENW	1858-09-01		A1
3466	" "	4	SWNE	1858-09-01		A1
3467	" "	4	W½SE	1858-09-01		A1
3482	RABURN, Joseph	7	NENE	1837-05-20		A1
3505	RHAME, Ransom H	18	E½NW	1852-02-02		A1
3506	" "	18	W½NW	1858-11-01		A1

ID	Individual in Patent	Sec.	Sec. Part	Date Issued	Other Counties	For More Info . . .
3507	RHAME, Ransom H (Cont'd)	8	SESE	1858-11-01		A1
3415	ROACH, David C	9	SWNW	1850-08-10		A1
3412	" "	8	SENE	1858-09-01		A1
3413	" "	9	S½SW	1858-09-01		A1
3414	" "	9	SENW	1858-09-01		A1
3402	SCARBOROUGH, Addison	6	SESE	1852-02-02		A1
3399	SHOWS, Abbie	32	NENW	1902-09-02		A1 G41
3399	SHOWS, James Z	32	NENW	1902-09-02		A1 G41
3403	SMITH, Ambrose A	9	SESE	1858-09-01		A1
3468	SMITH, John	18	E½SE	1832-08-08		A1
3469	" "	18	W½SE	1833-08-02		A1
3470	" "	6	S½SW	1849-09-01		A1
3471	" "	7	NWSW	1852-02-02		A1
3472	" "	7	SWNW	1852-02-02		A1
3474	SMYTH, John	19	SENW	1838-07-28		A1
3476	" "	19	W½SW	1838-07-28		A1
3473	" "	19	NENW	1858-11-01		A1
3475	" "	19	W½NW	1858-11-01		A1
3517	SPURLOCK, Samuel	21	NWSE	1850-08-10		A1
3432	STAGGERS, Henry S	9	E½NE	1858-11-01		A1
3433	" "	9	SWSE	1858-11-01		A1
3457	STAGGERS, John H	7	E½SE	1832-08-08		A1
3460	" "	8	SW	1837-08-12		A1
3458	" "	7	W½SE	1838-07-28		A1
3459	" "	8	E½NW	1838-07-28		A1
3461	" "	8	SWNW	1838-07-28		A1
3478	STAGGERS, Joseph H	7	SENE	1858-11-01		A1
3479	" "	8	NWNW	1858-11-01		A1
3480	" "	8	NWSE	1858-11-01		A1
3549	STAGGERS, William	17	SENE	1838-07-28		A1
3550	" "	17	W½NE	1838-07-28		A1
3548	" "	17	NENE	1847-05-01		A1
3400	TATOM, Abel	31	E½SW	1858-11-01		A1
3401	" "	31	NW	1858-11-01		A1
3451	THOMAS, John F	10	NESE	1858-09-01	Crenshaw	A1
3452	" "	10	SENE	1858-09-01	Crenshaw	A1
3434	WARD, Henry W	17	SESE	1835-04-02		A1
3483	WILKERSON, Joshua H	31	SWSE	1858-11-01		A1
3537	WILLIAMSON, Wiley	28	SENW	1858-11-01		A1
3538	" "	28	W½NW	1858-11-01		A1
3539	" "	28	W½SW	1858-11-01		A1
3540	" "	29	S½SE	1858-11-01		A1
3418	WREN, Davis B	7	E½NW	1858-11-01		A1
3419	" "	7	NWNW	1858-11-01		A1

Patent Map

T9-N R16-E
St Stephens Meridian

Map Group 15

Township Statistics

Parcels Mapped	:	162
Number of Patents	:	103
Number of Individuals	:	68
Patentees Identified	:	67
Number of Surnames	:	49
Multi-Patentee Parcels	:	1
Oldest Patent Date	:	7/10/1826
Most Recent Patent	:	9/2/1902
Block/Lot Parcels	:	0
Parcels Re - Issued	:	0
Parcels that Overlap	:	0
Cities and Towns	:	0
Cemeteries	:	4

Section 6
PHELPS Terrell 1848 · PHELPS Terrell 1849 · BISHOP Matthew 1852
COOK Stephen H 1848 · RABUN Joseph 1840 · AMBROSE Ashley 1852
AMBROSE Ashley 1848 · BOLLING John 1848 · AMBROSE Ashley 1858
SCARBOROUGH Addison 1852
SMITH John 1849

Section 5
PHELPS Lorenzo D 1858 · PHELPS Lorenzo D 1858
MCALLISTER Colin 1852
MCCORMACK Maxfield 1837
BLACK Thomas J 1858

Section 4
PHELPS Lorenzo D 1858 · PHELPS Terrel 1858 · PHELPS Terrel 1858 · RABURN John 1858
BELL James W 1852 · PHELPS Lorenzo D 1858 · RABURN John 1858 · RABURN John 1858
ARMSTRONG Elisha J 1852 · RABURN John 1858 · ARMSTRONG Jesse M 1858
RABURN John 1858
BELL James W 1852

Section 7
WREN Davis B 1858 · BOLLING John 1848 · RABURN Joseph 1837
WREN Davis B 1858
SMITH John 1852 · STAGGERS Joseph H 1858
SMITH John 1852 · STAGGERS John H 1838 · STAGGERS John H 1832

Section 8
STAGGERS Joseph H 1858 · STAGGERS John H 1838
STAGGERS John H 1838
STAGGERS John H 1837

Section 9
BLACK Andrew M 1852 · HANSON Herndon 1849 · STAGGERS Henry S 1858
ELLINGTON Joseph 1837 · ROACH David C 1858 · ROACH David C 1850 · ROACH David C 1858
STAGGERS Joseph H 1858
RHAME Ransom H 1858 · ROACH David C 1858 · STAGGERS Henry S 1858 · SMITH Ambrose A 1858

Section 18
RHAME Ransom H 1858
RHAME Ransom H 1852
KETTLER Thomas S 1858 · KETLER Thomas S 1858 · SMITH John 1833 · SMITH John 1832
KETLER Thomas S 1860

Section 17

Section 16
STAGGERS William 1847
STAGGERS William 1838 · STAGGERS William 1838
GREEN Rolla A 1848 · BAILEY Singleton 1837
WARD Henry W 1835

Butler County

Section 19
SMYTH John 1858 · SMYTH John 1858 · QUARLES Samuel 1832
SMYTH John 1838 · QUARLES Samuel 1832
COOK Isaac 1835
SMYTH John 1838 · COOK Isaac 1832 · KETLER Thomas S 1858

Section 20
COOK Isaac 1837 · COOK Isaac 1832
COOK Isaac 1832
COOK Isaac M 1848 · COOK Isaac 1837
GREEN Rolla A 1848 · COOK Francis M 1841
COOK Francis M 1841

Section 21
GREEN Rolla A 1849 · HARRISON Williamson 1837 · BEDGOOD Richmond 1843 · RABUN Richard 1848
LONG Jacob 1852 · LONG Jacob 1843
PERRY Hiram 1837 · SPURLOCK Samuel 1850

Section 30
DAVENPORT Palmore P 1858 · KETLER Thomas S 1858 · KETTLER Thomas S 1852
DAVENPORT Palmore P 1858 · KETTLER Thomas S 1852 · KETLER Thomas S 1858
MCCALL Reuel E 1858 · HARRISON John H 1858
HARRISON John H 1858
HARRISON John H 1858 · BREWER Edward 1858

Section 29
KETTLER Thomas S 1852 · KETLER Peter 1858
QUARLES Samuel 1826
KETLER Thomas S 1858 · MOORE Littleton J 1854 · MOORE Littleton J 1858
HARRISON John H 1858 · MOORE Littleton J 1858
BREWER Edward 1858 · BREWER Edward 1858 · WILLIAMSON Wiley 1858

Section 28
WILLIAMSON Wiley 1858 · KETTLER Thomas S 1854 · HASTING John P 1854 · HASTING Benjamin 1858
WILLIAMSON Wiley 1858 · COE William A 1858
WILLIAMSON Wiley 1858 · LONG William T 1858 · COE William A 1858 · LONG William T 1858
LONG William T 1858

Section 31
TATOM Abel 1858 · BREWER Edward 1858
BREWER Edward 1858 · JACKSON Littleberry 1858
JACKSON Littleberry 1858
TATOM Abel 1858 · WILKERSON Joshua H 1858 · JACKSON Littleberry 1858

Section 32
BREWER Edward 1858 · SHOWS [4] Abbie 1902 · DIXON Zebulon 1858
JACKSON Littleberry 1858 · DIXON Zebulon 1858
JACKSON Littleberry 1858 · DIXON Zebulon 1858 · DIXON Zebulon 1858
JACKSON Littleberry 1858 · MOORMAN David J 1858

Section 33
HARBIN William P 1858
LONG William T 1858 · LONG William T 1858 · KENNINGTON Arnold 1858
HARBIN William P 1858 · HARBIN William P 1858 · KENNINGTON Arnold 1858
MOORMAN David J 1858 · HARBIN William P 1858 · HARBIN William P 1858

| 3 | 2 | 1 |

BURNS Lauchlin 1858	BURNS Lauchlin 1858	BURNS Lauchlin 1858	
		THOMAS John F 1858	12
BLACK Francis M 1858	BLACK Francis M 1858	THOMAS John F 1858	
		BLACK Francis M 1858	

10

11

Crenshaw County

| 15 | 14 | 13 |

| 22 | 23 | 24 |

| 27 | 26 | 25 |

| 34 | 35 | 36 |

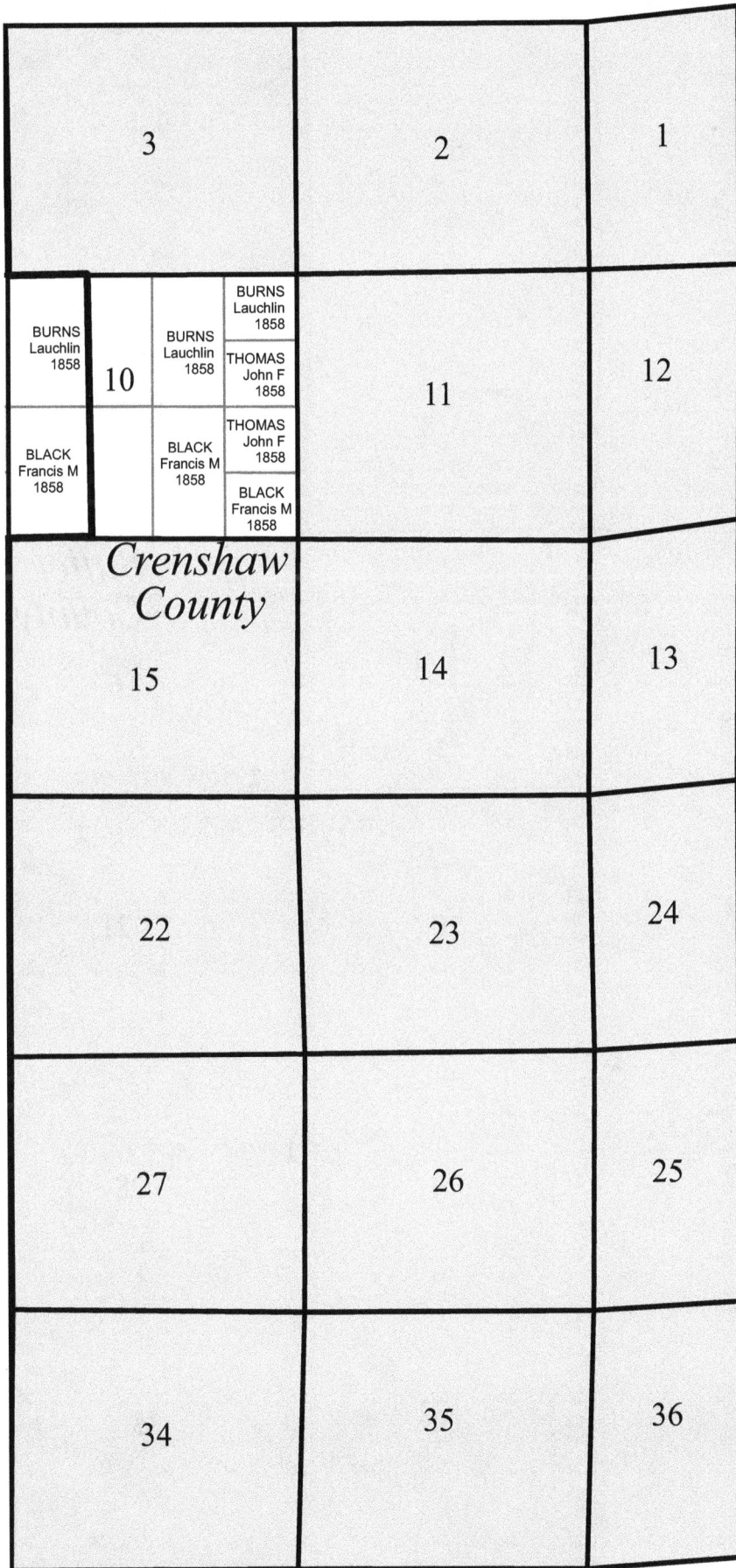

Helpful Hints

1. This Map's INDEX can be found on the preceding pages.

2. Refer to Map "C" to see where this Township lies within Butler County, Alabama.

3. Numbers within square brackets [ ] denote a multi-patentee land parcel (multi-owner). Refer to Appendix "C" for a full list of members in this group.

4. Areas that look to be crowded with Patentees usually indicate multiple sales of the same parcel (Re-issues) or Overlapping parcels. See this Township's Index for an explanation of these and other circumstances that might explain "odd" groupings of Patentees on this map.

Legend

——— Patent Boundary

▬▬▬ Section Boundary

No Patents Found
(or Outside County)

1., 2., 3., ...   Lot Numbers
(when beside a name)

[ ]   Group Number
(see Appendix "C")

Scale: Section = 1 mile X 1 mile
(generally, with some exceptions)

Road Map

T9-N R16-E
St Stephens Meridian

Map Group 15

Cities & Towns
None

Cemeteries
Bedgood Cemetery
Butler Cemetery
Howard Cemetery
Wren Cemetery

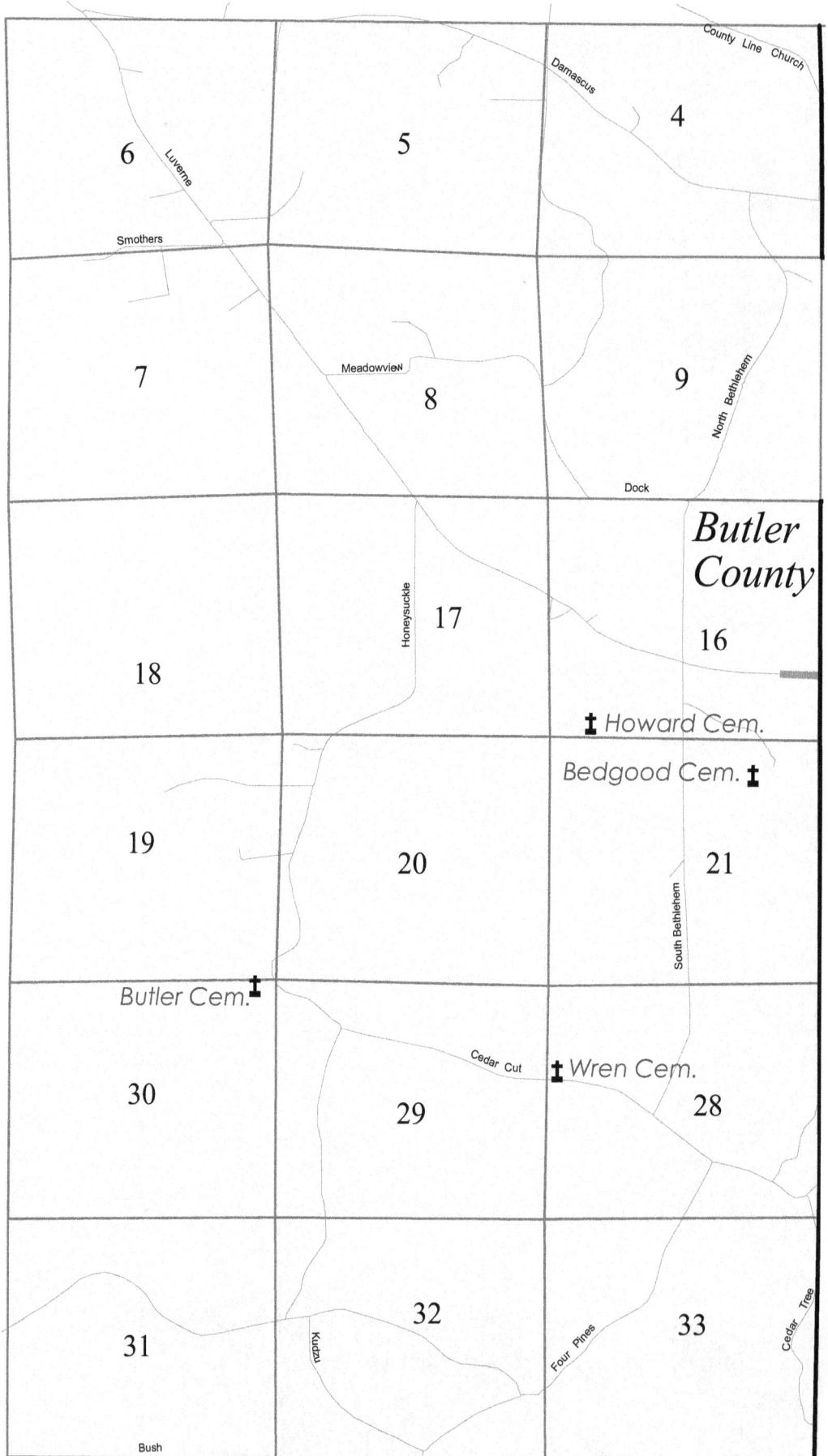

County Line Church

Damascus

4

6

Luverne

5

Smothers

7

Meadowview

8

North Bethlehem

9

Dock

Butler County

Honeysuckle

17

16

✝ *Howard Cem.*

18

Bedgood Cem. ✝

19

20

South Bethlehem

21

✝ *Butler Cem.*

Cedar Cut

✝ *Wren Cem.*

30

29

28

31

Kudzu

32

Four Pines

Cedar Tree

33

Bush

| 3 | 2 | 1 |
| 10 | 11 | 12 |

Crenshaw County

15	14	13
22	23	24
27	26	25
34	35	36

Copyright 2006 Boyd IT, Inc. All Rights Reserved

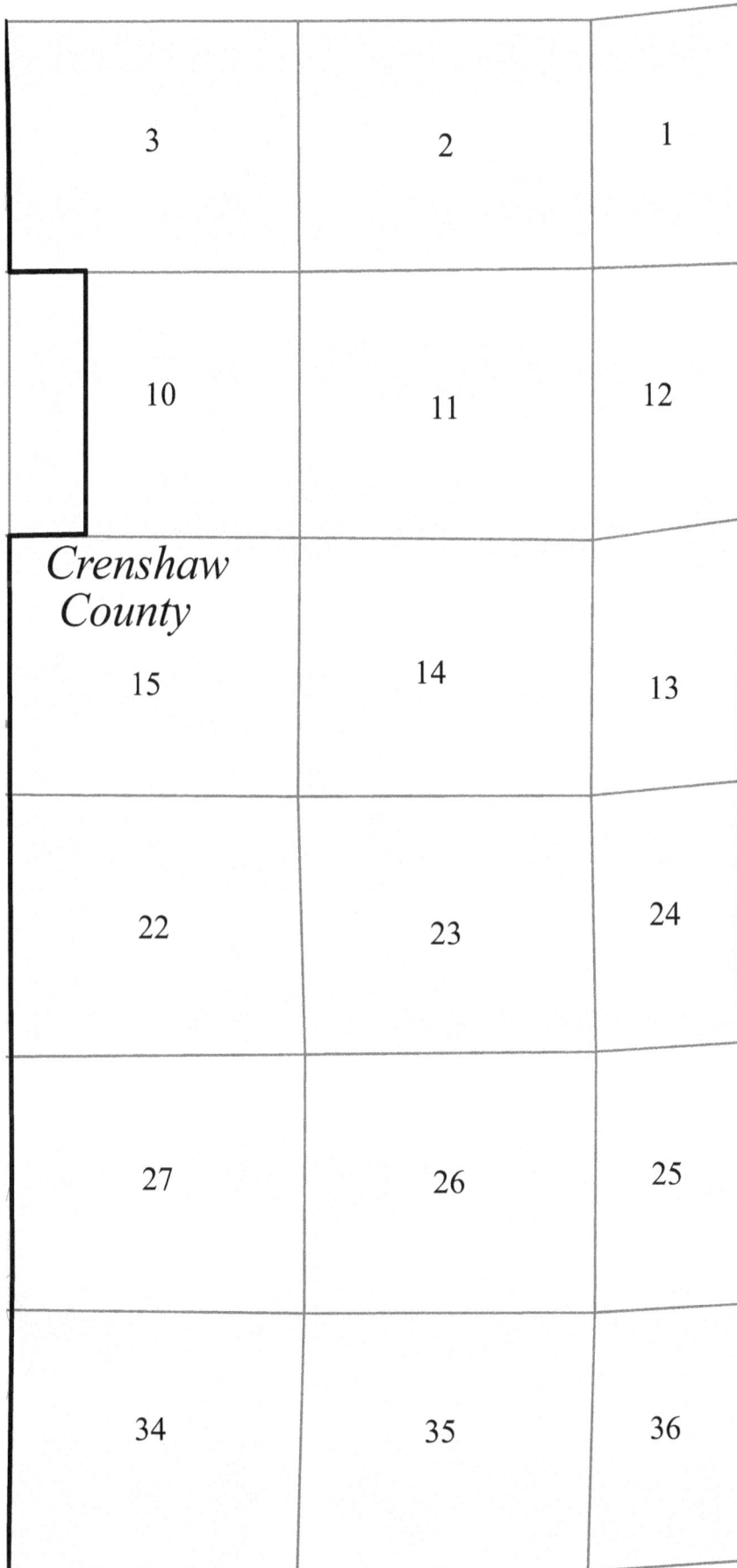

Legend

- Section Lines
- Interstates
- Highways
- Other Roads
- ● Cities/Towns
- ✝ Cemeteries

Scale: Section = 1 mile X 1 mile
(generally, with some exceptions)

Historical Map

T9-N R16-E
St Stephens Meridian

Map Group 15

Cities & Towns
None

Cemeteries
Bedgood Cemetery
Butler Cemetery
Howard Cemetery
Wren Cemetery

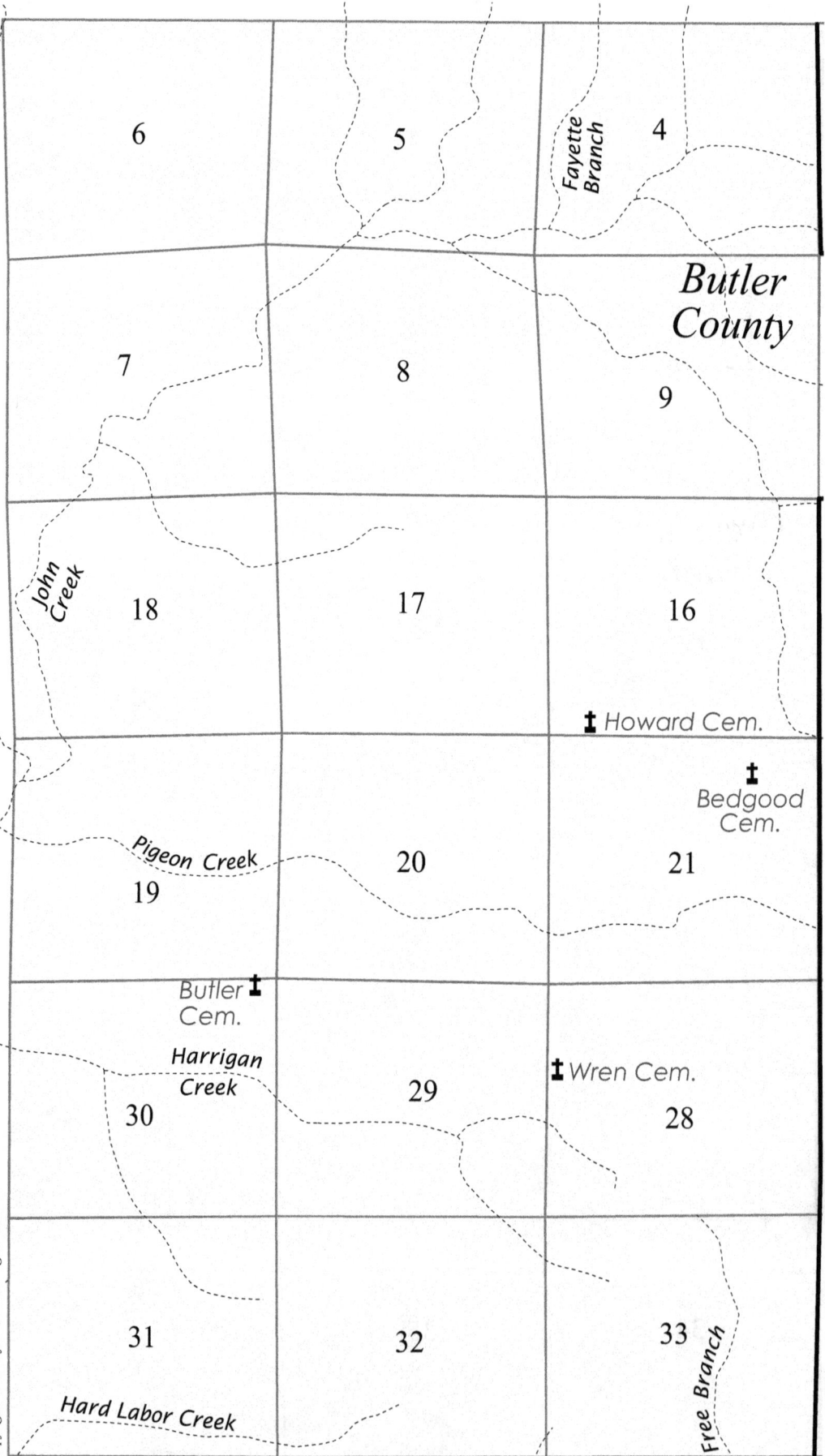

Butler County

6	5	4
7	8	9
18	17	16
19	20	21
30	29	28
31	32	33

Fayette Branch

John Creek

✝ Howard Cem.

✝ Bedgood Cem.

Pigeon Creek

Butler ✝
Cem.

Harrigan Creek

✝ Wren Cem.

Hard Labor Creek

Free Branch

3	2	1
Crenshaw County 10	11	12
15	14	13
22	23	24
27	26	25
34	35	36

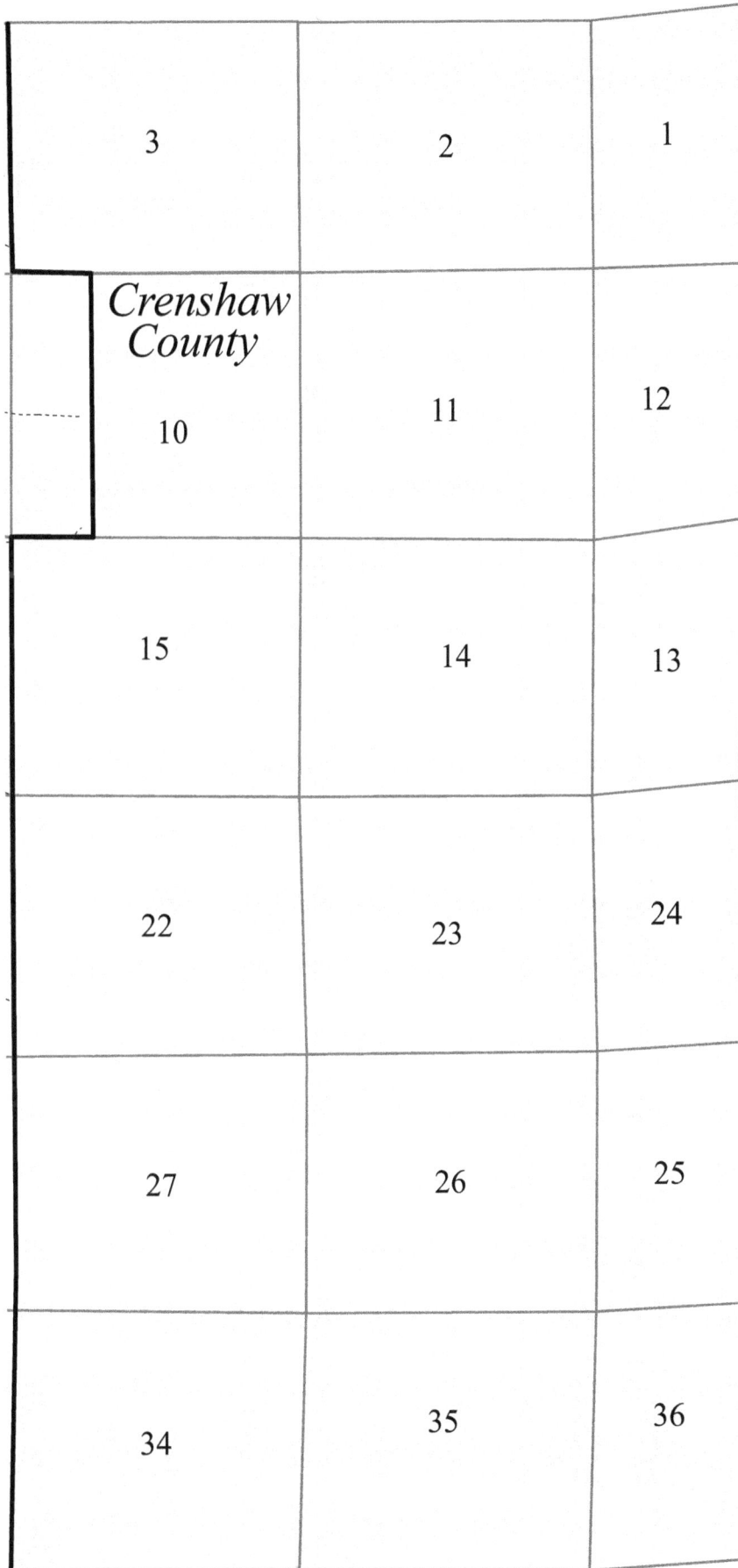

Helpful Hints

1. This Map takes a different look at the same Congressional Township displayed in the preceding two maps. It presents features that can help you better envision the historical development of the area: a) Water-bodies (lakes & ponds), b) Water-courses (rivers, streams, etc.), c) Railroads, d) City/town center-points (where they were oftentimes located when first settled), and e) Cemeteries.

2. Using this "Historical" map in tandem with this Township's Patent Map and Road Map, may lead you to some interesting discoveries. You will often find roads, towns, cemeteries, and waterways are named after nearby landowners: sometimes those names will be the ones you are researching. See how many of these research gems you can find here in Butler County.

Legend

———————— Section Lines

+++++++++ Railroads

▭ Large Rivers & Bodies of Water

----------- Streams/Creeks & Small Rivers

● Cities/Towns

✝ Cemeteries

Scale: Section = 1 mile X 1 mile
(there are some exceptions)

Map Group 16: Index to Land Patents

Township 8-North Range 12-East (St Stephens)

After you locate an individual in this Index, take note of the Section and Section Part then proceed to the Land Patent map on the pages immediately following. You should have no difficulty locating the corresponding parcel of land.

The "For More Info" Column will lead you to more information about the underlying Patents. See the *Legend* at right, and the "How to Use this Book" chapter, for more information.

ID	Individual in Patent	Sec.	Sec. Part	Date Issued	Other Counties	For More Info . . .
3685	AINESWORTH, Joseph	9	SENW	1837-08-02		A1
3662	AINSWORTH, Joab	4	SWNE	1852-02-02		A1
3580	AMASON, Benjamin	28	N½SE	1858-11-01		A1
3581	" "	28	N½SW	1858-11-01		A1
3582	" "	28	S½NW	1858-11-01		A1
3756	BENNETT, Thomas	26	S½SW	1858-11-01		A1
3757	" "	33	SESE	1858-11-01		A1
3758	" "	33	SWSE	1858-11-01		A1
3759	" "	34	NENE	1858-11-01		A1
3760	" "	34	SWNW	1858-11-01		A1
3761	" "	36	NESE	1858-11-01		A1
3762	" "	36	SENE	1858-11-01		A1
3763	" "	36	SWNE	1858-11-01		A1
3814	BILLINGSLEA, Winston	12	W½SE	1858-11-01		A1
3815	" "	13	E½SW	1858-11-01		A1
3816	" "	13	W½NE	1858-11-01		A1
3817	" "	22	S½NE	1858-11-01		A1
3818	" "	22	SE	1858-11-01		A1
3819	" "	23	N½SE	1858-11-01		A1
3820	" "	23	SESE	1858-11-01		A1
3821	" "	23	W½SW	1858-11-01		A1
3822	" "	24	E½SE	1858-11-01		A1 V3809
3823	" "	24	S½NE	1858-11-01		A1
3824	" "	24	SWSE	1858-11-01		A1
3825	" "	24	W½	1858-11-01		A1
3826	" "	25	E½NW	1858-11-01		A1
3827	" "	25	W½NE	1858-11-01		A1
3828	" "	29	S½SE	1858-11-01		A1
3829	" "	32	E½NW	1858-11-01		A1
3830	" "	32	N½SE	1858-11-01		A1
3831	" "	32	NE	1858-11-01		A1
3832	" "	33	S½NW	1858-11-01		A1
3620	BRANSFORD, James A	35	SWNW	1850-08-10		A1
3724	BRANSFORD, Nathan	34	SENE	1850-08-10		A1
3683	BREWER, John W	7	S½SE	1860-09-01		A1
3679	BROOKS, John S	36	NW	1858-11-01		A1
3663	BRYAN, John A	13	W½NW	1858-11-01		A1
3664	" "	14	E½NE	1858-11-01		A1
3781	BRYANT, William	20	E½SW	1858-11-01		A1
3782	" "	29	SENW	1858-11-01		A1
3562	BUFFINGTON, Alfred E	10	NWNW	1850-08-10		A1
3563	" "	4	SESE	1850-08-10		A1
3561	BURKET, Alfred	3	NENW	1858-11-01		A1
3590	BURKETT, Caleb	2	N½SE	1858-11-01		A1
3591	" "	2	S½NE	1858-11-01		A1
3625	BURKETT, James	11	SWNW	1837-05-20		A1

ID	Individual in Patent	Sec.	Sec. Part	Date Issued	Other Counties	For More Info . . .
3624	BURKETT, James (Cont'd)	11	NWNW	1838-07-28		A1
3623	" "	1	E½NE	1858-09-01		A1
3626	" "	12	NENE	1858-09-01		A1
3686	BURKETT, Joseph	2	SWNW	1838-07-28		A1
3688	" "	3	SENE	1838-07-28		A1
3687	" "	3	NENE	1858-11-01		A1
3689	" "	3	W½NE	1858-11-01		A1
3779	BURKETT, Wiley	1	NWNW	1858-11-01		A1
3780	" "	2	NENE	1858-11-01		A1
3783	BURKETT, William	2	SWSW	1837-08-12		A1
3784	" "	3	SESE	1837-08-12		A1
3778	BUTLER, Whitmill	35	W½SE	1837-08-18		A1
3777	" "	35	SESE	1838-07-28		A1
3745	COLEMAN, Richard	11	SENW	1838-07-28		A1
3622	CONE, James B	34	SWSW	1837-08-18		A1
3621	" "	34	SWSE	1838-07-28		A1
3660	CONE, Jesse	14	E½NW	1838-07-28		A1
3661	" "	14	W½NE	1838-07-28		A1
3801	COPELAND, William J	31	NWSW	1852-02-02	Conecuh	A1
3796	DANIEL, William F	27	E½NW	1838-07-28		A1
3797	" "	27	E½SW	1838-07-28		A1
3798	" "	27	W½NE	1838-07-28		A1
3799	" "	27	W½SE	1838-07-28		A1
3785	DEAN, William	10	NESW	1852-12-01		A1
3786	" "	10	W½SE	1854-10-02		A1
3659	DEEN, Jeremiah	15	SESW	1837-08-15		A1
3792	DEEN, William	15	NESW	1837-08-08		A1
3787	" "	10	NWSW	1850-08-10		A1
3788	" "	10	S½SW	1850-08-10		A1
3791	" "	15	E½NW	1850-08-10		A1
3793	" "	9	NESE	1850-08-10		A1
3789	" "	10	SENW	1858-11-01		A1
3790	" "	10	W½NE	1858-11-01		A1
3794	" "	9	SESE	1858-11-01		A1
3795	EASTERS, William	33	NWSW	1850-08-10		A1 V3751
3583	ELLIS, Benjamin C	35	NESE	1837-08-12		A1
3584	" "	35	SENE	1838-07-28		A1
3585	" "	36	W½SW	1838-07-28		A1
3693	ELLIS, Josiah	31	NWNW	1838-07-28	Conecuh	A1
3694	" "	30	SE	1840-01-13	Conecuh	A1 G16
3676	FAIL, John O	26	NW	1858-11-01		A1
3725	FAIL, Nathan	23	NENW	1858-11-01		A1
3726	" "	23	SENW	1858-11-01		A1
3727	" "	23	SWNW	1858-11-01		A1
3735	FAIL, Osborn	22	NWNE	1837-08-12		A1
3734	" "	11	SESW	1858-11-01		A1
3736	FAIL, Osborne	11	W½SE	1852-02-02		A1
3737	FAIL, Osburn	23	NWNW	1837-08-14		A1
3617	FINKLEA, Hugh	4	NWSW	1837-08-18		A1
3618	" "	5	W½NE	1837-08-18		A1
3605	FRANKLIN, Edmond	2	S½SE	1858-09-01		A1
3606	FRANKLIN, Edmun	1	SESW	1858-11-01		A1
3607	" "	1	SWSE	1858-11-01		A1
3608	" "	1	W½SW	1858-11-01		A1
3715	FRANKLIN, Mark	11	NENW	1837-05-20		A1
3716	" "	11	NWNE	1838-07-28		A1
3717	" "	12	NWNW	1858-11-01		A1
3673	FULLER, John M	19	E½SE	1896-10-28		A1
3674	" "	19	NE	1896-10-28		A1
3675	" "	20	W½SW	1896-10-28		A1
3805	FULLER, William R	15	NWNW	1852-02-02		A1
3806	" "	17	E½NW	1858-11-01		A1
3807	" "	17	W½NE	1858-11-01		A1
3564	GANDY, Allford	5	SENE	1858-11-01		A1
3565	" "	5	SENW	1858-11-01		A1
3566	" "	5	SW	1858-11-01		A1
3567	" "	5	SWSE	1858-11-01		A1
3568	" "	5	W½NW	1858-11-01		A1
3738	GANDY, Oxford	7	N½SE	1858-11-01		A1
3739	" "	7	S½NE	1858-11-01		A1
3740	" "	8	NENW	1858-11-01		A1
3741	" "	8	NWSW	1858-11-01		A1
3742	" "	8	W½NW	1858-11-01		A1

ID	Individual in Patent	Sec.	Sec. Part	Date Issued	Other Counties	For More Info . . .
3627	GARNER, James E	19	S½NW	1913-09-12		A2
3700	GARNER, Levi	30	SESW	1852-02-02	Conecuh	A1
3702	" "	31	SWNW	1852-02-02	Conecuh	A1
3698	" "	29	NWSW	1858-11-01		A1
3701	" "	31	NENW	1858-11-01	Conecuh	A1
3697	" "	29	E½SW	1860-04-02		A1
3699	" "	29	SWSW	1860-04-02		A1
3703	" "	33	N½SE	1875-04-20		A1
3704	" "	33	SWNE	1875-04-20		A1
3705	" "	34	NWSW	1875-04-20		A1
3722	GARNER, Nathan B	29	N½SE	1858-11-01		A1
3723	" "	29	W½NE	1858-11-01		A1
3754	GARNER, Stephen W	18	S½NW	1904-07-15		A2
3611	GIBSON, Henry T	21	E½NE	1858-11-01		A1
3612	" "	21	NENW	1858-11-01		A1
3613	" "	21	SW	1858-11-01		A1
3614	" "	21	W½NW	1858-11-01		A1
3615	" "	28	N½NW	1858-11-01		A1
3616	" "	29	E½NE	1858-11-01		A1
3628	GIBSON, James G	19	E½SW	1858-11-01		A1
3629	" "	19	SWSW	1858-11-01		A1
3630	" "	23	SESW	1858-11-01		A1
3631	" "	23	SWSE	1858-11-01		A1
3632	" "	25	W½NW	1858-11-01		A1
3633	" "	26	NE	1858-11-01		A1
3634	" "	30	NWNW	1858-11-01	Conecuh	A1
3635	" "	30	SENW	1858-11-01	Conecuh	A1
3636	" "	34	NWNW	1858-11-01		A1
3753	GIBSON, Springer S	27	E½NE	1860-04-02		A1
3666	GILMORE, John	32	N½SW	1854-07-15		A1
3667	" "	32	S½SE	1858-11-01		A1
3668	" "	32	S½SW	1858-11-01		A1
3800	GILMORE, William	31	N½NE	1854-07-15	Conecuh	A1
3593	GRACE, Christopher	31	SWSE	1851-04-10	Conecuh	A1
3594	" "	31	SWSW	1852-02-02	Conecuh	A1
3592	" "	31	SESW	1854-07-15	Conecuh	A1
3718	HATCHER, Mary	21	W½SE	1838-07-28		A1
3719	" "	28	NE	1838-07-28		A1
3746	HATCHER, Richard J	22	SW	1838-07-28		A1
3747	" "	34	E½NW	1838-07-28		A1
3748	" "	34	W½NE	1838-07-28		A1
3713	HAYNIE, Luke	36	E½SW	1838-07-28		A1
3714	" "	36	W½SE	1838-07-28		A1
3721	HOLLIS, Moses P	28	SWSE	1861-05-01		A1
3643	HOWARD, James T	3	SENW	1858-11-01		A1
3644	" "	8	SWNE	1858-11-01		A1
3645	" "	9	NWSE	1858-11-01		A1
3646	" "	9	SENE	1858-11-01		A1
3604	HUSON, Dawson	22	NW	1838-07-28		A1
3619	HUSON, Isaiah	32	W½NW	1854-07-15		A1
3569	JACKSON, Andrew E	30	NESW	1858-11-01	Conecuh	A1
3749	JOHNSON, Robert	15	SESE	1837-08-18		A1
3750	" "	22	NENE	1837-08-18		A1
3670	KEEBLER, John	28	SESE	1854-07-15		A1
3672	" "	33	NWNE	1854-07-15		A1
3669	" "	28	S½SW	1858-11-01		A1
3671	" "	33	N½NW	1858-11-01		A1
3751	KEEBLER, Samuel	33	SW	1858-11-01		A1 V3795
3695	KENDRICK, Josiah	31	SENW	1851-04-10	Conecuh	A1
3752	KENDRICKE, Shilldrake	19	NWSW	1896-10-21		A1
3589	LEE, Briant	26	SWSE	1858-11-01		A1
3595	LEE, David B	23	NE	1858-11-01		A1
3767	LEE, Thomas	13	SESE	1858-11-01		A1
3768	" "	13	W½SE	1858-11-01		A1
3769	" "	24	N½NE	1858-11-01		A1
3836	LEE, Young	14	NWSW	1850-08-10		A1
3833	" "	13	W½SW	1858-11-01		A1
3834	" "	14	E½SE	1858-11-01		A1
3835	" "	14	E½SW	1858-11-01		A1
3837	" "	14	SWSE	1858-11-01		A1
3838	" "	14	SWSW	1858-11-01		A1
3770	MAHONE, Thomas	10	SESE	1858-11-01		A1
3771	" "	15	SWNE	1858-11-01		A1

ID	Individual in Patent	Sec.	Sec. Part	Date Issued	Other Counties	For More Info . . .
3772	MAHONE, Thomas (Cont'd)	15	W½SE	1858-11-01		A1
3773	" "	20	SE	1858-11-01		A1
3774	" "	4	SWSE	1858-11-01		A1
3775	" "	9	N½NE	1858-11-01		A1
3596	MCBRIDE, David	12	E½SE	1858-11-01		A1
3640	MCWILLIAMS, James	14	W½NW	1837-08-12		A1
3641	" "	15	E½NE	1837-08-12		A1
3642	" "	15	NWNE	1837-08-15		A1
3720	MILLER, Mary M	34	SESE	1858-11-01		A1
3812	MILNER, Willis J	27	E½SE	1858-09-01		A1
3808	" "	13	NESE	1858-11-01		A1
3809	" "	24	NESE	1858-11-01		A1 V3822
3810	" "	26	N½SW	1858-11-01		A1
3811	" "	26	NWSE	1858-11-01		A1
3813	" "	27	W½SW	1858-11-01		A1
3570	MOORE, Andrew J	21	E½SE	1858-09-01		A1
3571	" "	27	W½NW	1858-09-01		A1
3764	MOORE, Thomas D	3	NWSW	1858-11-01		A1
3765	" "	3	W½NW	1858-11-01		A1
3766	" "	4	N½SE	1858-11-01		A1
3586	NORRIS, Benjamin	1	NWNE	1858-11-01		A1
3743	OWENS, Phil	6	NW	1860-09-01		A1
3744	" "	6	W½NE	1860-09-01		A1
3587	PAGE, Bennet	31	NESW	1851-04-10	Conecuh	A1
3588	" "	31	SENE	1851-04-10	Conecuh	A1
3654	PAGE, James W	12	E½NW	1858-11-01		A1
3655	" "	12	E½SW	1858-11-01		A1
3656	" "	12	SENE	1858-11-01		A1
3657	" "	12	SWNW	1858-11-01		A1
3658	" "	12	W½NE	1858-11-01		A1
3677	PAGE, John	31	NWSE	1851-04-10	Conecuh	A1
3597	PARKER, David	11	SWSW	1837-08-12		A1
3678	PARKER, John	5	NENW	1837-08-18		A1
3729	PARKER, Noah	35	E½SW	1858-11-01		A1
3730	" "	35	N½NW	1858-11-01		A1
3731	" "	35	NWNE	1858-11-01		A1
3732	" "	35	SENW	1858-11-01		A1
3733	" "	35	SWNE	1858-11-01		A1
3755	PARKER, Sterling	14	NWSE	1837-08-12		A1
3804	PARKER, William	36	SESE	1837-08-12		A1
3637	PIGGOT, James M	19	W½SE	1858-11-01		A1
3638	" "	29	W½NW	1858-11-01		A1
3639	" "	30	NE	1858-11-01	Conecuh	A1
3802	POLLARD, William P	25	E½SE	1858-11-01		A1
3803	" "	36	N½NE	1858-11-01		A1
3609	PRICE, George W	25	E½NE	1858-11-01		A1
3598	PURVIS, David	2	NWSW	1858-11-01		A1
3599	" "	3	E½SW	1858-11-01		A1
3600	" "	3	NESE	1858-11-01		A1
3601	" "	3	W½SE	1858-11-01		A1
3602	" "	4	SENE	1858-11-01		A1
3603	" "	4	SWSW	1858-11-01		A1
3776	RILEY, Travis M	13	E½NE	1858-11-01		A1
3579	SIMS, Arthur	15	NESE	1838-07-28		A1
3576	" "	11	NESW	1848-05-03		A1
3575	" "	11	E½SE	1850-08-10		A1
3577	" "	12	NWSW	1852-02-02		A1
3578	" "	12	SWSW	1858-09-01		A1
3711	SIRMON, Levi	9	E½SW	1837-08-18		A1
3712	" "	9	SWSE	1852-02-02		A1
3706	" "	8	N½SE	1858-09-01		A1
3707	" "	8	NESW	1858-11-01		A1
3708	" "	8	S½SE	1858-11-01		A1
3709	" "	8	S½SW	1858-11-01		A1
3710	" "	8	SENW	1858-11-01		A1
3680	SMITH, John	34	N½SE	1837-08-18		A1
3681	" "	34	NESW	1837-08-18		A1
3682	" "	35	W½SW	1838-07-28		A1
3696	STINSON, Leander	2	NWNE	1858-09-01		A1
3728	STUCKEY, Nathan	30	NENW	1837-08-10	Conecuh	A1
3610	SWEETEN, Goodman	10	SWNW	1854-10-02		A1
3647	THOMAS, James T	11	SWNE	1858-11-01		A1
3648	" "	17	E½NE	1858-11-01		A1

ID	Individual in Patent	Sec.	Sec. Part	Date Issued	Other Counties	For More Info . . .
3649	THOMAS, James T (Cont'd)	3	SWSW	1858-11-01		A1
3650	"	8	NWNE	1858-11-01		A1
3651	"	8	SENE	1858-11-01		A1
3652	"	9	NWNW	1858-11-01		A1
3653	"	9	SWNE	1858-11-01		A1
3574	THOMPSON, Andrew	4	W½NW	1837-08-12		A1
3572	"	4	E½NW	1837-08-15		A1
3573	"	4	E½SW	1838-07-28		A1
3665	THOMPSON, John C	5	NENE	1837-08-15		A1
3690	TIPTON, Joseph	10	E½NE	1858-11-01		A1
3691	"	10	NESE	1858-11-01		A1
3692	"	11	NWSW	1858-11-01		A1
3684	WHITHERINGTON, John	30	W½SW	1837-08-02	Conecuh	A1
3694	WITHERINGTON, John	30	SE	1840-01-13	Conecuh	A1 G16

Patent Map

T8-N R12-E
St Stephens Meridian

Map Group 16

Township Statistics

Parcels Mapped	:	278
Number of Patents	:	193
Number of Individuals	:	104
Patentees Identified	:	104
Number of Surnames	:	68
Multi-Patentee Parcels	:	1
Oldest Patent Date	:	5/20/1837
Most Recent Patent	:	9/12/1913
Block/Lot Parcels	:	0
Parcels Re - Issued	:	0
Parcels that Overlap	:	4
Cities and Towns	:	2
Cemeteries	:	2

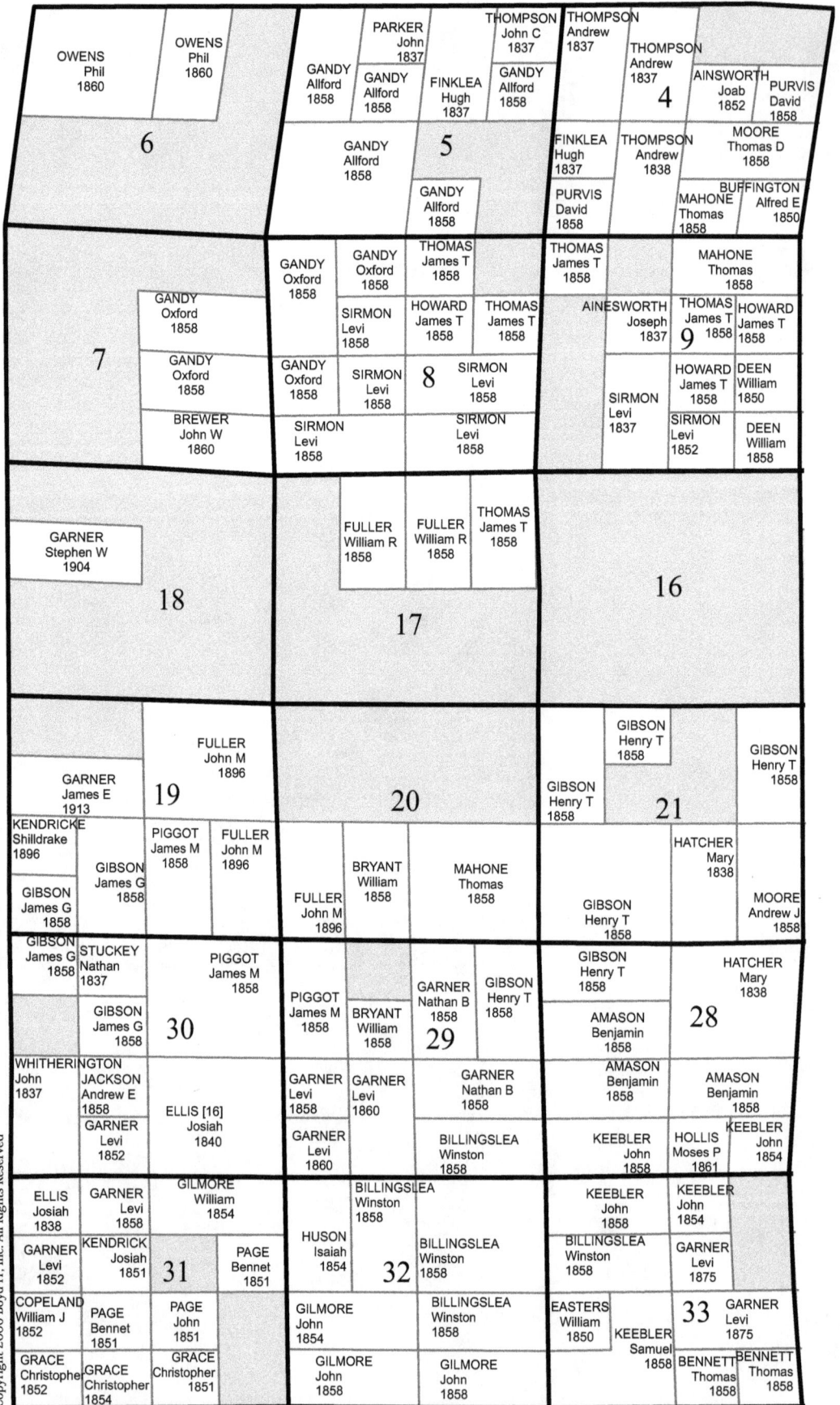

Section 6

OWENS Phil 1860 — OWENS Phil 1860

Section 5

GANDY Allford 1858 — GANDY Allford 1858 — PARKER John 1837 — FINKLEA Hugh 1837 — GANDY Allford 1858 — THOMPSON John C 1837 — THOMPSON Andrew 1837
GANDY Allford 1858 — GANDY Allford 1858

Section 4

THOMPSON Andrew 1837 — AINSWORTH Joab 1852 — PURVIS David 1858 — FINKLEA Hugh 1837 — THOMPSON Andrew 1838 — MOORE Thomas D 1858 — PURVIS David 1858 — MAHONE Thomas 1858 — BUFFINGTON Alfred E 1850

Section 7

GANDY Oxford 1858 — GANDY Oxford 1858 — BREWER John W 1860

Section 8

GANDY Oxford 1858 — GANDY Oxford 1858 — THOMAS James T 1858 — SIRMON Levi 1858 — HOWARD James T 1858 — THOMAS James T 1858 — GANDY Oxford 1858 — SIRMON Levi 1858 — SIRMON Levi 1858 — SIRMON Levi 1858 — SIRMON Levi 1858

Section 9

THOMAS James T 1858 — MAHONE Thomas 1858 — AINESWORTH Joseph 1837 — THOMAS James T 1858 — HOWARD James T 1858 — SIRMON Levi 1837 — HOWARD James T 1858 — DEEN William 1850 — SIRMON Levi 1852 — DEEN William 1858

Section 18

GARNER Stephen W 1904

Section 17

FULLER William R 1858 — FULLER William R 1858 — THOMAS James T 1858

Section 16

Section 19

FULLER John M 1896 — GARNER James E 1913 — KENDRICKE Shilldrake 1896 — GIBSON James G 1858 — PIGGOT James M 1858 — FULLER John M 1896 — GIBSON James G 1858

Section 20

BRYANT William 1858 — MAHONE Thomas 1858 — FULLER John M 1896

Section 21

GIBSON Henry T 1858 — GIBSON Henry T 1858 — GIBSON Henry T 1858 — HATCHER Mary 1838 — GIBSON Henry T 1858 — MOORE Andrew J 1858

Section 30

GIBSON James G 1858 — STUCKEY Nathan 1837 — PIGGOT James M 1858 — GIBSON James G 1858 — WHITHERINGTON John 1837 — JACKSON Andrew E 1858 — GARNER Levi 1852 — ELLIS [16] Josiah 1840

Section 29

PIGGOT James M 1858 — BRYANT William 1858 — GARNER Nathan B 1858 — GIBSON Henry T 1858 — GARNER Levi 1858 — GARNER Levi 1860 — GARNER Nathan B 1858 — GARNER Levi 1860 — BILLINGSLEA Winston 1858

Section 28

GIBSON Henry T 1858 — AMASON Benjamin 1858 — AMASON Benjamin 1858 — HATCHER Mary 1838 — AMASON Benjamin 1858 — KEEBLER John 1858 — HOLLIS Moses P 1861 — KEEBLER John 1854

Section 31

ELLIS Josiah 1838 — GARNER Levi 1858 — GILMORE William 1854 — GARNER Levi 1852 — KENDRICK Josiah 1851 — PAGE Bennet 1851 — COPELAND William J 1852 — PAGE Bennet 1851 — PAGE John 1851 — GRACE Christopher 1852 — GRACE Christopher 1854 — GRACE Christopher 1851

Section 32

BILLINGSLEA Winston 1858 — HUSON Isaiah 1854 — BILLINGSLEA Winston 1858 — GILMORE John 1854 — BILLINGSLEA Winston 1858 — GILMORE John 1858 — GILMORE John 1858

Section 33

KEEBLER John 1858 — KEEBLER John 1854 — BILLINGSLEA Winston 1858 — GARNER Levi 1875 — EASTERS William 1850 — KEEBLER Samuel 1858 — GARNER Levi 1875 — BENNETT Thomas 1858 — BENNETT Thomas 1858

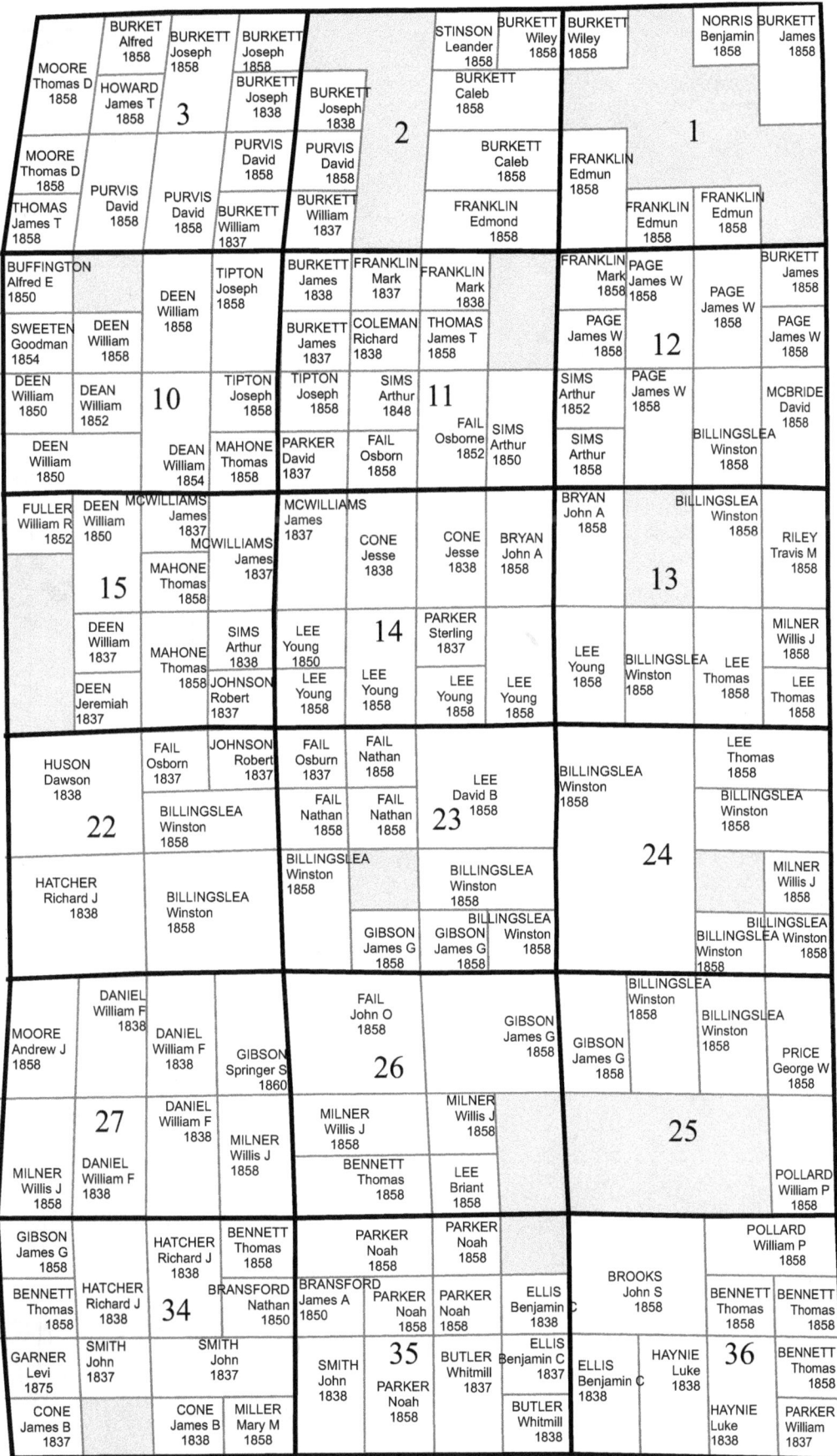

Map (Township grid)

Section 3
- MOORE Thomas D 1858
- BURKET Alfred 1858
- HOWARD James T 1858
- BURKETT Joseph 1858
- BURKETT Joseph 1858
- BURKETT Joseph 1838
- BURKETT Joseph 1838
- MOORE Thomas D 1858
- THOMAS James T 1858
- PURVIS David 1858
- PURVIS David 1858
- PURVIS David 1858
- BURKETT William 1837

Section 2
- STINSON Leander 1858
- BURKETT Joseph 1838
- BURKETT Caleb 1858
- BURKETT Caleb 1858
- BURKETT William 1837
- FRANKLIN Edmond 1858

Section 1
- BURKETT Wiley 1858
- BURKETT Wiley 1858
- NORRIS Benjamin 1858
- BURKETT James 1858
- FRANKLIN Edmun 1858
- FRANKLIN Edmun 1858
- FRANKLIN Edmun 1858

Section 10
- BUFFINGTON Alfred E 1850
- SWEETEN Goodman 1854
- DEEN William 1850
- DEEN William 1852
- DEEN William 1850
- DEEN William 1858
- DEEN William 1858
- TIPTON Joseph 1858
- TIPTON Joseph 1858
- DEAN William 1854
- MAHONE Thomas 1858

Section 11
- BURKETT James 1838
- FRANKLIN Mark 1837
- FRANKLIN Mark 1838
- BURKETT James 1837
- COLEMAN Richard 1838
- THOMAS James T 1858
- TIPTON Joseph 1858
- SIMS Arthur 1848
- PARKER David 1837
- FAIL Osborn 1858
- FAIL Osborne 1852
- SIMS Arthur 1850

Section 12
- FRANKLIN Mark 1858
- PAGE James W 1858
- PAGE James W 1858
- PAGE James W 1858
- PAGE James W 1858
- SIMS Arthur 1852
- PAGE James W 1858
- SIMS Arthur 1858
- BILLINGSLEA Winston 1858
- BURKETT James 1858
- PAGE James W 1858
- MCBRIDE David 1858

Section 15
- FULLER William R 1852
- DEEN William 1850
- MCWILLIAMS James 1837
- MCWILLIAMS James 1837
- MAHONE Thomas 1858
- DEEN William 1837
- MAHONE Thomas 1858
- DEEN Jeremiah 1837

Section 14
- MCWILLIAMS James 1837
- CONE Jesse 1838
- SIMS Arthur 1838
- JOHNSON Robert 1837
- LEE Young 1850
- LEE Young 1858
- LEE Young 1858
- PARKER Sterling 1837
- LEE Young 1858
- LEE Young 1858

Section 13
- CONE Jesse 1838
- BRYAN John A 1858
- BRYAN John A 1858
- BILLINGSLEA Winston 1858
- RILEY Travis M 1858
- LEE Young 1858
- BILLINGSLEA Winston 1858
- LEE Thomas 1858
- MILNER Willis J 1858
- LEE Thomas 1858

Section 22
- HUSON Dawson 1838
- FAIL Osborn 1837
- JOHNSON Robert 1837
- BILLINGSLEA Winston 1858
- HATCHER Richard J 1838
- BILLINGSLEA Winston 1858

Section 23
- FAIL Osborn 1837
- FAIL Nathan 1858
- FAIL Nathan 1858
- FAIL Nathan 1858
- LEE David B 1858
- BILLINGSLEA Winston 1858
- GIBSON James G 1858
- GIBSON James G 1858
- BILLINGSLEA Winston 1858

Section 24
- BILLINGSLEA Winston 1858
- LEE Thomas 1858
- BILLINGSLEA Winston 1858
- MILNER Willis J 1858
- BILLINGSLEA Winston 1858
- BILLINGSLEA Winston 1858

Section 27
- MOORE Andrew J 1858
- DANIEL William F 1838
- DANIEL William F 1838
- GIBSON Springer S 1860
- DANIEL William F 1838
- MILNER Willis J 1858
- DANIEL William F 1838
- MILNER Willis J 1858

Section 26
- FAIL John O 1858
- MILNER Willis J 1858
- BENNETT Thomas 1858
- MILNER Willis J 1858
- LEE Briant 1858

Section 25
- BILLINGSLEA Winston 1858
- GIBSON James G 1858
- BILLINGSLEA Winston 1858
- GIBSON James G 1858
- PRICE George W 1858
- POLLARD William P 1858

Section 34
- GIBSON James G 1858
- BENNETT Thomas 1858
- HATCHER Richard J 1838
- BENNETT Thomas 1858
- HATCHER Richard J 1838
- BRANSFORD Nathan 1850
- GARNER Levi 1875
- SMITH John 1837
- SMITH John 1837
- CONE James B 1837
- CONE James B 1838
- MILLER Mary M 1858

Section 35
- BRANSFORD James A 1850
- PARKER Noah 1858
- PARKER Noah 1858
- PARKER Noah 1858
- PARKER Noah 1858
- SMITH John 1838
- PARKER Noah 1858
- BUTLER Whitmill 1837
- ELLIS Benjamin C 1838
- ELLIS Benjamin C 1837
- BUTLER Whitmill 1838

Section 36
- BROOKS John S 1858
- ELLIS Benjamin C 1838
- HAYNIE Luke 1838
- POLLARD William P 1858
- BENNETT Thomas 1858
- BENNETT Thomas 1858
- BENNETT Thomas 1858
- HAYNIE Luke 1838
- PARKER William 1837

Helpful Hints

1. This Map's INDEX can be found on the preceding pages.

2. Refer to Map "C" to see where this Township lies within Butler County, Alabama.

3. Numbers within square brackets [ ] denote a multi-patentee land parcel (multi-owner). Refer to Appendix "C" for a full list of members in this group.

4. Areas that look to be crowded with Patentees usually indicate multiple sales of the same parcel (Re-issues) or Overlapping parcels. See this Township's Index for an explanation of these and other circumstances that might explain "odd" groupings of Patentees on this map.

Legend

- —— Patent Boundary
- —— Section Boundary
- No Patents Found (or Outside County)
- 1., 2., 3., ... Lot Numbers (when beside a name)
- [ ] Group Number (see Appendix "C")

Scale: Section = 1 mile X 1 mile (generally, with some exceptions)

217

Road Map

T8-N   R12-E
St Stephens Meridian

Map Group 16

Copyright 2006 Boyd IT, Inc. All Rights Reserved

Cities & Towns

Grace
Starlington

Cemeteries

Old Bethel Cemetery
Stamps Cemetery

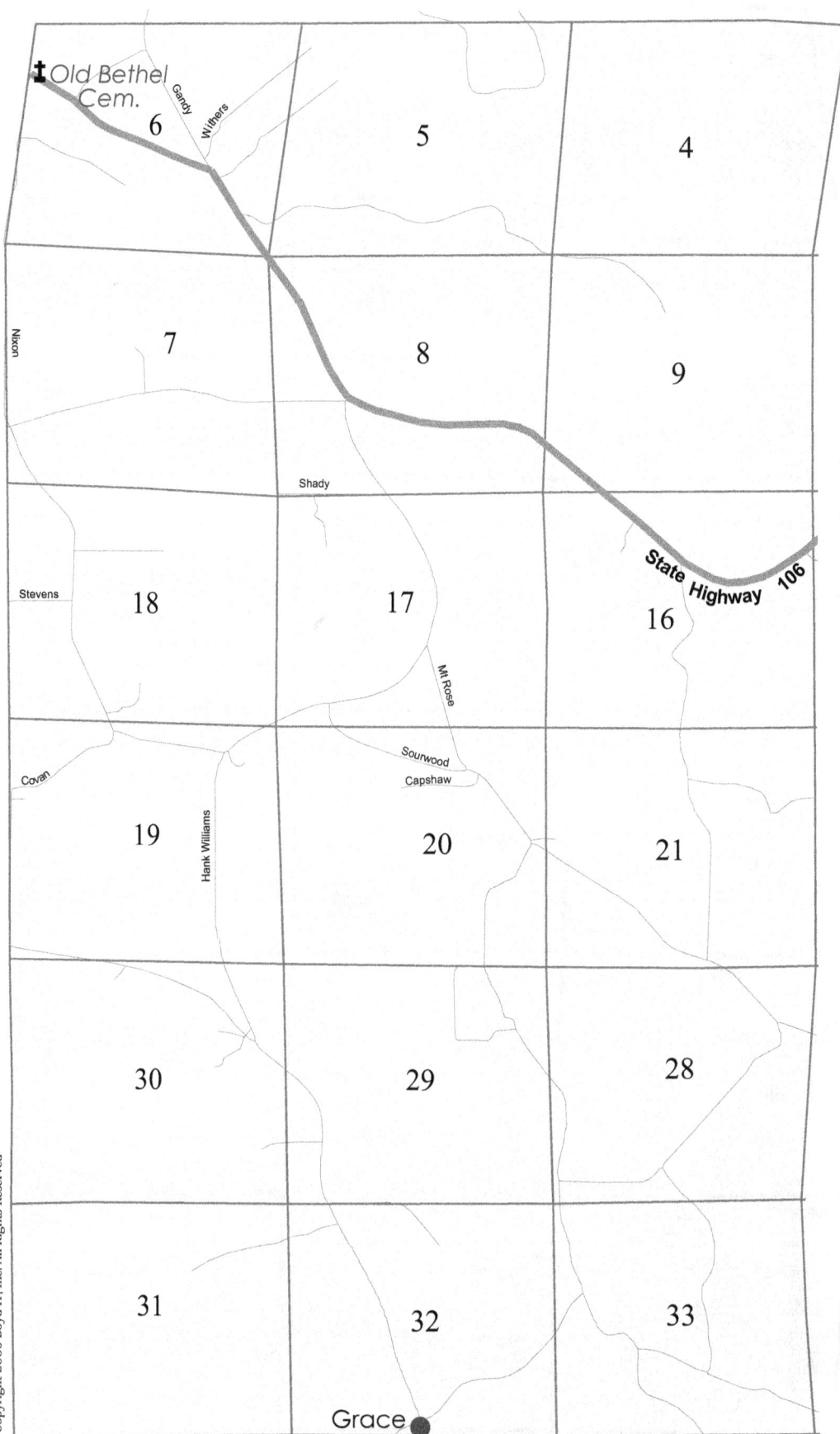

Old Bethel Cem.

6

5

4

Gandy

Withers

Nixon

7

8

9

Shady

Stevens

18

17

16

Mt Rose

State Highway 106

Covan

Sourwood

Capshaw

Hank Williams

19

20

21

30

29

28

31

32

33

Grace

3

Mt Pisgah

Huggins

2

Starlington

Stinson

1

10

11

Starlington

12

15

14

Stamps Cem.

13

22

23

Blue Round

24

Lilac

County Road 16

Shows

Hall

27

26

25

Mill

34

35

Beverly

36

I-65

Helpful Hints

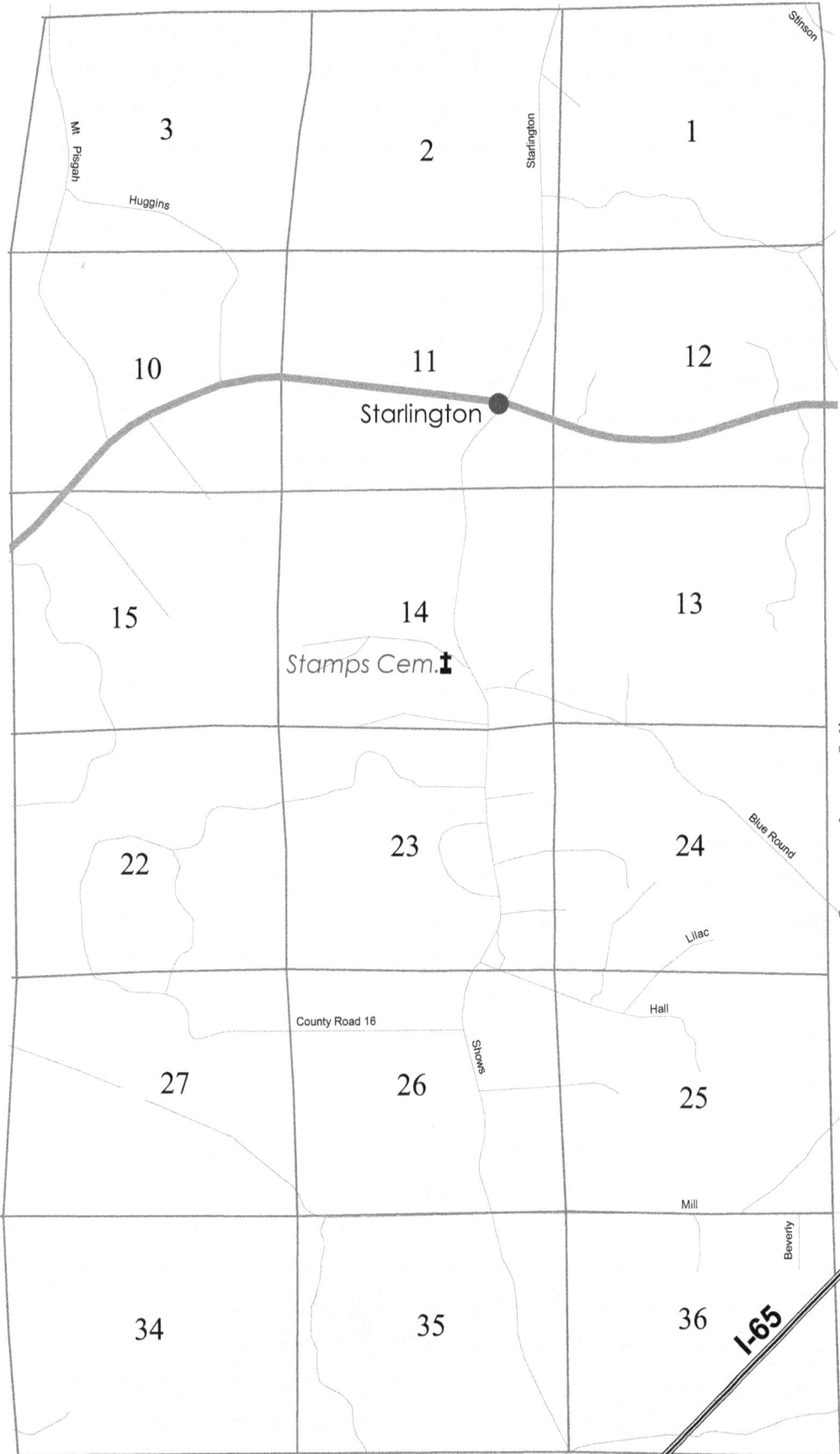

1. This road map has a number of uses, but primarily it is to help you: a) find the present location of land owned by your ancestors (at least the general area), b) find cemeteries and city-centers, and c) estimate the route/roads used by Census-takers & tax-assessors.

2. If you plan to travel to Butler County to locate cemeteries or land parcels, please pick up a modern travel map for the area before you do. Mapping old land parcels on modern maps is not as exact a science as you might think. Just the slightest variations in public land survey coordinates, estimates of parcel boundaries, or road-map deviations can greatly alter a map's representation of how a road either does or doesn't cross a particular parcel of land.

Legend

——— Section Lines

═══ Interstates

▬▬▬ Highways

——— Other Roads

● Cities/Towns

✝ Cemeteries

Scale: Section = 1 mile X 1 mile
(generally, with some exceptions)

219

Historical Map

T8-N R12-E
St Stephens Meridian

Map Group 16

Cities & Towns

Grace
Starlington

Cemeteries

Old Bethel Cemetery
Stamps Cemetery

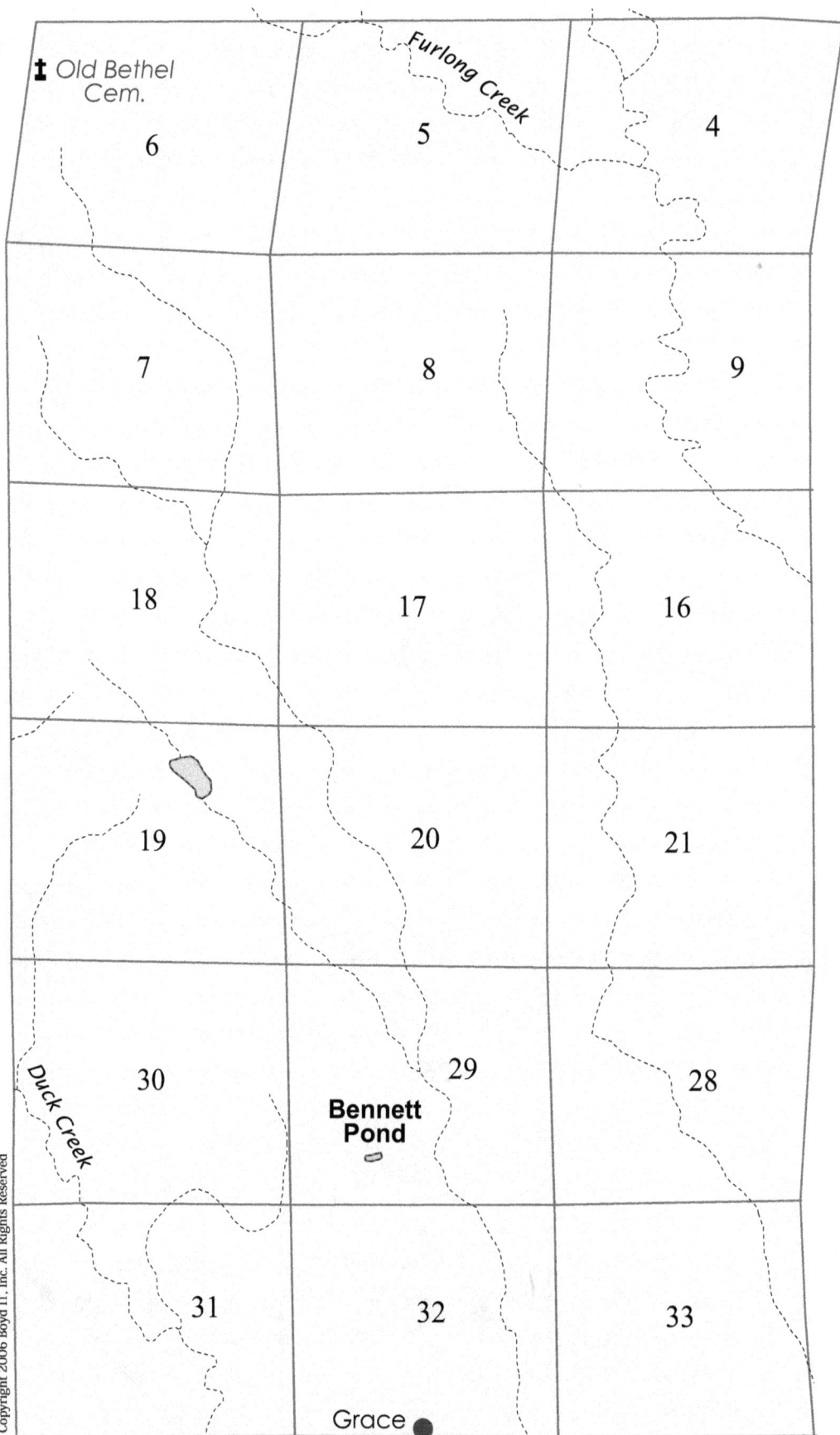

✝ *Old Bethel Cem.*

Furlong Creek

6	5	4
7	8	9
18	17	16
19	20	21
30	29	28
31	32	33

Duck Creek

Bennett Pond

Grace ●

3

2

1

10

11

Starlington ●

12

15

Long Creek

14

✝
Stamps Cem.

Panther Creek

13

22

23

24

27

26

25

34

35

36

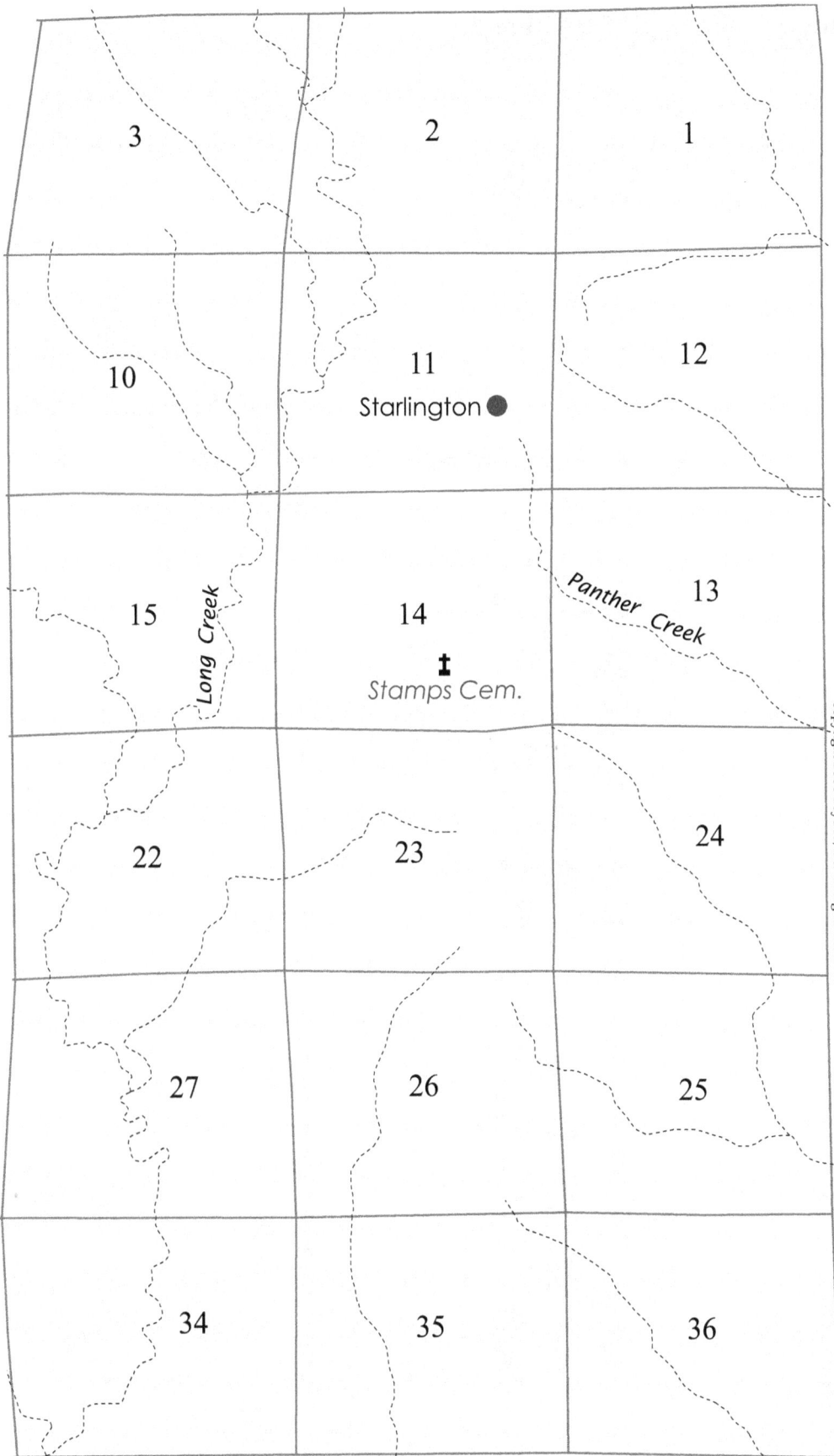

Helpful Hints

1. This Map takes a different look at the same Congressional Township displayed in the preceding two maps. It presents features that can help you better envision the historical development of the area: a) Water-bodies (lakes & ponds), b) Water-courses (rivers, streams, etc.), c) Railroads, d) City/town center-points (where they were oftentimes located when first settled), and e) Cemeteries.

2. Using this "Historical" map in tandem with this Township's Patent Map and Road Map, may lead you to some interesting discoveries. You will often find roads, towns, cemeteries, and waterways are named after nearby landowners: sometimes those names will be the ones you are researching. See how many of these research gems you can find here in Butler County.

Legend

———	Section Lines
—+—+—+—	Railroads
▭	Large Rivers & Bodies of Water
---------	Streams/Creeks & Small Rivers
●	Cities/Towns
✝	Cemeteries

Scale: Section = 1 mile X 1 mile
(there are some exceptions)

Map Group 17: Index to Land Patents

Township 8-North Range 13-East (St Stephens)

After you locate an individual in this Index, take note of the Section and Section Part then proceed to the Land Patent map on the pages immediately following. You should have no difficulty locating the corresponding parcel of land.

The "For More Info" Column will lead you to more information about the underlying Patents. See the *Legend* at right, and the "How to Use this Book" chapter, for more information.

```
                        LEGEND
               "For More Info . . . " column
A = Authority (Legislative Act, See Appendix "A")
B = Block or Lot (location in Section unknown)
C = Cancelled Patent
F = Fractional Section
G = Group (Multi-Patentee Patent, see Appendix "C")
V = Overlaps another Parcel
R = Re-Issued (Parcel patented more than once)

(A & G items require you to look in the Appendixes referred
to above. All other Letter-designations followed by a number
require you to locate line-items in this index that possess
the ID number found after the letter).
```

ID	Individual in Patent	Sec.	Sec. Part	Date Issued	Other Counties	For More Info . . .
3919	AINSWORTH, Frank L	6	N½NE	1885-08-05		A2
4032	ARDIS, John	36	E½SE	1860-10-01		A1
4033	" "	36	W½NE	1860-10-01		A1
4034	" "	36	W½SE	1860-10-01		A1
3930	BARNES, Henry	23	W½SW	1858-11-01		A1
3916	BECK, Everett	24	E½NW	1858-11-01		A1
3917	" "	24	N½SE	1858-11-01		A1
3918	" "	24	NESW	1858-11-01		A1
4067	BELL, Jonathan E	26	S½NW	1884-12-05		A2
4127	BENNETT, Thomas	31	N½SW	1858-11-01		A1
4128	" "	31	S½NW	1858-11-01		A1
4124	BINION, Temus	8	E½SE	1896-04-28		A1
3955	BLACK, Hugh L	4	N½SE	1858-11-01		A1
3956	" "	4	SENW	1858-11-01		A1
3957	" "	4	SWNE	1858-11-01		A1
4003	BLACK, James M	4	N½SW	1858-11-01		A1
4004	" "	4	S½SW	1858-11-01		A1
4005	" "	5	E½SE	1858-11-01		A1
4006	" "	9	N½NW	1858-11-01		A1
4114	BLACK, Robert L	10	NESW	1858-11-01		A1
4115	" "	10	S½NW	1858-11-01		A1
4097	BLACKMON, Peter F	25	NENE	1913-06-21		A2
3848	BOGGAN, Anderson	1	NWSW	1837-08-18		A1
3849	" "	2	W½SE	1837-08-18		A1
4043	BRANSFORD, John H	29	W½NW	1858-11-01		A1
4044	" "	30	SENE	1858-11-01		A1
4092	BRANSFORD, Nathan	30	NENE	1837-08-14		A1
4091	" "	19	SESE	1858-11-01		A1
4093	" "	30	NWNE	1858-11-01		A1
3888	BROOKS, Drewry W	33	N½SE	1858-11-01		A1
3889	" "	33	SWNE	1858-11-01		A1
3890	" "	33	SWSW	1858-11-01		A1
4060	BROXSON, John W	12	SWNW	1858-11-01		A1
4061	" "	13	NWNW	1896-10-26		A1
3986	BURKETT, James	7	NWNW	1858-09-01		A1
3982	" "	23	NENE	1858-11-01		A1
3984	" "	23	W½NE	1858-11-01		A1
3985	" "	24	NWNW	1858-11-01		A1
3983	" "	23	NW	1875-04-20		A1
3931	BURNS, Henry	22	E½SW	1858-11-01		A1
3932	" "	22	N½SE	1858-11-01		A1
4143	CALDWELL, William C	1	SESW	1858-11-01		A1
4144	" "	1	W½NE	1858-11-01		A1
4145	" "	1	W½SE	1858-11-01		A1
4146	" "	12	E½NW	1858-11-01		A1 F
4147	" "	12	NWNE	1858-11-01		A1 F

ID	Individual in Patent	Sec.	Sec. Part	Date Issued	Other Counties	For More Info . . .
3929	CARTER, Harbert	30	E½NW	1880-02-20		A2
4094	CLOPTON, Nathaniel V	3	NWNW	1858-11-01		A1
4095	" "	9	E½NE	1858-11-01		A1
4024	COLEMAN, Joab	6	N½NW	1858-11-01		A1
4076	COOK, Laurence E	29	E½SW	1858-11-01		A1
4077	" "	29	W½SE	1858-11-01		A1
4078	" "	32	N½NW	1858-11-01		A1
4079	" "	32	W½NE	1858-11-01		A1
4037	CORLEY, John	36	W½	1858-11-01		A1
3988	CROSBY, James	34	NWSW	1860-12-01		A1
4040	ELLIS, John G	17	SESW	1860-04-02		A1
4041	" "	17	SWNW	1860-04-02		A1
4042	" "	17	W½SW	1860-04-02		A1
3978	ENGLISH, James B	7	SESE	1875-04-20		A1
3979	" "	7	W½SE	1875-04-20		A1
4080	ETHEREGE, Lewis	31	SESE	1858-11-01		A1
4081	" "	31	W½SE	1858-11-01		A1
3870	FAIL, Bryan	14	E½NE	1837-08-14		A1
4014	FAIL, Jeremiah	26	NWSW	1854-07-15		A1
4015	" "	27	E½SE	1854-07-15		A1
4016	" "	27	NWSE	1854-07-15		A1
4017	" "	27	SWNE	1854-07-15		A1
4018	" "	34	E½SW	1854-07-15		A1
4019	" "	34	N½NE	1854-07-15		A1
4020	" "	34	N½SE	1854-07-15		A1
4021	" "	35	NWNW	1854-07-15		A1
4083	FAIL, Loveard	2	NWNE	1858-11-01		A1
4096	FAIL, Ozbon	11	SWSE	1838-07-28		A1
4154	FAIL, William	9	SESE	1852-02-02		A1
4153	" "	10	SESW	1858-11-01		A1
3843	FAILES, Alexander	18	NWNW	1882-10-20		A2
4038	FAILS, John	21	NWSE	1858-11-01		A1
4039	" "	22	SWSW	1858-11-01		A1
4082	FAILS, Lewis	25	NWNE	1837-08-14		A1
4062	FREEMAN, John W	1	E½NE	1858-11-01		A1
4063	" "	1	E½SE	1858-11-01		A1
4064	" "	12	E½NE	1858-11-01		A1
4065	" "	12	NESE	1858-11-01		A1
4066	" "	12	SWNE	1858-11-01		A1
3972	FUNDERBURKE, Isham G	36	E½NE	1860-10-01		A1
4111	GARDNER, Richard S	26	N½NW	1858-11-01		A1
4112	" "	26	NWNE	1858-11-01		A1
4110	" "	22	S½SE	1860-04-02		A1
4113	" "	27	N½NE	1860-04-02		A1
4120	GAY, Solomon	8	E½NW	1858-11-01		A1
3989	GIBSON, James G	19	NESE	1858-11-01		A1
3990	" "	19	SWNE	1858-11-01		A1
3991	" "	19	W½SE	1858-11-01		A1
3992	" "	25	E½NW	1858-11-01		A1
3993	" "	25	E½SE	1858-11-01		A1
3994	" "	25	NWSE	1858-11-01		A1
3995	" "	25	SW	1858-11-01		A1
3996	" "	25	W½NW	1858-11-01		A1
3997	" "	29	SESE	1858-11-01		A1
3998	" "	33	NWNW	1858-11-01		A1
4089	HAMMONDS, Nancy	11	SENE	1858-11-01		A1
4090	" "	12	NWNW	1858-11-01		A1
3867	HARPER, Berry	29	NENE	1858-11-01		A1
3868	" "	29	NENW	1858-11-01		A1
3869	" "	29	NWNE	1858-11-01		A1
3935	HARRISON, Henry	6	NWSE	1852-02-02		A1
3938	" "	6	SENW	1852-02-02		A1
3939	" "	6	SWNE	1852-02-02		A1
3934	" "	6	NESE	1858-11-01		A1
3936	" "	6	NWSW	1858-11-01		A1
3940	" "	6	SWNW	1858-11-01		A1
3933	" "	6	NESE	1860-12-01		A1
3937	" "	6	SENE	1860-12-01		A1
4158	HARRISON, William M	1	NESW	1858-11-01		A1
4138	HASSEY, William B	23	SENE	1858-11-01		A1
4139	" "	24	NWSW	1858-11-01		A1
4140	" "	24	SWNW	1858-11-01		A1
4155	HEAP, William J	9	N½SW	1858-11-01		A1

223

ID	Individual in Patent	Sec.	Sec. Part	Date Issued	Other Counties	For More Info . . .
4156	HEAP, William J (Cont'd)	9	S½NW	1858-11-01		A1
4157	" "	9	SWNE	1858-11-01		A1
4051	HENDERSON, John M	35	S½SE	1860-04-02		A1
3913	HOBBS, Elijah J	33	NESW	1858-11-01		A1
3914	" "	33	SWNW	1858-11-01		A1
3976	HOBBS, Jacob	31	SESW	1858-11-01		A1
3977	" "	31	SWSW	1858-11-01		A1
4047	HOOD, John	1	SENW	1837-08-18		A1
4118	HOWEL, Sherod S	1	NENW	1837-05-15		A1
4119	HOWELL, Sherod S	1	NWNW	1837-08-15		A1
3958	INGRAM, Irad	17	NESW	1858-11-01		A1
3959	" "	17	NWSE	1858-11-01		A1
3963	INGRAM, Isaac	17	SENW	1858-11-01		A1
3964	" "	17	SWNE	1858-11-01		A1
3941	JOHNSON, Henry	34	SENE	1875-11-20		A2
3965	KENDALL, Isaac J	24	SWSE	1858-11-01		A1
3966	" "	25	SWNE	1858-11-01		A1
3967	" "	30	SWNW	1858-11-01		A1 V3928
4022	KUYKENDAL, Jesse H	25	SWSE	1858-11-01		A1
3969	KUYKENDALL, Isaac J	25	SENE	1854-05-11		A1
3968	" "	24	SESW	1858-11-01		A1
3904	LARKINS, Eleazar	26	E½SE	1885-06-12		A2
3905	" "	26	NESW	1885-06-12		A2
3906	" "	26	NWSE	1885-06-12		A2
3859	LEE, Benjamin N	17	S½SE	1858-11-01		A1
3860	" "	20	NENE	1858-11-01		A1
3861	" "	20	SWNE	1858-11-01		A1 R4161
3892	LEE, Edward	14	E½NW	1841-05-20		A1
3896	" "	14	W½NE	1841-05-20		A1
3893	" "	14	NWSE	1858-11-01		A1
3894	" "	14	SESW	1858-11-01		A1
3895	" "	14	SWSE	1858-11-01		A1
3897	" "	14	W½NW	1858-11-01		A1
3898	" "	14	W½SW	1858-11-01		A1
3899	" "	15	NESE	1860-04-02		A1
3900	" "	15	W½SE	1860-04-02		A1
3915	LEE, Emily H	18	SESE	1885-03-30		A2
3960	LEE, Irvin	10	N½SE	1858-11-01		A1
3961	" "	10	S½SE	1858-11-01		A1
3962	" "	11	N½SW	1858-11-01		A1
3970	LEE, Isaac	34	SENW	1858-11-01		A1
3971	" "	34	SWNE	1858-11-01		A1
3973	LEE, Jackson	13	SWNW	1858-11-01		A1
3974	" "	13	W½SW	1858-11-01		A1
3975	" "	14	E½SE	1858-11-01		A1
4025	LEE, Joel W	21	NENE	1837-08-12		A1
4026	" "	27	SWSW	1858-11-01		A1
4027	" "	33	NENE	1858-11-01		A1
4028	" "	34	NENW	1858-11-01		A1
4029	" "	34	NWNW	1858-11-01		A1
4048	LEE, John	19	E½NW	1858-11-01		A1
4049	" "	19	E½SW	1858-11-01		A1
4050	" "	19	NWNW	1858-11-01		A1
4045	LEE, John H	10	E½NE	1858-11-01		A1
4046	" "	11	W½NW	1858-11-01		A1
4162	LEE, Young	11	NENE	1837-04-10		A1
4163	" "	11	W½NE	1838-07-28		A1
4001	LOURY, James	4	N½NE	1858-11-01		A1
4002	" "	4	NENW	1858-11-01		A1
4141	MARSHALL, William B	18	E½NW	1858-11-01		A1
4142	" "	18	W½NE	1858-11-01		A1
3925	MASSINGILL, George W	11	E½NW	1837-08-18		A1
3926	" "	2	E½NW	1837-08-18		A1
3927	" "	2	E½SW	1837-08-18		A1
4125	MATHENY, Thomas B	10	N½NW	1858-11-01		A1
4126	" "	10	W½NE	1858-11-01		A1
3884	MAY, Drewry B	30	NWSW	1858-11-01		A1
3885	" "	30	W½SE	1858-11-01		A1
3886	" "	31	N½NW	1858-11-01		A1
3887	" "	31	NE	1858-11-01		A1
3891	MAY, Drury B	32	SESE	1861-05-01		A1
3881	MCBRIDE, David	7	W½SW	1858-11-01		A1
4098	MILNER, Pitt S	27	E½NW	1858-11-01		A1

ID	Individual in Patent	Sec.	Sec. Part	Date Issued	Other Counties	For More Info . . .
4099	MILNER, Pitt S (Cont'd)	27	NWNW	1858-11-01		A1
4100	" "	28	NWSW	1858-11-01		A1
4101	" "	28	SWSW	1858-11-01		A1
4102	MILNER, Pitts S	27	NWSW	1858-11-01		A1
4103	" "	28	E½SE	1858-11-01		A1
4104	" "	28	E½SW	1858-11-01		A1
4105	" "	28	NWNE	1858-11-01		A1
4106	" "	28	SENE	1858-11-01		A1
4107	" "	28	W½NW	1858-11-01		A1
4108	" "	33	NWNE	1858-11-01		A1
4117	MILNER, Sang	34	S½SE	1875-11-20		A2
3845	MOORE, Allen W	15	SWSW	1854-10-02		A1
3847	" "	22	SWNW	1854-10-02		A1
3846	" "	22	SENW	1858-11-01		A1
4087	MOORE, Mosley J	15	SESW	1860-04-02		A1
4088	" "	22	N½NW	1860-04-02		A1
3841	MORROW, Abraham	20	W½	1858-09-01		A1
3842	MORROW, Abraham S	6	SESE	1891-06-19		A2
3920	MORROW, George H	20	E½SE	1858-11-01		A1
3921	" "	20	NWSE	1858-11-01		A1
3922	" "	20	SWSE	1858-11-01		A1
3923	" "	21	W½SW	1858-11-01		A1
3880	MYERS, David B	4	SESE	1858-11-01		A1
3862	NORRIS, Benjamin	7	E½SW	1858-11-01		A1
3863	" "	7	S½NW	1858-11-01		A1
3864	PARKER, Benjamin	4	SWSE	1838-07-28		A1
3865	" "	8	W½NW	1838-07-28		A1
3866	" "	9	NWNE	1838-07-28		A1
3903	PARKER, Eldridge	7	NENE	1838-07-28		A1
4116	PARKER, Samuel	24	NE	1891-06-08		A2
4149	PARMER, William F	12	SESE	1858-11-01		A1
4150	" "	12	W½SE	1858-11-01		A1
4151	" "	13	NE	1858-11-01		A1
4152	" "	13	NENW	1858-11-01		A1
3999	POLLARD, James L	3	NWSE	1858-11-01		A1
4000	" "	3	SW	1858-11-01		A1
4052	POWELL, John	33	SESE	1837-08-18		A1
3882	PRICE, David S	30	E½SW	1858-11-01		A1
3883	" "	30	SWSW	1858-11-01		A1
3928	PRICE, George W	30	W½NW	1858-11-01		A1 V3967
4084	PUGH, Masten B	4	NWNW	1858-11-01		A1
4085	" "	4	SWNW	1858-11-01		A1
4086	PUGH, Mastin B	5	NENE	1858-11-01		A1
4035	PULASKI, John C	23	E½SW	1858-11-01		A1
4036	" "	24	SESE	1885-11-13		A1
4073	RILEY, Larkin G	19	NWNE	1850-08-10		A1
4074	" "	19	SENE	1850-08-10		A1
4071	" "	18	E½SW	1858-11-01		A1
4072	" "	18	W½SE	1858-11-01		A1
4075	RILEY, Larkind G	19	NENE	1858-11-01		A1
4134	RILEY, Travis M	18	NWSW	1858-11-01		A1
4135	" "	18	SWNW	1858-11-01		A1
4136	" "	18	SWSW	1858-11-01		A1
4109	ROBINSON, Reubin	26	NENE	1885-06-20		A2
3901	RUSTIN, Eldridge C	32	E½SW	1858-11-01		A1
3902	" "	32	W½SE	1858-11-01		A1
3912	SANDERS, Elijah A	26	SWSW	1875-11-20		A2
3856	SAUCER, Benjamin F	11	E½SE	1858-11-01		A1
3857	" "	11	NWSE	1858-11-01		A1
4008	SHEPARD, James	3	E½NW	1858-11-01		A1
4009	" "	3	S½NE	1858-11-01		A1
3980	SHEPARD, James B	3	SWNW	1858-11-01		A1
3981	" "	4	SENE	1858-11-01		A1
4129	SHEPHEARD, Thomas	2	SWSW	1860-04-02		A1
3987	SHEPHERD, James C	2	NWNW	1858-11-01		A1
4054	SHEPHERD, John	15	E½NW	1854-07-15		A1
4055	" "	15	NE	1858-11-01		A1
4056	" "	15	W½NW	1858-11-01		A1
4030	SHEPHERD, John A	15	SESE	1858-11-01		A1
4031	" "	22	NE	1858-11-01		A1
4053	SHEPHERD, John S	9	SWSE	1837-08-12		A1
4130	SHEPHERD, Thomas	2	NWSW	1858-11-01		A1
4131	" "	2	SWNW	1858-11-01		A1

ID	Individual in Patent	Sec.	Sec. Part	Date Issued	Other Counties	For More Info . . .
4132	SHEPHERD, Thomas (Cont'd)	3	E½SE	1858-11-01		A1
4133	" "	3	SWSE	1858-11-01		A1
4148	SHEPHERD, William C	3	N½NE	1858-11-01		A1
4010	SHEPPARD, James	9	SESW	1837-05-15		A1
3924	SIMPSON, George	24	SWSW	1885-06-12		A2
3850	SIMS, Arthur	17	NENW	1858-11-01		A1
3851	" "	17	NWNE	1858-11-01		A1
3852	" "	17	NWNW	1858-11-01		A1
3853	" "	8	NESW	1858-11-01		A1
3854	" "	8	S½SW	1858-11-01		A1
3855	" "	8	W½SE	1858-11-01		A1
3907	SIMS, Elihu	6	SESW	1858-11-01		A1
3908	" "	6	SWSE	1858-11-01		A1
3909	" "	7	NENW	1858-11-01		A1
3910	" "	7	NWNE	1858-11-01		A1
3911	" "	7	SWNE	1858-11-01		A1
4121	SIMS, Stephen	7	NESE	1858-11-01		A1
4122	" "	7	SENE	1858-11-01		A1
4123	" "	8	NWSW	1858-11-01		A1
4068	SINGLETARY, Joseph	28	SENW	1890-07-03		A2
4069	" "	28	SWNE	1890-07-03		A2
4070	" "	28	W½SE	1890-07-03		A2
3945	SMITH, Henry	21	NWNE	1858-09-01		A1
3942	" "	20	SENE	1858-11-01		A1
3943	" "	21	E½NW	1858-11-01		A1
3944	" "	21	NESW	1858-11-01		A1
3946	" "	21	NWNW	1858-11-01		A1
3947	" "	21	SENE	1858-11-01		A1
3948	" "	21	SESW	1858-11-01		A1
3949	" "	21	SWNE	1858-11-01		A1
3950	" "	21	SWNW	1858-11-01		A1
3951	" "	21	SWSE	1858-11-01		A1
4007	SMITH, James M	30	E½SE	1888-01-21		A2
4057	SMITH, John	33	SENE	1854-07-15		A1
4058	" "	34	SWNW	1854-07-15		A1
4160	SMITH, William T	15	NESW	1858-11-01		A1
4161	" "	20	SWNE	1858-11-01		A1 R3861
3952	SNELGROVE, Henry	26	SESW	1885-03-16		A2
3953	" "	26	SWSE	1885-03-16		A2
3954	SNELGROVE, Hezekiah	26	S½NE	1889-03-01		A2
3858	SORCER, Benjamin F	12	SW	1858-11-01		A1
4011	STAMPS, James	14	NESW	1882-11-20		A2
4159	STAMPS, William	28	NENE	1890-07-03		A2
3840	STOTT, Abdiel	2	NENE	1858-11-01		A1
3844	TAYLOR, Alfred S	28	NENW	1919-09-29		A1
4023	THOMAS, Jim	8	NE	1891-06-19		A2
3839	THOMASON, Aaron M	2	SWNE	1848-04-01		A1
4137	TYNES, Wiley	34	SWSW	1858-11-01		A1
4012	WALKER, James	18	E½NE	1858-11-01		A1
4013	" "	18	NESE	1858-11-01		A1
3871	WALTERS, Bryant D	5	NENW	1858-11-01		A1
3872	" "	5	NWNE	1858-11-01		A1
3873	" "	5	SWNE	1858-11-01		A1
3874	WARD, Cornie H	32	S½NW	1858-11-01		A1
3875	" "	32	W½SW	1858-11-01		A1
4059	WHITTINGTON, John T	9	NESE	1854-07-15		A1
3876	WILLIAMS, Daniel B	1	SWNW	1858-11-01		A1
3877	" "	1	SWSW	1858-11-01		A1
3878	" "	2	E½SE	1858-11-01		A1
3879	" "	2	SENE	1858-11-01		A1

Patent Map

T8-N R13-E
St Stephens Meridian

Map Group 17

Township Statistics

Parcels Mapped	:	325
Number of Patents	:	217
Number of Individuals	:	139
Patentees Identified	:	139
Number of Surnames	:	94
Multi-Patentee Parcels	:	0
Oldest Patent Date	:	4/10/1837
Most Recent Patent	:	9/29/1919
Block/Lot Parcels	:	0
Parcels Re - Issued	:	1
Parcels that Overlap	:	2
Cities and Towns	:	2
Cemeteries	:	5

Section 6
COLEMAN Joab 1858
AINSWORTH Frank L 1885
HARRISON Henry 1858
HARRISON Henry 1852
HARRISON Henry 1852
HARRISON Henry 1860
HARRISON Henry 1858
HARRISON Henry 1852
HARRISON Henry 1858
HARRISON Henry 1860
SIMS Elihu 1858
SIMS Elihu 1858
MORROW Abraham S 1891

Section 5
WALTERS Bryant D 1858
WALTERS Bryant D 1858
PUGH Mastin B 1858
WALTERS Bryant D 1858
BLACK James M 1858

Section 4
PUGH Masten B 1858
LOURY James 1858
LOURY James 1858
PUGH Masten B 1858
BLACK Hugh L 1858
BLACK Hugh L 1858
SHEPARD James B 1858
BLACK James M 1858
BLACK Hugh L 1858
BLACK James M 1858
PARKER Benjamin 1838
MYERS David B 1858

Section 7
BURKETT James 1858
SIMS Elihu 1858
SIMS Elihu 1858
PARKER Eldridge 1838
NORRIS Benjamin 1858
SIMS Elihu 1858
SIMS Stephen 1858
MCBRIDE David 1858
NORRIS Benjamin 1858
ENGLISH James B 1875
SIMS Stephen 1858
ENGLISH James B 1875

Section 8
PARKER Benjamin 1838
GAY Solomon 1858
THOMAS Jim 1891
SIMS Stephen 1858
SIMS Arthur 1858
SIMS Arthur 1858
SIMS Arthur 1858
BINION Temus 1896

Section 9
BLACK James M 1858
PARKER Benjamin 1838
CLOPTON Nathaniel V 1858
HEAP William J 1858
HEAP William J 1858
HEAP William J 1858
WHITTINGTON John T 1854
SHEPPARD James 1837
SHEPHERD John S 1837
FAIL William 1852

Section 18
FAILES Alexander 1882
MARSHALL William B 1858
WALKER James 1858
RILEY Travis M 1858
MARSHALL William B 1858
RILEY Travis M 1858
RILEY Larkin G 1858
WALKER James 1858
RILEY Travis M 1858
RILEY Larkin G 1858
LEE Emily H 1885

Section 17
SIMS Arthur 1858
SIMS Arthur 1858
SIMS Arthur 1858
ELLIS John G 1860
INGRAM Isaac 1858
INGRAM Isaac 1858
INGRAM Irad 1858
INGRAM Irad 1858
ELLIS John G 1860
ELLIS John G 1860
LEE Benjamin N 1858

Section 16

Section 19
LEE John 1858
LEE John 1858
RILEY Larkin G 1850
RILEY Larkind G 1858
GIBSON James G 1858
RILEY Larkin G 1850
GIBSON James G 1858
GIBSON James G 1858
LEE John 1858
BRANSFORD Nathan 1858

Section 20
MORROW Abraham 1858

Section 21
LEE Benjamin N 1858
SMITH William T 1858
LEE Benjamin N 1858
SMITH Henry 1858
MORROW George H 1858
MORROW George H 1858
MORROW George H 1858
SMITH Henry 1858
SMITH Henry 1858
SMITH Henry 1858
SMITH Henry 1858
SMITH Henry 1858
LEE Joel W 1837
SMITH Henry 1858
SMITH Henry 1858
SMITH Henry 1858
FAILS John 1858
SMITH Henry 1858

Section 30
PRICE George W 1858
CARTER Harbert 1880
BRANSFORD Nathan 1858
BRANSFORD Nathan 1837
KENDALL Isaac J 1858
BRANSFORD John H 1858
MAY Drewry B 1858
PRICE David S 1858
PRICE David S 1858
MAY Drewry B 1858
SMITH James M 1888

Section 29
HARPER Berry 1858
HARPER Berry 1858
HARPER Berry 1858
BRANSFORD John H 1858
COOK Laurence E 1858
COOK Laurence E 1858

Section 28
TAYLOR Alfred S 1919
MILNER Pitts S 1858
STAMPS William 1890
MILNER Pitts S 1858
SINGLETARY Joseph 1890
SINGLETARY Joseph 1890
MILNER Pitts S 1858
MILNER Pitt S 1858
SINGLETARY Joseph 1890
GIBSON James G 1858
MILNER Pitt S 1858
MILNER Pitts S 1858
MILNER Pitts S 1858

Section 31
MAY Drewry B 1858
MAY Drewry B 1858
BENNETT Thomas 1858
BENNETT Thomas 1858
ETHEREGE Lewis 1858
HOBBS Jacob 1858
HOBBS Jacob 1858
ETHEREGE Lewis 1858

Section 32
COOK Laurence E 1858
WARD Cornie H 1858
COOK Laurence E 1858
WARD Cornie H 1858
RUSTIN Eldridge C 1858
RUSTIN Eldridge C 1858
MAY Drury B 1861

Section 33
GIBSON James G 1858
MILNER Pitts S 1858
LEE Joel W 1858
HOBBS Elijah J 1858
BROOKS Drewry W 1858
SMITH John 1854
HOBBS Elijah J 1858
BROOKS Drewry W 1858
BROOKS Drewry W 1858
POWELL John 1837

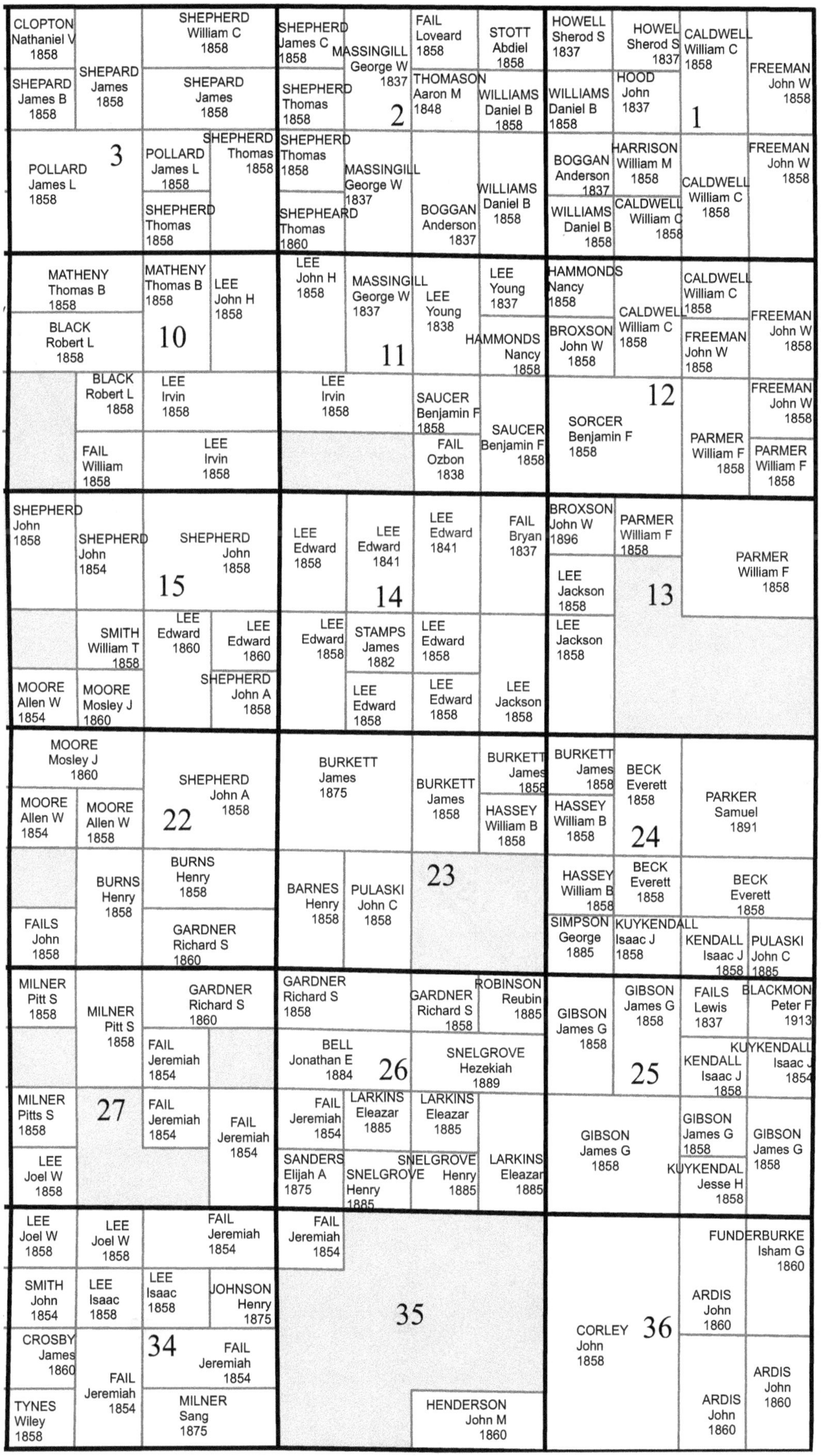
CLOPTON Nathaniel V 1858
SHEPARD James 1858
SHEPHERD William C 1858
SHEPARD James B 1858
SHEPARD James 1858
3
POLLARD James L 1858
SHEPHERD Thomas 1858
POLLARD James L 1858
SHEPHERD Thomas 1858
SHEPHERD James C 1858
MASSINGILL George W 1837
FAIL Loveard 1858
STOTT Abdiel 1858
SHEPHERD Thomas 1858
THOMASON Aaron M 1848
WILLIAMS Daniel B 1858
2
SHEPHERD Thomas 1858
MASSINGILL George W 1837
WILLIAMS Daniel B 1858
SHEPHEARD Thomas 1860
BOGGAN Anderson 1837
HOWELL Sherod S 1837
HOWEL Sherod S 1837
CALDWELL William C 1858
FREEMAN John W 1858
WILLIAMS Daniel B 1858
HOOD John 1837
1
BOGGAN Anderson 1837
HARRISON William M 1858
FREEMAN John W 1858
CALDWELL William C 1858
WILLIAMS Daniel B 1858
CALDWELL William C 1858
MATHENY Thomas B 1858
MATHENY Thomas B 1858
LEE John H 1858
BLACK Robert L 1858
10
BLACK Robert L 1858
LEE Irvin 1858
FAIL William 1858
LEE Irvin 1858
LEE John H 1858
MASSINGILL George W 1837
LEE Young 1838
LEE Young 1837
HAMMONDS Nancy 1858
11
LEE Irvin 1858
SAUCER Benjamin F 1858
SAUCER Benjamin F 1858
FAIL Ozbon 1838
HAMMONDS Nancy 1858
CALDWELL William C 1858
CALDWELL William C 1858
BROXSON John W 1858
FREEMAN John W 1858
FREEMAN John W 1858
12
SORCER Benjamin F 1858
FREEMAN John W 1858
PARMER William F 1858
PARMER William F 1858
SHEPHERD John 1858
SHEPHERD John 1854
SHEPHERD John 1858
15
SMITH William T 1858
LEE Edward 1860
LEE Edward 1860
MOORE Allen W 1854
MOORE Mosley J 1860
SHEPHERD John A 1858
LEE Edward 1858
LEE Edward 1841
LEE Edward 1841
FAIL Bryan 1837
14
LEE Edward 1858
STAMPS James 1882
LEE Edward 1858
LEE Edward 1858
LEE Edward 1858
LEE Jackson 1858
BROXSON John W 1896
PARMER William F 1858
PARMER William F 1858
LEE Jackson 1858
13
LEE Jackson 1858
MOORE Mosley J 1860
SHEPHERD John A 1858
MOORE Allen W 1854
MOORE Allen W 1858
22
BURNS Henry 1858
BURNS Henry 1858
FAILS John 1858
GARDNER Richard S 1860
BURKETT James 1875
BURKETT James 1858
BURKETT James 1858
HASSEY William B 1858
23
BARNES Henry 1858
PULASKI John C 1858
BURKETT James 1858
BECK Everett 1858
HASSEY William B 1858
24
PARKER Samuel 1891
HASSEY William B 1858
BECK Everett 1858
BECK Everett 1858
SIMPSON George 1885
KUYKENDALL Isaac J 1858
KENDALL Isaac J 1858
PULASKI John C 1885
MILNER Pitt S 1858
MILNER Pitt S 1858
GARDNER Richard S 1860
FAIL Jeremiah 1854
MILNER Pitts S 1858
27
FAIL Jeremiah 1854
FAIL Jeremiah 1854
LEE Joel W 1858
GARDNER Richard S 1858
GARDNER Richard S 1858
ROBINSON Reubin 1885
BELL Jonathan E 1884
26
SNELGROVE Hezekiah 1889
FAIL Jeremiah 1854
LARKINS Eleazar 1885
LARKINS Eleazar 1885
SANDERS Elijah A 1875
SNELGROVE Henry 1885
SNELGROVE Henry 1885
LARKINS Eleazar 1885
GIBSON James G 1858
GIBSON James G 1858
FAILS Lewis 1837
BLACKMON Peter F 1913
KUYKENDALL Isaac J 1854
KENDALL Isaac J 1858
25
GIBSON James G 1858
GIBSON James G 1858
GIBSON James G 1858
KUYKENDAL Jesse H 1858
LEE Joel W 1858
LEE Joel W 1858
FAIL Jeremiah 1854
SMITH John 1854
LEE Isaac 1858
LEE Isaac 1858
JOHNSON Henry 1875
CROSBY James 1860
34
FAIL Jeremiah 1854
FAIL Jeremiah 1854
TYNES Wiley 1858
MILNER Sang 1875
FAIL Jeremiah 1854
35
HENDERSON John M 1860
FUNDERBURKE Isham G 1860
ARDIS John 1860
CORLEY John 1858
36
ARDIS John 1860
ARDIS John 1860

Helpful Hints

1. This Map's INDEX can be found on the preceding pages.
2. Refer to Map "C" to see where this Township lies within Butler County, Alabama.
3. Numbers within square brackets [ ] denote a multi-patentee land parcel (multi-owner). Refer to Appendix "C" for a full list of members in this group.
4. Areas that look to be crowded with Patentees usually indicate multiple sales of the same parcel (Re-issues) or Overlapping parcels. See this Township's Index for an explanation of these and other circumstances that might explain "odd" groupings of Patentees on this map.

Legend

- Patent Boundary
- Section Boundary
- No Patents Found (or Outside County)
- 1., 2., 3., ... Lot Numbers (when beside a name)
- [ ] Group Number (see Appendix "C")

Scale: Section = 1 mile X 1 mile (generally, with some exceptions)

Road Map

T8-N R13-E
St Stephens Meridian

Map Group 17

Cities & Towns
Chapman
Georgiana

Cemeteries
Ebenezer Cemetery
Friendship Cemetery
Miller Cemetery
Oak Grove Cemetery
Oakwood Cemetery

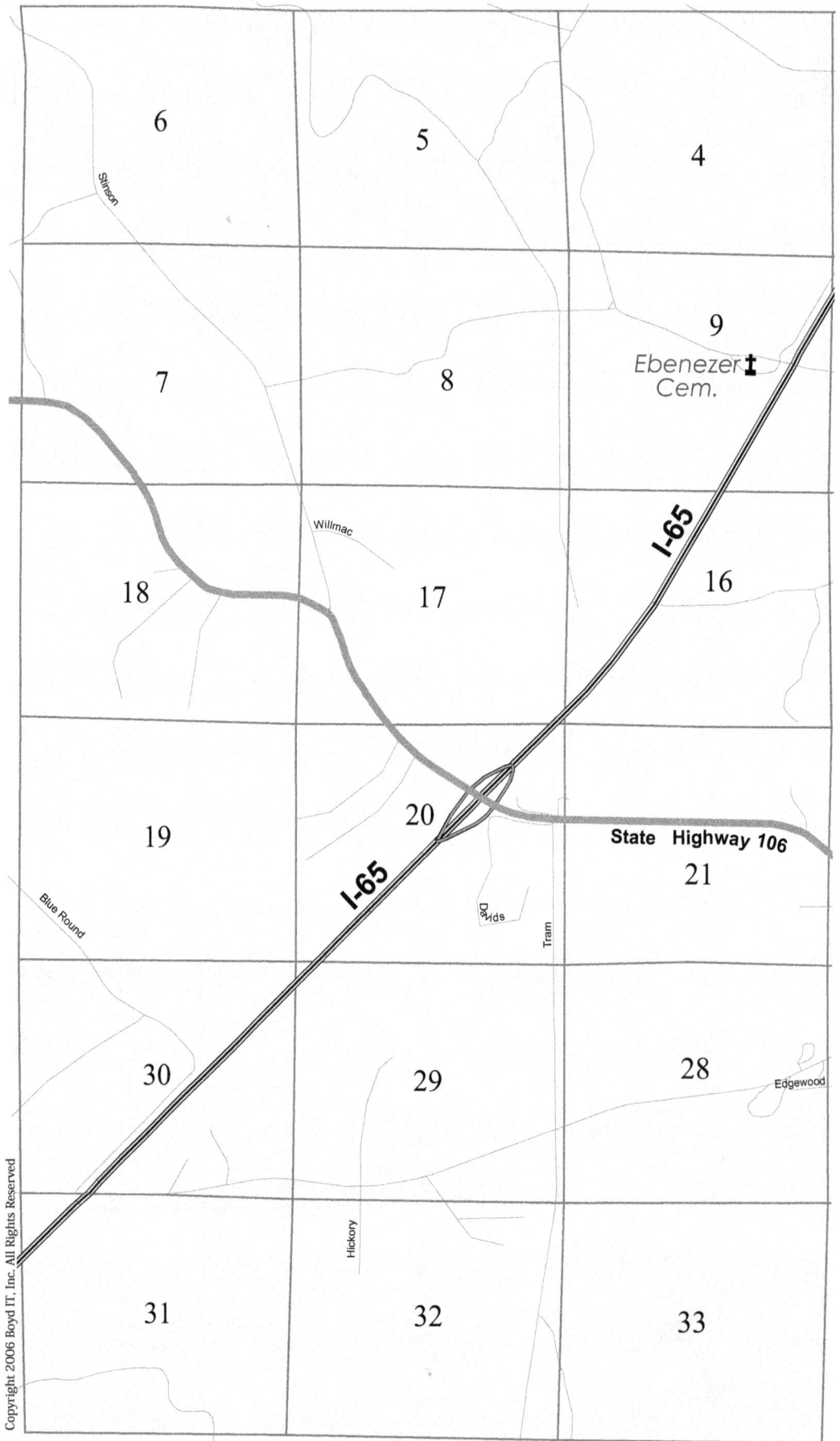

6   5   4

7   8   9

Ebenezer Cem.

18   17   16

Willmac

I-65

19   20   21

State Highway 106

Blue Round

Davids   Tram

30   29   28

Edgewood

Hickory

31   32   33

Stinson

3

2

1

Bolling

Helpful Hints

1. This road map has a number of uses, but primarily it is to help you: a) find the present location of land owned by your ancestors (at least the general area), b) find cemeteries and city-centers, and c) estimate the route/roads used by Census-takers & tax-assessors.

2. If you plan to travel to Butler County to locate cemeteries or land parcels, please pick up a modern travel map for the area before you do. Mapping old land parcels on modern maps is not as exact a science as you might think. Just the slightest variations in public land survey coordinates, estimates of parcel boundaries, or road-map deviations can greatly alter a map's representation of how a road either does or doesn't cross a particular parcel of land.

10

11

12

● Chapman

Spann

Royal Crest

Dogwood

Gravel
Hill

15

Ebenezer

14

13

Ripley

Hill

Clipper

Windchime

Railroad

Mobile

White

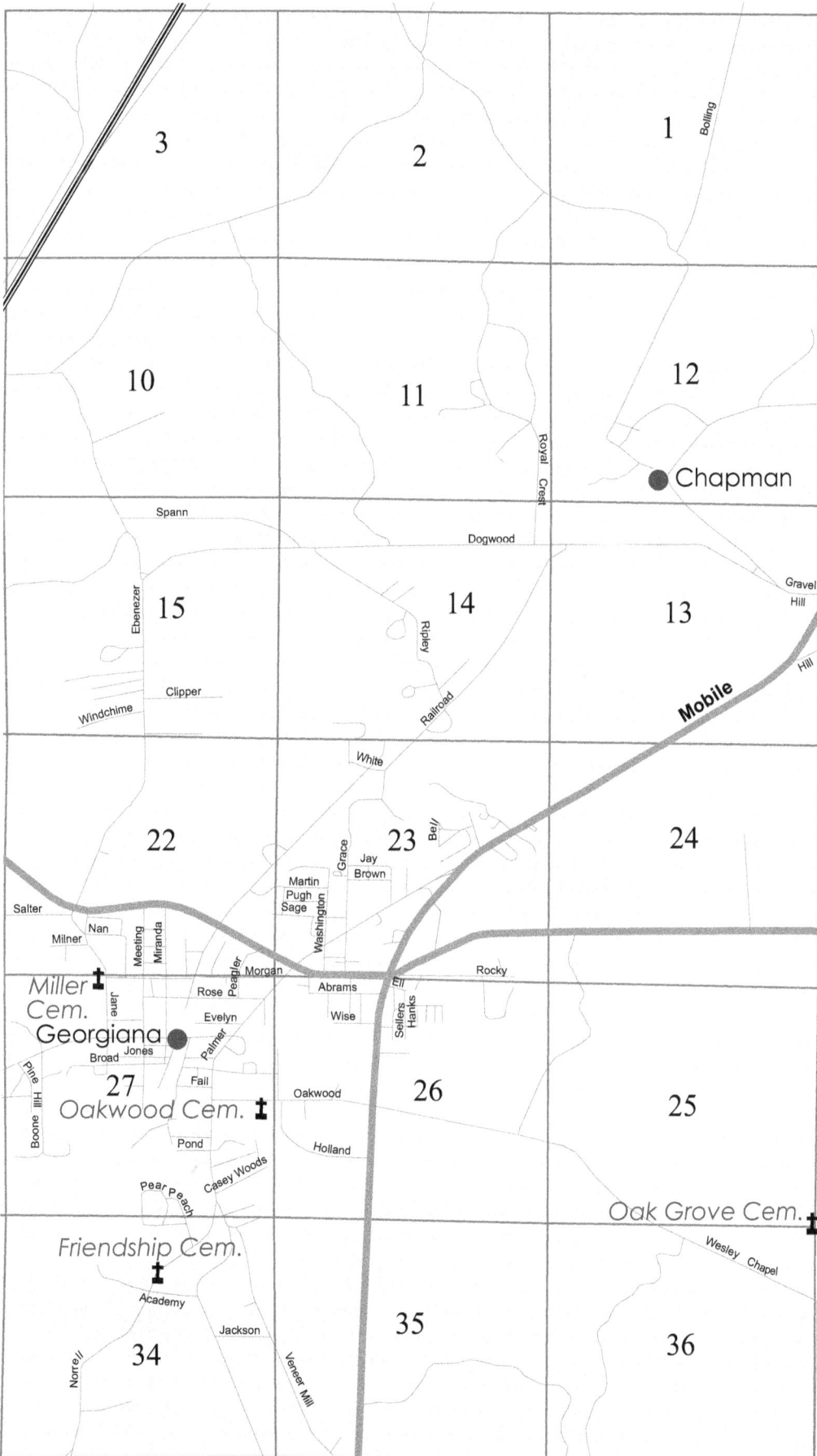

22

Grace

23

Bell

24

Jay
Brown

Martin
Pugh
Sage

Washington

Salter

Nan

Miranda
Meeting

Milner

Morgan

Rocky

Peagler

Rose

Abrams

Ell

L e g e n d

Miller
Cem. ✝

Jane

Evelyn

Wise

Sellers
Hanks

Section Lines

Georgiana ●

Jones

Palmer

Broad

Interstates

Pine Hill

27

Fail

Oakwood

26

25

Highways

Boone

Oakwood Cem. ✝

Pond

Holland

Other Roads

Casey Woods

Pear Peach

Oak Grove Cem. ✝

● Cities/Towns

Friendship Cem.

✝

Wesley Chapel

✝ Cemeteries

Academy

Jackson

Scale: Section = 1 mile X 1 mile
(generally, with some exceptions)

Norrell

34

Veneer Mill

35

36

Historical Map

T8-N R13-E
St Stephens Meridian

Map Group 17

Cities & Towns
Chapman
Georgiana

Cemeteries
Ebenezer Cemetery
Friendship Cemetery
Miller Cemetery
Oak Grove Cemetery
Oakwood Cemetery

Oaklog Creek

Panther Creek

6

5

4

7

8

9

Ebenezer Cem. ‡

18

17

16

19

20

21

Wise Pond

30

29

28

Panther Creek

31

32

33

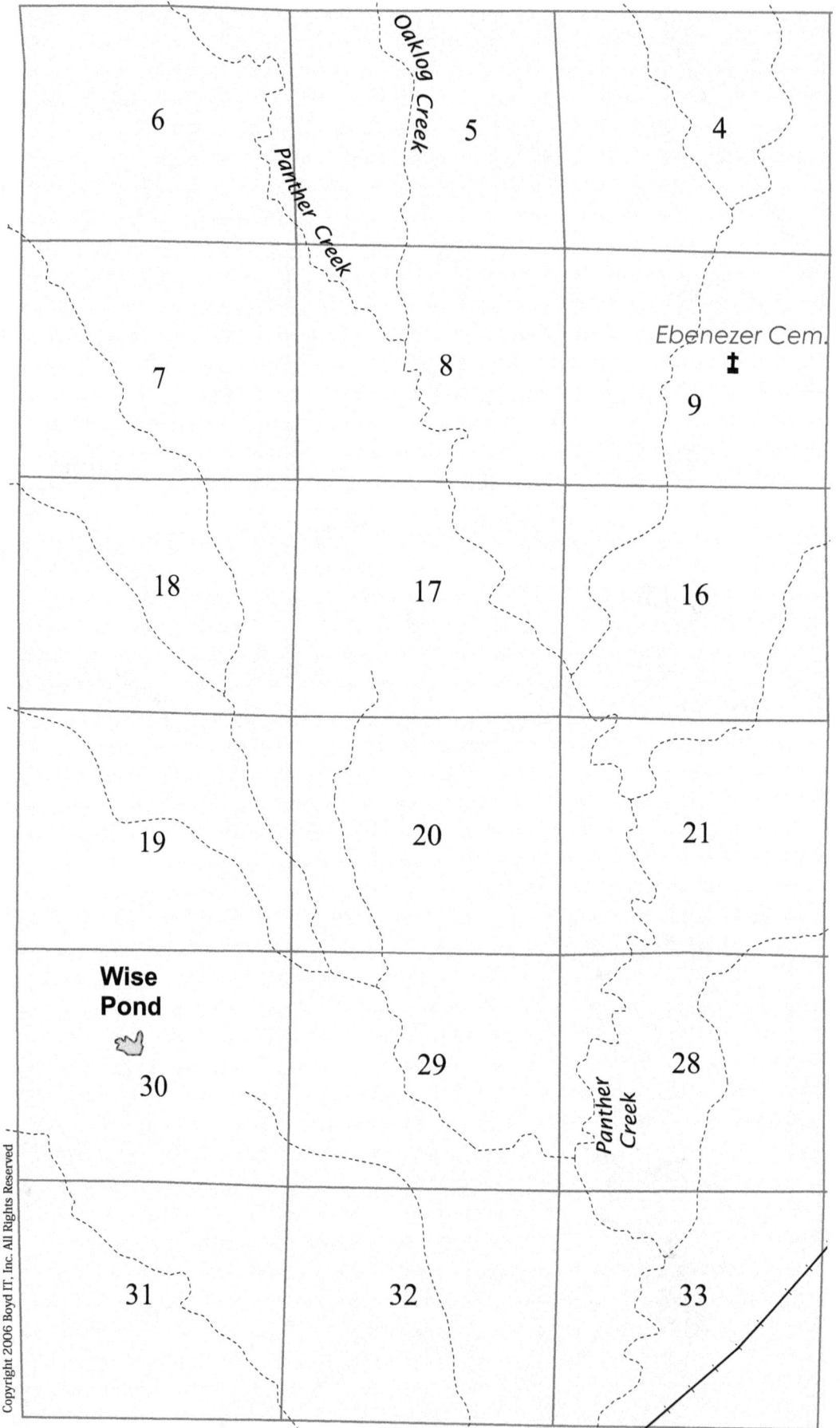

3

2

Rocky Creek

1

11

12

10

Chapman

15

14

Martin Creek

13

22

23

24

Miller Cem.

Georgiana

27

Oakwood Cem.

26

25

Oak Grove Cem.

Friendship Cem.

35

36

34

Helpful Hints

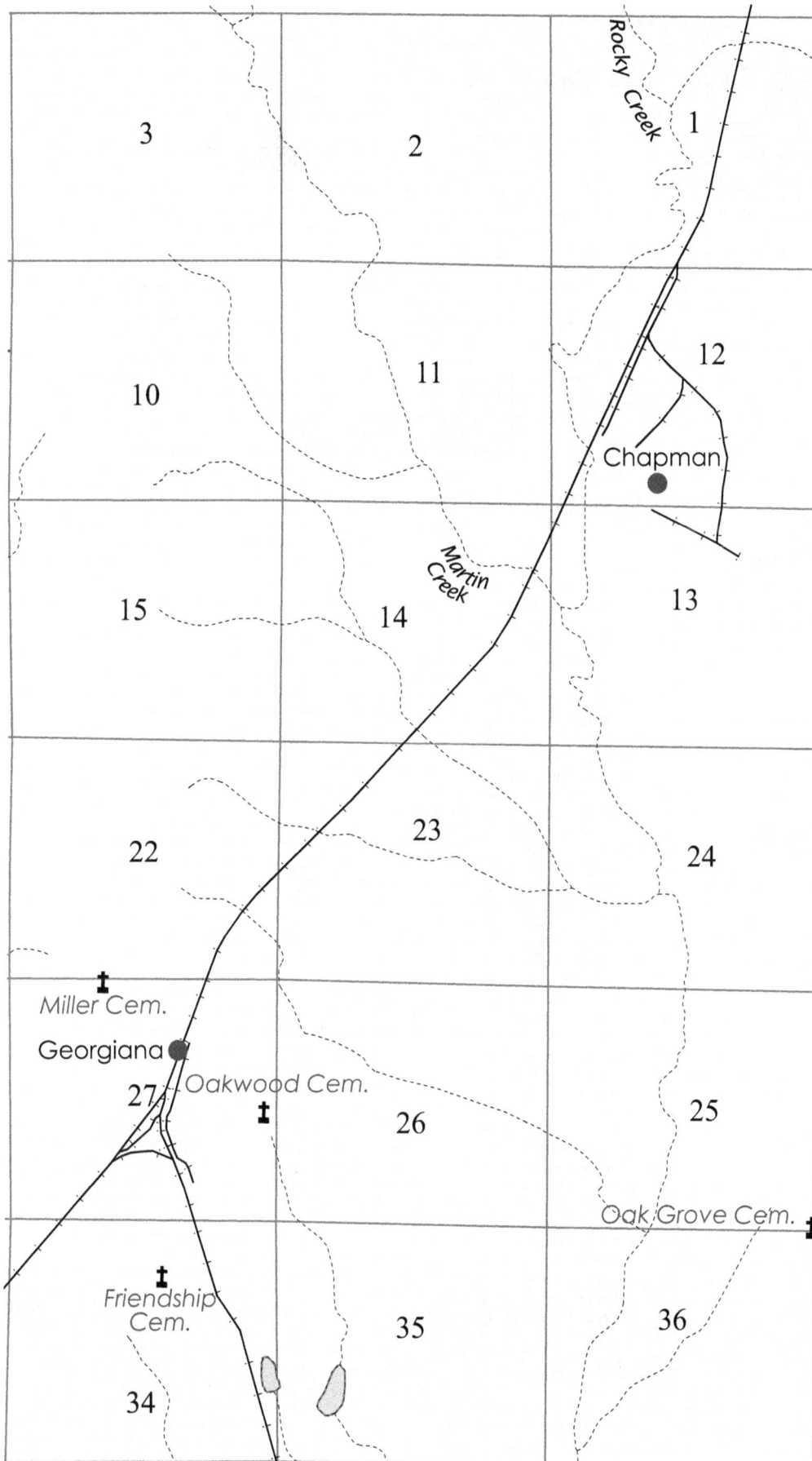

1. This Map takes a different look at the same Congressional Township displayed in the preceding two maps. It presents features that can help you better envision the historical development of the area: a) Water-bodies (lakes & ponds), b) Water-courses (rivers, streams, etc.), c) Railroads, d) City/town center-points (where they were oftentimes located when first settled), and e) Cemeteries.

2. Using this "Historical" map in tandem with this Township's Patent Map and Road Map, may lead you to some interesting discoveries. You will often find roads, towns, cemeteries, and waterways are named after nearby landowners: sometimes those names will be the ones you are researching. See how many of these research gems you can find here in Butler County.

Legend

——	Section Lines
+++++	Railroads
▨	Large Rivers & Bodies of Water
- - - -	Streams/Creeks & Small Rivers
●	Cities/Towns
✝	Cemeteries

Scale: Section = 1 mile X 1 mile
(there are some exceptions)

233

Map Group 18: Index to Land Patents

Township 8-North Range 14-East (St Stephens)

After you locate an individual in this Index, take note of the Section and Section Part then proceed to the Land Patent map on the pages immediately following. You should have no difficulty locating the corresponding parcel of land.

The "For More Info" Column will lead you to more information about the underlying Patents. See the *Legend* at right, and the "How to Use this Book" chapter, for more information.

```
                        LEGEND
              "For More Info . . . " column
  A = Authority (Legislative Act, See Appendix "A")
  B = Block or Lot (location in Section unknown)
  C = Cancelled Patent
  F = Fractional Section
  G = Group (Multi-Patentee Patent, see Appendix "C")
  V = Overlaps another Parcel
  R = Re-Issued (Parcel patented more than once)

  (A & G items require you to look in the Appendixes referred
  to above. All other Letter-designations followed by a number
  require you to locate line-items in this index that possess
  the ID number found after the letter).
```

ID	Individual in Patent	Sec.	Sec. Part	Date Issued	Other Counties	For More Info . . .
4323	ADAMS, Samuel	34	S½NE	1860-10-01		A1
4324	" "	34	SENW	1860-10-01		A1
4325	" "	34	SWSE	1860-10-01		A1
4190	ARANT, Elvin P	24	NENW	1860-10-01		A1
4191	" "	24	W½NW	1860-10-01		A1
4192	" "	24	W½SW	1860-10-01		A1
4224	ARANT, Jacob	23	SE	1858-11-01		A1
4225	" "	26	NENW	1858-11-01		A1
4226	" "	26	NWNE	1858-11-01		A1
4227	" "	27	N½NE	1858-11-01		A1
4223	" "	22	W½SE	1860-10-01		A1
4255	ARDIS, John	14	W½NE	1860-10-01		A1
4256	" "	20	SESW	1860-10-01		A1
4257	" "	20	W½SW	1860-10-01		A1
4193	BECK, Everett	19	NWSW	1858-11-01		A1
4206	BENDER, Griffin M	28	W½SW	1837-04-10		A1 V4328, 4362
4203	BENNETT, George W	20	E½NE	1891-06-08		A2
4318	BERRY, Rhoda	34	NWSE	1858-11-01		A1
4228	BLACKMAN, James	22	NWSW	1891-12-01		A1
4229	" "	22	W½NW	1891-12-01		A1
4247	BLACKMON, James S	22	SWSW	1904-05-05		A2
4241	BLAIR, James M	7	SW	1858-11-01		A1
4242	" "	7	SWNE	1858-11-01		A1
4243	" "	7	SWNW	1858-11-01		A1
4244	" "	7	W½SE	1858-11-01		A1
4335	BLAIR, William	6	N½SW	1858-11-01		A1
4336	" "	6	NWSE	1858-11-01		A1
4337	" "	6	S½NE	1858-11-01		A1
4338	" "	6	S½NW	1858-11-01		A1
4168	BRADLEY, Alsey	32	NENE	1858-11-01		A1
4181	BRADLEY, Austin	32	NWNE	1885-06-12		A2
4182	" "	32	S½NE	1885-06-12		A2
4230	BRASSWELL, James	1	NENE	1897-03-18		A1
4167	BRIGHT, Alfred	18	SESW	1885-03-16		A2
4180	BRIGHT, Ashley	18	W½SW	1883-09-15		A2
4171	BROWN, Andrew J	22	E½SE	1858-11-01		A1
4172	" "	23	NW	1858-11-01		A1
4173	" "	23	W½SW	1858-11-01		A1
4198	BROWN, Francis M	2	NWSE	1875-04-20		A1
4199	" "	2	W½NE	1875-04-20		A1
4209	BURKE, Henry F	8	E½SW	1860-10-01		A1
4210	" "	8	W½NW	1860-10-01		A1
4211	" "	8	W½SW	1860-10-01		A1
4258	BURKE, John	15	W½NW	1858-11-01		A1
4354	BUSH, William P	2	E½NE	1858-11-01		A1
4355	" "	2	E½SE	1858-11-01		A1

ID	Individual in Patent	Sec.	Sec. Part	Date Issued	Other Counties	For More Info . . .
4356	BUSH, William P (Cont'd)	2	SESW	1858-11-01		A1
4357	" "	2	SWSE	1858-11-01		A1
4303	BUTLER, Madison	32	S½SW	1885-06-12		A2
4304	" "	32	SWSE	1901-11-16		A2
4284	COHRON, Leonidas B	8	E½SE	1890-07-03		A2
4169	COX, Andrew	15	N½NE	1913-06-21		A2
4170	" "	15	NENW	1913-06-21		A2
4215	CRENSHAW, Howel	20	SE	1885-04-27		A2
4207	DAVIDSON, Henry	30	SENW	1885-11-13		A1
4208	" "	30	SWNE	1885-11-13		A1
4165	DEMING, Albert	4	SWSW	1854-07-15		A1
4166	" "	5	NWSE	1854-07-15		A1
4194	DEMING, Ezra	4	E½SW	1858-11-01		A1
4195	" "	4	NWSW	1858-11-01		A1
4196	" "	4	SE	1858-11-01		A1
4197	" "	4	SWNW	1858-11-01		A1
4185	DENDY, Buford W	12	SESE	1860-09-01		A1
4186	" "	36	E½NE	1860-09-01		A1
4290	DUKE, Lewis D	4	N½NW	1897-07-03		A2
4291	" "	4	SENW	1897-07-03		A2
4292	" "	4	SWNE	1897-07-03		A2
4253	EVANS, Jim	14	N½SW	1893-05-26		A2
4254	" "	14	S½NW	1893-05-26		A2
4283	FAIL, Leonard	6	E½SE	1860-10-01		A1
4295	FAIL, Loveard	6	S½SW	1858-11-01		A1
4296	" "	6	SWSE	1858-11-01		A1
4297	" "	7	N½NW	1858-11-01		A1
4298	" "	7	NWNE	1858-11-01		A1
4299	" "	7	SENW	1858-11-01		A1
4245	FORTUNE, James M	32	N½SW	1885-03-30		A2
4262	FRIDDLE, John	23	NENE	1852-12-01		A1
4259	" "	14	E½SE	1858-11-01		A1
4261	" "	14	SWSE	1858-11-01		A1
4260	" "	14	NWSE	1860-04-02		A1
4234	GIBSON, James G	26	NWSW	1858-11-01		A1
4235	" "	27	NESW	1858-11-01		A1
4236	" "	27	SENW	1858-11-01		A1
4237	" "	27	SWNE	1858-11-01		A1
4238	" "	27	SWSE	1858-11-01		A1 V4346
4276	GREEN, Joseph E	10	E½NW	1891-05-29		A2
4277	" "	10	W½SW	1897-11-22		A2
4306	HALL, Martha E	32	S½NW	1883-10-01		A2
4267	HALLFORD, John	23	E½SW	1837-08-14		A1
4268	" "	26	NWNW	1837-08-14		A1
4312	HALLFORD, Owen	11	NESE	1838-07-28		A1
4269	HAMMONDS, John	1	SWSW	1848-04-01		A1
4308	HAMMONDS, Meshack G	11	N½SW	1858-11-01		A1
4309	" "	11	NWSE	1858-11-01		A1
4310	" "	11	W½NE	1858-11-01		A1
4231	HARRISON, James E	7	E½NE	1858-11-01		A1
4232	" "	7	NESE	1858-11-01		A1
4246	HARRISON, James P	5	SESW	1858-11-01		A1
4233	HEATHCOCK, James F	2	W½SW	1885-03-30		A2
4179	HINSON, Asa	27	NESE	1837-08-14		A1
4177	HINSON, Asa E	26	SWNW	1858-11-01		A1
4178	" "	27	SENE	1858-11-01		A1
4331	HINSON, Tilmon G	11	E½NE	1858-11-01		A1
4332	" "	12	NWSW	1858-11-01		A1
4333	" "	12	S½NW	1858-11-01		A1
4334	" "	12	SWSW	1858-11-01		A1
4239	HODGES, James	1	SENW	1858-11-01		A1
4240	" "	1	W½NW	1858-11-01		A1
4346	JACKSON, William	27	S½SE	1858-11-01		A1 V4238
4347	" "	27	SESW	1858-11-01		A1
4348	" "	34	NENE	1858-11-01		A1
4349	" "	34	NENW	1858-11-01		A1
4263	JOHNSON, John H	24	SENW	1885-03-16		A2
4264	" "	24	SWNE	1885-03-16		A2
4342	JOINER, William H	24	E½NE	1883-03-01		A2
4343	" "	24	W½SE	1883-03-01		A2
4285	JONES, Levi	9	NESE	1858-11-01		A1
4286	" "	9	S½NE	1858-11-01		A1
4287	" "	9	SENW	1858-11-01		A1

ID	Individual in Patent	Sec.	Sec. Part	Date Issued	Other Counties	For More Info . . .
4288	JONES, Levi (Cont'd)	9	SWNW	1858-11-01		A1
4350	JONES, William	12	SESW	1860-04-02		A1
4351	" "	12	SWSE	1860-04-02		A1
4352	" "	13	NENW	1860-04-02		A1
4353	" "	13	NWNE	1860-04-02		A1
4320	JOYNER, Robert J	26	SENW	1885-05-25		A2
4321	" "	26	SWNE	1885-05-25		A2
4175	KELSOE, Angus	33	E½SE	1858-11-01		A1
4176	" "	34	SWSW	1858-11-01		A1
4319	LANCASTER, Riley A	20	W½NE	1890-03-19		A2
4344	LANE, William H	34	NESE	1860-09-01		A1
4248	LEONARD, James S	23	W½NE	1841-05-20		A1
4307	LUDLAM, Mary J	18	SESE	1891-11-23		A2 G28
4307	LUDLAM, Samuel	18	SESE	1891-11-23		A2 G28
4183	MAJORS, Benjamin S	4	N½NE	1891-11-23		A2
4184	" "	4	SENE	1891-11-23		A2
4187	MAJORS, David	30	SE	1885-06-12		A2
4265	MCCALL, John H	10	E½SW	1895-02-23		A2
4300	MCCANN, Lucinda A	5	NW	1858-11-01		A1
4301	" "	6	N½NE	1858-11-01		A1
4302	" "	6	N½NW	1858-11-01		A1
4222	MERCER, Jacob A	28	N½SW	1884-03-10		A2 C
4221	" "	28	N½NE	1891-06-08		A2
4164	MOORE, Acy	10	NE	1891-11-23		A2
4217	MOORE, Isham	34	NWNE	1858-09-01		A1
4216	" "	34	NESW	1858-11-01		A1
4266	MOORE, John H	8	E½NW	1888-01-21		A2 G32
4293	MOORE, Lewis	12	NENW	1858-11-01		A1
4294	" "	12	NWNW	1858-11-01		A1
4266	MOORE, Nancy A	8	E½NW	1888-01-21		A2 G32
4270	NICHOLAS, John I	2	S½NW	1885-04-27		A2
4249	NICHOLES, Jasper N	10	W½SE	1891-05-29		A2
4271	NICHOLS, John J	2	N½NW	1891-06-08		A2
4345	NICHOLS, William H	10	E½SE	1891-11-23		A2
4326	OVERSTREET, Samuel	3	E½NW	1858-11-01		A1
4218	PARKER, Israel	24	E½NE	1860-10-01		A1
4219	" "	24	E½SE	1860-10-01		A1
4220	" "	24	NWNE	1860-10-01		A1
4202	PATTON, George	12	NWNE	1888-01-21		A2
4289	PEARCE, Levi	14	N½NW	1858-11-01		A1
4311	PERRITT, Needham	13	E½NE	1858-11-01		A1
4305	PETTY, Marion E	8	S½NE	1919-06-25		A2
4328	PORTER, Thomas M	28	NWSW	1884-03-10		A2 V4206
4330	" "	28	SWNW	1884-03-10		A2
4327	" "	28	NESW	1884-12-05		A2
4329	" "	28	SENW	1884-12-05		A2
4361	PORTER, William	28	S½SW	1891-10-07		A1
4362	" "	28	S½SW	1891-10-07		A1 V4206
4316	RIGSBY, Philo D	26	SWSW	1885-11-13		A1 G40
4317	RIGSBY, Ransom M	26	E½SW	1883-08-13		A2
4358	ROUTON, William P	18	N½NE	1860-10-01		A1
4359	" "	18	NENW	1860-10-01		A1
4360	" "	18	SWSE	1860-10-01		A1
4250	RYALS, Jesse	5	NESE	1853-11-15		A1
4251	" "	5	NESW	1858-11-01		A1
4252	" "	5	SWNE	1858-11-01		A1
4339	SARTOR, William C	33	SWSE	1858-11-01		A1
4200	SEXTON, Gabriel	28	N½SE	1891-06-18		A1
4201	" "	28	S½NE	1891-06-18		A1
4212	SHINE, Henry	20	E½NW	1886-04-10		A2
4314	SIMS, Peter	2	NESW	1897-10-05		A1
4322	SIMS, Sam	10	W½NW	1891-11-23		A2
4280	SINGLETON, Joseph T	18	W½NW	1858-11-01		A1
4278	" "	18	NESW	1860-04-02		A1
4279	" "	18	SENW	1860-04-02		A1
4188	SMITH, Eliza A	36	SW	1860-10-01		A1
4272	SMITH, John	1	SESW	1852-02-02		A1
4273	" "	1	W½SE	1852-02-02		A1
4189	TILLMAN, Elizabeth	12	NESW	1880-02-20		A2
4213	TILMAN, Henry	30	SW	1885-12-10		A2 G43
4213	TILMAN, Susan	30	SW	1885-12-10		A2 G43
4313	TOBIAS, Peter C	30	NWNE	1885-08-05		A1
4340	TURNER, William D	1	NENW	1858-11-01		A1

ID	Individual in Patent	Sec.	Sec. Part	Date Issued	Other Counties	For More Info . . .
4341	TURNER, William D (Cont'd)	1	NWNE	1858-11-01		A1
4363	WALKER, William W	30	N½NW	1891-06-19		A2
4214	WATERS, Henry	20	NESW	1891-06-19		A2
4174	WATSON, Andrew J	30	E½NE	1890-07-03		A2
4204	WATSON, Gilbert	29	SWSE	1858-11-01		A1
4205	" "	32	N½NW	1885-07-27		A1
4315	WATSON, Peter W	32	N½SE	1894-11-21		A2
4316	WATSON, William S	26	SWSW	1885-11-13		A1 G40
4364	WATSON, Willoby	20	W½NW	1884-03-10		A2
4275	WILLIAMS, John	14	E½NE	1837-08-14		A1
4274	" "	11	SESE	1838-07-28		A1
4281	WILLIAMS, Joseph	18	N½SE	1860-04-02		A1
4282	" "	18	S½NE	1860-04-02		A1
4365	WILLIAMS, Winney	25	NESE	1858-11-01		A1 C

Patent Map

T8-N R14-E
St Stephens Meridian

Map Group 18

Township Statistics

Parcels Mapped	:	202
Number of Patents	:	138
Number of Individuals	:	111
Patentees Identified	:	107
Number of Surnames	:	79
Multi-Patentee Parcels	:	4
Oldest Patent Date	:	4/10/1837
Most Recent Patent	:	6/25/1919
Block/Lot Parcels	:	0
Parcels Re - Issued	:	0
Parcels that Overlap	:	5
Cities and Towns	:	3
Cemeteries	:	5

Map parcels:

Section 6: MCCANN Lucinda A 1858; MCCANN Lucinda A 1858; BLAIR William 1858; BLAIR William 1858; BLAIR William 1858; BLAIR William 1858; FAIL Leonard 1860; FAIL Loveard 1858; FAIL Loveard 1858

Section 5: MCCANN Lucinda A 1858; RYALS Jesse 1858; RYALS Jesse 1858; DEMING Albert 1854; RYALS Jesse 1853; HARRISON James P 1858

Section 4: DUKE Lewis D 1897; MAJORS Benjamin S 1891; DEMING Ezra 1858; DUKE Lewis D 1897; DUKE Lewis D 1897; MAJORS Benjamin S 1891; DEMING Ezra 1858; DEMING Ezra 1858; DEMING Ezra 1858; DEMING Albert 1854

Section 7: FAIL Loveard 1858; FAIL Loveard 1858; HARRISON James E 1858; BLAIR James M 1858; FAIL Loveard 1858; BLAIR James M 1858; BLAIR James M 1858; HARRISON James E 1858; BLAIR James M 1858

Section 8: MOORE [32] John H 1888; PETTY Marion E 1919; BURKE Henry F 1860; BURKE Henry F 1860; BURKE Henry F 1860; COHRON Leonidas B 1890

Section 9: JONES Levi 1858; JONES Levi 1858; JONES Levi 1858; JONES Levi 1858

Section 18: ROUTON William P 1860; ROUTON William P 1860; SINGLETON Joseph T 1858; SINGLETON Joseph T 1860; WILLIAMS Joseph 1860; SINGLETON Joseph T 1860; WILLIAMS Joseph 1860; BRIGHT Ashley 1883; BRIGHT Alfred 1885; ROUTON William P 1860; LUDLAM [28] Mary J 1891

Section 17

Section 16

Section 19: BECK Everett 1858

Section 20: LANCASTER Riley A 1890; BENNETT George W 1891; WATSON Willoby 1884; SHINE Henry 1886; WATERS Henry 1891; CRENSHAW Howel 1885; ARDIS John 1860; ARDIS John 1860

Section 21

Section 30: WALKER William W 1891; TOBIAS Peter C 1885; WATSON Andrew J 1890; DAVIDSON Henry 1885; DAVIDSON Henry 1885; TILMAN [43] Henry 1885; MAJORS David 1885

Section 29: WATSON Gilbert 1858

Section 28: MERCER Jacob A 1891; PORTER Thomas M 1884; PORTER Thomas M 1884; SEXTON Gabriel 1891; PORTER Thomas M 1884; PORTER Thomas M 1884; MERCER Jacob A 1884; SEXTON Gabriel 1891; BENDER Griffin M 1837; PORTER William 1891; PORTER William 1891

Section 31

Section 32: WATSON Gilbert 1885; BRADLEY Austin 1885; BRADLEY Alsey 1858; HALL Martha E 1883; BRADLEY Austin 1885; FORTUNE James M 1885; WATSON Peter W 1894; BUTLER Madison 1885; BUTLER Madison 1901

Section 33: KELSOE Angus 1858; SARTOR William C 1858

OVERSTREET Samuel 1858	NICHOLS John J 1891	BROWN Francis M 1875	BUSH William P 1858	HODGES James 1858	TURNER William D 1858	TURNER William D 1858	BRASSWELL James 1897

3

NICHOLAS John I 1885

2

HEATHCOCK James F 1885 / SIMS Peter 1897 / BROWN Francis M 1875

BUSH William P 1858 / BUSH William P 1858 / BUSH William P 1858

HODGES James 1858

1

HAMMONDS John 1848 / SMITH John 1852

SMITH John 1852

SIMS Sam 1891 | GREEN Joseph E 1891 | MOORE Acy 1891 | **10**

MCCALL John H 1895

GREEN Joseph E 1897 | NICHOLES Jasper N 1891 | NICHOLS William H 1891

HAMMONDS Meshack G 1858 | **11** | HINSON Tilmon G 1858

HAMMONDS Meshack G 1858 | HAMMONDS Meshack G 1858 | HALLFORD Owen 1838

WILLIAMS John 1838

MOORE Lewis 1858 | MOORE Lewis 1858 | PATTON George 1888

HINSON Tilmon G 1858 | **12**

HINSON Tilmon G 1858 | TILLMAN Elizabeth 1880

HINSON Tilmon G 1858 | JONES William 1860 | JONES William 1860 | DENDY Buford W 1860

BURKE John 1858 | COX Andrew 1913 | COX Andrew 1913 | **15**

PEARCE Levi 1858 | EVANS Jim 1893 | EVANS Jim 1893 | **14**

ARDIS John 1860 | FRIDDLE John 1860 | FRIDDLE John 1858 | FRIDDLE John 1858

WILLIAMS John 1837

JONES William 1860 | JONES William 1860

13

PERRITT Needham 1858

BLACKMAN James 1891 | BLACKMAN James 1891 | BLACKMON James S 1904 | **22** | ARANT Jacob 1860 | BROWN Andrew J 1858

BROWN Andrew J 1858 | **23** | LEONARD James S 1841 | FRIDDLE John 1852

HALLFORD John 1837 | BROWN Andrew J 1858 | ARANT Jacob 1858

ARANT Elvin P 1860 | ARANT Elvin P 1860 | ARANT Elvin P 1860

JOHNSON John H 1885 | **24** | JOINER William H 1883

ARANT Elvin P 1860 / PARKER Israel 1860

JOHNSON John H 1885 / PARKER Israel 1860

PARKER Israel 1860

JOINER William H 1883

ARANT Jacob 1858

GIBSON James G 1858 | GIBSON James G 1858 | HINSON Asa E 1858 | **27** | HINSON Asa 1837

GIBSON James G 1858 | GIBSON James G 1858 | JACKSON William 1858

HALLFORD John 1837 | ARANT Jacob 1858 | ARANT Jacob 1858

HINSON Asa E 1858 | JOYNER Robert J 1885 | JOYNER Robert J 1885

GIBSON James G 1858 | RIGSBY Ransom M 1883 | **26**

RIGSBY [40] Philo D 1885

25

WILLIAMS Winney 1858

JACKSON William 1858 | MOORE Isham 1858 | JACKSON William 1858

ADAMS Samuel 1860 | **34** | ADAMS Samuel 1860

MOORE Isham 1858 | BERRY Rhoda 1858 | LANE William H 1860

KELSOE Angus 1858 | ADAMS Samuel 1860

35

SMITH Eliza A 1860

36

DENDY Buford W 1860

Copyright 2006 Boyd IT, Inc. All Rights Reserved

Helpful Hints

1. This Map's INDEX can be found on the preceding pages.

2. Refer to Map "C" to see where this Township lies within Butler County, Alabama.

3. Numbers within square brackets [ ] denote a multi-patentee land parcel (multi-owner). Refer to Appendix "C" for a full list of members in this group.

4. Areas that look to be crowded with Patentees usually indicate multiple sales of the same parcel (Re-issues) or Overlapping parcels. See this Township's Index for an explanation of these and other circumstances that might explain "odd" groupings of Patentees on this map.

Legend

———— Patent Boundary

━━━━ Section Boundary

No Patents Found (or Outside County)

1., 2., 3., ... Lot Numbers (when beside a name)

[ ] Group Number (see Appendix "C")

Scale: Section = 1 mile X 1 mile (generally, with some exceptions)

Road Map

T8-N R14-E
St Stephens Meridian

Map Group 18

Cities & Towns

Avant
Brushy Creek
East Chapman

Cemeteries

Brushy Creek Cemetery
Hopewell Cemetery
Mount Pleasant Cemetery
Union Cemetery
Wesley Chapel Cemetery

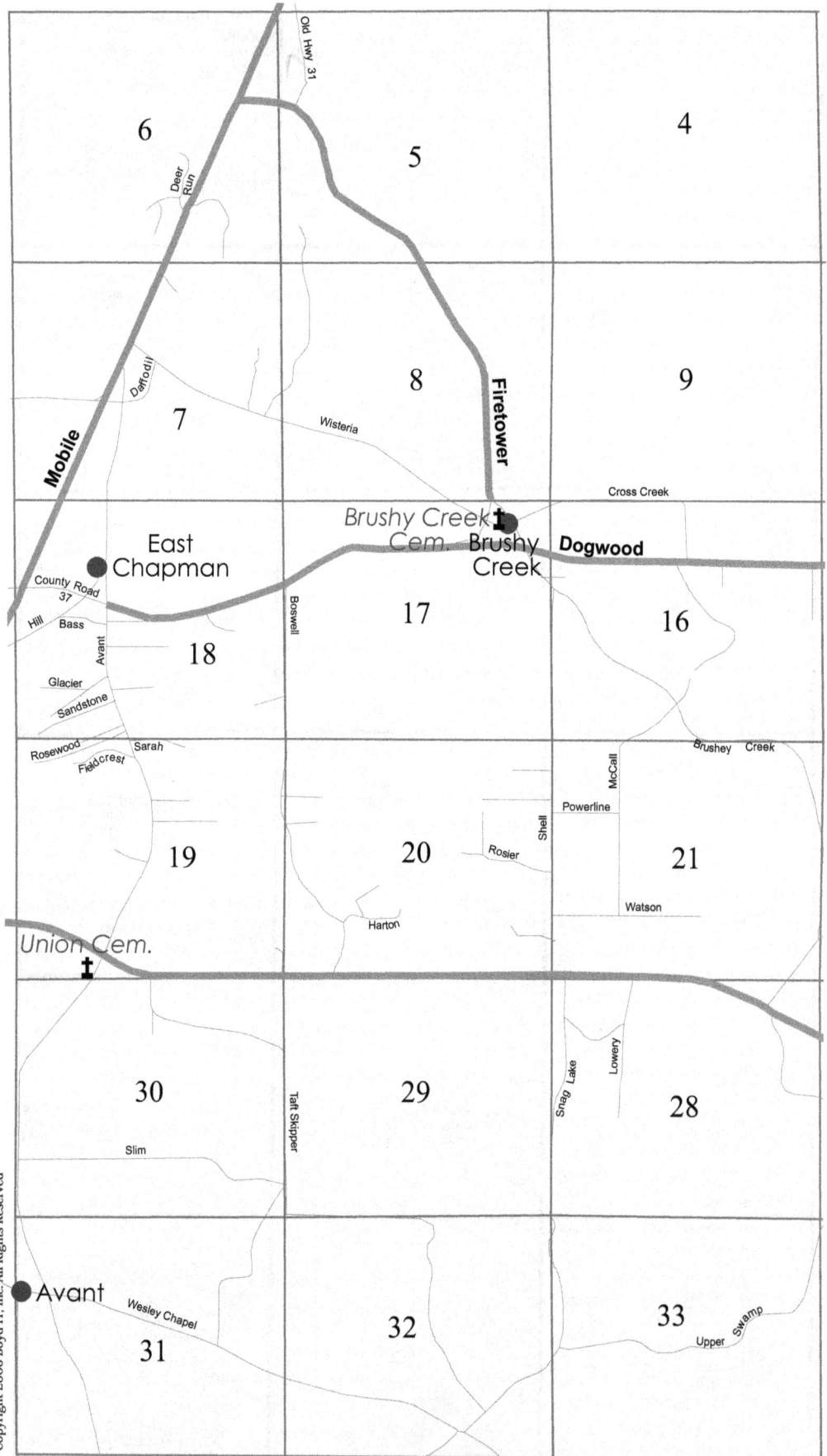

6

5

4

Old Hwy 31

Deer Run

7

Daffodil

Mobile

Wisteria

8

Firetower

9

Cross Creek

Brushy Creek Cem.

East Chapman

County Road 37

Hill

Bass

Avant

18

Boswell

Brushy Creek

Dogwood

17

16

Glacier

Sandstone

Rosewood

Fieldcrest

Sarah

19

20

Rosier

Shell

Powerline

McCall

Brushey Creek

21

Watson

Harton

Union Cem.

30

Slim

Taft Skipper

29

Snag Lake

Lowery

28

Avant

Wesley Chapel

31

32

33

Upper Swamp

Wildfork

Ballpark

3

2

Ashley

1

County Road 45

Hopewell
Cem.

Greenmoore

Dusty

10

11

12

15

14

Friendship

13

Sarah

Laurel Hill

Jones

McKenzie Grade

22

23

24

Mount Pleasant
Cem.

Mt Pleasant

Cedar

27

26

State Highway 106

25

Bluebird Acres

34

Cook Bridge

35

Wesley Chapel

36

Wesley Chapel
Cem.

Helpful Hints

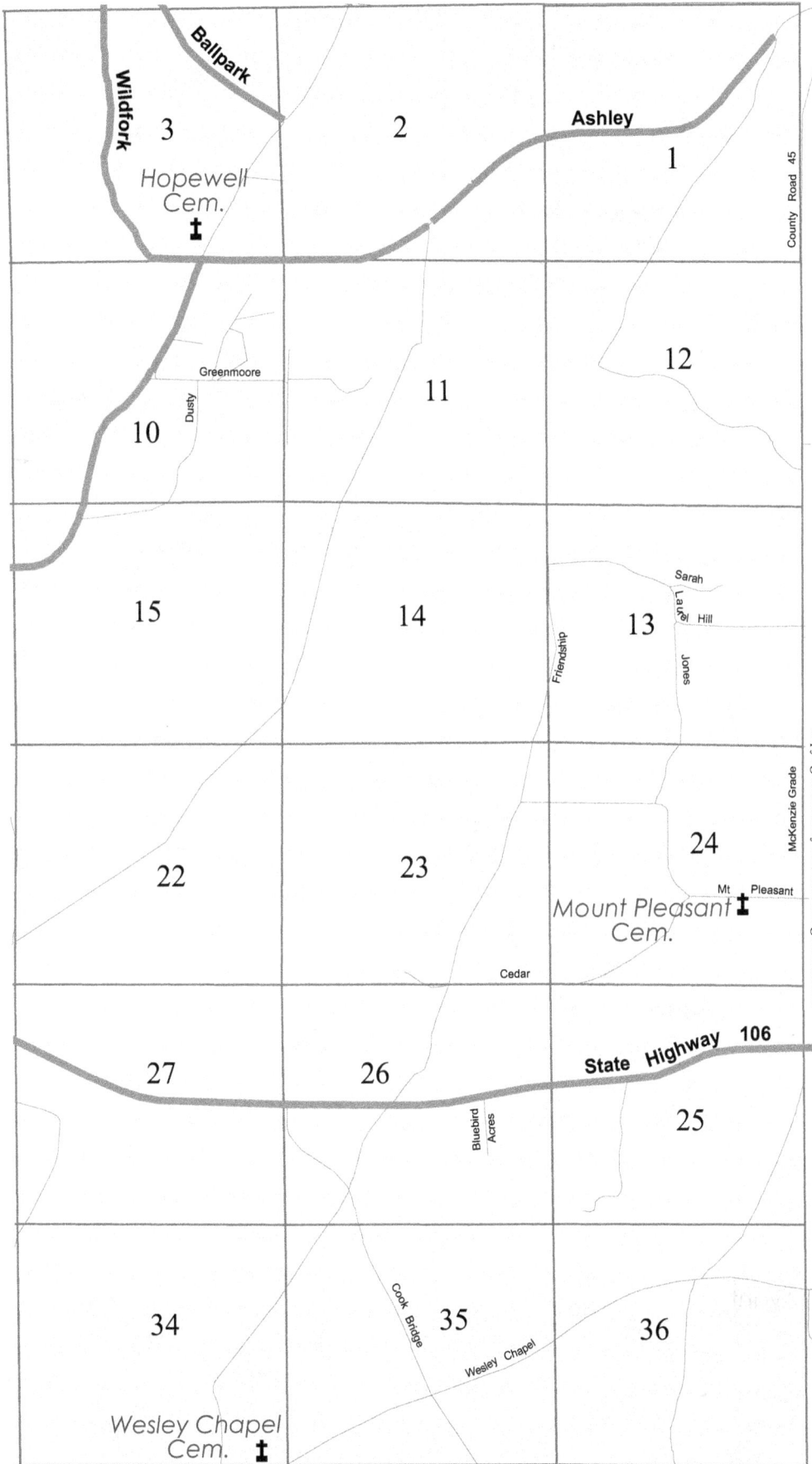

1. This road map has a number of uses, but primarily it is to help you: a) find the present location of land owned by your ancestors (at least the general area), b) find cemeteries and city-centers, and c) estimate the route/roads used by Census-takers & tax-assessors.

2. If you plan to travel to Butler County to locate cemeteries or land parcels, please pick up a modern travel map for the area before you do. Mapping old land parcels on modern maps is not as exact a science as you might think. Just the slightest variations in public land survey coordinates, estimates of parcel boundaries, or road-map deviations can greatly alter a map's representation of how a road either does or doesn't cross a particular parcel of land.

Legend

————— Section Lines

═════ Interstates

━━━━ Highways

————— Other Roads

● Cities/Towns

✝ Cemeteries

Scale: Section = 1 mile X 1 mile
(generally, with some exceptions)

241

Historical Map

T8-N R14-E
St Stephens Meridian

Map Group 18

Cities & Towns
Avant
Brushy Creek
East Chapman

Cemeteries
Brushy Creek Cemetery
Hopewell Cemetery
Mount Pleasant Cemetery
Union Cemetery
Wesley Chapel Cemetery

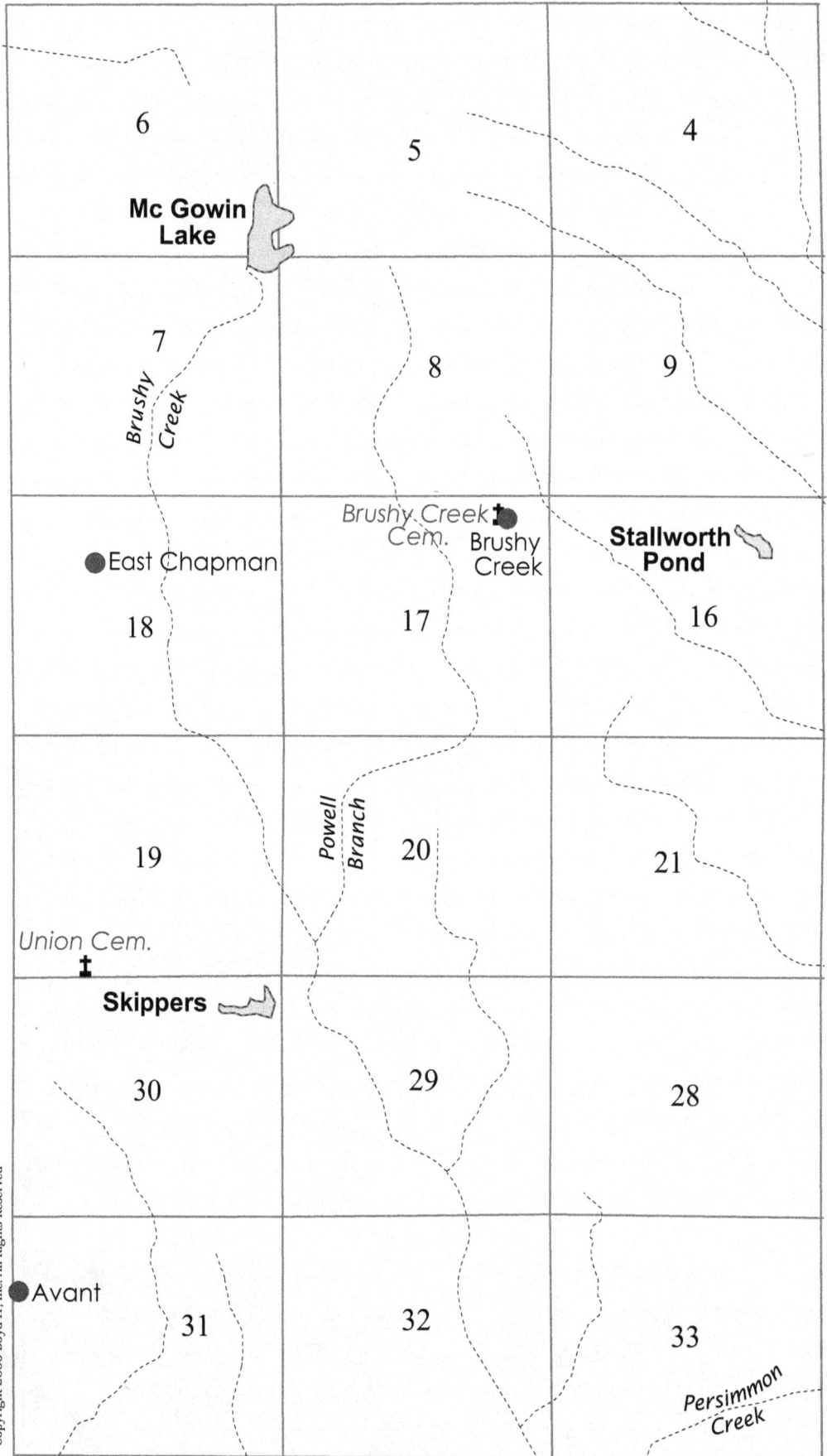

6

5

4

Mc Gowin Lake

7

8

9

Brushy Creek Brushy Creek Cem. **Brushy Creek** **Stallworth Pond**

● East Chapman

18

17

16

19

Powell Branch

20

21

Union Cem. ✝

Skippers

30

29

28

● Avant

31

32

33

Persimmon Creek

3

2

1

Hopewell
Cem.
†

10

11

12

Persimmon
Creek

15

14

13

Mashy Creek

22

23

24

Mount Pleasant †
Cem.

27

26

25

34

35

36

Nall
Pond

Tiger Branch

Wyrosdick
Pond

Wesley Chapel Cem. †

Helpful Hints

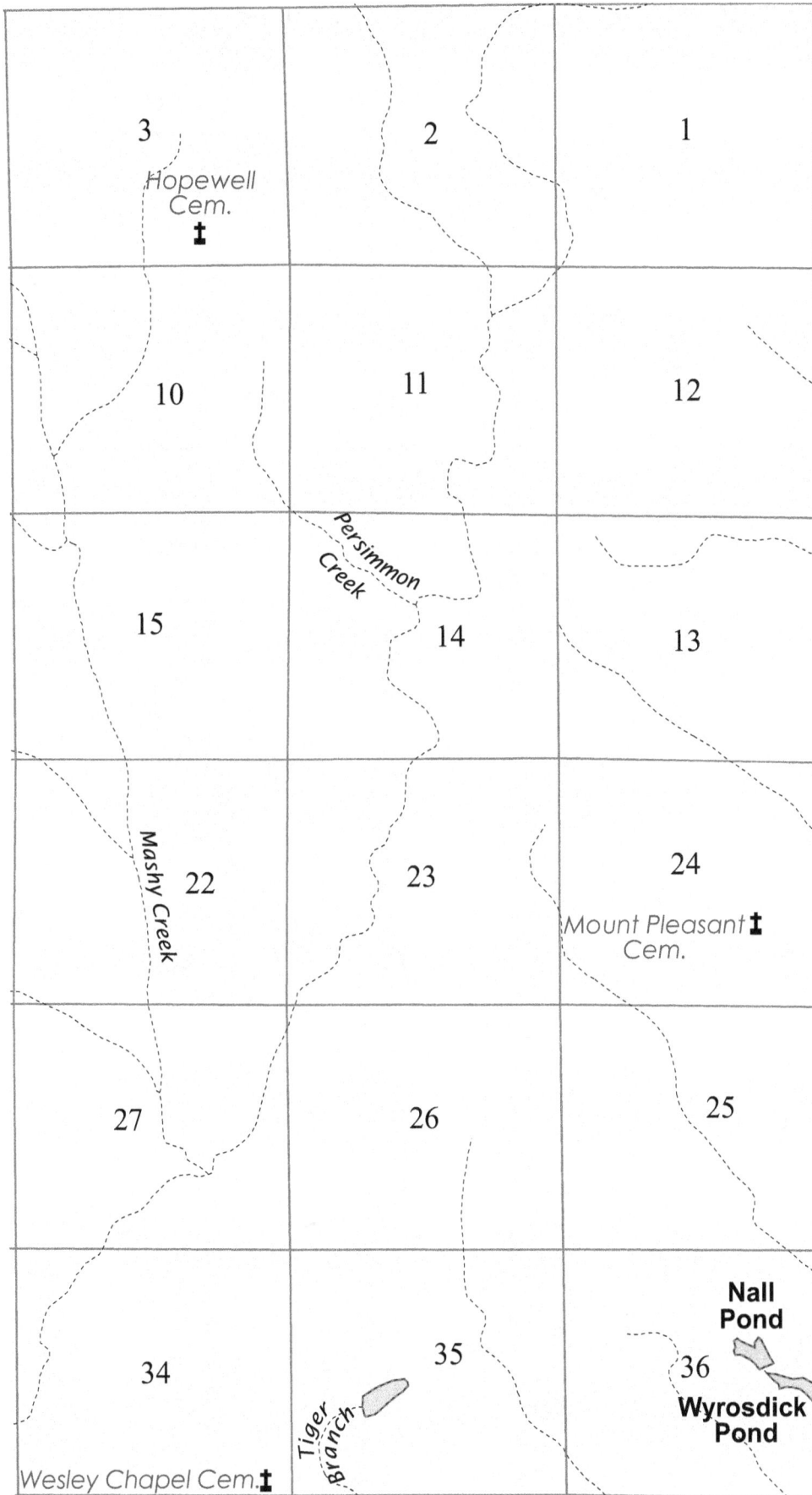

1. This Map takes a different look at the same Congressional Township displayed in the preceding two maps. It presents features that can help you better envision the historical development of the area: a) Water-bodies (lakes & ponds), b) Water-courses (rivers, streams, etc.), c) Railroads, d) City/town center-points (where they were oftentimes located when first settled), and e) Cemeteries.

2. Using this "Historical" map in tandem with this Township's Patent Map and Road Map, may lead you to some interesting discoveries. You will often find roads, towns, cemeteries, and waterways are named after nearby landowners: sometimes those names will be the ones you are researching. See how many of these research gems you can find here in Butler County.

Legend

———— Section Lines

++++++ Railroads

▨ Large Rivers & Bodies of Water

------- Streams/Creeks & Small Rivers

● Cities/Towns

† Cemeteries

Scale: Section = 1 mile X 1 mile
(there are some exceptions)

Map Group 19: Index to Land Patents

Township 8-North Range 15-East (St Stephens)

After you locate an individual in this Index, take note of the Section and Section Part then proceed to the Land Patent map on the pages immediately following. You should have no difficulty locating the corresponding parcel of land.

The "For More Info" Column will lead you to more information about the underlying Patents. See the *Legend* at right, and the "How to Use this Book" chapter, for more information.

ID	Individual in Patent	Sec.	Sec. Part	Date Issued	Other Counties	For More Info . . .
4528	ALLEN, Lovick P	14	NWSW	1858-11-01		A1
4529	" "	15	E½SW	1858-11-01		A1
4530	" "	15	NESE	1858-11-01		A1
4531	" "	15	NWSE	1858-11-01		A1
4532	" "	22	NENW	1858-11-01		A1
4533	" "	22	NWNE	1858-11-01		A1
4534	" "	22	SWNW	1858-11-01		A1
4478	ANDREWS, John	36	N½	1860-10-01		A1
4448	ANSLEY, Francis A	14	N½SE	1860-10-01		A1
4584	BRIGHTWELL, William	6	N½	1858-11-01		A1
4545	BROOK, Preston	32	SESE	1837-08-12		A1
4441	BRYANT, Elisha	4	NESW	1858-11-01		A1
4442	" "	4	SESW	1858-11-01		A1 R4471
4425	CAMPBELL, David	1	NESE	1858-11-01		A1
4426	" "	1	NWSE	1858-11-01		A1
4427	" "	1	SWNE	1858-11-01		A1
4543	CAMPBELL, Philip	35	SWNW	1858-11-01		A1
4544	CAMPBELL, Phillip J	25	W½SW	1858-11-01		A1
4497	DEES, John T	15	SWSW	1858-11-01		A1
4382	DENDY, Buford W	10	SENE	1860-09-01		A1
4383	" "	14	NWNW	1860-09-01		A1
4400	DICKEN, Clinton	1	W½NW	1860-09-01		A1
4443	DICKEN, Elisha T	2	E½NE	1858-11-01		A1
4593	DUKE, William	9	N½SE	1852-12-01		A1 R4458
4594	" "	9	S½NE	1852-12-01		A1 V4459
4599	EDWARDS, William J	34	SESW	1858-11-01		A1
4523	FRANKLIN, Josiah	11	SE	1875-04-20		A1
4465	GALLOPS, Isom	12	NWSE	1858-11-01		A1 G18
4466	" "	13	N½SE	1858-11-01		A1 G18
4467	" "	13	SWNE	1858-11-01		A1 G18
4447	GANDY, Evander	28	W½NE	1843-02-01		A1
4596	GANDY, William	34	W½SW	1880-02-20		A2
4595	" "	26	SWSW	1882-10-30		A1
4581	GRAVES, William B	10	SWNW	1860-10-01		A1
4582	" "	18	NESE	1860-10-01		A1
4583	" "	4	NWSW	1860-10-01		A1
4464	GREEN, Isaac	27	NW	1875-04-20		A1
4469	GREGORY, James G	32	NESE	1838-07-28		A1
4470	" "	32	W½SE	1838-07-28		A1
4505	HALSO, John W	1	SWSW	1854-10-02		A1
4508	" "	12	SENW	1854-10-02		A1
4504	" "	1	SESW	1858-11-01		A1
4506	" "	12	N½NW	1858-11-01		A1
4507	" "	12	NESW	1858-11-01		A1
4509	" "	12	SWNE	1858-11-01		A1
4510	" "	12	SWNW	1858-11-01		A1

ID	Individual in Patent	Sec.	Sec. Part	Date Issued	Other Counties	For More Info . . .
4480	HAMMONDS, John	21	W½NE	1848-04-01		A1
4481	" "	22	NWNW	1849-09-01		A1
4514	HAMMONDS, Joseph	34	S½SE	1860-04-02		A1
4515	"	35	SWSW	1860-04-02		A1
4598	HAMMONDS, William	21	E½NE	1837-05-20		A1
4558	HENDERSON, Shadrick M	26	NESW	1861-05-01		A1
4559	" "	26	SE	1861-05-01		A1
4468	HICKS, James A	8	NWNE	1885-06-30		A1
4366	HORTMAN, Abraham	4	W½NW	1858-11-01		A1
4367	" "	5	NE	1858-11-01		A1
4368	" "	5	NESW	1858-11-01		A1
4369	" "	5	SENW	1858-11-01		A1
4438	HUDSON, Eli	28	SENE	1843-02-01		A1
4574	HUGHS, Tirey M	30	SWSE	1858-11-01		A1
4575	"	31	NENW	1858-11-01		A1
4576	" "	31	W½NE	1858-11-01		A1
4577	" "	32	E½NW	1858-11-01		A1
4578	" "	32	SWNE	1858-11-01		A1
4449	HUGULEY, George	10	E½NW	1858-11-01		A1
4450	" "	10	NENE	1858-11-01		A1
4451	" "	10	W½NE	1858-11-01		A1
4452	" "	3	S½SE	1858-11-01		A1
4453	" "	3	SESW	1858-11-01		A1
4432	JERNIGAN, David P	34	E½NW	1861-05-01		A1
4433	" "	34	N½SE	1861-05-01		A1
4434	" "	34	NESW	1861-05-01		A1
4435	" "	34	SWNW	1861-05-01		A1
4436	" "	34	W½NE	1861-05-01		A1
4465	JOHNSON, Joseph B	12	NWSE	1858-11-01		A1 G18
4511	" "	12	SWSE	1858-11-01		A1
4466	" "	13	N½SE	1858-11-01		A1 G18
4512	" "	13	NWNE	1858-11-01		A1
4513	" "	13	SENE	1858-11-01		A1
4467	" "	13	SWNE	1858-11-01		A1 G18
4535	JOHNSTON, Matilda D	13	SWSW	1860-04-02		A1
4536	" "	14	S½SE	1860-04-02		A1
4537	" "	14	SESW	1860-04-02		A1
4552	JONES, Samuel J	33	SWSE	1858-11-01		A1
4410	KEITH, Daniel	3	NESW	1858-09-01		A1
4411	" "	3	NWNW	1858-09-01		A1
4412	" "	3	NWSE	1858-09-01		A1
4413	" "	3	SENW	1858-09-01		A1
4407	" "	13	SWNW	1860-04-02		A1
4408	" "	14	SENE	1860-04-02		A1
4409	" "	14	W½NE	1860-04-02		A1
4485	KEITH, John	3	NENW	1843-02-01		A1
4482	" "	12	SWSW	1875-04-20		A1
4483	" "	13	N½NW	1875-04-20	'	A1
4484	" "	14	NENE	1875-04-20		A1
4560	KEITH, Silas	4	SENE	1848-05-03		A1
4371	KITE, Bankston	26	NW	1860-04-02		A1
4391	KITE, Caswell	20	SENE	1860-09-01		A1
4392	" "	28	SENW	1860-09-01		A1
4393	" "	28	W½NW	1860-09-01		A1
4388	" "	18	E½SW	1860-12-01		A1
4389	" "	18	SESE	1860-12-01		A1
4390	" "	18	W½SE	1860-12-01		A1
4428	KITE, David	14	NENW	1860-04-02		A1
4429	" "	14	S½NW	1860-04-02		A1
4430	" "	15	SENE	1860-04-02		A1
4597	LANE, William H	12	SESW	1860-09-01		A1
4395	LEWIS, Charles	13	NENE	1858-09-01		A1
4394	" "	12	NESE	1858-11-01		A1
4396	" "	34	E½NE	1858-11-01		A1
4397	" "	35	N½SW	1858-11-01		A1
4498	LONG, John T	28	W½SW	1858-11-01		A1
4499	" "	29	E½SE	1858-11-01		A1
4500	" "	29	SWSE	1858-11-01		A1
4501	" "	32	E½NE	1858-11-01		A1
4502	" "	32	NWNE	1858-11-01		A1
4503	" "	34	NWNW	1858-11-01		A1
4375	MAJORS, Benjamin	18	E½NW	1884-03-20		A2
4376	" "	18	W½NE	1884-03-20		A2

ID	Individual in Patent	Sec.	Sec. Part	Date Issued	Other Counties	For More Info . . .
4445	MAJORS, Ella	7	E½SW	1912-08-08		A2 G29
4446	" "	7	W½SE	1912-08-08		A2 G29
4445	MAJORS, Jesse H	7	E½SW	1912-08-08		A2 G29
4446	" "	7	W½SE	1912-08-08		A2 G29
4431	MARTIN, David	21	E½NW	1845-06-01		A1
4487	MARTIN, John R	6	N½SE	1860-09-01		A1
4488	" "	6	N½SW	1860-09-01		A1
4370	MAXEY, Allen	35	SENW	1858-11-01		A1
4486	MAXEY, John	33	S½SW	1837-08-15		A1
4546	MCCALL, Reuel E	2	SENW	1858-11-01		A1
4547	" "	2	SW	1858-11-01		A1
4548	" "	3	NESE	1858-11-01		A1
4401	MCLAIN, Columbus	22	E½SW	1858-11-01		A1
4402	" "	22	SENW	1858-11-01		A1
4403	" "	22	W½SE	1858-11-01		A1
4404	" "	27	NWNE	1858-11-01		A1
4554	MERCER, Seth	5	NESE	1858-11-01		A1
4555	" "	5	NWSE	1858-11-01		A1
4556	" "	8	NENE	1858-11-01		A1
4557	" "	9	W½NW	1858-11-01		A1
4572	MINIARD, Thomas	21	NWNW	1858-11-01		A1
4573	MINYARD, Thomas	20	NENE	1854-07-15		A1
4463	MONTGOMERY, Hugh B	2	SWNE	1860-10-01		A1
4462	" "	2	NWSE	1862-04-10		A1
4527	MOORE, Lewis	21	E½SW	1837-08-12		A1
4516	MUNCHUS, Joseph K	12	NWSW	1860-09-01		A1
4474	NICHOLS, Joel	23	E½SW	1858-11-01		A1
4475	" "	23	SESE	1858-11-01		A1
4476	" "	23	W½SE	1858-11-01		A1
4477	" "	24	SWSW	1858-11-01		A1
4600	NORSWORTHY, William J	14	NESW	1860-10-01		A1
4405	PARKER, Daniel C	6	S½SE	1860-04-02		A1
4406	" "	6	S½SW	1860-04-02		A1
4456	PARKER, Henry E	17	N½NE	1858-11-01		A1
4457	" "	8	S½SE	1858-11-01		A1
4458	" "	9	N½SE	1858-11-01		A1 R4593
4459	" "	9	SWNE	1858-11-01		A1 V4594
4460	" "	9	SWSW	1858-11-01		A1
4461	PARKER, Henry J	8	SENE	1861-05-01		A1
4517	PARMER, Joseph M	15	NWSW	1858-11-01		A1
4518	" "	15	SWNW	1858-11-01		A1
4519	" "	17	SE	1858-11-01		A1
4520	" "	20	W½NE	1858-11-01		A1
4521	" "	27	NWSW	1858-11-01		A1
4522	" "	28	NENE	1858-11-01		A1
4601	PARMER, William K	18	E½NE	1858-11-01		A1
4602	" "	8	E½NW	1858-11-01		A1
4603	PARMER, William R	17	NW	1858-11-01		A1
4604	" "	17	S½NE	1858-11-01		A1
4605	" "	8	E½SW	1858-11-01		A1
4606	" "	8	W½NW	1858-11-01		A1
4607	" "	8	W½SW	1858-11-01		A1
4541	PERRITT, Needham	18	SWNW	1858-11-01		A1
4540	" "	18	NWNW	1860-10-01		A1
4542	" "	18	W½SW	1860-10-01		A1
4561	PERRY, Simeon	1	S½SE	1858-11-01		A1
4562	" "	12	E½NE	1862-01-01		A1
4563	" "	12	NWNE	1862-01-01		A1
4479	PITTS, John F	26	S½NE	1891-06-30		A2
4553	REDDOCK, Sarah	5	SESE	1848-05-03		A1
4586	REDDOCK, William C	3	SWSW	1848-05-03		A1
4589	" "	4	SESE	1848-05-03		A1
4585	" "	10	NWNW	1858-11-01		A1
4588	" "	4	N½NE	1858-11-01		A1
4591	" "	4	SWSE	1858-11-01		A1
4587	" "	4	E½NW	1860-04-02		A1
4590	" "	4	SWNE	1860-04-02		A1
4489	REID, John	26	SESW	1897-11-22		A2 G39
4489	REID, Racael	26	SESW	1897-11-22		A2 G39
4592	RIDDOCK, William C	9	NENE	1848-05-03		A1
4378	SANDERS, Bluford B	10	SW	1858-11-01		A1
4379	" "	15	NWNW	1858-11-01		A1
4380	" "	9	S½SE	1858-11-01		A1

ID	Individual in Patent	Sec.	Sec. Part	Date Issued	Other Counties	For More Info . . .
4381	SANDERS, Bluford B (Cont'd)	9	SESW	1858-11-01		A1
4377	SIMMONS, Benjamin	4	NESE	1848-05-03		A1
4444	SIMMONS, Elizabeth	3	NWSW	1848-05-03		A1
4579	SIMS, Wiley	4	NWSE	1848-05-03		A1
4580	" "	9	NENW	1848-05-03		A1
4495	SMITH, John	33	NENE	1850-04-01		A1
4494	" "	12	SESE	1854-10-02		A1
4566	SMITH, Stephen	27	E½SW	1858-11-01		A1
4567	" "	27	SE	1858-11-01		A1
4568	" "	27	SWNE	1858-11-01		A1
4569	" "	27	SWSW	1858-11-01		A1
4496	SMYTH, John	28	W½SE	1843-02-01		A1
4490	SORRELLS, John S	14	SWSW	1860-04-02		A1
4491	" "	15	SESE	1860-04-02		A1
4492	" "	22	NENE	1860-04-02		A1
4493	" "	23	NWNW	1860-04-02		A1
4471	STEVENS, James	4	SESW	1858-11-01		A1 R4442
4422	THOMAS, Daniel	3	E½NE	1852-02-02		A1
4423	" "	3	NWNE	1854-10-02		A1
4419	" "	2	NENW	1858-11-01		A1
4420	" "	2	NWNW	1858-11-01		A1
4421	" "	2	SWNW	1858-11-01		A1
4424	" "	3	SWNE	1858-11-01		A1
4415	THOMAS, Daniel L	22	S½NE	1858-11-01		A1
4416	" "	23	SWNW	1858-11-01		A1
4418	" "	27	NENE	1858-11-01		A1
4414	" "	22	E½SE	1875-04-20		A1
4417	" "	23	W½SW	1875-04-20		A1
4570	THOMAS, Thomas C	9	NESW	1858-11-01		A1
4571	" "	9	SENW	1858-11-01		A1
4538	TRAMMELL, Nancy	23	E½NW	1860-04-02		A1
4539	" "	23	W½NE	1860-04-02		A1
4439	TYNER, Elijah S	26	N½NE	1860-09-01		A1
4440	" "	26	NWSW	1860-09-01		A1
4524	TYNER, Keeland	24	E½SW	1860-09-01		A1
4525	" "	24	NWSW	1860-09-01		A1
4526	" "	24	SE	1860-09-01		A1
4564	TYNER, Simeon	24	NE	1860-09-01		A1
4565	" "	24	NW	1860-10-01		A1
4372	WILKERSON, Benjamin F	2	NESE	1858-11-01		A1
4373	" "	2	SESE	1858-11-01		A1
4374	" "	2	SWSE	1858-11-01		A1
4384	WILLIAMS, Calvin D	21	NWSE	1858-11-01		A1
4385	" "	21	SWSE	1858-11-01		A1
4386	" "	22	NWSW	1858-11-01		A1
4387	" "	22	SWSW	1858-11-01		A1
4398	WILLIAMS, Chatmon L	20	SW	1860-04-02		A1
4399	" "	20	W½NW	1860-04-02		A1
4454	WILLIAMS, George	28	E½SE	1845-07-01		A1
4455	" "	28	E½SW	1845-07-01		A1
4472	WILLIAMS, Jethro L	33	NWSE	1858-11-01		A1
4473	WILLIAMS, Jethro S	33	SESE	1858-11-01		A1
4549	WILLIAMS, Richard	33	N½SW	1843-02-01		A1
4550	" "	33	NW	1845-07-01		A1
4551	" "	33	W½NE	1845-07-01		A1
4608	WILLIAMS, Winney	30	NWSW	1858-11-01		A1 C
4437	WOOD, David	1	SENW	1858-11-01		A1

Patent Map

T8-N R15-E
St Stephens Meridian

Map Group 19

Township Statistics

Parcels Mapped	:	243
Number of Patents	:	148
Number of Individuals	:	101
Patentees Identified	:	99
Number of Surnames	:	69
Multi-Patentee Parcels	:	6
Oldest Patent Date	:	5/20/1837
Most Recent Patent	:	8/8/1912
Block/Lot Parcels	:	0
Parcels Re - Issued	:	2
Parcels that Overlap	:	2
Cities and Towns	:	2
Cemeteries	:	4

Section 6
BRIGHTWELL William 1858
MARTIN John R 1860
MARTIN John R 1860
PARKER Daniel C 1860
PARKER Daniel C 1860

Section 5
HORTMAN Abraham 1858
HORTMAN Abraham 1858
HORTMAN Abraham 1858
MERCER Seth 1858
MERCER Seth 1858
REDDOCK Sarah 1848

Section 4
HORTMAN Abraham 1858
REDDOCK William C 1860
REDDOCK William C 1858
REDDOCK William C 1860
KEITH Silas 1848
GRAVES William B 1860
BRYANT Elisha 1858
SIMS Wiley 1848
SIMMONS Benjamin 1848
STEVENS James 1858
BRYANT Elisha 1858
REDDOCK William C 1858
REDDOCK William C 1848

Section 7
MAJORS [29] Ella 1912
MAJORS [29] Ella 1912

Section 8
HICKS James A 1885
PARMER William R 1858
PARMER William K 1858
PARKER Henry J 1861
PARMER William R 1858
PARMER William R 1858
PARKER Henry E 1858

Section 9
MERCER Seth 1858
MERCER Seth 1858
SIMS Wiley 1848
THOMAS Thomas C 1858
THOMAS Thomas C 1858
RIDDOCK William C 1848
PARKER Henry E 1858
DUKE William 1852
PARKER Henry E 1858
DUKE William 1852
PARKER Henry E 1858
SANDERS Bluford B 1858
SANDERS Bluford B 1858

Section 18
PERRITT Needham 1860
PERRITT Needham 1858
MAJORS Benjamin 1884
MAJORS Benjamin 1884
PARMER William K 1858
PERRITT Needham 1860
KITE Caswell 1860
KITE Caswell 1860

Section 17
PARMER William R 1858
GRAVES William B 1860
KITE Caswell 1860
PARKER Henry E 1858
PARMER William R 1858
PARMER Joseph M 1858

Section 16

Section 19

Section 20
WILLIAMS Chatmon L 1860
PARMER Joseph M 1858
WILLIAMS Chatmon L 1860

Section 21
MINYARD Thomas 1854
MINIARD Thomas 1858
KITE Caswell 1860
MARTIN David 1845
HAMMONDS John 1848
HAMMONDS William 1837
WILLIAMS Calvin D 1858
WILLIAMS Calvin D 1858
MOORE Lewis 1837

Section 30
WILLIAMS Winney 1858
HUGHS Tirey M 1858
HUGHS Tirey M 1858
HUGHS Tirey M 1858

Section 29
LONG John T 1858
LONG John T 1858

Section 28
GANDY Evander 1843
PARMER Joseph M 1858
KITE Caswell 1860
KITE Caswell 1860
HUDSON Eli 1843
LONG John T 1858
WILLIAMS George 1845
SMYTH John 1843
WILLIAMS George 1845

Section 31

Section 32
HUGHS Tirey M 1858
HUGHS Tirey M 1858
GREGORY James G 1838

Section 33
LONG John T 1858
LONG John T 1858
WILLIAMS Richard 1845
WILLIAMS Richard 1845
WILLIAMS Jethro L 1858
SMITH John 1850
GREGORY James G 1838
BROOK Preston 1837
WILLIAMS Richard 1843
MAXEY John 1837
JONES Samuel J 1858
WILLIAMS Jethro S 1858

248

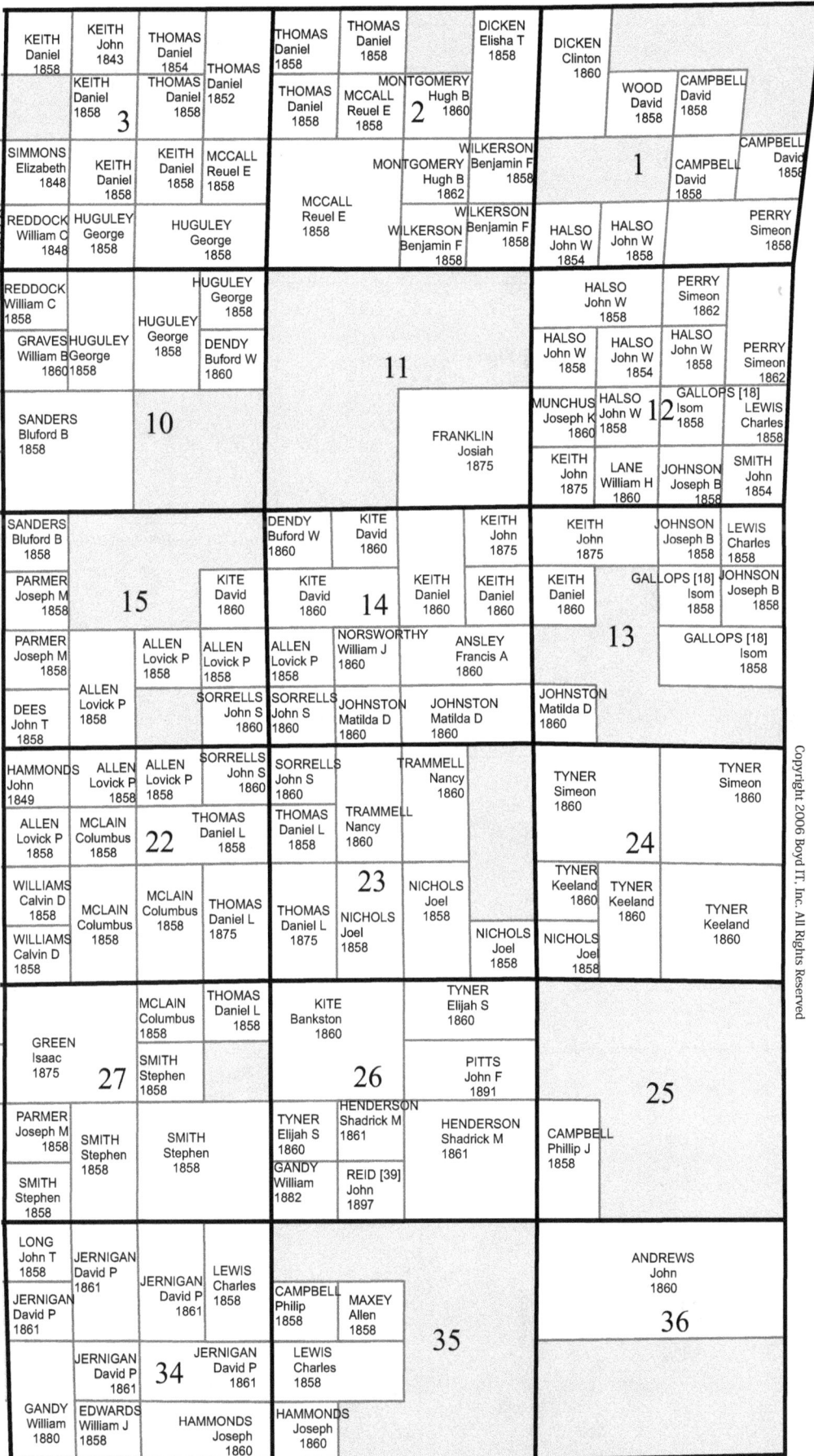

Section 3
- KEITH Daniel 1858
- KEITH John 1843
- THOMAS Daniel 1854
- THOMAS Daniel 1852
- KEITH Daniel 1858
- THOMAS Daniel 1858
- SIMMONS Elizabeth 1848
- KEITH Daniel 1858
- KEITH Daniel 1858
- MCCALL Reuel E 1858
- REDDOCK William C 1848
- HUGULEY George 1858
- HUGULEY George 1858

Section 2
- THOMAS Daniel 1858
- THOMAS Daniel 1858
- DICKEN Elisha T 1858
- THOMAS Daniel 1858
- MCCALL Reuel E 1858
- MONTGOMERY Hugh B 1860
- MCCALL Reuel E 1858
- MONTGOMERY Hugh B 1862
- WILKERSON Benjamin F 1858
- WILKERSON Benjamin F 1858
- WILKERSON Benjamin F 1858

Section 1
- DICKEN Clinton 1860
- WOOD David 1858
- CAMPBELL David 1858
- CAMPBELL David 1858
- CAMPBELL David 1858
- HALSO John W 1854
- HALSO John W 1858
- PERRY Simeon 1858

Section 10
- REDDOCK William C 1858
- HUGULEY George 1858
- HUGULEY George 1858
- GRAVES William B 1860
- HUGULEY George 1858
- DENDY Buford W 1860
- SANDERS Bluford B 1858

Section 11
- FRANKLIN Josiah 1875

Section 12
- HALSO John W 1858
- PERRY Simeon 1862
- HALSO John W 1858
- HALSO John W 1854
- HALSO John W 1858
- PERRY Simeon 1862
- MUNCHUS Joseph K 1860
- HALSO John W 1858
- GALLOPS [18] Isom 1858
- LEWIS Charles 1858
- KEITH John 1875
- LANE William H 1860
- JOHNSON Joseph B 1858
- SMITH John 1854

Section 15
- SANDERS Bluford B 1858
- PARMER Joseph M 1858
- PARMER Joseph M 1858
- KITE David 1860
- DEES John T 1858
- ALLEN Lovick P 1858

Section 14
- DENDY Buford W 1860
- KITE David 1860
- KEITH John 1875
- KITE David 1860
- KITE David 1860
- KEITH Daniel 1860
- KEITH Daniel 1860
- ALLEN Lovick P 1858
- ALLEN Lovick P 1858
- ALLEN Lovick P 1858
- NORSWORTHY William J 1860
- ANSLEY Francis A 1860
- SORRELLS John S 1860
- SORRELLS John S 1860
- JOHNSTON Matilda D 1860
- JOHNSTON Matilda D 1860

Section 13
- KEITH John 1875
- JOHNSON Joseph B 1858
- LEWIS Charles 1858
- KEITH Daniel 1860
- GALLOPS [18] Isom 1858
- JOHNSON Joseph B 1858
- GALLOPS [18] Isom 1858
- JOHNSTON Matilda D 1860

Section 22
- HAMMONDS John 1849
- ALLEN Lovick P 1858
- ALLEN Lovick P 1858
- SORRELLS John S 1860
- ALLEN Lovick P 1858
- MCLAIN Columbus 1858
- THOMAS Daniel L 1858
- WILLIAMS Calvin D 1858
- MCLAIN Columbus 1858
- MCLAIN Columbus 1858
- THOMAS Daniel L 1875
- WILLIAMS Calvin D 1858

Section 23
- SORRELLS John S 1860
- TRAMMELL Nancy 1860
- THOMAS Daniel L 1858
- TRAMMELL Nancy 1860
- THOMAS Daniel L 1875
- NICHOLS Joel 1858
- NICHOLS Joel 1858
- NICHOLS Joel 1858

Section 24
- TYNER Simeon 1860
- TYNER Simeon 1860
- TYNER Keeland 1860
- TYNER Keeland 1860
- TYNER Keeland 1860

Section 27
- GREEN Isaac 1875
- MCLAIN Columbus 1858
- THOMAS Daniel L 1858
- SMITH Stephen 1858
- PARMER Joseph M 1858
- SMITH Stephen 1858
- SMITH Stephen 1858
- SMITH Stephen 1858

Section 26
- KITE Bankston 1860
- TYNER Elijah S 1860
- PITTS John F 1891
- TYNER Elijah S 1860
- HENDERSON Shadrick M 1861
- HENDERSON Shadrick M 1861
- GANDY William 1882
- REID [39] John 1897

Section 25
- CAMPBELL Phillip J 1858

Section 34
- LONG John T 1858
- JERNIGAN David P 1861
- LEWIS Charles 1858
- JERNIGAN David P 1861
- JERNIGAN David P 1861
- JERNIGAN David P 1861
- JERNIGAN David P 1861
- GANDY William 1880
- EDWARDS William J 1858

Section 35
- CAMPBELL Philip 1858
- MAXEY Allen 1858
- LEWIS Charles 1858
- HAMMONDS Joseph 1860
- HAMMONDS Joseph 1860

Section 36
- ANDREWS John 1860

Helpful Hints

1. This Map's INDEX can be found on the preceding pages.

2. Refer to Map "C" to see where this Township lies within Butler County, Alabama.

3. Numbers within square brackets [ ] denote a multi-patentee land parcel (multi-owner). Refer to Appendix "C" for a full list of members in this group.

4. Areas that look to be crowded with Patentees usually indicate multiple sales of the same parcel (Re-issues) or Overlapping parcels. See this Township's Index for an explanation of these and other circumstances that might explain "odd" groupings of Patentees on this map.

Legend

- Patent Boundary
- Section Boundary
- No Patents Found (or Outside County)
- 1., 2., 3., ... Lot Numbers (when beside a name)
- [ ] Group Number (see Appendix "C")

Scale: Section = 1 mile X 1 mile (generally, with some exceptions)

Road Map

T8-N R15-E
St Stephens Meridian

Map Group 19

Cities & Towns
Pigeon Creek
Sardis

Cemeteries
Ebenezer Cemetery
New Prospect Cemetery
Sardis Cemetery
Shiloh Cemetery

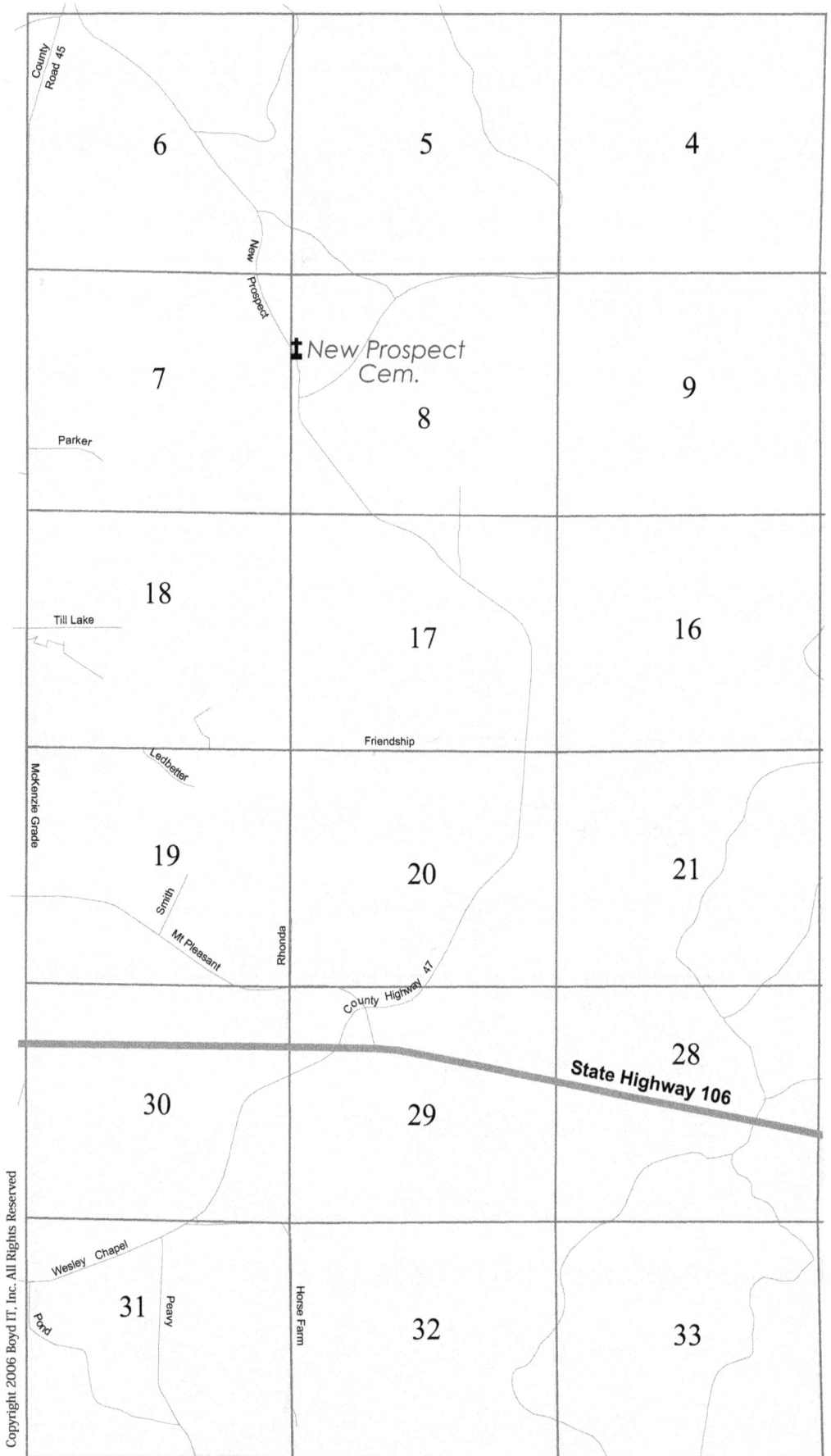

County Road 45

New Prospect

6

5

4

7

Parker

✝ New Prospect Cem.

8

9

18

Till Lake

17

16

Ledbetter

Friendship

McKenzie Grade

19

Smith

Mt Pleasant

Rhonda

20

County Highway 47

21

County Highway 47

28

State Highway 106

30

29

Wesley Chapel

31

Peavy

Pond

Horse Farm

32

33

3

2

1

Bush

Hugely Bridge

Hugley Bridge

10

11

Sardis Cem.
Sardis

12

15

14

13
Shiloh Cem.
Greybeard
Cook
Ebenezer Cem.
Pigeon Creek

22

23

24

Halso Mill

27

26
Peachtree

25

Pigeon Creek

34
Jernigan

35
Shine

36

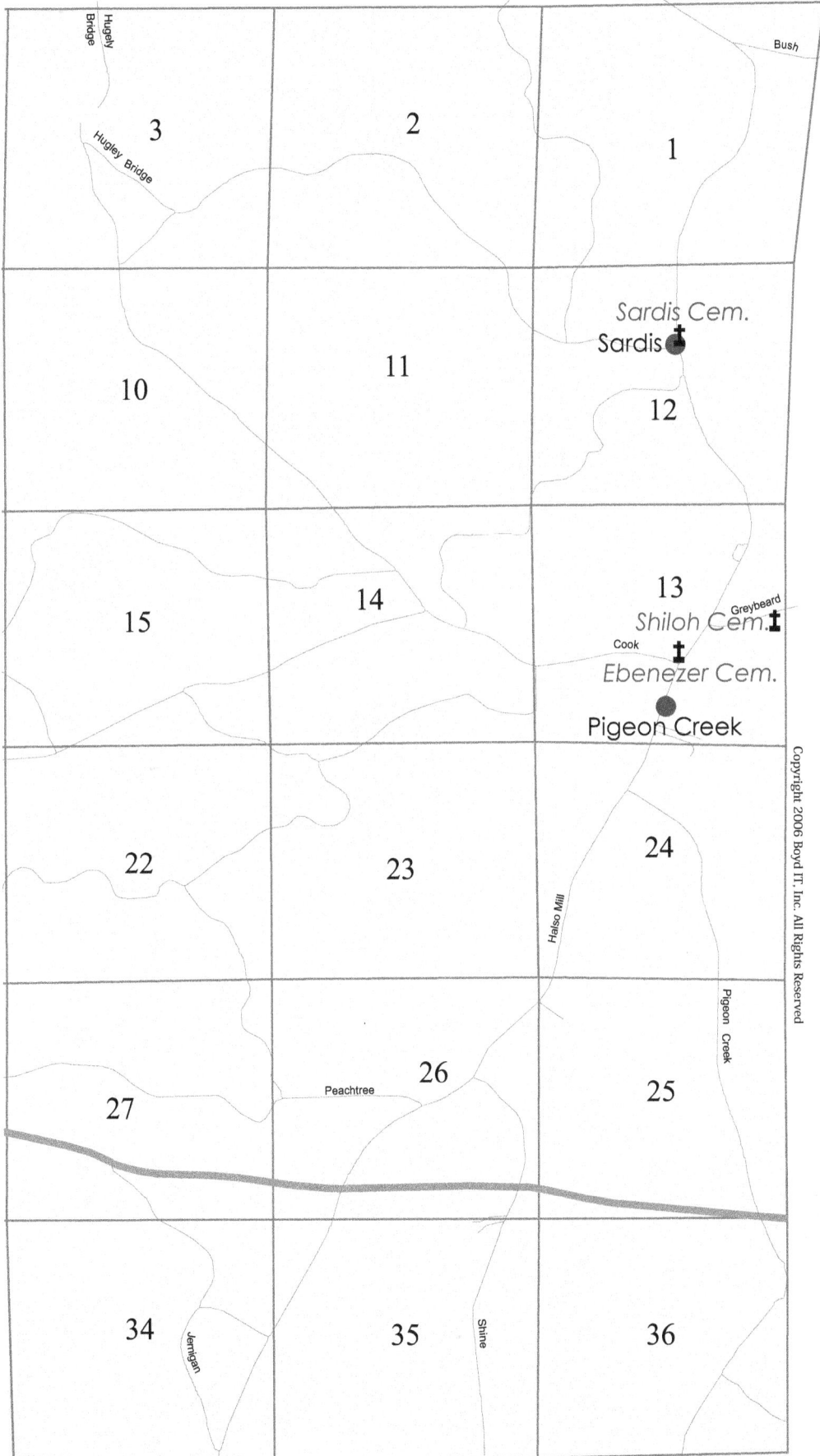

Helpful Hints

1. This road map has a number of uses, but primarily it is to help you: a) find the present location of land owned by your ancestors (at least the general area), b) find cemeteries and city-centers, and c) estimate the route/roads used by Census-takers & tax-assessors.

2. If you plan to travel to Butler County to locate cemeteries or land parcels, please pick up a modern travel map for the area before you do. Mapping old land parcels on modern maps is not as exact a science as you might think. Just the slightest variations in public land survey coordinates, estimates of parcel boundaries, or road-map deviations can greatly alter a map's representation of how a road either does or doesn't cross a particular parcel of land.

Legend

——————— Section Lines

═══════ Interstates

▬▬▬▬▬▬ Highways

——————— Other Roads

● Cities/Towns

✝ Cemeteries

Scale: Section = 1 mile X 1 mile
(generally, with some exceptions)

Historical Map

T8-N R15-E
St Stephens Meridian

Map Group 19

Cities & Towns
Pigeon Creek
Sardis

Cemeteries
Ebenezer Cemetery
New Prospect Cemetery
Sardis Cemetery
Shiloh Cemetery

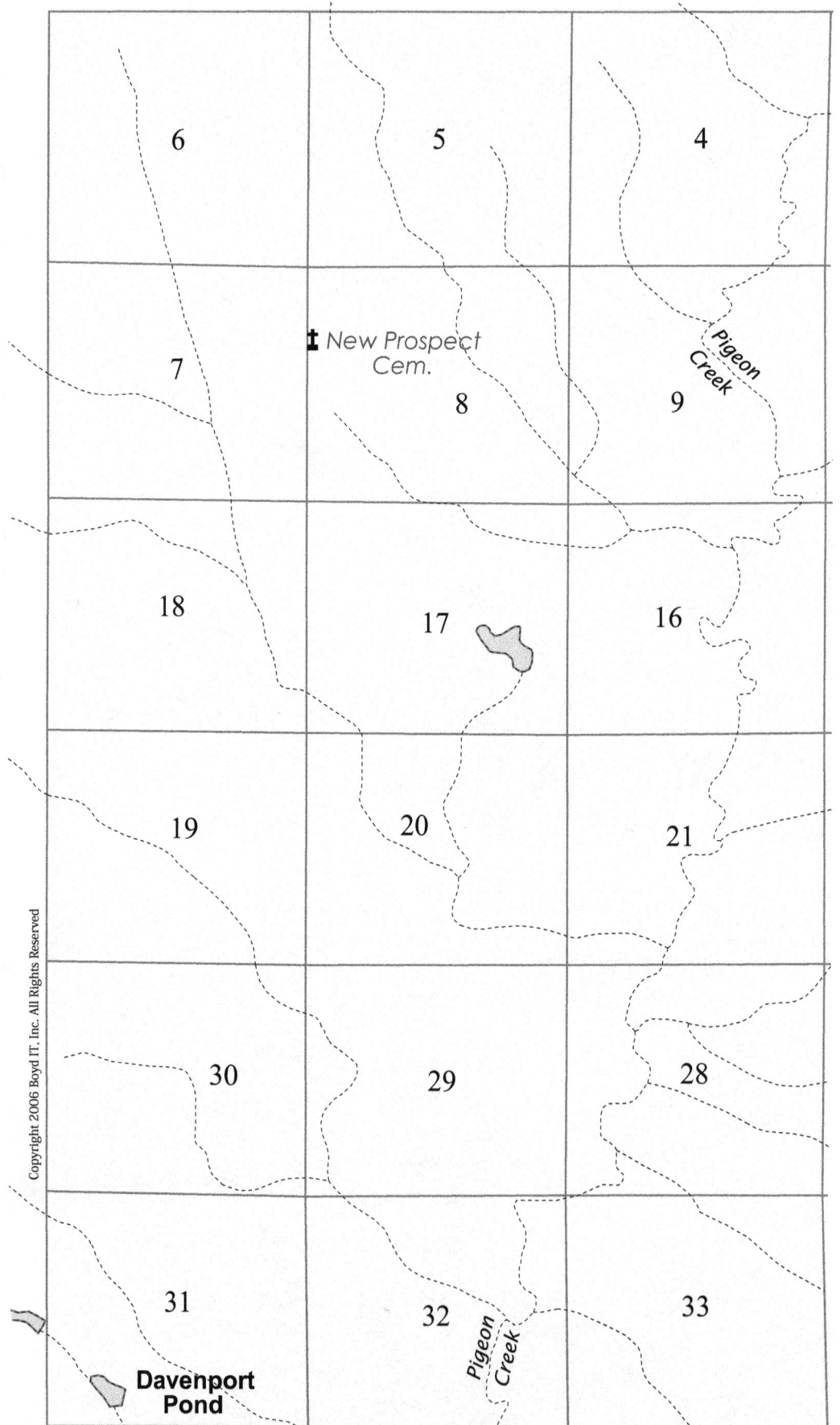

6	5	4
7	✝ New Prospect Cem. 8	Pigeon Creek 9
18	17	16
19	20	21
30	29	28
31 Davenport Pond	32 Pigeon Creek	33

3

2

1

Hard Labor Creek

10

11

Sardis Cem. ✝
● Sardis

12

15

14

13

Shiloh Cem. ✝

Ebenezer ✝
Cem.

● Pigeon Creek

22

23

24

27

26

25

34

35

Orange Branch

Flat Branch

36

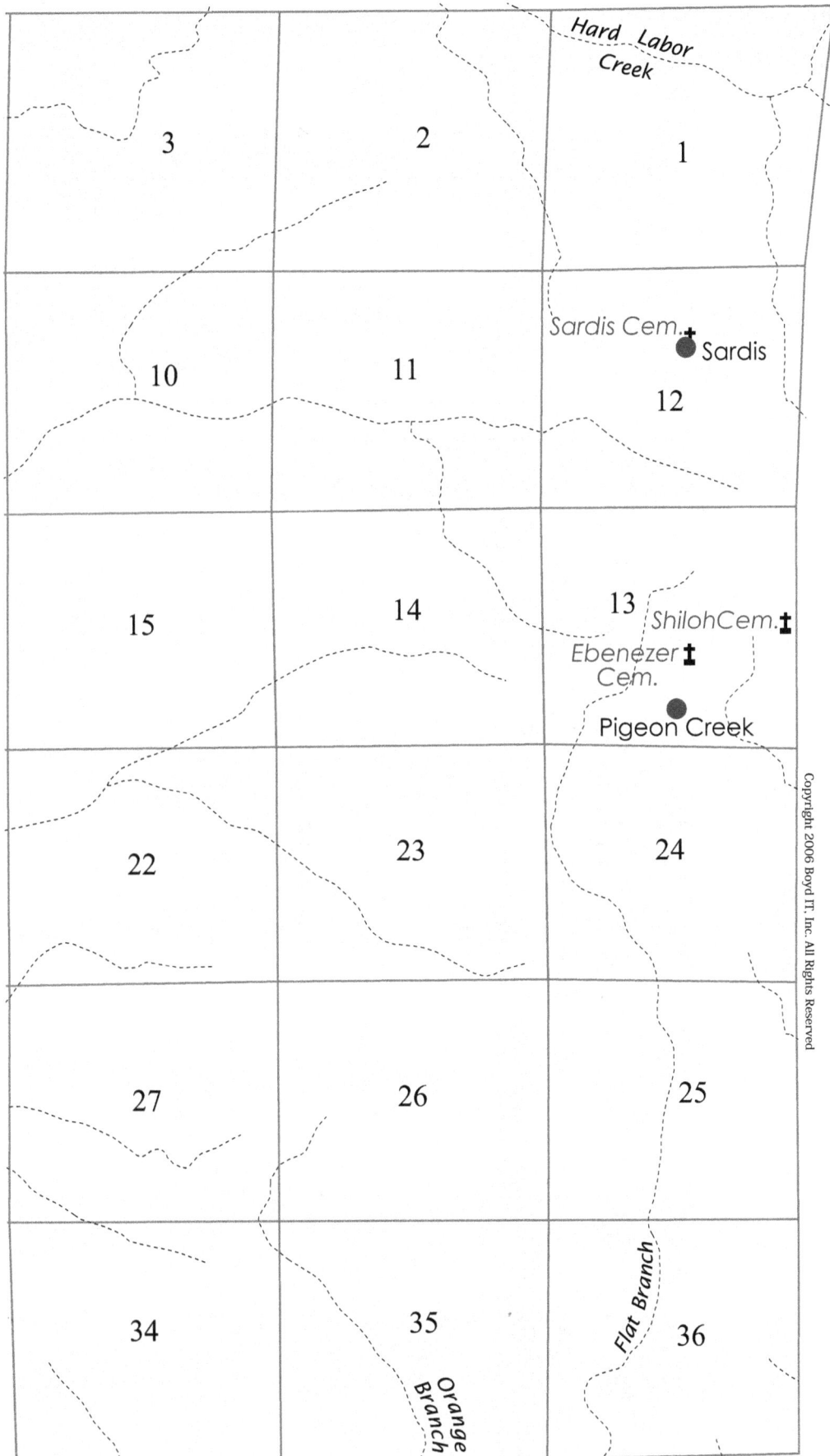

Helpful Hints

1. This Map takes a different look at the same Congressional Township displayed in the preceding two maps. It presents features that can help you better envision the historical development of the area: a) Water-bodies (lakes & ponds), b) Water-courses (rivers, streams, etc.), c) Railroads, d) City/town center-points (where they were oftentimes located when first settled), and e) Cemeteries.

2. Using this "Historical" map in tandem with this Township's Patent Map and Road Map, may lead you to some interesting discoveries. You will often find roads, towns, cemeteries, and waterways are named after nearby landowners: sometimes those names will be the ones you are researching. See how many of these research gems you can find here in Butler County.

Legend

————	Section Lines
┼┼┼┼┼┼	Railroads
▭	Large Rivers & Bodies of Water
- - - - -	Streams/Creeks & Small Rivers
●	Cities/Towns
✝	Cemeteries

Scale: Section = 1 mile X 1 mile
(there are some exceptions)

Map Group 20: Index to Land Patents

Township 8-North Range 16-East (St Stephens)

After you locate an individual in this Index, take note of the Section and Section Part then proceed to the Land Patent map on the pages immediately following. You should have no difficulty locating the corresponding parcel of land.

The "For More Info" Column will lead you to more information about the underlying Patents. See the *Legend* at right, and the "How to Use this Book" chapter, for more information.

```
                          LEGEND
               "For More Info . . . " column

A = Authority (Legislative Act, See Appendix "A")
B = Block or Lot (location in Section unknown)
C = Cancelled Patent
F = Fractional Section
G = Group  (Multi-Patentee Patent, see Appendix "C")
V = Overlaps another Parcel
R = Re-Issued (Parcel patented more than once)

(A & G items require you to look in the Appendixes referred
to above. All other Letter-designations followed by a number
require you to locate line-items in this index that possess
the ID number found after the letter).
```

ID	Individual in Patent	Sec.	Sec. Part	Date Issued	Other Counties	For More Info . . .
4651	ALLEN, Washington	8	SW	1860-10-01		A1
4657	BROWDER, William T	4	SWNW	1891-06-29		A2
4644	CAMPBELL, Richard J	18	NENE	1885-07-27		A1
4632	CODY, John	4	NE	1861-05-01		A1
4633	" "	4	NESE	1861-05-01		A1
4640	DRAKE, Patrick H	6	E½SE	1858-11-01		A1
4641	" "	6	NWSE	1858-11-01		A1
4642	" "	6	SWSE	1858-11-01		A1
4626	GALLOPS, Isom	18	NWSW	1858-11-01		A1 G18
4625	GARRETT, Henry L	8	SENW	1861-05-01		A1
4653	HESTER, William	7	W½NW	1858-11-01		A1
4643	HICKMAN, Pinkney N	8	SWSE	1891-06-29		A1
4629	HUGULEY, John A	5	N½NW	1858-11-01		A1
4630	" "	5	NENE	1858-11-01		A1
4631	" "	5	NWNE	1858-11-01		A1
4626	JOHNSON, Joseph B	18	NWSW	1858-11-01		A1 G18
4635	" "	18	W½NW	1858-11-01		A1
4611	LEWIS, Charles	7	NESW	1858-11-01		A1
4612	" "	7	NWSW	1858-11-01		A1
4627	MCLAIN, James	18	N½SE	1860-12-01		A1
4628	" "	18	S½SE	1860-12-01		A1
4655	MERCER, William	6	SENW	1852-02-02		A1
4656	" "	6	SWNW	1854-10-02		A1
4654	" "	6	NESW	1858-11-01		A1
4613	MOORMAN, David J	4	E½NW	1858-11-01		A1
4614	" "	4	E½SW	1858-11-01		A1
4615	" "	4	NWNW	1858-11-01		A1
4618	NIX, Edward	6	N½NW	1858-11-01		A1
4645	PERRY, Simeon	6	NWSW	1858-11-01		A1
4646	" "	7	N½SE	1858-11-01		A1
4647	" "	8	W½NW	1858-11-01		A1
4619	SANFORD, Henry H	4	W½SW	1858-11-01		A1
4620	" "	5	N½SE	1858-11-01		A1
4621	" "	5	NESW	1858-11-01		A1
4622	" "	5	SENE	1858-11-01		A1
4623	" "	5	SENW	1858-11-01		A1
4624	" "	5	SWNE	1858-11-01		A1
4609	SELLARS, Calvin K	4	S½SE	1861-05-01		A1
4610	SELLERS, Calvin K	4	NWSE	1861-05-01		A1
4648	SLATON, Thomas	6	S½SW	1858-11-01		A1
4649	" "	7	E½NW	1858-11-01		A1
4650	" "	7	NE	1858-11-01		A1
4634	SMITH, John	7	SWSW	1854-10-02		A1
4636	WILKERSON, Joshua A	5	NWSW	1858-11-01		A1
4637	" "	5	SWNW	1858-11-01		A1
4638	WILKERSON, Joshua H	6	E½NE	1858-11-01		A1

ID	Individual in Patent	Sec.	Sec. Part	Date Issued	Other Counties	For More Info . . .
4639	WILKERSON, Joshua H (Cont'd)	6	NWNE	1858-11-01		A1
4652	WILKERSON, William F	8	NENW	1862-04-10		A1
4616	WOOD, David	8	N½SE	1860-12-01		A1
4617	" "	8	NE	1860-12-01		A1

Patent Map

T8-N R16-E
St Stephens Meridian

Map Group 20

Township Statistics

Parcels Mapped	:	49
Number of Patents	:	36
Number of Individuals	:	26
Patentees Identified	:	26
Number of Surnames	:	24
Multi-Patentee Parcels	:	1
Oldest Patent Date	:	2/2/1852
Most Recent Patent	:	6/29/1891
Block/Lot Parcels	:	0
Parcels Re - Issued	:	0
Parcels that Overlap	:	0
Cities and Towns	:	0
Cemeteries	:	0

Note: the area contained in this map amounts to far less than a full Township. Therefore, its contents are completely on this single page (instead of a "normal" 2-page spread).

Legend

——— Patent Boundary

━━━ Section Boundary

░░ No Patents Found (or Outside County)

1., 2., 3., ... Lot Numbers (when beside a name)

[ ] Group Number (see Appendix "C")

Scale: Section = 1 mile X 1 mile (generally, with some exceptions)

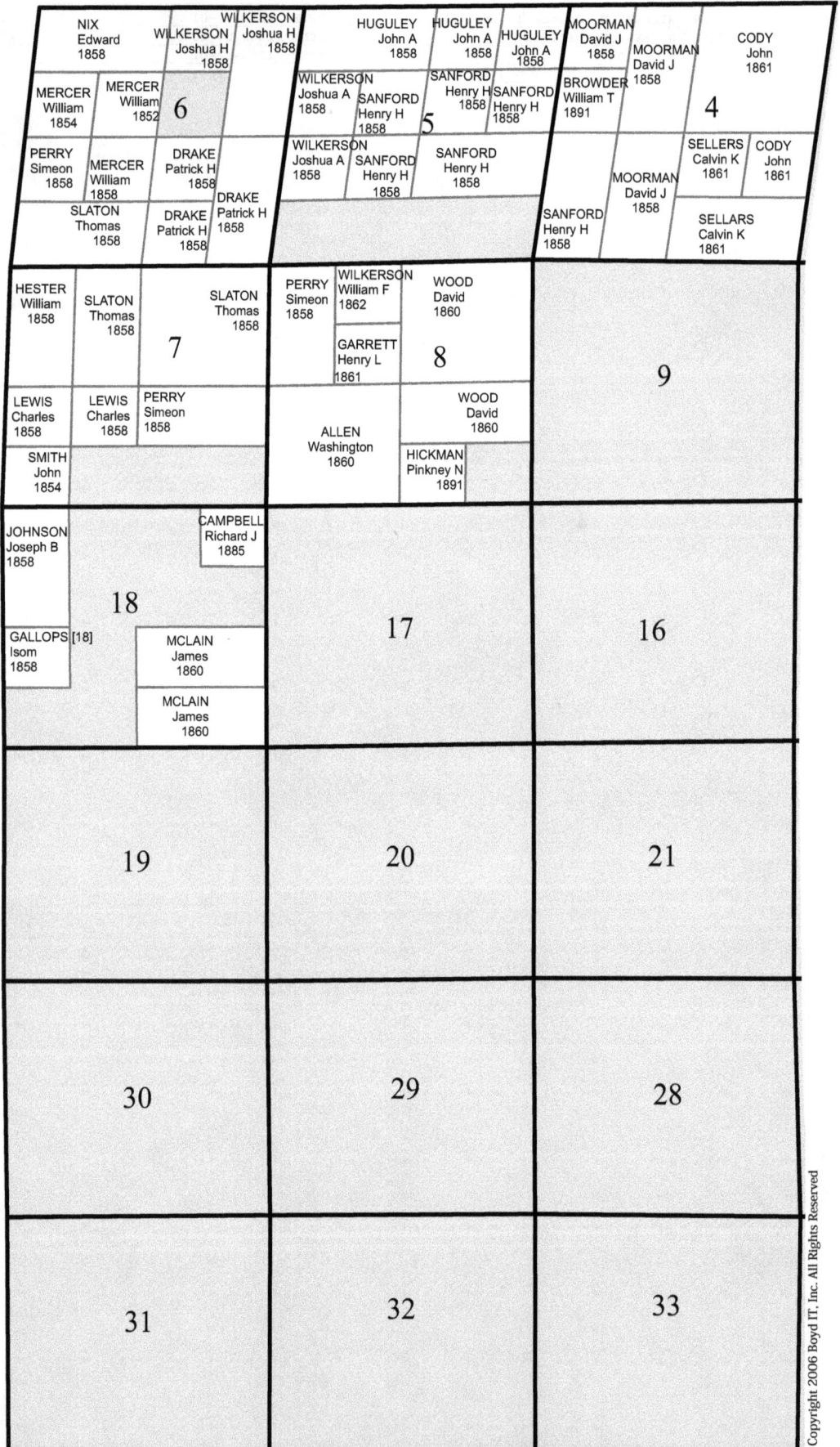

Section 6
NIX Edward 1858
WILKERSON Joshua H 1858
WILKERSON Joshua H 1858
MERCER William 1854
MERCER William 1852
PERRY Simeon 1858
MERCER William 1858
DRAKE Patrick H
DRAKE Patrick H 1858
SLATON Thomas 1858
DRAKE Patrick H 1858

Section 5
HUGULEY John A 1858
HUGULEY John A 1858
HUGULEY John A 1858
WILKERSON Joshua A 1858
SANFORD Henry H 1858
SANFORD Henry H 1858
SANFORD Henry H 1858
WILKERSON Joshua A 1858
SANFORD Henry H 1858
SANFORD Henry H 1858

Section 4
MOORMAN David J 1858
MOORMAN David J 1858
CODY John 1861
BROWDER William T 1891
MOORMAN David J 1858
SANFORD Henry H 1858
SELLERS Calvin K 1861
CODY John 1861
SELLARS Calvin K 1861

Section 7
HESTER William 1858
SLATON Thomas 1858
SLATON Thomas 1858
LEWIS Charles 1858
LEWIS Charles 1858
PERRY Simeon 1858
SMITH John 1854

Section 8
PERRY Simeon 1858
WILKERSON William F 1862
WOOD David 1860
GARRETT Henry L 1861
ALLEN Washington 1860
WOOD David 1860
HICKMAN Pinkney N 1891

Section 9

Section 18
JOHNSON Joseph B 1858
CAMPBELL Richard J 1885
GALLOPS [18] Isom 1858
MCLAIN James 1860
MCLAIN James 1860

Section 17
Section 16
Section 19
Section 20
Section 21
Section 30
Section 29
Section 28
Section 31
Section 32
Section 33

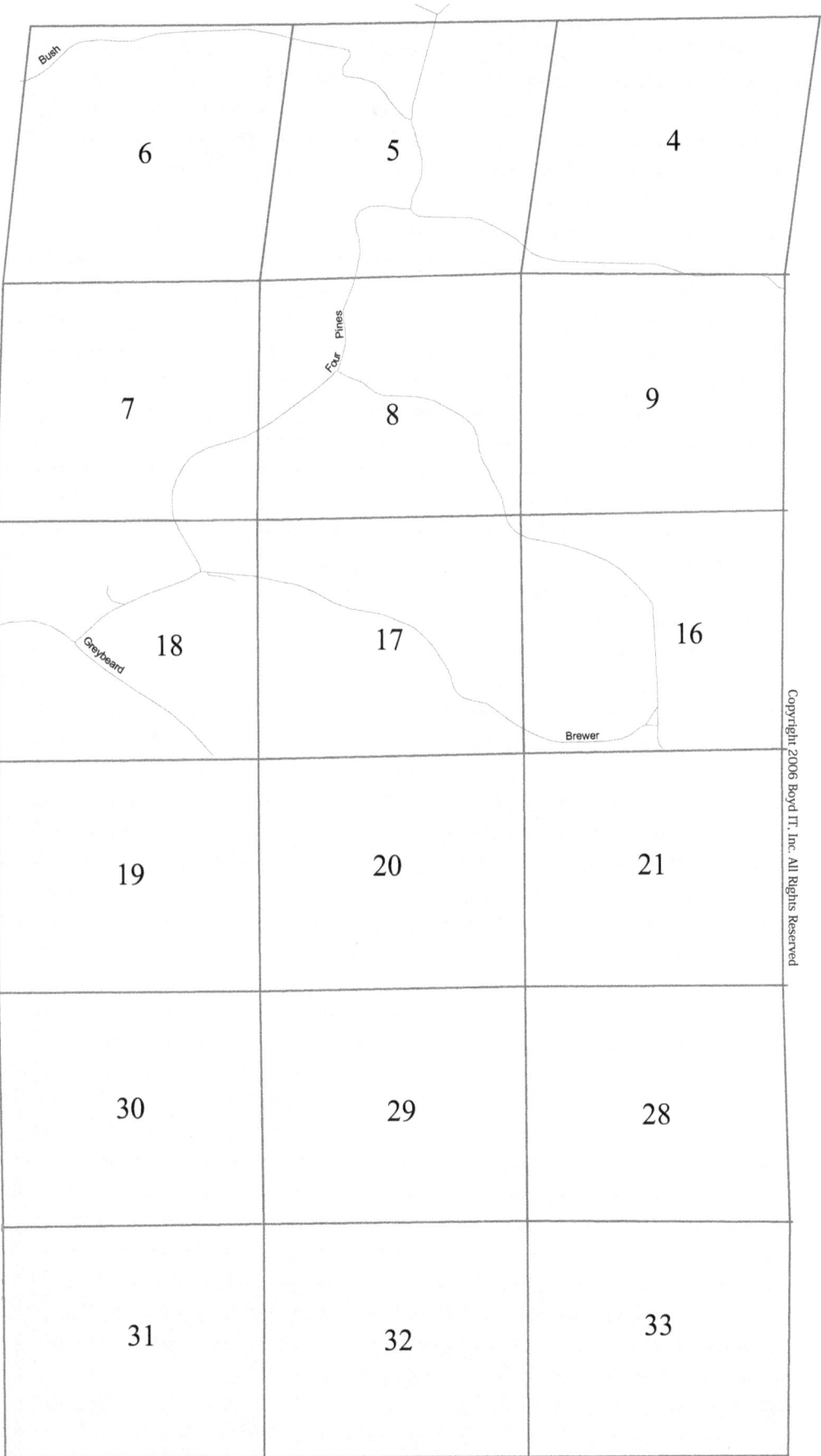

Road Map

T8-N R16-E
St Stephens Meridian

Map Group 20

Note: the area contained in this map amounts to far less than a full Township. Therefore, its contents are completely on this single page (instead of a "normal" 2-page spread).

Cities & Towns
None

Cemeteries
None

Legend

——— Section Lines
═══ Interstates
▬▬▬ Highways
——— Other Roads
● Cities/Towns
✝ Cemeteries

Scale: Section = 1 mile X 1 mile
(generally, with some exceptions)

Historical Map

T8-N R16-E
St Stephens Meridian

Map Group 20

Note: the area contained in this map amounts to far less than a full Township. Therefore, its contents are completely on this single page (instead of a "normal" 2-page spread).

Cities & Towns
None

Cemeteries
None

Legend

——————	Section Lines
++++++++	Railroads
▭	Large Rivers & Bodies of Water
- - - - - -	Streams/Creeks & Small Rivers
●	Cities/Towns
†	Cemeteries

Scale: Section = 1 mile X 1 mile
(there are some exceptions)

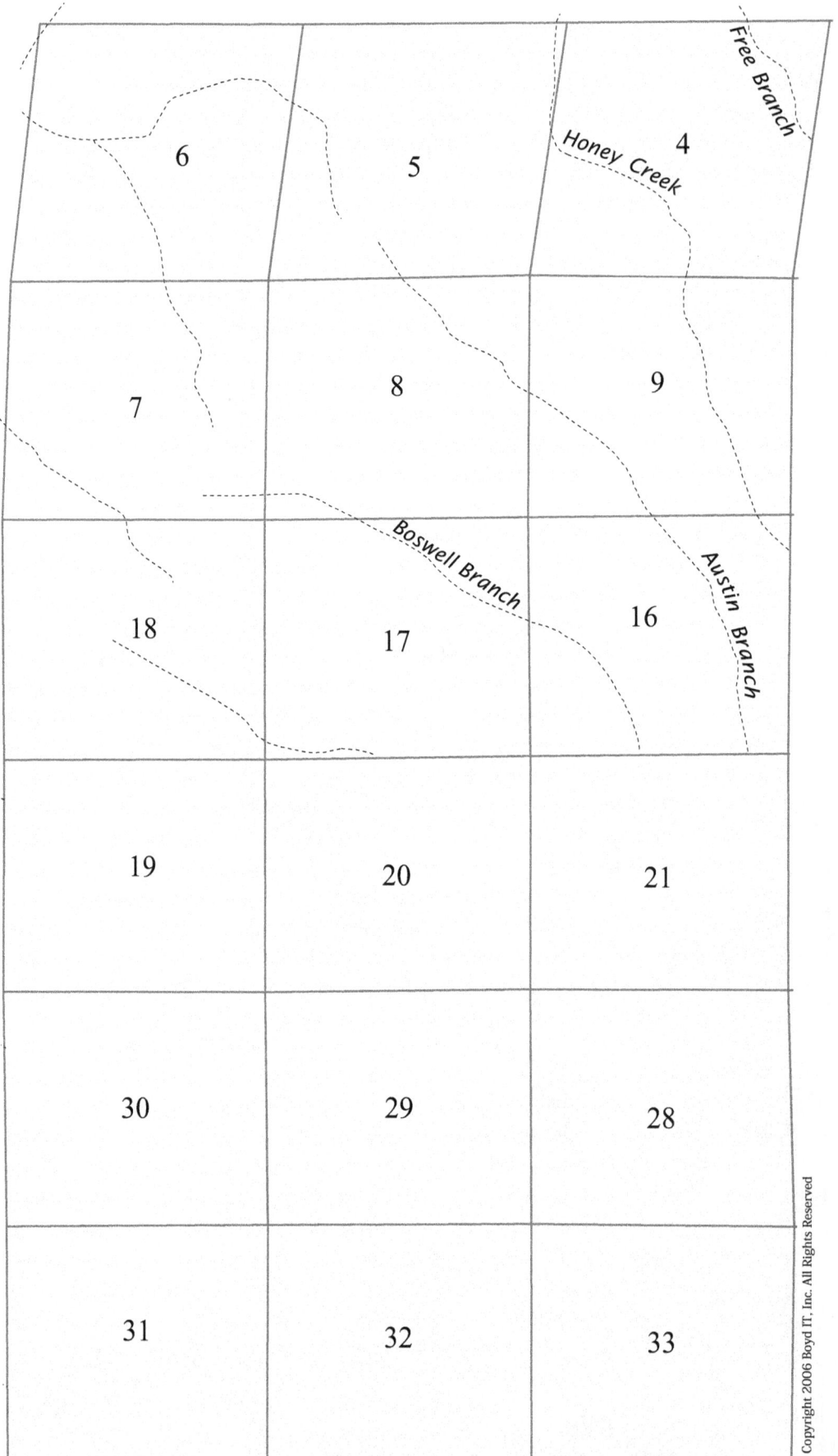

6

5

4

Free Branch

Honey Creek

7

8

9

18

17

Boswell Branch

16

Austin Branch

19

20

21

30

29

28

31

32

33

Map Group 21: Index to Land Patents

Township 7-North Range 12-East (St Stephens)

After you locate an individual in this Index, take note of the Section and Section Part then proceed to the Land Patent map on the pages immediately following. You should have no difficulty locating the corresponding parcel of land.

The "For More Info" Column will lead you to more information about the underlying Patents. See the *Legend* at right, and the "How to Use this Book" chapter, for more information.

```
                    LEGEND
            "For More Info . . . " column

A = Authority (Legislative Act, See Appendix "A")
B = Block or Lot (location in Section unknown)
C = Cancelled Patent
F = Fractional Section
G = Group (Multi-Patentee Patent, see Appendix "C")
V = Overlaps another Parcel
R = Re-Issued (Parcel patented more than once)

(A & G items require you to look in the Appendixes referred
to above. All other Letter-designations followed by a number
require you to locate line-items in this index that possess
the ID number found after the letter).
```

ID	Individual in Patent	Sec.	Sec. Part	Date Issued	Other Counties	For More Info . . .
4860	ANTONY, Thomas	10	SWSE	1858-11-01		A1
4861	" "	11	E½SW	1858-11-01		A1
4862	" "	14	W½SW	1858-11-01		A1 V4869
4863	" "	15	N½NE	1858-11-01		A1
4864	" "	15	SESE	1858-11-01		A1
4773	BALDWIN, Jesse	34	E½SW	1884-12-05	Conecuh	A2
4884	BAYZIER, William B	20	NWSE	1862-04-10	Conecuh	A1
4725	BEASLEY, Elijah	35	S½SW	1837-08-14		A1
4865	BENNETT, Thomas	3	NENE	1858-11-01		A1
4900	BILLINGSLEA, Winston	15	SW	1858-11-01		A1
4901	" "	15	SWNE	1858-11-01		A1
4902	" "	15	W½SE	1858-11-01		A1
4903	" "	5	E½NE	1858-11-01	Conecuh	A1
4904	" "	5	E½SW	1858-11-01	Conecuh	A1
4905	" "	5	NESE	1858-11-01	Conecuh	A1
4906	" "	5	SWNE	1858-11-01	Conecuh	A1
4907	" "	5	SWSE	1858-11-01	Conecuh	A1
4724	BOWDEN, Elias W	35	SENW	1860-04-02		A1
4696	BROOKS, Drury W	34	SENE	1860-12-01	Conecuh	A1
4703	BROOKS, Edward P	23	E½SE	1858-11-01		A1
4704	" "	23	NWSE	1858-11-01		A1
4705	" "	23	SWSE	1858-11-01		A1
4706	" "	25	E½SW	1858-11-01		A1
4707	" "	25	NWNW	1858-11-01		A1
4708	" "	25	SENW	1858-11-01		A1
4709	" "	36	NENW	1858-11-01		A1
4763	BROWN, James	33	SENE	1860-04-02	Conecuh	A1
4849	BROWN, Presley	28	NWSE	1838-07-28	Conecuh	A1
4850	BROWN, Pressley	28	NESE	1837-08-18	Conecuh	A1
4859	BROWN, Sterling	28	S½SE	1837-08-12	Conecuh	A1
4660	BUTLER, Albert	2	NESE	1838-07-28		A1
4880	BUTLER, Whitmill	2	NW	1837-08-18		A1
4881	" "	2	W½NE	1837-08-18		A1
4876	" "	11	E½NE	1838-07-28		A1
4877	" "	12	SW	1838-07-28		A1
4878	" "	12	W½NW	1838-07-28		A1
4879	" "	2	E½NE	1838-07-28		A1
4851	CANTELOO, Ransom	20	S½SW	1885-03-16	Conecuh	A2
4741	CHANCELLOR, Gillum	9	NWNE	1837-04-10		A1
4740	" "	4	W½SE	1837-08-12		A1
4752	CHANCELLOR, Jackson	10	NWSW	1858-11-01		A1
4753	" "	9	E½NE	1858-11-01		A1
4754	" "	9	SE	1858-11-01		A1
4759	CLARK, James B	12	E½NE	1837-08-14		A1
4760	" "	12	NWNE	1837-08-14		A1
4761	" "	13	E½SE	1837-08-15		A1 G8

ID	Individual in Patent	Sec.	Sec. Part	Date Issued	Other Counties	For More Info . . .
4762	CLARK, James B (Cont'd)	13	S½NE	1837-08-15		A1 G8
4675	COKER, Daniel	23	SW	1858-11-01		A1
4837	COKER, Nelson	22	N½NW	1890-03-19		A2
4866	COKER, Thomas	10	E½SE	1838-07-28		A1
4867	" "	11	W½SW	1838-07-28		A1
4868	" "	14	E½NW	1838-07-28		A1
4869	" "	14	SWSW	1838-07-28		A1 V4862
4789	COLEMAN, John	3	NWNW	1837-05-20		A1
4788	" "	3	NENW	1838-07-28		A1
4790	" "	3	NWSE	1858-09-01		A1 R4793
4886	COLEMAN, William	3	W½NE	1838-07-28		A1 V4792
4778	CONE, Jesse	36	SW	1837-08-12		A1
4774	" "	10	E½NW	1838-07-28		A1
4775	" "	10	NE	1838-07-28		A1
4776	" "	11	W½NW	1838-07-28		A1
4777	" "	24	NE	1838-07-28		A1
4779	" "	4	NENE	1838-07-28		A1
4780	" "	6	NESE	1838-07-28	Conecuh	A1
4781	" "	6	W½SE	1838-07-28	Conecuh	A1
4782	" "	8	NW	1838-07-28	Conecuh	A1
4783	" "	8	SE	1838-07-28	Conecuh	A1
4784	" "	8	W½NE	1838-07-28	Conecuh	A1
4829	CONE, Lewis	12	SWNE	1837-08-12		A1
4893	CONE, William N	36	W½SE	1837-08-15		A1
4892	" "	2	W½SE	1837-08-18		A1
4887	" "	11	E½NW	1838-07-28		A1
4888	" "	11	SE	1838-07-28		A1
4889	" "	11	W½NE	1838-07-28		A1
4890	" "	14	E½SW	1838-07-28		A1
4891	" "	2	SESE	1838-07-28		A1
4755	CUNNINGHAM, James A	34	SWSW	1860-04-02	Conecuh	A1
4764	DEWBERRY, James	34	NESE	1837-08-12	Conecuh	A1
4882	DEWBERRY, Wiley	25	SWNW	1837-08-15		A1
4883	" "	25	W½SW	1837-08-15		A1
4872	DOZIER, Thomas R	25	SESE	1858-11-01		A1
4873	" "	25	SWSE	1858-11-01		A1
4744	DUKE, Henry L	36	NWNW	1837-08-12		A1
4745	" "	36	SENW	1837-08-18		A1
4662	DUNNAM, Andrew J	13	NWSW	1858-11-01		A1
4663	" "	14	SWNE	1858-11-01		A1
4822	ELLIS, Kinchen	6	SESE	1838-07-28	Conecuh	A1
4819	" "	25	E½NE	1858-11-01		A1
4820	" "	25	NWSE	1858-11-01		A1
4821	" "	25	SWNE	1858-11-01		A1
4855	EMANUEL, Samuel	28	W½SW	1888-01-21	Conecuh	A2
4701	ETHEREDGE, Edmund	28	SENW	1837-05-15	Conecuh	A1
4702	" "	28	SWNE	1837-08-14	Conecuh	A1
4697	" "	21	SWSE	1858-11-01	Conecuh	A1
4698	" "	26	NENW	1858-11-01		A1
4699	" "	28	E½NE	1858-11-01	Conecuh	A1
4700	" "	28	NWNE	1858-11-01	Conecuh	A1
4791	GILMER, John	5	NENW	1850-08-10	Conecuh	A1
4792	GILMON, John	3	NWNE	1852-02-02		A1 V4886
4793	" "	3	NWSE	1852-02-02		A1 R4790
4794	GILMORE, John	5	SENW	1854-07-15	Conecuh	A1
4795	" "	5	W½NW	1858-11-01	Conecuh	A1
4796	" "	5	W½SW	1858-11-01	Conecuh	A1
4668	GOSS, Benajah	10	W½NW	1838-07-28		A1
4798	HAMMETT, John	14	E½NE	1837-08-14		A1
4799	" "	14	NWNE	1837-08-14		A1
4695	HAMN, Dora	4	NWSW	1915-04-17		A1
4797	HAMN, John H	4	SESW	1915-04-17		A1
4800	HARE, John	36	NE	1858-11-01		A1
4801	" "	36	NESE	1858-11-01		A1
4830	HAYNIE, Luke	1	E½NW	1838-07-28		A1
4831	" "	1	W½NE	1838-07-28		A1
4665	HAYS, Archibald S	8	SENE	1858-11-01	Conecuh	A1
4666	" "	9	SWNW	1858-11-01		A1
4765	HENDERSON, James	4	SESE	1837-05-15		A1
4766	" "	9	E½NW	1837-05-15		A1
4768	" "	9	SWSW	1837-08-12		A1
4767	" "	9	E½SW	1837-08-18		A1
4728	HOBBS, Elijah	14	NESE	1838-07-28		A1

ID	Individual in Patent	Sec.	Sec. Part	Date Issued	Other Counties	For More Info . . .
4688	HUSON, Dawson	4	NESE	1837-08-02		A1
4692	" "	4	SENE	1837-08-02		A1
4686	" "	3	SWNW	1837-08-12		A1
4693	" "	4	SWNE	1841-05-20		A1
4691	" "	4	NWNW	1852-02-02		A1
4687	" "	4	E½NW	1858-11-01		A1
4689	" "	4	NESW	1858-11-01		A1
4690	" "	4	NWNE	1858-11-01		A1
4694	" "	4	SWNW	1858-11-01		A1
4802	HUSON, John	9	NWSW	1837-08-18		A1
4803	" "	9	SWNE	1837-08-18		A1
4769	JAMES, James	25	NENW	1852-12-01		A1
4679	JAY, David	20	N½SW	1858-11-01	Conecuh	A1
4770	JAY, James W	20	N½NW	1858-11-01	Conecuh	A1
4771	" "	20	S½NW	1858-11-01	Conecuh	A1
4785	JAY, Jesse	17	NESW	1875-04-20	Conecuh	A1
4786	" "	17	NWSE	1875-04-20	Conecuh	A1
4787	" "	17	SENW	1875-04-20	Conecuh	A1
4742	KEEBLER, Hamilton	15	NW	1858-11-01		A1
4818	KENDRICK, Josiah	2	E½SW	1837-08-12		A1
4885	LYNCH, William B	25	NWNE	1843-02-01		A1
4737	MCCLURE, George H	24	NESE	1858-11-01		A1
4738	" "	24	SESE	1858-11-01		A1
4739	" "	24	SWSE	1858-11-01		A1
4804	MCMULLINS, John	4	SWSW	1858-11-01		A1
4805	" "	5	SESE	1858-11-01	Conecuh	A1
4676	MCPHERSON, Daniel	3	N½SW	1875-04-20		A1
4677	" "	3	SESW	1875-04-20		A1
4678	" "	3	SWSE	1875-04-20		A1
4670	MIMS, Chappell	22	S½SW	1892-01-20		A2
4671	" "	22	W½SE	1892-01-20		A2
4806	MURPHEY, John	3	SENE	1840-10-10		A1
4807	MYERS, John	13	W½SE	1837-08-12		A1
4809	MYERS, John P	12	SESE	1837-08-07		A1 R4713
4811	" "	13	NENE	1837-08-07		A1
4808	" "	12	E½NW	1837-08-14		A1
4810	" "	13	E½NW	1858-11-01		A1
4812	MYRES, John P	13	W½NW	1837-08-18		A1
4669	PAGE, Bennet	14	NWNW	1837-08-18		A1
4673	PAGE, Curtis	8	NESW	1858-11-01	Conecuh	A1
4674	" "	8	SESW	1858-11-01	Conecuh	A1
4826	PAGE, Kinchin	6	S½NW	1837-08-18	Conecuh	A1
4827	" "	6	SWSW	1851-04-10	Conecuh	A1
4828	" "	6	W½NE	1851-04-10	Conecuh	A1
4823	" "	6	E½NE	1858-11-01	Conecuh	A1
4824	" "	6	NENW	1860-04-02	Conecuh	A1
4825	" "	6	NWSW	1860-04-02	Conecuh	A1
4894	PARKER, William	1	E½NE	1837-08-12		A1
4842	PEACOCK, Nicholas	34	NWSW	1880-02-20	Conecuh	A2
4843	" "	34	SWNW	1880-02-20	Conecuh	A2
4844	PEACOCK, Noah B	27	E½NW	1858-11-01		A1
4845	" "	27	E½SW	1858-11-01		A1
4846	" "	27	NWSE	1858-11-01		A1
4847	" "	27	SWNE	1858-11-01		A1
4848	" "	27	W½SE	1858-11-01		A1
4856	PIPKIN, Stephen W	34	NENW	1840-10-10	Conecuh	A1
4857	" "	34	SENW	1840-10-10	Conecuh	A1
4858	" "	34	W½NE	1840-10-10	Conecuh	A1
4713	PRESLAR, Elias	12	SESE	1837-08-12		A1 R4809
4714	" "	12	W½SE	1837-08-12		A1
4715	" "	13	NWNE	1837-08-12		A1
4716	" "	13	SESW	1837-08-18		A1
4717	" "	24	E½NW	1837-08-18		A1
4661	PRESLEY, Alfred	26	SENW	1883-09-15		A2
4664	PRESLEY, Anthony	1	SE	1837-08-14		A1
4718	PRESLEY, Elias	13	SWSW	1858-11-01		A1
4719	" "	14	SESE	1858-11-01		A1
4720	" "	14	W½SE	1858-11-01		A1
4721	" "	2	SWSW	1858-11-01		A1
4722	" "	23	E½NE	1858-11-01		A1
4723	" "	24	W½NW	1858-11-01		A1
4711	PRESLEY, Elias B	22	NENE	1858-11-01		A1
4712	" "	23	NW	1858-11-01		A1

ID	Individual in Patent	Sec.	Sec. Part	Date Issued	Other Counties	For More Info . . .
4750	PRESLEY, Hosey S	2	NWSW	1858-11-01		A1
4751	" "	3	E½SE	1858-11-01		A1
4756	PRESLEY, James A	10	E½SW	1858-11-01		A1
4757	" "	10	NWSE	1858-11-01		A1
4758	" "	10	SWSW	1858-11-01		A1
4833	PRESSLEY, Martin	26	E½SW	1883-07-03		A2
4749	PRUETT, Henry W	20	SWSE	1920-01-19	Conecuh	A1
4735	ROBERTS, Franklin	26	SWNW	1891-06-29		A2
4736	" "	26	W½SW	1891-06-29		A2
4734	" "	26	NWNW	1892-01-18		A2
4729	ROGERS, Francis	34	SWSE	1858-11-01	Conecuh	A1
4730	" "	35	N½SE	1858-11-01		A1
4731	" "	35	N½SW	1858-11-01		A1
4732	" "	35	SENE	1858-11-01		A1
4733	" "	36	SWNW	1858-11-01		A1
4895	ROGERS, William	21	NENW	1858-11-01	Conecuh	A1
4896	" "	21	SENE	1858-11-01	Conecuh	A1
4897	" "	21	SENW	1858-11-01	Conecuh	A1
4898	" "	21	SWNE	1858-11-01	Conecuh	A1
4672	SALTER, Charles P	6	NWNW	1837-08-18	Conecuh	A1
4658	SCARBOROUGH, Addison	17	E½SE	1837-08-18	Conecuh	A1
4659	" "	17	NE	1837-08-18	Conecuh	A1
4874	SCIPPER, Wesley	33	E½SE	1860-04-02	Conecuh	A1
4875	" "	33	SWSE	1860-04-02	Conecuh	A1
4813	SHELL, John	8	W½SW	1852-02-02	Conecuh	A1
4838	SIMPSON, Nicholas L	17	SESE	1858-11-01	Conecuh	A1
4839	" "	17	SWSE	1858-11-01	Conecuh	A1
4840	" "	20	NE	1858-11-01	Conecuh	A1
4841	" "	21	W½NW	1858-11-01	Conecuh	A1
4667	SKINNER, Asa	26	E½SE	1841-05-20		A1
4710	SMITH, Edwin R	1	SW	1837-08-15		A1
4899	SMITH, Wilson	26	SWSE	1915-07-20		A2
4836	STILL, Nathaniel	34	NWNW	1895-06-03	Conecuh	A2 R4854
4853	STILL, Robert	22	SESE	1892-05-19		A2
4814	STINSON, Jordan B	13	NESW	1858-11-01		A1
4815	" "	23	W½NE	1858-11-01		A1
4816	" "	24	N½SW	1858-11-01		A1
4817	" "	24	S½SW	1858-11-01		A1
4681	STOTT, David	21	SW	1837-05-20	Conecuh	A1
4684	" "	28	W½NW	1837-05-20	Conecuh	A1
4682	" "	28	NENW	1837-08-12	Conecuh	A1
4683	" "	28	SESW	1837-08-12	Conecuh	A1
4685	" "	33	NWNW	1837-08-12	Conecuh	A1
4680	" "	20	E½SE	1838-07-28	Conecuh	A1
4832	STOTT, Marshall	28	NESW	1837-08-02	Conecuh	A1
4834	WALLACE, Mitchell	22	N½SW	1894-11-21		A2
4835	" "	22	S½NW	1894-11-21		A2
4746	WARD, Henry R	17	NENW	1858-09-01	Conecuh	A1
4747	" "	17	W½NW	1858-09-01	Conecuh	A1
4748	" "	17	W½SW	1858-09-01	Conecuh	A1
4852	WEAVER, Rebecca	8	NENE	1895-07-17	Conecuh	A2
4743	WEST, Harry	1	W½NW	1838-07-28		A1
4761	WEST, Henry	13	E½SE	1837-08-15		A1 G8
4762	" "	13	S½NE	1837-08-15		A1 G8
4726	WILLIAMS, Elijah H	15	NESE	1852-02-02		A1
4727	" "	15	SENE	1852-02-02		A1
4854	WILLIAMS, Samuel D	34	NWNW	1837-08-18	Conecuh	A1 R4836
4772	WRIGHT, James	6	E½SW	1851-04-10	Conecuh	A1
4870	WRIGHT, Thomas G	27	SWSW	1840-10-10		A1
4871	" "	34	NWSE	1840-10-10	Conecuh	A1

Patent Map

T7-N R12-E
St Stephens Meridian

Map Group 21

Township Statistics

Parcels Mapped	:	250
Number of Patents	:	171
Number of Individuals	:	106
Patentees Identified	:	106
Number of Surnames	:	74
Multi-Patentee Parcels	:	2
Oldest Patent Date	:	4/10/1837
Most Recent Patent	:	1/19/1920
Block/Lot Parcels	:	0
Parcels Re - Issued	:	3
Parcels that Overlap	:	4
Cities and Towns	:	2
Cemeteries	:	4

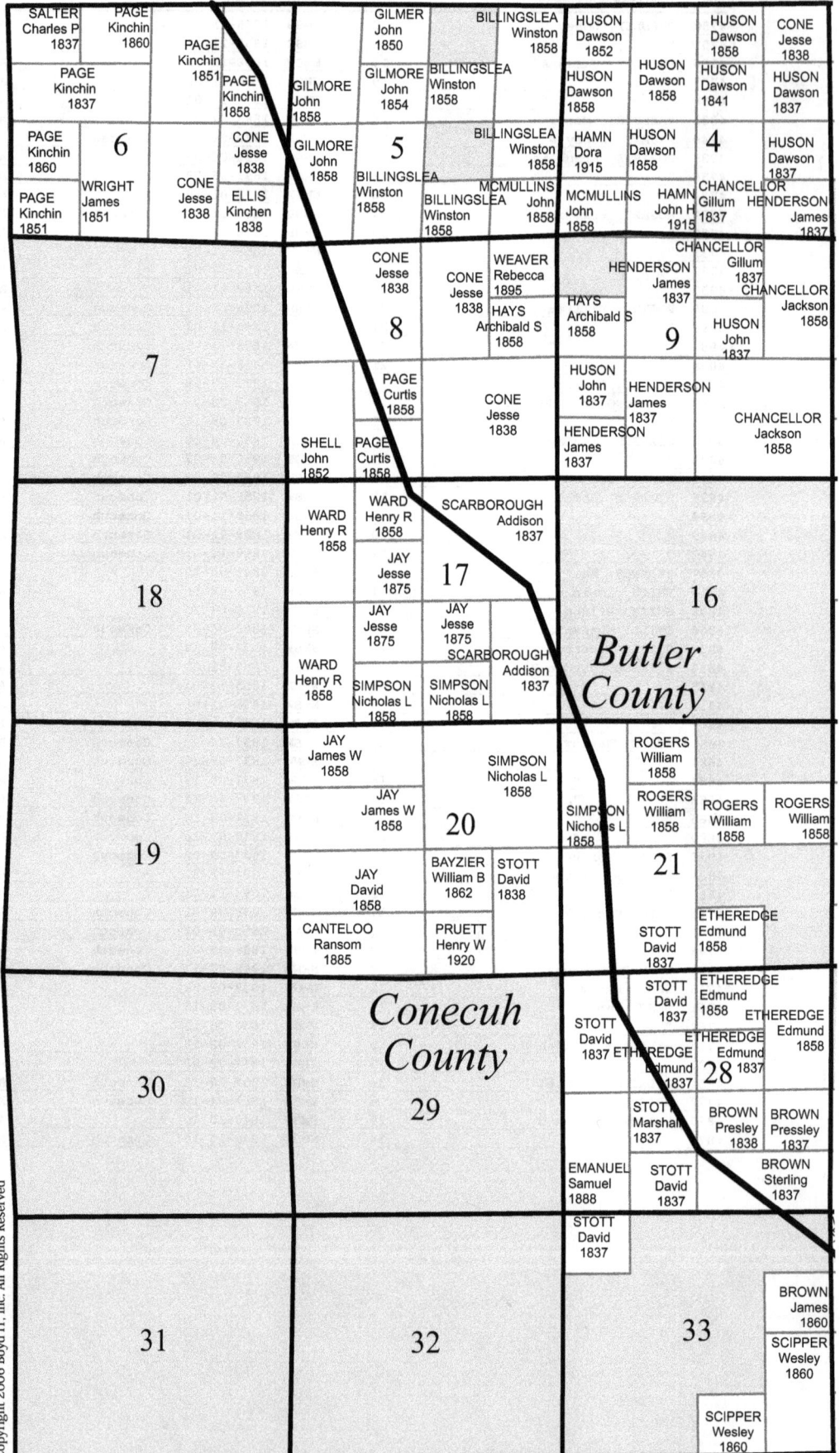

Map content (parcels):

Section 6:
SALTER Charles P 1837 | PAGE Kinchin 1860 | PAGE Kinchin 1851
PAGE Kinchin 1837
PAGE Kinchin 1860 | WRIGHT James 1851 | CONE Jesse 1838 | CONE Jesse 1838 | ELLIS Kinchen 1838
PAGE Kinchin 1851
PAGE Kinchin 1858

Section 5:
GILMER John 1850 | BILLINGSLEA Winston 1858
GILMORE John 1858 | GILMORE John 1854 | BILLINGSLEA Winston 1858
GILMORE John 1858
BILLINGSLEA Winston 1858 | BILLINGSLEA Winston 1858 | MCMULLINS John 1858

Section 4:
HUSON Dawson 1852 | HUSON Dawson 1858 | CONE Jesse 1838
HUSON Dawson 1858 | HUSON Dawson 1858 | HUSON Dawson 1841 | HUSON Dawson 1837
HAMN Dora 1915 | HUSON Dawson 1858 | HUSON Dawson 1837
MCMULLINS John 1858 | HAMN John H 1915 | CHANCELLOR Gillum 1837 | HENDERSON James 1837

Section 7

Section 8:
CONE Jesse 1838 | CONE Jesse 1838 | WEAVER Rebecca 1895
HAYS Archibald S 1858
PAGE Curtis 1858 | CONE Jesse 1838
SHELL John 1852 | PAGE Curtis 1858

Section 9:
CHANCELLOR Gillum 1837
HENDERSON James 1837 | CHANCELLOR Jackson 1858
HAYS Archibald S 1858 | HUSON John 1837
HUSON John 1837 | HENDERSON James 1837 | CHANCELLOR Jackson 1858
HENDERSON James 1837

Section 18

Section 17:
WARD Henry R 1858 | WARD Henry R 1858 | SCARBOROUGH Addison 1837
JAY Jesse 1875
JAY Jesse 1875 | JAY Jesse 1875
WARD Henry R 1858 | SIMPSON Nicholas L 1858 | SIMPSON Nicholas L 1858 | SCARBOROUGH Addison 1837

Section 16 — Butler County

Section 19

Section 20:
JAY James W 1858
JAY James W 1858
JAY David 1858 | BAYZIER William B 1862 | STOTT David 1838
CANTELOO Ransom 1885 | PRUETT Henry W 1920
SIMPSON Nicholas L 1858

Section 21:
ROGERS William 1858
SIMPSON Nicholas L 1858 | ROGERS William 1858 | ROGERS William 1858 | ROGERS William 1858
STOTT David 1837 | ETHEREDGE Edmund 1858

Section 29 — Conecuh County

Section 28:
STOTT David 1837 | ETHEREDGE Edmund 1858 | ETHEREDGE Edmund 1858
STOTT David 1837 | ETHEREDGE Edmund 1837 | ETHEREDGE Edmund 1837
STOTT Marshall 1837 | BROWN Presley 1838 | BROWN Pressley 1837
EMANUEL Samuel 1888 | STOTT David 1837 | BROWN Sterling 1837
STOTT David 1837

Section 30

Section 31

Section 32

Section 33:
BROWN James 1860
SCIPPER Wesley 1860
SCIPPER Wesley 1860

COLEMAN John 1837	COLEMAN John 1838	GILMON John 1852	BENNETT Thomas 1858	BUTLER Whitmill 1837		BUTLER Whitmill 1837	BUTLER Whitmill 1838	WEST Harry 1838	HAYNIE Luke 1838	HAYNIE Luke 1838	PARKER William 1837

Section 3
- COLEMAN John 1837
- COLEMAN John 1838
- GILMON John 1852
- BENNETT Thomas 1858
- HUSON Dawson 1837
- COLEMAN William 1838
- MURPHEY John 1840
- MCPHERSON Daniel 1875
- COLEMAN John 1858
- GILMON John 1852
- MCPHERSON Daniel 1875
- MCPHERSON Daniel 1875
- PRESLEY Hosey S 1858

Section 2
- BUTLER Whitmill 1837
- BUTLER Whitmill 1837
- BUTLER Whitmill 1838
- PRESLEY Hosey S 1858
- KENDRICK Josiah 1837
- CONE William N 1837
- BUTLER Albert 1838
- PRESLEY Elias 1858
- CONE William N 1838

Section 1
- WEST Harry 1838
- HAYNIE Luke 1838
- HAYNIE Luke 1838
- PARKER William 1837
- SMITH Edwin R 1837
- PRESLEY Anthony 1837

Section 10
- GOSS Benajah 1838
- CONE Jesse 1838
- CONE Jesse 1838
- CHANCELLOR Jackson 1858
- PRESLEY James A 1858
- PRESLEY James A 1858
- PRESLEY James A 1858
- ANTONY Thomas 1858
- COKER Thomas 1838

Section 11
- CONE Jesse 1838
- CONE William N 1838
- CONE William N 1838
- BUTLER Whitmill 1838
- COKER Thomas 1838
- ANTONY Thomas 1858
- CONE William N 1838

Section 12
- MYERS John P 1837
- CLARK James B 1837
- CLARK James B 1837
- CONE Lewis 1837
- BUTLER Whitmill 1838
- PRESLAR Elias 1837
- PRESLAR Elias 1837
- MYERS Elias 1837
- MYERS John P 1837

Section 15
- KEEBLER Hamilton 1858
- ANTONY Thomas 1858
- BILLINGSLEA Winston 1858
- WILLIAMS Elijah H 1852
- BILLINGSLEA Winston 1858
- WILLIAMS Elijah H 1852
- BILLINGSLEA Winston 1858
- ANTONY Thomas 1858

Section 14
- PAGE Bennet 1837
- HAMMETT John 1837
- COKER Thomas 1838
- DUNNAM Andrew J 1858
- ANTONY Thomas 1858
- COKER Thomas 1838
- CONE William N 1838
- PRESLEY Elias 1858
- HOBBS Elijah 1838
- PRESLEY Elias 1858

Section 13
- HAMMETT John 1837
- MYRES John P 1837
- MYERS John P 1858
- PRESLAR Elias 1837
- MYERS John P 1837
- CLARK [8] James B 1837
- DUNNAM Andrew J 1858
- STINSON Jordan B 1858
- PRESLEY Elias 1858
- PRESLAR Elias 1837
- MYERS John 1837
- CLARK [8] James B 1837

Section 22
- COKER Nelson 1890
- PRESLEY Elias B 1858
- WALLACE Mitchell 1894
- WALLACE Mitchell 1894
- MIMS Chappell 1892
- MIMS Chappell 1892
- STILL Robert 1892

Section 23
- PRESLEY Elias B 1858
- PRESLEY Elias B 1858
- STINSON Jordan B 1858
- COKER Daniel 1858
- BROOKS Edward P 1858
- BROOKS Edward P 1858
- BROOKS Edward P 1858

Section 24
- PRESLEY Elias 1858
- PRESLEY Elias 1858
- PRESLAR Elias 1837
- CONE Jesse 1838
- STINSON Jordan B 1858
- STINSON Jordan B 1858
- MCCLURE George H 1858
- MCCLURE George H 1858
- MCCLURE George H 1858

Section 27
- PEACOCK Noah B 1858
- PEACOCK Noah B 1858
- PEACOCK Noah B 1858
- PEACOCK Noah B 1858
- PEACOCK Noah B 1858
- WRIGHT Thomas G 1840

Section 26
- ROBERTS Franklin 1892
- ETHEREDGE Edmund 1858
- ROBERTS Franklin 1891
- PRESLEY Alfred 1883
- ROBERTS Franklin 1891
- PRESSLEY Martin 1883
- SKINNER Asa 1841
- SMITH Wilson 1915

Section 25
- BROOKS Edward P 1858
- JAMES James 1852
- LYNCH William B 1843
- ELLIS Kinchen 1858
- DEWBERRY Wiley 1837
- BROOKS Edward P 1858
- ELLIS Kinchen 1858
- ELLIS Kinchen 1858
- DEWBERRY Wiley 1837
- BROOKS Edward P 1858
- DOZIER Thomas R 1858
- DOZIER Thomas R 1858

Section 34
- WILLIAMS Samuel D 1837
- STILL Nathaniel 1858
- PIPKIN Stephen W 1840
- PIPKIN Stephen W 1840
- PEACOCK Nicholas 1880
- PIPKIN Stephen W 1840
- BROOKS Drury W 1860
- PEACOCK Nicholas 1880
- WRIGHT Thomas G 1840
- DEWBERRY James 1837
- BALDWIN Jesse 1884
- CUNNINGHAM James A 1860
- ROGERS Francis 1858

Section 35
- BOWDEN Elias W 1860
- ROGERS Francis 1858
- ROGERS Francis 1858
- ROGERS Francis 1858
- BEASLEY Elijah 1837

Section 36
- DUKE Henry L 1837
- BROOKS Edward P 1858
- ROGERS Francis 1858
- ROGERS Francis 1858
- DUKE Henry L 1837
- HARE John 1858
- CONE Jesse 1837
- CONE William N 1837
- HARE John 1858

Helpful Hints

1. This Map's INDEX can be found on the preceding pages.

2. Refer to Map "C" to see where this Township lies within Butler County, Alabama.

3. Numbers within square brackets [ ] denote a multi-patentee land parcel (multi-owner). Refer to Appendix "C" for a full list of members in this group.

4. Areas that look to be crowded with Patentees usually indicate multiple sales of the same parcel (Re-issues) or Overlapping parcels. See this Township's Index for an explanation of these and other circumstances that might explain "odd" groupings of Patentees on this map.

Legend

- ——— Patent Boundary
- ▬▬▬ Section Boundary
- No Patents Found (or Outside County)
- 1., 2., 3., ... Lot Numbers (when beside a name)
- [ ] Group Number (see Appendix "C")

Scale: Section = 1 mile X 1 mile (generally, with some exceptions)

Road Map

T7-N R12-E
St Stephens Meridian

Map Group 21

Cities & Towns
Garland
Mount Olive

Cemeteries
Garland Cemetery
Maye Cemetery
Mount Olive West Cemetery
Pressley Cemetery

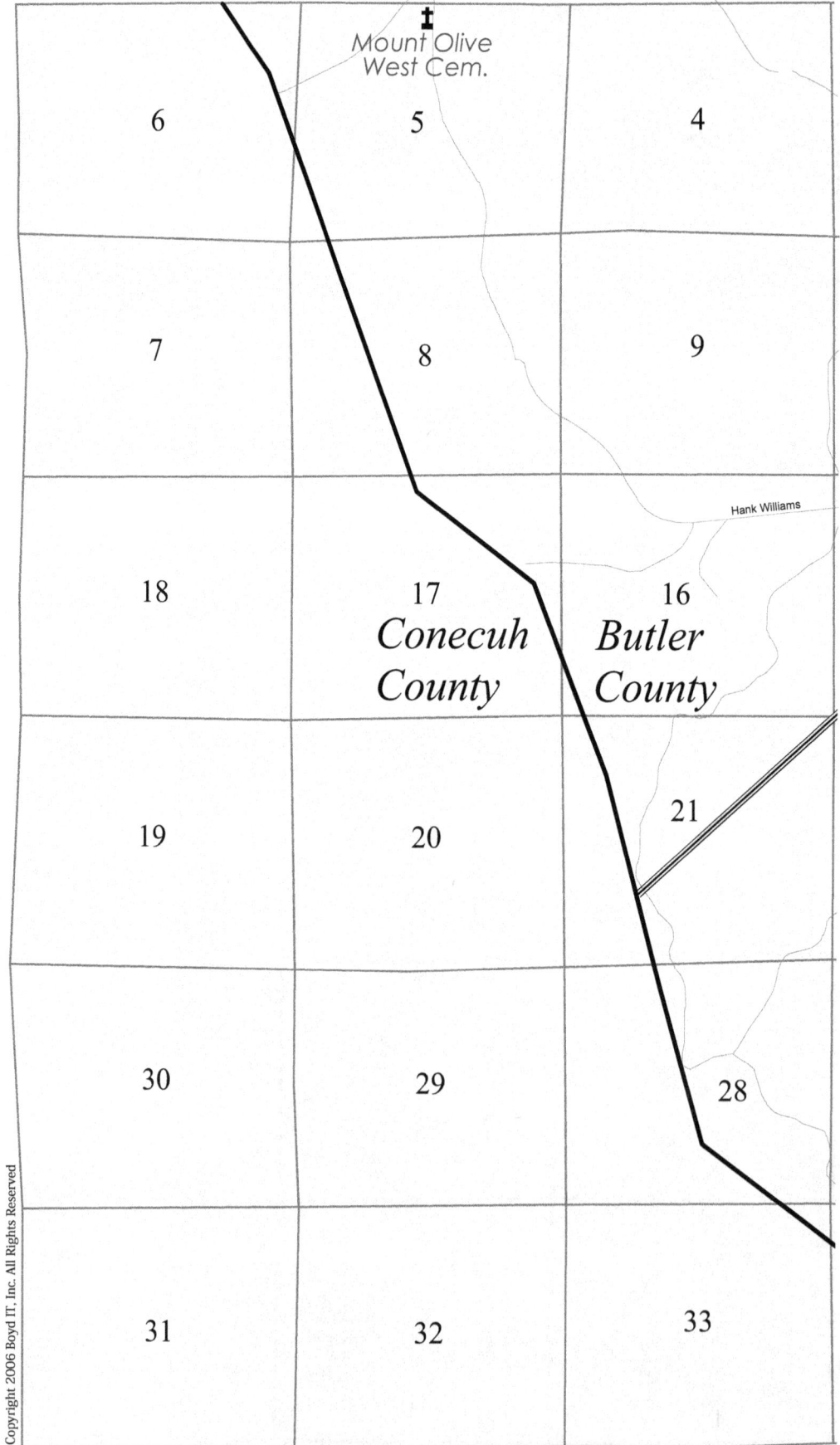

Mount Olive
West Cem.

6

5

4

7

8

9

Hank Williams

18

17
*Conecuh
County*

16
*Butler
County*

19

20

21

30

29

28

31

32

33

3

2

1

± Maye Cem.

Pressley Cem. ±

I-65

10

11

12

Shows

Mount Olive ●

Garland Cem. ±

15

14

13

22

Hank Williams

23

24

Garland ●

Garland

27

26

25

34

35

36

Mill Creek

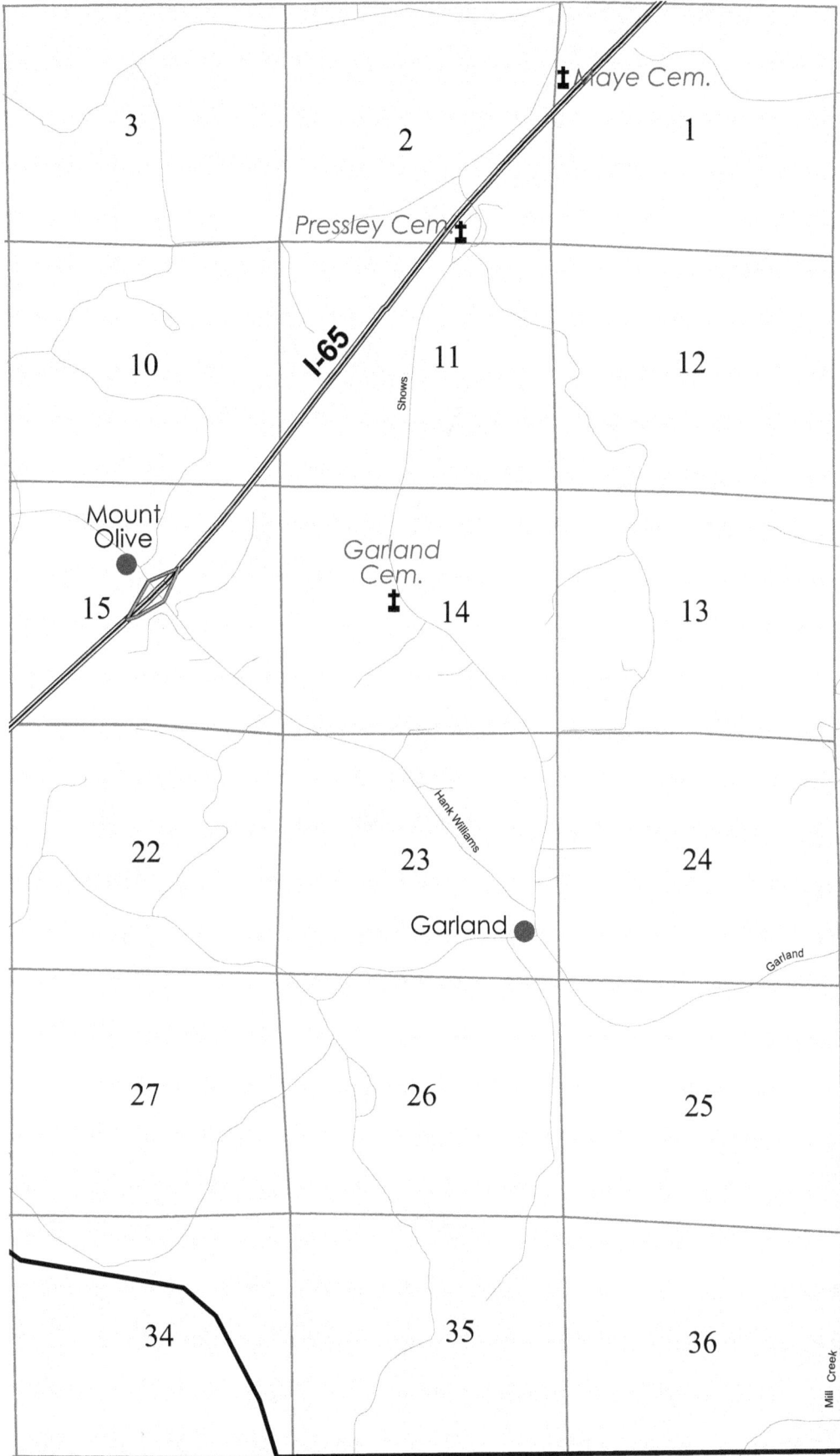

Helpful Hints

1. This road map has a number of uses, but primarily it is to help you: a) find the present location of land owned by your ancestors (at least the general area), b) find cemeteries and city-centers, and c) estimate the route/roads used by Census-takers & tax-assessors.

2. If you plan to travel to Butler County to locate cemeteries or land parcels, please pick up a modern travel map for the area before you do. Mapping old land parcels on modern maps is not as exact a science as you might think. Just the slightest variations in public land survey coordinates, estimates of parcel boundaries, or road-map deviations can greatly alter a map's representation of how a road either does or doesn't cross a particular parcel of land.

Legend

———— Section Lines

═══════ Interstates

▬▬▬▬▬▬ Highways

———— Other Roads

● Cities/Towns

± Cemeteries

Scale: Section = 1 mile X 1 mile
(generally, with some exceptions)

Historical Map

T7-N R12-E
St Stephens Meridian

Map Group 21

Cities & Towns
Garland
Mount Olive

Cemeteries
Garland Cemetery
Maye Cemetery
Mount Olive West Cemetery
Pressley Cemetery

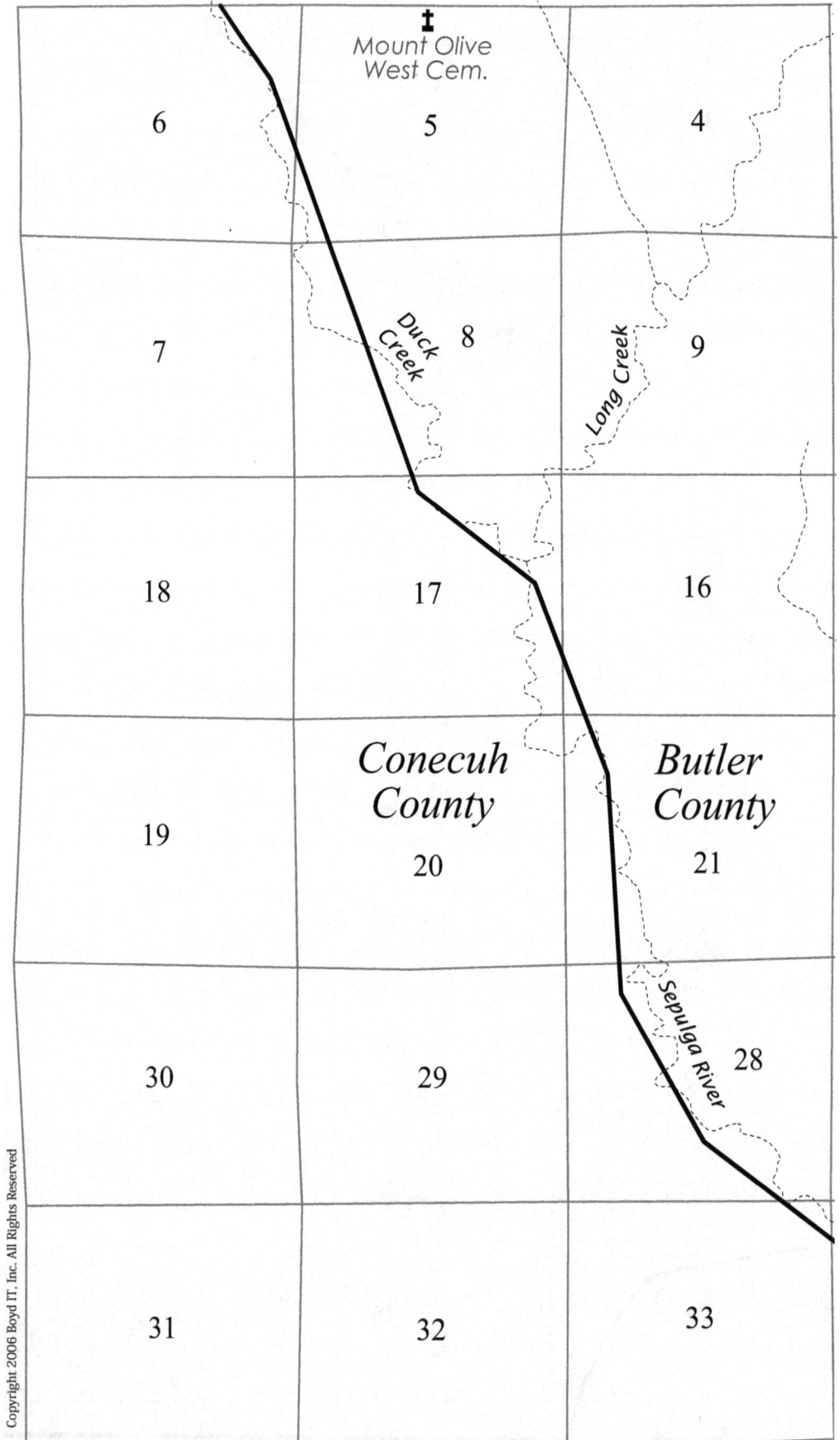

Mount Olive
West Cem.

| 6 | 5 | 4 |

| 7 | 8 | 9 |

Duck Creek

Long Creek

| 18 | 17 | 16 |

Conecuh County

Butler County

| 19 | 20 | 21 |

Sepulga River

| 30 | 29 | 28 |

| 31 | 32 | 33 |

‡ Maye Cem.

3　　　2　　　1

Pressley Cem. ‡

10　　　11　　　12

Mount Olive
●
15

Garland Cem.
‡
14　　　13

22　　　23　　　24

Persimmon Creek

Garland ●

27　　　26　　　25

34　　　35　　　36

Helpful Hints

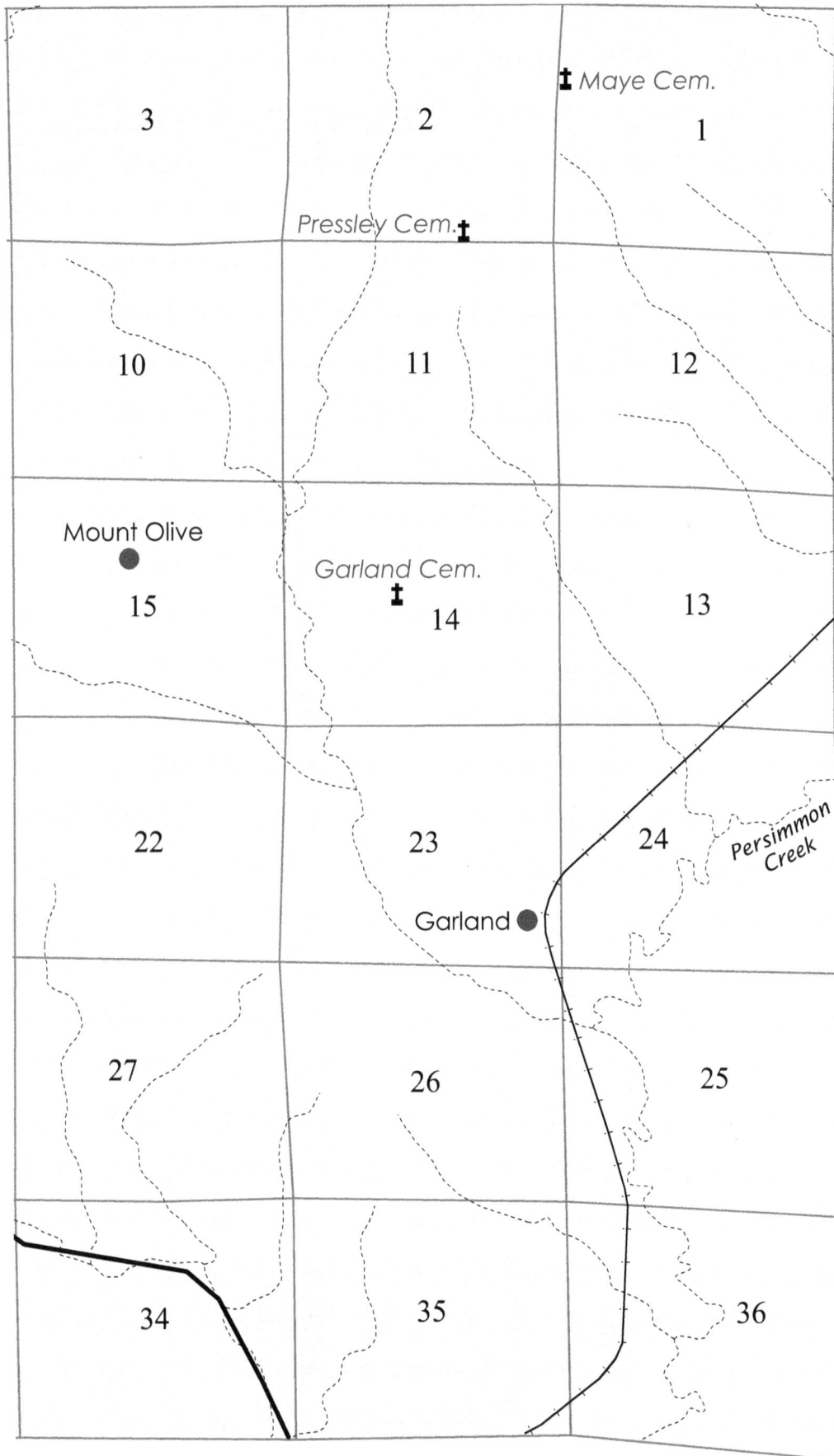

1. This Map takes a different look at the same Congressional Township displayed in the preceding two maps. It presents features that can help you better envision the historical development of the area: a) Water-bodies (lakes & ponds), b) Water-courses (rivers, streams, etc.), c) Railroads, d) City/town center-points (where they were oftentimes located when first settled), and e) Cemeteries.

2. Using this "Historical" map in tandem with this Township's Patent Map and Road Map, may lead you to some interesting discoveries. You will often find roads, towns, cemeteries, and waterways are named after nearby landowners: sometimes those names will be the ones you are researching. See how many of these research gems you can find here in Butler County.

Legend

————————	Section Lines
+++++++++	Railroads
▭	Large Rivers & Bodies of Water
- - - - - - -	Streams/Creeks & Small Rivers
●	Cities/Towns
‡	Cemeteries

Scale: Section = 1 mile X 1 mile
(there are some exceptions)

Map Group 22: Index to Land Patents

Township 7-North Range 13-East (St Stephens)

After you locate an individual in this Index, take note of the Section and Section Part then proceed to the Land Patent map on the pages immediately following. You should have no difficulty locating the corresponding parcel of land.

The "For More Info" Column will lead you to more information about the underlying Patents. See the *Legend* at right, and the "How to Use this Book" chapter, for more information.

```
                          LEGEND
             "For More Info . . . " column
A = Authority (Legislative Act, See Appendix "A")
B = Block or Lot (location in Section unknown)
C = Cancelled Patent
F = Fractional Section
G = Group  (Multi-Patentee Patent, see Appendix "C")
V = Overlaps another Parcel
R = Re-Issued (Parcel patented more than once)

(A & G items require you to look in the Appendixes referred
to above. All other Letter-designations followed by a number
require you to locate line-items in this index that possess
the ID number found after the letter).
```

ID	Individual in Patent	Sec.	Sec. Part	Date Issued	Other Counties	For More Info . . .
4911	ADAMS, Absalom J	20	E½NW	1891-06-08		A2
4934	ARANT, Calvin L	22	W½NW	1882-10-20		A2
4935	" "	22	W½SW	1882-10-20		A2
5016	ARANT, John F	21	NENE	1912-08-08		A2
4952	AUSTIN, Davis	4	SWSW	1837-05-15		A1
4953	" "	9	NENW	1837-05-15		A1
5096	BAILEY, Warner	7	W½	1837-08-12		A1
4918	BAKER, Amos C	6	NE	1838-07-28		A1
5014	BALDWIN, John A	24	E½NE	1884-03-20		A2
4964	BEASLEY, Enoch	9	NESW	1841-05-20		A1
4985	BEASLEY, Hillory	12	S½SE	1875-06-01		A2
5032	BEASLEY, John K	26	NENE	1891-05-29		A2
5033	" "	26	NWSE	1891-05-29		A2
5034	" "	26	W½NE	1891-05-29		A2
4936	BEESLEY, Celia	9	SESE	1858-11-01		A1
4965	BEESLEY, Enoch	10	W½NW	1858-11-01		A1
4966	" "	9	SENE	1858-11-01		A1
4912	BINION, Adam	26	NESW	1892-06-10		A2
4969	BINION, Eugene M	30	SWSE	1901-10-23		A2
5052	BINION, John T	30	W½SW	1883-10-20		A1
5050	" "	30	E½NE	1888-02-04		A2
5051	" "	30	E½SE	1888-02-04		A2
5086	BINION, Romaldus F	30	E½SW	1888-02-04		A2
5087	" "	30	NWSE	1888-02-04		A2
5088	" "	30	SWNE	1888-02-04		A2
5089	BINION, Rufus	26	N½NW	1893-05-26		A2
5073	BRANSFORD, Nathan	4	E½SW	1837-05-20		A1
4917	BROOKS, Allen	24	W½NE	1880-02-20		A2
4916	" "	24	E½NW	1883-04-10		A2
4941	BROOKS, Christopher	14	SESW	1884-03-20		A2
4942	" "	14	SWSE	1884-03-20		A2
4954	BROOKS, Drewry W	4	NESE	1858-11-01		A1
4955	" "	4	W½NE	1858-11-01		A1
4956	" "	4	W½SE	1858-11-01		A1
4957	BROOKS, Drury W	18	E½SW	1860-10-01		A1
4958	" "	18	W½SW	1860-10-01		A1
4959	" "	20	E½NE	1860-10-01		A1
5045	BROOKS, John S	20	NWNW	1858-11-01		A1
5046	" "	20	SWNW	1858-11-01		A1
5047	" "	5	S½SW	1858-11-01		A1
5048	" "	8	NW	1858-11-01		A1
5049	" "	8	W½NE	1858-11-01		A1
5057	BROOKS, Joseph S	34	SW	1891-09-01		A2
5067	BROOKS, Marshall	26	SENE	1894-05-08		A1
5077	BROOKS, Rachel	11	NENW	1858-11-01		A1
5078	" "	11	NWSE	1858-11-01		A1

ID	Individual in Patent	Sec.	Sec. Part	Date Issued	Other Counties	For More Info . . .
5079	BROOKS, Rachel (Cont'd)	11	S½NE	1858-11-01		A1
5080	" "	11	SWNW	1858-11-01		A1
5081	" "	12	W½NW	1858-11-01		A1
4960	BRYAN, Edward	14	SENE	1840-10-10		A1 G6
4995	BURKETT, James	28	SE	1858-11-01		A1 V5003
4996	" "	28	SESW	1858-11-01		A1 R5004
4922	CARPENTER, Benjamin D	2	S½SE	1889-11-21		A2
4994	CLARK, James B	17	NW	1837-08-15		A1 G8
5013	CONE, Jesse	7	W½NE	1838-07-28		A1
4998	CRAIG, James D	18	E½	1837-08-14		A1 G12
4997	" "	18	NW	1837-08-14		A1
4967	DANIEL, Ephraim F	10	NE	1858-11-01		A1
4968	" "	10	NESE	1858-11-01		A1
4920	DARBY, Armstead D	32	E½NW	1883-03-10		A1
4921	" "	32	W½NE	1883-03-10		A1
5061	DAVIS, Lancelott C	13	E½NE	1837-08-12		A1
4923	DEASE, Benjamin	21	SENW	1837-08-12		A1
4976	DEASE, George J	13	NESE	1837-08-12		A1
5010	DEEN, Jeptha J	14	NENW	1860-12-01		A1
5002	DRISKELL, James J	28	NESW	1891-06-30		A2 V5070
5003	" "	28	NWSE	1891-06-30		A2 V4995
5004	" "	28	SESW	1891-06-30		A2 R4996
4981	DRIVER, Giles	10	SW	1858-11-01		A1
4939	EDDINS, Charles M	32	S½SW	1890-01-08		A2
4940	" "	32	SWSE	1890-01-08		A2
5063	ETHEREDGE, Lewis	6	E½SE	1858-11-01		A1
5064	" "	6	SENW	1858-11-01		A1
5065	" "	6	W½SE	1858-11-01		A1
5011	FAIL, Jeremiah	2	E½SW	1854-07-15		A1
5012	" "	2	S½NW	1854-07-15		A1
5074	GALLAWAY, Nathan	4	W½NW	1858-11-01		A1
5075	GALLOWAY, Nathan	4	SENW	1858-11-01		A1
5076	" "	4	SESE	1860-10-01		A1
5095	GANUS, Walter A	32	SESE	1905-12-30		A2
5094	GARRETT, Thomas	14	SWNE	1837-08-12		A1
4982	GARUM, Halley D	5	NWNE	1916-11-15		A2 C R4988
4988	GORUM, Holley D	5	NWNE	1920-01-24		A2 R4982
5108	GRAHAM, William P	4	NWSW	1903-05-12		A1
5019	GREEN, John	8	SW	1838-07-28		A1
5020	" "	8	W½SE	1838-07-28		A1
5021	GREENE, John	7	SE	1837-08-15		A1
5028	HALL, John J	2	NESE	1910-11-25		A2
5029	" "	2	SENE	1910-11-25		A2
5027	" "	14	NWNE	1919-04-22		A1
5069	HARRISON, Mary J	5	NENW	1913-03-18		A2 G24
5069	HARRISON, William M	5	NENW	1913-03-18		A2 G24
4998	HARVEY, Thomas P	18	E½	1837-08-14		A1 G12
4943	HECKS, Cicero	2	W½SW	1883-03-01		A2
5037	HENDERSON, John M	2	N½NE	1860-04-02		A1
5038	" "	2	NWSE	1885-03-16		A2
5039	" "	2	SWNE	1885-03-16		A2
5035	HENRY, John K	12	NESW	1860-10-01		A1
5036	" "	12	W½NE	1860-10-01		A1
4938	HESTER, Charles J	36	NE	1891-06-19		A2
4963	HOBBS, Elijah	6	SESW	1838-07-28		A1
4992	HOBBS, Jacob	6	NWSW	1837-08-07		A1
4993	" "	6	W½NW	1837-08-07		A1
4991	" "	6	NENW	1858-11-01		A1
4927	HORN, Benjamin M	28	SWSW	1895-10-22		A2
4951	HOWELL, David	14	E½SE	1875-06-01		A2
5090	HUGGINS, Sarah	24	SWNW	1884-12-05		A2
5091	" "	24	W½SW	1884-12-05		A2
5005	JAMES, James	30	NWNW	1858-11-01		A1
4933	JONES, Caleb	34	NE	1891-06-08		A2
4971	JONES, Frank X	12	NWSW	1891-06-19		A2
4972	" "	12	S½SW	1891-06-19		A2
4913	LEE, Alexander	1	SENW	1835-10-15		A1
4914	" "	1	SWNE	1835-10-15		A1
4915	LEE, Alfred Y	34	SE	1891-06-19		A2
5084	LEE, Robert C	36	NW	1891-05-29		A2
4937	LONTZ, Charity E	2	N½NW	1885-03-16		A2
5053	MAY, Joseph J	5	N½SW	1858-11-01		A1
5054	" "	5	SE	1858-11-01		A1

ID	Individual in Patent	Sec.	Sec. Part	Date Issued	Other Counties	For More Info . . .
5055	MAY, Joseph J (Cont'd)	8	E½NE	1858-11-01		A1
5056	" "	9	NWNW	1858-11-01		A1
4974	MCCLURE, George H	19	SWSW	1849-09-01		A1
4973	" "	19	SESW	1858-11-01		A1
4975	" "	30	NENW	1858-11-01		A1
4977	MCCLURE, George L	28	NWNW	0012-00-00		A2
5100	MCCLURE, William D	19	NENW	1837-08-12		A1
5101	" "	19	NWNE	1858-11-01		A1
5102	" "	19	SENW	1858-11-01		A1
5103	" "	19	SWSE	1858-11-01		A1
5104	" "	19	W½NW	1858-11-01		A1
5105	" "	30	NWNE	1858-11-01		A1
5018	MCPHERSON, John F	9	SWNW	1852-02-02		A1
5017	" "	17	SW	1858-11-01		A1
5022	MCPHERSON, John H	20	NWSE	1888-02-04		A2
5023	" "	20	W½NE	1888-02-04		A2
5106	MCPHERSON, William L	20	NESE	1888-02-04		A2
5107	" "	20	S½SE	1888-02-04		A2
4919	MILLER, Andrew J	10	E½NW	1885-03-16		A1
5068	MILLS, Martha A	30	S½NW	1882-10-30		A1
5007	MINIARD, James T	22	E½SE	1888-02-04		A2
5008	" "	22	SESW	1888-02-04		A2
5009	" "	22	SWSE	1888-02-04		A2
4930	MITCHELL, Bud D	24	E½SW	1884-12-05		A2
4931	" "	24	N½SE	1884-12-05		A2
5083	MITCHELL, Ricey M	15	W½SE	1858-11-01		A1
5030	MORRIS, John J	32	E½NE	1890-03-19		A2
5031	" "	32	N½SE	1890-03-19		A2
5085	NORTHCUTT, Robert	13	N½SW	1838-07-28		A1
4989	OWENS, Isaiah	14	SENW	1885-03-16		A2
4990	" "	14	W½NW	1885-03-16		A2
4908	PACKER, Aaron	12	E½NW	1860-10-01		A1
4909	" "	12	N½SE	1860-10-01		A1
4910	" "	12	SENE	1860-10-01		A1
5040	PARKER, John	21	NENW	1858-11-01		A1
5042	PEACOCK, John R	20	SW	1883-10-20		A1
5041	POWELL, John	4	NENE	1837-08-18		A1
5109	POWELL, William	8	NESE	1837-08-18		A1
5110	" "	9	NWSW	1837-08-18		A1
5111	" "	9	SENW	1837-08-18		A1
5112	" "	9	SESW	1837-08-18		A1
4970	PRESLAR, Floyd	13	NENW	1837-08-12		A1
4986	PRESLAR, Holden	13	NWNW	1837-08-01		A1
4987	" "	14	NENE	1837-08-01		A1
4960	" "	14	SENE	1840-10-10		A1 G6
5006	PRICE, James	6	SWSW	1838-07-28		A1
5024	PRUETT, John H	32	N½SW	1889-11-21		A2
5025	" "	32	W½NW	1889-11-21		A2
5113	QUINNELLY, William	13	SWSW	1837-08-12		A1
5114	" "	24	NWNW	1837-08-12		A1
4949	RHODES, Daniel H	22	NESW	1899-08-14		A2
5099	ROBERTS, William C	10	SESE	1912-08-19		A2
5043	RUSHTON, John	8	SESE	1837-04-10		A1
5044	" "	9	SWSW	1837-04-10		A1
4950	SANFORD, Daniel	10	W½SE	1860-10-01		A1
4947	SELLERS, Daniel B	22	NWSE	1885-06-30		A2
4948	" "	22	S½NE	1885-06-30		A2
4978	SELLERS, George O	28	N½NE	1888-02-04		A2
4979	" "	28	NENW	1888-02-04		A2
4980	" "	28	SENE	1888-02-04		A2
5015	SELLERS, John D	9	NENE	1854-07-15		A1 C
5098	SELLERS, William A	28	SWNE	1891-06-18		A1
5062	STUART, Lewis C	22	NENE	1882-12-20		A1
5072	TALLENT, Minerva E	36	SE	1891-06-19		A2
5082	TALLENT, Rachel E	36	SW	1891-06-19		A2
5070	THOMAS, Maston H	28	N½SW	1888-01-21		A2 V5002
5071	" "	28	S½NW	1888-01-21		A2
4932	TOLIN, Burrell	24	S½SE	1885-12-10		A2
4983	TYNES, Henry	3	SWNW	1858-11-01		A1
4984	" "	4	SENE	1858-11-01		A1
5097	TYNES, Wiley	3	NWNW	1858-11-01		A1
4961	WALLACE, Elias A	22	NENW	1852-02-02		A1
4962	" "	22	NWNE	1852-02-02		A1

ID	Individual in Patent	Sec.	Sec. Part	Date Issued	Other Counties	For More Info . . .
5026	WALLER, John H	15	SESE	1921-08-26		A1
4944	WARD, Cornie H	5	NWNW	1858-11-01		A1
4945	" "	5	S½NW	1858-11-01		A1
4946	" "	5	SWNE	1858-11-01		A1
5058	WEAVER, Josephus L	34	NW	1888-02-04		A2
4994	WEST, Henry	17	NW	1837-08-15		A1 G8
4928	WHIDDON, Bennett	14	N½SW	1858-11-01		A1
4929	" "	14	NWSE	1858-11-01		A1
5115	WHITTED, William	17	E½	1837-08-14		A1
4924	WIGGINS, Benjamin J	26	E½SE	1888-02-04		A2
4925	" "	26	SESW	1888-02-04		A2
4926	" "	26	SWSE	1888-02-04		A2
5059	WIGGINS, Joshua	15	SWSW	1858-11-01		A1
5060	" "	22	SENW	1875-11-20		A2
4999	WILLIAMS, James E	1	E½SE	1858-11-01		A1
5000	" "	1	SENE	1858-11-01		A1
5001	" "	12	NENE	1858-11-01		A1
5066	WILLIAMS, Malissa C	14	SWSW	1891-06-08		A2
5092	WILLIAMS, Thomas A	26	S½NW	1888-02-04		A2
5093	" "	26	W½SW	1888-02-04		A2

Patent Map

T7-N R13-E
St Stephens Meridian

Map Group 22

Township Statistics

Parcels Mapped	:	208
Number of Patents	:	152
Number of Individuals	:	124
Patentees Identified	:	122
Number of Surnames	:	88
Multi-Patentee Parcels	:	4
Oldest Patent Date	:	10/15/1835
Most Recent Patent	:	8/26/1921
Block/Lot Parcels	:	0
Parcels Re - Issued	:	2
Parcels that Overlap	:	4
Cities and Towns	:	3
Cemeteries	:	5

Section 6: HOBBS Jacob 1858; BAKER Amos C 1838; HOBBS Jacob 1837; ETHEREDGE Lewis 1858; HOBBS Jacob 1837; ETHEREDGE Lewis 1858; ETHEREDGE Lewis 1858; PRICE James 1838; HOBBS Elijah 1838

Section 5: WARD Cornie H 1858; HARRISON [24] Mary J 1913; GARUM Halley D 1916; GORUM Holley D 1920; WARD Cornie H 1858; WARD Cornie H 1858; MAY Joseph J 1858; MAY Joseph J 1858; BROOKS John S 1858

Section 4: GALLAWAY Nathan 1858; BROOKS Drewry W 1858; POWELL John 1837; GALLOWAY Nathan 1858; TYNES Henry 1858; GRAHAM William P 1903; BRANSFORD Nathan 1837; BROOKS Drewry W 1858; BROOKS Drewry W 1858; AUSTIN Davis 1837; GALLOWAY Nathan 1860

Section 7: BAILEY Warner 1837; CONE Jesse 1838; GREENE John 1837

Section 8: BROOKS John S 1858; BROOKS John S 1858; MAY Joseph J 1858; GREEN John 1838; POWELL William 1837; GREEN John 1838; RUSHTON John 1837

Section 9: MAY Joseph J 1858; AUSTIN Davis 1837; SELLERS John D 1854; MCPHERSON John F 1852; POWELL William 1837; BEESLEY Enoch 1858; POWELL William 1837; BEASLEY Enoch 1841; RUSHTON John 1837; POWELL William 1837; BEESLEY Celia 1858

Section 18: CRAIG James D 1837; CRAIG [12] James D 1837; BROOKS Drury W 1860; BROOKS Drury W 1860

Section 17: CLARK [8] James B 1837; WHITTED William 1837; MCPHERSON John F 1858

Section 16: (empty)

Section 19: MCCLURE William D 1858; MCCLURE William D 1837; MCCLURE William D 1858; MCCLURE William D 1858; MCCLURE George H 1849; MCCLURE George H 1858; MCCLURE William D 1858

Section 20: BROOKS John S 1858; MCPHERSON John H 1888; BROOKS John S 1858; ADAMS Absalom J 1891; BROOKS Drury W 1860; PEACOCK John R 1883; MCPHERSON John H 1888; MCPHERSON William L 1888; MCPHERSON William L 1888

Section 21: PARKER John 1858; ARANT John F 1912; DEASE Benjamin 1837

Section 30: JAMES James 1858; MCCLURE George H 1858; MCCLURE William D 1858; BINION John T 1888; MILLS Martha A 1882; BINION Romaldus F 1888; BINION John T 1883; BINION Romaldus F 1888; BINION Romaldus F 1888; BINION Eugene M 1901; BINION John T 1888

Section 29: (empty)

Section 28: MCCLURE George L 0012; SELLERS George O 1888; SELLERS George O 1888; THOMAS Maston H 1888; SELLERS William A 1891; SELLERS George O 1888; THOMAS Maston H 1888; DRISKELL James J 1891; DRISKELL James J 1891; HORN Benjamin M 1895; BURKETT James 1858; DRISKELL James J 1891; BURKETT James 1858

Section 31: (empty)

Section 32: PRUETT John H 1889; DARBY Armstead D 1883; MORRIS John J 1890; DARBY Armstead D 1883; PRUETT John H 1889; MORRIS John J 1890; EDDINS Charles M 1890; EDDINS Charles M 1890; GANUS Walter A 1905

Section 33: (empty)

TYNES Wiley 1858			LONTZ Charity E 1885	HENDERSON John M 1860			
TYNES Henry 1858	**3**		FAIL Jeremiah 1854	HENDERSON John M 1885 **2**	HALL John J 1910	LEE Alexander 1835	LEE Alexander 1835	WILLIAMS James E 1858
			FAIL Jeremiah 1854	HENDERSON John M 1885	HALL John J 1910	**1**	WILLIAMS James E 1858
			HECKS Cicero 1883	CARPENTER Benjamin D 1889			

BEESLEY Enoch 1858	MILLER Andrew J 1885	DANIEL Ephraim F 1858	BROOKS Rachel 1858			BROOKS Rachel 1858	PACKER Aaron 1860	HENRY John K 1860	WILLIAMS James E 1858
	10		BROOKS Rachel 1858	**11**	BROOKS Rachel 1858			**12**	PACKER Aaron 1860
DRIVER Giles 1858		DANIEL Ephraim F 1858			BROOKS Rachel 1858	JONES Frank X 1891	HENRY John K 1860	PACKER Aaron 1860
	SANFORD Daniel 1860	ROBERTS William C 1912				JONES Frank X 1891		BEASLEY Hillory 1875

				DEEN Jeptha J 1860	HALL John J 1919	PRESLAR Holden 1837	PRESLAR Holden 1837	PRESLAR Floyd 1837		DAVIS Lancelott C 1837
15		OWENS Isaiah 1885	OWENS Isaiah 1885	GARRETT Thomas 1837	BRYAN [6] Edward 1840		**13**	
	MITCHELL Ricey M 1858		WHIDDON Bennett 1858 **14**	WHIDDON Bennett 1858	HOWELL David 1875	NORTHCUTT Robert 1838		DEASE George J 1837
WIGGINS Joshua 1858		WALLER John H 1921	WILLIAMS Malissa C 1891	BROOKS Christopher 1884	BROOKS Christopher 1884	QUINNELLY William 1837		

ARANT Calvin L 1882	WALLACE Elias A 1852	WALLACE Elias A 1852	STUART Lewis C 1882			QUINNELLY William 1837	BROOKS Allen 1883		BALDWIN John A 1884
	WIGGINS Joshua 1875	**22** SELLERS Daniel B 1885		**23**	HUGGINS Sarah 1884	**24**	BROOKS Allen 1880	
	RHODES Daniel H 1899	SELLERS Daniel B 1885	MINIARD James T 1888				MITCHELL Bud D 1884	MITCHELL Bud D 1884
ARANT Calvin L 1882	MINIARD James T 1888	MINIARD James T 1888			HUGGINS Sarah 1884		TOLIN Burrell 1885

	BINION Rufus 1893	BEASLEY John K 1891	BEASLEY John K 1891	
27	WILLIAMS Thomas A 1888	**26**	BROOKS Marshall 1894	**25**
	BINION Adam 1892	BEASLEY John K 1891	WIGGINS Benjamin J 1888	
	WILLIAMS Thomas A 1888	WIGGINS Benjamin J 1888	WIGGINS Benjamin J 1888	

WEAVER Josephus L 1888	JONES Caleb 1891		LEE Robert C 1891	HESTER Charles J 1891
34		**35**	**36**	
BROOKS Joseph S 1891	LEE Alfred Y 1891		TALLENT Rachel E 1891	TALLENT Minerva E 1891

Legend

- ————— Patent Boundary
- ▬▬▬▬▬ Section Boundary
- No Patents Found (or Outside County)
- 1., 2., 3., ... Lot Numbers (when beside a name)
- [ ] Group Number (see Appendix "C")

Scale: Section = 1 mile X 1 mile (generally, with some exceptions)

Road Map

T7-N R13-E
St Stephens Meridian

Map Group 22

Cities & Towns
McKenzie
Odom Crossroads
Salter

Cemeteries
Elizabeth Cemetery
McClure Cemetery
Pleasant Hill Cemetery
Sellers Cemetery
South Butler Cemetery

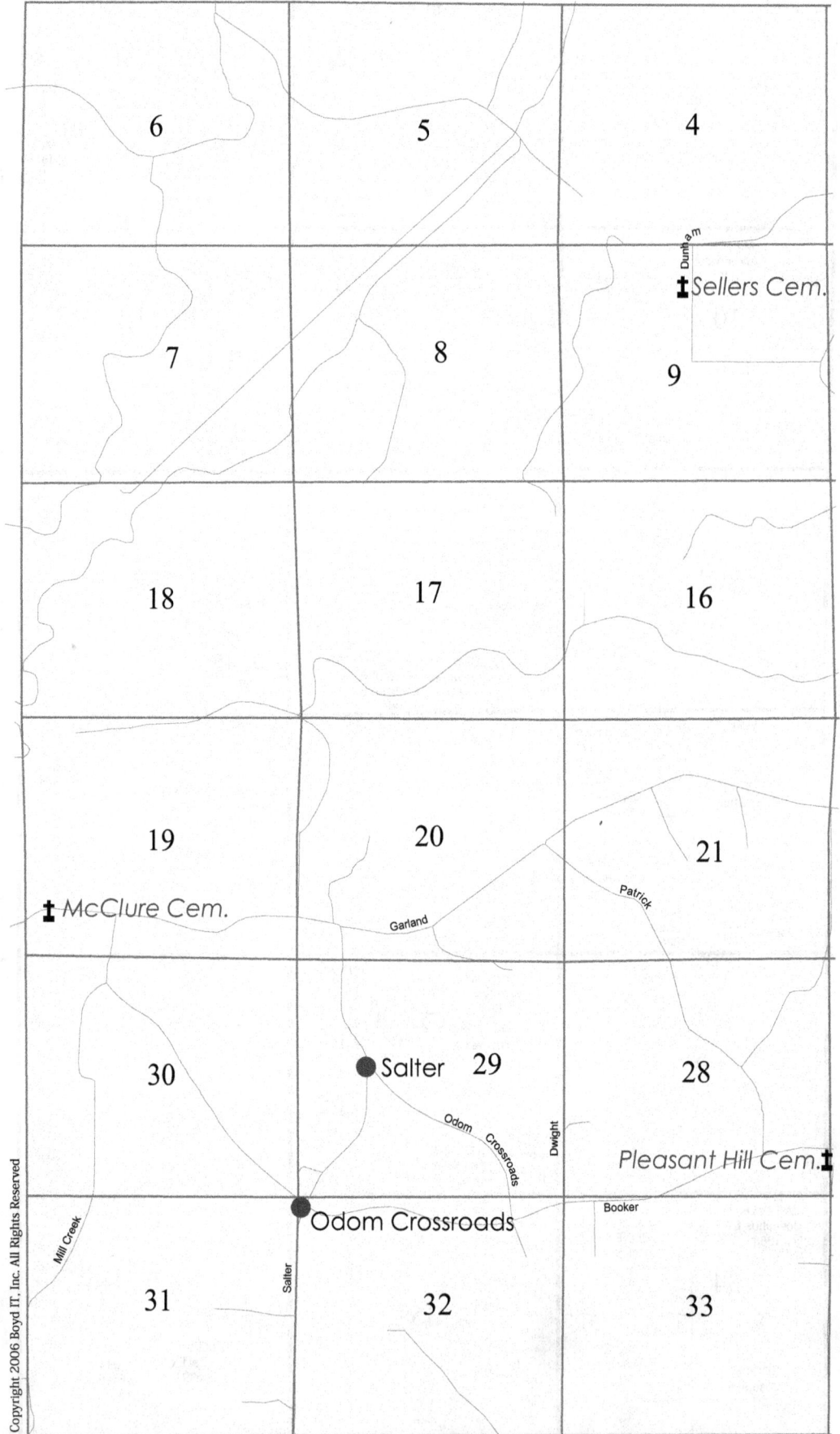

6

5

4

Dunham

✝ *Sellers Cem.*

7

8

9

18

17

16

19

20

21

Patrick

✝ *McClure Cem.*

Garland

30

● Salter   29

28

Odom Crossroads

Dwight

Pleasant Hill Cem. ✝

● Odom Crossroads

Booker

Mill Creek

Salter

31

32

33

3

Dove

Palmer

Mobile

2

New Home

1

Avant

Norrell

Kokomo

Nushone

10

11

12

15

14

13

Rhodes

Station

Helpful Hints

1. This road map has a number of uses, but primarily it is to help you: a) find the present location of land owned by your ancestors (at least the general area), b) find cemeteries and city-centers, and c) estimate the route/roads used by Census-takers & tax-assessors.

2. If you plan to travel to Butler County to locate cemeteries or land parcels, please pick up a modern travel map for the area before you do. Mapping old land parcels on modern maps is not as exact a science as you might think. Just the slightest variations in public land survey coordinates, estimates of parcel boundaries, or road-map deviations can greatly alter a map's representation of how a road either does or doesn't cross a particular parcel of land.

✝ South Butler Cem.

Elizabeth

22

County Road 9

23

24

Gorum

Goodwin

✝ Elizabeth Cem.

North

McKenzie

Grade

27

Scott

26

Walsh

Ivy

Sellers

Hester

25

Brogden

Wise

Garland

Lee

Mill

McKenzie

Mancil

Church

Legend

———— Section Lines

═══ Interstates

━━━ Highways

——— Other Roads

● Cities/Towns

✝ Cemeteries

Harvey

Main

34

County Highway 33

35

Crum Foshee

Faust

Huggins

36

Hayes

Armstrong

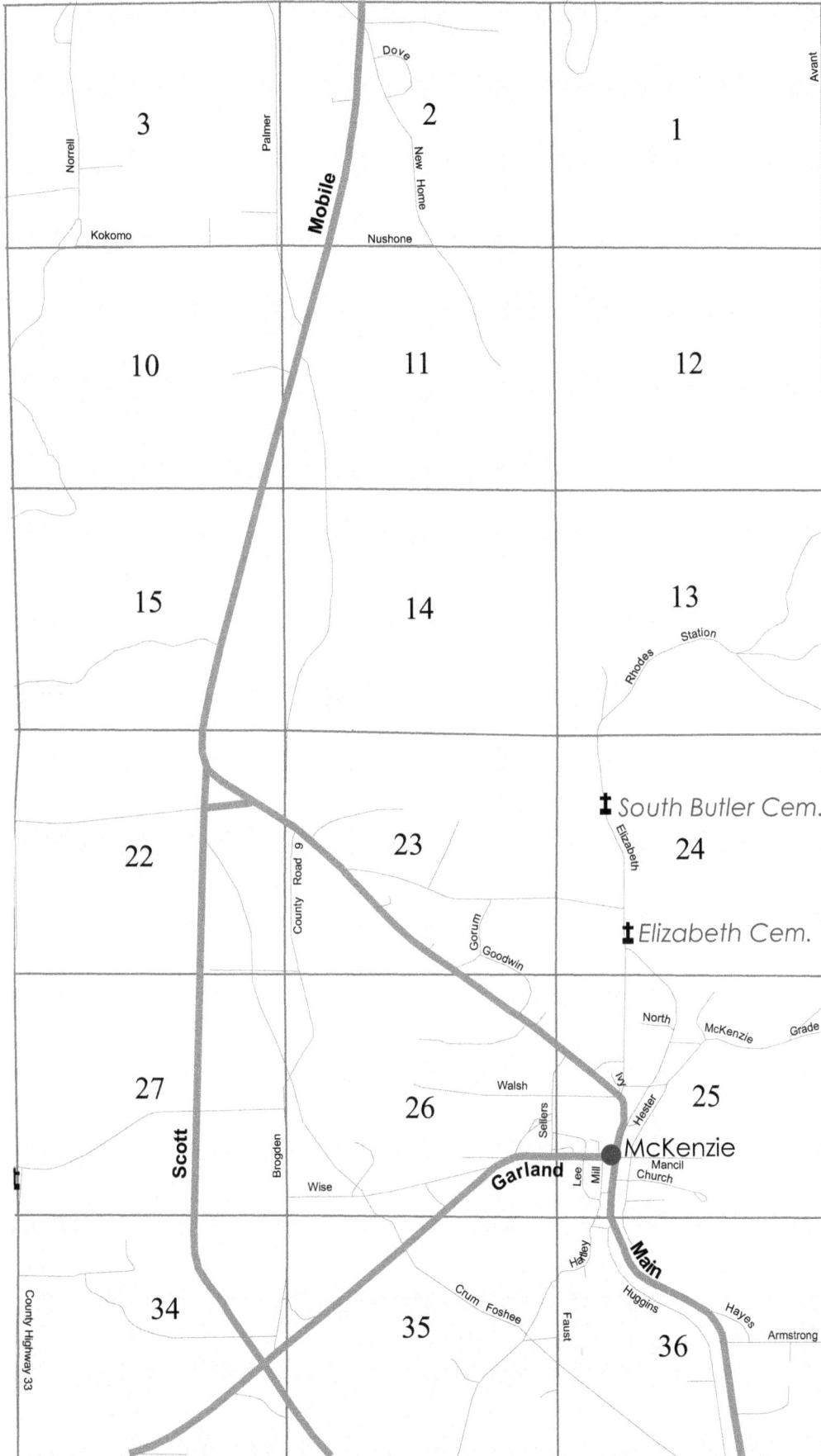

Scale: Section = 1 mile X 1 mile
(generally, with some exceptions)

Historical Map

T7-N R13-E
St Stephens Meridian

Map Group 22

Cities & Towns

Cities & Towns
McKenzie
Odom Crossroads
Salter

6

5

4

✝
Sellers Cem.

7

8

Panther Creek

9

18

17

16

Persimmon Creek

19

20

21

✝ *McClure Cem.*

Cemeteries
Elizabeth Cemetery
McClure Cemetery
Pleasant Hill Cemetery
Sellers Cemetery
South Butler Cemetery

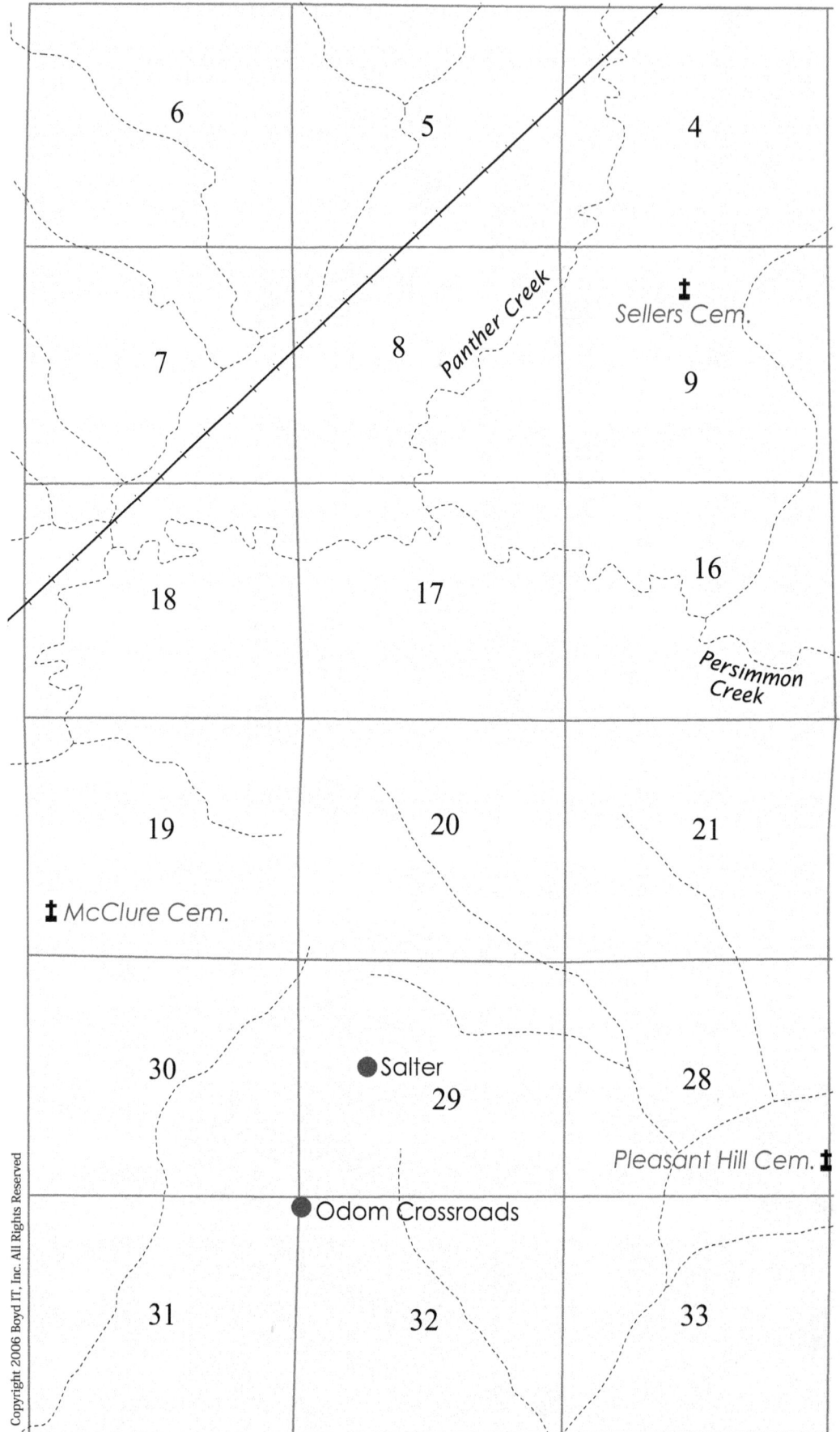

30

● Salter

29

28

Pleasant Hill Cem. ✝

● Odom Crossroads

31

32

33

3

2

Alexander Pond

1

10

11

Rocky Creek

12

15

14

13

22

23

‡*South Butler Cem.*

24

‡ *Elizabeth Cem.*

27

26

25

● McKenzie *Mill Creek*

34

35

36

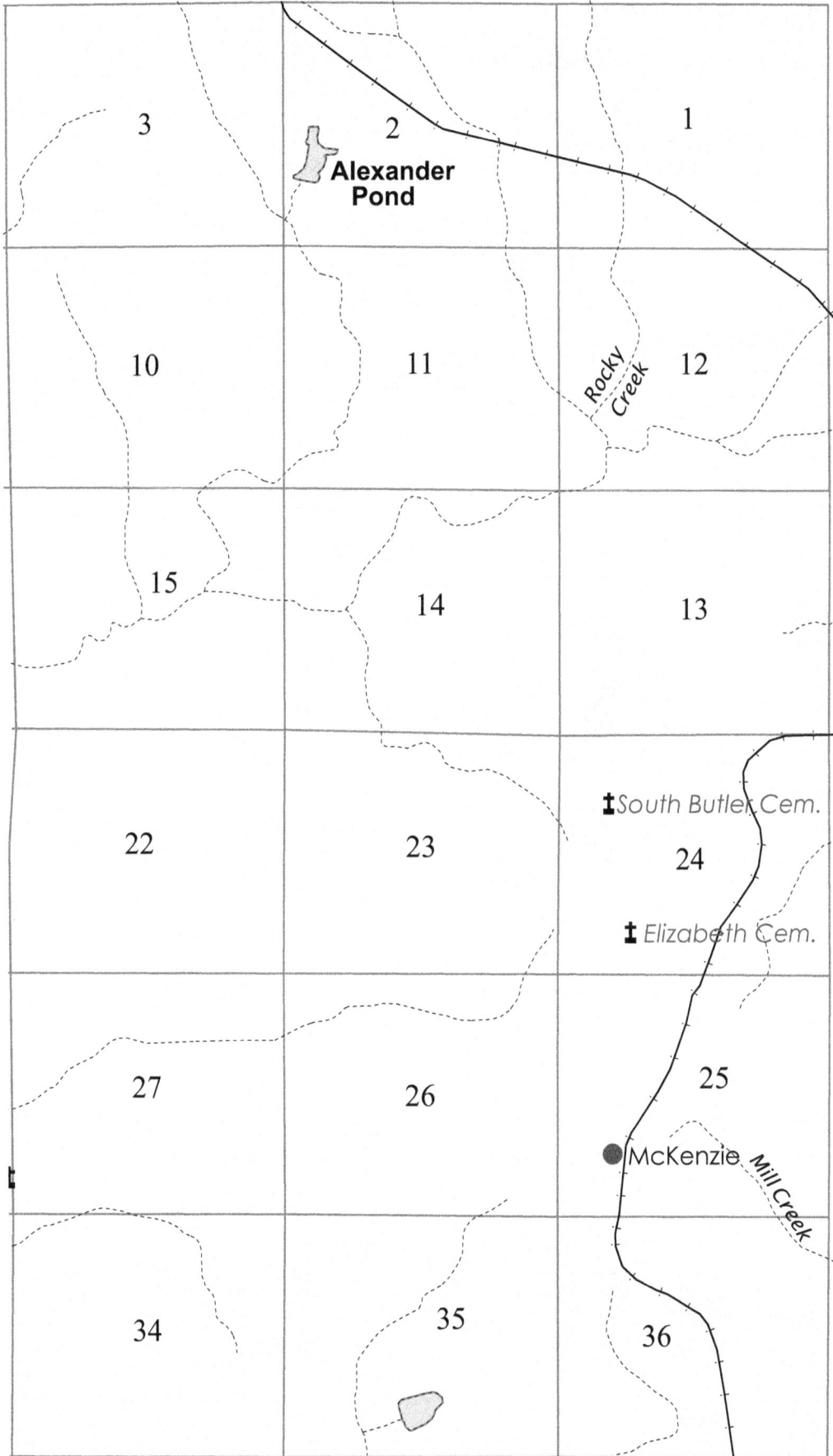

Helpful Hints

1. This Map takes a different look at the same Congressional Township displayed in the preceding two maps. It presents features that can help you better envision the historical development of the area: a) Water-bodies (lakes & ponds), b) Water-courses (rivers, streams, etc.), c) Railroads, d) City/town center-points (where they were oftentimes located when first settled), and e) Cemeteries.

2. Using this "Historical" map in tandem with this Township's Patent Map and Road Map, may lead you to some interesting discoveries. You will often find roads, towns, cemeteries, and waterways are named after nearby landowners: sometimes those names will be the ones you are researching. See how many of these research gems you can find here in Butler County.

Legend

———	Section Lines
+++++	Railroads
▭	Large Rivers & Bodies of Water
------	Streams/Creeks & Small Rivers
●	Cities/Towns
‡	Cemeteries

Scale: Section = 1 mile X 1 mile
(there are some exceptions)

Map Group 23: Index to Land Patents

Township 7-North Range 14-East (St Stephens)

After you locate an individual in this Index, take note of the Section and Section Part then proceed to the Land Patent map on the pages immediately following. You should have no difficulty locating the corresponding parcel of land.

The "For More Info" Column will lead you to more information about the underlying Patents. See the *Legend* at right, and the "How to Use this Book" chapter, for more information.

```
                        LEGEND
            "For More Info . . . " column
A = Authority (Legislative Act, See Appendix "A")
B = Block or Lot (location in Section unknown)
C = Cancelled Patent
F = Fractional Section
G = Group (Multi-Patentee Patent, see Appendix "C")
V = Overlaps another Parcel
R = Re-Issued (Parcel patented more than once)

(A & G items require you to look in the Appendixes referred
to above. All other Letter-designations followed by a number
require you to locate line-items in this index that possess
the ID number found after the letter).
```

ID	Individual in Patent	Sec.	Sec. Part	Date Issued	Other Counties	For More Info . . .
5324	ABNEY, William	15	SENW	1837-08-18		A1
5187	ATKINSON, Jason E	14	SESW	1838-07-28		A1
5188	ATKINSON, Jesse	17	SWNW	1837-08-12		A1
5190	" "	8	N½NE	1837-08-12		A1
5189	" "	27	NWNW	1852-02-02		A1
5211	BANISTER, John J	12	NESW	1858-11-01		A1
5212	" "	12	NWSE	1858-11-01		A1
5213	" "	12	SENW	1858-11-01		A1
5214	" "	12	SWNE	1858-11-01		A1
5362	BARRETT, Willis T	10	SENW	1852-02-02		A1
5134	BEESLEY, Blackston	6	N½NW	1891-05-29		A2
5296	BEESLEY, Solomon	14	NESW	1852-02-02		A1
5200	BENNETT, John	10	SENE	1875-04-20		A1
5201	" "	11	NESW	1875-04-20		A1
5202	" "	11	S½NW	1875-04-20		A1 V5245
5203	" "	30	NW	1885-03-30		A2
5308	BENNETT, Thomas	14	W½SE	1837-08-12		A1
5309	" "	23	E½NW	1837-08-12		A1
5310	" "	23	NWNW	1837-08-12		A1
5307	" "	14	NWSW	1849-09-01		A1
5305	BENNETT, Thomas B	23	S½SE	1858-11-01		A1
5306	" "	26	NWNE	1858-11-01		A1
5359	BENNETT, William M	23	NWNE	1848-04-01		A1
5285	BOLLING, Samuel J	12	SENE	1860-10-01		A1
5152	BROOKS, Drury J	8	SWNW	1860-10-01		A1
5155	BRYAN, Edward	18	W½NE	1837-08-14		A1
5156	" "	7	E½SW	1837-08-14		A1
5157	" "	7	SWSW	1837-08-14		A1
5132	CARPENTER, Benjamin D	20	NWNW	1875-11-20		A2
5193	CARPENTER, Jiles B	30	W½SW	1890-03-19		A2
5273	CATLIN, Richard	13	E½	1858-11-01		A1
5174	CRAIG, James	26	NENW	1858-11-01		A1
5175	CRAIG, James D	27	E½NW	1837-08-18		A1
5176	" "	27	W½NE	1837-08-18		A1
5123	CRAVEY, Amos	21	NE	1837-08-18		A1
5238	DAVIS, Lancelott C	18	S½	1837-08-12		A1
5239	" "	19	E½NE	1837-08-12		A1
5240	" "	19	W½NE	1837-08-18		A1
5295	DAVIS, Silas P	6	SESW	1891-06-08		A2
5133	DEASE, Benjamin	18	E½NW	1837-08-12		A1
5164	DEASE, George J	18	W½NW	1837-08-12		A1
5135	DENDY, Buford W	24	SWNE	1860-09-01		A1
5136	" "	24	SWNW	1860-09-01		A1
5137	" "	26	NESW	1860-09-01		A1
5138	" "	26	SESE	1860-09-01		A1
5139	" "	26	SWNE	1860-09-01		A1

ID	Individual in Patent	Sec.	Sec. Part	Date Issued	Other Counties	For More Info . . .
5140	DENDY, Buford W (Cont'd)	30	E½SW	1860-09-01		A1
5248	GALLAWAY, Nathan	7	E½SE	1837-08-12		A1
5249	" "	7	SWSE	1837-08-12		A1
5250	" "	8	NWSW	1837-08-12		A1
5364	GALLAWAY, Zacheus	17	NENW	1837-08-12		A1
5365	" "	8	NESW	1837-08-12		A1
5267	GRISWOLD, Obadiah	2	NW	1861-05-01		A1
5128	HINSON, Asa	4	NENE	1849-09-01		A1
5162	HINSON, Elijah	13	SWNW	1860-04-02		A1
5178	HINSON, James	20	SENW	1850-08-10		A1
5160	HUDSON, Eli	8	S½NE	1852-02-02		A1
5159	" "	8	NENW	1860-10-01		A1
5224	HUDSON, John T	10	N½NE	1875-04-20		A1
5225	" "	10	SWNE	1875-04-20		A1
5226	" "	3	SWSE	1875-04-20		A1
5246	HUDSON, Morning	10	SWNW	1858-11-01		A1
5251	HUDSON, Nelson	3	SWSW	1858-11-01		A1
5252	" "	4	SESE	1858-11-01		A1
5253	" "	9	NENE	1858-11-01		A1
5363	HUGHES, Young	14	SWSW	1848-04-01		A1
5245	JACKSON, Matthew	11	NW	1837-08-10		A1 V5202
5268	JACKSON, Pleasant G	17	NWNW	1837-05-20		A1 F
5269	" "	18	SENE	1837-08-12		A1
5270	" "	20	E½SE	1845-07-01		A1
5271	" "	20	SWNE	1850-04-01		A1
5318	JACKSON, Wiley P	17	NESW	1838-07-28		A1
5179	JAMES, James	20	SWNW	1837-08-18		A1
5158	JONES, Elbert	22	NESE	1850-08-10		A1
5215	JONES, John	3	SESW	1858-11-01		A1
5293	JONES, Seaborn G	14	E½NW	1875-04-20		A1
5294	" "	14	S½NW	1875-04-20		A1
5337	JONES, William H	22	SESE	1891-06-08		A2
5126	KELSOE, Angus	3	NWNW	1858-11-01		A1
5247	KIRVIN, Morris	34	SESE	1858-11-01		A1
5116	KNOWLES, Abraham A	24	NESE	1845-07-01		A1
5154	KNOWLES, Edmund	24	E½NE	1843-02-01		A1
5196	KORNEGAY, John B	17	W½SW	1837-08-12		A1
5197	" "	29	E½NW	1837-08-12		A1
5198	" "	29	E½SE	1837-08-12		A1
5199	" "	29	NE	1837-08-12		A1
5338	LANE, William H	10	NENW	1860-09-01		A1
5340	" "	28	NESW	1860-09-01		A1
5339	" "	2	NENE	1896-11-21		A1
5311	LITTLE, Thomas	10	NESE	1852-02-02		A1
5312	" "	11	W½SW	1852-02-02		A1
5314	" "	14	NWNW	1852-12-01		A1
5313	" "	14	E½SE	1858-11-01		A1
5315	" "	23	NENE	1858-11-01		A1
5316	" "	23	SWNE	1858-11-01		A1
5317	" "	24	NWNW	1858-11-01		A1
5184	MCCORMICK, James	4	NWSW	1847-05-01		A1
5185	" "	4	SWNW	1847-05-01		A1
5183	" "	4	NWSE	1858-11-01		A1
5180	" "	4	E½NW	1862-01-01		A1
5181	" "	4	NESW	1862-01-01		A1
5182	" "	4	NWNW	1862-01-01		A1
5186	" "	4	SWSW	1862-01-01		A1
5232	MCDANIEL, Joseph	20	NENW	1891-11-23		A2
5233	" "	20	NWNE	1891-11-23		A2
5125	MCKINZIE, Anguish	17	SENW	1838-07-28		A1
5205	MCPHERSON, John F	9	NWSW	1845-07-01		A1
5204	" "	26	NENE	1850-04-01		A1
5335	MENEES, William D	20	SWSE	1850-08-10		A1
5332	" "	20	NWSE	1852-02-02		A1
5336	" "	21	NWSW	1852-02-02		A1
5331	" "	20	NESW	1854-07-15		A1
5333	" "	20	NWSW	1858-11-01		A1
5334	" "	20	SESW	1858-11-01		A1
5171	MITCHELL, Holland W	26	NESE	1921-03-25		A2
5272	MITCHELL, Ricey M	30	W½NE	1883-04-10		A2
5242	MOSELEY, Mark	36	NWSW	1858-09-01		A1
5241	" "	35	SENW	1858-11-01		A1
5127	NORTHCUT, Ann W	28	NENW	1850-04-01		A1

ID	Individual in Patent	Sec.	Sec. Part	Date Issued	Other Counties	For More Info . . .
5165	NORTHCUT, Henrietta F	28	NWNW	1850-08-10		A1
5206	NORTHCUT, John G	28	SENW	1850-04-01		A1
5319	NORTHCUT, William A	21	E½NW	1852-02-02		A1
5163	OPRY, George A	8	S½SW	1837-08-12		A1
5260	PARKER, Noah	24	NWSE	1858-11-01		A1
5261	" "	24	NWSW	1858-11-01		A1
5262	" "	24	SESW	1858-11-01		A1
5263	" "	25	N½NW	1858-11-01		A1
5264	" "	25	SWNE	1858-11-01		A1
5265	" "	25	SWNW	1858-11-01		A1
5266	" "	26	SENE	1858-11-01		A1
5286	PARKER, Samuel	33	S½SE	1858-09-01		A1
5287	" "	33	SESW	1858-09-01		A1
5288	" "	33	W½SW	1858-09-01		A1
5143	PEARY, Charles	9	SWNW	1849-09-01		A1
5131	PEAVY, Asa	22	NWSW	1854-10-02		A1
5144	PEAVY, Charles	17	W½NE	1837-08-12		A1
5145	" "	8	SENW	1837-08-12		A1
5172	PEAVY, Isaac	19	NESE	1837-08-12		A1
5353	PEAVY, William J	28	SWNE	1852-02-02		A1
5348	" "	21	E½SW	1858-11-01		A1
5349	" "	21	W½SE	1858-11-01		A1
5350	" "	28	E½NE	1858-11-01		A1
5351	" "	28	NESE	1858-11-01		A1
5352	" "	28	NWNE	1858-11-01		A1
5354	" "	34	E½NE	1858-11-01		A1
5355	" "	34	NWNE	1858-11-01		A1
5356	" "	34	S½NW	1860-09-01		A1
5357	" "	34	SWNE	1860-09-01		A1
5117	PEEVY, Abraham	22	W½NW	1837-08-12		A1
5129	PEEVY, Asa M	21	E½SE	1858-11-01		A1
5130	" "	22	SWSW	1858-11-01		A1
5146	PEEVY, Charles	22	E½SW	1837-08-12		A1
5150	PEEVY, Daniel	10	SESE	1838-07-28		A1
5168	PEEVY, Hiram	22	SENW	1849-09-01		A1
5358	PEEVY, William J	28	NWSW	1849-09-01		A1
5320	PERRY, William A	20	E½NE	1875-06-01		A2
5169	PEVEY, Hiram	10	NWSE	1849-09-01		A1
5151	PEVY, Daniel	10	N½SW	1858-11-01		A1
5121	PRESLAR, Allen	23	NWSW	1837-05-20		A1
5122	" "	23	SWNW	1837-05-20		A1
5118	" "	15	NENE	1837-08-14		A1
5119	" "	15	SESE	1837-08-14		A1
5120	" "	15	W½NE	1837-08-14		A1
5170	PRESLAR, Holden	19	NW	1837-08-12		A1
5276	PRESLAR, Robert A	13	NESW	1858-11-01		A1
5277	" "	13	SENW	1858-11-01		A1
5321	PRESLAR, William A	15	SW	1858-11-01		A1
5322	" "	15	W½NW	1858-11-01		A1
5278	PRESLEY, Robert A	13	NENW	1852-02-02		A1
5279	" "	13	W½SW	1852-02-02		A1
5281	PRESSLAR, Robert	15	NESE	1837-08-12		A1
5282	" "	15	SENE	1837-08-12		A1
5297	PRUETT, Stephen T	36	NENE	1895-06-19		A2
5298	" "	36	W½NE	1895-06-19		A2
5216	QUINNELLY, John R	19	SESE	1837-08-14		A1
5217	" "	20	SWSW	1837-08-14		A1
5191	REAVES, Jesse	22	E½NE	1840-10-10		A1
5192	" "	23	E½SW	1840-10-10		A1
5254	RHODES, Newton M	5	SESE	1848-05-03		A1
5255	" "	9	NWNW	1854-07-15		A1
5141	RILEY, Chapman	9	E½SW	1837-08-12		A1
5166	RILEY, Henry C	9	SWNE	1837-08-12		A1
5167	" "	9	SWSE	1837-08-12		A1
5207	RILEY, John H	9	E½SE	1858-11-01		A1
5208	" "	9	NWSE	1858-11-01		A1
5209	" "	9	SENE	1858-11-01		A1
5361	RILEY, William	23	SWSW	1848-05-03		A1
5274	SARTOR, Richard F	4	SWSE	1837-08-12		A1
5275	" "	9	NWNE	1837-08-12		A1
5330	SARTOR, William C	4	SWNE	1852-02-02		A1
5325	" "	3	NWSW	1858-11-01		A1
5326	" "	3	SWNW	1858-11-01		A1

ID	Individual in Patent	Sec.	Sec. Part	Date Issued	Other Counties	For More Info . . .
5327	SARTOR, William C (Cont'd)	4	NESE	1858-11-01		A1
5328	" "	4	NWNE	1858-11-01		A1
5329	" "	4	SENE	1858-11-01		A1
5124	SEARCY, Andrew J	36	NW	1875-07-01		A2
5194	SEEGAR, John A	2	E½SE	1858-11-01		A1
5195	" "	2	SENE	1858-11-01		A1
5289	SEEGAR, Samuel	1	SE	1858-11-01		A1
5290	" "	12	NENW	1858-11-01		A1
5291	" "	12	NWNE	1858-11-01		A1
5153	SELLERS, Duncan	8	W½SE	1837-08-12		A1
5218	SELLERS, John	8	SESE	1852-02-02		A1
5280	SMALLWOOD, Robert J	14	N½NE	1861-05-01		A1
5219	SMITH, John	24	NESW	1852-02-02		A1
5220	" "	24	SENW	1852-02-02		A1
5221	" "	26	SESW	1852-02-02		A1
5222	" "	26	SWSE	1852-02-02		A1
5223	" "	35	NENW	1852-02-02		A1
5235	STANFORD, Kizziah	36	E½SE	1893-03-03		A2
5236	" "	36	SENE	1893-03-03		A2
5237	" "	36	SWSE	1893-03-03		A2
5142	STANLEY, Charles F	26	SWSW	1919-01-18		A1
5147	STEWART, Charles	17	NESE	1837-08-12		A1
5148	" "	17	SENE	1837-08-12		A1
5149	" "	17	W½SE	1837-08-12		A1
5256	STEWART, Nimrod	28	SWNW	1858-11-01		A1
5257	" "	28	SWSW	1858-11-01		A1
5258	" "	29	NWSE	1858-11-01		A1
5259	" "	32	NENE	1858-11-01		A1
5342	STEWART, William H	28	SESW	1850-08-10		A1
5341	" "	28	SESE	1858-11-01		A1
5343	" "	33	NENE	1858-11-01		A1
5284	STUART, Robert W	14	SWNW	1852-12-01		A1
5347	STUART, William H	33	NWNE	1850-08-10		A1
5344	" "	27	SESW	1858-09-01		A1
5345	" "	27	W½SE	1858-09-01		A1
5346	" "	27	W½SW	1858-09-01		A1
5292	TISDALE, Samuel	18	NENE	1860-10-01		A1
5243	TORRENCE, Matilda	6	NWSW	1891-06-08		A2
5244	" "	6	SWNW	1891-06-08		A2
5173	WATSON, James A	6	E½SE	1891-06-19		A2
5323	WATSON, William A	6	E½NE	1891-09-01		A2
5360	WATSON, William R	6	W½NE	1886-04-10		A2
5227	WHEELER, John	12	SWSW	1838-07-28		A1
5228	" "	13	NWNW	1858-11-01		A1
5210	WHEELER, John H	15	W½SE	1837-08-12		A1
5229	WILKERSON, John	22	NENW	1858-11-01		A1
5230	" "	4	SESW	1858-11-01		A1
5231	" "	9	NENW	1858-11-01		A1
5161	WILLIAMS, Eli	1	S½NW	1860-04-02		A1
5177	WILLIAMS, James E	6	SWSW	1858-11-01		A1
5234	WILLIAMS, Joshua F	1	SW	1858-11-01		A1
5299	WILLIAMS, Theophilus	5	SWSW	1858-11-01		A1
5300	" "	6	NESW	1858-11-01		A1
5301	" "	6	SENW	1858-11-01		A1
5302	" "	6	W½SE	1858-11-01		A1
5303	" "	7	N½NE	1858-11-01		A1
5304	" "	8	NWNW	1858-11-01		A1
5283	WRIGHT, Robert R	8	NESE	1858-09-01		A1

Patent Map

T7-N R14-E
St Stephens Meridian

Map Group 23

Township Statistics

Parcels Mapped	:	250
Number of Patents	:	179
Number of Individuals	:	123
Patentees Identified	:	123
Number of Surnames	:	71
Multi-Patentee Parcels	:	0
Oldest Patent Date	:	5/20/1837
Most Recent Patent	:	3/25/1921
Block/Lot Parcels	:	0
Parcels Re - Issued	:	0
Parcels that Overlap	:	2
Cities and Towns	:	3
Cemeteries	:	2

Section 6
BEESLEY Blackston 1891
TORRENCE Matilda 1891
WATSON William R 1886
WATSON William A 1891
WILLIAMS Theophilus 1858
TORRENCE Matilda 1891
WILLIAMS Theophilus 1858
WILLIAMS James E 1858
DAVIS Silas P 1891
WILLIAMS Theophilus 1858
WATSON James A 1891

Section 5
WILLIAMS Theophilus 1858
RHODES Newton M 1848

Section 4
MCCORMICK James 1862
MCCORMICK James 1862
SARTOR William C 1858
HINSON Asa 1849
MCCORMICK James 1847
SARTOR William C 1852
SARTOR William C 1858
MCCORMICK James 1847
MCCORMICK James 1862
MCCORMICK James 1858
SARTOR William C 1858
MCCORMICK James 1862
WILKERSON John 1858
SARTOR Richard F 1837
HUDSON Nelson 1858

Section 7
WILLIAMS Theophilus 1858
BRYAN Edward 1837
BRYAN Edward 1837
GALLAWAY Nathan 1837
GALLAWAY Nathan 1837

Section 8
WILLIAMS Theophilus 1858
HUDSON Eli 1860
ATKINSON Jesse 1837
BROOKS Drury J 1860
PEAVY Charles 1837
HUDSON Eli 1852
GALLAWAY Nathan 1837
GALLAWAY Zacheus 1837
SELLERS Duncan 1837
WRIGHT Robert R 1858
OPRY George A 1837
SELLERS John 1852

Section 9
RHODES Newton M 1854
WILKERSON John 1858
SARTOR Richard F 1837
HUDSON Nelson 1858
PEARY Charles 1849
RILEY Henry C 1837
RILEY John H 1858
MCPHERSON John F 1845
RILEY John H 1858
RILEY Chapman 1837
RILEY Henry C 1837
RILEY John H 1858

Section 18
DEASE George J 1837
DEASE Benjamin 1837
BRYAN Edward 1837
DAVIS Lancelott C 1837

Section 17
TISDALE Samuel 1860
JACKSON Pleasant G 1837
JACKSON Pleasant G 1837
ATKINSON Jesse 1837
JACKSON Wiley P 1838
KORNEGAY John B 1837
GALLAWAY Zacheus 1837
PEAVY Charles 1837
MCKINZIE Anguish 1838
STEWART Charles 1837
STEWART Charles 1837
STEWART Charles 1837

Section 16

Section 19
PRESLAR Holden 1837
DAVIS Lancelott C 1837
DAVIS Lancelott C 1837
PEAVY Isaac 1837
QUINNELLY John R 1837

Section 20
CARPENTER Benjamin D 1875
MCDANIEL Joseph 1891
MCDANIEL Joseph 1891
PERRY William A 1875
JAMES James 1837
HINSON James 1850
JACKSON Pleasant G 1850
MENEES William D 1858
MENEES William D 1854
MENEES William D 1852
JACKSON Pleasant G 1845
QUINNELLY John R 1837
MENEES William D 1858
MENEES William D 1850

Section 21
NORTHCUT William A 1852
CRAVEY Amos 1837
MENEES William D 1852
PEAVY William J 1858
PEAVY William J 1858
PEEVY Asa M 1858

Section 30
BENNETT John 1885
MITCHELL Ricey M 1883
CARPENTER Jiles B 1890
DENDY Buford W 1860

Section 29
KORNEGAY John B 1837
KORNEGAY John B 1837
STEWART Nimrod 1858
KORNEGAY John B 1837

Section 28
NORTHCUT Henrietta F 1850
NORTHCUT Ann W 1850
PEAVY William J 1858
PEAVY William J 1858
STEWART Nimrod 1858
NORTHCUT John G 1850
PEAVY William J 1852
PEEVY William J 1849
LANE William H 1860
PEAVY William J 1858
STEWART Nimrod 1858
STEWART William H 1850
STEWART William H 1858

Section 31

Section 32
STEWART Nimrod 1858

Section 33
STEWART Nimrod 1858
STUART William H 1850
STEWART William H 1858
PARKER Samuel 1858
PARKER Samuel 1858
PARKER Samuel 1858

KELSOE Angus 1858				LANE William H 1896	
SARTOR William C 1858	3	GRISWOLD Obadiah 1861		SEEGAR John A 1858	WILLIAMS Eli 1860	1
SARTOR William C 1858		2	WILLIAMS Joshua F 1858	SEEGAR Samuel 1858
HUDSON Nelson 1858	JONES John 1858	HUDSON John T 1875	SEEGAR John A 1858		

Helpful Hints

1. This Map's INDEX can be found on the preceding pages.

2. Refer to Map "C" to see where this Township lies within Butler County, Alabama.

3. Numbers within square brackets [ ] denote a multi-patentee land parcel (multi-owner). Refer to Appendix "C" for a full list of members in this group.

4. Areas that look to be crowded with Patentees usually indicate multiple sales of the same parcel (Re-issues) or Overlapping parcels. See this Township's Index for an explanation of these and other circumstances that might explain "odd" groupings of Patentees on this map.

LANE William H 1860	HUDSON John T 1875	JACKSON Matthew 1837	SEEGAR Samuel 1858	SEEGAR Samuel 1858
HUDSON Morning 1858	BARRETT Willis T 1852	HUDSON John T 1875	BENNETT John 1875	BENNETT John 1875	BANISTER John J 1858 12	BANISTER John J 1858	BOLLING Samuel J 1860
PEVY Daniel 1858	10	PEVEY Hiram 1849	LITTLE Thomas 1852	BENNETT John 1875	BANISTER John J 1858	BANISTER John J 1858
		PEEVY Daniel 1838	LITTLE Thomas 1852	WHEELER John 1838

PRESLAR William A 1858	PRESLAR Allen 1837	PRESLAR Allen 1837	LITTLE Thomas 1852	SMALLWOOD Robert J 1861	WHEELER John 1858	PRESLEY Robert A 1852
	ABNEY William 1837	PRESSLAR Robert 1837	STUART Robert W 1852	JONES Seaborn G 1875	14	JONES Seaborn G 1875	HINSON Elijah 1860	PRESLAR Robert A 1858	13	CATLIN Richard 1858
PRESLAR William A 1858	15	PRESSLAR Robert 1837	BENNETT Thomas 1849	BEESLEY Solomon 1852	BENNETT Thomas 1837	PRESLAR Robert A 1858
	WHEELER John H 1837	PRESLAR Allen 1837	HUGHES Young 1848	ATKINSON Jason E 1838	LITTLE Thomas 1858	PRESLEY Robert A 1852

PEEVY Abraham 1837	WILKERSON John 1858		BENNETT Thomas 1837	BENNETT William M 1848	LITTLE Thomas 1858	LITTLE Thomas 1858		KNOWLES Edmund 1843
	PEEVY Hiram 1849	REAVES Jesse 1840	PRESLAR Allen 1837	BENNETT Thomas 1837	LITTLE Thomas 1858	DENDY Buford W 1860	SMITH John 1852 24	DENDY Buford W 1860	
PEAVY Asa 1854	PEEVY Charles 1837	JONES Elbert 1850	PRESLAR Allen 1837	23	PARKER Noah 1858	SMITH John 1852	PARKER Noah 1858	KNOWLES Abraham A 1845
PEEVY Asa M 1858		JONES William H 1891	RILEY William 1848	REAVES Jesse 1840	BENNETT Thomas B 1858		PARKER Noah 1858		

ATKINSON Jesse 1852	CRAIG James D 1837	CRAIG James D 1837	CRAIG James 1858	BENNETT Thomas B 1858	MCPHERSON John F 1850	PARKER Noah 1858	
				DENDY Buford W 1860	PARKER Noah 1858	PARKER Noah 1858	PARKER Noah 1858
	27	STUART William H 1858	26	DENDY Buford W 1860	MITCHELL Holland W 1921	25
STUART William H 1858	STUART William H 1858	STANLEY Charles F 1919	SMITH John 1852	SMITH John 1852	DENDY Buford W 1860	

	PEAVY William J 1858	PEAVY William J 1858	SMITH John 1852		SEARCY Andrew J 1875	PRUETT Stephen T 1895	PRUETT Stephen T 1895
PEAVY William J 1860	PEAVY William J 1860	MOSELEY Mark 1858			STANFORD Kizziah 1893
	34	35	MOSELEY Mark 1858	36	STANFORD Kizziah 1893
	KIRVIN Morris 1858			STANFORD Kizziah 1893

Legend

————	Patent Boundary
▬▬▬▬	Section Boundary
	No Patents Found (or Outside County)
1., 2., 3., ...	Lot Numbers (when beside a name)
[ ]	Group Number (see Appendix "C")

Scale: Section = 1 mile X 1 mile (generally, with some exceptions)

Road Map

T7-N R14-E
St Stephens Meridian

Map Group 23

Cities & Towns
Industry
Rhodes
Shell

Cemeteries
Macedonia Cemetery
Riley Cemetery

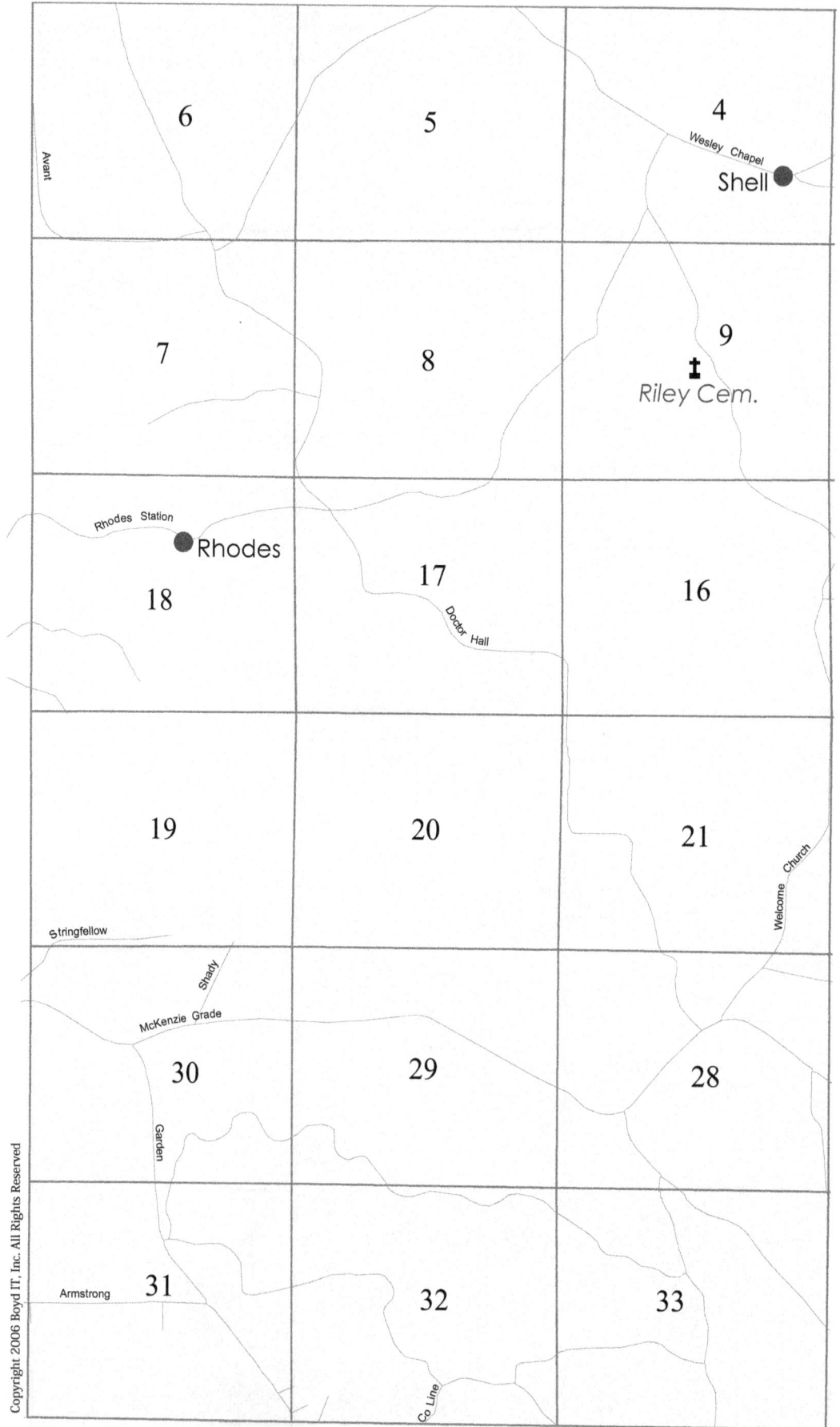

6	5	4
		Wesley Chapel
		Shell ●
7	8	9
		Riley Cem.
18	17	16
Rhodes Station ● Rhodes	Doctor Hall	
19	20	21
Stringfellow		Welcome Church
Shady		
McKenzie Grade		
30	29	28
Garden		
31	32	33
Armstrong		
	Co. Line	

Avant

3

2

1
● Industry   Peavy

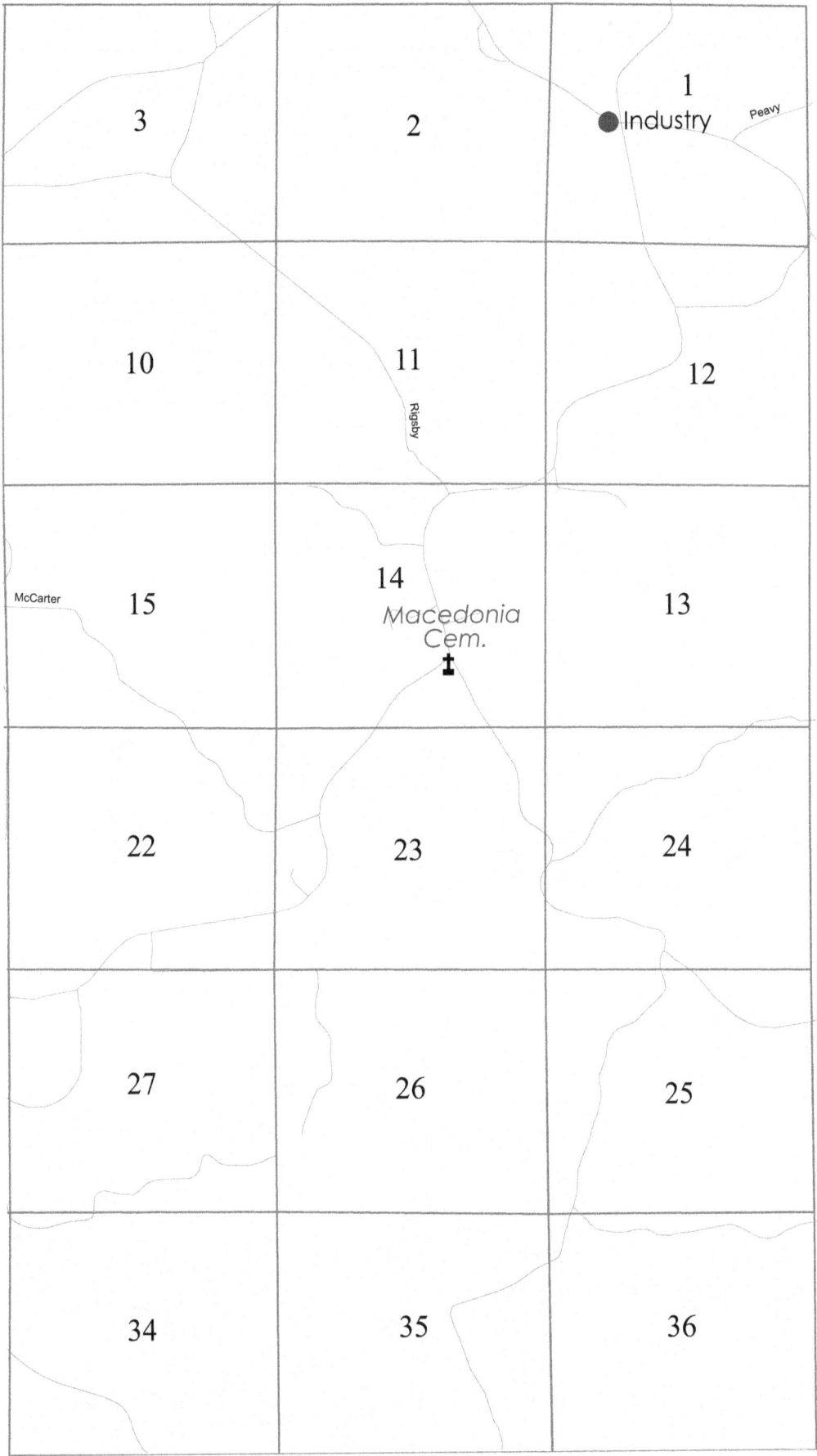

10

11
Rigsby

12

McCarter

15

14
Macedonia
Cem.
✝

13

22

23

24

27

26

25

34

35

36

Legend

———— Section Lines

═══ Interstates

▬▬▬ Highways

———— Other Roads

● Cities/Towns

✝ Cemeteries

Scale: Section = 1 mile X 1 mile
(generally, with some exceptions)

Historical Map

T7-N R14-E
St Stephens Meridian

Map Group 23

Cities & Towns
Industry
Rhodes
Shell

Cemeteries
Macedonia Cemetery
Riley Cemetery

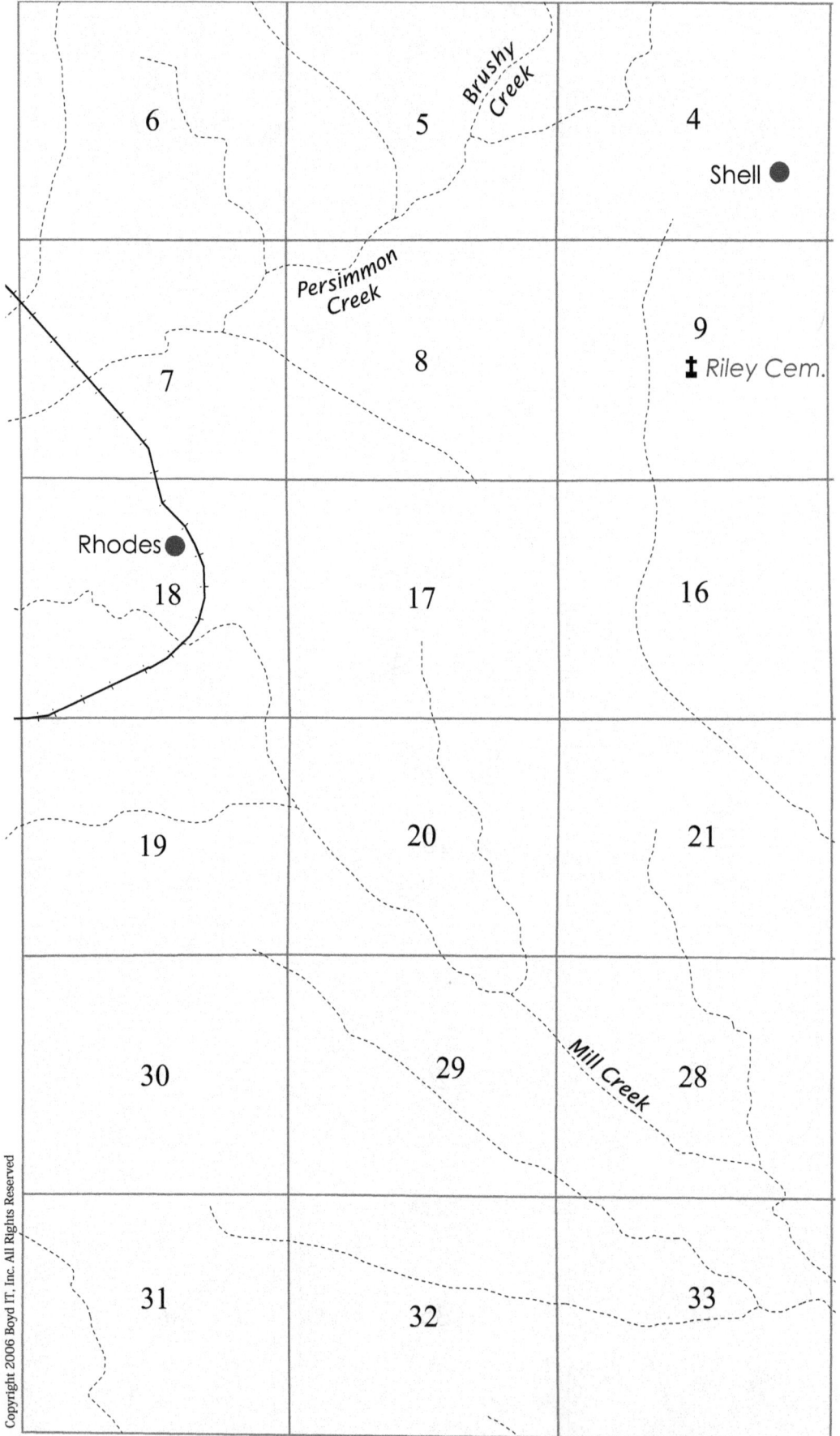

6

5

Brushy Creek

4

Shell ●

Persimmon Creek

7

8

9

✝ *Riley Cem.*

Rhodes ●

18

17

16

19

20

21

30

29

Mill Creek

28

31

32

33

3

2

● Industry

1

10

11

12

Tiger Branch

15

Bennett
Branch

14

Macedonia †
Cem.

13

22

23

24

27

26

Pigeon
Creek

25

Riley Creek

34

35

36

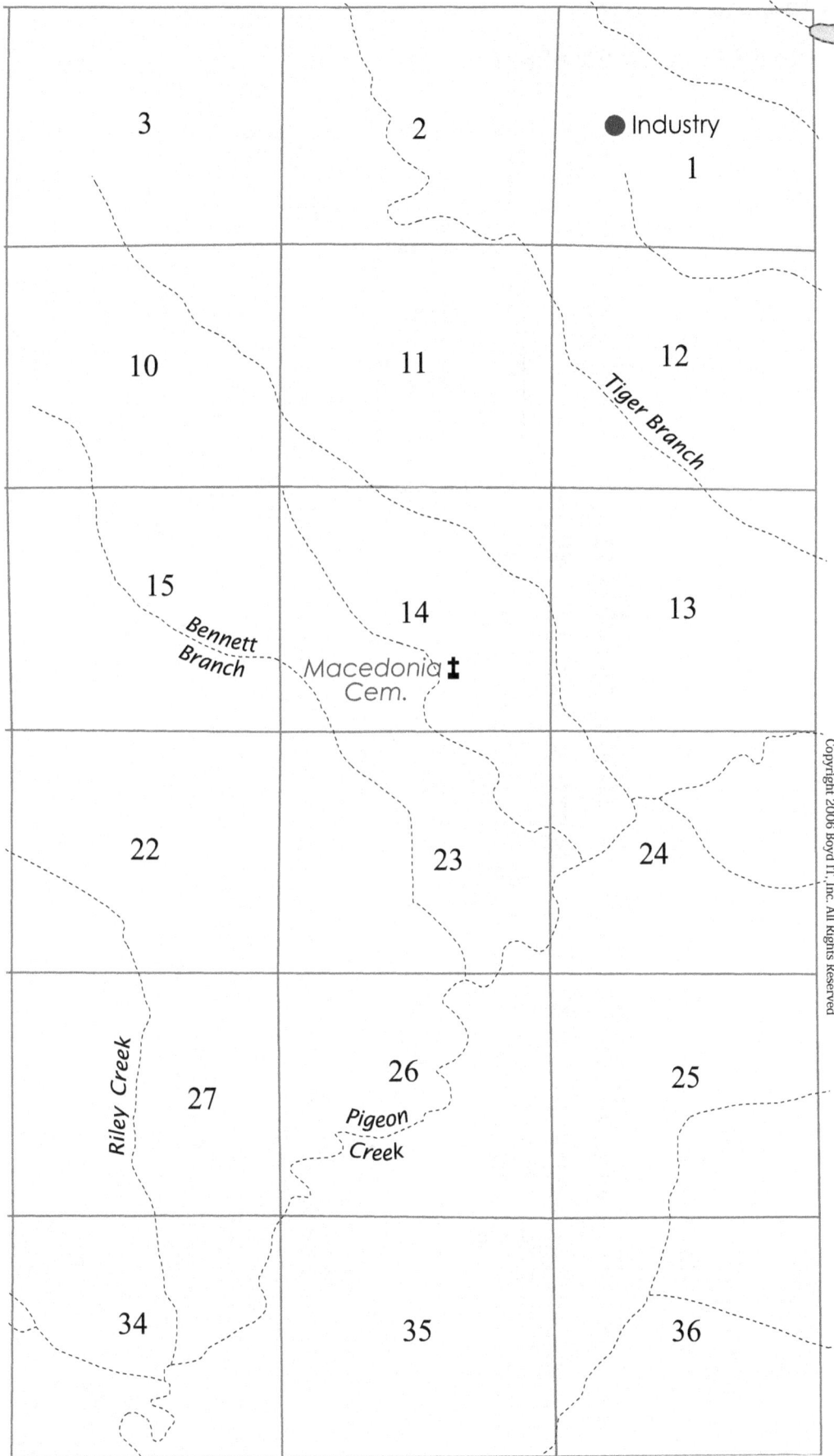

Helpful Hints

1. This Map takes a different look at
the same Congressional Township
displayed in the preceding two
maps. It presents features that
can help you better envision the
historical development of the area:
a) Water-bodies (lakes & ponds),
b) Water-courses (rivers, streams,
etc.), c) Railroads, d) City/town
center-points (where they were
oftentimes located when first
settled), and e) Cemeteries.

2. Using this "Historical" map in
tandem with this Township's
Patent Map and Road Map, may
lead you to some interesting
discoveries. You will often find
roads, towns, cemeteries, and
waterways are named after nearby
landowners: sometimes those
names will be the ones you are
researching. See how many of
these research gems you can find
here in Butler County.

Legend

————————	Section Lines
┼┼┼┼┼┼┼	Railroads
▭	Large Rivers & Bodies of Water
- - - - - - - -	Streams/Creeks & Small Rivers
●	Cities/Towns
†	Cemeteries

Scale: Section = 1 mile X 1 mile
(there are some exceptions)

Map Group 24: Index to Land Patents

Township 7-North Range 15-East (St Stephens)

After you locate an individual in this Index, take note of the Section and Section Part then proceed to the Land Patent map on the pages immediately following. You should have no difficulty locating the corresponding parcel of land.

The "For More Info" Column will lead you to more information about the underlying Patents. See the *Legend* at right, and the "How to Use this Book" chapter, for more information.

```
                        LEGEND
              "For More Info . . . " column
   A = Authority (Legislative Act, See Appendix "A")
   B = Block or Lot (location in Section unknown)
   C = Cancelled Patent
   F = Fractional Section
   G = Group  (Multi-Patentee Patent, see Appendix "C")
   V = Overlaps another Parcel
   R = Re-Issued (Parcel patented more than once)

   (A & G items require you to look in the Appendixes referred
   to above. All other Letter-designations followed by a number
   require you to locate line-items in this index that possess
   the ID number found after the letter).
```

ID	Individual in Patent	Sec.	Sec. Part	Date Issued	Other Counties	For More Info . . .
5426	ADAMS, Frederick	9	SESE	1843-02-01		A1
5490	BANISTER, John A	30	N½SE	1892-01-18		A2
5491	"	30	S½NE	1892-01-18		A2
5388	BARRETT, Benjamin J	13	NWNW	1852-02-02		A1
5577	BARRETT, Timothy	12	N½SW	1858-11-01		A1
5578	" "	12	NWSE	1858-11-01		A1
5579	" "	12	S½NE	1858-11-01		A1
5580	" "	12	SENW	1858-11-01		A1
5581	" "	12	SESW	1860-10-01		A1
5582	" "	12	SWSE	1860-12-01		A1
5626	BERRY, William T	6	SW	1860-04-02		A1
5573	BOAN, Ted S	30	S½SE	1891-11-23		A2
5574	" "	30	S½SW	1891-11-23		A2
5445	BRILEY, Jacob	5	SENE	1837-08-02		A1
5444	" "	4	SWNW	1837-08-15		A1
5446	" "	5	SESE	1837-08-15		A1
5588	BROGDEN, William	27	NENW	1858-11-01		A1
5589	" "	27	W½NW	1858-11-01		A1
5590	" "	28	E½NE	1858-11-01		A1
5447	BROGDON, James C	9	SESW	1849-09-01		A1
5540	BROOK, Preston	5	NENE	1837-08-12		A1
5448	CALLIN, James	18	E½	1837-08-18		A1
5549	CALLIN, Richard	7	W½SE	1837-08-18		A1
5449	CATLIN, James	17	SWNW	1837-08-18		A1
5450	" "	17	W½SW	1837-08-18		A1
5452	" "	18	W½NW	1837-08-18		A1
5453	" "	18	W½SW	1837-08-18		A1
5455	" "	19	NE	1837-08-18		A1
5456	" "	22	E½NW	1837-08-18		A1
5458	" "	22	W½NE	1837-08-18		A1
5461	" "	7	NESE	1837-08-18		A1
5462	" "	8	NENW	1837-08-18		A1
5463	" "	8	NWNE	1837-08-18		A1
5464	" "	8	SWNW	1837-08-18		A1
5451	" "	18	E½SW	1838-07-28		A1
5454	" "	19	E½NW	1838-07-28		A1
5457	" "	22	E½SW	1838-07-28		A1
5459	" "	7	E½SW	1838-07-28		A1
5460	" "	7	NE	1838-07-28		A1
5550	CATLIN, Richard	18	E½NW	1858-11-01		A1
5537	COLEMAN, Peter E	8	SENW	1834-08-12		A1
5538	" "	9	SWNW	1834-08-12		A1
5533	COOK, Milton J	8	NWNW	1835-10-08		A1
5534	" "	8	SWNE	1835-10-08		A1
5598	COOK, William H	32	NW	1894-10-22		A2
5492	CRITTENDEN, John	4	NWSE	1861-05-01		A1

ID	Individual in Patent	Sec.	Sec. Part	Date Issued	Other Counties	For More Info . . .
5419	CURRY, Ebenezer	33	NESW	1860-04-02		A1
5420	" "	33	NWSE	1860-04-02		A1
5421	" "	33	S½NW	1860-04-02		A1
5523	DAVIS, Lewis C	6	E½NE	1860-04-02		A1
5524	" "	6	N½SE	1860-04-02		A1
5525	" "	6	SWSE	1860-04-02		A1
5509	DEES, John T	11	S½SE	1858-11-01		A1
5510	" "	11	SESW	1858-11-01		A1
5511	" "	13	SWNW	1858-11-01		A1
5512	" "	14	NE	1858-11-01		A1
5513	" "	14	NENW	1858-11-01		A1
5389	DENDY, Buford W	26	NWNE	1860-09-01		A1
5390	" "	26	NWNW	1860-09-01		A1
5391	" "	34	N½SE	1860-09-01		A1
5392	" "	34	SENW	1860-09-01		A1
5393	" "	36	NWNW	1860-09-01		A1
5606	EDWARDS, William J	3	N½NE	1858-11-01		A1
5607	" "	3	N½NW	1858-11-01		A1
5366	FEAGIN, Aaron P	17	S½SE	1858-11-01		A1
5367	" "	20	NENE	1858-11-01		A1
5368	" "	20	NENW	1860-10-01		A1
5369	" "	20	NWNE	1860-10-01		A1
5596	FERRELL, William	2	N½NE	1884-12-05		A2
5597	" "	2	NENW	1884-12-05		A2
5585	FLORENCE, Toliver	35	N½SW	1858-11-01		A1
5586	" "	35	SE	1858-11-01		A1
5587	" "	35	W½NE	1858-11-01		A1
5413	GILL, David	7	W½NW	1823-12-01		A1
5572	GORUM, Shelton D	17	NESW	1840-10-10		A1
5417	GREGORY, Dudley S	5	W½NE	1837-08-18		A1
5418	" "	5	W½SE	1837-08-18		A1
5466	GREGORY, James G	5	E½SW	1838-07-28		A1
5519	HAMMONDS, Joseph	2	NWNW	1860-04-02		A1
5520	HAMMONDS, Joseph W	27	SESW	1850-08-10		A1
5604	HAMMONDS, William	27	NWSW	1850-08-10		A1
5605	" "	27	SENW	1854-07-15		A1
5603	" "	27	NWSE	1858-11-01		A1
5516	HART, Jordan	4	NESW	1858-11-01		A1
5517	" "	4	SENE	1858-11-01		A1
5518	" "	4	SENW	1858-11-01		A1
5521	HART, Jurdin	4	SESW	1858-11-01		A1
5522	" "	9	NENE	1858-11-01		A1
5387	HUGHES, Benjamin	24	SWNW	1835-10-01		A1
5552	HUGHES, Richard S	21	SESE	1853-08-01		A1
5553	HUGHS, Richard S	21	N½SW	1858-11-01		A1
5554	" "	21	SWSW	1858-11-01		A1
5555	" "	28	N½NW	1858-11-01		A1
5556	" "	28	S½NW	1860-10-01		A1
5629	HUGHS, Wilson	11	E½NW	1858-11-01		A1
5630	" "	11	N½SW	1858-11-01		A1
5627	" "	10	NWSE	1896-10-21		A1
5628	" "	10	SENW	1896-10-21		A1
5609	JERNIGAN, William	3	NESW	1854-10-02		A1
5608	" "	10	NWNE	1858-11-01		A1
5610	" "	3	NWSW	1858-11-01		A1
5611	" "	3	S½NW	1858-11-01		A1
5612	" "	3	SESE	1858-11-01		A1
5613	" "	3	SWNE	1858-11-01		A1
5614	" "	3	W½SE	1858-11-01		A1
5474	JONES, James W	28	SW	1891-06-30		A2
5541	JONES, Raleigh	5	NESE	1835-09-12		A1
5565	JONES, Samuel J	4	N½NE	1858-11-01		A1
5566	" "	4	NENW	1858-11-01		A1
5567	" "	4	SWNE	1858-11-01		A1
5469	JOSEY, James S	21	SENE	1848-05-03		A1
5468	" "	21	NENE	1858-11-01		A1
5470	" "	21	SWNE	1858-11-01		A1
5471	" "	22	NWNW	1858-11-01		A1
5475	JOSEY, James W	15	SWSW	1840-10-10		A1
5560	JOSEY, Robert M	28	W½SE	1860-04-02		A1
5561	" "	33	W½NE	1860-04-02		A1
5493	KENNEDY, John D	30	N½SW	1893-09-23		A2
5494	" "	30	S½NW	1893-09-23		A2

ID	Individual in Patent	Sec.	Sec. Part	Date Issued	Other Counties	For More Info . . .
5473	LANE, James T	36	NENW	1837-08-18		A1
5485	LANE, Jesse C	13	SWSW	1860-04-02		A1
5486	" "	14	NESE	1860-04-02		A1
5487	" "	23	NESW	1860-04-02		A1
5488	" "	25	NW	1860-04-02		A1
5489	" "	26	NENE	1860-04-02		A1
5599	LANE, William H	20	SESE	1860-09-01		A1
5514	LE FLORE, JOHN W	30	N½NE	1875-10-01		A2
5515	" "	30	N½NW	1875-10-01		A2
5437	LEE, Hillary	11	NENE	1858-11-01		A1
5438	" "	12	W½NW	1858-11-01		A1
5443	LEE, Jackson	11	N½SE	1858-11-01		A1
5528	LEE, Marion	2	SE	1884-12-05		A2
5496	MAXCEY, John	4	NWNW	1843-02-01		A1
5551	MERCHANT, Richard	33	NWSW	1850-04-01		A1
5617	MOORE, William	23	E½SE	1837-08-14		A1
5401	NICHOLS, Daniel R	12	SWSW	1882-10-30		A1
5422	NIX, Edward	20	NWSE	1862-04-10		A1
5576	PEARY, Thomas W	26	NWSE	1850-08-10		A1
5394	PITTS, Chaney	10	NWNW	1852-02-02		A1
5398	PITTS, Creed T	2	E½SW	1884-03-10		A2
5412	PITTS, David D	10	NENE	1852-02-02		A1
5414	PITTS, David W	10	SENE	1860-04-02		A1
5415	" "	11	W½NW	1860-04-02		A1
5500	PITTS, John S	35	SESW	1858-11-01		A1
5631	PREWETT, Winnefred	34	NWNW	1858-11-01		A1
5557	PRUETT, Richard W	34	SWNW	1838-07-28		A1
5558	PRUITT, Richard W	34	NENW	1850-08-10		A1
5465	RAINEE, James D	22	NWSE	1860-10-01		A1
5529	RAINER, Martha A	22	SWSE	1904-08-16		A2
5370	REID, Archey M	17	NENW	1852-02-02		A1
5371	" "	8	SESW	1852-02-02		A1
5374	REID, Archibald M	15	E½NW	1837-08-15		A1
5376	" "	23	E½NE	1837-08-15		A1
5379	" "	23	W½NW	1837-08-15		A1
5382	" "	24	W½SW	1837-08-15		A1
5380	" "	24	NWNW	1840-10-10		A1
5373	" "	14	W½SE	1841-05-20		A1
5377	" "	23	E½NW	1845-07-01		A1
5375	" "	17	SENW	1848-04-01		A1
5386	" "	33	NESE	1848-04-01		A1
5378	" "	23	W½NE	1848-05-03		A1
5384	" "	28	E½SE	1848-05-03		A1
5385	" "	33	E½NE	1848-05-03		A1
5383	" "	27	NWNE	1850-08-10		A1
5372	" "	14	SESE	1858-11-01		A1
5381	" "	24	SESW	1860-10-01		A1
5539	REID, Peter	2	S½NE	1885-08-05		A1
5547	REID, Reuben	7	SESE	1837-04-10		A1
5548	" "	8	W½SW	1837-04-10		A1
5546	" "	17	NWNW	1837-08-12		A1
5563	REID, Sam	26	SENE	1884-12-05		A2
5497	ROGERS, John	24	NESW	1843-02-01		A1
5498	" "	24	SENW	1843-02-01		A1
5499	" "	24	SWNE	1843-02-01		A1
5530	ROSE, Mary	19	NESE	1848-05-03		A1
5531	" "	20	NWNW	1850-04-01		A1
5532	" "	20	NWSW	1858-11-01		A1
5600	ROSE, William H	20	NESW	1860-09-01		A1
5601	" "	20	SENW	1860-09-01		A1
5602	" "	20	SWNE	1860-09-01		A1
5400	SHINE, Daniel B	25	W½SE	1845-07-01		A1
5399	" "	25	SESE	1858-11-01		A1
5411	SHINE, David B	25	S½NE	1837-08-15		A1
5423	SHINE, Elizabeth	25	N½SW	1837-08-15		A1
5424	" "	25	S½SW	1858-11-01		A1
5425	" "	26	SESE	1858-11-01		A1
5478	SHINE, James W	14	NWSW	1847-05-01		A1
5479	" "	14	S½SW	1848-05-03		A1
5481	" "	15	E½SE	1849-09-01		A1
5476	" "	14	NESW	1850-04-01		A1
5480	" "	14	SWNW	1850-04-01		A1
5483	" "	15	SWSE	1850-08-10		A1

ID	Individual in Patent	Sec.	Sec. Part	Date Issued	Other Counties	For More Info . . .
5477	SHINE, James W (Cont'd)	14	NWNW	1854-07-15		A1
5482	" "	15	SWNE	1854-07-15		A1
5484	" "	25	N½NE	1858-11-01		A1
5618	SHINE, William P	24	E½NE	1858-11-01		A1
5619	" "	24	NESE	1858-11-01		A1
5564	SIMMONS, Samuel A	8	E½NE	1834-08-20		A1
5395	SMITH, Clarissa W	35	SENE	1858-11-01		A1
5396	" "	36	N½SW	1858-11-01		A1
5397	" "	36	SWNW	1858-11-01		A1
5439	SMITH, Isaac R	36	N½SE	1858-11-01		A1
5441	" "	36	SENW	1858-11-01		A1
5442	" "	36	W½NE	1858-11-01		A1
5440	" "	36	NENE	1860-12-01		A1
5501	SMITH, John	10	SWNE	1850-04-01		A1
5568	SMITH, Samuel T	26	NWSW	1860-12-01		A1
5569	" "	26	SWNW	1860-12-01		A1
5570	" "	26	SWSW	1861-05-01		A1
5506	SMYTH, John	4	W½SW	1841-05-20		A1
5507	" "	9	NWNW	1841-05-20		A1
5505	" "	4	E½SE	1848-05-03		A1
5502	" "	10	NENW	1849-09-01		A1
5503	" "	3	SESW	1849-09-01		A1
5504	" "	3	SWSW	1849-09-01		A1
5575	SMYTH, Thomas	36	SESE	1849-09-01		A1
5615	SOLOMON, William L	2	S½NW	1860-04-02		A1
5616	" "	2	W½SW	1860-04-02		A1
5416	SPEARS, Demsey G	32	SE	1891-07-28		A2
5403	STALLINGS, Daniel	13	E½NW	1837-08-15		A1
5405	" "	13	NENE	1837-08-15		A1
5409	" "	24	NENW	1843-02-01		A1
5404	" "	13	E½SE	1848-05-03		A1
5406	" "	13	SENE	1858-11-01		A1
5407	" "	13	SESW	1858-11-01		A1
5408	" "	13	W½SE	1858-11-01		A1
5410	" "	24	NWNE	1858-11-01		A1
5402	" "	12	SESE	1860-10-01		A1
5472	STALLINGS, James	17	SESW	1850-08-10		A1
5542	STALLINGS, Reuben R	21	NESE	1853-11-15		A1
5543	" "	21	SESE	1858-11-01		A1
5544	" "	22	SWNW	1858-11-01		A1
5545	" "	22	SWSW	1858-11-01		A1
5591	STALLINGS, William D	34	NESW	1858-11-01		A1
5592	" "	34	SESW	1858-11-01		A1
5593	" "	34	W½SW	1858-11-01		A1
5508	SULLIVAN, John	22	E½NE	1837-08-15		A1
5427	TILMAN, George	26	NESW	1850-08-10		A1
5428	" "	26	SWNE	1850-08-10		A1
5430	TILMON, George	26	NESE	1838-07-28		A1
5432	" "	26	SWSE	1850-08-10		A1
5429	" "	26	E½NW	1858-11-01		A1
5431	" "	26	SESW	1858-11-01		A1
5583	TYNES, Timothy	20	S½SW	1860-12-01		A1
5584	" "	20	SWSE	1860-12-01		A1
5594	WADE, William F	22	E½SE	1858-11-01		A1
5595	" "	23	W½SW	1858-11-01		A1
5620	WALL, William R	10	E½SW	1858-11-01		A1
5621	" "	10	NWSW	1858-11-01		A1
5622	" "	10	SWSW	1858-11-01		A1
5623	" "	9	E½NW	1858-11-01		A1
5624	" "	9	NESW	1858-11-01		A1
5625	" "	9	W½NE	1858-11-01		A1
5562	WEAVER, Robert M	9	SENE	1848-05-03		A1
5467	WELLS, James M	32	SW	1891-11-23		A2
5495	WHEELER, John H	23	W½SE	1837-08-14		A1
5535	WILLIAMS, Nancy L	6	NW	1861-05-01		A1
5536	" "	6	W½NE	1861-05-01		A1
5559	WILLIAMS, Richard	9	NESE	1848-05-03		A1
5571	WILLIAMSON, Shadrach	34	S½SE	1860-12-01		A1
5433	WILSON, George W	8	NESE	1834-10-21		A1
5435	" "	9	SWSE	1837-04-15		A1
5434	" "	8	SESE	1849-09-01		A1
5436	" "	9	W½SW	1852-02-02		A1
5526	WILSON, Louisa H	17	NENE	1858-11-01		A1

ID	Individual in Patent	Sec.	Sec. Part	Date Issued	Other Counties	For More Info . . .
5527	WILSON, Lovett	36	SENE	1841-05-20		A1

Patent Map

T7-N R15-E
St Stephens Meridian

Map Group 24

Township Statistics

Parcels Mapped	:	266
Number of Patents	:	200
Number of Individuals	:	111
Patentees Identified	:	111
Number of Surnames	:	70
Multi-Patentee Parcels	:	0
Oldest Patent Date	:	12/1/1823
Most Recent Patent	:	8/16/1904
Block/Lot Parcels	:	0
Parcels Re - Issued	:	0
Parcels that Overlap	:	0
Cities and Towns	:	1
Cemeteries	:	2

Section 6
WILLIAMS Nancy L 1861
WILLIAMS Nancy L 1861
DAVIS Lewis C 1860
DAVIS Lewis C 1860
BERRY William T 1860
DAVIS Lewis C 1860

Section 5
GREGORY Dudley S 1837
BROOK Preston 1837
GREGORY James G 1838
JONES Raleigh 1835
GREGORY Dudley S 1837
BRILEY Jacob 1837
BRILEY Jacob 1837

Section 4
MAXCEY John 1843
JONES Samuel J 1858
JONES Samuel J 1858
BRILEY Jacob 1837
HART Jordan 1858
JONES Samuel J 1858
HART Jordan 1858
SMYTH John 1841
HART Jordan 1858
CRITTENDEN John 1861
HART Jurdin 1858
SMYTH John 1848

Section 7
GILL David 1823
CATLIN James 1838
CATLIN James 1838
CALLIN Richard 1837
CATLIN James 1837
REID Reuben 1837

Section 8
COOK Milton J 1835
CATLIN James 1837
CATLIN James 1837
CATLIN James 1837
COLEMAN Peter E 1834
CATLIN James 1837
COOK Milton J 1835
8
WILSON George W 1834
REID Reuben 1837
REID Archey M 1852
WILSON George W 1849
SIMMONS Samuel A 1834

Section 9
SMYTH John 1841
COLEMAN Peter E 1834
WILSON George W 1852
9
WALL William R 1858
WALL William R 1858
WALL William R 1858
BROGDON James C 1849
WILSON George W 1837
HART Jurdin 1858
WEAVER Robert M 1848
WILLIAMS Richard 1848
ADAMS Frederick 1843

Section 18
CATLIN Richard 1858
CATLIN James 1837
18
CATLIN James 1837
CATLIN James 1838
CALLIN James 1837

Section 17
REID Reuben 1837
REID Archey M 1852
CATLIN James 1837
REID Archibald M 1848
CATLIN James 1837
GORUM Shelton D 1840
17
CATLIN James 1837
STALLINGS James 1850
FEAGIN Aaron P 1858
WILSON Louisa H 1858

Section 16
16

Section 19
CATLIN James 1838
CATLIN James 1837
19
ROSE Mary 1848

Section 20
ROSE Mary 1850
FEAGIN Aaron P 1860
FEAGIN Aaron P 1860
FEAGIN Aaron P 1858
ROSE William H 1860
ROSE William H 1860
20
ROSE Mary 1858
ROSE William H 1860
NIX Edward 1862
TYNES Timothy 1860
TYNES Timothy 1860
LANE William H 1860

Section 21
21
HUGHS Richard S 1858
HUGHS Richard S 1858
HUGHES Richard S 1853
JOSEY James S 1858
JOSEY James S 1858
JOSEY James S 1848
STALLINGS Reuben R 1853
STALLINGS Reuben R 1858

Section 30
FLORE John W Le 1875
FLORE John W Le 1875
KENNEDY John D 1893
BANISTER John A 1892
30
KENNEDY John D 1893
BANISTER John A 1892
BOAN Ted S 1891
BOAN Ted S 1891

Section 29
29

Section 28
HUGHS Richard S 1858
HUGHS Richard S 1860
28
JONES James W 1891
BROGDEN William 1858
REID Archibald M 1848
JOSEY Robert M 1860

Section 31
31

Section 32
COOK William H 1894
32
WELLS James M 1891
SPEARS Demsey G 1891

Section 33
CURRY Ebenezer 1860
33
MERCHANT Richard 1850
CURRY Ebenezer 1860
CURRY Ebenezer 1860
JOSEY Robert M 1860
REID Archibald M 1848
REID Archibald M 1848

EDWARDS William J 1858
EDWARDS William J 1858
HAMMONDS Joseph 1860
FERRELL William 1884
FERRELL William 1884

JERNIGAN William 1858
3
JERNIGAN William 1858
SOLOMON William L 1860
2
REID Peter 1885

JERNIGAN William 1858
JERNIGAN William 1854
JERNIGAN William 1858
JERNIGAN William 1858
SOLOMON William L 1860
PITTS Creed T 1884
LEE Marion 1884

SMYTH John 1849
SMYTH John 1849

1

PITTS Chaney 1852
SMYTH John 1849
JERNIGAN William 1858
PITTS David D 1852
LEE Hillary 1858

HUGHS Wilson 1896
SMITH John 1850
PITTS David W 1860
PITTS David W 1860
HUGHS Wilson 1858
11
LEE Hillary 1858
BARRETT Timothy 1858
BARRETT Timothy 1858

WALL William R 1858
10
HUGHS Wilson 1896
HUGHS Wilson 1858
LEE Jackson 1858
BARRETT Timothy 1858
12
BARRETT Timothy 1858

WALL William R 1858
WALL William R 1858
DEES John T 1858
DEES John T 1858
NICHOLS Daniel R 1882
BARRETT Timothy 1860
BARRETT Timothy 1860
STALLINGS Daniel 1860

REID Archibald M 1837
SHINE James W 1854
DEES John T 1858
DEES John T 1858
BARRETT Benjamin J 1852
STALLINGS Daniel 1837
STALLINGS Daniel 1837

SHINE James W 1854
SHINE James W 1850
14
STALLINGS Daniel 1837
DEES John T 1858
STALLINGS Daniel 1858

15
SHINE James W 1849
SHINE James W 1847
SHINE James W 1850
REID Archibald M 1841
LANE Jesse C 1860
13
STALLINGS Daniel 1848

SHINE James W 1850
SHINE James W 1848
REID Archibald M 1858
LANE Jesse C 1860
STALLINGS Daniel 1858
STALLINGS Daniel 1858

JOSEY James W 1840
SHINE James W 1850

JOSEY James S 1858
CATLIN James 1837
REID Archibald M 1837
REID Archibald M 1837
STALLINGS Daniel 1843
STALLINGS Daniel 1858

STALLINGS Reuben R 1858
CATLIN James 1837
SULLIVAN John 1837
REID Archibald M 1845
REID Archibald M 1837
HUGHES Benjamin 1835
ROGERS John 1843
24
ROGERS John 1843
SHINE William P 1858

22
REID Archibald M 1848

CATLIN James 1838
RAINEE James D 1860
WADE William F 1858
WADE William F 1858
LANE Jesse C 1860
23
MOORE William 1837
REID Archibald M 1837
ROGERS John 1843
REID Archibald M 1860
SHINE William P 1858

STALLINGS Reuben R 1858
RAINER Martha A 1904
WHEELER John H 1837

BROGDEN William 1858
REID Archibald M 1850
DENDY Buford W 1860
DENDY Buford W 1860
LANE Jesse C 1860
SHINE James W 1858

BROGDEN William 1858
HAMMONDS William 1854
27
SMITH Samuel T 1860
TILMON George 1858
TILMAN George 1850
LANE Jesse C 1860
25
SHINE David B 1837

REID Sam 1884

HAMMONDS William 1850
HAMMONDS William 1858
SMITH Samuel T 1860
TILMAN George 1850
PEARY Thomas W 1850
TILMON George 1838
SHINE Elizabeth 1837
SHINE Daniel B 1845

HAMMONDS Joseph W 1850
SMITH Samuel T 1861
TILMON George 1858
TILMON George 1850
SHINE Elizabeth 1858
SHINE Elizabeth 1858
SHINE Daniel B 1858

PREWETT Winnefred 1858
PRUITT Richard W 1850
FLORENCE Toliver 1858
DENDY Buford W 1860
LANE James T 1837
SMITH Isaac R 1858
SMITH Isaac R 1860

PRUETT Richard W 1838
DENDY Buford W 1860
34
35
SMITH Clarissa W 1858
SMITH Clarissa W 1858
SMITH Isaac R 1858
36
WILSON Lovett 1841

STALLINGS William D 1858
STALLINGS William D 1858
DENDY Buford W 1860
FLORENCE Toliver 1858
SMITH Clarissa W 1858
SMITH Isaac R 1858

STALLINGS William D 1858
WILLIAMSON Shadrach 1860
PITTS John S 1858
FLORENCE Toliver 1858
SMYTH Thomas 1849

Helpful Hints

1. This Map's INDEX can be found on the preceding pages.

2. Refer to Map "C" to see where this Township lies within Butler County, Alabama.

3. Numbers within square brackets [ ] denote a multi-patentee land parcel (multi-owner). Refer to Appendix "C" for a full list of members in this group.

4. Areas that look to be crowded with Patentees usually indicate multiple sales of the same parcel (Re-issues) or Overlapping parcels. See this Township's Index for an explanation of these and other circumstances that might explain "odd" groupings of Patentees on this map.

Legend

———— Patent Boundary

━━━━ Section Boundary

No Patents Found (or Outside County)

1., 2., 3., ... Lot Numbers (when beside a name)

[ ] Group Number (see Appendix "C")

Scale: Section = 1 mile X 1 mile (generally, with some exceptions)

Road Map

T7-N R15-E
St Stephens Meridian

Map Group 24

Cities & Towns
Oaky Streak

Cemeteries
Consolation Cemetery
Oaky Streak Cemetery

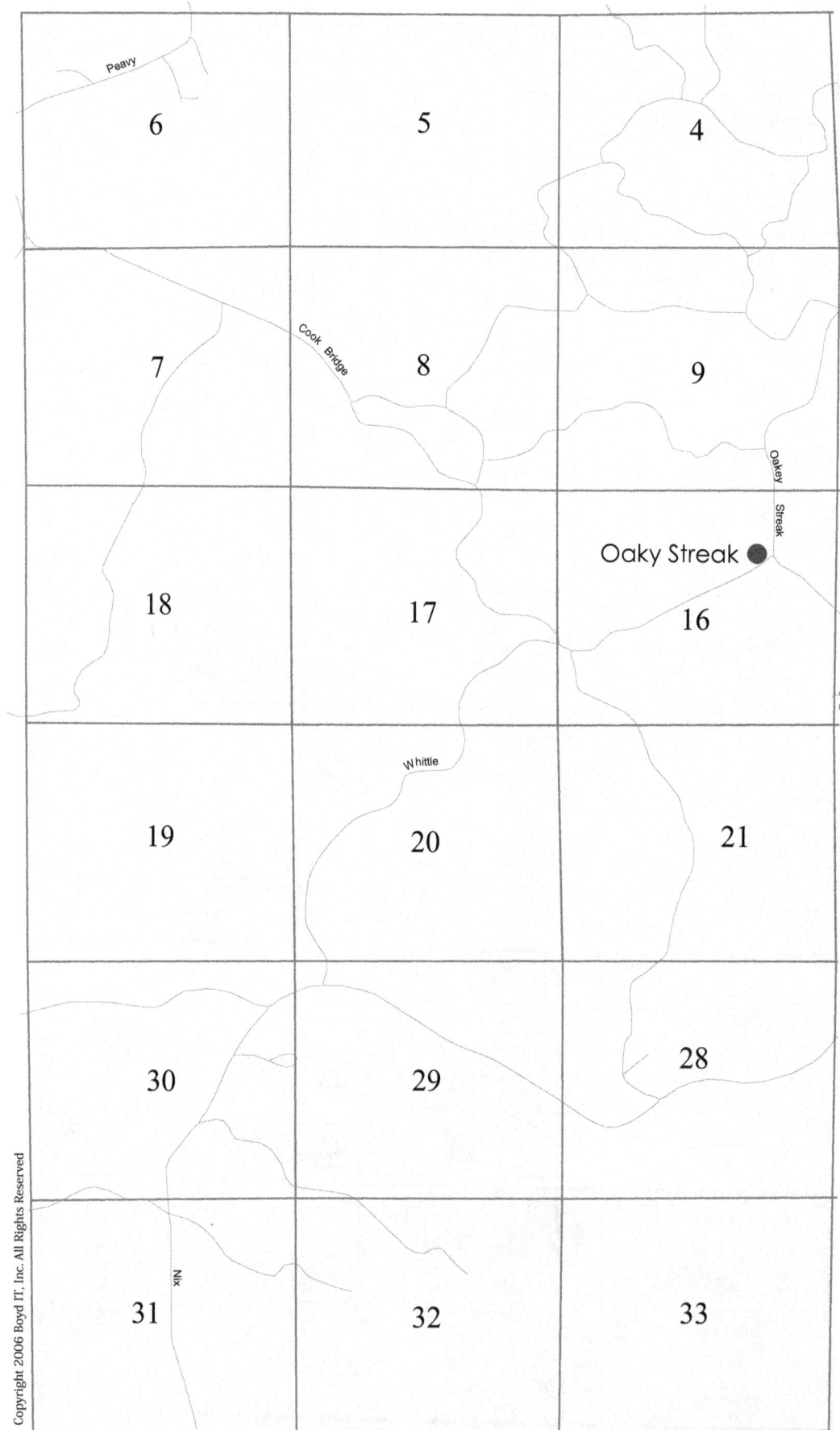

6	5	4
7	8	9
18	17	16
19	20	21
30	29	28
31	32	33

Peavy

Cook Bridge

Oakey Streak

Oaky Streak ●

Whittle

Nix

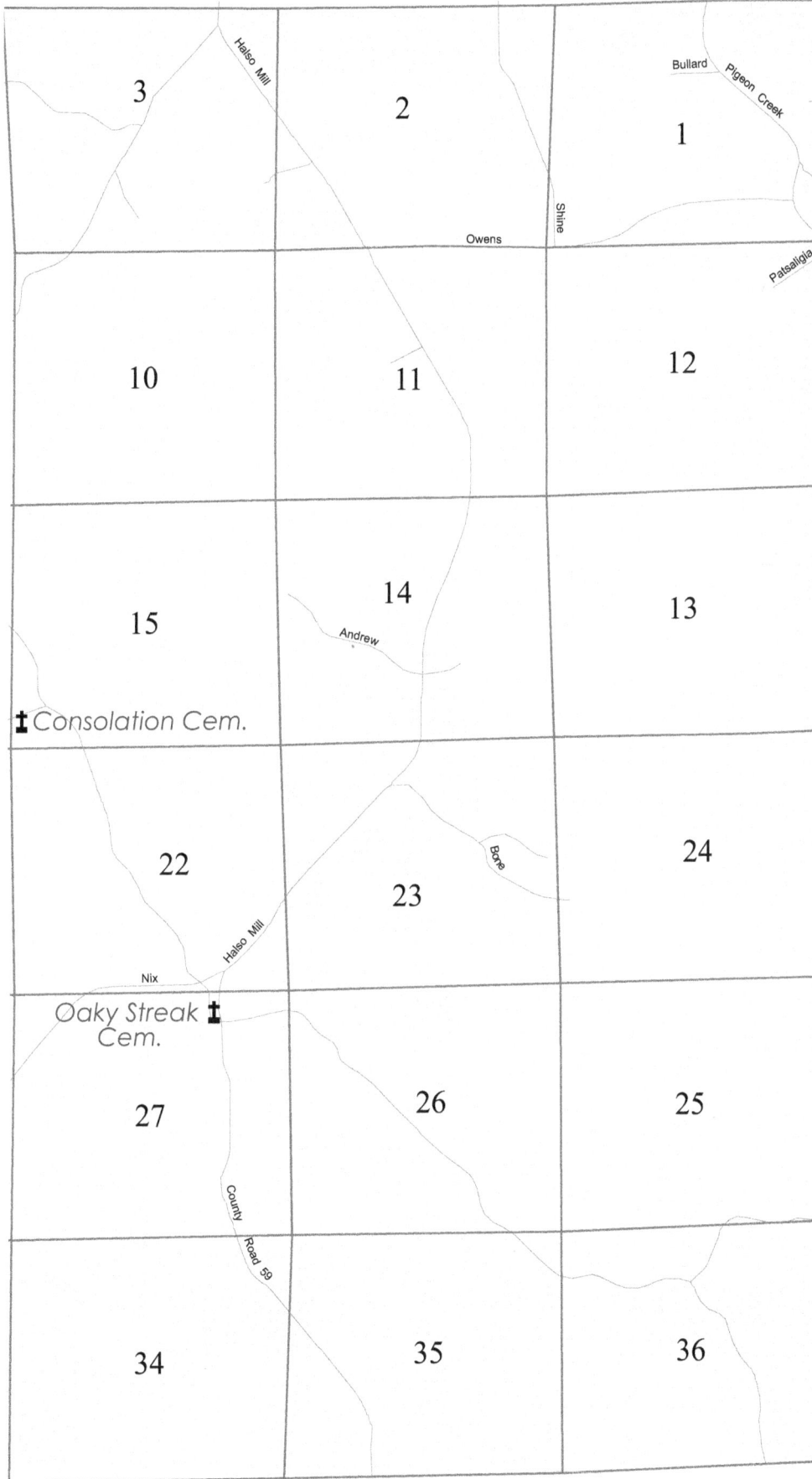

Helpful Hints

1. This road map has a number of uses, but primarily it is to help you: a) find the present location of land owned by your ancestors (at least the general area), b) find cemeteries and city-centers, and c) estimate the route/roads used by Census-takers & tax-assessors.

2. If you plan to travel to Butler County to locate cemeteries or land parcels, please pick up a modern travel map for the area before you do. Mapping old land parcels on modern maps is not as exact a science as you might think. Just the slightest variations in public land survey coordinates, estimates of parcel boundaries, or road-map deviations can greatly alter a map's representation of how a road either does or doesn't cross a particular parcel of land.

Legend

- Section Lines
- Interstates
- Highways
- Other Roads
- Cities/Towns
- Cemeteries

Scale: Section = 1 mile X 1 mile (generally, with some exceptions)

Historical Map

T7-N R15-E
St Stephens Meridian

Map Group 24

Cities & Towns
Oaky Streak

Cemeteries
Consolation Cemetery
Oaky Streak Cemetery

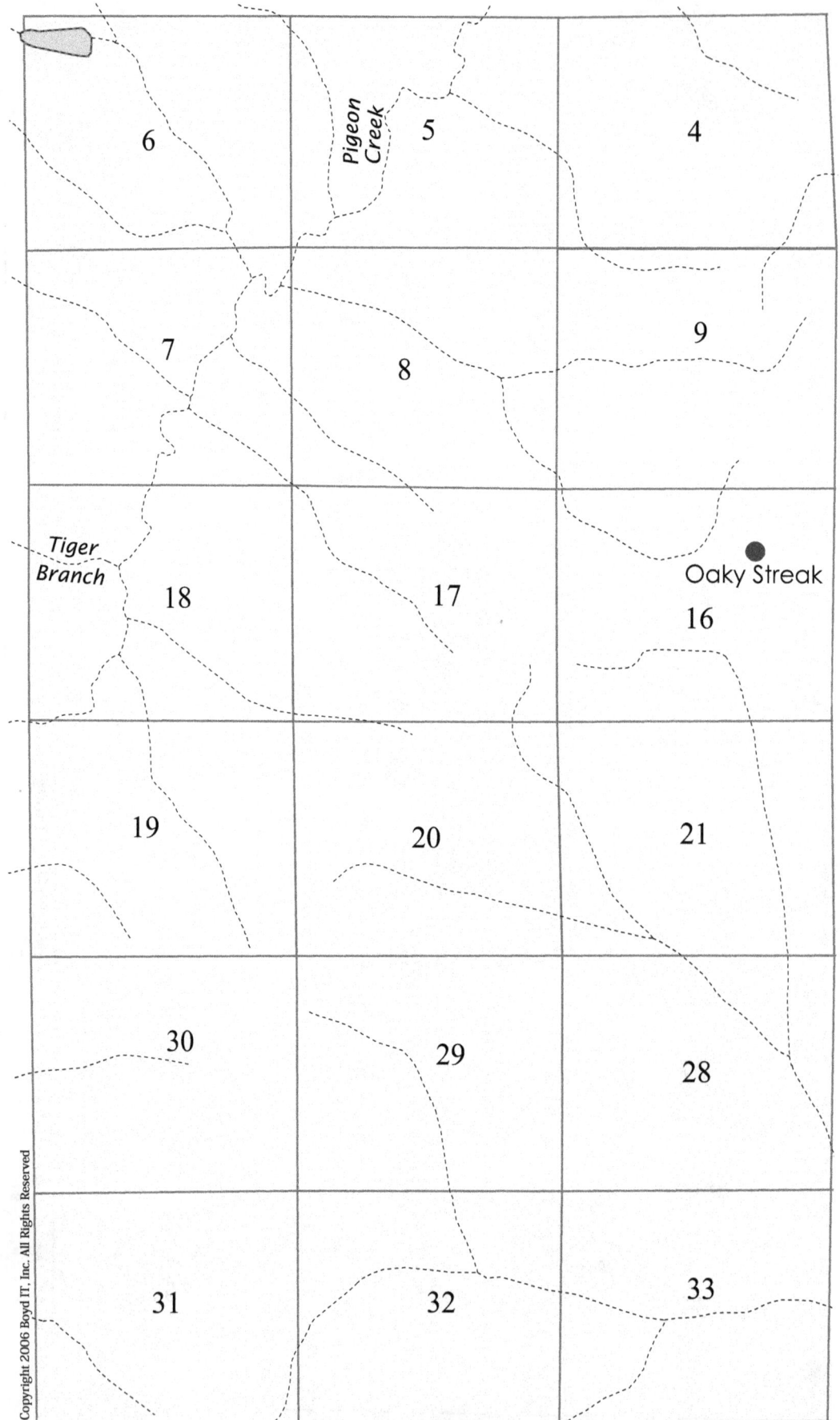

6	5 Pigeon Creek	4
7	8	9
18 Tiger Branch	17	16 • Oaky Streak
19	20	21
30	29	28
31	32	33

3

2

1

Hughes Branch

Flat Branch

Orange Branch

10

11

12

Sawyer Creek

15

14

13

✝Consolation Cem.

Oaky Creek

Woods

22

23

24

Oaky Streak ✝
Cem.

27

26

25

34

35

36

Helpful Hints

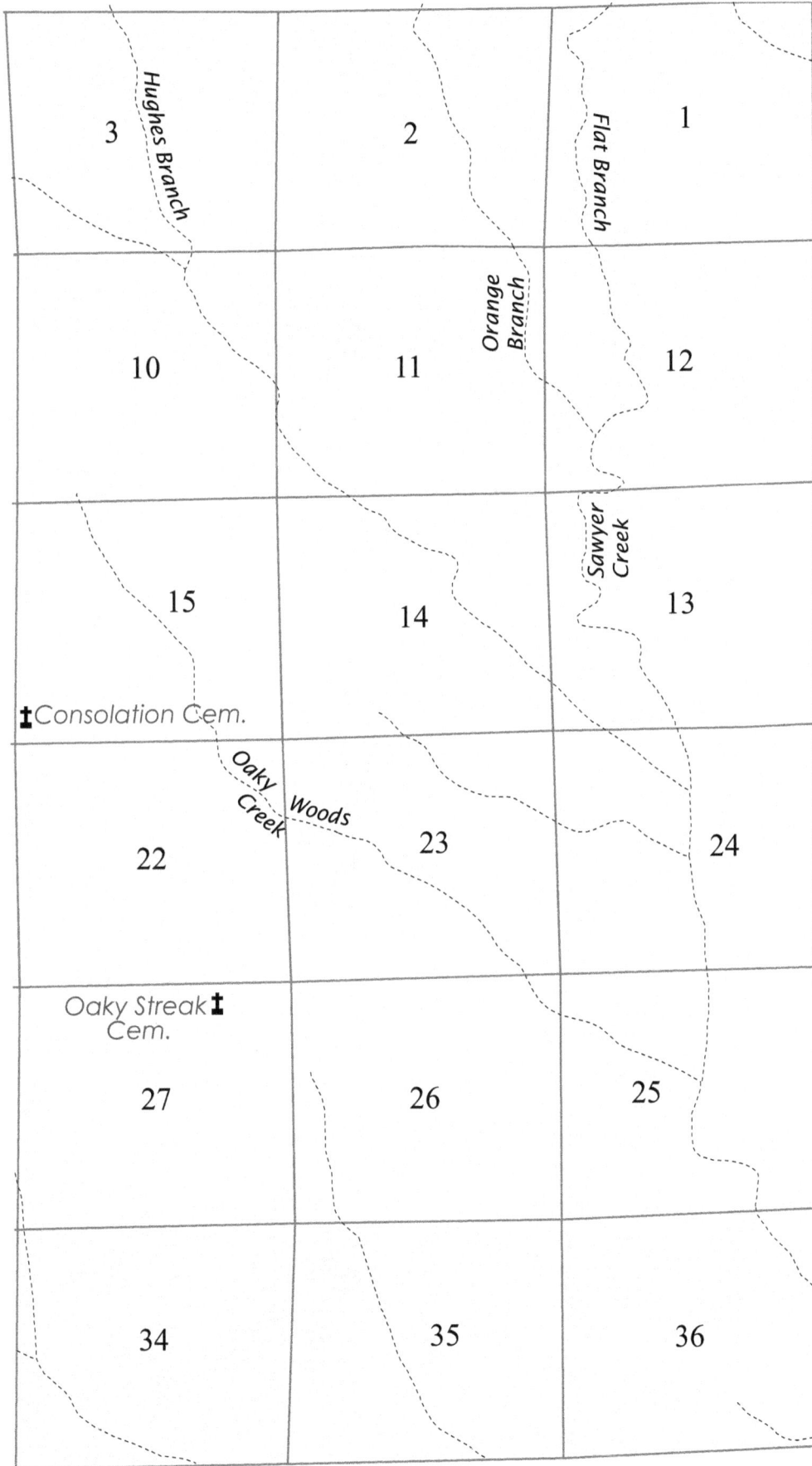

1. This Map takes a different look at
the same Congressional Township
displayed in the preceding two
maps. It presents features that
can help you better envision the
historical development of the area:
a) Water-bodies (lakes & ponds),
b) Water-courses (rivers, streams,
etc.), c) Railroads, d) City/town
center-points (where they were
oftentimes located when first
settled), and e) Cemeteries.

2. Using this "Historical" map in
tandem with this Township's
Patent Map and Road Map, may
lead you to some interesting
discoveries. You will often find
roads, towns, cemeteries, and
waterways are named after nearby
landowners: sometimes those
names will be the ones you are
researching. See how many of
these research gems you can find
here in Butler County.

L e g e n d

—————— Section Lines

+++++++ Railroads

▭ Large Rivers &
Bodies of Water

------- Streams/Creeks
& Small Rivers

● Cities/Towns

✝ Cemeteries

Scale: Section = 1 mile X 1 mile
(there are some exceptions)

Appendices

Appendix A - Acts of Congress Authorizing the Patents Contained in this Book

The following Acts of Congress are referred to throughout the Indexes in this book. The text of the Federal Statutes referred to below can usually be found on the web. For more information on such laws, check out the publishers's web-site at *www.arphax.com*, go to the "Research" page, and click on the "Land-Law" link.

Ref. No.	Date and Act of Congress	Number of Parcels of Land
1	April 24, 1820: Sale-Cash Entry (3 Stat. 566)	5280
2	May 20, 1862: Homestead EntryOriginal (12 Stat. 392)	351

Appendix B - Section Parts (Aliquot Parts)

The following represent the various abbreviations we have found thus far in describing the parts of a Public Land Section. Some of these are very obscure and rarely used, but we wanted to list them for just that reason. A full section is 1 square mile or 640 acres.

Section Part	Description	Acres
\<none\>	Full Acre (if no Section Part is listed, presumed a full Section)	640
\<1-??\>	A number represents a Lot Number and can be of various sizes	?
E½	East Half-Section	320
E½E½	East Half of East Half-Section	160
E½E½SE	East Half of East Half of Southeast Quarter-Section	40
E½N½	East Half of North Half-Section	160
E½NE	East Half of Northeast Quarter-Section	80
E½NENE	East Half of Northeast Quarter of Northeast Quarter-Section	20
E½NENW	East Half of Northeast Quarter of Northwest Quarter-Section	20
E½NESE	East Half of Northeast Quarter of Southeast Quarter-Section	20
E½NESW	East Half of Northeast Quarter of Southwest Quarter-Section	20
E½NW	East Half of Northwest Quarter-Section	80
E½NWNE	East Half of Northwest Quarter of Northeast Quarter-Section	20
E½NWNW	East Half of Northwest Quarter of Northwest Quarter-Section	20
E½NWSE	East Half of Northwest Quarter of Southeast Quarter-Section	20
E½NWSW	East Half of Northwest Quarter of Southwest Quarter-Section	20
E½S½	East Half of South Half-Section	160
E½SE	East Half of Southeast Quarter-Section	80
E½SENE	East Half of Southeast Quarter of Northeast Quarter-Section	20
E½SENW	East Half of Southeast Quarter of Northwest Quarter-Section	20
E½SESE	East Half of Southeast Quarter of Southeast Quarter-Section	20
E½SESW	East Half of Southeast Quarter of Southwest Quarter-Section	20
E½SW	East Half of Southwest Quarter-Section	80
E½SWNE	East Half of Southwest Quarter of Northeast Quarter-Section	20
E½SWNW	East Half of Southwest Quarter of Northwest Quarter-Section	20
E½SWSE	East Half of Southwest Quarter of Southeast Quarter-Section	20
E½SWSW	East Half of Southwest Quarter of Southwest Quarter-Section	20
E½W½	East Half of West Half-Section	160
N½	North Half-Section	320
N½E½NE	North Half of East Half of Northeast Quarter-Section	40
N½E½NW	North Half of East Half of Northwest Quarter-Section	40
N½E½SE	North Half of East Half of Southeast Quarter-Section	40
N½E½SW	North Half of East Half of Southwest Quarter-Section	40
N½N½	North Half of North Half-Section	160
N½NE	North Half of Northeast Quarter-Section	80
N½NENE	North Half of Northeast Quarter of Northeast Quarter-Section	20
N½NENW	North Half of Northeast Quarter of Northwest Quarter-Section	20
N½NESE	North Half of Northeast Quarter of Southeast Quarter-Section	20
N½NESW	North Half of Northeast Quarter of Southwest Quarter-Section	20
N½NW	North Half of Northwest Quarter-Section	80
N½NWNE	North Half of Northwest Quarter of Northeast Quarter-Section	20
N½NWNW	North Half of Northwest Quarter of Northwest Quarter-Section	20
N½NWSE	North Half of Northwest Quarter of Southeast Quarter-Section	20
N½NWSW	North Half of Northwest Quarter of Southwest Quarter-Section	20
N½S½	North Half of South Half-Section	160
N½SE	North Half of Southeast Quarter-Section	80
N½SENE	North Half of Southeast Quarter of Northeast Quarter-Section	20
N½SENW	North Half of Southeast Quarter of Northwest Quarter-Section	20
N½SESE	North Half of Southeast Quarter of Southeast Quarter-Section	20

Section Part	Description	Acres
N½SESW	North Half of Southeast Quarter of Southwest Quarter-Section	20
N½SESW	North Half of Southeast Quarter of Southwest Quarter-Section	20
N½SW	North Half of Southwest Quarter-Section	80
N½SWNE	North Half of Southwest Quarter of Northeast Quarter-Section	20
N½SWNW	North Half of Southwest Quarter of Northwest Quarter-Section	20
N½SWSE	North Half of Southwest Quarter of Southeast Quarter-Section	20
N½SWSE	North Half of Southwest Quarter of Southeast Quarter-Section	20
N½SWSW	North Half of Southwest Quarter of Southwest Quarter-Section	20
N½W½NW	North Half of West Half of Northwest Quarter-Section	40
N½W½SE	North Half of West Half of Southeast Quarter-Section	40
N½W½SW	North Half of West Half of Southwest Quarter-Section	40
NE	Northeast Quarter-Section	160
NEN½	Northeast Quarter of North Half-Section	80
NENE	Northeast Quarter of Northeast Quarter-Section	40
NENENE	Northeast Quarter of Northeast Quarter of Northeast Quarter	10
NENENW	Northeast Quarter of Northeast Quarter of Northwest Quarter	10
NENESE	Northeast Quarter of Northeast Quarter of Southeast Quarter	10
NENESW	Northeast Quarter of Northeast Quarter of Southwest Quarter	10
NENW	Northeast Quarter of Northwest Quarter-Section	40
NENWNE	Northeast Quarter of Northwest Quarter of Northeast Quarter	10
NENWNW	Northeast Quarter of Northwest Quarter of Northwest Quarter	10
NENWSE	Northeast Quarter of Northwest Quarter of Southeast Quarter	10
NENWSW	Northeast Quarter of Northwest Quarter of Southwest Quarter	10
NESE	Northeast Quarter of Southeast Quarter-Section	40
NESENE	Northeast Quarter of Southeast Quarter of Northeast Quarter	10
NESENW	Northeast Quarter of Southeast Quarter of Northwest Quarter	10
NESESE	Northeast Quarter of Southeast Quarter of Southeast Quarter	10
NESESW	Northeast Quarter of Southeast Quarter of Southwest Quarter	10
NESW	Northeast Quarter of Southwest Quarter-Section	40
NESWNE	Northeast Quarter of Southwest Quarter of Northeast Quarter	10
NESWNW	Northeast Quarter of Southwest Quarter of Northwest Quarter	10
NESWSE	Northeast Quarter of Southwest Quarter of Southeast Quarter	10
NESWSW	Northeast Quarter of Southwest Quarter of Southwest Quarter	10
NW	Northwest Quarter-Section	160
NWE½	Northwest Quarter of Eastern Half-Section	80
NWN½	Northwest Quarter of North Half-Section	80
NWNE	Northwest Quarter of Northeast Quarter-Section	40
NWNENE	Northwest Quarter of Northeast Quarter of Northeast Quarter	10
NWNENW	Northwest Quarter of Northeast Quarter of Northwest Quarter	10
NWNESE	Northwest Quarter of Northeast Quarter of Southeast Quarter	10
NWNESW	Northwest Quarter of Northeast Quarter of Southwest Quarter	10
NWNW	Northwest Quarter of Northwest Quarter-Section	40
NWNWNE	Northwest Quarter of Northwest Quarter of Northeast Quarter	10
NWNWNW	Northwest Quarter of Northwest Quarter of Northwest Quarter	10
NWNWSE	Northwest Quarter of Northwest Quarter of Southeast Quarter	10
NWNWSW	Northwest Quarter of Northwest Quarter of Southwest Quarter	10
NWSE	Northwest Quarter of Southeast Quarter-Section	40
NWSENE	Northwest Quarter of Southeast Quarter of Northeast Quarter	10
NWSENW	Northwest Quarter of Southeast Quarter of Northwest Quarter	10
NWSESE	Northwest Quarter of Southeast Quarter of Southeast Quarter	10
NWSESW	Northwest Quarter of Southeast Quarter of Southwest Quarter	10
NWSW	Northwest Quarter of Southwest Quarter-Section	40
NWSWNE	Northeast Quarter of Southwest Quarter of Northeast Quarter	10
NWSWNW	Northwest Quarter of Southwest Quarter of Northwest Quarter	10
NWSWSE	Northwest Quarter of Southwest Quarter of Southeast Quarter	10
NWSWSW	Northwest Quarter of Southwest Quarter of Southwest Quarter	10
S½	South Half-Section	320
S½E½NE	South Half of East Half of Northeast Quarter-Section	40
S½E½NW	South Half of East Half of Northwest Quarter-Section	40
S½E½SE	South Half of East Half of Southeast Quarter-Section	40

Section Part	Description	Acres
S½E½SW	South Half of East Half of Southwest Quarter-Section	40
S½N½	South Half of North Half-Section	160
S½NE	South Half of Northeast Quarter-Section	80
S½NENE	South Half of Northeast Quarter of Northeast Quarter-Section	20
S½NENW	South Half of Northeast Quarter of Northwest Quarter-Section	20
S½NESE	South Half of Northeast Quarter of Southeast Quarter-Section	20
S½NESW	South Half of Northeast Quarter of Southwest Quarter-Section	20
S½NW	South Half of Northwest Quarter-Section	80
S½NWNE	South Half of Northwest Quarter of Northeast Quarter-Section	20
S½NWNW	South Half of Northwest Quarter of Northwest Quarter-Section	20
S½NWSE	South Half of Northwest Quarter of Southeast Quarter-Section	20
S½NWSW	South Half of Northwest Quarter of Southwest Quarter-Section	20
S½S½	South Half of South Half-Section	160
S½SE	South Half of Southeast Quarter-Section	80
S½SENE	South Half of Southeast Quarter of Northeast Quarter-Section	20
S½SENW	South Half of Southeast Quarter of Northwest Quarter-Section	20
S½SESE	South Half of Southeast Quarter of Southeast Quarter-Section	20
S½SESW	South Half of Southeast Quarter of Southwest Quarter-Section	20
S½SESW	South Half of Southeast Quarter of Southwest Quarter-Section	20
S½SW	South Half of Southwest Quarter-Section	80
S½SWNE	South Half of Southwest Quarter of Northeast Quarter-Section	20
S½SWNW	South Half of Southwest Quarter of Northwest Quarter-Section	20
S½SWSE	South Half of Southwest Quarter of Southeast Quarter-Section	20
S½SWSE	South Half of Southwest Quarter of Southeast Quarter-Section	20
S½SWSW	South Half of Southwest Quarter of Southwest Quarter-Section	20
S½W½NE	South Half of West Half of Northeast Quarter-Section	40
S½W½NW	South Half of West Half of Northwest Quarter-Section	40
S½W½SE	South Half of West Half of Southeast Quarter-Section	40
S½W½SW	South Half of West Half of Southwest Quarter-Section	40
SE	Southeast Quarter Section	160
SEN½	Southeast Quarter of North Half-Section	80
SENE	Southeast Quarter of Northeast Quarter-Section	40
SENENE	Southeast Quarter of Northeast Quarter of Northeast Quarter	10
SENENW	Southeast Quarter of Northeast Quarter of Northwest Quarter	10
SENESE	Southeast Quarter of Northeast Quarter of Southeast Quarter	10
SENESW	Southeast Quarter of Northeast Quarter of Southwest Quarter	10
SENW	Southeast Quarter of Northwest Quarter-Section	40
SENWNE	Southeast Quarter of Northwest Quarter of Northeast Quarter	10
SENWNW	Southeast Quarter of Northwest Quarter of Northwest Quarter	10
SENWSE	Souteast Quarter of Northwest Quarter of Southeast Quarter	10
SENWSW	Southeast Quarter of Northwest Quarter of Southwest Quarter	10
SESE	Southeast Quarter of Southeast Quarter-Section	40
SESENE	SoutheastQuarter of Southeast Quarter of Northeast Quarter	10
SESENW	Southeast Quarter of Southeast Quarter of Northwest Quarter	10
SESESE	Southeast Quarter of Southeast Quarter of Southeast Quarter	10
SESESW	Southeast Quarter of Southeast Quarter of Southwest Quarter	10
SESW	Southeast Quarter of Southwest Quarter-Section	40
SESWNE	Southeast Quarter of Southwest Quarter of Northeast Quarter	10
SESWNW	Southeast Quarter of Southwest Quarter of Northwest Quarter	10
SESWSE	Southeast Quarter of Southwest Quarter of Southeast Quarter	10
SESWSW	Southeast Quarter of Southwest Quarter of Southwest Quarter	10
SW	Southwest Quarter-Section	160
SWNE	Southwest Quarter of Northeast Quarter-Section	40
SWNENE	Southwest Quarter of Northeast Quarter of Northeast Quarter	10
SWNENW	Southwest Quarter of Northeast Quarter of Northwest Quarter	10
SWNESE	Southwest Quarter of Northeast Quarter of Southeast Quarter	10
SWNESW	Southwest Quarter of Northeast Quarter of Southwest Quarter	10
SWNW	Southwest Quarter of Northwest Quarter-Section	40
SWNWNE	Southwest Quarter of Northwest Quarter of Northeast Quarter	10
SWNWNW	Southwest Quarter of Northwest Quarter of Northwest Quarter	10

Section Part	Description	Acres
SWNWSE	Southwest Quarter of Northwest Quarter of Southeast Quarter	10
SWNWSW	Southwest Quarter of Northwest Quarter of Southwest Quarter	10
SWSE	Southwest Quarter of Southeast Quarter-Section	40
SWSENE	Southwest Quarter of Southeast Quarter of Northeast Quarter	10
SWSENW	Southwest Quarter of Southeast Quarter of Northwest Quarter	10
SWSESE	Southwest Quarter of Southeast Quarter of Southeast Quarter	10
SWSESW	Southwest Quarter of Southeast Quarter of Southwest Quarter	10
SWSW	Southwest Quarter of Southwest Quarter-Section	40
SWSWNE	Southwest Quarter of Southwest Quarter of Northeast Quarter	10
SWSWNW	Southwest Quarter of Southwest Quarter of Northwest Quarter	10
SWSWSE	Southwest Quarter of Southwest Quarter of Southeast Quarter	10
SWSWSW	Southwest Quarter of Southwest Quarter of Southwest Quarter	10
W½	West Half-Section	320
W½E½	West Half of East Half-Section	160
W½N½	West Half of North Half-Section (same as NW)	160
W½NE	West Half of Northeast Quarter	80
W½NENE	West Half of Northeast Quarter of Northeast Quarter-Section	20
W½NENW	West Half of Northeast Quarter of Northwest Quarter-Section	20
W½NESE	West Half of Northeast Quarter of Southeast Quarter-Section	20
W½NESW	West Half of Northeast Quarter of Southwest Quarter-Section	20
W½NW	West Half of Northwest Quarter-Section	80
W½NWNE	West Half of Northwest Quarter of Northeast Quarter-Section	20
W½NWNW	West Half of Northwest Quarter of Northwest Quarter-Section	20
W½NWSE	West Half of Northwest Quarter of Southeast Quarter-Section	20
W½NWSW	West Half of Northwest Quarter of Southwest Quarter-Section	20
W½S½	West Half of South Half-Section	160
W½SE	West Half of Southeast Quarter-Section	80
W½SENE	West Half of Southeast Quarter of Northeast Quarter-Section	20
W½SENW	West Half of Southeast Quarter of Northwest Quarter-Section	20
W½SESE	West Half of Southeast Quarter of Southeast Quarter-Section	20
W½SESW	West Half of Southeast Quarter of Southwest Quarter-Section	20
W½SW	West Half of Southwest Quarter-Section	80
W½SWNE	West Half of Southwest Quarter of Northeast Quarter-Section	20
W½SWNW	West Half of Southwest Quarter of Northwest Quarter-Section	20
W½SWSE	West Half of Southwest Quarter of Southeast Quarter-Section	20
W½SWSW	West Half of Southwest Quarter of Southwest Quarter-Section	20
W½W½	West Half of West Half-Section	160

Appendix C - Multi-Patentee Groups

The following index presents groups of people who jointly received patents in Butler County, Alabama. The Group Numbers are used in the Patent Maps and their Indexes so that you may then turn to this Appendix in order to identify all the members of the each buying group.

Group Number 1
BABCOCK, Joseph; CONOLEY, John F; EVANS, George R; GAYLE, Matt

Group Number 2
BARNES, John C; WRIGHT, William

Group Number 3
BAXLEY, Martha A; DAWSON, Martha A

Group Number 4
BOLLING, Samuel J; LEWIS, John B

Group Number 5
BOLLING, Samuel J; MARSHALL, William B

Group Number 6
BRYAN, Edward; PRESLAR, Holden

Group Number 7
BURKETT, Florence L; DREADEN, Florence L

Group Number 8
CLARK, James B; WEST, Henry

Group Number 9
CLOPTON, Allford; CLOPTON, Sally

Group Number 10
COLLINS, Isaac; SHEPPARD, Andrew

Group Number 11
COLLINS, William; TAYLOR, Joseph M

Group Number 12
CRAIG, James D; HARVEY, Thomas P

Group Number 13
CRENSHAW, Charles E; CRENSHAW, Frederick W

Group Number 14
CROCKER, Benjamin; TILLERY, William

Group Number 15
DRAKE, William; YELDELL, Robert

Group Number 16
ELLIS, Josiah; WITHERINGTON, John

Group Number 17
FUTCH, Isaac; FUTCH, Jacob

Group Number 18
GALLOPS, Isom; JOHNSON, Joseph B

Group Number 19
GASTON, David; POWELL, William

Group Number 20
GODWIN, Daniel; GODWIN, Jane

Group Number 21
GRAYSON, Emily S; GRAYSON, James T

Group Number 22
GREGORY, Ossian; GREGORY, Susan

Group Number 23
HARRELL, German B; WHITE, John P

Group Number 24
HARRISON, Mary J; HARRISON, William M

Group Number 25
HARTLEY, Henry G; RABUN, Bud

Group Number 26
HOLAWAY, John F; HOLAWAY, Mary J

Group Number 27
LOGAN, George A; PAYNE, William

Group Number 28
LUDLAM, Mary J; LUDLAM, Samuel

Group Number 29
MAJORS, Ella; MAJORS, Jesse H

Group Number 30
MCDANIEL, Thomas; RUGELEY, Henry

Group Number 31
MCMULLEN, Charles; PEARMON, Orrin

Group Number 32
MOORE, John H; MOORE, Nancy A

Group Number 33
OLIVER, Henry P; OLIVER, Samuel

Group Number 34
OLIVER, Henry; OLIVER, Samuel

Group Number 35
PARMER, Joseph M; PARMER, William K

Group Number 36
PEAGLER, Artemous; PEAGLER, John

Group Number 37
PEVY, Michael; WALLER, James

Group Number 38
PHILLIPS, Thomas C; PORTERFIELD, Charles

Group Number 39
REID, John; REID, Racael

Group Number 40
RIGSBY, Philo D; WATSON, William S

Group Number 41
SHOWS, Abbie; SHOWS, James Z

Group Number 42
SMITH, Henry; TRAWEEK, William H; YELDELL,
James R; YELDELL, Jonathan M

Group Number 43
TILMAN, Henry; TILMAN, Susan

Group Number 44
TINSLEY, James; TINSLEY, Mary

Group Number 45
TRAWEEK, Thomas M; WATTS, Jeremiah

Group Number 46
WOMACK, George; WOMACK, John

Extra! Extra! (about our Indexes)

We purposefully do not have an all-name index in the back of this volume so that our readers do not miss one of the best uses of this book: finding misspelled names among more specialized indexes.

Without repeating the text of our "How-to" chapter, we have nonetheless tried to assist our more anxious researchers by delivering a short-cut to the two county-wide Surname Indexes, the second of which will lead you to all-name indexes for each Congressional Township mapped in this volume :

Surname Index (whole county, with number of parcels mapped) ....page 18
Surname Index (township by township) ....just following

For your convenience, the "How To Use this Book" Chart on page 2 is repeated on the reverse of this page.

We should be releasing new titles every week for the foreseeable future. We urge you to write, fax, call, or email us any time for a current list of titles. Of course, our web-page will always have the most current information about current and upcoming books.

Arphax Publishing Co.
2210 Research Park Blvd.
Norman, Oklahoma 73069
(800) 681-5298 toll-free
(405) 366-6181 local
(405) 366-8184 fax
info@arphax.com

www.arphax.com

How to Use This Book - A Graphical Summary

Part I
"The Big Picture"

Map A ▸ *Counties in the State*

Map B ▸ *Surrounding Counties*

Map C ▸ *Congressional Townships (Map Groups) in the County*

Map D ▸ *Cities & Towns in the County*

Map E ▸ *Cemeteries in the County*

Surnames in the County ▸ *Number of Land-Parcels for Each Surname*

Surname/Township Index ▸ *Directs you to Township Map Groups in Part II*

The <u>*Surname/Township Index*</u> *can direct you to any number of* **Township Map Groups**

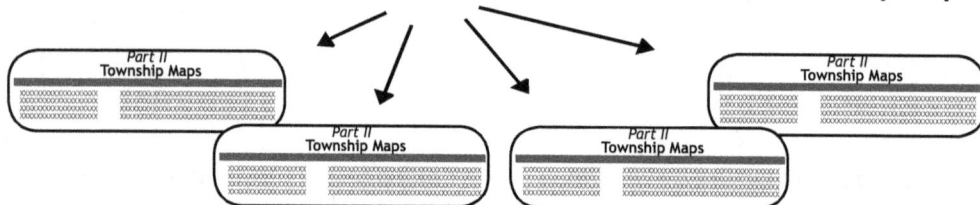

Part II Township Maps	Part II Township Maps

Part II Township Maps	Part II Township Maps

Part II
Township Map Groups
(1 for each Township in the County)

Each Township Map Group contains all four of of the following tools . . .

Land Patent Index ▸ *Every-name Index of Patents Mapped in this Township*

Land Patent Map ▸ *Map of Patents as listed in above Index*

Road Map ▸ *Map of Roads, City-centers, and Cemeteries in the Township*

Historical Map ▸ *Map of Railroads, Lakes, Rivers, Creeks, City-Centers, and Cemeteries*

Appendices

Appendix A ▸ *Congressional Authority enabling Patents within our Maps*

Appendix B ▸ *Section-Parts / Aliquot Parts (a comprehensive list)*

Appendix C ▸ *Multi-patentee Groups (Individuals within Buying Groups)*